W9-CEM-068

BRIEF TABLE OF CONTENTS

OB SKILLS WORKBOOK

The **OB Skills Workbook** is an end-of-text learning resource complete with a wide variety of cases, experiential exercises, and self-assessments to enrich and extend student learning.

JOSSEY-BASS/PFEIFFER CLASSROOM COLLECTION

Selected from the best of the Jossey-Bass and Pfeiffer publications, this collection includes the Kouzes and Posner Leadership Practices Inventory, and exercise selections from the Pfeiffer Annual Editions.

CASES FOR CRITICAL THINKING

The **Cases for Critical Thinking** section contains 19 cases, with each developed to explore issues, concepts and applications for a text chapter.

CROSS-FUNCTIONAL CASES

A **Cross-Functional Case** extends critical thinking case analysis across management functions.

EXPERIENTIAL EXERCISES

A portfolio of 42 **Experiential Exercises** helps students engage in teamwork and experience practical aspects of each chapter.

SELF-ASSESSMENTS

A set of 22 **Self-assessments** that involves students in exploring their personal managerial tendencies and perspectives.

eGrade Plus

www.wiley.com/college/schermerhorn
Based on the Activities You Do Every Day

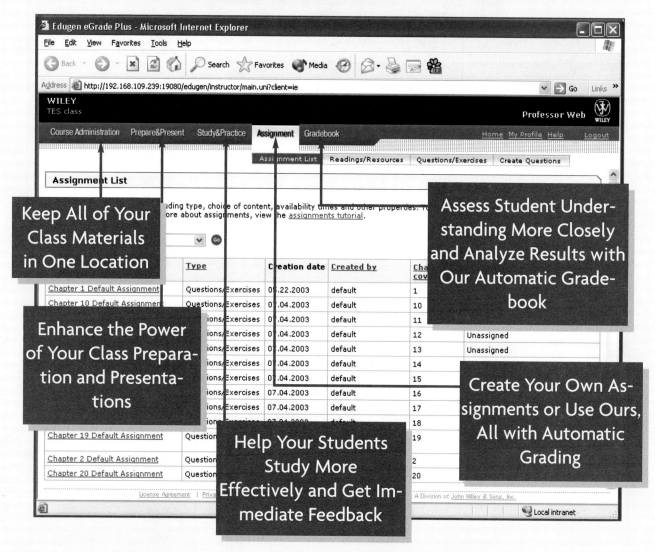

Keep All of Your Class Materials in One Location

Enhance the Power of Your Class Preparation and Presentations

Help Your Students Study More Effectively and Get Immediate Feedback

Assess Student Understanding More Closely and Analyze Results with Our Automatic Gradebook

Create Your Own Assignments or Use Ours, All with Automatic Grading

All the content and tools you need, all in one location, in an easy-to-use browser format.
Choose the resources you need, or rely on the arrangement supplied by us.

Now, many of Wiley's textbooks are available with eGrade Plus, a powerful online tool that provides a completely integrated suite of teaching and learning resources in one easy-to-use website. eGrade Plus integrates Wiley's world-renowned content with media, including a multimedia version of the text, PowerPoint slides, and more. Upon adoption of eGrade Plus, you can begin to customize your course with the resources shown here.

See for yourself! Go to **www.wiley.com/college/egradeplus** for an online demonstration of this powerful new software.

Keep All of Your Class Materials in One Location

Course Administration tools allow you to manage your class and integrate your eGrade Plus resources with most Course Management Systems, allowing you to keep all of your class materials in one location.

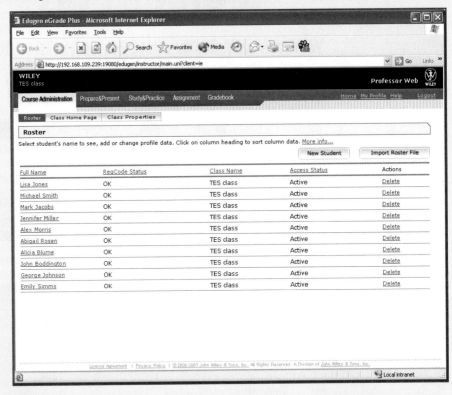

Enhance the Power of Your Class Preparation and Presentations

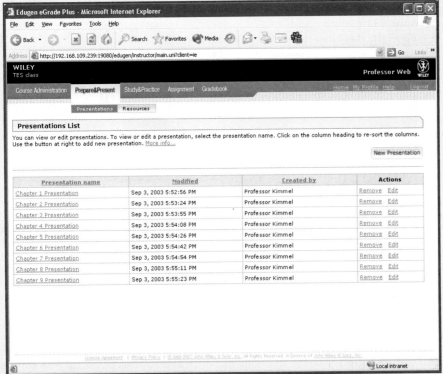

A **Prepare and Present tool** contains all of the Wiley-provided resources, such as **PowerPoint slides** and **student activities,** making your preparation time more efficient. You may easily adapt, customize, and add to Wiley content to meet the needs of your course.

Create Your Own Assignments or Use Ours, All with Automatic Grading

An **Assignment** area allows you to create **student homework** and **quizzes** by using **Wiley-provided question banks,** or by writing your own. You may also assign readings, activities and other work you want your students to complete. One of the most powerful features of eGrade Plus is that student assignments will be automatically graded and recorded in your gradebook. This will not only save you time but will provide your students with immediate feedback on their work.

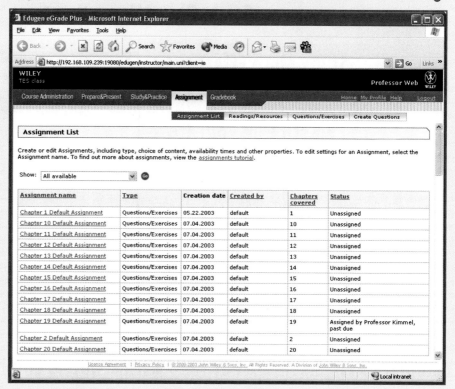

Assess Student Understanding More Closely

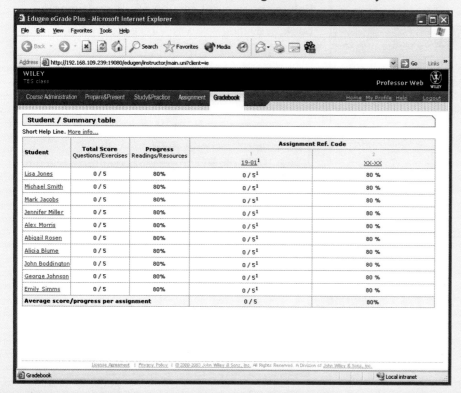

An **Instructor's Gradebook** will keep track of your students' progress and allow you to analyze individual and overall class results to determine their progress and level of understanding

Students,
eGrade Plus Allows You to:

Study More Effectively

Get Immediate Feedback When You Practice on Your Own

eGrade Plus problems link directly to relevant sections of the **electronic book content,** so that you can review the text while you study and complete homework online. Additional resources include **the OB Skills Workbook,** including **the Jossey-Bass/Pfeiffer Classroom Collection, Cases, Experiential Exercises,** and **interactive Self-Assessments.**

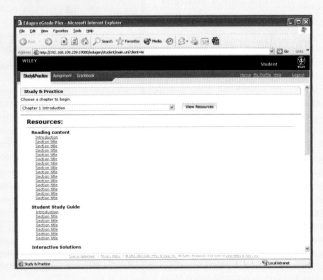

Complete Assignments / Get Help with Problem Solving

An **Assignment** area keeps all your assigned work in one location, making it easy for you to stay "on task." In addition, many homework problems contain a **link** to the relevant section of the **multimedia book,** providing you with a text explanation to help you conquer problem-solving obstacles as they arise.

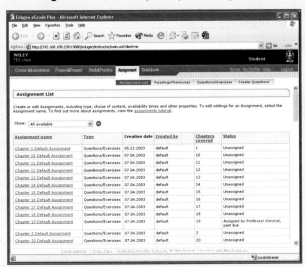

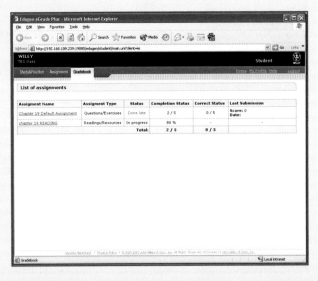

Keep Track of How You're Doing

A **Personal Gradebook** allows you to view your results from past assignments at any time.

Organizational Behavior

Ninth Edition

Organizational Behavior
Ninth Edition

John R. Schermerhorn, Jr.
OHIO UNIVERSITY

James G. Hunt
TEXAS TECH UNIVERSITY

Richard N. Osborn
WAYNE STATE UNIVERSITY

WILEY

John Wiley & Sons, Inc.

Associate Publisher	Judy Joseph
Senior Acquisitions Editor	Jayme Heffler
Developmental Editor	David Kear
Marketing Manager	Heather King
Media Editor	Allie Morris
Senior Production Editor	Sandra Dumas
Senior Designer	Madelyn Lesure
Illustration Editor	Anna Melhorn
Text Designer	Laura C. Ierardi
Front Cover Images	Top: ©Susan C. Bourgoin/Foodpix/PictureArts Corp.
	Center left: ©Dimitri Lundt/Corbis Images
	Center right: ©David Madison/The Image Bank/Getty Images
	Bottom: ©Dan Lim/Masterfile
Back Cover Images	Top: ©Susan C. Bourgoin/Foodpix/PictureArts Corp.
	Center top: ©David Madison/The Image Bank/Getty Images
	Center bottom: ©Dan Lim/Masterfile
	Bottom: ©Dimitri Lundt/Corbis Images
Senior Photo Editor	Sara Wight
Photo Researcher	Ramón Rivera-Moret
Production Management Services	Ingrao Associates

This book was set in 10/12 ITC Garamond Light by LCI Design and printed and bound by Von Hoffmann. The cover was printed by Von Hoffmann, Inc.

This book is printed on acid-free paper. ∞

To order books or for customer service please, call 1(800)-CALL-WILEY (225-5945).

Schermerhorn, John R. Jr., Hunt, James G., Osborn, Richard N.
    Organizational Behavior, Ninth Edition

ISBN 0-471-68170-9
ISBN 0-471-70150-5 (Wiley International Edition - paperback)

Printed in the United States of America.

10 9 8 7 6 5 4 3 2

About the Authors

Dr. John R. Schermerhorn Jr. is the Charles G. O'Bleness Professor of Management in the College of Business Administration at Ohio University. He holds a PhD in organizational behavior from Northwestern University, an MBA (with distinction) from New York University, and a BS from the State University of New York at Buffalo. He received an honorary doctorate from the University of Pecs (Hungary) in recognition of his international contributions to management research and education, and presently serves as Adjunct Professor of Management at the National University of Ireland at Galway and a member of the graduate faculty at Bangkok University in Thailand. He has also held appointments as the Kohei Miura Visiting Professor at Chubu University Japan, Visiting Professor of Management at the Chinese University of Hong Kong, and Visiting Scholar at Liaoning University in China and the Technical University of Wroclaw in Poland. At Ohio University he has been Director of the Center for Southeast Asia Studies and on-site Coordinator of EMBA and MBA programs in Malaysia. Dr. Schermerhorn has won awards for teaching excellence at Tulane University, the University of Vermont, and Ohio University, where he has been named a University Professor, the university's leading award for undergraduate teaching. He is the author or co-author of numerous journal articles, book chapters, and proceedings. His other Wiley books include *Management* (Eighth Edition, 2005), *Core Concepts of Management* (2004), and *Core Concepts of Organizational Behavior* (Wiley, 2004).

Dr. James G. (Jerry) Hunt is the Paul Whitfield Horn Professor of Management, Trinity Company Professor in Leadership, Professor of Health Organization Management, Director, Institute for Leadership Research, and former department chair of Management, Texas Tech University. He received his PhD and master's degrees from the University of Illinois after completing a BS (with honors) at Michigan Technological University. Dr. Hunt has co-authored an organization theory text and *Basic Organizational Behavior* (Wiley, 1998) and has authored or co-authored three leadership monographs. He founded the Leadership Symposia Series and co-edited the eight volumes based on the series. He has presented or published nearly 200 articles, papers, and book chapters, and among his most recent books are *Leadership: A New Synthesis*, published by Sage, and *Out-of-the-Box Leadership*, published by JAI. The former was a finalist for the Academy of Management's 1993 Terry Distinguished Book Award. Recently, Dr. Hunt received the Distinguished Service Award from the Academy of Management, the Sustained Outstanding Service Award from the Southern Management Association, and the Barnie E. Rushing. Jr. Distinguished Researcher Award from Texas Tech University for his long-term contributions to management research and scholarship. He has lived and taught in England and Finland, and taught in China.

Dr. Richard N. Osborn is a Distinguished Professor at Wayne State University in the School of Business Administration and formerly a Board of Governors Faculty Fellow. He has received teaching awards at Southern Illinois University at Carbondale and Wayne State University, and he has also taught at Monash University (Australia), Tulane University, and the University of Washington. He received a DBA from Kent State University after earning an MBA at Washington State University and a BS from Indiana University. With over 175 presentations and publications, he is a charter member of the Academy of Management Journals Hall of Fame. Dr. Osborn is a leading authority on international alliances in technology-intensive industries and is co-author of an organization theory text and *Basic Organizational Behavior* (John Wiley & Sons, 1995, 1998). He has served as a member of the editorial boards of the *Academy of Management Journal, Technology Studies, Journal of High Technology Management, The Academy of Management Review, The Journal of Management* and editor of international strategy for the *Journal of World Business*. He is very active in the Academy of Management, having served as divisional program chair and president, as well as the Academy representative for the International Federation of Scholarly Associations of Management. Dr. Osborn's research has been sponsored by the Department of Defense, Ford Motor Company, National Science Foundation, Nissan, and the Nuclear Regulatory Commission, among others. In addition to teaching, Dr. Osborn spent a number of years in private industry, including a position as a senior research scientist with the Battelle Memorial Institute in Seattle, where he worked on improving the safety of commercial nuclear power.

Preface

People working individually and together are what should come to mind when looking at the beautiful hands on the cover and throughout this book. They are not just artistic expressions; they symbolize a basic fact of organizations and careers—people do the work of our society and its organizations. The lesson for students of organizational behavior is an important one: in your hands anything and everything is possible. Our job, as educators, is to bring to them the great power of knowledge, understanding, and inquiry that characterizes our discipline and its commitment to understanding human behavior in organizations.

Organizational Behavior, Ninth Edition, deals with the opportunities and challenges faced by those who must help themselves and their organizations meet the demanding tests of new and sometimes very difficult times. While retaining an emphasis on the fundamentals of organizational behavior, the theme for the new edition is one of personal and organizational transformation. It recognizes that today's students must build career success in an ever-changing environment and that they must do so while achieving a positive balance between work and personal lives and goals. We all live, work, and learn in a society that expects high performance and high quality of work life to go hand in hand, that considers ethics and social responsibility paramount measures of individual and organizational performance, that respects the talents of workforces increasingly rich in demographic and cultural diversity, and that knows the imprint of globalization.

The ninth edition was created with these realities in mind. It also applies the insights of OB across organizational and career settings—be they business, government, education, or public service. No matter what the reference point, we must all be prepared to perform in organizations challenged by uncertainty, bound for continuous change, and affected by the forces of high technology. What our students do with their talents will not only shape the contributions of the institutions of society but also fundamentally alter lives around the globe. Our goal must be to help them gain the understanding that can help them become leaders of tomorrow's organizations.

In content and design, this book can serve the needs of your OB course and help you to inform and enthuse students who will face the challenges of tomorrow's workplace, not yesterday's. We have written it for those who want to understand the discipline of OB in full awareness of its practical value and importance to their future careers. And, we have written it for educators who want to give their students a solid introduction to the discipline, a rich array of alternative learning activities, and a strong emphasis on and commitment to personal development.

Organizational Behavior, Ninth Edition, is our contribution to the study of a dynamic discipline that becomes increasingly relevant as our society and its institutions rush forward into an uncertain future. It is dedicated to our students, those whose hands hold the real keys to the future.

John R. Schermerhorn Jr.
Ohio University

James G. (Jerry) Hunt
Texas Tech University

Richard N. Osborn
Wayne State University

About This Book

Organizational Behavior, Ninth Edition, brings to its readers the solid and complete content core of prior editions, the exciting "OB Skills Workbook," and many revisions, updates, and enhancements that reflect today's dynamic times.

New Organization

The most significant change that past users will note is a rearrangement of the table of contents. In this edition, and in response to feedback, we have moved the section on organizations to Part 5 and thus allow for instructors and students to cover all of the "micro" OB topics before moving to the "macro" topics. The book still covers the discipline in an orderly progression that allows for major parts and/or chapters to be used out of sequence at the instructor's prerogative. We do suggest that the first two chapters in Part 1—Chapter 1, "Organizational Behavior Today," and Chapter 2, "Current Issues in Organizational Behavior"—be used in sequence to set the context for the course.

New Chapter

Chapter 2, "Current Issues in Organizational Behavior," is new to this edition. It retains the emphasis of its predecessor on high-performance organizations, while engaging the student reader in special discussions of multiculturalism and diversity, ethical behavior and moral management, corporate governance, positive organizational behavior, globalization and job migration, organizational transformation, and career planning. This chapter places the study of organizational behavior in the context of issues, directions, and transitions of today's realities and work environments.

New Chapter Content

In addition to the new Chapter 2, the OB foundations have been substantially updated. Revisions to several chapters included a change of title to better focus attention on the subject matter. In addition to updates throughout the text, look for these redesigned chapters in the new edition.

- Chapter 3: Organizational Behavior Across Cultures
- Chapter 4: Personality and Individual Differences
- Chapter 6: Motivation Theories
- Chapter 7: Motivation and Job Design
- Chapter 8: Performance Management and Rewards

New Research Insights

To better communicate the timely research foundations of OB, a new feature—*Research Insights*—has been added to each chapter. This feature overviews a recent journal article of relevance to chapter content. Examples include articles dealing with attitudes and performance, ethical behavior, cross-cultural intelligence, and workplace identities, among others. A special primer on Research Methods in Organizational Behavior is also included after the last text chapter.

New Leadership Focus

To remind students that there are many positive leadership role models available for study, a new *Leaders on Leadership* feature has been added to each chapter. This feature offers short examples of real leaders, their experiences and perspectives—including Rudy Giuliani, Carly Fiorina, Earl Graves, Colleen Barret, Richard Branson, and others. Each vignette is followed by a study question that asks students to further consider the implications of the leadership example.

New Chapter Pedagogy

As always, a primary goal in writing this book is to create a textbook that appeals to the student reader, while still offering solid content. Through market research surveys and focus groups with students and professors, we continue to learn what features worked best from previous editions, what can be improved, and what can be added to accomplish this goal both effectively and efficiently. Our response is a selection of pedagogical elements that include popular elements from the last edition and new additions.

- **Chapter Opening**—includes a *Planning Ahead* section with *study questions/learning objectives*—linked to end-of-chapter Summary, and a *short opening vignette* that leads the reader into chapter text.

- **Inside the Chapter**—includes *thematic embedded boxes* that highlight current events and examples relating to ethics and social responsibility, people and technology, and cultures and the global workforce—with each box followed by a reflection question posed to the reader; *leaders on leadership boxes* that introduce a leader's views and actions relating to chapter content, also followed by a reflection question; *effective manager boxes* that provide handy summaries and action guidelines on chapter content; *margin photo essays*—short examples highlighting events and issues; running *margin glossary* and *margin list identifiers*.

- **End of Chapter**—includes a Study Guide to help students review and test their mastery of chapter content. Key components are: Chapter Summary (keyed to opening Planning Ahead questions), Key Terms listing, and a Self-Test—with multiple choice, short response and essay questions. Also included is *OB in Action*, a guide to selections of cases, exercises and assessments from the OB Skills Workbook that link to chapter material. Students can access on the web site for interactive versions of self-tests, cases and assessments, as well as to obtain self-test answers.

New Update to *The OB Skills Workbook:* *Featuring The Jossey-Bass/Pfeiffer Collection*

The end-of-text **OB Skills Workbook** has become a hallmark feature of the text-book, and it has been updated and expanded for the new edition. In addition to a selection of *cases, exercises* and *assessments* that can be used at the instructor's convenience, *The Jossey-Bass Pfeiffer Collection* is new. This collection offers the popular Kouzes and Posner *Student Leadership Practices Inventory* and six other selections from recent Pfeiffer training annuals. These materials are further op-portunities to extend the OB learning experience in creative and helpful ways.

New Student and Instructor Support

Organizational Behavior, Ninth Edition is supported by a comprehensive learn-ing package that assists the instructor in creating a motivating and enthusiastic environment.

Student Resources (www.wiley.com/college/schermerhorn) An updated inter-active web site contains a rich variety of student and instructor resources. Stu-dents benefit from engaging in on-line activities based on *Interactive Self-Testing, On-line Study Guide, On-Line Cases,* and *Interactive Self-Assessments.*

Instructor Resources Rich and substantive, the special instructors resources in-clude:

The Creative Classroom (www.wiley.com/college/schermerhorn) by Robert E. (Lenie) Holbrook—a variety of ready-to-use enrichments to build creative learning opportunities ranging from social responsibility projects to special in-class exercises and activities.

Lecture Launcher Videos—Brief video clips, ranging from 2-5 minutes in length from the Films for the Humanities, are tied to the major topics in Organiza-tional Behavior. These videos provide an excellent starting point for lectures.

The Author's Classroom—additional PowerPoint selections from the authors' classrooms.

Instructor's Resource Guide—compendium of numerous resources for each chapter, including Course Syllabi, Sample Assignments, Lecture Outlines, Lec-ture Notes, Teaching Suggestions for using multi-media components, and much more.

Test Bank—An expanded and revised Test Bank includes multiple choice, True/False and essay questions for each chapter, with questions keyed to major headings in the text.

Course Management Tools—Both WebCT and Blackboard are fully supported.

eGrade Plus—provides an integrated suite of teaching and learning re-sources, along with a complete online version of the text, in one easy-to-use website. *eGrade Plus* will help you create class presentations, create assign-ments and automate the assigning and grading of homework or quizzes, track your students' progress, and administer your course. For more informa-tion, go to www.wiley.com/college/egradeplus

Contributors

Cases for Critical Thinking

Barry R. Armandi, *State University of New York*, Forrest F. Aven, *University of Houston, Downtown*, Kim Cameron, *Brigham Young University*, David S. Chappell, *Ohio University*, Anne C. Cowden, *California State University, Sacramento*, Bernardo M. Ferdman, *Alliant International University*, Placido L. Gallegos, *Southwest Communications Resources, Inc.* and the *Kaleel Jamison Consulting Group. Inc.*, Carol Harvey, *Assumption College*; Ellen Ernst Kossek, *Michigan State University*, Barbara McCain, *Oklahoma City University*, Mary McGarry, *Empire State College*, Aneil Mishra, *Pennsylvania State University*, Karen Mishra, *Pennsylvania State University*, Marc Osborn, *R&R Partners Phoenix, AZ*, V. Jean Ramsey, *Texas Southern University*, Franklin Ramsoomair, *Wilfrid Laurier University*, Hal Babson and John Bowen of *Columbus State Community College*.

Experiential Exercises and Self-Assessment Inventories

Barry R. Armandi, *State University of New York, Old Westbury*, Ariel Fishman, *The Wharton School, University of Pennsylvania*, Barbara K. Goza, *University of California, Santa Cruz*, D.T. Hall, *Boston University*, F.S. Hall, *University of New Hampshire*, Lady Hanson, *California State Polytechnic University, Pomona*, Conrad N. Jackson, *MPC, Inc.*, Mary Khalili, *Oklahoma City University*, Robert Ledman, *Morehouse College*, Paul Lyons, *Frostburg State University*, J. Marcus Maier, *Chapman University*, Michael R. Manning, *New Mexico State University*, Barbara McCain, *Oklahoma City University*, Annie McKee, *The Wharton School, University of Pennsylvania*, Bonnie McNeely, *Murray State University*, W. Alan Randolph, *University of Baltimore*, Joseph Raelin, *Boston College*, Paula J. Schmidt, *New Mexico State University*, Susan Schor, *Pace University*, Timothy T. Serey, *Northern Kentucky University*, Barbara Walker, *Diversity Consultant*, Paula S. Weber, *New Mexico Highlands University*, Susan Rawson Zacur, *University of Baltimore*.

Acknowledgments

Organizational Behavior, Ninth Edition benefits from insights provided by a dedicated group of management educators from around the globe who carefully read and critiqued draft chapters of this edition. We are pleased to express our appreciation to the following colleagues for their contributions to this new edition.

David Baldridge, *Oregon State University*
Melinda Blackman, *California State University, Fullerton*
Lisa Bleich, *Whittier College*
Pat Buhler, *Goldey Beacom College*
Roosevelt Butler, *The College of New Jersey*
Ken Butterfield, *Washington State University - Pullman*
Tom Callahan, *University of Michigan - Dearborn*
Emmeline De Pillis, *University of Hawaii - Hilo*
Robert Delprino, *Buffalo State College*
Pam Dobies, *University of Missouri - Kansas City*
Norb Elbert, *Eastern Kentucky University*
Claudia Ferrante, *U.S. Air Force Academy*
Virginia Geurin, *University of North Carolina - Charlotte*
Leslie Korb, *University of Nebraska - Kearney*
Jim Lessner, *Scott Community College*
Robert Liden, *University of Illinois - Chicago*
Michael Lounsbury, *Cornell University*
Tom Mayes, *California State University - Fullerton*
Jeanne McNett, *Assumption College*
David Morand, *Pennsylvania State University - Harrisburg*
Regina O'Neill, *Suffolk University*
Prudence Pollard, *LaSierra University*
Clint Relyea, *Arkansas State University*
Bobby Remington, *Chapman University - Orange*
Robert Salitore, *Keller Graduate School of Management*
Terri Scandura, *University of Miami*
Mel Schnake, *Valdosta State University*
Holly Schroth, *University of California - Berkeley*
William Sharbrough, *The Citadel Military College of South Carolina*
Mary Alice Smith, *Tarrant County College*
Ron Stone, *DeVry University - Arlington*
Tom Thompson, *University of Maryland University College*
Nicholas Twigg, *Lamar University*

Andy Wagstaff, *University of Phoenix*
Edward Ward, *St. Cloud State University*
Fred Ware, *Valdosta State University*
Robert Whitcomb, *University of Wisconsin - Eau Claire*
Kimberly Young, *St. Bonaventure University*

We also thank those reviewers who contributed to the success of previous editions:

Merle Ace	Robert Giambatista	Dennis Pappas
Chi Anyansi-Archibong	Manton Gibbs	Edward B. Parks
Terry Armstrong	Eugene Gomolka	Robert F. Pearse
Leanne Atwater	Barbara Goodman	Lawrence Peters
Forrest Aven	Stephen Gourlay	Joseph Porac
Steve Axley	Frederick Greene	Samuel Rabinowitz
Abdul Aziz	Richard Grover	Franklin Ramsoomair
Richard Babcock	Bengt Gustafsson	Charles L. Roegiers
Michael Banutu-Gomez	Peter Gustavson	Steven Ross
Robert Barbato	Lady Alice Hanson	Michael Rush
Richard Barrett	Don Hantula	L. David Schuelke
Nancy Bartell	Kristi Harrison	Richard J. Sebastian
Anna Bavetta	William Hart	Anson Seers
Robb Bay	Nell Hartley	R. Murray Sharp
Hrach Bedrosian	Neil J. Humphreys	Allen N. Shub
Bonnie Betters-Reed	David Hunt	Sidney Siegal
Gerald Biberman	Eugene Hunt	Dayle Smith
Mauritz Blonder	Howard Kahn	Walter W. Smock
Dale Blount	Harriet Kandelman	Pat Sniderman
G. B. Bohn	Paul N. Keaton	Ritch L. Sorenson
Joseph F. Byrnes	Andrew Klein	Shanthi Srinivas
Gene E. Burton	Peter Kreiner	Paul L. Starkey
Michal Cakrt	Donald Lantham	Ronni Stephens
Daniel R. Cillis	Les Lewchuk	Romuald Stone
Nina Cole	Kristi M. Lewis	Sharon Tucker
Paul Collins	Beverly Linnell	Ted Valvoda
Ann Cowden	Kathy Lippert	Joyce Vincelette
Deborah Crown	Michael London	David Vollrath
Roger A. Dean	Carol Lucchesi	W. Fran Waller
Delf Dodge	David Luther	Charles Wankel
Dennis Duchon	Lorna Martin	Fred A. Ware, Jr.
Michael Dumler	Douglas McCabe	Andrea F. Warfield
Ken Eastman	James McFillen	Harry Waters, Jr.
Theresa Feener	Charles Milton	Joseph W. Weiss
Janice M. Feldbauer	Herff L. Moore	Deborah Wells
Dalmar Fisher	David Morean	Donald White
J. Benjamin Forbes	Sandra Morgan	Bobbie Williams
Cynthia V. Fukami	Paula Morrow	Barry L. Wisdom
Normandie Gaitley	Richard Mowday	Wayne Wormley
Daniel Ganster	Linda Neider	Barry Wright
Joe Garcia	Judy C. Nixon	Raymond Zammuto

Efforts to extend *Organizational Behavior*, Ninth Edition in new directions have benefited greatly from those educators whose materials are represented in The OB Skills Workbook. These colleagues are identified in the workbook with their contributions, and we greatly appreciate the range of innovative pedagogical options they help provide users of this book.

We are grateful for all the hard work of the supplements authors, who worked to develop the comprehensive ancillary package described above. We thank Michael McCuddy for preparing the Instructor's Resource Guide and Test Bank, John Stark for creating the eGrade quizzes, Joan Rentsch for developing the Lecture Launch Video, and Hal Babson and John Bowen for case revisions. Thanks are also due to David Cavazos, Adrienne Haan and Donna Hunt for finding, typing, and checking important material for various chapters. Robert E. (Lenie) Holbrook of Ohio University deserves a special acknowledgement for his contributions of The Creative OB Classroom and assistance with The Jossey-Bass Pfeiffer Collection.

As always, the support staff at John Wiley & Sons was most helpful in the various stages of developing and producing this edition. We would especially like to thank Jayme Heffler (Acquisitions Editor), Judith Joseph (Associate Publisher), and David Kear (Project Editor) for their extraordinary efforts in support of this project. They took OB to heart and did their very best to build a high performance team in support of this book. We thank everyone at Wiley for maintaining the quest for quality and timeliness in all aspects of the book's content and design. Special gratitude goes to Maddy Lesure as the creative force behind the new design, while Sara Wight's special talent as photo researcher resulted in the beautiful use of photography that enhances this edition. We also thank Sandra Dumas, Laura Ierardi, and Ingrao Associates for their excellent production and design assistance, Allie Morris for overseeing the media development, and Heather King for leading the marketing campaign. Thank you everyone!!

Brief Contents

Contents

Chapter 8
Performance Management and Rewards   162

Part 3
Group Dynamics and Teamwork

Chapter 9
How Groups Work   192

Chapter 10
Teamwork and Team Performance   216

Chapter 1

Introducing Organizational Behavior

Chapter at a Glance

People are an organization's most important assets. Chapter 1 introduces the field of organizational behavior as a useful knowledge base for success in today's dynamic environments. As you read Chapter 1, *keep in mind these study questions.*

WHAT IS ORGANIZATIONAL BEHAVIOR AND WHY IS IT IMPORTANT?

- What Is Organizational Behavior
- Scientific Foundations of Organizational Behavior
- Shifting Paradigms of Organizational Behavior

WHAT ARE ORGANIZATIONS LIKE AS WORK SETTINGS?

- Organizational Purpose, Mission, and Strategy
- Organizational Environments and Stakeholders
- Organizational Cultures and Diversity
- Organizational Effectiveness

WHAT IS THE NATURE OF MANAGERIAL WORK?

- The Management Process
- The Nature of Managerial Work
- Managerial Roles, Networks, and Mind-Sets
- Managerial Skills and Competencies

HOW DO WE LEARN ABOUT ORGANIZATIONAL BEHAVIOR?

- Learning and Experience
- Learning Guide to *Organizational Behavior /9E*

REVIEW IN END-OF-CHAPTER STUDY GUIDE

Of all the advice on high-performing organizations, one message stands above them all: "People are an organization's most important assets!" Stanford scholar Jeffrey Pfeffer points out that such beliefs aren't based on emotional or sentimental attachments to the human factor; the bottom-line returns are there, too. Organizations with positive human resource practices gain competitive advantage through higher productivity and lower turnover. Pfeffer argues that organizations do best when leaders treat people well, valuing them as assets to be nurtured and developed rather than costs to be controlled.

Consider the case of Malden Mills, a maker of Polartec fleece for clothing. When the plant burned down several years ago, CEO Aaron Feurstein refused to lay off the workers. He paid them while rebuilding, even though insurance picked up only 75 percent of the cost. But just after the firm got back on its feet, the economy turned down. Facing large debts, Feurstein had to file for Chapter 11 bankruptcy while reorganizing. His employees stood by the company. Says one engineer: "I would never leave him at a time like this, not for what he's done for me." Nine hundred workers gave up their paid personal days for a year to help cut expenses and agreed to freeze salaries for two years. Saving the company became a shared goal. As Malden Mills fought for survival, it did so with the best possible support—a highly committed workforce. And they won the fight, just as Pfeffer would have expected.[1]

> "People are an organization's most important assets!"

Introducing Organizational Behavior

Aaron Feurstein's leadership at Malden Mills provides an important lesson. If you act ethically and treat people in organizations well, you can expect them to treat you well in return. The example also shows that the pathways to high performance today are complex, challenging, and full of pitfalls; nothing is ever guaranteed. Yet even in a time of crisis, Feurstein was able to face the future and its risks with confidence—he had earned the trust and respect of Malden's employees. Whether your career unfolds in entrepreneurship, corporate enterprise, public service, or any other occupational setting, this lesson must be remembered. Success in any work setting depends on a respect for people and an understanding of human behavior in complex organizational systems. It also depends on your commitment to flexibility, creativity, learning, and willingness to change with the challenges of time. That is the message of today, and it will be the message of tomorrow.

People at work in organizations today are part of a new era. The institutions of society and the people who make them work are challenged in many and

Leaders on Leadership

LEADERSHIP BEGINS WITH BELIEVING IN YOURSELF

Earl G. Graves Sr., is known for believing that anything is possible. When he founded *Black Enterprise* magazine in 1970, his goal was to mobilize support for business entrepreneurship and success among African-Americans. At the time he saw them "lacking in capital, managerial and technical knowledge, and crippled by prejudice." Starting with a $175,000 loan, Graves says his vision was to serve as a catalyst for black economic development. His magazine was a great success, and Graves has gone on to a high-profile business career, becoming a role model for minority business success. The business school at Morgan State University, his alma mater, is now named after him. Among his words of advice is the importance of believing in yourself and having a positive attitude. "If you tell someone you're going to do something, do it," says Graves, adding: "You have to live by your word."

Question: How does the record of minority leadership in Fortune 500 companies compare with minority participation in entrepreneurship and small business?

very special ways. The public at large increasingly expects high performance and high quality of life to go hand in hand, considers ethics and social responsibility core values, respects the vast potential of demographic and cultural diversity among people, and recognizes the imprint of globalization on everyday living and organizational competitiveness.

What Is Organizational Behavior?

In this new era of work and organizations, the body of knowledge we call "organizational behavior" offers many insights of great value. **Organizational behavior**, OB for short, is the study of human behavior in organizations. It is a multidisciplinary field devoted to understanding individual and group behavior, interpersonal processes, and organizational dynamics. Learning about OB will help you develop a better work-related understanding about yourself and other people. It can also expand your potential for career success in the dynamic, shifting, complex, and challenging new workplaces of today—and tomorrow.

    Organizational Behavior 9/E is about people, everyday people like you and us, who work and pursue careers in today's new and highly demanding settings. It is about people who seek fulfillment in their lives and jobs in a variety of ways and in uncertain times. It is about common themes that now characterize the modern workplace—ethical behavior, globalization, technology utilization, diversity, high performance, work–life balance, and more. *OB 9/E* is also about how our complex environment challenges people and organizations to change,

■ **Organizational behavior** is the study of individuals and groups in organizations.

learn, and continuously develop themselves in the quest for high performance and promising futures.

Scientific Foundations of Organizational Behavior

As far back as a century ago, consultants and scholars were giving increased attention to the systematic study of management. Although the early focus was initially on physical working conditions, principles of administration, and industrial engineering principles, the interest had broadened by the 1940s to include the essential human factor. This gave impetus to research dealing with individual attitudes, group dynamics, and the relationships between managers and workers. Eventually, the discipline of organizational behavior emerged as a broader and encompassing approach. Today, it continues to evolve as a discipline devoted to scientific understanding of individuals and groups in organizations and of the performance implications of organizational processes, systems, and structures.[2]

Interdisciplinary Body of Knowledge   Organizational behavior is an interdisciplinary body of knowledge with strong ties to the behavioral sciences—psychology, sociology, and anthropology—as well as to allied social sciences, such as economics and political science. OB is unique, however, in its goals of integrating the diverse insights of these other disciplines and applying them to real-world problems and opportunities. The ultimate goal of OB is to improve the performance of people, groups, and organizations and to improve the quality of work life overall.

Use of Scientific Methods   OB uses scientific methods to develop and empirically test generalizations about behavior in organizations. Figure 1.1 describes re-

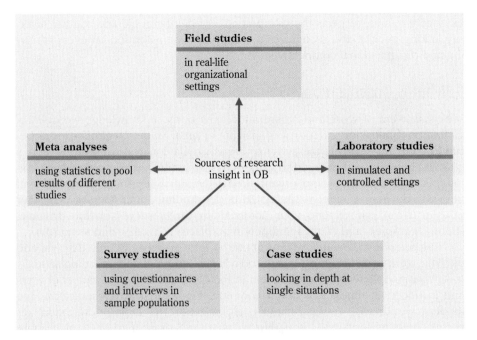

Figure 1.1   Research methods in organizational behavior.

search methods commonly used. Scientific thinking is important to OB researchers and scholars for these reasons: (1) the process of data collection is controlled and systematic; (2) proposed explanations are carefully tested; and (3) only explanations that can be scientifically verified are accepted. Research concepts and designs in OB are explained further in the end-of-book primer on "Research Methods in Organizational Behavior."

Focus on Application   The field of organizational behavior focuses on applications that can make a real difference in how organizations and people in them perform. The outcome or dependent variables studied by researchers, for example, include task performance, job satisfaction, job involvement, absenteeism, and turnover. Among the practical questions addressed by the discipline of OB and in this book are: How should rewards such as merit pay raises be allocated? How can jobs be designed for high performance? What are the ingredients of successful teamwork? How can organizational cultures be changed? Should decisions be made by individual, consultative, or group methods? In a negotiation, what is the best way to achieve "win–win" outcomes? What creates job satisfaction for people at work? How can ethical and socially responsible behavior in and by organizations be ensured?

Contingency Thinking   Rather than assuming that there is one "best" or universal way to manage people and organizations, OB recognizes that management practices must be tailored to fit the exact nature of each situation. Using a **contingency approach**, researchers try to identify how different situations can best be understood and handled. In Chapter 3, for example, we recognize that culture can affect how OB theories and concepts apply in different countries.[3] What works well in one culture may not work as well in another. Other important contingency variables addressed in this book include environment, technology, task, structure, and people.

Shifting Paradigms of Organizational Behavior

Progressive workplaces today look and act very differently from those of the past. They have new features, they approach work processes in new ways, and they serve different customer and client markets. The last decade of the twentieth century was especially dramatic in both the nature and pace of change. One observer called it a "revolution that feels something like this: scary, guilty, painful, liberating, disorienting, exhilarating, empowering, frustrating, fulfilling, confusing, challenging. In other words, it feels very much like chaos."[4]

This sense of revolution has become everyday reality. Intense global competition, job migration due to outsourcing and offshoring, highly interdependent national economies, constantly emerging computer and information technologies, new forms of organizations, and shifting population demographics are now part of the norm. Today we are surrounded by change and uncertainty, and their implications for organizations (just look at the new economic realities and the world of electronic commerce) and for individuals (look also at the demand for competencies with new technologies and commitment to continuous personal improvement).[5] What remains is the struggle to best deal with these changes, individually and institutionally, and to keep up the pace as further challenges emerge in the new workplace.

MIT's Center for Coordination Science

Researchers at MIT's Center for Coordination Science study how information technology and computer networks are changing commerce and organizations. A current initiative focuses on designing computer systems that help people work together in teams.

■■■ The **contingency approach** seeks ways to meet the needs of different management situations.

In an article entitled "The Company of the Future," Brandeis University professor and former secretary of labor Robert Reich says: "Everybody works for somebody or something—be it a board of directors, a pension fund, a venture capitalist, or a traditional boss. Sooner or later you're going to have to decide who you want to work for."[6] In making this decision, you will want to join a progressive workplace that reflects values consistent with your own. This book can help you prepare for such choices in full recognition that the realities of working today include these trends:[7]

Trends in the new workplace

- *Commitment to ethical behavior:* Highly publicized scandals involving unethical and illegal business practices highlight concerns for ethical behavior in the workplace; there is growing intolerance for breaches of public faith by organizations and those who run them.
- *Importance of human capital:* A dynamic and complex environment poses continuous challenges; sustained success places a premium on the knowledge, experience, and commitments of people as valuable human assets of organizations.
- *Demise of "command-and-control":* Traditional hierarchical structures are proving incapable of handling new environmental pressures and demands; they are being replaced by flexible structures and participatory work settings that fully value human capital.
- *Emphasis on teamwork:* Organizations today are less vertical and more horizontal in focus; driven by complex environments and customer demands, work is increasingly team-based with a focus on peer contributions.
- *Pervasive influence of information technology:* As computers increasingly penetrate all aspects of the workplace, implications for workflows, work arrangements, and organizational systems and processes are far-reaching.
- *Respect for new workforce expectations:* The new generation of workers is less tolerant of hierarchy, more informal, and less concerned about status; organizations are paying more attention to helping members balance work responsibilities and personal affairs.
- *Changing definition of "jobs" and "career":* The new realities of a global economy find employers using more "offshoring" and "outsourcing" of jobs and more individuals working as independent contractors rather than traditional full-time employees.

Organizations as Work Settings

Organizations are collections of people working together to achieve a common purpose.

The study of organizational behavior must be framed in an understanding of organizations as work settings. An **organization** is defined as a collection of people working together in a division of labor to achieve a common purpose. This definition describes a wide variety of clubs, voluntary organizations, and religious bodies, as well as entities such as small and large businesses, labor unions, schools, hospitals, and government agencies. The insights and applications of OB can be applied to help all such organizations perform up to expectations as social institutions.

**GREAT EMPLOYERS CREATE A
HIGH QUALITY OF WORK LIFE**

Once you start work for SAS Institute in Cary, North Carolina, the world's largest closely held software company, you're unlikely to quit to take a better job with a competitor. Under the leadership of entrepreneur and co-founder James H. Goodnight, SAS offers impressive benefits. Goodnight says, "I like happy people." Headquarters employees have a free health clinic, a recreation facility, daily performances by musicians during lunch, and private offices. SAS promotes families by offering flexible hours, a 35-hour work schedule, and two on-site day-care centers. Employees get an extra week of paid vacation over the Christmas holiday and receive a year-end bonus and profit sharing. Not surprisingly, SAS's turnover is a low 4 percent.

Question: What criteria will you use when screening potential employers for your next full-time job?

Organizational Purpose, Mission, and Strategy

The core *purpose* of an organization may be stated as the creation of goods or services for customers. Nonprofit organizations produce services with public benefits, such as health care, education, judicial processing, and highway maintenance. Large and small for-profit businesses produce consumer goods and services such as automobiles, banking, travel, gourmet dining, and accommodations. *Missions* and *mission statements* focus the attention of organizational members and external constituents on the core purpose.[8] For example, the pharmaceutical giant Merck states that its purpose is to "discover, develop, manufacture and market a broad range of innovative products to improve human and animal health." The Maytag Corporation's mission is "to improve the quality of home life by designing, building, marketing and servicing the best appliances in the world." Apple Computer, Inc., says that its mission is "bringing the best possible personal computing experience to students, educators, creative professionals, businesses and consumers around the world."[9] These and other mission statements are written to communicate to employees, customers, and other audiences a clear sense of the domain in which the organization's products and services fit, as well as a vision and sense of future aspiration.[10] As Robert Reich states in his description of the company of the future: "Talented people want to be part of something that they can believe in, something that confers meaning on their work, on their lives—something that involves a mission."[11]

Given a sense of purpose and a vision, organizations pursue *strategies* to accomplish them. A **strategy** is a comprehensive plan that guides organizations to operate in ways that allow them to outperform their competitors. The variety of mergers, acquisitions, joint ventures, global alliances, and even restructurings and divestitures found in business today are examples of corporate strategies to achieve and sustain advantage in highly competitive environments. In this challenging context however, strategic management responsibilities always include

Strategy guides organizations to operate in ways that outperform competitors.

executive leadership in both formulating and implementing strategies.[12] Although all organizations need good strategies, strategy alone is no guarantee of success; sustainable high performance is achieved only when strategies are well implemented. And, it is in respect to implementation that a knowledge of organizational behavior is especially important. After all, things happen in organizations because people working individually and in groups make them happen. Armed with an understanding of the dynamics of behavior in organizations provided by OB, managers are well prepared to mobilize and activate human capital and talents to fully implement strategies.

Organizational Environments and Stakeholders

Open systems transform human and material resource inputs into finished goods and services.

Today's strategic emphasis on customer-driven and market-driven organizations places great significance on the relationship between an organization and its external environment. As shown in Figure 1.2, organizations are dynamic **open systems** that obtain resource inputs from the environment and transform them into finished goods or services that are returned to the environment as outputs. If everything works right, customers and clients in the environment value the organization's outputs and create a continuing demand for them; suppliers value the organization as their customer and continue to provide needed resources; employees value their work opportunities and continue to infuse the transformation processes with their energies and intellects. All of this allows the organization to sustain operations and, hopefully, prosper over the long run. But if and when any aspect of this value chain breaks down, an organization's performance can suffer and its livelihood may become threatened. In the extreme case, as well illustrated by corporate ethics scandals that beset the once highly regarded accounting giant Arthur Andersen, it can even be forced out of existence. [13]

Stakeholders are people and groups with an interest or "stake" in the performance of the organization.

One way to describe and analyze the complex environment of organizations is in terms of **stakeholders**—people, groups, and institutions that are affected

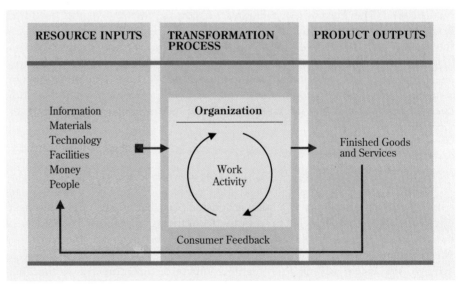

Figure 1.2   Organization and environment relationships.

by and thus have an interest or "stake" in an organization's performance. It is common in OB to recognize customers, owners, employees, suppliers, regulators, and local communities among the key stakeholders of organizations. In stakeholder analysis, an important question becomes: What do the various stakeholders want? Ideally, an organization should operate in ways that best serve the interests of all stakeholders. But, the reality is that conflicting interests among multiple stakeholders often create challenges for organizational decision makers. For example, customers increasingly want value pricing and high-quality products; owners are concerned about profits and returns on investments; employees are concerned about jobs, security, and employment conditions; suppliers are interested in contracts and on-time payments; regulators are interested in legal compliance; and local communities are concerned about organizational citizenship and community support.

ETHICS AND SOCIAL RESPONSIBILITY

GIVING BACK TO COMMUNITY: THE REAL TEST OF RESPONSIBILITY

With all the worry about outsourcing and the loss of jobs to foreign countries, you would think that corporate executives would be worrying about their home communities. It might do them well to remember the Ben & Jerry's story. When starting their firm years ago in Burlington, Vermont, Ben Cohen and Jerry Greenfield did more than focus on making and selling high-quality ice cream with all-natural ingredients. They made a commitment to their community, beginning with buying as much as possible from Vermont dairy farmers. Even when they first sold stock to raise capital for expansion, Vermonters were given first preference. They called their model "caring capitalism" and set up a foundation to support social change, funded by 7.5 percent of the firm's pre-tax profits.

Question: What do you think—should companies redefine "success" to mean community welfare plus business profits?

Organizational Cultures and Diversity

In the internal environment of organizations, the shared beliefs and values that influence the behavior of organizational members create what is called the **organizational culture**.[14] As discussed further in Chapters 2 and 19, organizations with "strong cultures" operate with a clear vision of the future that is supported by well-developed and well-communicated beliefs and values. The internal environments of organizations with strong and positive cultures typically include a high performance orientation, emphasis on teamwork, encouragement of risk taking, and emphasis on innovation.[15] They also display an underlying respect for people and for **workforce diversity**—the presence of individual differences based on gender, race and ethnicity, age, able-bodiedness, and sexual orientation.[16] *Valuing diversity* is a core OB theme that is central to this book and criti-

Organizational culture is the shared beliefs and values that influence the behavior of organizational members.

Workforce diversity involves differences based on gender, race and ethnicity, age, able-bodiedness, and sexual orientation.

THE EFFECTIVE MANAGER 1.1

How to Make Diversity Stick

- Focus on getting the best talent.
- Develop career plans for all employees.
- Provide career mentoring by diversity cohorts.
- Promote minorities to responsible positions.
- Maintain accountability for diversity goals.
- Make diversity part of organizational strategy.
- Build diversity into senior management.

cal to the new workplace.[17] In organizational cultures that fully value diversity, one would expect to find management priorities and practices such as those described in The Effective Manager 1.1. Such practices help build an internal climate of inclusiveness, one that respects diversity and provides opportunities for all members, not just a privileged few. Members of such organizations are skilled at working successfully with people from different racial and ethnic backgrounds, of different ages and genders, different ethnic and national cultures, and different life styles.

Organizational Effectiveness

Organizational effectiveness is sustainable high performance in accomplishing mission and objectives.

The concept of **organizational effectiveness** is used in OB as an indicator of how well organizations perform as the open systems described in Figure 1.2. The analysis of performance, however, can be done from different perspectives.[19] The *systems resource approach* looks at the input side of the figure and defines effectiveness in terms of success in acquiring needed resources from the organization's external environment. The *internal process approach* looks at the transformation process and examines how efficiently resources are utilized to produce goods and/or services. The *goal approach* looks at the output side to measure achievement of key operating objectives such as product quality, innovation, and profits. And the *strategic constituencies approach* analyzes the impact of the organization on key stakeholders and their interests.

When evaluating organizational effectiveness, furthermore, it is also necessary to consider short-term and longer-term performance considerations.[20] In the short run, the performance assessment often focuses on effectiveness in goal accomplishment and efficiency in resource utilization, as well as stakeholder satisfaction—including customers, employees, owners, and society at large. Over a slightly longer time frame, the organization's ability to adapt to changing environmental conditions and its ability to develop people and systems to meet new challenges gain importance. In the long run, the primary criterion of organizational effectiveness becomes survival under conditions of environmental uncertainty. And, an important contributor to the effectiveness of any organization is the quality of its management.

Organizational Behavior and Management

Managers are formally responsible for supporting the work efforts of other people.

Regardless of your career direction, the field of organizational behavior will someday become especially important as you try to master the special challenges of working as a **manager**. In all organizations, managers perform jobs that involve directly supporting the work efforts of others. Being a manager is a unique challenge that carries distinct performance responsibilities. Managers help other people get important things done in timely, high-quality, and personally satisfying ways. In the new workplace, this is accomplished more through "helping" and "supporting" than through traditional notions of "directing" and "control-

Research Insight
Women Might Make Better Leaders

No one doubts there are good and bad leaders of both genders. But research by Alice Eagley and her colleagues at Northwestern University suggests that women may be more likely than men to use leadership styles that result in high performance by followers. In a meta-analysis of 45 studies dealing with male and female leadership styles, the researchers found that women are more likely than men to lead by inspiring, exciting, mentoring, and stimulating creativity. These behaviors have "transformational" qualities that build stronger organizations through innovation and teamwork. Women also score higher on rewarding positive performance,

POSSIBLE LEADERSHIP STRENGTHS OF WOMEN

- More "transformational"
- Good at mentoring
- Very inspiring
- Encourage creativity
- Show excitement about goals
- Reward positive performance

while men score higher in punishing and correcting mistakes. Eagley and her colleagues explain these findings in part by the fact that followers are more accepting of a transformational style when the leader is female and that the style comes more naturally to women because of its emphasis on nurturing. They also suggest that because women may have to work harder than men to succeed, their leadership skills are better developed.

Reference: Alice H. Eagley, Mary C. Johannesen-Smith, and Marloes L. van Engen, "Transformational, Transactional and Laissez-Faire Leadership Styles: A Meta-Analysis Comparison," *Psychological Bulletin* 124(4): 2003, 569–591.

ling." Indeed, the word "manager" is increasingly being linked in the new workplace to roles described by such titles as "coordinator," "coach," or "team leader."

The Management Process

An **effective manager** is one whose organizational unit, group, or team consistently achieves its goals while members remain capable, committed, and enthusiastic. This definition focuses attention on two key results. The first is **task performance**—the quality and quantity of the work produced or the services provided by the work unit as a whole. The second is **job satisfaction**—how people feel about their work and the work setting. Just as a valuable machine should not be allowed to break down for lack of proper maintenance, the performance contributions of human resources should never be lost or compromised for lack of proper care. Accordingly, OB directs a manager's attention to such matters as job satisfaction, job involvement, and organizational commitment, as well as measures of actual task performance.

The job of any manager or team leader is largely one of adding value to the work setting by doing things that help others to accomplish their tasks. A traditional and still relevant way of describing this job is as a set of tasks or functions performed constantly and often simultaneously. As shown in Figure 1.3, these four functions of management are planning, organizing, leading, and controlling. They form a framework for managerial action that can be described as follows:[21]

An **effective manager** is one whose team consistently achieves high-performance goals.

Task performance is the quantity and quality of work produced.

Job satisfaction is a positive feeling about one's work and work setting.

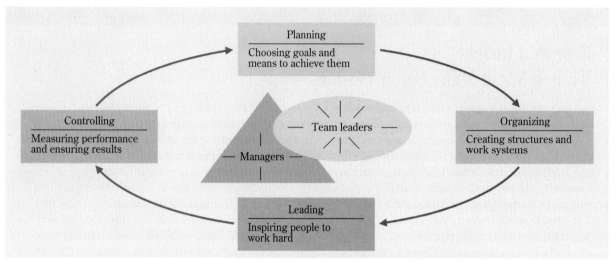

Figure 1.3   The management process of planning, organizing, leading, and controlling.

Four functions of management

Planning sets objectives and identifies the actions needed to achieve them.

Organizing divides up tasks and arranges resources to accomplish them.

Leading creates enthusiasm to work hard to accomplish tasks successfully.

Controlling monitors performance and takes any needed corrective action.

- **Planning**—defining goals, setting specific performance objectives, and identifying the actions needed to achieve them
- **Organizing**—creating work structures and systems, and arranging resources to accomplish goals and objectives
- **Leading**—instilling enthusiasm by communicating with others, motivating them to work hard, and maintaining good interpersonal relations
- **Controlling**—ensuring that things go well by monitoring performance and taking corrective action as necessary

The Nature of Managerial Work

Anyone who serves as a manager or team leader assumes a unique responsibility for work that is accomplished largely through the efforts of other people. The result is a very demanding and complicated job that has been described by researchers in the following terms.[22] Managers work long hours. A workweek of more than the standard 40 hours is typical. The length of the workweek tends to increase as one advances to higher managerial levels; heads of organizations often work the longest hours. Managers are busy people. Their work is intense and involves doing many different things on any given workday. The busy day of a manager includes a shifting mix of incidents that require attention, with the number of incidents being greatest for lower-level managers. Managers are often interrupted. Their work is fragmented and variable; many tasks must be completed quickly; and managers work mostly with other people. In fact, they spend little time working alone. Time spent with others includes working inside the organization with bosses, peers, subordinates, and subordinates of their subordinates. Externally, it includes working with outsiders such as customers, suppliers, and the like. Managers are communicators. Managers spend a lot of time getting, giving, and processing information in both face-to-face and electronic communications. They participate in frequent formal and informal meetings, with higher-level managers typically spending more time in scheduled meetings.

Managerial Roles, Networks, and Mind-Sets

In what has become a classic study of managerial behavior, Henry Mintzberg moved beyond this functional approach to describe what managers do. He identified 10 roles, falling into three categories, as shown in Figure 1.4, that managers must be prepared to perform on a daily basis.[23] The *interpersonal roles* involve working directly with other people. They include hosting and attending official ceremonies (figurehead), creating enthusiasm and serving people's needs (leader), and maintaining contacts with important people and groups (liaison). The *informational roles* involve exchanging information with other people. They include seeking out relevant information (monitor), sharing relevant information with insiders (disseminator), and sharing relevant information with outsiders (spokesperson). The *decisional roles* involve making decisions that affect other people. They include seeking out problems to solve and opportunities to explore (entrepreneur), helping to resolve conflicts (disturbance handler), allocating resources to various uses (resource allocator), and negotiating with other parties (negotiator).

Good interpersonal relationships are essential to success in these roles and to all managerial work. Managers and team leaders should be able to develop, maintain, and work well with a wide variety of people, both inside and outside the organization.[24] They must seek out and work with others in task networks (of specific job-related contacts), career networks (of career guidance and opportunity resources), and social networks (of trustworthy friends and peers).[25]

Recently, Henry Mintzberg and his colleague Jonathon Gosling asked another question: What does it mean to think like a manager?[26] They raise this question because of the inherent complexity of managerial work and with the goal of helping managers develop attitudes and ways of thinking that can im-

Adena Health System

To fill staff shortages in critical skill areas, Adena Health System offers employees an innovative educational option—free books and tuition, plus full salary and benefits. Employees pay back with three years employment for each year they spend in school.

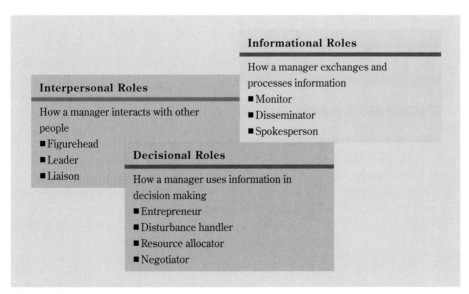

Interpersonal Roles

How a manager interacts with other people
- Figurehead
- Leader
- Liaison

Informational Roles

How a manager exchanges and processes information
- Monitor
- Disseminator
- Spokesperson

Decisional Roles

How a manager uses information in decision making
- Entrepreneur
- Disturbance handler
- Resource allocator
- Negotiator

Figure 1.4   Ten roles of effective managers.

▓▓ A **managerial mind-set** is an attitude or frame of mind about management.

prove their effectiveness. Based on their experience, Mintzberg and Gosling define a **managerial mind-set** as "an attitude, a frame of mind that opens up new vistas.[27] They also describe five mind-sets as important to success in managerial work—reflective, analytic, worldly, collaborative, and action. An organization achieves its common purpose, say Gosling and Mintzberg, when its "managers collaborate to combine their reflective actions in analytic, worldly ways."[28] All five mind-sets must work together, ideally being interwoven in the daily stream of managerial decisions.

Five mind-sets of managers.

The *reflective mindset* deals with being able to manage oneself.
The *analytic mindset* deals with managing organizational operations and decisions.
The *worldly mind-set* deals with managing in the global context.
The *collaborative mind-set* deals with managing relationships.
The *action mind-set* deals with managing change.

Managerial Skills and Competencies

A skill is an ability to translate knowledge into action that results in a desired performance. Robert Katz divides the essential managerial skills into three categories: technical, human, and conceptual.[29] He further suggests that the relative importance of these skills varies across the different levels of management. Technical skills are considered more important at entry levels of management, where supervisors and team leaders must deal with job-specific problems. Senior executives are concerned more with issues of organizational purpose, mission, and strategy. Broader, more ambiguous, and longer-term decisions dominate attention at these higher levels, and conceptual skills gain in relative importance. Human skills, which are strongly grounded in the foundations of organizational behavior, are consistent in their importance across all managerial levels.

▓▓ **Technical skill** is an ability to perform specialized tasks.

Technical Skills   A **technical skill** is an ability to perform specialized tasks. Such ability derives from knowledge or expertise gained from education or experience. This skill involves proficiency at using select methods, processes, and procedures to accomplish tasks. Perhaps the best current example is skill in using the latest communication and information technologies. In the high-tech workplaces of today, technical proficiency in word processing, database management, spreadsheet analysis, e-mail, and communications networks is often a hiring prerequisite. Some technical skills require preparatory education, whereas others are acquired through specific training and on-the-job experience.

▓▓ **Human skill** is the ability to work well with other people.

Human Skills   Central to managerial work and team leadership are **human skills**, or the ability to work well with other people. They emerge as a spirit of trust, enthusiasm, and genuine involvement in interpersonal relationships. A person with good human skills will have a high degree of self-awareness and a capacity for understanding or empathizing with the feelings of others. People with this skill are able to interact well with others, engage in persuasive communications, deal successfully with disagreements and conflicts, and more.

▓▓ **Emotional intelligence** is the ability to manage oneself and one's relationships effectively.

An important new emphasis in this area of human skills is **emotional intelligence** (EI), defined by Daniel Goleman as the ability to understand and deal with emotions. EI, with its emphasis on managing emotions both personally and in relationships with others, is now considered an important leadership competency.[30] Goleman's research suggests that a leader's emotional intelligence contributes significantly to his or her leadership effectiveness. Important dimensions of emotional intelligence that can and should be developed by any manager are shown in The Effective Manager 1.2. Human skills such as EI are indispensable in the new age of organizations, where traditions of hierarchy and vertical structures are giving way to lateral relations and peer structures.

Conceptual Skills   All good managers are able to view the organization or situation as a whole and to solve problems to the benefit of everyone concerned. This capacity to analyze and solve complex and interrelated problems is a **conceptual skill**. It involves the ability to see and understand how the whole organizational system works and how the parts are interrelated. Conceptual skill is used to identify problems and opportunities, gather and interpret relevant information, and make good problem-solving decisions that serve the organization's purpose.

> **THE EFFECTIVE MANAGER 1.2**
> ## Developing Your Emotional Intelligence
> - Self-awareness—ability to understand your own moods and emotions
> - Self-regulation—ability to think before acting and control disruptive impulses
> - Motivation—ability to work hard and persevere
> - Empathy—ability to understand the emotions of others
> - Social skill—ability to gain rapport with others and build good relationships

Conceptual skill is the ability to analyze and solve complex problems.

Learning About Organizational Behavior

Learning is usually defined as an enduring change of behavior that results from experience. Our new and rapidly developing knowledge-based economy places a great premium on learning by organizations as well as individuals. Only the learners, so to speak, will be able to maintain the pace and succeed in a constantly changing environment. Consultants and scholars emphasize **organizational learning** as the process of acquiring knowledge and utilizing information to adapt successfully to changing circumstances.[31] Organizations must be able to change continuously and positively while searching for new ideas and opportunities. The same is true for each of us. Individually, we must also pursue continuous improvement to achieve career success in a dynamic and complex environment.

Learning is an enduring change in behavior that results from experience.

Organizational learning is the process of acquiring knowledge and using information to adapt successfully to changing circumstances.

CULTURES AND THE GLOBAL WORKFORCE

GAP LEARNS THAT TRANSPARENCY IS BEST APPROACH TO FOREIGN FACTORIES

U.S. apparel retailers often find themselves criticized for poor working conditions and human rights violations in the foreign factories that make their products. The Gap, Inc., which contracts with suppliers in more than 50 countries, has felt the sting of such complaints. But the firm has also learned from its experience. It recently released a report card that describes problems at some of its factories. Among the findings were: 10 to 25 percent of factories of

its Chinese suppliers had problems with physical coercion or verbal abuse; 50 percent or more in sub-Saharan Africa had plant safety problems. Gap cut contracts with 136 factories; it is also investing in training and development to train factory managers in better practices. Activist groups have called its report "a major step forward" in efforts to improve working conditions in foreign factories.

Question: What examples can you find of successes and failures with organizational learning?

Learning and Experience

Your learning about OB only begins with the pages of this book. It will continue in the future as you benefit more from actual work experiences. The challenges of learning from both classroom and experience are substantial enough that it is worth considering how to derive maximum advantages from them.

Figure 1.5 shows how the content and activities of the typical OB course fit together as part of an experiential learning cycle.[32] The learning sequence begins with initial experience and subsequent reflection. It builds further as theory building takes place to try to explain what has happened. This theory is then tested in future behavior. *OB/9E* and your course activities should complement one another and help you move through the phases of this learning cycle. With practice, you can make it part of your personal commitment to continued personal and career development. This figure assigns you a substantial responsibility for learning. Along with your instructor, we can offer examples, cases, and exercises to provide you with initial experience. We can even stimulate your reflection and theory building by presenting concepts and discussing their research and practical implications. Sooner or later, however, you must become an active

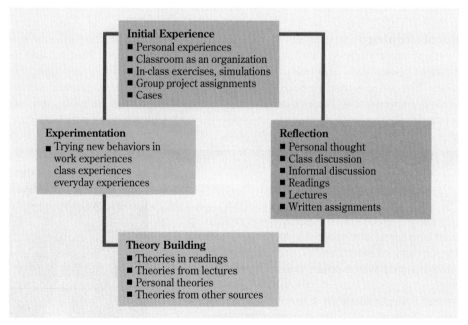

Figure 1.5   Experiential learning in an OB course.

participant in the process; you and only you can do the active experimentation required to complete the learning cycle.

Lifelong learning is a popular concept these days, and the message is relevant. You can and must learn continuously from day-to-day work experiences, conversations with colleagues and friends, counseling and advice from mentors, success models, training seminars and workshops, and the information available in the popular press and mass media. This book contains a special section, the *OB Skills Workbook*, designed specifically to help you with this process. Included in the workbook are many opportunities for you, individually and in study groups, to analyze readings and cases, participate in experiential exercises, and complete skills-assessment inventories to advance your learning. The OB in Action feature at the end of each chapter guides you to the workbook and learning activities that fit the chapter themes and content.

Learning Guide to *Organizational Behavior 9/E*

The parts and chapters in *Organizational Behavior 9/E* progress logically in the following order. *Part 1* introduces the discipline and context of OB—including current issues and the implications of globalization. *Part 2* and *Part 3* provide in-depth explorations of theories and concepts relating to individual and group behavior in organizations. *Part 4* focuses on leadership and the processes of OB—including power and politics, information and communication, decision making, conflict and negotiation, change and stress. *Part 5* examines the nature of organizations themselves—including structures, designs, and cultures. As you proceed now with your study of organizational behavior, remember:

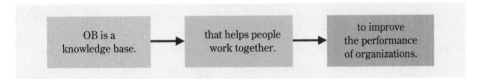

OB is a knowledge base. → that helps people work together. → to improve the performance of organizations.

Chapter 1   Study Guide

What is organizational behavior and why is it important?

Summary

- Organizational behavior is the study of individuals and groups in organizations.

- OB is an applied discipline based on scientific methods that uses a contingency approach, recognizing that management practices must fit the situation.

- Dramatic changes signal the emergence of a new workplace with high-technology, global competition, demanding customers, high-performance systems, and concerns for ethical behavior and social responsibility.

What are organizations like as work settings?

- An organization is a collection of people working together in a division of labor for a common purpose—to produce goods or services for society.

- As open systems, organizations interact with their environments to obtain resources that are transformed into outputs returned to the environment for consumption.

- The resources of organizations are material—such as technology, capital, and information, as well as human—the people who do the required work.

- Organizations pursue strategies that facilitate the accomplishment of purpose and mission; the field of OB is an important foundation for effective strategy implementation.

- Key stakeholders in the external environments of organizations include customers, owners, suppliers, regulators, local communities, and employees.

- The organizational culture is the internal "personality" of the organization, including the beliefs and values that are shared by members.

- Positive organizational cultures place a high value on inclusiveness of all members, showing respect for all aspects of workforce diversity.

- Organizational effectiveness can be measured from different perspectives, including the systems resource, internal process, goal, and strategic constituencies approaches.

What is the nature of managerial work?

- Managers in the new workplace are expected to act more like "coaches" and "facilitators" than as "bosses" and "controllers."

- An effective manager is one whose work unit, team, or group accomplishes high levels of performance that are sustainable over the long term by enthusiastic workers.

- The four functions of management are (1) planning—to set directions, (2) organizing—to assemble resources and systems, (3) leading—to create workforce enthusiasm, and (4) controlling—to ensure desired results.

- Managers fulfill a variety of interpersonal, informational, and decisional roles while working with networks of people both inside and outside of the organization.

- Managers should understand and be comfortable with five mind-sets that guide and activate their work: collaborative, action, reflective, worldly, and analytic.

- Managerial performance is based on a combination of essential technical, human, and conceptual skills.

How do we learn about organizational behavior?

- Learning is an enduring change in behavior that results from experience.

- Organization learning is the process of acquiring knowledge and utilizing information to adapt successfully to changing circumstances.

- Most organizational behavior courses use multiple methods and approaches that take advantage of the experiential learning cycle.

- True learning about organizational behavior involves more than just reading a textbook; it requires a commitment to continuous and lifelong learning from one's work and everyday experiences.

Key Terms

Conceptual skill (p. 15)
Contingency approach
  (p. 5)
Controlling (p. 12)
Effective manager (p. 11)
Emotional intelligence
  (p. 14)
Human skill (p. 14)
Job satisfaction (p. 11)
Leading (p. 12)

Learning (p. 15)
Managerial mind-set (p. 14)
Managers (p. 10)
Open system (p. 8)
Organizational behavior
  (p. 3)
Organizational culture
  (p. 9)
Organizational
  effectiveness (p. 10)

Organizational learning
  (p. 15)
Organizations (p. 6)
Organizing (p. 12)
Planning (p. 12)
Stakeholders (p. 8)
Strategy (p. 7)
Task performance (p. 11)
Technical skills (p. 14)
Workforce diversity (p. 9)

Self-Test 1

Multiple Choice

1. Which of the following issues is most central to the field of organizational behavior? (a) ways to improve advertising for a new product (b) ways to increase job satisfaction and performance among employees (c) creation of new strategy for organizational growth (d) design of a new management information system

2. What is the best description of the setting facing organizational behavior today? (a) Command-and-control is in. (b) The new generation expects much the same as the old. (c) Empowerment is out. (d) Work–life balance concerns are in.

3. The term "workforce diversity" refers to differences in race, age, gender, ethnicity, and _____ among people at work. (a) social status (b) personal wealth (c) able-bodiedness (d) political preference.

4. Which statement about OB is most correct? (a) OB seeks "one-best-way" solutions to management problems. (b) OB is a unique science that has little relationship to other scientific disciplines. (c) OB is focused on using knowledge for practical applications. (d) OB is so modern that it has no historical roots.

5. In the open-systems view of organizations, such things as technology, information, and money are considered _____. (a) transformation elements (b) feedback (c) inputs (d) outputs

6. In strategic management, the discipline of organizational behavior is most essential in terms of _____. (a) developing strategies (b) clarifying mission statements (c) implementing strategies (d) identifying organizational purpose

7. A strategic constituencies analysis of organizational effectiveness would focus on evaluating _____. (a) long-term survival effectiveness (b) performance efficiency (c) stakeholder satisfactions (d) resource acquisition

8. Which of the following words best describes an organizational culture in which

workforce diversity is highly valued? (a) inclusive (b) effective (c) dynamic (d) predictable

9. The management function of _____ is concerned with creating enthusiasm for hard work among organizational members. (a) planning (b) motivating (c) controlling (d) leading

10. In the management process, _____ is concerned with measuring performance results and taking action to improve future performance. (a) disciplining (b) organizing (c) leading (d) controlling

11. A manager who is extremely skilled at developing and maintaining good working relationships with other people displays strength in what Gosling and Mintzberg call the _____ mind-set. (a) worldly (b) collaborative (c) action (d) reflective

12. According to current views of managerial work, it is highly unlikely that an effective manager will _____. (a) engage in extensive networking (b) have good interpersonal skills (c) spend a lot of time working alone (d) be good at solving problems

13. When a manager moves upward in responsibility, Katz suggests that _____ skills decrease in importance and the _____ skills increase in importance. (a) human, conceptual (b) conceptual, emotional (c) technical, conceptual (d) emotional, human

14. A person with high emotional intelligence would be strong in_____, the ability to think before acting and control disruptive impulses. (a) motivation (b) perseverance (c) self-regulation (d) empathy

15. Which statement about learning is *not* correct? (a) Learning is a change in behavior that results from experience. (b) People learn; organizations do not. (c) Experiential learning is common in OB courses. (d) Lifelong learning is an important personal responsibility for career development.

Short Response

16. What are the key characteristics of OB as a scientific discipline?

17. What does "valuing diversity" mean in the workplace?

18. What is an effective manager?

19. How would Henry Mintzberg describe a typical executive's workday?

Applications Essay

20. Carla, a college junior, is participating in a special "elementary education outreach" project in her local community. Along with other students from the business school, she is going to spend the day with fourth- and fifth-grade students and introduce them to the opportunities of going to college. One of her tasks is to lead a class of sixth graders in a discussion of the question: "How is the world of work changing today?" Help Carla out by creating an outline for her of the major points that she should try to develop with the students.

These learning activities from *The OB Skills Workbook* are suggested for Chapter 1.

CASE	EXPERIENTIAL EXERCISES	SELF-ASSESSMENTS
■ 1. Drexler's Bar-B-Que	■ 1. My Best Manager ■ 2. Graffiti Needs Assessment ■ 3. My Best Job	■ 1. Managerial Assumptions ■ 2. A Twenty-First-Century Manager

Plus—special learning experiences from *The Jossey-Bass/Pfeiffer Classroom Collection*

Chapter 2

Current Issues in Organizational Behavior

Chapter at a Glance

Society needs and deserves the best from our organizations. Chapter 2 examines current issues in organizational behavior to establish the high-performance context within which people and organizations are expected to contribute to our society. As you read Chapter 2, *keep in mind these study questions.*

WHAT IS A HIGH-PERFORMANCE ORGANIZATION?

- Stakeholders, Value Creation, and Customer Satisfaction
- Human Capital and Empowerment
- Learning and High-Performance Cultures

WHAT IS MULTICULTURALISM, AND HOW CAN WORKFORCE DIVERSITY BE MANAGED?

- Multiculturalism and Inclusivity
- Diversity Issues and Challenges
- Managing Diversity

HOW DO ETHICS AND SOCIAL RESPONSIBILITY INFLUENCE HUMAN BEHAVIOR IN ORGANIZATIONS?

- Moral Management and Ethics Mindfulness
- Ways of Thinking About Ethical Behavior
- Ethical Failures and Dilemmas
- Organizational Social Responsibility

WHAT ARE KEY OB TRANSITIONS IN THE NEW WORKPLACE?

- Corporate Governance and Ethics Leadership
- Quality of Work Life and Positive Organizational Behavior
- Globalization, Job Migration, and Organizational Transformation
- Personal Management and Career Planning

REVIEW IN END-OF-CHAPTER STUDY GUIDE

We live and work in an age of increasing global competition, new technologies, shifting demographics, and changing social values. A crucial reaction to these kinds of forces has been the emergence of a new breed of organization, the high-performance organization, or HPO. These are organizations intentionally designed to bring out the best in people and create an extraordinary capability that consistently delivers high-performance results. HPOs are fast, agile, and market driven. They emphasize respect for people, as evidenced by the involvement of workers and managers at all levels. Richard Kovacevic, former president and CEO of Wells Fargo, once said: "Our success has to do with execution...talented, professional, motivated people who care...that's our competitive advantage."[1]

The study of organizational behavior is a search for practical ideas on how to help organizations achieve high performance. Central to this search is a commitment to valuing the people who do the real work of organizations. Indeed, the needs, satisfactions, and growth of people should be

> **"Talented, professional, motivated people who care...that's our competitive advantage."**

at the top of any list of management and leadership priorities. OB scholar Jeffrey Pfeffer poses this challenge to leaders everywhere:[2]

The key to managing people in ways that lead to profits, productivity, innovation, and real organizational learning ultimately lies in how you think about your organization and its people.... When you look at your people, do you see costs to be reduced?... Or, when you look at your people do you see intelligent, motivated, trustworthy individuals—the most critical and valuable strategic assets your organization can have?

Organizations today operate in a social context that is unforgiving in its expectations for high performance while also being demanding in respect to ethical behavior and social responsibility. As they face new and sometimes very difficult times, leaders of organizations aspiring to high performance must understand the new significance of an old concept: the keys to meeting these challenges rest with the intellect, talents, experience, and commitments of their members[3]

High-Performance Organizations

There is no doubt that developments over the last few years have brought about many significant changes in organizations and in the ways in which people work.[4] We have become reacquainted with the challenges of a struggling economy, experienced the stresses of organizations downsizing and restructuring, and become increasingly comfortable with an increasingly "Net-centric" world driven by electronic communication. As the forces of globalization continue to influence the world economy, we have had to face not just the opportunities of the global marketplace but problems of job losses to foreign countries. Unfortunately, we have also had to deal with a rash of ethics scandals that revealed wrongdoing by business executives and raised serious questions about the governance of large corporations. Yet, as always, one of the great strengths of our society, its institutions, and its people gives us confidence about the future—our ability to learn and to seek positive change. By facing challenges with transparency and public debate, we have a unique capacity for self-regulation and learning, using today's experiences to build a better tomorrow.

There is no doubt that truly progressive organizations are meeting the challenges of the new century by doing much more than simply cutting employees, utilizing new technologies, and joining the global economy.[5] They are changing the very essence of the way things get done, the settings in which people work, and the value delivered to customers and clients. We are well into an era that gives primacy to the **high-performance organization**—one that operates in a way that brings out the best in people and produces sustainable high-performance results while creating high quality-of-work-life environments.[6] These HPOs tend to share the five components listed below.[7] Each of these distinguishing features is well represented in the concepts, theories, and issues you will be studying throughout *OB/9e*. The question of the moment is: Are you ready to work, contribute, and provide leadership in organizations with these high-performance characteristics?

> ▮ **High-performance organizations** are designed to bring out the best in people and produce sustainable organizational results.

- Value people as human assets, respect diversity, and empower all members to fully use talents to advance organizational and personal performance
- Mobilize teams that build synergy from the talents of members and that have the freedom to exercise self-direction and initiative to maximize their performance contributions
- Utilize the latest in information and production technologies, achieving success in bringing people and technology together in a performance context
- Thrive on learning, with norms and cultures that encourage knowledge sharing and enable members to experience continuous growth and development
- Are achievement oriented, sensitive to the external environment, and focused on total quality management and being the best in delivering customer satisfaction

> **Characteristics of high-performance organizations**

Stakeholders, Value Creation, and Customer Satisfaction

Chapter 1 introduced **stakeholders** as the customers and clients, owners, suppliers, regulators, communities, and employees affected by an organization's performance.[8] The interests of key stakeholders can be described in terms of the organization's multiple responsibilities for **value creation**—the extent to which it satisfies the needs of these strategic constituencies. In respect to product outputs, for example, businesses create value for customers through product price and quality; for their owners, value is represented by realized profits and investment returns. In respect to inputs, businesses create value for suppliers through the benefits of long-term business relationships; value for communities derives from the citizenship displayed in using and contributing to public services and

> ▮ **Stakeholders** are the individuals, groups, and other organizations affected by an organization's performance.

> ▮ **Value creation** is the extent to which an organization satisfies the needs of strategic constituencies.

positive impact on the natural environment. And in respect to throughputs, businesses create value for employees through wages, satisfaction, and development opportunities through their work.

Today, perhaps more than ever before, organizations are being asked to operate in ways that create value for and satisfy the needs of these many stakeholders, even as they overlap and potentially conflict among one another. And importantly, it is only when organizations deliver quality products that satisfy customers and clients that they can hope to sustain performance success in highly competitive environments. Figure 2.1 expresses this notion in the form of an *upside-down pyramid* view of organizations. The figure focuses attention on value creation for customers and clients by placing them at the top of the organization. Managing from this point of view requires that workers operate in ways that deliver value to customers and clients; it requires that team leaders and middle managers do things that directly support these workers; and it requires that top managers clarify the organizational mission and objectives, set strategies, and make adequate resources available.[9]

This continues to be an age of **total quality management** (TQM)—management dedicated to ensuring that an organization and all of its members are committed to high-quality results, continuous improvement, and customer satis-

Total quality management is total commitment to high-quality results, continuous improvement, and meeting customer needs.

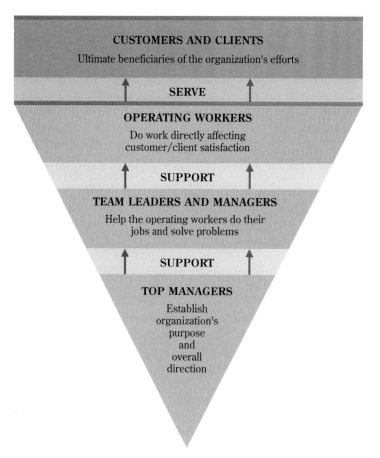

CUSTOMERS AND CLIENTS
Ultimate beneficiaries of the organization's efforts

SERVE

OPERATING WORKERS
Do work directly affecting customer/client satisfaction

SUPPORT

TEAM LEADERS AND MANAGERS
Help the operating workers do their jobs and solve problems

SUPPORT

TOP MANAGERS
Establish organization's purpose and overall direction

Figure 2.1   The upside-down pyramid view of organizations and management.

Leaders on Leadership

GREAT LEADERS TREAT EMPLOYEES AS THEIR CUSTOMERS

According to an interview with *BizEd* magazine, Southwest Airlines president and CEO, Colleen Barrett, believes success begins with leadership commitment to all employees. She says the firm has three types of customers: employees, passengers, and shareholders. Barrett says an important purpose is served by defining employees as customers: "If senior leaders regularly communicate with employees, if we're truthful and factual, if we show them that we care, and we do our best to respond to their needs, they'll feel good about their work environment and they'll be better at serving the passenger." Everyone is expected to be great at "TLC"— tender loving care for employees and customers. "We tell job applicants we're in the customer service business," says Barrett. "We just happen to provide airline transportation." Southwest is rich with leadership classes and seminars, outside speakers, meetings with senior managers, roundtable discussions, and brown-bag meetings with employees. Barrett describes herself as a mentor, willing to work with "anyone who seems to have a passion for what he or she does, or who has a desire to learn."

Question: If you adopt this view of employees as a leader's customers, what difference will it make in your behavior as a team leader or as the leader of a large company?

---

faction.[10] *Quality* in a TQM context means that customers' needs are met and that all tasks are done right the first time. An important hallmark of TQM is **continuous improvement**—the belief that anything and everything done in the workplace should be continually evaluated by asking two questions: (1) Is this necessary? (2) If so, can it be done better?[11]

Human Capital and Empowerment

Long-term performance success for any organization begins with strong foundations of **human capital**—the economic value of people with job-relevant abilities, knowledge, experience, ideas, energies, creativity, and dedication.[12] When managers give priority to human capital, they are recognizing that even in this age of high technology, people are indispensable resources. Only through human efforts can the great advantages be realized from other material resources of organizations such as technology, information, raw materials, and money.

Critical among the many players in our new economy are **knowledge workers**, people whose minds rather than physical capabilities become critical assets for organizations. Human capital in this respect becomes **intellectual capital** represented in the performance potential of the expertise, competencies, creativity, and commitment within an organization's workforce.[13] The primacy of intellectual capital is another hallmark of the high-performance organization. A

■ **Continuous improvement** is the belief that anything and everything done in the workplace should be continually improved.

■ **Human capital** is the economic value of people with job-relevant abilities, knowledge, ideas, energies, and commitments.

■ **Knowledge workers** use their minds rather than physical capabilities to bring value to organizations.

■ **Intellectual capital** consists of the expertise, competencies, and commitment of an organization's workforce.

Research Insight
Linking Employee Attitudes and Firm Performance

One of the important lines of inquiry in organizational behavior research has dealt with the relationship between work attitudes and performance. Recent research by Benjamin Schneider and his associates with aggregated organizational data indicates that the causal priorities in this relationship are complex and deserving of further research attention. Using longitudinal data collected from large companies during 1987–1995, they measured return on assets (ROA), earnings per share (EPS), and various components of job satisfaction. Analysis showed that satisfaction with pay and security and overall job satisfaction were related with subsequent firm performance. But also, firm performance appeared to cause overall job satisfaction and satisfaction with security. Schneider and colleagues interpret these results as indicating a complex relationship between employee attitudes

and firm performance that includes elements of reciprocity. They call attention to the abbreviated model shown in the accompanying figure. In this model, high-performance work practices (such as employee involvement, total quality management, and human resource systems) lead to better firm performance which leads to better working conditions (pay, benefits, reputation); better conditions create positive employee attitudes that encourage employee behaviors that contribute further to firm performance.

Reference: Benjamin Schneider, Paul. J. Hanghes, D. Brent Smith, and Amy Nicole Salvaggio, "Which Comes First: Employee Attitudes or Organizational Financial and Market Performance?" *Journal of Applied Psychology*, 88 (5)(2003): 836–851.

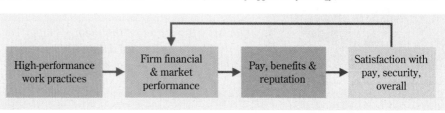

Empowerment allows people, individually and in groups, to use their talents to make decisions that affect their work.

Social capital is the performance potential represented in the relationships maintained among people at work.

Fortune magazine survey of America's most admired firms, for example, has gone so far as to report that "the single best predictor of overall success was a company's ability to attract, motivate, and retain talented people."[14] HPOs unlock intellectual capital through **empowerment** by allowing people, individually and in groups, to use their talents and know-how to make decisions that affect their work.

The value of people as human assets is also mobilized through **social capital**—the performance potential represented in the relationships maintained among people at work.[15] When relationships are strong, positive, genuine, and reciprocal, everyone involved gains performance advantages by working with others, not just alone. HPOs mobilize social capital through a commitment to teams and teamwork, arranging the flow of work around key business processes and then empowering teams to fully implement them. Focusing on teams, they achieve greater flexibility, internal coordination, innovation, and speed. They also use fewer levels of management and change the way managers operate. In team settings, managers become much less directive and instead emphasize coaching that facilitates teamwork and work results that meet customer expectations.[16]

Learning and High-Performance Cultures

As noted in the last chapter, our new and fast-paced world of uncertainty highlights the importance of *organizational learning*. It is a way for organizations to achieve positive adaptation through constant knowledge acquisition and utilization in change environments.[17] High-performance organizations are designed for organizational learning. They have value-driven organizational cultures that emphasize information sharing, teamwork, empowerment, participation, and learning. Importantly, the leaders of learning organizations set the example for others by embracing change and communicating enthusiasm to all members for solving problems and growing with new opportunities. About this leadership role, John Rogers, president of the international health and sciences firm MDS says: "We keep driving home the vision.... You can't lose sight of where you want to go.... You have to make sure you have the right people in the right positions."[18]

An important characteristic of any learning organization is a strong and positive culture, or internal climate, that values human capital and invigorates learning in a high-performance context. *Organizational culture* was discussed in Chapter 1, and is further discussed in Chapter 19, as a system of beliefs and values that shapes the attitudes of members, guides their behaviors at work, and influences their performance goals and aspirations.[19] In organizations with strong and positive cultures, the effect on members is substantial and enduring; in organizations with weak cultures, the effect is dispersed and less consequential.[20] High-performance organizations tend to be those that have cultures that provide members with a clear vision of the organization's purpose and goals, encourage learning and positive behaviors that support those goals, and discourage dysfunctional behaviors.[21]

Figure 2.2 shows an approach for mapping organizational cultures developed by Human Synergistics.[22] Using an instrument called the Organizational Culture Inventory, or OCI, people describe the behaviors and expectations that make up the prevailing cultures of their organizations.[23] The OCI mapsuse these results to describe three alternative types of organizational cultures: (1) In a *constructive culture*, members are encouraged to work together in ways that meet higher order human needs. (2) In a *passive/defensive culture*, members tend to

Whole Foods Market, Inc.

Whole Foods Market, Inc., has a compensation policy designed to encourage employees, or "team members," to feel in partnership with the firm. No executive can earn in salary and bonus more than 14 times what the average worker makes. Co-founder and CEO John Mackey says, "We have a philosophy of shared fate, that we're in this together."

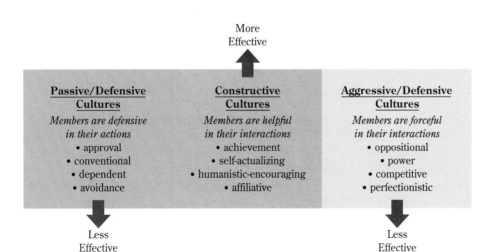

Figure 2.2 **Understanding organizational cultures: Insights from the Organizational Culture Inventory.** *Source:* This diagram is developed with permission from "The Organizational Culture Inventory," published by Human Synergistics International (Plymouth, Michigan).

act defensively in their working relationships, seeking to protect their security. (3) In an *aggressive/defensive culture*, members tend to act forcefully in their working relationships to protect their status and positions.

Among these three types of organizational cultures, the constructive culture would be most associated with the high-performance organization. In constructive cultures, researchers find that people tend to work with greater motivation, satisfaction, teamwork, and performance. In passive/defensive and aggressive/defensive cultures, motivation tends to be lower and work attitudes less positive.[24] The expectation is that people prefer constructive cultures and behave within them in ways that fully tap the value of human capital, promoting both high-performance results and personal satisfaction.

Multiculturalism and Diversity

Workforce diversity describes how people differ in such respects as age, race, ethnicity, gender, physical ability, and sexual orientation.

When it comes to the importance of human capital and positive cultures to high-performance organizations, the discussion naturally leads to a reconsideration of **workforce diversity**, first described in Chapter 1 as how people differ in such respects as age, race, ethnicity, gender, physical ability, and sexual orientation.[25] Rather than focus immediately on the notion of "difference," however, it is important to consider diversity in a broader perspective: we are all unique; thus, we are each different. And in this respect, author and consultant R. Roosevelt Thomas makes an important point when he says that "diversity includes everyone."[26] Thomas also suggests that when it comes to people and their diversity, positive organizational cultures tap the talents, ideas, and creative potential of all members.

Multiculturalism and Inclusivity

Multiculturalism refers to pluralism and respect for diversity in the workplace.

One of the major forces behind the growing diversity of the workforce is a strong demographic trend in American society.[27] In respect to gender differences, there are more women working than ever before in our history—almost 50 percent of the workforce is now female. And interestingly, 72 percent of women with children under the age of 18 are in the workforce.[28] In respect to racial and ethnic differences, the proportion of African-Americans, Hispanics, and Asians in the labor force is increasing. By the year 2060, projections are that people of color will constitute the majority of the U.S. population, with close to 30 percent of the population being Hispanic.[29]

Inclusivity is the degree to which the culture respects and values diversity and is open to anyone who can perform a job, regardless of their diversity attributes.

But although changing demographics may bring diversity to an organization's workforce, it does not guarantee that the diversity is fully valued, respected, and utilized. In OB, the term **multiculturalism** refers to pluralism and respect for diversity and individual differences in the workplace.[30] A key element in any organization that embraces multiculturalism is **inclusivity**—the degree to which the culture respects and values diversity and is open to anyone who can perform a job, regardless of their diversity attributes.[31] HPOs with positive organizational cultures that set high expectations of inclusion and respect for diversity, versus exclusion and disrespect, are best positioned to unlock the full potential of intellectual and social capital. In so doing, they also bring themselves into better alignment with the challenges and opportunities of the external environment. As Michael R. Losey, president of the Society for Human Resource Management (SHRM), says: "Companies must realize that the talent pool includes people of all types, including older workers; persons with disabilities; persons of various religious, cultural, and national backgrounds; persons who are not heterosexual; minorities; and women."[32]

Diversity Issues and Challenges

Notwithstanding the new demographics, and even though diversity is now widely discussed in our books and classrooms, much remains to be accomplished in our society in respect to inclusion and valuing diversity. In someone's place of employment, for example, what does it mean when individual differences are distributed unequally across organizational levels or among work functions? What are the implications of some members holding majority status while others are minorities in respect to representation with the organization? The daily work challenges faced by minority cultures or populations in organizations can range from having to deal with misunderstandings and lack of sensitivity on the one hand to suffering harassment and discrimination, active or subtle, on the other. In respect to race relations in the workplace, a *Fortune* magazine article once concluded: "The good news is, there's plenty of progress for companies and employees to talk about.... But what often doesn't get said, especially in mixed-race settings, is how much remains to get done."[33] A recent study revealed that when résumés are sent to potential employers, those with white-sounding first names, such as Brett, received 50 percent more responses than those with black-sounding first names, such as Kareem.[34]

The fact is that such bias can still be limiting factors in too many work settings. *Prejudice*, or the holding of negative, irrational opinions and attitudes regarding members of diverse populations, sets the stage for diversity bias in the workplace. Such bias can result in *discrimination* that actively disadvantages individuals by treating them unfairly and denying them the full benefits of organizational membership. Take a look at the situation described by Figure 2.3. It shows a potential **glass ceiling** effect—the existence of an invisible barrier or "ceiling" that prevents women and minorities from rising above a certain level of organizational responsibility.[35] Even though organizations are changing today, for example, most senior executives in large organizations are older, white, and male. There is still likely to be more workforce diversity at lower and middle levels of most organizations than at the top. How likely is it that minority members, such as women, persons of color, and gays and lesbians will have difficulty with career advancement in organizations traditionally dominated by a majority culture, such as heterosexual white males?

The discrimination that occurs under the glass ceiling effect can take additional forms. *Sexual harassment* in the form of unwanted sexual advances, requests for sexual favors, and other sexually laced communications is a problem female employees in particular may face. Minority workers can also be targets of *verbal abuse* in the form of cultural jokes. One survey reports that some 45 percent of respondents had been the targets of such abuse. And *pay discrimination* remains an issue in our society. A senior executive in the computer industry reported her surprise at finding out that the top performer in her work group, an African-American male, was paid 25 percent less than anyone else. This wasn't because his pay had been cut to that level, she said, but because his pay in-

Chubb Group

At this New Jersey insurance company, same-sex couples are given several days off to celebrate civil unions and domestic partnerships. The head of the firm's network of 120 gay and lesbian employees said the policy "has energized people like you wouldn't believe."

The **glass ceiling** is an invisible barrier preventing career advancements for women and minorities.

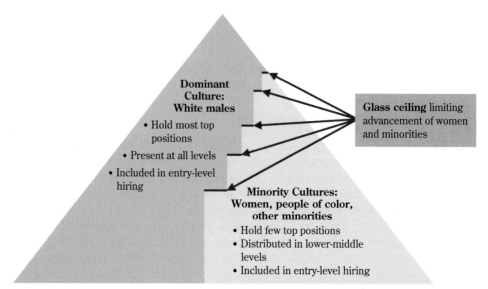

Figure 2.3   The glass ceiling effect as a barrier to career advancement of women and minorities. *Source*: John R. Schermerhorn Jr., *Management*, 8th ed. (Hoboken, NJ: John Wiley & Sons, 2005), p. 102. Used by permission.

creases over time had always trailed those given to his white co-workers. The differences added up significantly over time, but no one noticed or stepped forward to make the appropriate adjustment.[36]

Managing Diversity

The management and leadership implications of this discussion can be summed up in the concept of *managing diversity*. Thomas defines this as the process of comprehensively developing a work environment that is for everyone, that allows "all kinds of people to reach their full potential."[37] To help guide others in managing diversity, he poses these questions: (1) "What do I as a manager need to do to ensure the effective and efficient utilization of employees in pursuit of the corporate mission?" (2) "What are the implications of diversity for the way I manage?" When all managers can answer these questions positively, Thomas calls the organization "diversity mature." In such organizations, there is a diversity mission as well as an organizational mission; diversity is viewed as a strategic imperative and the members understand diversity concepts.[38] Ultimately, he considers the basic building block of a diversity-mature organization to be the *diversity-mature individual*—someone who can positively and honestly answer the questions posed in The Effective Manager 2.1.[39]

Business leaders today find that managing diversity makes good business sense as a strategic imperative, not just a legal and moral one. A diverse workforce offers a rich pool of talents, ideas, and viewpoints useful for solving the complex problems of highly competitive and often-uncertain environments. Well-managed workforce diversity increases human capital. Research reported in the *Gallup Management Journal*, for example, shows that establishing a racially and ethnically inclusive workplace is good for morale.[40] In a study of 2014 American workers, those who felt included were more likely to stay with their employers and recommend them to others. Survey questions asked such things as: "Do you always trust your company to be fair to all employees?" "At work, are all employees always treated with respect?" "Does your supervisor always make the best use of employees' skills?" An organizational culture of inclusivity counts both in terms of respect for people and in building organizational capacities for sustainable high performance.

A diverse workforce is also well aligned with the needs and expectations of a diverse customer and supplier base, including those increasingly distributed around the world and among its cultures. If you do the right things in organizational leadership, Thomas suggests, you will gain competitive advantage through diversity. If you don't, you'll lose it. This message is backed, with qualification, by recent research on the diversity and performance relationship. In a study of the business case for diversity, Thomas Kochan and his colleagues at MIT found that the presence of diversity alone does not guarantee a positive performance impact. Only when diversity is leveraged through training and supportive human resource practices are the advantages gained. The study offers this guidance:[41]

> ### THE EFFECTIVE MANAGER 2.1
> ### Are You Mature on Diversity?
>
> 1. Do you accept personal responsibility for improving your performance?
> 2. Do you accept personal responsibility for improving your organization's performance?
> 3. Do you understand yourself and your organization?
> 4. Do you understand important diversity concepts?
> 5. Do you make decisions involving differences based on ability to meet job requirements?
> 6. Do you understand that diversity is complex and accompanied by tensions?
> 7. Are you able to cope with complexity and tensions in addressing diversity?
> 8. Are you willing to challenge the way things are?
> 9. Are you willing to learn continuously?

> To be successful in working with and gaining value from diversity requires a sustained, systemic approach and long-term commitment. Success is facilitated by a perspective that considers diversity to be an opportunity for everyone in an organization to learn from each other how better to accomplish their work and an occasion that requires a supportive and cooperative organizational culture as well as group leadership and process skills that can facilitate effective group functioning.

Ethics and Social Responsibility

WORLDCOM FACING CHARGES OF FRAUD—HOW ENRON BOSSES CREATED A CULTURE OF PUSHING LIMITS—ANDERSEN'S WRONG TURNS GREW OBVIOUS—A 'STELLAR REPUTATION' SHATTERED.[42] Who can read such headlines or listen to news reports about failures by prominent businesses leaders without being concerned? The word "ethics" is important in OB, as it is to society at large.[43] We can generally agree that **ethical behavior** is that accepted as morally "good" and "right," as opposed to "bad" or "wrong," in a particular setting. But to agree on whether or not a specific action or decision is ethical is not always an easy matter. For example, is it ethical to withhold information that might discourage a well-qualified job candidate from joining your organization? Is it ethical to ask someone to take a job you know will not be good for his or her career progress? Is it ethical to ask so much of people that they continually have to choose between having a career and having a life? Although the list of such questions can go on and on, an important point remains: the public is demanding that people in organizations act in accordance with high moral standards.

■ **Ethical behavior** is morally accepted as "good" and "right."

Moral Management and Ethics Mindfulness

When it comes to morality, management scholar Archie B. Carroll draws a distinction between immoral managers, amoral managers, and moral managers.[44] The *immoral manager* doesn't subscribe to any ethical principles, making decisions and acting in any situation to simply take best personal advantage. This manager essentially chooses to behave unethically. One might describe the disgraced executives behind the earlier headlines on these terms. The *amoral manager*, by contrast, fails to consider the ethics of a decision or behavior. This manager acts unethically at times, but unintentionally. Common forms of unintentional ethics lapses that we all must guard against include prejudice that derives from unconscious stereotypes and attitudes, showing bias based on in-group favoritism, claiming too much personal credit for one's performance contributions, and favoring those who can benefit you.[45] Finally, the *moral manager* is one who incorporates ethics principles and goals into his or her personal behavior. For this manager, ethical behavior is a goal, a standard, and even a matter of routine.

Carroll believes that the majority of managers tend to act amorally, being well intentioned but often failing to take ethical considerations into account when taking action and making decisions. A review article by Terry Thomas and his colleagues suggests that this pattern most likely applies to the general membership of organizations.[46] They describe the "ethics center of gravity" shown in Figure 2.4 as one that can be moved positively through moral leadership—a "virtuous" shift—or negatively through amoral leadership. The authors also present the concept of **ethics mindfulness** as an "enriched awareness" that causes one to behave with an ethical consciousness from one decision or behavioral event to another. They describe a leader's responsibilities for communicating ethics values that help build organizational cultures within which ethics mindfulness is the norm. In this view, a moral manager or moral leader always acts as an ethical role model, communicates ethics values and messages, and champions ethics mindfulness. This results in the "virtuous shift" shown in the figure and an organizational culture within which people act ethically as a matter of routine.

▨ **Ethics mindfulness** is an enriched awareness that causes one to consistently behave with ethical consciousness.

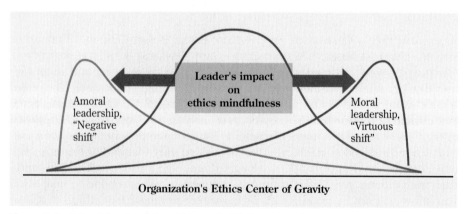

Figure 2.4   Moral leadership, ethics mindfulness, and the virtuous shift. *Source*: Developed from Terry Thomas, John R. Schermerhorn Jr., and John W. Dinehart, "Strategic Leadership of Ethical Behavior in Business," *Academy of Management Executive*, Vol. 18 (May 2004), pp. 56–66.

**MAKING PRINCIPLED DECISIONS
IN A HIGH-TECH WORLD**

Google! What a search engine and what a story. Founded in 1998 by Stanford graduate students Larry Page and Sergey Brin, the firm is now the premier global site for Web searches. Experiencing rapid growth and many new business opportunities, the firm hired Eric Schmidt as CEO to develop strategy and add business discipline. Schmidt says that no major decisions are made without at least two top people in agreement and that "we try to make decisions in as large a group as possible." He also reiterates his commitment to uphold the founders' goal of "do no evil." When an employee made a proposal to mine the firm's extensive information base in an "iffy" way for financial gain, it was turned down immediately. "No, that's completely counter to our principles, there's no way to do this, it's completely unacceptable," said the founders.

Question: If guiding "principles" are not clear from the top, how can you maintain a sense of personal ethics in business decision making?

Ways of Thinking about Ethical Behavior

Ethical behavior conforms not only to the dictates of law but also to a broader moral code that is common to society as a whole. But as suggested earlier, just exactly what moral code governs a person's decisions and actions is a subject of debate and disagreement. At least four ways of thinking about ethical behavior in and by organizations can be identified.[47] In the **utilitarian view**, ethical behavior is behavior that delivers the greatest good to the greatest number of people. Those who subscribe to the results-oriented utilitarian logic assess the moral aspects of their decisions in terms of the consequences they create. In utilitarianism, the needs of the many outweigh the needs of the few. From such a perspective, it may be ethical to close a factory in one town in order to keep the parent corporation profitable and operating in several other towns.

The **individualism view** considers ethical behavior as behavior that is best for an individual's long-term self-interests. In principle, at least, someone who acts unethically in the short run—such as by denying a qualified minority employee a promotion—should not succeed in the long run because the short-run actions will not be tolerated. Thus, if everyone operated with long-term self-interest in mind, their short-run actions would be ethical. By contrast, the **moral-rights view** considers ethical behavior to be behavior that respects the fundamental rights shared by all human beings. This view is tied very closely to the principle of basic human rights, such as those of life, liberty, and fair treatment by the law. In an organization, this principle is reflected in such issues as rights to privacy, due process, and freedom of speech. Ethical behavior does not violate any of these fundamental human rights.

The **justice view** considers behavior to be ethical when it is fair and impartial in the treatment of people. It is based on the concept of equitable treatment

■ In the **utilitarian view,** ethical behavior creates the greatest good for the most people.

■ In the **individualism view,** ethical behavior advances long-term self-interests.

■ In the **moral-rights view,** ethical behavior respects and protects human rights.

■ In the **justice view,** ethical behavior treats people impartially and fairly.

■■■ **Procedural justice** is the degree to which policies and procedures are properly followed.

■■■ **Distributive justice** is the degree to which all people are treated the same under a policy.

■■■ **Interactional justice** is the degree to which people are treated with dignity and respect.

■■■ An **ethical dilemma** requires a person to choose among actions that offer possible benefits while also violating ethical standards.

Ways to rationalize unethical behavior

for all concerned. In OB, two issues address this view of ethical behavior.[48] **Procedural justice** is the degree to which the rules and procedures specified by policies are properly followed in all cases to which they are applied. In a sexual harassment case, for example, this may mean that required formal hearings are held for every case submitted for administrative review. **Distributive justice** is the degree to which all people are treated the same under a policy, regardless of race, ethnicity, gender, age, or any other demographic characteristic. In a sexual harassment case, this might mean that a complaint filed by a man against a woman would receive the same consideration as one filed by a woman against a man. **Interactional justice** is the degree to which the people affected by a decision are treated with dignity and respect.[49] In a sexual harassment case, this may mean that both the accused and accusing parties believe they have received a complete explanation of any decision made.

Ethical Failures and Dilemmas

An **ethical dilemma** is a situation in which a person must decide whether or not to do something that—although benefiting him- or herself, or the organization, or both—may be considered unethical. It is difficult to predict exactly what ethical dilemmas you will someday face. However, research suggests that people at work often encounter such dilemmas in their relationships with superiors, subordinates, customers, competitors, suppliers, and regulators. Common issues underlying the dilemmas involve honesty in communications and contracts, gifts and entertainment, kickbacks, pricing practices, and employee terminations.[50] Unfortunately, persons caught up in such situations may find themselves behaving unethically and trying to justify it through use of these common rationalizations for ethical misconduct:[51]

- Pretending the behavior is not really unethical or illegal
- Excusing the behavior by saying it's really in the organization's or your own best interest
- Assuming the behavior is OK because no one else is expected to find out about it
- Presuming your superiors will support and protect you if anything should go wrong

The reality is that all of us will face ethical dilemmas. In one survey, 56 percent of respondents reported feeling pressured to act unethically in their jobs; 48 percent admitted that they had committed questionable acts within the past year.[52] Another survey, by the Ethics Resource Center, reports that some 44 percent of workers in the United States still fail to report the wrongdoing they observe at work. The top reasons for not reporting are "(1) the belief that no corrective action would be taken and (2) the fear that reports would not be kept confidential."[53] Personal values that give priority to such virtues as honesty, fairness, integrity, and self-respect provide *ethical anchors* that help people make correct decisions even when circumstances are ambiguous and situational pressures are difficult. In addition, many organizations now have *ethics codes* that spell out how employees are expected to behave in circumstances that may present ethical quandaries and dilemmas. More and more organizations are also offering *ethics training* to help employees learn how to handle situations that challenge them ethically. Sample guidelines for ethical decision making are offered in The Effective Manager 2.2.

Organizational Social Responsibility

Closely related to the ethics of workplace behavior is **social responsibility**—the obligation of organizations to behave in ethical and moral ways as institutions of the broader society.[54] This concept suggests that members must ensure that their ethical frameworks extend to the organization as a whole. Managers and leaders should commit organizations to actions that are consistent with both the quest for high productivity and the objective of corporate social responsibility.[55] Unfortunately, it doesn't always turn out this way.

Some years ago, for example, two Beechnut senior executives were sentenced to jail for their roles in a notorious case of organizational wrongdoing. The scandal involved the sale of adulterated apple juice for infants. Although the bottles were labeled "100% fruit juice," the contents turned out to be a blend of chemical ingredients. This case came to public awareness because of a **whistleblower**—someone within the organization who exposes the wrongdoing of others in order to preserve high ethical standards.[56] More recently we have had the Enron case.[57] Employees kept buying shares in the firm for their retirement accounts, unaware that a complex series of limited partnerships were creating financial instability. Those who lost most of their retirement savings when Enron went bankrupt are now probably wishing that someone had earlier "blown the whistle" on the firm's questionable practices. They had a right to expect, furthermore, that Enron's auditor, Arthur Andersen, would have disclosed these practices at the time. By failing to do so and thereby violating its public trust, Andersen—a long-standing and highly reputed accounting firm—lost credibility and went out of business when major customers canceled contracts with the firm.[58]

THE EFFECTIVE MANAGER 2.2
How to Deal with Ethical Dilemmas

1. Recognize and clarify the dilemma.
2. Get all the possible facts.
3. List all of your options.
4. Test each option by asking: Is it legal? Is it right? Is it beneficial?
5. Make your decision.
6. Double check your decision by asking the *spotlight questions*:
   a. How will I feel if my family finds out?
   b. How will I feel if this is printed in the newspaper?
7. Then, and only then, take action.

Social responsibility is the obligation of organizations to behave in ethical and moral ways.

A **whistleblower** exposes the wrongdoing of others.

Issues and Transitions in the New Workplace

The new economy is competitive, global, digital, Net-centric, and knowledge based. High-performance organizations in this economy are ones with leadership that understands new developments, sets high moral standards, unlocks the full productive potential of human capital, and embraces opportunities for creativity and innovation in the very organization of work itself. As we move forward now to study organizational behavior in this dynamic context, it is helpful to identify issues and transitions that presently influence people at work.

Corporate Governance and Ethics Leadership

Let there be no doubt about it—society is now very impatient with the perceived arrogance and lack of ethics among some business and government leaders. It is becoming strict in requiring businesses and other social institutions to operate according to high moral standards. On the regulatory side, the U.S. government has passed legislation that attempts to substitute for any lack of ethics leadership at the firm and industry levels.[59] The Sarbanes-Oxley Act of 2002 now makes it easier for corporate executives to be tried and sentenced to jail for financial misconduct. By law, businesses must also have boards of directors that are elected by stockholders to represent their interests.[60]

We have also witnessed the reemergence of interest in **corporate governance**, the active oversight of management decisions, corporate strategy, and financial reporting by boards of directors.[61] Many argue that corporate governance failed in cases like Enron and Andersen. The result is more emphasis today on restoring the strength of corporate governance in hiring, firing, and compensating CEOs; assessing business strategies; and verifying financial records. One board says that corporate governance "is really about setting and maintaining high standards."[62]

But even though its purpose is clear, reports on corporate governance are often critical on such matters as CEO pay. Complaints are that it is both too high and too often high when firms perform poorly.[63] All of this prompts renewed calls for **ethics leadership**, whereby business and organizational decisions are made with high moral standards that meet the ethical test of being "good," not "bad," and of being "right," not "wrong." A foundation for ethics in leadership, yours or anyone else's, is personal **integrity**.[64] It is displayed when people act in ways that are always honest and credible, and consistent in putting one's values into practice.

When a leader has integrity, he or she earns the trust of followers. And when followers believe leaders are trustworthy, they are willing to commit themselves to behave in ways that live up to the leader's expectations. Even though integrity may be listed among the core values espoused by organizations and be widely publicized in corporate mission statements, the real test is whether or not it is firmly embedded in organizational culture. Mere testimonies to ethics values are not enough; the values must be real, shared, modeled, and reinforced by leaders from top to bottom. At Tom's of Maine, for example, CEO Tom Chappell didn't hesitate to recall a new all-natural deodorant when customers were dissatisfied.[65] Even though it cost the company some $400,000, Chappell confidently did the "right" thing. His company is founded on values that include "fairness" and "honesty" and he lived up to them, even to the point of personally answering many telephone calls from customers.

Quality of Work Life and Positive Organizational Behavior

It is a natural extension of this discussion of corporate governance and ethics leadership to discuss the nature of the work climate that leaders and managers establish in organizations. A key question that should be asked of any employer is: What quality of work life does your organization provide the people upon whose labor its performance ultimately depends? In OB, the term **quality of work life**, or QWL, is used as a prominent indicator of the overall quality of human experience in the workplace.[66] A commitment to QWL can be considered a cornerstone value of organizational behavior. Theorists with a strong human orientation, such as Douglas McGregor, set the stage for this value very early in the life of the discipline.[67] He contrasted what he called *Theory X assumptions*—that people basi-

---

Corporate governance is the oversight of management decisions by boards of directors.

Ethics leadership is leadership with high moral standards.

Integrity involves acting honestly and credibly, with consistency.

Quality of work life is the overall quality of human experiences in the workplace.

cally dislike work, need direction, and avoid responsibility—with *Theory Y assumptions*—that people like work, are creative, and accept responsibility. For McGregor, Theory Y was the most appropriate; when people were treated well at work, he believed they would respond positively and as expected.

ETHICS AND SOCIAL RESPONSIBILITY

SOCIAL RESPONSIBILITY BEGINS WITH BUILDING A GREAT WORKPLACE

After learning that The Container Store made the list of *Fortune* magazine's list of "100 Best Companies to Work For" for the fifth straight year, CEO and co-founder Kip Tindell said: "We are so proud to foster a place where people enjoy getting up and coming to work every morning, working alongside great people—truly making a difference every single day." Tindell places credit for the firm's success on the employees, emphasizing the importance of offering them training, good pay, and equal treatment. All financial information about the company is shared with employees, full time and part time. Among other things, *Fortune* praised the firm for helping employees reduce stress.

Question: What are the top five items on your list of human resource practices that create a high quality-of-work-life environment?

Today the many concepts and theories discussed in OB reflect Theory Y themes. The hallmarks of excellence in management and organizations include *empowerment*—involving people from all levels of responsibility in decision making; *trust*—redesigning jobs, systems, and structures to give people more personal discretion in their work; *performance-based rewards*—building reward systems that are fair, relevant, and consistent, while contingent on work performance; *responsiveness*—making the work setting more pleasant and supportive of individual needs and family responsibilities; and **work–life balance**—making sure that the demands of the job are a reasonable fit with one's personal life and nonwork responsibilities.

A recent development in OB that builds from and extends these directions is known as **positive organizational behavior (POB)**. Scholar Fred Luthans defines POB as "the study and application of positively oriented human resource strengths and psychological capacities that can be measured, developed, and effectively managed for performance improvement in today's workplace."[68] Taking insight from the broader positive psychology movement,[69] he warns managers against negative perspectives that concentrate attention on people's weaknesses and the search for ways to fix what is wrong with them. Instead, he advocates positive practices that value human capacities and encourage their full utilization. Like McGregor's earlier work, POB focuses attention on the positive attributes of people that make living and working worthwhile, thus pushing the field of OB in a positive and promising direction.[70] The concept itself reinforces McGregor's inherent belief in people and the importance for leaders of building high-QWL work settings rich in human capital.[71] Specifically, Luthans directs the attention of managers and scholars alike toward core POB states such as *confidence, hope, optimism*, and *resilience*.

Work–life balance deals with the demands from one's work and personal affairs.

Positive Organizational Behavior is the study and application of positive human strengths and capacities for performance improvements.

These POB states are considered keys to high-performance systems and, importantly, Luthans suggests that these states can be nurtured through training and development; performance in organizations can be advanced when leaders develop these states personally and assist others to do so as well. The first task of a leader armed with POB insights is to build followers' *confidence* regarding their ability to achieve success on a task. The POB state of *hope* reflects belief in one's capacity to set goals and make plans for their achievement. In respect to *optimism*, the focus is on helping people to avoid pessimism and become more self-confident in experiencing and creating positive outcomes. Finally, *resilience* in POB involves the capacity for positive adaptation, for making dynamic adjustments to achieve progress even when facing setbacks and adversity.

Globalization, Job Migration, and Organizational Transformation

It wasn't too long ago that it seemed rather radical for Japanese management consultant Kenichi Ohmae to suggest that the national boundaries of world business were disappearing.[72] Today, even the most conservative among us would have to admit that they are at least fast disappearing. Who can state with confidence where their favorite athletic shoes or the parts for their personal computer were manufactured? More and more products are designed in one country, while their component parts are made in others and the assembly of the final product takes place in still another. Top managers at Toyota, IBM, Unilever, Nestlé, and other global corporations have no real need for the word "overseas" in everyday business vocabulary; they operate as global businesses in a global marketplace of customers, suppliers, and employees. All of this ties to the processes and forces of **globalization**, the worldwide interdependence of resource flows, product markets, and business competition that characterizes our new economy.[73] There is no escaping the fact that countries, cultures, and peoples around the world are increasingly interconnected. This is reflected in the news, in travel and lifestyles, in labor markets and employment patterns, and in business dealings, not just in the affairs of governments. And it has brought to each of us an appreciation of the diversity among global cultures.

Globalization is the worldwide interdependence of resource flows, product markets, and business competition that characterizes our new economy.

CULTURES AND THE GLOBAL WORKFORCE

FENG SHUI CONSULTANTS ADVISE ON OFFICE DESIGN

The ancient Chinese tradition of feng shui emphasizes the role of energy, or "chi," as an influence on our lives. Feng shui consultants are very popular now—just talk to executives at firms like Coca-Cola, Procter & Gamble, Ford, and more. The goal is to design one's work and living spaces to maximize good chi and minimize the bad. According to Zahjong Shen, founder of Feng Shui New York, the three C's of design according to feng shui are: clean, clear, and comfort. Among the feng shui principles in office layout and design are: don't sit with a window behind you; avoid clutter on desks; in a high-tech setting, decorate with pieces of nature; and try to get an office on the eighth floor—a number in Chinese that signifies wealth.

> *Question: What about the chi in your work and personal spaces—are you taking best advantage of "good" chi?*

Government leaders now worry about the competitiveness of nations just as corporate leaders worry about business competitiveness.[74] And in this respect, no issue looms larger than the growing implications of **job migration**, or the shifting of jobs from one country to another. A key aspect of this is **global outsourcing**, in which employers cut back domestic jobs and replace them with contract workers hired in other countries. An analysis of job losses in the United States over a three-month period, for example, identified that three out of ten layoffs were caused by global outsourcing; the remaining seven were the result of jobs being shifted to American sources.[75]

Job migration and global sourcing loomed large in the 2004 presidential campaigns for the United States, as both parties had to face voters concerned about the loss of both manufacturing and white-collar jobs to other countries. Countries like India, the Philippines, and Russia are among popular outsourcing destinations for the IT industry. Highly trained workers in these countries are available at as much as one-fifth the cost of an equivalent American worker. With the ease of communication made possible in the virtual workspaces of the Internet age, it is easy for employers to contract for work anywhere in the world the talent exists to perform it at the lowest price. The result is **organizational transformation**, as businesses, government institutions, and nonprofits alike react to globalization by redesigning themselves for high performance in a changed world. They are cutting employment and streamlining in the search for operational efficiencies; they are becoming more horizontal and flexible in structures; they are ever more virtual and technology driven; and their workforces are not just multicultural, they are globally dispersed. Such transformations are the reality of the new workplace, and we must each understand and prepare to best deal with them.

Job migration is the transferring of jobs from one country to another.

Global outsourcing occurs when domestic jobs are replaced with contract workers hired in other countries.

Organizational transformation is the redesign of organizations to streamline, gain flexibility, and utilize new technologies for high performance.

Personal Management and Career Planning

It is not only organizations that are being transformed; the nature of careers is changing, too. We are in the midst of what some call a *free-agent economy* in which more and more people contract their services to a shifting mix of employers over time.[76] British scholar and consultant Charles Handy describes the implications of what he calls the **shamrock organization**.[77] Each leaf of the shamrock represents a different group of people. The first leaf is a core group of workers made up of permanent, full-time employees with critical skills who follow standard career paths. The second leaf is a group of outside operators who are engaged contractually by the core group to perform a variety of jobs essential to the daily functioning of the organization. Many of these jobs are ones that would be performed by full-time staff (e.g., human resource personnel) in a more traditional organization. The third leaf is a group of part-timers who can be hired temporarily by the core group as the needs of the business grow and who can just as easily be let go when business needs decline. Today's college graduates must be prepared to succeed in the second and third leaves, not just the first.

Shamrock organizations operate with a core group of permanent workers supplemented by outside contractors and part-time workers.

■■■ **Personal management** is the ability to understand one's self individually and in the social context, and to continually learn from experience.

■■■ **Self-monitoring** is when a person observes and reflects on his or her behavior and adapts it to the situation.

In this challenging career setting, **personal management** becomes an essential skill. It is the ability to understand one's self individually and in the social context, to exercise initiative, to accept responsibility for accomplishments, to work well with others, and to continually learn from experience in the quest for self-improvement. Such understanding and discipline facilitates **self-monitoring**, in which a person makes the effort to observe and reflect on his or her own behavior and act in ways that adapt it to best fit the needs of the situation. One way to achieve improved self-awareness is by using structured assessment devices such as the Life Styles Inventory developed by Human Synergistics.[78] This particular inventory helps people gain insight into their ways of thinking and the behaviors they are likely to engage in when working with others. The goal is greater self-awareness that enables positive change in future behavior. Many similar learning resources are available to you in the end-of-book *OB Skills Workbook*.

An introductory course in organizational behavior offers great opportunities to explore your skills and capabilities and to engage in personal development activities that set strong foundations for future career readiness. But even as you take advantage of them, you must remember that one fact remains true in today's challenging times: what happens in your career is up to you. And there is no better time than the present to take charge of your learning and development. You must create, refine, and market what author and consultant Tom Peters has called the "brand called 'you'"—a unique and timely package of skills and capabilities. In his words, your personal brand should be "remarkable, measurable, distinguished, and distinctive" relative to the competition—others who want the same career opportunities that you do.[79]

Chapter 2   Study Guide

Summary

What is a high-performance organization?

- A high-performance organization is designed to bring out the best in people and achieve sustained high performance while creating high quality-of-work-life environments.

- The key components of HPOs include valuing people as human assets, mobilizing synergy from teams, utilizing appropriate technology, focusing on learning, and being customer driven.

- Customer-driven organizations that focus on customer service and product quality as foundations of competitive advantage can be viewed as upside-down pyramids where workers operate in ways directly affecting customers and managers directly support the workers.

- Total quality management deals with meeting the customer's needs, making sure all tasks are done right the first time, and emphasizing continuous improvement.

- Human capital in the form of the productive potential of people is a foundation for HPOs; both intellectual capital (the intellect and talents of people) and social capital (the value of working relationships) are major contributors to human capital.

- In organizations with strong and positive cultures, members behave with shared norms and beliefs that support high-performance goals.

What is multiculturalism, and how can workforce diversity be managed?

- Multicultural organizations operate with a commitment to pluralism and respect for diversity and individual differences.

- A key aspect to multiculturalism is inclusivity, the degree to which the culture respects and values diversity and is open to anyone who can perform a job, regardless of their diversity attributes.

- Diversity bias in organizations includes prejudice, in the form of negative attitudes, and discrimination—active disenfranchisement of minorities from rights of organizational membership.

- Challenges faced by diverse populations in the workplace include sexual harassment, pay discrimination, job discrimination, and the glass ceiling effect—a hidden barrier that limits career advancement by women and minorities.

- Managing diversity is the process of developing a work environment that is fully inclusive and allows everyone to reach his or her full work potential.

How do ethics and social responsibility influence human behavior in organizations?

- Ethical behavior is that which is accepted as morally "good" and "right" instead of "bad" or "wrong."

- Managers and people in organizations may be amoral—prone to unintentional ethical lapses; immoral—intentionally pursuing unethical courses of action; or moral—consistently acting according to ethics principles.

- Ethics leaders can create a virtuous shift in the ethics center of gravity of organizations and help members to develop ethics mindfulness as an "enriched awareness" that causes one to behave with an ethical consciousness from one decision or behavioral event to another.

- Ways of thinking about an ethical behavior include the utilitarian, individualism, moral-rights, and justice views.

- The workplace is a source of possible ethical dilemmas in which someone must decide whether or not to pursue a course of action that, although offering the potential for personal or organizational benefit or both, may be considered potentially unethical.

- Managers report that their ethical dilemmas often involve conflicts with superiors, customers, and subordinates over such matters as dishonesty in advertising and communications as well as pressure from their bosses to do unethical things.

- Common rationalizations for unethical behavior include believing the behavior is not illegal, is in everyone's best interests, will never be noticed, or will be supported by the organization.

- Corporate social responsibility is an obligation of the organization to act in ways that serve both its own interests and the interest of its many external publics, often called stakeholders.

- Whistleblowers actively expose wrongdoing in organizations and help further the obligations of organizations and their members to act in ethical ways.

What are key OB issues and transitions in the new workplace?

- In the wake of major ethics scandals, there is renewed emphasis in our society on corporate governance, the active oversight of management decisions, corporate strategy, and financial reporting by boards of directors.

- There are corresponding expectations for more ethics leadership, whereby business and organizational decisions are made with high moral standards, and for leaders to act with greater integrity by always being honest, credible, and consistent in putting values into practice.

- A historical value underlying the field of OB has been a commitment to fully valuing and respecting people as human beings and to building high quality-of-work-life environments for them.

- Positive organizational behavior is a new development that directs managerial attention toward nurturing confidence, hope, optimism, and resiliency as positive states that build individual performance capacities.

- The forces of globalization are bringing increased interdependencies among nations and economies as customer markets and resource flows create intense business competition.

- Job migration through global outsourcing of manufacturing and white-collar jobs is one of the areas of current concern and controversy; it is associated with organization transformations including workforce reductions, new structures, and creative use of technology in the quest for greater operating efficiencies.

- The new economy and organizational transformations are resulting in changes to the traditional notion of a career and employer–employee relationships; more people today are working as independent contractors rather than full-time employees.

- To sustain career success in our challenging times, everyone must engage in personal management to continually learn and improve from experiences and to build skill portfolios that are always up to date and valuable to employers challenged by the intense competition and opportunities of the information age.

Key Terms

Continuous improvement (p. 27)	Ethics leadership (p. 38)	Inclusivity (p. 30)
Corporate governance (p. 38)	Ethics mindfulness (p. 34)	Individualism view of ethics (p. 35)
Distributive justice (p. 36)	Glass ceiling (p. 31)	Integrity (p. 38)
Empowerment (p. 28)	Globalization (p. 40)	Intellectual capital (p. 27)
Ethical behavior (p. 33)	Global outsourcing (p. 41)	Interactional justice (p. 36)
Ethical dilemma (p. 36)	High-performance organization (p. 25)	Job migration (p. 41)
	Human capital (p. 27)	Justice view of ethics (p. 35)

Knowledge workers
(p. 27)
Moral-rights view of ethics
(p. 35)
Multiculturalism (p. 30)
Organizational
transformation (p. 41)
Personal management
(p. 42)

Positive Organizational
Behavior (p. 39)
Procedural justice (p. 36)
Quality of work life (p. 38)
Self-monitoring (p. 42)
Shamrock organizations
(p. 41)
Social capital (p. 28)
Social responsibility (p. 37)

Stakeholders (p. 25)
Total quality management
(p. 26)
Utilitarian view of ethics
(p. 35)
Value creation (p. 25)
Whistleblower (p. 37)
Workforce diversity (p. 30)
Work–life balance (p. 39)

Multiple Choice

Self-Test 2

1. In a true high-performance organization one would expect to find _____. (a) norms and beliefs that emphasis individual achievement (b) a concentration of decision-making power in top management (c) a goal of placing people with technology (d) a commitment to teams and teamwork

2. The performance potential of an organization based on the value of people and their job-relevant abilities, knowledge, and experience is called _____. (a) knowledge management (b) human capital (c) organizational learning (d) empowerment

3. Members of organizations with _____ cultures could be expected to value working together and meeting higher-order needs. (a) constructive (b) defensive (c) aggressive (d) passive

4. The manager's role in the upside-down pyramid view of organizations is best described as providing _____ so that operating workers can directly serve _____. (a) direction; top management (b) leadership; organizational goals (c) support; customers (d) agendas; networking

5. A leader who wanted to build an organizational culture that respected diversity and was open to all persons capable of performing jobs well would emphasize norms and beliefs that supported _____. (a) inclusivity (b) prejudice (c) self-monitoring (d) job migration

6. The glass ceiling effect in organizations is _____. (a) a hidden barrier limiting career advancement of minorities and women (b) an informal commitment to advancement of minorities and women (c) an unpublicized limit on wages paid to non-managerial employees (d) a restriction on the hiring of full-time permanent workers

7. Whereas a(n)_____ manager essentially chooses to act unethically, a(n) _____ manager sometimes acts unethically but unintentionally. (a) moral; amoral (b) immoral; amoral (c) amoral; moral (d) immoral; moral

8. Research on ethical dilemmas indicates that _____ is often the cause of unethical behavior by people at work. (a) a decline in morals in society (b) lack of religious beliefs (c) the absence of whistleblowers (d) pressure from bosses and superiors

9. A manager who justifies a decision as ethical because it will result in the greatest good for the most people is using the _____ approach to ethical reasoning. (a) utilitarian (b) individualism (c) moral-rights (d) justice

10. Someone who excuses unethical behavior by pointing out that it is really in the organization's best interest is _____. (a) doing the right thing for him- or herself

(b) doing the right thing for society (c) rationalizing the unethical conduct (d) following the rule of procedural justice

11. When facing an ethical dilemma, ethics training programs typically recommend that final action should be taken only after _____. (a) rationalizing the dilemma (b) making sure the action is not illegal (c) making sure no one will find out if the action is wrong (d) double-checking to make sure that you are personally comfortable with the decision

12. The Sarbanes-Oxley Act of 2002 makes it easier for corporate executives to _____. (a) protect themselves from shareholder lawsuits (b) sue employees who commit illegal acts (c) be tried and sentenced to jail for financial misconduct (d) shift blame for wrongdoing to boards of directors

13. Customers, investors, employees, and regulators are examples of _____ that are important in the analysis of corporate social responsibility. (a) special-interest groups (b) stakeholders (c) ethics advocates (d) whistleblowers

14. Present concerns for the migration of jobs to other countries is one of the controversies associated with _____. (a) quality-of-work-life concerns (b) whistleblowing (c) globalization (d) personal management

15. If Charles Handy's concept of the shamrock organization is correct, more people in the future will be _____. (a) working as independent contractors (b) employed in low-wage jobs (c) unemployed because technology has taken over most traditional jobs (d) secure in the growing number of jobs in the permanent full-time core of the organization's workforce

Short Response

16. What is the difference between the moral-rights and individualism approaches to ethical reasoning?

17. Explain the major difference between the moral-rights and individualism approaches to ethical reasoning.

18. What is the connection between Douglas McGregor's Theory Y and positive organizational behavior?

19. Why is integrity an essential component of ethics leadership?

Applications Essay

20. Juanita Perez faces a dilemma in her role as the accounts manager for a local social service agency. An employee has reported to her that another employee is charging meals to his travel expense account even when he is attending a conference where meals are provided. What should Juanita do in this situation to set the stage so that (a) similar problems will not arise in the future and (b) the criteria of both procedural and distributive justice are satisfied?

These learning activities from *The OB Skills Workbook* are suggested for Chapter 2.

OB in Action

CASE	EXPERIENTIAL EXERCISES	SELF-ASSESSMENTS
■ 2. The Panera Bread Case—Not by Bread Alone	■ 3. My Best Job ■ 4. What Do You Value in Work? ■ 5. My Asset Base	■ 2. A Twenty-First-Century Manager ■ 3. Turbulence Tolerance Test

Plus—special learning experiences from *The Jossey-Bass/Pfeiffer Classroom Collection*

Chapter 3

Organizational Behavior across Cultures

Chapter at a Glance

Cultures bring rich variety to our world and workplaces. This chapter will broaden your understanding of people and organizations operating across cultures and in a complex global economy. As you read Chapter 3, *keep in mind these study questions*.

WHAT IS THE GLOBAL CONEXT OF ORGANIZATIONAL BEHAVIOR?

- Forces of Globalization
- Regional Economic Alliances
- Global Outsourcing and Offshoring
- Global Managers

WHAT IS CULTURE, AND HOW CAN WE UNDERSTAND CULTURAL DIFFERENCES?

- Popular Dimensions of Culture
- Values and National Cultures
- Understanding Cultural Differences

HOW DOES CULTURAL DIVERSITY AFFECT PEOPLE AT WORK?

- Multinational Employers
- Multicultural Workforces and Expatriates
- Ethical Behavior Across Cultures

WHAT IS A GLOBAL VIEW OF ORGANIZATIONAL LEARNING?

- Are Management Theories Universal?
- Best Practices Around the World

REVIEW IN END-OF-CHAPTER STUDY GUIDE

It seems like everyone must have heard of Wal-Mart. The firm is the largest company in the world by total sales (over $200 billion annually). It is also the world's largest private employer—sending paychecks to over 1.2 million "associates," as its employees are proudly called. And like other businesses of the day, Wal-Mart's future is an international one. Starting just over a dozen years ago, Wal-Mart's first venture abroad was a Sam's Club in Mexico City. After a slow start, the firm became Mexico's biggest retailer. But finding success internationally is a lesson in crossing cultures. Critics claim Wal-Mart was at first too quick to export its culture—and America's. The popular morning "Wal-Mart cheer" was a bust in Germany, where the firm also had trouble understanding German trade unions, distribution systems, and customer preferences. But Wal-Mart executives learned one of the top lessons of international business—you've got to understand the local culture.[1]

> **"Today's organizations need managers with global awareness and cultural sensitivity."**

Today's organizations need managers with global awareness and cultural sensitivity.[2] This doesn't mean that they all must work in foreign lands, although many will certainly do so. It does mean that managers must be aware of how international events may affect the well-being of organizations. They must know how to deal with people from other countries and cultures. And they must be inquisitive and willing to learn quickly from management practices around the globe. Insights into effective management and high-performance organizations are not restricted to any one location or culture. Contributions to our understanding about people and organizations can be found from Africa to Asia and from Europe to North and South America. The variety of issues and topics in the present chapter will help you to understand the important global dimensions of organizational behavior.

Global Context of
Organizational Behavior

Most organizations today must achieve high performance in the context of a competitive and complex global environment.[3] All around the globe, people working in large and small businesses alike are facing the many challenges and opportunities associated with business competition in an increasingly interconnected and "borderless" but also very complex world.[4] The ability to recognize, understand, and respect differences and value global diversity is an important key to success in managing organizational behavior across cultures.

As we begin the twenty-first century, we find ourselves fully in the age of **globalization**, with its complex economic networks of international competition, resource supplies, and product markets.[5] No one can deny its impact on organizations, the people who work in them, and our everyday lives. Consider globalization in terms of your own life and career: (1) you already purchase many products made by foreign firms (2) and may someday work overseas in the foreign operation of a domestic firm; (3) you may someday work overseas as an expatriate employee of a foreign firm; and (4) you may someday work as a domestic employee of a foreign firm operating in your home country. The field of organizational behavior recognizes these realities and seeks to help you understand the performance implications of work in the global economy.

Globalization involves growing worldwide interdependence of resource suppliers, product markets, and business competition.

Forces of Globalization

The rapid growth of information technology and electronic communications has heightened the average person's awareness of the global economy. The international news brings the entire world into our homes and our thoughts daily. An explosion of opportunities on the Internet allows us to share and gather information from global sources at low cost and from the convenience of our desktops, laptops, palmtops, and cell phones—at home, while traveling, or at work. And, always, the transnational movement of products, trends, values, and innovations continues to change lifestyles at a rapid pace. Just think of the "foreign" films that attract our attention and how "our" films attract viewers in other countries. Think also of how easily valuable skills and investments move from country to country and how the cultural diversity among their populations is increasing. Immigration is having profound implications for many nations, and job migration continues to create change and opportunity in an interconnected global economy. Employers increasingly deal with **multicultural workforces**—with members from nontraditional labor sources and from ethnic backgrounds representing all corners of the globe.[6]

Multicultural workforces include workers from diverse ethnic backgrounds and nationalities.

With the realities of globalization, domestic self-sufficiency is no longer a viable option for nations or businesses.[7] Commercial investments and jobs now easily and routinely travel the trade routes of the world. Germany's Daimler now owns the once-great American firm of Chrysler. Honda recently produced its 10 millionth car—in America. The Japanese own stakes in over 1500 U.S. factories, employing over 350,000 people. Global supplier networks play significant roles in the operations of most major industries. Information technology creates opportunities to work in virtual space with people and teams located around the world. Truly, the forces of globalization today affect working more than ever before, and the time to best understand the implications is right now.

Regional Economic Alliances

One impact of globalization is the emergence of regional economic alliances.[8] The European Union (EU) is moving forward with its agendas of political, economic, and monetary union among member countries. It has seen the advent of a new world currency, the *euro*, which has replaced the traditional currencies of many member nations. Within the EU, businesses from 25 member countries have a combined gross domestic product (GDP) larger than that of the United

Research Insight
Human Resource Executives Stress Importance of Global Mindset

Organizations operating in a world of globalization increasingly find themselves dealing with global workforces. With an interest in how well these workforces are mobilized and managed, Thomas M. Begley and David P. Boyd conducted interviews with 39 human resource executives involved in the international operations of high-technology multinational companies. Their interests focused on how well human resource policies were received and implemented in corporate locations around the world. Begley and Boyd conclude that success was associated with the presence of a "global mind-set," defined as "the ability to develop and interpret criteria for business performance that are not dependent on the assumptions of a single country, culture, or con-

text and to implement those criteria appropriately in different countries, cultures and contexts." They suggest that although this concept is recognized in the world of international business, it is not truly embedded in the operations of enough companies. As suggested in the accompanying figure, getting to a fully integrated corporate global mind-set involves balancing the needs for global consistency and for local responsiveness. The most common error, say Begley and Boyd, is to favor global consistency. Also shown in the figure are the components identified with executive success in avoiding this error and achieving a global–local balance.

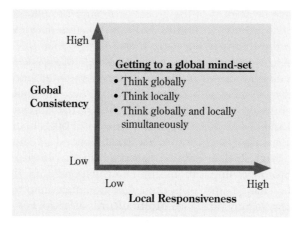

Getting to a global mind-set
- Think globally
- Think locally
- Think globally and locally simultaneously

Reference: Thomas M. Begley and David P. Boyd, "The Need for a Corporate Global Mindset," *Sloan Management Review* (Winter 2003):25–32.

States. Agreements to eliminate border controls and trade barriers, create uniform technical product standards, open government procurement contracts, and unify financial regulations are all designed to bring economic benefit to EU members.

The EU's counterpart in North America, the North American Free Trade Agreement (NAFTA), links the economies and customer markets of Canada, the United States, and Mexico in freer trade. NAFTA has been praised for uniting in trade a region with more potential customers than the European Union. It now looks forward to a future of expanded membership to other countries of the Americas. Some business and government leaders even speak of an all-encompassing Free Trade Agreement for the Americas (FTAA). At present, the Caribbean Community (CARICOM) is seeking to negotiate free-trade agreements with Latin American countries. In addition, the Andean Pact (linking Venezuela, Colombia, Ecuador, Peru, and Bolivia) and Mercosur (linking Brazil, Paraguay, Uruguay, and Argentina) are already active in South America.

Similar regional economic partnerships are being forged in other parts of the globe as well. In Asia, the Asia-Pacific Economic Co-operation Forum

(APEC) is designed for joint economic development among member countries. Asia's overall significance and economic power, with China and Japan at the center, continue to grow, and the continent is the home of an increasing number of world-class business competitors. Recent events have further confirmed the importance of other Asian countries, especially Taiwan, Singapore, South Korea, Malaysia, Thailand, and Indonesia. India, with its huge population, is an economy on the move and is recognized as a world-class supplier of software expertise.

A whole new world of opportunity is unfolding in Africa. Led by developments in post-apartheid South Africa, the continent's nations are becoming important members of the global economy. Countries like Uganda, Ivory Coast, Botswana, South Africa, and Ghana are recognized for their positive business prospects. Since the end of apartheid, for example, South Africa has steadily advanced in the IMD world competitiveness rankings.[9] A report on sub-Saharan Africa concluded that the region's contextual problems are manageable and that the continent presents investment opportunities.[10]

And ultimately, one has to wonder: What might and could happen in the Middle East if the turmoil and conflicts and animosities of the region can ever be put to rest?

Global Outsourcing and Offshoring

One important fact of working life today is that wherever you are employed, the likelihood is that you will be competing for jobs with persons in different countries. **Outsourcing**, or the contracting out of work rather than accomplishing it within a full-time permanent workforce, has grown in popularity in recent years. In today's economy, with the forces of globalization in full play, a form of outsourcing known popularly as "offshoring" has emerged as a major force and challenge to employers, workers, and even governments. **Offshoring** involves contracting out work to persons in other countries. A major controversy associated with its growing use is **job migration**, discussed in Chapter 1 as the movement of jobs from one location or country to another. Job migration hurts domestic workers and their communities as local jobs are lost to foreign countries. The driving force behind most offshoring decisions is the competitive push for ever-greater operating efficiencies and cost reductions. Through offshoring, employers reduce costs by taking advantage of foreign labor that has equivalent or better skills and costs a fraction of the price of domestic labor. The great facilitator, of course, is information technology, which allows continual "virtual" contact with one's labor force or contractors no matter where in the world they may be located.

Global outsourcing, offshoring, and job migration, of course, are here to stay. Their significance in the workplace will surely grow in the future. The implications for organizations and their members will continue to be studied, analyzed, and addressed in the years to come. Importantly, whereas one used to think of job migration in terms of manufacturing and traditional blue-collar work, things are very different today. In a digital world, information technology is enabling a whole new class of outsourcing and offshoring that includes white-collar work as well—engineering, research, professional services such as accounting and law, and technology support, among a growing list of possibilities.

Starbucks

Starbucks performance guidelines for its overseas suppliers require wages that address the basic needs of workers and their families and practices that help them get safe housing, health facilities, and services.

Outsourcing is the contracting out of work as an alternative to accomplishing it with one's own workforce.

Offshoring is contracting out or outsourcing to workers in foreign countries.

Job migration is the movement of jobs from one location or country to another.

TECHNOLOGY CROSSES BORDERS TO FUEL ENTREPRENEURSHIP

There is a lot of publicity being given these days to India's emergence as a new center of technology and entrepreneurship in the global economy. But whether one is talking of India or somewhere else, one thing is clear—the right use of technology is a major advantage in international business. At Infosys, one of India's premier and largest high-tech firms, CEO Nandan Nilekani harnesses the latest in technology to integrate his firm with the world. A global conference room in Bangalore has a wall-sized screen and ceiling cameras that allow videoconferencing with its global partners. He says: "We can have our whole global supply chain on the screen at the same time." Distance is no challenge to Infosys and its virtual worldwide teams.

Question: Granted that technology has a long reach and great capabilities, but what does it take to make a real success out of a virtual team?

A major facilitator of global sourcing by businesses is growing adherence around the world to total quality, perhaps best represented in the designation *ISO*. This certification is earned by meeting quality standards set by the International Standards Organization in Geneva, Switzerland, and is now considered a "must-have" by companies around the world that want to win reputations as total-quality world-class manufacturers. With the availability of a growing number of ISO-certified manufacturers around the world, it is ever easier for companies to outsource contracts and engage in offshoring relationships with the assurance that international quality standards will be upheld.

▨ A **global manager** has the international awareness and cultural sensitivity needed to work well across national borders.

Global Managers

Along with prior developments in globalization, the search is now also on for a new breed of manager—the **global manager**. This is a manager who knows how to conduct business in multiple countries, is culturally adaptable, and is often multilingual.[11] A global manager thinks with a worldview; appreciates diverse beliefs, values, behaviors, and practices; and is able to map strategy in the global context. Fred Hanson, chairman and CEO of Schering-Plough, describes this type of manager as someone who embraces work in a globalized world with a *global attitude*—"a willingness to accept good ideas no matter where they come from."[12] If you fit the description in The Effective Manager 3.1, or soon will, get ready. Corporate recruiters are scrambling to find people with a global attitude and strong cross-cultural skills and interests.

The global dimension in business and management, though pervasive, poses many complications

THE EFFECTIVE MANAGER 3.1

Attributes of the Global Manager

- Adapts well to different business environments
- Respects different beliefs, values, and practices
- Solves problems quickly in new circumstances
- Communicates well with people from different cultures
- Speaks more than one language
- Understands different government and political systems
- Conveys respect and enthusiasm when dealing with others
- Possesses high technical expertise for a job

to be overcome. A global manager has to work especially hard, be open to learning, and strive to embrace diversity to succeed in the global marketplace. Even high performers with proven technical skills at home may find that their styles and attitudes just don't work well overseas. Experienced international managers indicate that a "global mind-set" of cultural adaptability, patience, flexibility, and tolerance is indispensable.[13] The failure rate for Americans in overseas assignments has been measured as high as 25 percent, and a study criticizes British and German companies for giving inadequate preparation to staff sent abroad.[14]

Cultures and Cross-Cultural Understanding

The word "culture" is frequently used in organizational behavior in connection with the concept of corporate culture, the growing interest in workforce diversity, and the broad differences among people around the world. Specialists tend to agree that **culture** is the learned, shared way of doing things in a particular society. It is the way, for example, in which its members eat, dress, greet and treat one another, teach their children, solve everyday problems, and so on.[15] Geert Hofstede, a Dutch scholar and consultant, refers to culture as the "software of the mind," making the analogy that the mind's "hardware" is universal among human beings.[16] But the software of culture takes many different forms. We are not born with a culture; we are born into a society that teaches us its culture. And because culture is shared among people, it helps to define the boundaries between different groups and affect how their members relate to one another. Recently the term **cultural intelligence** has been used to describe a person's ability to identify, understand, and act with sensitivity and effectiveness in cross-cultural situations.[17]

> ▪ **Culture** is the learned and shared way of thinking and acting among a group of people or society.

> ▪ **Cultural intelligence** is the ability to identify, understand, and act effectively in cross-cultural situations.

CULTURES AND THE GLOBAL WORKFORCE

UBUNTU UNDERLIES WORKPLACE VALUES IN SOUTH AFRICA

The link between the individual and community is central to the African principle of *ubuntu*. It signifies humaneness and the values of caring, belonging, respect, and interacting with and through one's community rather than separate from it. *Ubuntu* underlies an initiative by the nonprofit group Vukani-Ubuntu to foster business development in South Africa. The firm works with big businesses to provide seed capital for promising young entrepreneurs. But the capital doesn't go to them individually; it is targeted toward clusters of small businesses in the same industry. New businesses are owned 50 percent by the cluster and 50 percent by the individuals who run them. This design for business development emphasizes interdependence; individuals work within clusters to grow their businesses to the benefit of everyone.

Question: Can the values underlying ubuntu *be mobilized to facilitate entrepreneurship in other areas of the world?*

Popular Dimensions of Culture

Cultural diversity emerges in many forms as the richness of cultures varies from one part of our world to the next. To begin, it is helpful to recognize differences in what might be called the popular dimensions of culture. These are things that are most apparent to the individual when traveling abroad—for example, language, time orientation, use of space, and religion.[18]

Language   Perhaps the most conspicuous aspect of culture, and certainly the one the traveler notices first, is language. The languages of the world number in the thousands; some, such as English and Chinese, are spoken by millions and others, such as Maltese, are spoken by only a handful of people. Some countries, such as France and Malaysia, have one official language; others, such as Canada, Switzerland, and India, have more than one; and still others, like the United States, have none.

The centrality of language to culture is represented by the *Whorfian hypothesis*, which considers language as a major determinant of our thinking.[19] The vocabulary and structure of a language reflect the history of a society and can also reveal how members relate to the environment. Arabic, for example, has many different words for the camel, its parts, and related equipment. As you might expect, English is very poor in its ability to describe camels. The fact that many people apparently speak the same language, such as English, doesn't mean that they share the same culture. Some words spoken in one language fail to carry the same meaning from culture to culture or region to region. A "truck" in Chicago is a "lorry" in London; "hydro" in Calgary is "electric power" in Boston; grocery shoppers in the American Midwest put "pop" in their "sacks," but East Coast shoppers put "soda" in their "bags."

The anthropologist Edward T. Hall notes important differences in the ways different cultures use language.[20] Members of **low-context cultures** are very explicit in using the spoken and written word. In these cultures, such as those of Australia, Canada, and United States, the message is largely conveyed by the words someone uses, and not particularly by the "context" in which they are spoken. In contrast, members of **high-context cultures** use words to convey only a limited part of the message. The rest must be inferred or interpreted from the context, which includes body language, the physical setting, and past relationships—all of which add meaning to what is being said. Many Asian and Middle Eastern cultures are considered high context, according to Hall, whereas most Western cultures are low context.

Time Orientation   Hall also uses time orientation to classify cultures.[21] In **polychronic cultures** people hold a traditional view of time that may be described as a "circle." This suggests repetition in the sense that time is cyclical and goes around and around. In this view, time does not create pressures for immediate action or performance. After all, one will have another chance to pass the same way again. If an opportunity is lost today—no problem, it may return again tomorrow. Members of polychronic cultures tend to emphasize the present and often do more than one thing at a time.[22] An important business or government official in a Mediterranean country, for example, may have a large reception area outside his or her office. Visitors wait in this area and may transact business with the official and others who move in and out and around the room, conferring as they go.

Members of **monochronic cultures** view time more as a straight line. In this linear view of time, the past is gone, the present is here briefly, and the future is

■ In **low-context cultures** messages are expressed mainly by the spoken and written word.

■ In **high-context cultures** words convey only part of a message, while the rest of the message must be inferred from body language and additional contextual cues.

■ In a **polychronic culture** people tend to do more than one thing at a time.

■ In a **monochronic culture** people tend to do one thing at a time.

almost upon us. In monochronic cultures time is measured precisely and creates pressures for action and performance. People appreciate schedules and appointments and talk about "saving" and "wasting" time. Long-range goals become important, and planning is a way of managing the future. In contrast to the Mediterranean official in the last example, a British manager will typically allot a certain amount of time in his or her daily calendar to deal with a business visitor. During this time the visitor receives the manager's complete attention. Only after one visitor leaves will another one be received, again based on the daily schedule.

Use of Space   *Proxemics*, the study of how people use space to communicate, reveals important cultural differences.[23] Personal space can be thought of as the "bubble" that surrounds us, and its preferred size tends to vary from one culture to another. When others invade or close in on our personal space, we tend to feel uncomfortable. Then again, if people are too far away, communication becomes difficult. Arabs and South Americans seem more comfortable talking at closer distances than do North Americans; Asians seem to prefer even greater distances. When a Saudi moves close to speak with a visiting Canadian executive, the visitor may back away to keep more distance between them. But the same Canadian may approach a Malaysian too closely when doing business in Kuala Lumpur, causing his or her host to back away. Cross-cultural misunderstandings due to different approaches to personal space are quite common.

In some cultures, often polychronic ones, space is organized in such a way that many activities can be carried out simultaneously. Spanish and Italian towns are organized around central squares (plazas or piazzas), whereas American towns typically have a traditional "Main Street" laid out in linear fashion. Similar cultural influences are seen in the layout of workspace. Americans, who seem to prefer individual offices, may have difficulty adjusting to Japanese employers, who prefer open floor plans.

Religion   Religion is also a major element of culture and can be one of its more visible manifestations. The influence of religion often prescribes rituals, holy days, and foods that can be eaten. Codes of ethics and moral behavior often have their roots in religious beliefs. The influence of religion on economic matters can also be significant.[24] In the Middle East, one finds interest-free Islamic banks that operate based on principles set forth in the Koran. In Malaysia, business dinners are scheduled after 8:00 P.M. so that Muslim guests can first attend to their evening prayers.

Values and National Cultures

Cultures vary in their underlying patterns of values and attitudes. The way people think about such matters as achievement, wealth and material gain, and risk and change may influence how they approach work and their relationships with organizations. A framework developed by Geert Hofstede offers one approach for understanding how value differences across national cultures can influence human behavior at work. The five dimensions of national culture in his framework can be described as follows.[25]

1. **Power distance** is the willingness of a culture to accept status and power differences among its members. It reflects the degree to which people are likely to respect hierarchy and rank in organizations. Indonesia is consid-

Social Accountability International

Social Accountability International evaluates firms on use of child labor, health and safety, freedom of association, discrimination, disciplinary practices, working hours, and compensation systems.

Hofstede's dimensions of national cultures

▰▰ **Power distance** is the willingness of a culture to accept status and power differences among its members.

▓ Uncertainty avoidance is the cultural tendency to be uncomfortable with uncertainty and risk in everyday life.

▓ Individualism–collectivism is the tendency of a culture's members to emphasize individual self-interests or group relationships.

▓ Masculinity–femininity is the degree to which a society values assertiveness or relationships.

▓ Long-term/short-term orientation is the degree to which a culture emphasizes long-term or short-term thinking.

ered a high power distance culture, whereas Sweden is considered a relatively low power distance culture.

2. **Uncertainty avoidance** is a cultural tendency toward discomfort with risk and ambiguity. It reflects the degree to which people are likely to prefer structured versus unstructured organizational situations. France is considered a high uncertainty avoidance culture, whereas Hong Kong is considered a low uncertainty avoidance culture.

3. **Individualism–collectivism** is the tendency of a culture to emphasize either individual or group interests. It reflects the degree to which people are likely to prefer working as individuals or working together in groups. The United States is a highly individualistic culture, whereas Mexico is a more collectivist one.

4. **Masculinity–femininity** is the tendency of a culture to value stereotypical masculine or feminine traits. It reflects the degree to which organizations emphasize competition and assertiveness versus interpersonal sensitivity and concerns for relationships. Japan is considered a very masculine culture, whereas Thailand is considered a more feminine culture.

5. **Long-term/short-term orientation** is the tendency of a culture to emphasize values associated with the future, such as thrift and persistence, or values that focus largely on the present. It reflects the degree to which people and organizations adopt long-term or short-term performance horizons. South Korea is high on long-term orientation, whereas the United States is a more short-term-oriented country.

The first four dimensions in Hofstede's framework were identified in an extensive study of thousands of employees of a multinational corporation operating in more than 40 countries.[26] The fifth dimension of long-term/short-term orientation was added from research using the Chinese Values Survey conducted by cross-cultural psychologist Michael Bond and his colleagues.[27] Their research suggested the cultural importance of Confucian dynamism, with its emphasis on persistence, the ordering of relationships, thrift, sense of shame, personal steadiness, reciprocity, protection of "face," and respect for tradition.[28]

Figure 3.1   Sample country clusters on Hofstede's dimensions of individualism–collectivism and power distance.

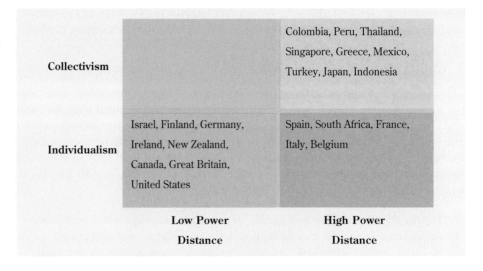

When using the Hofstede framework, it is important to remember that the five dimensions are interrelated, not independent.[29] National cultures may best be understood in terms of cluster maps or collages that combine multiple dimensions. For example, Figure 3.1 shows a sample grouping of countries based on individualism–collectivism and power distance. Note that high power distance and collectivism are often found together, as are low power distance and individualism. Whereas high collectivism may lead us to expect a work team in Indonesia to operate by consensus, the high power distance may cause the consensus to be heavily influenced by the desires of a formal leader. A similar team operating in more individualist and low power distance Great Britain or America might make decisions with more open debate, including expressions of disagreement with a leader's stated preferences.

Understanding Cultural Differences

To work well with people from different cultures, you must first understand your own culture. We are usually unaware of our own culture until we come into contact with a very different one. Knowing your own culture will help guard you against two problems that frequently arise in international dealings. One is the danger of **parochialism**—assuming that the ways of your culture are the only ways of doing things. The other is the danger of **ethnocentrism**—assuming that the ways of your culture are the best ways of doing things.[30] It is parochial for a traveling American businesswoman to insist that all of her business contacts speak English, whereas it is ethnocentric for her to think that anyone who dines with a spoon rather than a knife and fork lacks proper table manners.

A framework developed by Fons Trompenaars offers a useful vantage point for better understanding and, hopefully, dealing with cultural differences.[31] Working from a databank of respondents from 47 national cultures, he suggests that cultures vary in the way their members solve problems of three major types: (1) relationships with people, (2) attitudes toward time, and (3) attitudes toward the environment. Trompenaars identifies five major cultural differences in how people handle relationships with other people. The orientations, as illustrated in Figure 3.2, are:

1. *Universalism versus particularism*—relative emphasis on rules and consistency or on relationships and flexibility.
2. *Individualism versus collectivism*—relative emphasis on individual freedom and responsibility or on group interests and consensus.

Parochialism is assuming that ways of your culture are the only ways of doing things.

Ethnocentrism is assuming that the ways of your culture are the best ways of doing things.

How cultures deal with relationships among people

Canada, USA, Ireland	**Universalism vs. Particularism**	Indonesia, China, Venezuela
USA, Hungary, Russia	**Individualism vs. Collectivism**	Thailand, Japan, Mexico
Indonesia, Germany, Japan	**Neutral vs. Affective**	Italy, France, USA
Spain, Poland, USA	**Specific vs. Diffuse**	India, Great Britain, Egypt
Australia, Canada, Norway	**Achievement vs. Ascription**	Philippines, Pakistan, Brazil
Great Britain, Belgium, USA	**Sequential vs. Synchronic**	Malaysia, Venezuela, France

Figure 3.2 Sample country clusters on Trompenaars's framework for understanding cultural differences.

3. *Neutral versus affective*—relative emphasis on objectivity and detachment or on emotion and expressed feelings.

4. *Specific versus diffuse*—relative emphasis on focused and narrow involvement or on involvement with the whole person.

5. *Achievement versus ascription*—relative emphasis on performance-based and earned status or on ascribed status.

With regard to problems based on attitudes toward time, Trompenaars distinguishes between cultures with sequential versus synchronic orientations. Time in a sequential view is a passing series of events; in a synchronic view, it consists of an interrelated past, present, and future. With regard to problems based on attitudes toward the environment, he contrasts how different cultures may relate to nature in inner-directed versus outer-directed ways. Members of an inner-directed culture tend to view themselves separate from nature and believe they can control it. Those in an outer-directed culture view themselves as part of nature and believe they must go along with it.

Cultural Diversity and People at Work

OB scholars are increasingly sensitive to the need to better understand how management and organizational practices vary among the world's cultures. In this sense, we must be familiar with the importance of multinational employers, the diversity of multicultural workforces, and the special demands of international work assignments.

Multinational Employers

▨ A **multinational corporation** is a business with extensive international operations in more than one country.

A **multinational corporation** (MNC) is a business firm that has extensive international operations in more than one foreign country. MNCs are more than just companies that "do business abroad"; they are global concerns—exemplified by Xerox, Ford, Sony, Hewlett-Packard, and many others. The missions, strategies, and stakeholders of MNCs are worldwide in scope. In the public sector, multinational organizations (MNOs) are those with nonprofit missions whose operations also span the globe. Examples are Amnesty International, the International Red Cross, the United Nations, and the World Wildlife Fund.

Today, more and more businesses are seeking to shift from multinational operations into becoming truly *global corporations*—ones that operate with a total worldview and do not have primary identification with one national "home." Futurist Alvin Toffler labels them transnational organizations that "may do research in one country, manufacture components in another, assemble them in a third, sell the manufactured goods in a fourth, deposit surplus funds in a fifth, and so on."[32] Although the pure transnational corporation may not yet exist, large MNCs like Nestlé, Gillette, and Ford are striving hard to move in that direction. Jeffrey Immelt, chairman and CEO of the global giant GE, describes a global company this way: "(1) a global sales company with customers around the world, (2) a global products company using technology and factories to make products around the world, and (3) a global people company that uses brainpower from around the world."[33]

Leaders on Leadership

LEADING AROUND THE WORLD VALUES PEOPLE

When Xerox needed to change its ways or go out of business, its board of directors turned to an experienced insider for leadership. Their choice was Anne Mulcahy, a company veteran who worked her way to the top in a 27-year career. With an undergraduate degree in English and journalism, Mulcahy brought a charismatic and hands-on style of leadership to the struggling firm. She also brought a global vision. Mulcahy began by flying around the world to personally visit Xerox employees in all locations. Her goal was to communicate a positive message; through her personal presence she strove to raise morale and refocus attention on the company's future and away from its past. And she succeeded. Now considered one of the most powerful women in the corporate world by *Fortune* magazine, Mulcahy has excelled by placing a high leadership priority on valuing people and trying to build morale and motivation no matter where in the world they might work. She says: "People have to feel engaged, motivated and feel they are making a contribution to something that is important."

Question: How can a leader with a personal commitment to people create an organizational culture that embraces and fully values cultural diversity?

MNCs and the emerging global corporations have enormous economic power and impact. One estimate is that of the world's 100 largest economies, 51 are actually corporations; the largest among them is Exxon Mobil, whose economic wealth is greater than that of 181 nations.[34] Toffler warns that "the size, importance, and political power of this new player in the global game has skyrocketed." Another observer states: "Multinational corporations play an increasingly important role in wealth creation, resource use, employment, environmental and cultural impact, fulfillment of human needs, technology transfer, and governance."[35]

There is no doubt that the MNCs bring both benefits and potential controversies to the host countries in which they operate. One example is in Mexico, where many *maquiladoras*, or foreign-owned plants, assemble imported parts and ship finished products to the United States. Inexpensive labor is an advantage for the foreign operators. Mexico benefits from industrial development, reduced unemployment, and increased foreign exchange earnings. But some complain about the downsides of *maquiladoras*—stress on housing and public services in Mexican border towns, inequities in the way Mexican workers are treated (wages, working conditions, production quotas) relative to their foreign counterparts, and the environmental impact of pollution from the industrial sites.

Multicultural Workforces and Expatriates

What is the best way to deal with a multicultural workforce? There are no easy answers. Styles of leadership, motivation, decision making, planning, organizing, leading, and controlling vary from country to country.[36] Managing a construction project in Saudi Arabia with employees from Asia, the Middle East, Europe, and North America working side by side will clearly present challenges different from those involved in a domestic project. Similarly, establishing and successfully operating a joint venture in Kazakhstan, Nigeria, or Vietnam will require a great deal of learning and patience. In these and other international settings, political risks and bureaucratic difficulties further complicate the already difficult process of working across cultural boundaries.

Domestic multiculturalism is cultural diversity within a national population.

The challenges of managing across cultures, however, are not limited to international operations. In this connection, a new term has been coined—**domestic multiculturalism**, which describes cultural diversity within a given national population: this diversity will be reflected in the workforces of local organizations.[37] Los Angeles, for example, is home to many immigrant groups, with a large and growing percentage of the city's schoolchildren speaking other languages more fluently than they speak English.

An expatriate works and lives in a foreign country for an extended time.

People who work and live abroad for extended periods of time are referred to as **expatriates**. The cost of an expatriate worker can be very expensive for the employer. In addition to salary differentials, these costs typically include added benefits as well as transfer and other relocation expenses. To get the most out of the investment, progressive employers will maximize the potential of expatriate performance by taking a variety of supportive actions.[38] They carefully recruit employees who have the right sensitivities and skills, provide them with good training and orientation to the foreign culture, actively support them while they are working abroad, give extra attention to the needs of the expatriate's family members, and pay careful attention to relocation when the expatriate and family return home.

Expatriates usually face their greatest problems when entering a foreign culture and when experiencing repatriation on the return home.[39] Figure 3.3 illustrates phases in the typical expatriate work assignment, beginning with the initial assignment shock the person experiences upon being informed of a foreign posting. The ways in which recruitment, selection, and orientation are handled during this stage can have an important influence on the assignment's eventual success. Ideally, the employee, along with his or her spouse and family, is allowed to choose whether or not to accept the opportunity. Also ideally, proper pre-departure support and counseling are given to provide "realistic expectations" of what is to come.

The expatriate undergoes three phases of adjustment to the new country. First is the tourist stage, in which the expatriate enjoys discovering the new culture. Second is the disillusionment stage, in which his or her mood is dampened as difficulties become more evident. Typical problems include conversing well in the local language and obtaining personal products and food supplies of preference. Third, the expatriate's mood often hits bottom in the stage of culture shock. Here confusion, disorientation, and frustration about the ways of the local culture and living in the foreign environment set in. If culture shock is well handled, the expatriate begins to feel better, function more effectively, and lead a reasonably normal life. If it isn't, work performance may suffer, even deteriorating to the point where a reassignment home may be necessary.

Kola Real

Started with a $30,000 investment, Peru's Kola Real is shaking up the soft-drink markets south of the border; its low prices and aggressive marketing are creating growing competitive pressures for giants Coke and Pepsi.

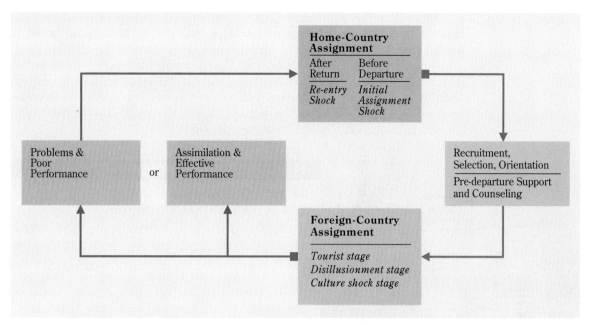

Figure 3.3   Stages in the expatriate international career cycle: potential adjustment problems in the home and foreign countries.

At the end of the expatriate assignment, perhaps after two to four years, the reentry process can also be stressful. After an extended period away, the expatriate and his or her family have changed and the home country has changed as well. One does not simply "fall back in"; rather, it takes time to get used to living at home again. In too many instances, little thought may be given to assigning the returned expatriate a job that matches his or her current skills and abilities. While abroad, the expatriate has often functioned with a great degree of independence—something that may or may not be possible at home. Problems caused by reentry shock can be minimized through careful planning. This includes maintaining adequate contact with the home office during the expatriate assignment as well as having all possible support for the move back. Employers should also identify any new skills and abilities, and assign returned expatriates to jobs commensurate with their abilities. As organizations make more and more expatriate assignments, their career planning and development systems must also operate on a global scale.

Ethical Behavior Across Cultures

The importance of ethical issues in organizational behavior and management was first introduced in Chapter 1. In the international arena, special ethical challenges arise as a result of cultural diversity and the variation in governments and legal systems that characterize our world. Prominent current issues include corruption and bribery in international business practices, poor working conditions and the employment of child and prison labor in some countries, and the role of international business in supporting repressive governments that fail to protect and respect the basic human rights of citizens.[40]

In the United States, the Foreign Corrupt Practices Act of 1977 makes it illegal for firms to engage in corrupt practices overseas, such as giving bribes to government officials in order to obtain business contracts. More broadly, countries of the Organization for Economic Development have now also agreed to ban payoffs to foreign officials by their countries' businesses. The U.S. government is pushing for more countries to join the movement against bribe giving and taking, and suggestions have been made that the World Bank consider corruption as a criterion when making loan decisions.

ETHICS AND SOCIAL RESPONSIBILITY

BRIBERY CREATES PROBLEMS FOR INTERNATIONAL BUSINESSES

It is against U.S. law for American companies to pay bribes to foreign officials or to engage in corrupt practices in other countries. But IBM ran into difficulty when executives of its Korean subsidiary were accused of paying bribes to receive government contracts. Although the executives were immediately fired, IBM was targeted for inquiry by the U.S. Justice Department. It also faced sanctions in Korea under the country's strict ethics laws. An IBM statement said: "We regret the actions by several individuals.... Such activity was neither approved or condoned by IBM Korea...[we] will work to restore the faith placed in us by our customers and Korean society."

Question: In what other ways can executives get caught in the ethical challenges of international business?

■■■ **Sweatshops** employ people that must work under adverse labor conditions.

The term **sweatshop**, increasingly in the news these days, refers to organizations that force workers to labor under adverse conditions that may include long workdays, involve unsafe conditions, and even make use of child labor. A variety of advocacy groups are now active in campaigning against sweatshops, and a number of well-recognized firms have been the targets of their attention—including such well-recognized multinationals as Nike, Mattel, and Disney. Watchdog groups in Asia, for example, have in the past criticized Disney for allowing some of its contract manufacturers in China to force workers to labor seven days a week, up to 16 hours a day, and at no overtime; Mattel has been accused of engaging subcontractors who run "sweatshop Barbie" assembly lines that include extra-long work hours and heavy fines for workers' mistakes. In response to such criticisms, more multinational employers are engaging outside consultants to conduct social audits of their international operations, adopting formal codes of ethical practices governing subcontractors, and backing external codes of conduct such as Social Accountability 8000—a certificate awarded by the Council on Economic Priorities. Worth considering is the following comment by Jack Sheinkman, president emeritus of the Amalgamated Clothing and Textile Workers Unions and member of the Council on Economic Priorities advisory board:

As business becomes ever more global in scope and its links in the chain of production extend further, the task of rating corporate social responsibility has be-

Cultural relativism	Ethical imperialism
←	→
No culture's ethics are superior. **The values and practices of the local setting determine what is right or wrong.**	**Certain absolute truths apply everywhere.** **Universal values transcend cultures in determining what is right or wrong.**
When in Rome, do as the Romans do.	*Don't do anything you wouldn't do at home.*

Figure 3.4 **The extremes of cultural relativism and ethical absolutism in international business ethics.**

come more complex. So, too, has the safeguarding of workers' rights...especially when responsibility is shared among manufacturers, contractors, subcontractors, buying agents...and other parties to business agreements which transcend time-zones, language barriers, and developing and industrialized country borders alike.[41]

A continuing issue for debate in this area of international business and management practices is the influence of culture on ethical behavior. Figure 3.4 presents a continuum that contrasts cultural relativism with ethical absolutism. Business ethicist Thomas Donaldson describes **cultural relativism** as the position that there is no universal right way to behave and that ethical behavior is determined by its cultural context.[42] In other words, international business behavior is justified on the argument "When in Rome, do as the Romans do." If one accepts cultural relativism, a sweatshop operation would presumably be OK as long as it was consistent with the laws and practices of the local culture. The opposite extreme on the continuum in Figure 3.4 reflects **ethical absolutism**, a universalistic assumption that there is a single moral standard that fits all situations, regardless of culture and national location. In other words, if a practice such as child labor is not acceptable in one's home environment, it shouldn't be engaged in elsewhere. Critics of the absolutist approach claim that it is a form of ethical imperialism because it attempts to impose external ethical standards unfairly or inappropriately on local cultures and fails to respect their needs and unique situations.

■ **Cultural relativism** suggests that ethical behavior is determined by its cultural context.

■ **Ethical absolutism** assumes that a single moral standard applies to all cultures.

Donaldson suggests that there is no simple answer to this debate and warns against the dangers of both cultural relativism and ethical absolutism. He makes the case that multinational businesses should adopt core or threshold values to guide behavior in ways that respect and protect fundamental human rights in any situation. However, he also suggests that there is room beyond the threshold to adapt and tailor one's actions in ways that respect the traditions, foundations, and needs of different cultures.[43]

A Global View of Organizational Learning

Organizational learning was first defined in Chapter 1 as the process of acquiring the knowledge necessary to adapt to a changing environment. In the context and themes of this chapter, the concept can be extended to **global organizational learning**—the ability to gather from the world at large the knowledge re-

■ **Global organizational learning** is the ability to gather from the world at large the knowledge required for long-term organizational adaptation.

quired for long-term organizational adaptation. Simply stated, people from different cultures and parts of the world have a lot to learn from one another about organizational behavior and management.

Are Management Theories Universal?

One of the most important questions to be asked and answered in this age of globalization is whether or not management theories are universal. That is, can and should a theory developed in one cultural context be transferred and used in another? The answer according to Geert Hofstede is "no," at least not without careful consideration of cultural influences.[44] Culture can influence both the development of a theory or concept and its application. As an example, Hofstede cites the issue of motivation. He notes that Americans have historically addressed motivation from the perspective of individual performance and rewards—consistent with their highly individualistic culture. However, concepts such as merit pay and job enrichment may not fit well in other cultures where high collectivism places more emphasis on teamwork and groups. Hofstede's point, and one well worth remembering, is that although we can and should learn from what is taking place in other cultures, we should be informed consumers of that knowledge. We should always factor cultural considerations into account when transferring theories and practices from one setting to the next.

A good case in point relates to the interest generated some years ago in Japanese management approaches, based on the success experienced at the time by Japanese industry.[45] Japanese firms have traditionally been described as favoring lifetime employment with strong employee–employer loyalty, seniority pay, and company unions. Their operations have emphasized a quality commitment, the use of teams and consensus decision making, and career development based on slow promotions and cross-functional job assignments.[46]

Although the Japanese economy and many of its firms have had problems of their own recently, management scholars and consultants recognize that many lessons can still be learned from their practices. However, we also recognize that cultural differences must be considered in the process. Specifically, what works in Japan may not work as well elsewhere, at least not without some modifications. Japan's highly collectivist society, for example, contrasts markedly with the highly individualistic cultures of the United States and other Western nations. It is only reasonable to expect differences in their management and organizational practices. Insights into Japanese culture from management scholar Makoto Ohtso are provided in The Effective Manager 3.2.[47]

THE EFFECTIVE MANAGER 3.2

Influences of Confucian values on Japanese culture

- *Harmony*—works well in a group, doesn't disrupt group order, puts group before self-interests.
- *Hierarchy*—views hierarchical nature of organizations as natural, accepts authority, doesn't challenge superiors.
- *Benevolence*—willing to help, acts kind and understanding toward others, paternalistic, willing to teach and help subordinates.
- *Loyalty*—loyal to organization and supervisor, dedicated to job, grateful for job and benevolence of superior.
- *Learning*—loves to learn, eager for new knowledge, works hard to learn new job skills, strives to be a high performer.

Best Practices Around the World

An appropriate goal in global organizational learning is to identify the "best practices" found around the world. What is being done well in other settings may be of great value at home, whether that home is in Africa, Asia, Europe, North America, or anywhere else. Whereas the world at large once looked mainly to North Americans and Europeans for management insights, today we recognize that potential benchmarks of excellence for high-performance organizations can be discovered anywhere. For example, as discussed above, the influence of the Japanese approaches as a stimulus to global organizational learning is evident in many of the workplace themes with which you will become familiar in this book. They include growing attention to the value of teams and workgroups, consensus decision making, employee involvement, flatter structures, and strong corporate cultures.

As the field of organizational behavior continues to mature in its global research and understanding, we will all benefit from an expanding knowledge base that is enriched by cultural diversity. Organizational behavior is a science of contingencies, and one of them is culture. No one culture possesses all of the "right" answers to today's complex management and organizational problems. But a sincere commitment to global organizational learning can give us fresh ideas while still permitting locally appropriate solutions to be implemented with cultural sensitivity. This search for global understanding will be reflected in the following chapters as we move further into the vast domain of OB.

Chapter 3   Study Guide

Why is globalization significant for organizational behavior?

Summary

- Globalization, with its complex worldwide economic networks of business competition, resource supplies, and product markets, is having a major impact on businesses, employers, and workforces around the world.

- Nations in Europe, North America, and Asia are forming regional trade agreements, such as the EU, NAFTA, and APEC, to gain economic strength in the highly competitive global economy.

- More and more organizations, large and small, do an increasing amount of business abroad; more and more local employers are foreign owned, in whole or in part; the domestic workforce is becoming multicultural and more diverse.

- One of the important trends today is increasing use by businesses of global outsourcing, or offshoring, with the result that many jobs previously performed by domestic workers are migrating to foreign countries.

- All organizations need global managers with the special interests and talents needed to excel in international work and cross-cultural relationships.

What is culture, and how can we understand cultural differences?

- Culture is the learned and shared way of doing things in a society; it represents deeply ingrained influences on the way people from different societies think, behave, and solve problems.

- Popular dimensions of culture include observable differences in language, time orientation, use of space, and religion.

- Hofstede's five national culture dimensions are power distance, individualism–collectivism, uncertainty avoidance, masculinity–femininity, and long-term/short-term orientation.

- Trompenaars's framework for understanding cultural differences focuses on relationships among people, attitudes toward time, and attitudes toward the environment.

- Cross-cultural awareness requires a clear understanding of one's own culture and the ability to overcome the limits of parochialism and ethnocentrism.

How does cultural diversity affect people at work?

- Among multinational corporations (MNCs), truly global businesses operate with a worldwide scope; the largest of the world's MNCs are powerful forces in the global economy.

- Multiculturalism in the domestic workforce requires everyone to work well with people of different cultural backgrounds.

- Expatriate employees who work abroad for extended periods of time face special challenges, including possible adjustment problems abroad and reentry problems upon returning home.

- The international dimensions of business create unique ethical challenges; ethical behavior across cultures can be viewed from the perspectives of cultural relativism and ethical absolutism.

What is a global view on organizational learning?

- A global view on learning about OB seeks to understand the best practices from around the world, with due sensitivity to cultural differences.

- Management concepts and theories must always be considered relative to the cultures in which they are developed and applied.

- Interest in Japanese management practices continues, with the traditional focus on long-term employment, emphasis on teams, quality commitment, careful career development, and consensus decision making.

- Global learning will increasingly move beyond North America, Europe, and Japan to include best practices anywhere in the world.

Key Terms

Cultural intelligence (p. 55)
Cultural relativism (p. 65)
Culture (p. 55)

Domestic multiculturalism
(p. 62)
Ethical absolutism (p. 65)

Ethnocentrism (p. 59)
Expatriates (p. 62)
Globalization (p. 51)

Global manager (p. 54)
Global organizational
   learning (p. 65)
High-context culture (p. 56)
Individualism–collectivism
   (p. 58)
Job migration (p. 53)
Long-term/short-term
   orientation (p. 58)

Low-context culture (p. 56)
Masculinity–femininity
   (p. 58)
Monochronic culture (p. 56)
Multicultural workforces
   (p. 51)
Multinational corporation
   (p. 60)

Offshoring (p. 53)
Outsourcing (p. 53)
Parochialism (p. 59)
Polychronic culture (p. 56)
Power distance (p. 57)
Sweatshops (p. 64)
Uncertainty avoidance
   (p. 58)

Self-Test 3

Multiple Choice

1. NAFTA, APEC, and the EU are examples of _____. (a) MNCs (b) agencies of the United Nations (c) regional economic groupings (d) transnational organizations

2. The term used to describe global outsourcing of jobs is _____. (a) globalization (b) offshoring (c) virtual work (d) privatization

3. When scholar and consultant Geert Hofstede speaks about "software of the mind," he is referring to _____. (a) culture (b) absolutism (c) ethnocentrism (d) global organizational learning

4. _____is the study of how people in different cultures use space to communicate. (a) Confucian dynamism (b) the Whorfian hypothesis (c) Proxemics (d) Domestic multiculturalism

5. In _____ cultures, people tend to complete one activity at a time. (a) high-context (b) low-context (c) polychronic (d) monochronic

6. A culture in which an important part of communication takes place through nonverbal and situational cues is said to be a _____ culture. (a) monochronic (b) polychronic (c) high-context (d) low-context

7. Cultural values emphasizing respect for tradition, ordering of relationships, and protecting one's "face" are associated with _____. (a) religious differences (b) uncertainty avoidance (c) masculinity–femininity (d) Confucian dynamism

8. One would expect to find respect for authority and acceptance of status differences in cultures with high _____. (a) power distance (b) individualism (c) uncertainty avoidance (d) aggressiveness

9. Asian countries like Japan and China are described on Hofstede's dimensions of national culture as generally high in _____. (a) uncertainty avoidance (b) short-term orientation (c) long-term orientation (d) individualism

10. In Trompenaars's framework for understanding cultural differences, _____ is used to describe different orientations toward nature. (a) inner directed versus outer directed (b) sequential versus polychronic (c) universal versus particular (d) neutral versus emotional

11. When someone is traveling or working in a foreign country, the stage where one becomes uncomfortable and possibly upset with "new" local ways and customs is called _____. (a) culture shock (b) xenophobia (c) expatriatism (d) ethnocentrism

12. In international business, justifying one's practices in a foreign country by saying "When in Rome do as the Romans do" is a sign of _____. (a) ethical absolutism (b) universalism (c) cultural relativism (d) protectionism

13. Management practices such as participative decision making and an emphasis on teamwork are often characteristic of organizations in _____ cultures. (a) monochronic (b) collectivist (c) paternalistic (d) uncertain

14. Which of the following is most characteristic of stereotypical Japanese management practices? (a) consensus decisions (b) fast promotion (c) highly specialized career paths (d) low emphasis on quality

15. Use the concept of global organizational learning in response to this question posed by an American business executive: Should I be using Japanese business practices in America? (a) No, the best approach is to stick with the American ways. (b) Neither yes nor no; the best management these days is found in China. (c) Yes, the Japanese approaches should be implemented without question. (d) Yes and no; try to learn from the Japanese but realize their practices may not fit perfectly in American culture.

Short Response

16. Why is the individualism–collectivism dimension of national culture important in OB?

17. How do power distance values affect management practices across cultures?

18. Define ethnocentrism and give examples of ethnocentric behavior on campus or in your community.

19. An organization trying to operate with Japanese management practices would do what?

Applications Essay

20. Stephen Bachand, the CEO of Canadian Tire, wants to keep his company "ahead of the pack" as foreign retailers try to penetrate the Canadian market. It used to be that American firms such as Wal-Mart and Home Depot were the major threats; now he has learned that the Asian giant Yaohan and the well-known Sainsbury's from Britain are considering operations in Canada. Bachand has heard of your special consulting expertise in "global organizational learning." He is on the telephone now and wants you to explain how the concept can help him keep his company a world-class competitor. With a large consulting contract at stake, what do you tell him about this concept?

OB in Action

These learning activities from *The OB Skills Workbook* are suggested for Chapter 3

CASE	EXPERIENTIAL EXERCISES	SELF-ASSESSMENTS
■ 3. Crossing Borders	■ 6. Expatriate Assignments	■ 4. Global Readiness Index
	■ 7. Cultural Cues	■ 5. Personal Values
	■ 8. Prejudice in Our Lives	

Plus—special learning experiences from *The Jossey-Bass/Pfeiffer Classroom Collection*

Chapter 4

Personality and Individual Differences

Chapter at a Glance

Chapter 4 introduces the importance of personality, values, and attitudes, along with individual differences and further treatment of diversity in the study of today's increasingly diverse work settings. As you read Chapter 4, *keep in mind these study questions.*

WHAT IS PERSONALITY?

HOW DO PERSONALITIES DIFFER?

WHAT ARE VALUE AND ATTITUDE DIFFERENCES AMONG INDIVIDUALS, AND WHY ARE THEY IMPORTANT?

WHAT ARE INDIVIDUAL DIFFERENCES, AND HOW ARE THEY RELATED TO WORKFORCE DIVERSITY?

REVIEW IN END-OF-CHAPTER STUDY GUIDE

More than 39 million Hispanics are changing the face of banking—especially for mega Bank of America (nearly $50 billion in revenues in a recent year). Maria Hijar personifies one such change. She came to America 10 years ago from a tiny bean-growing village in Mexico with a promise to send money back to her mother and nine siblings.

A major problem was that she had a one-hour metro ride from the houses she cleaned to a cut-rate money changing and transmittal shop in central Los Angeles. Then she stood in line another hour and paid up to $35 for each remittance. Similarly, in Mexico, her sister would take a three-hour bus ride to collect funds at a bank, then spend three hours traveling back.

However, recently things changed: Maria came upon Bank of America's SafeSend. Now all Maria has to do is grab the phone and punch buttons to transfer money from her checking to her SafeSend account. From there, Bank of America zips the money to a special ATM account for Maria in Mexico. Her sister travels only 15 minutes to the nearest ATM and withdraws the funds in pesos using her SafeSend card. "This changed my life," says Maria. She is now thinking about getting a Bank of America credit card. In this she epitomizes the new face of banking, and Bank of America is right in the middle of it. The bank dominates the Sunbelt states and is gearing up to grab some 80 percent of its future banking growth through aggressively servicing the fast-growing Hispanic market. A key part of its plan for doing this is to target its own customers, many of whom are Hispanics, who currently use SafeSend. "Hispanics are considered incredibly loyal to brands and to people," says Eusebio Rivera, Bank of America's Chief of Hispanic Initiatives.[1]

> "Hispanics are considered incredibly loyal to brands and to people."

What we have described is becoming more and more characteristic of our rapidly changing economy—diversity at both the employee and customer levels. With diversity comes differences, and with differences come a mix of potential opportunities and problems. Along with diversity and other individual differences come personality, values, and attitudes—all together comprising the bedrock of OB concepts examined in this chapter.

Personality

As the chapter opening suggests, a key individual attribute in the workforce is personality.

What Is Personality?

The term **personality** encompasses the overall combination of characteristics that captures the unique nature of a person as that person reacts and interacts with others. As an example, think of a person who was the billionaire founder of

■ **Personality** represents the overall profile, or combination of characteristics, that captures the unique nature of a person as that person reacts and interacts with others.

a fast-growing, high-tech computer company by the time he was 30; who in his senior year in high school had turned selling newspapers into enough of a business to buy a BMW; who told his management team that his daughter's first words were "Daddy—kill-IBM, Gateway, Compaq"; who learned from production mistakes and brought in senior managers to help his firm; and who is so private he seldom talks about himself. In other words, think of Michael Dell, the founder of Dell Computer, and his personality.[2]

Personality combines a set of physical and mental characteristics that reflect how a person looks, thinks, acts, and feels. Sometimes attempts are made to measure personality with questionnaires or special tests. Frequently, personality can be inferred from behavior alone, such as by the actions of Michael Dell. Either way, personality is an important individual characteristic for managers to understand. An understanding of personality contributes to an understanding of organizational behavior in that we expect a predictable interplay between an individual's personality and his or her tendency to behave in certain ways.

Personality and Development

Just what determines personality? Is personality inherited or genetically determined, or is it formed by experience? You may have heard someone say something like, "She acts like her mother." Similarly, someone may argue that "Bobby is the way he is because of the way he was raised." These two arguments illustrate the nature/nurture controversy: Is personality determined by heredity—that is, by genetic endowment—or by one's environment? As Figure 4.1 shows, these two forces actually operate in combination. Heredity consists of those factors that are determined at conception, including physical characteristics, gender, and personality factors. Environment consists of cultural, social, and situational factors.

The impact of heredity on personality continues to be the source of considerable debate. Perhaps the most general conclusion we can draw is that heredity sets the limits on just how much personality characteristics can be developed; environment determines development within these limits. For instance, a person could be born with a tendency toward authoritarianism, and that tendency could be reinforced in an authoritarian work environment. These limits appear to vary

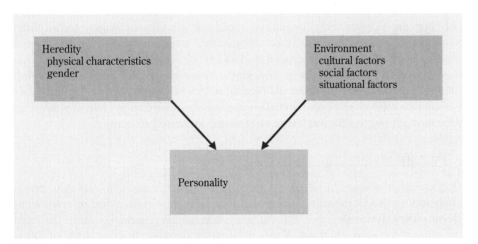

Figure 4.1   Heredity and environmental linkage with personality.

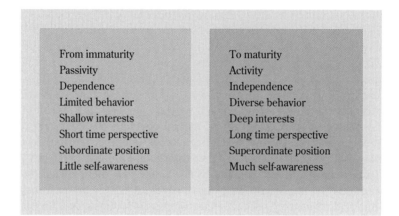

Figure 4.2   Argyris's maturity–immaturity continuum.

from one characteristic to the next, and across all characteristics there is about a 50–50 heredity–environment split.[3]

As we show throughout this book, *cultural values and norms* play a substantial role in the development of an individual's personality and behaviors. Contrast the individualism of U.S. culture with the collectivism of Mexican culture, for example.[4] Social factors reflect such things as family life, religion, and the many kinds of formal and informal groups in which people participate throughout their lives—friendship groups, athletic groups, as well as formal workgroups. Finally, the demands of differing *situational factors* emphasize or constrain different aspects of an individual's personality. For example, in class you are likely to rein in your high spirits and other related behaviors encouraged by your personality. However, at a sporting event, you may be jumping up, cheering, and loudly criticizing the referees.

The **developmental approaches** of Chris Argyris, Daniel Levinson, and Gail Sheehy systematically examine the ways personality develops across time. Argyris notes that people develop along a continuum of dimensions from immaturity to maturity, as shown in Figure 4.2. He believes that many organizations treat mature adults as if they were still immature and that this creates many problems in terms of bringing out the best in employees. Levinson and Sheehy maintain that an individual's personality unfolds in a series of stages across time. Sheehy's model, for example, talks about three stages—ages 18–30, 30–45, and 45–85+. Each of these has a crucial impact on the worker's employment and career, as we show in Chapter 7. The implications are that personalities develop over time and require different managerial responses. Thus, the needs and other personality aspects of people initially entering an organization change sharply as they move through different stages or toward increased maturity.[5]

■ **Developmental approaches** are systematic models of ways in which personality develops across time.

Personality and the Self-Concept

Collectively, the ways in which an individual integrates and organizes the previously mentioned personality aspects and the traits they contain are referred to as **personality dynamics**. It is this category that makes personality more than just the sum of the separate traits. A key personality dynamic in your study of OB is the self-concept.

■ **Personality dynamics** are the ways in which an individual integrates and organizes social traits, values and motives, personal conceptions, and emotional adjustment.

We can describe the **self-concept** as the view individuals have of themselves as physical, social, and spiritual or moral beings.[6] It is a way of recognizing oneself as a distinct human being. A person's self-concept is greatly influenced by his or her culture. For example, Americans tend to disclose much more about themselves than do the English; that is, an American's self-concept is more assertive and talkative.[7]

Two related—and crucial—aspects of the self-concept are self-esteem and self-efficacy. *Self-esteem* is a belief about one's own worth based on an overall self-evaluation.[8] People high in self-esteem see themselves as capable, worthwhile, and acceptable and tend to have few doubts about themselves. The opposite is true of a person low in self-esteem. Some OB research suggests that whereas high self-esteem generally can boost performance and human resource maintenance, when under pressure, people with high self-esteem may become boastful and act egotistically. They may also be overconfident at times and fail to obtain important information.[9]

ETHICS AND SOCIAL RESPONSIBILITY

NICKLAUS AND THE FIRST TEE

Jack Nicklaus's father introduced him to golf and, within the game's context, Jack learned respect, integrity, and sportsmanship lessons. Jack, often acknowledged as the greatest player in history, wanted to teach these same lessons to current youths. Thus, he eagerly embraced The First Tee, a World Golf Foundation initiative that gives America's youth a chance to develop life-enhancing values through golf and character education. He passes on what he learned from his father.

The immediate goal is to introduce half a million kids to golf by December 2005. Nicklaus speaks throughout the country to promote the $50 million effort. He also raises money for Mended Hearts, a cardiovascular patient support group.

Question: How would you relate Nicklaus's behavior and values to your estimate of his self-concept?

Self-efficacy, sometimes called the "effectance motive," is a more specific version of self-esteem; it is an individual's belief about the likelihood of successfully completing a specific task. You could be high in self-esteem yet have a feeling of low self-efficacy about performing a certain task, such as public speaking.

How Personalities Differ

Big Five Personality Traits

Numerous lists of personality traits—enduring characteristics describing an individual's behavior—have been developed, many of which have been used in OB research and can be looked at in different ways. A key starting point is to con-

> **Self-concept** is the view individuals have of themselves as physical, social, and spiritual or moral beings.

sider the personality dimensions that recent research has distilled from extensive lists into what is called the "Big Five":[10]

The Big Five personality dimensions

- *Extraversion*—outgoing, sociable, assertive
- *Agreeableness*—good-natured, trusting, cooperative
- *Conscientiousness*—responsible, dependable, persistent
- *Emotional stability*—unworried, secure, relaxed
- *Openness to experience*—imaginative, curious, broad-minded

Standardized personality tests determine how positively or negatively an individual scores on each of these dimensions. For instance, a person scoring high on openness to experience tends to ask lots of questions and to think in new and unusual ways. You can consider a person's individual personality profile across the five dimensions. In terms of job performance, research has shown that conscientiousness predicts job performance across five occupational groups of professions—engineers, police, managers, salespersons, and skilled and semiskilled employees. Predictability of the other dimensions depends on the occupational group. For instance, not surprisingly, extraversion predicts performance for sales and managerial positions.

A second approach to looking at OB personality traits is to divide them into social traits, personal conception traits, and emotional adjustment traits, and then to consider how those categories come together dynamically.[11]

Social Traits

Social traits are surface-level traits that reflect the way a person appears to others when interacting in various social settings.

Social traits are surface-level traits that reflect the way a person appears to others when interacting in various social settings. Problem-solving style, based on the work of Carl Jung, a noted psychologist, is one measure representing social traits.[12] It reflects the way a person goes about gathering and evaluating information in solving problems and making decisions.

Information gathering involves getting and organizing data for use. Styles of information gathering vary from sensation to intuitive. *Sensation-type individuals* prefer routine and order and emphasize well-defined details in gathering information; they would rather work with known facts than look for possibilities. By contrast, *intuitive-type individuals* prefer the "big picture." They like solving new problems, dislike routine, and would rather look for possibilities than work with facts.

The second component of problem solving, *evaluation*, involves making judgments about how to deal with information once it has been collected. Styles of information evaluation vary from an emphasis on feeling to an emphasis on thinking. *Feeling-type individuals* are oriented toward conformity and try to accommodate themselves to other people. They try to avoid problems that may result in disagreements. *Thinking-type individuals* use reason and intellect to deal with problems and downplay emotions.

When these two dimensions (information gathering and evaluation) are combined, four basic problem-solving styles result: sensation–feeling (SF), intuitive–feeling (IF), sensation–thinking (ST), and intuitive–thinking (IT), together with summary descriptions, as shown in Figure 4.3.

Research indicates that there is a fit between the styles of individuals and the kinds of decisions they prefer. For example, STs (sensation–thinkers) prefer analytical strategies—those that emphasize detail and method. IFs (intuitive–feelers)

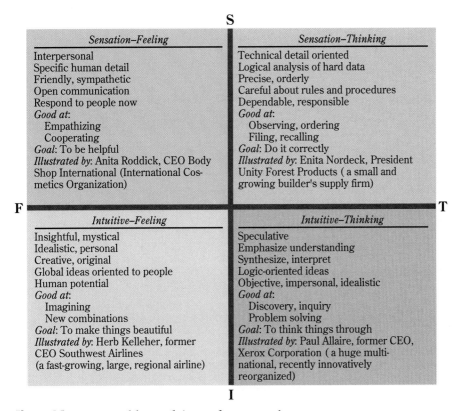

S

Sensation–Feeling	Sensation–Thinking
Interpersonal	Technical detail oriented
Specific human detail	Logical analysis of hard data
Friendly, sympathetic	Precise, orderly
Open communication	Careful about rules and procedures
Respond to people now	Dependable, responsible
Good at:	*Good at*:
Empathizing	Observing, ordering
Cooperating	Filing, recalling
Goal: To be helpful	*Goal*: Do it correctly
Illustrated by: Anita Roddick, CEO Body Shop International (International Cosmetics Organization)	*Illustrated by*: Enita Nordeck, President Unity Forest Products (a small and growing builder's supply firm)

F ─────────────────────────────────── **T**

Intuitive–Feeling	Intuitive–Thinking
Insightful, mystical	Speculative
Idealistic, personal	Emphasize understanding
Creative, original	Synthesize, interpret
Global ideas oriented to people	Logic-oriented ideas
Human potential	Objective, impersonal, idealistic
Good at:	*Good at*:
Imagining	Discovery, inquiry
New combinations	Problem solving
Goal: To make things beautiful	*Goal*: To think things through
Illustrated by: Herb Kelleher, former CEO Southwest Airlines (a fast-growing, large, regional airline)	*Illustrated by*: Paul Allaire, former CEO, Xerox Corporation (a huge multi-national, recently innovatively reorganized)

I

Figure 4.3   Four problem-solving style summaries.

prefer intuitive strategies—those that emphasize an overall pattern and fit. Not surprisingly, mixed styles (sensation–feelers or intuitive–thinkers) select both analytical and intuitive strategies. Other findings also indicate that thinkers tend to have higher motivation than do feelers and that individuals who emphasize sensations tend to have higher job satisfaction than do intuitives. These and other findings suggest a number of basic differences among different problem-solving styles, emphasizing the importance of fitting such styles with a task's information processing and evaluation requirements.[13]

Problem-solving styles are most frequently measured by the (typically 100-item) *Myers–Briggs Type Indicator (MBTI)*, which asks individuals how they usually act or feel in specific situations. Firms such as Apple, AT&T, and Exxon, as well as hospitals, educational institutions, and military organizations, have used the Myers–Briggs for various aspects of management development.[14]

Personal Conception Traits

The *personal conception traits* represent the way individuals tend to think about their social and physical setting as well as their major beliefs and personal orientation concerning a range of issues.

Locus of Control   The extent to which a person feels able to control his or her own life is concerned with a person's internal–external orientation and is measured

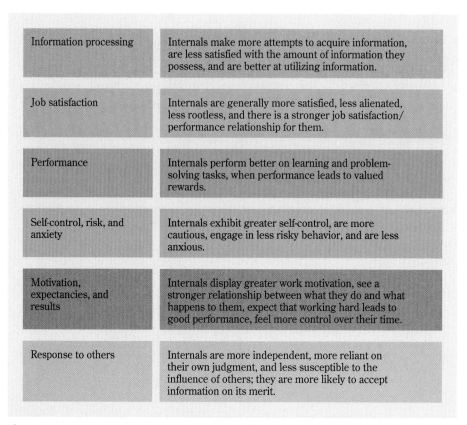

Information processing	Internals make more attempts to acquire information, are less satisfied with the amount of information they possess, and are better at utilizing information.
Job satisfaction	Internals are generally more satisfied, less alienated, less rootless, and there is a stronger job satisfaction/performance relationship for them.
Performance	Internals perform better on learning and problem-solving tasks, when performance leads to valued rewards.
Self-control, risk, and anxiety	Internals exhibit greater self-control, are more cautious, engage in less risky behavior, and are less anxious.
Motivation, expectancies, and results	Internals display greater work motivation, see a stronger relationship between what they do and what happens to them, expect that working hard leads to good performance, feel more control over their time.
Response to others	Internals are more independent, more reliant on their own judgment, and less susceptible to the influence of others; they are more likely to accept information on its merit.

Figure 4.4   Some ways in which internals differ from externals.

by Rotter's locus of control instrument.[15] People have personal conceptions about whether events are controlled primarily by themselves, which indicates an internal orientation, or by outside forces, such as their social and physical environment, which indicates an external orientation. Internals, or persons with an internal locus of control, believe that they control their own fate or destiny. In contrast, externals, or persons with an external locus of control, believe that much of what happens to them is beyond their control and is determined by environmental forces.

In general, externals are more extraverted in their interpersonal relationships and are more oriented toward the world around them. Internals tend to be more introverted and are more oriented toward their own feelings and ideas. Figure 4.4 suggests that internals tend to do better on tasks requiring complex information processing and learning as well as initiative. Many managerial and professional jobs have these kinds of requirements.

Authoritarianism/Dogmatism   Both "authoritarianism" and "dogmatism" deal with the rigidity of a person's beliefs. A person high in **authoritarianism** tends to adhere rigidly to conventional values and to obey recognized authority. This person is concerned with toughness and power and opposes the use of subjective feelings. An individual high in **dogmatism** sees the world as a threatening place. This person regards legitimate authority as absolute and accepts or rejects others according to how much they agree with accepted authority. Supe-

Authoritarianism is a tendency to adhere rigidly to conventional values and to obey recognized authority.

Dogmatism leads a person to see the world as a threatening place and regard authority as absolute.

riors who possess these latter traits tend to be rigid and closed. At the same time, dogmatic subordinates tend to want certainty imposed upon them.[16]

From an ethical standpoint, we can expect highly authoritarian individuals to present a special problem because they are so susceptible to authority that in their eagerness to comply they may behave unethically.[17] For example, we might speculate that many of the Nazis who were involved in war crimes during World War II were high in authoritarianism or dogmatism; they believed so strongly in authority that they followed their unethical orders without question.

Machiavellianism   The third personal conceptions dimension is Machiavellianism, which owes its origins to Niccolo Machiavelli. The very name of this sixteenth-century author evokes visions of a master of guile, deceit, and opportunism in interpersonal relations. Machiavelli earned his place in history by writing *The Prince*, a nobleman's guide to the acquisition and use of power.[18] The subject of Machiavelli's book is manipulation as the basic means of gaining and keeping control of others. From its pages emerges the personality profile of a Machiavellian— someone who views and manipulates others purely for personal gain.

Psychologists have developed a series of instruments called Mach scales to measure a person's Machiavellian orientation.[19] A high-Mach personality is someone who tends to behave in ways consistent with Machiavelli's basic principles. Such individuals approach situations logically and thoughtfully and are even capable of lying to achieve personal goals. They are rarely swayed by loyalty, friendships, past promises, or the opinions of others, and they are skilled at influencing others.

Research using the Mach scales provides insight into the way high and low Machs may be expected to behave in various situations. A person with a "cool" and "detached" high-Mach personality can be expected to take control and try to exploit loosely structured environmental situations but will perform in a perfunctory, even detached, manner in highly structured situations. Low Machs tend to accept direction imposed by others in loosely structured situations; they work hard to do well in highly structured ones. For example, we might expect that, where the situation permitted, a high Mach would do or say whatever it took to get his or her way. In contrast, a low Mach would tend to be much more strongly guided by ethical considerations and would be less likely to lie or cheat or to get away with lying or cheating.

Self-Monitoring   A final personal conceptions trait of special importance to managers is self-monitoring. **Self-monitoring** reflects a person's ability to adjust his or her behavior to external, situational (environmental) factors.[20]

High self-monitoring individuals are sensitive to external cues and tend to behave differently in different situations. Like high Machs, high self-monitors can present a very different appearance from their true self. In contrast, low self-monitors, like their low-Mach counterparts, aren't able to disguise their behaviors—"what you see is what you get." There is also evidence that high self-monitors are closely attuned to the behavior of others and conform more readily than do low self-monitors.[21] Thus, they appear flexible and may be especially good at responding to the kinds of situational contingencies emphasized throughout this book. For example, high self-monitors should be especially good at changing their leadership behavior to fit subordinates with high or low experience, tasks with high or low structure, and so on.

> **Self-monitoring** reflects a person's ability to adjust his or her behavior to external, situational (environmental) factors.

Emotional Adjustment Traits

■ Emotional adjustment traits measure how much an individual experiences emotional distress or displays unacceptable acts.

The **emotional adjustment traits** measure how much an individual experiences emotional distress or displays unacceptable acts. Often the person's health is affected. Although numerous such traits are cited in the literature, a frequently encountered one especially important for OB is the Type A/Type B orientation.

Type A and Type B Orientation   To get a feel for this orientation, take the following quiz and then read on.[22] Circle the number that best characterizes you on each of the following pairs of characteristics.

Casual about appointments	1 2 3 4 5 6 7 8	Never late
Not competitive	1 2 3 4 5 6 7 8	Very competitive
Never feel rushed	1 2 3 4 5 6 7 8	Always feel rushed
Take one thing at a time	1 2 3 4 5 6 7 8	Try to do many things
Do things slowly	1 2 3 4 5 6 7 8	Do things fast
Express my feelings	1 2 3 4 5 6 7 8	Hold in my feelings
Many outside interests	1 2 3 4 5 6 7 8	Few outside interests

Total your points for the seven items in the quiz. Multiply this total by 3 to arrive at a final score. Use this total to locate your Type A/Type B orientation on the following list.

FINAL POINTS	A/B ORIENTATION
Below 90	B
90–99	B+
100–105	A-
106–119	A
120 or more	A+

■ Type A orientations are characterized by impatience, desire for achievement and less competitive nature than Type A.

■ Type B orientations are characterized by an easygoing and less competitive nature than Type A.

Individuals with a **Type A orientation** are characterized by impatience, desire for achievement, and perfectionism. In contrast, those with a **Type B orientation** are characterized as more easygoing and less competitive in relation to daily events.[23]

Type A people tend to work fast and to be abrupt, uncomfortable, irritable, and aggressive. Such tendencies indicate "obsessive" behavior, a fairly widespread—but not always helpful—trait among managers. Many managers are hard-driving, detail-oriented people who have high performance standards and thrive on routine. But when such work obsessions are carried to the extreme, they may lead to greater concerns for details than for results, resistance to change, overzealous control of subordinates, and various kinds of interpersonal difficulties, which may even include threats and physical violence. In contrast, Type B managers tend to be much more laid back and patient in their dealings with co-workers and subordinates.

Values and Attitudes

Joining personality characteristics as important individual difference characteristics are values and attitudes.

Leaders on Leadership

FOCUSING ON VALUES THROUGH PRAGMATIC INQUIRY

F. Byron (Ron) Nahser owns three businesses, all built around his ethical leadership beliefs while fitting both his Chicago-area and global clients. He has developed an activity called "pragmatic inquiry," which helps to determine a "belief" or "truth" in terms of the direct behavior that results from embracing that belief or truth. He and what is called the "Globe Group" use this approach for both clients and their own people to ensure that values are used to drive decisions. A major leadership challenge is how to have people live the values in tough times; for example, "Are we doing the right thing as we downsize"? "Is the way we are treating people a sustainable relationship?"

Question: How are ethics and morality played out in leadership such as Nahser's?

Values

Values can be defined as broad preferences concerning appropriate courses of action or outcomes. As such, values reflect a person's sense of right and wrong or what "ought" to be.[24] "Equal rights for all" and "People should be treated with respect and dignity" are representative of values. Values tend to influence attitudes and behavior. For example, if you value equal rights for all and you go to work for an organization that treats its managers much better than it does its workers, you may form the attitude that the company is an unfair place to work; consequently, you may not produce well or may perhaps leave the company. It's likely that if the company had had a more egalitarian policy, your attitude and behaviors would have been more positive.

Sources and Types of Values   Parents, friends, teachers, and external reference groups are all value sources that can influence individual values. Indeed, peoples' values develop as a product of the learning and experience they encounter from various sources in the cultural setting in which they live. As learning and experiences differ from one person to another, value differences result. Such differences are likely to be deep seated and difficult (though not impossible) to change; many have their roots in early childhood and the way a person has been raised.[25]

The noted psychologist Milton Rokeach has developed a well-known set of values classified into two broad categories.[26] **Terminal values** reflect a person's preferences concerning the "ends" to be achieved; they are the goals individuals would like to achieve during their lifetime. Rokeach divides values into 18 terminal values and 18 instrumental values, as summarized in Figure 4.5. **Instrumental values** re-

Values can be defined as broad preferences concerning appropriate courses of action or outcomes.

Sources and types of values Parents, friends, teachers, and external reference groups can all influence individual values.

Terminal values reflect a person's preferences concerning the "ends" to be achieved.

Instrumental values reflect a person's beliefs about the means for achieving desired ends.

Terminal Values	Instrumental Values
A comfortable life (and prosperous)	Ambitious (hardworking)
An exciting life (stimulating)	Broad-minded (open-minded)
A sense of accomplishment (lasting contibution)	Capable (competent, effective)
A world at peace (free of war and conflict)	Cheerful (lighthearted, joyful)
A world of beauty (beauty of nature and the arts)	Clean (neat, tidy)
Equality (brotherhood, equal opportunity)	Courageous (standing up for beliefs)
Family security (taking care of loved ones)	Forgiving (willing to pardon)
Freedom (independence, free choice)	Helpful (working for others' welfare)
Happiness (contentedness)	Honest (sincere, truthful)
Inner harmony (freedom from inner conflict)	Imaginative (creative, daring)
Mature love (sexual and spiritual intimacy)	Independent (self-sufficient, self-reliant)
National security (attack protection)	Intellectual (intelligent, reflective)
Pleasure (leisurely, enjoyable life)	Logical (rational, consistent)
Salvation (saved, eternal life)	Loving (affectionate, tender)
Self-respect (self-esteem)	Obedient (dutiful, respectful)
Social recognition (admiration, respect)	Polite (courteous, well mannered)
True friendship (close companionship)	Responsible (reliable, dependable)
Wisdom (mature understanding of life)	Self-controlled (self-disciplined)

Figure 4.5   Rokeach value survey.

flect the "means" for achieving desired ends. They represent how you might go about achieving your important end states, depending on the relative importance you attached to the instrumental values.

Illustrative research shows, not surprisingly, that both terminal and instrumental values differ by group (for example, executives, activist workers, and union members).[27] These preference differences can encourage conflict or agreement when different groups have to deal with each other.

Another frequently used classification of human values has been developed by psychologist Gordon Allport and his associates. These values fall into six major types:[28]

Allport's six value categories

- *Theoretical*—interest in the discovery of truth through reasoning and systematic thinking
- *Economic*—interest in usefulness and practicality, including the accumulation of wealth
- *Aesthetic*—interest in beauty, form, and artistic harmony
- *Social*—interest in people and love as a human relationship
- *Political*—interest in gaining power and influencing other people
- *Religious*—interest in unity and in understanding the cosmos as a whole

Once again, groups differ in the way they rank order the importance of these values, as shown in the following.[29]

- *Ministers*—religious, social, aesthetic, political, theoretical, economic
- *Purchasing executive*—economic, theoretical, political, religious, aesthetic, social
- *Industrial scientists*—theoretical, political, economic, aesthetic, religious, social

The previous value classifications have had a major impact on the values literature, but they were not specifically designed for people in a work setting. A
more recent values schema, developed by Bruce Maglino and associates, is
aimed at people in the workplace:[30]

- *Achievement*—getting things done and working hard to accomplish difficult
  things in life
- *Helping and concern for others*—being concerned with other people and
  helping others
- *Honesty*—telling the truth and doing what you feel is right
- *Fairness*—being impartial and doing what is fair for all concerned

These four values have been shown to be especially important in the workplace;
thus, the framework should be particularly relevant for studying values in OB.

In particular, values can be influential through **value congruence**, which
occurs when individuals express positive feelings upon encountering others who
exhibit values similar to their own. When values differ, or are *incongruent*, conflicts over such things as goals and the means to achieve them may result.
Maglino and colleagues' value schema was used to examine value congruence
between leaders and followers. The researchers found greater follower satisfaction with the leader when there was such congruence in terms of achievement,
helping, honesty, and fairness values.[31]

Value congruence oc-
curs when individuals ex-
press positive feelings
upon encountering others
who exhibit values similar
to their own.

Patterns and Trends in Values We should also be aware of applied research
and insightful analyses of values trends over time. Daniel Yankelovich, for example, is known for his informative public opinion polls among North American
workers, and William Fox has prepared a carefully reasoned book analyzing values trends.[32] Both Yankelovich and Fox note movements away from earlier values, with Fox emphasizing a decline in such shared values as duty, honesty, responsibility, and the like, while Yankelovich notes a movement away from
valuing economic incentives, organizational loyalty, and work-related identity.
The movement is toward valuing meaningful work, pursuit of leisure, and personal identity and self-fulfillment. Yankelovich believes that the modern manager
must be able to recognize value differences and trends among people at work.
For example, he reports finding higher productivity among younger workers
who are employed in jobs that match their values and/or who are supervised by
managers who share their values, reinforcing the concept of value congruence.

In a nationwide sample, managers and human resource professionals were
asked to identify the work-related values they believed to be most important to
individuals in the workforce, both now and in the near future.[33] The nine most
popular values named were recognition for competence and accomplishments,
respect and dignity, personal choice and freedom, involvement at work, pride in
one's work, lifestyle quality, financial security, self-development, and health and
wellness. These values are especially important for managers because they indicate some key concerns of the new workforce. Even though each individual
worker places his or her own importance on these values, and even though the
United States today has by far the most diverse workforce in its history, this overall characterization is a good place for managers to start when dealing with
workers in the new workplace. It is important to note, however, that although

values are individual preferences, many tend to be shared within cultures and organizations.

Attitudes

Attitudes are influenced by values and are acquired from the same sources as values: friends, teachers, parents, and role models. Attitudes focus on specific people or objects, whereas values have a more general focus and are more stable than attitudes. "Employees should be allowed to participate" is a value; your positive or negative feeling about your job because of the participation it allows is an attitude. Formally defined, an **attitude** is a predisposition to respond in a positive or negative way to someone or something in one's environment. For example, when you say that you "like" or "dislike" someone or something, you are expressing an attitude. It's important to remember that an attitude, like a value, is a hypothetical construct; that is, one never sees, touches, or actually isolates an attitude. Rather, attitudes are *inferred* from the things people say, informally or in formal opinion polls or through their behavior.

Figure 4.6 shows attitudes as accompanied by antecedents and results.[34] The beliefs and values antecedents in the figure form the **cognitive component** of an attitude: the beliefs, opinions, knowledge, or information a person possesses. **Beliefs** represent ideas about someone or something and the conclusions people draw about them; they convey a sense of "what is" to an individual. "My job lacks responsibility" is a belief shown in the figure. Note that the beliefs may or may not be accurate. "Job responsibility is important" is a corresponding aspect of the cognitive component, which reflects an underlying value.

The **affective component** of an attitude is a specific feeling regarding the personal impact of the antecedents. This is the actual attitude itself, such as "I don't like my job." The **behavioral component** is an intention to behave in a certain way based on your specific feelings or attitudes. This intended behavior is a result of an attitude and is a predisposition to act in a specific way, such as "I'm going to quit my job."

Attitudes and Behavior   You should recognize that the link between attitudes and behavior is tentative. An attitude results in *intended* behavior; this intention may or may not be carried out in a given circumstance.

Attitude is a predisposition to respond in a positive or negative way to someone or something in one's environment.

The cognitive component of an attitude reflects the beliefs, opinions, knowledge, or information a person possesses.

Beliefs represent ideas about someone or something and the conclusions people draw about them.

The affective component of an attitude is a specific feeling regarding the personal impact of the antecedents.

The behavioral component is an intention to behave in a certain way based on your specific feelings or attitudes.

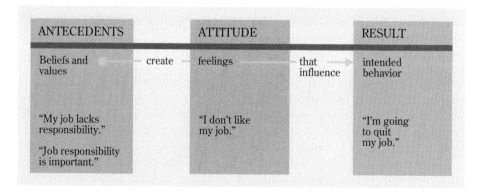

Figure 4.6   A world-related example of the three components of attitudes.

In general, the more specific attitudes and behaviors are, the stronger the relationship. For example, say you are a French-Canadian webmaster and you are asked about your satisfaction with your supervisor's treatment of French-Canadian webmasters. You also indicate the strength of your intent to look for another webmaster job in a similar kind of organization within the next six months. Here, both the attitude and the behavior are specifically stated (they refer to French-Canadian webmasters, and they identify a given kind of organization over a specific time period). Thus, we would expect to find a relatively strong relationship between these attitudes and how aggressively you actually start looking for another webmaster job.

It is also important that a good deal of freedom be available to carry out the intent. In the example just given, the freedom to follow through would be sharply restricted if the demand for webmasters dropped substantially.

Finally, the attitude and behavior linkage tends to be stronger when the person in question has had experience with the stated attitude. For example, assuming you are a business administration or management major, the relationship between your course attitude and/or your intent to drop the course and your later behavior of actually doing so would probably be stronger in your present OB course than in the first week of your enrollment in an advanced course in nuclear fission.[35]

Attitudes and the Workplace   Even though attitudes do not always predict behavior, the link between attitudes and potential or intended behavior is important for managers to understand. Think about your work experiences or conversations with other people about their work. It is not uncommon to hear concerns expressed about someone's "bad attitude." These concerns typically reflect displeasure with the behavioral consequences with which the poor attitude is associated. Unfavorable attitudes in the form of low job satisfaction can result in costly labor turnover, absenteeism, tardiness, and even impaired physical or mental health. One of the manager's responsibilities, therefore, is to recognize attitudes and to understand both their antecedents and their potential implications.

Attitudes and Cognitive Consistency   Leon Festinger, a noted social psychologist, uses the term **cognitive dissonance** to describe a state of inconsistency between an individual's attitudes and his or her behavior.[36] Let's assume that you have the attitude that recycling is good for the economy but you don't recycle. Festinger predicts that such an inconsistency results in discomfort and a desire to reduce or eliminate it by (1) changing the underlying attitude, (2) changing future behavior, or (3) developing new ways of explaining or rationalizing the inconsistency.

▪ **Cognitive dissonance** describes a state of inconsistency between an individual's attitude and behavior.

Two factors that influence which of the above choices tend to be made are the degree of control a person thinks he or she has over the situation and the magnitude of the rewards involved. In terms of control, if your boss won't let you recycle office trash, you would be less likely to change your attitude than if you voluntarily chose not to recycle. You might instead choose the rationalization option. In terms of rewards, if they are high enough, rewards tend to reduce your feeling of inconsistency: if I'm rewarded even though I don't recycle, the lack of recycling must not be so bad after all.

BASEBALL GLOBALIZATION

Welcome to the globalization of baseball. Not long ago, more than 25 percent of big league players came from outside our borders. The Dominican Republic, with players such as Alfonso Soriano, is today the largest contributor. Bruce Markusen, a historian at the National Baseball Hall of Fame, argues that soon we will be seeing players from such countries as Italy and Holland and that every team needs to have a global presence.

Question: How will the global presence affect personality and individual difference variables needed for successful baseball players?

Individual Differences and Diversity

Workforce diversity is differences based on gender, race and ethnicity, age, and able-bodiedness.

A majority of *Fortune* 500 companies, including Colgate Palmolive, Corning, and Quaker Oats, are now providing incentives for executives to deal successfully with workforce diversity.[37] **Workforce diversity** refers to the presence of individual human characteristics that make people different from one another.[38] More specifically, this diversity comprises key demographic differences among members of a given workforce, including gender, race and ethnicity, age, and able-bodiedness. Sometimes they also encompass other factors, such as marital status, parental status, and religion.[39] The challenge is how to manage workforce diversity in a way that both respects the individual's unique perspectives and contributions and promotes a shared sense of organization vision and identity.

Workforce diversity has increased in both the United States and Canada, as it has in much of the rest of the world. For example, in the United States, between 2000 and 2010, females in the workforce are expected to increase by 15 percent so that more than 62 percent of the women in the United States are expected to be working in 2010. Also, African-Americans are expected to increase by 26 percent and Hispanics by 43 percent. At the same time, those 40 and older are projected to make up more than one-half of the labor force.

Stereotyping occurs when one thinks of an individual as belonging to a group or category (e.g., elderly person) and the characteristics commonly associated with the group or category are assigned to the individual in question.

All of this is in sharp contrast to the traditionally younger, mostly white American male labor force. Canadian and U.K. trends for women are similar.[40]

As the workforce becomes increasingly diverse, the possibility of stereotyping and discrimination increases and managing diversity becomes more important. **Stereotyping** occurs when one thinks of an individual as belonging to a group or category—for instance, elderly person—and the characteristics commonly associated with the group or category are assigned to the individual in question—for instance, older people aren't creative. **Demographic characteristics** may serve as the basis of stereotypes that obscure individual differences and prevent people from getting to know others as individuals and accurately assessing their performance potential. If you believe that older people are not creative, for example, you may mistakenly decide not to assign a very inventive 60-year-old person to an important task force.

Demographic characteristics are the background variables (e.g., age, gender) that help shape what a person becomes over time.

Discrimination against certain people in the organization is not only a violation of U.S., Canadian, and European Union (EU) laws, but it is also counterproductive because it prevents the contributions of people who are discriminated against from being fully utilized. Many firms are increasingly recognizing that a diverse workforce that reflects societal differences helps bring them closer to their customers.

Equal Employment Opportunity

Equal employment opportunity involves both workplace nondiscrimination and affirmative action. Employment decisions are nondiscriminatory when there is no intent to exclude or disadvantage legally protected groups. *Affirmative action* is a set of remedial actions designed to compensate for proven discrimination or correct for statistical imbalances in the labor force (e.g., local workers are 90 percent Hispanic, and your organization employs only 10 percent Hispanics).[41]

The most comprehensive statute prohibiting employment discrimination is Title VII of the Civil Rights Act of 1964. This act prohibits employers from discriminating against any individual with respect to compensation, terms, or conditions of employment because of race, color, religion, sex, or national origin. Affirmative action plans are required of federal government agencies and federal contractors, as well as organizations found to be in noncompliance with equal employment opportunity provisions. Many organizations also have implemented voluntary affirmative action plans.[42]

Affirmative action is legally driven by federal, state and provincial, and local laws, as well as numerous court cases. It requires written reports containing plans and statistical goals for specific groups of people in terms of such employment practices as hiring, promotions, and layoffs.[43]

Demography and Individual Differences

Demographic characteristics are the background characteristics that help shape what a person becomes. Such attributes may be thought of in both current terms—for example, an employee's current medical status—and historical terms—for instance, where and how long a person has worked at various jobs. Demographic characteristics of special interest from equal employment opportunity and workplace diversity considerations include gender, age, able-bodiness, and race and ethnicity.

Gender   The research on working women in general tells us that there are very few differences between men and women that affect job performance (see The Effective Manager 4.1). Thus, men and women show no consistent differences in their problem-solving abilities, analytical skills, competitive drive, motivation, learning ability, or sociability. However, women are reported to be more conforming and to have lower expectations of success than men do. And women's absenteeism rates tend to be higher than those of men. This latter finding may change, however, as we see men starting to play a more active role in raising children; absenteeism is

THE EFFECTIVE MANAGER 4.1

Tips in Dealing with Male and Female Managers

- Do not assume that male and female managers differ in personal qualities.
- Make sure that policies, practices, and programs minimize gender differences in managers' job experiences.
- Do not assume that management success is more likely for either females or males.
- Recognize that there will be excellent, good, and poor managers within each gender.
- Understand that success requires the best use of human talent, regardless of gender.

Nothing Compares to Flying

In New Carlisle, Ohio, a Cherokee 140 single-engine plane lands. At the controls is Violet Blowers, age 84. She has been flying for 36 years. She also is one of only 12 women in the United Flying Octogenarians, a 420-member club for U.S. pilots age 80 and older.

also likely to be less frequent as telecommuting, flexible working hours, and the like become more prevalent.[44] In respect to pay, women's earnings have risen slowly from 59 percent of men's in 1975 to 76 percent more recently.[45] Certainly, this rise is not consistent with the large increase of women in the labor force since 1970.[46]

We have summarized a number of individual differences between men and women in the workplace and generally found few differences. Now, following recent researchers and recognizing the controversial nature of data, we summarize conclusions about differences between men and women as leaders.[47] We focus on three leadership questions: (1) What are differences in men's and women's leadership behaviors? (2) Is there prejudice against female leaders? (3) What are some leadership prospects for women?

Differences in Leader Behaviors   First, women tend to be more democratic and less autocratic than men, but not by much. Second, women tend to engage in more transformational behavior and deliver more rewards for good performance than do men.

Prejudice Against Females   Prejudice toward female leaders can come when conforming to their gender (communal) role would produce a failure to meet requirements of the leader role and conforming to the leader role would produce a failure to meet requirements of their gender role. The latter can result in lesser rewards for appropriate leadership behavior than a man would receive.

Leadership Prospects   In spite of the prejudice that still exists, the outlook for women's leadership participation is promising. More and more women are entering leadership positions in industrialized countries. Also, organizations can gain from putting women in leadership positions because it enhances the leadership pool.

Age   The research findings concerning age are particularly important given the aging of the workforce. People age 50 and older are expected to increase by nearly 50 percent between 2000 and 2010.[48] Older workers are susceptible to being stereotyped as inflexible and undesirable in other ways. In some cases, workers as young as age 40 are considered to be "old" and complain that their experience and skills are no longer valued. Age-discrimination lawsuits are increasingly common in the United States.[49] Such discrimination also operates in Britain, where 44 percent of older managers say they have experienced age discrimination.[50] On the other hand, small businesses in particular tend to value older workers for their experience, stability, and low turnover. Research is consistent with these preferences and also shows lower avoidable absences among older workers.[51] Finally, to the extent that age is linked to experience or job tenure, there is a positive relationship between seniority and performance. More experienced workers tend to have low absence rates and relatively low turnover.

Able-Bodiedness   Even though recent studies report that disabled workers do their jobs as well as, or better than, nondisabled workers, nearly three-quarters of severely disabled persons are reported to be unemployed. Almost 80 percent of those with disabilities say they want to work.[52] Once again, the expected shortage of traditional workers is predicted to lead to a reexamination of hiring policies. More firms are expected to give serious consideration to hiring disabled workers, particularly given that the cost of accommodating these workers has been shown to be low.[53]

TECH COMPANIES AND THE BOOMER GENERATION

To Annemarie Cooke, 50, the world looks somewhat like an impressionist painting. Anything beyond arm's length is almost impossible to make out. Once a newspaper reporter whose vision began to fail some 25 years ago, she now uses software that reads aloud what is on the screen. She is currently an executive at a nonprofit organization for the blind and dyslexic. However, she still has problems with cell phones and their tiny controls, which illustrates that technology companies are just beginning to work hard at making their tech equipment more user-friendly for people with disabilities.

Question: What might be some increasingly user-friendly developments to enhance contributions of older and/or disabled workers?

Racial and Ethnic Groups   Consistent with some current literature, we use the term "racial and ethnic groups" to reflect the broad spectrum of employees of differing ethnicities or races who make up an ever-increasing portion of the new workforce.[54] Of particular significance in the American workplace is diversity reflected in an increasing proportion of African-Americans, Asian-Americans, and Hispanic-Americans.[55] Projections by the Bureau of Labor Statistics estimate that they will constitute 27 percent of the workforce by 2005. The Hudson Institute extends this projection to 32 percent by 2020.[56] The potential for stereotypes and discrimination to adversely affect career opportunities and progress for members of these and other minority groups must be recognized.

Even though employment decisions based on demographic differences are allowable under Title VII if they can be justified as bona fide occupational qualifications reasonable to normal business operations, race cannot be one of these. Case law has shown that these qualifications are always extremely difficult to justify.[57] In any event, the job of flight attendant is a case in point. When the airlines failed to show why men could not perform flight attendant duties as well as females, gender restrictions on hiring were lifted.

Before leaving this section on demographic differences, it is important to reiterate the following:

• Demographic variables are important to consider in order to respect and best deal with the needs or concerns of people of different genders, ethnic backgrounds, ages, and so forth.

• However, these differences are too easily linked with stereotypes, which must be avoided.

• Demography is not a good indicator in seeking good individual–job fits. Rather, aptitude/ability, personality, and values and attitudes are what count.

Aptitude and Ability

■ Aptitude represents a person's capability of learning something.

■ Ability reflects a person's existing capacity to perform the various tasks needed for a given job.

Moving beyond demographic differences, let's consider aptitude and ability. **Aptitude** refers to a person's capability of learning something, whereas **ability** refers to a person's existing capacity to perform the various tasks needed for a given job and includes both relevant knowledge and skills.[58] In other words, aptitudes are potential abilities, whereas abilities are the knowledge and skills that an individual currently possesses.

Aptitudes and abilities are important considerations for a manager when initially hiring or selecting candidates for a job. We are all acquainted with various tests used to measure mental aptitudes and abilities. Some of these provide an overall intelligent quotient (IQ) score (e.g., the Stanford-Binet IQ Test). Others provide measures of more specific competencies that are required of people entering various educational programs or career fields. You have probably taken the ACT or SAT college entrance tests. Such tests are designed to facilitate the screening and selection of applicants for educational programs or jobs. In addition to mental aptitudes and abilities, some jobs, such as firefighters and police, require tests for physical abilities. Muscular strength and cardiovascular endurance are two of many physical ability dimensions.[59]

For legal purposes, demonstrated evidence must be presented that those scoring more favorably on the tests will tend to be more successful in their educational program, career field, or job performance than those with lower scores. In other words, there must be a fit between specific aptitudes and abilities and job requirements. If you want to be a surgeon, for instance, and cannot demonstrate good hand–eye coordination, there will not be a good ability–job fit. Such a fit is so important that it is a core concept in Chapter 8 on performance management and rewards.

Managing Diversity and Individual Differences

The concept of managing diversity in organizations emphasizes appreciation of differences in creating a setting where everyone feels valued and accepted. This is true not only in the United States but also in Canada, EU countries, and several countries in Asia.[60] Only the details differ. Managing diversity assumes that groups will retain their own characteristics and will shape the firm as well as be shaped by it, creating a common set of values that will strengthen ties with customers, enhance recruitment, and the like. Sometimes diversity management is resisted because of fear of change and discomfort with differences. To deal with this resistance, some countries, such as Canada, have laws designed to encourage the management of diversity at the provincial level through employment equity legislation.[61]

So how do managers deal with all this? To convey the flavor of what some of the more progressive employers have done in managing diversity, let's now consider Boston-based Harvard Pilgrim Health Care (HPHC). Barbara Stern is the Vice President of Diversity.[62] She argues that what has traditionally been a "soft" issue is now becoming a business necessity in terms of better serving customers, understanding markets, and obtaining full benefit from staff talents. Each year, HPHC attempts to increase its diversity in terms of the proportion of women and racial minorities by 0.5 percent, which allows for continuous improvement. Such improvement raised the proportion of minority new hires from 14 to 28 percent over four years, and the total minority employees went from 16 to 21 percent over the same period.

Research Insight
Do Social Skills and General Mental Ability Interact for Job Performance and Salary?

Social skills at work are becoming more widely considered and are recognized as quite different from general mental ability (GMA) in their relationship to job performance and salary, when controlling for personality and demographic characteristics. In a sample of computer programmers, the following linkages were found:

- The relationships between social skills and job performance were stronger among high-GMA programmers.

- The relationships between GMA and job performance were higher among high–social skill employees.

- Increases in social skills (or GMA) for high-GMA (or high–social skill) employees were associated with higher salaries.

- Surprisingly, increases in social skills (or GMA) for low-GMA (or low–social skill) individuals were associated with lower salaries.

Thus, social skills and GMA in most combinations contributed to performance and salary.

References: Gerald R. Ferris, L. A. Witt, and Wayne A. Hochwarter, "Interaction of Social Skill and General Mental Ability on Job Performance and Salary", *Journal of Applied Psychology* 86(6) (2001):1075–1082.

To ensure that diversity was more than just a fad, a corporate diversity council was established. This council set up specific actions to serve as the initial focus of the diversity efforts. The council determined it needed a vice presidential–level person to oversee the effort. The council's goals were (1) to create accountability for measuring diversity (tie meeting of diversity goals into salaries of the organization's top 85 managers); (2) to provide a custom-made education program; (3) to develop an explicit code of conduct and communication with a zero-tolerance policy (for example, the code spells out inappropriate behavior, such as racist jokes, and creates appropriate expectations and behavior standards); (4) to commit to creating diverse candidate pools for all managerial hiring and promotion decisions (traditional closed networks that were once used are no longer appropriate); and (5) to use cultural audits, surveys, focus groups, and broad networking groups to assess diversity.

HPHC also includes seven questions in a carefully phrased opinion survey. Questions such as how employees feel they are valued, what they feel their career opportunities are, and how well the organization supports work–life balance are asked. HPHC uses improvements in these areas as partial indicators of successful diversity.

The organization also relies on the Health Triangle—a networking group of more than 200 gay and lesbian employees—and the Disability Council to help the company keep abreast of issues relevant to each group of employees. These groups have also helped to attract additional customers.

Stern argues that simplicity and clarity are keys in diversity communication. She states that one should be able to communicate the information in 10 minutes and make it easy to understand, represent the data in a variety of ways, report on progress, and keep people at all levels informed about the progress. The Effective Manager 4.2 provides an example and illustrates insights suitable for diversity programs in general.

The following factors, encompassing and moving beyond those of HPHC, have been obtained from in-depth interviews and focus groups—they are important in tracking diversity programs: demographics, organizational culture, accountability, productivity, growth and profitability, benchmarking against the "best" programs, and measurement of the program.[63] Additionally, the Society for Human Resource Management (SHRM) has developed a survey instrument for focusing on a bottom-line analysis of diversity programs.[64]

Some firms, such as Microsoft, have moved far toward measurement and computerization of key diversity measures. Three Microsoft employees, Jonathan Stutz, Randy Massengale, and Andrea Gordon, developed the SMG Index acronym. It provides a separate bottom-line figure, encompassing both Microsoft's women and minorities; it allows managers to analyze goals and accomplishments for both affirmative action and diversity. The lower the SMG Index (zero is best), the lower the percentage of hires, promotions, and/or retentions needed to correct group disparities. The Index is compared across groups and time.[65]

Chapter 4   Study Guide

Summary

What is personality?

- Personality captures the overall profile, or combination of characteristics, that represents the unique nature of an individual as that individual interacts with others.
- Personality is determined by both heredity and environment; across all personality characteristics, the mix of heredity and environment is about 50–50.

How do personalities differ?

- The Big Five personality traits consist of extraversion, agreeableness, conscientiousness, emotional stability, and openness to experience.
- A useful personality framework consists of social traits, personal conception traits, emotional adjustment traits, and personality dynamics, where each category represents one or more personality dimensions.

- Personality characteristics are important because of their predictable interplay with an individual's behavior. Along with demographics and aptitude/ability differences, personality characteristics must be matched to organizations and jobs.

What are value and attitude differences among individuals, and why are they important?

- Values are broad preferences concerning courses of action or outcomes.
- Rokeach divides 18 values into terminal values (preferences concerning ends) and instrumental values (preferences concerning means).
- Allport and his associates identify six value categories, ranging from theoretical to religious.
- Maglino and his associates classify values into achievement, helping and concern for others, honesty, and fairness.
- There have been societal changes in value patterns away from economic and organizational loyalty and toward meaningful work and self-fulfillment.
- Attitudes are a predisposition to respond positively or negatively to someone or something in one's environment; they are influenced by values but are more specific.
- Individuals desire consistency between their attitudes and their behaviors.
- Values and attitudes are important because they indicate predispositions toward behaviors.
- Along with demographics, aptitude/ability, and personality differences, values and attitudes need to be matched to organizations and jobs.

What are individual differences, and how are they related to workforce diversity?

- Workforce diversity is the mix of gender, race and ethnicity, age, and able-bodiedness in the workforce.
- Workforces in the United States, Canada, and Europe are becoming more diverse, and valuing and managing such diversity is becoming increasingly more important to enhance organizational competitiveness and provide individual development.
- Demographic differences are background characteristics that help shape what a person has become.
- Gender, age, race and ethnicity, and able-bodiedness are particularly important demographic characteristics.
- The use of demographic differences in employment is covered by a series of federal, state/provincial, and local laws outlawing discrimination.
- Demographic differences can be the basis for inappropriate stereotyping that can influence workplace decisions and behaviors.
- Aptitude is a person's capability of learning something.
- Ability is a person's existing capacity to perform the various tasks needed for a given job.
- Aptitudes are potential abilities.
- Both mental and physical aptitudes and abilities are used in matching individuals to organizations and jobs.
- Managing diversity and individual differences involves striving for a match among the firm, specific jobs, and the people recruited, hired, and developed, while recognizing an increasingly diverse workforce.

- Increasing workforce diversity is provided by equal employment opportunity, through nondiscrimination and affirmative action; ethical considerations; local, national, and global competitive pressures; and a projected change in the nature of the workforce.
- Once a match between organizational and job requirements and individual characteristics is obtained, it is necessary to manage the increasing diversity in the workforce.
- Firms now use a wide variety of practices in managing workforce diversity; for example, interactive networks, recruitment, education, development, promotion, pay, and assessment.

Key Terms

Ability (p. 92)
Affective component (p. 86)
Aptitude (p. 92)
Attitude (p. 86)
Authoritarianism (p. 80)
Behavioral component (p. 86)
Beliefs (p. 86)
Cognitive component (p. 86)
Cognitive dissonance (p. 87)

Demographic characteristics (p. 88)
Developmental approaches (p. 76)
Dogmatism (p. 80)
Emotional adjustment traits (p. 82)
Instrumental values (p. 83)
Personality (p. 74)
Personality dynamics (p. 76)
Self-concept (p. 77)

Self-monitoring (p. 81)
Social traits (p. 78)
Sources and types of values (p. 83)
Stereotyping (p. 88)
Terminal values (p. 83)
Type A orientation (p. 82)
Type B orientation (p. 82)
Value congruence (p. 85)
Values (p. 83)
Workforce diversity (p. 88)

Self-Test 4

Multiple Choice

1. In the United States, Canada, the European Union, and much of the rest of the world, the workforce is _____. (a) becoming more homogeneous (b) more highly motivated than before (c) becoming more diverse (d) less motivated than before

2. Stereotyping occurs when one thinks of an individual _____. (a) as different from others in a given group (b) as possessing characteristics commonly associated with members of a given group (c) as like some members of a given group but different from others (d) as basically not very competent

3. Managing diversity and affirmative action are _____. (a) similar terms for the same thing (b) both mandated by law (c) different but complementary (d) becoming less and less important

4. Aptitudes and abilities are divided into _____. (a) stereotypes (b) physical and mental (c) mental and personality (d) aggressive and passive

5. The Big Five framework consists of _____. (a) five aptitudes and abilities (b) five demographic characteristics (c) extraversion, agreeableness, strength, emotional stability, and openness to experience (d) extraversion, agreeableness, conscientiousness, emotional stability, and openness to experience

6. Personality dynamics is represented by _____. (a) self-esteem and self-efficacy (b) Type A/Type B orientation (c) self-monitoring (d) Machiavellianism

7. Values and attitudes are _____. (a) similar to aptitudes and abilities (b) used interchangeably (c) related to each other (d) similar to demographic characteristics

8. Managing workforce diversity involves _____. (a) matching organizational and job requirements with increasingly diverse individuals (b) giving preference to tradi-

tional white American males (c) giving preference to nontraditional, nonwhite male workers (d) making sure quotas of workers in various categories are emphasized

9. Social traits are _____. (a) deep seated and difficult to understand (b) surface-level traits that reflect the way a person appears to others when interacting in various social settings (c) the single most important personality dimension (d) strongly endorsed by the U.S. government.

10. Locus of control _____. (a) is another name for authoritarianism/dogmatism (b) is another name for Machiavellianism (c) is similar to Type A/Type B orientation (d) is an important orientation toward internal or external control of events

11. Values in the United States _____. (a) are largely unchanged across time (b) have moved away from earlier values (c) are virtually the same as attitudes (d) tend not to be shared within cultures and organizations

12. A majority of *Fortune* 500 companies _____. (a) provide incentives for executives to deal successfully with workplace diversity (b) are moving away from workforce diversity (c) emphasize stereotyping (d) are hiring fewer females than before

13. Attitudes tend to _____. (a) follow values (b) either follow or precede behavior (c) be unrelated to behavior (d) be more general than values

14. Demographic differences _____. (a) are especially valuable in selecting workers (b) are based on aptitudes and abilities (c) are the background variables that help shape what a person becomes over time (d) are important personality aspects

15. Personality traits _____. (a) can sometimes be inferred by behavior (b) are unrelated to behavior (c) are mostly determined by environment (d) consist of behaviors, values, and attitudes

Short Response

16. What does managing diversity and individual differences mean in the workplace?
17. Why are diversity and individual differences important in the workplace?
18. In what ways are demographic characteristics important in the workplace?
19. Why are personality characteristics important in the workplace?

Applications Essay

20. Your boss is trying to figure out how to get the kinds of people she needs for her organization to do well, while at the same time dealing appropriately with an increasing number of nonwhite female and male workers. She has asked you to respond to this concern. Prepare a short report with specific suggestions for your boss.

These learning activities from *The OB Skills Workbook* are suggested for Chapter 4.

OB in Action

CASE	EXPERIENTIAL EXERCISE	SELF-ASSESSMENT
■ 4. Never on a Sunday	■ 8. Prejudice in Our Lives	■ 5. Personal Values

Plus—special learning experiences from *The Jossey-Bass/Pfeiffer Classroom Collection*

Chapter 5

Perception and Attribution

Chapter at a Glance

Like numerous big cities, Dallas is concerned about changing its perception and image among both residents and visitors. Such aspects of the overall perception process and related concepts are the topics of this chapter. As you read Chapter 5, *keep in mind these study questions*.

WHAT IS THE PERCEPTION PROCESS?

WHAT ARE COMMON PERCEPTUAL DISTORTIONS?

HOW CAN PERCEPTIONS BE MANAGED?

WHAT IS ATTRIBUTION THEORY?

REVIEW IN END-OF-CHAPTER STUDY GUIDE.

Dallas is undergoing an identity crisis. It has no singular defining characteristic—no Golden Gate Bridge, no St. Louis Arch. Indeed, a common perception of Dallas is J. R. Ewing, cowboys, and women with big hair. Phillip Jones is currently president and CEO of the Dallas Convention and Visitors Bureau; he argues that there is much more to Dallas and that an aggressive new branding campaign is needed.

The bureau has hired a nationally known advertising firm to bury lingering memories of the J. R. soap and bring back more conventions and tourists. Jones analyzed Dallas as a tourist destination that got bypassed a lot and noticed that people thought there was nothing to see and do there. He was especially concerned about the perceived lack of four- and five-star restaurants, of which Dallas has more than New Orleans.

John Bertter, a marketing executive with the advertising firm, argues, "Dallas is just an ill-defined brand at this stage." Hopefully, the rebranding and self-image presentation will make Dallas one of the top five tourist destinations in the United States, along with cities such as Orlando and Las Vegas.[1]

Perception and its cousins—attribution and impression management—are becoming more and more important for major cities such as Dallas, just as they are for managers and their followers, for whom perception is everything. This growing importance makes it necessary to understand the topics addressed in this chapter.

> **"Dallas is just an ill-defined brand at this stage."**

The Perception Process

A spectacular completed pass during the 1982 National Football Conference championship game helped propel Joe Montana, former San Francisco 49er quarterback, into the legendary status he enjoys today. The reverse effect apparently occurred for Danny White, the Dallas Cowboys' quarterback. He fumbled in the final minute of the same game and never obtained the status of his predecessor, Roger Staubach, even though White took the Cowboys to the championship game three years in a row.[2]

This example illustrates the notion of **perception**, the process by which people select, organize, interpret, retrieve, and respond to information from the world around them.[3] This information is gathered from the five senses of sight, hearing, touch, taste, and smell. As Montana, White, and Staubach can attest, perception and reality are not necessarily the same thing. The perceptions or responses of any two people are also not necessarily identical, even when they are describing the same event.

Through perception, people process information inputs into responses involving feelings and action. Perception is a way of forming impressions about oneself, other people, and daily life experiences. It also serves as a screen or filter through which information passes before it has an effect on people. The

Perception is the process through which people receive, organize, and interpret information from their environment.

100

quality or accuracy of a person's perceptions, therefore, has a major impact on his or her responses to a given situation.

PEOPLE AND TECHNOLOGY

WHERE HAVE ALL THE NERDS GONE?

Gone are the days of poker-faced space geeks with pocket protectors, crew cuts, and narrow ties. Instead, we now see rocket scientists at the Jet Propulsion Laboratory in Pasadena who are surfer dudes, skydivers, and even *Survivor* survivors. Indeed, these people look as varied as southern California itself. It seems that important parts of the physics community are undergoing an extreme geek makeover.

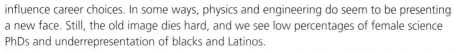

Even with the changes, the perception still persists. These images shape how people see themselves and thus influence career choices. In some ways, physics and engineering do seem to be presenting a new face. Still, the old image dies hard, and we see low percentages of female science PhDs and underrepresentation of blacks and Latinos.

Question: How important are perception and image in this situation and what can be done?

Perceptual responses are also likely to vary between managers and subordinates. Consider Figure 5.1, which depicts contrasting perceptions of a performance appraisal between managers and subordinates. Rather substantial differ-

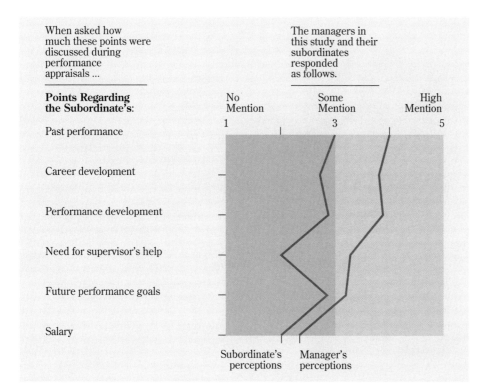

Figure 5.1 **Contrasting perceptions between managers and their subordinates: the case of the performance appraisal interview.**

ences exist in the two sets of perceptions; the responses can be significant. In this case, managers who perceive that they already give adequate attention to past performance, career development, and supervisory help are unlikely to give greater emphasis to these points in future performance appraisal interviews. In contrast, their subordinates are likely to experience continued frustration because they perceive that these subjects are not being given sufficient attention.

Factors Influencing Perception

The factors that contribute to perceptual differences and the perceptual process among people at work, which are summarized in Figure 5.2, include characteristics of the *perceiver*, the *setting*, and the *perceived*.

The Perceiver   A person's past experiences, needs or motives, personality, and values and attitudes may all influence the perceptual process. A person with a strong achievement need tends to perceive a situation in terms of that need. If you see doing well in class as a way to help meet your achievement need, for example, you will tend to emphasize that aspect when considering various classes. By the same token, a person with a negative attitude toward unions may react antagonistically even when local union officials make routine visits to the organization. These and other perceiver factors influence the various aspects of the perceptual process.

The Setting   The physical, social, and organizational context of the perceptual setting also can influence the perceptual process. Kim Jeffrey, the CEO of Nestlés Perrier, was perceived by his subordinates as a frightening figure when he gave vent to his temper and had occasional confrontations with them. Before he was

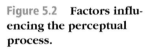

Figure 5.2   Factors influencing the perceptual process.

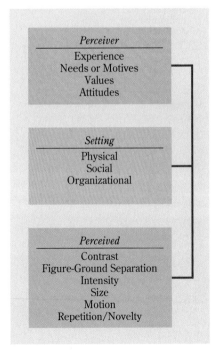

promoted, however, Jeffrey's flare-ups had been tolerable; now they caused intimidation, so his subordinates were afraid to express their opinions and recommendations. Fortunately, after he received feedback about this problem, he was able to change his subordinates' perceptions in the new setting.[4]

Figure 5.3
Figure–ground illustration.

The Perceived   Characteristics of the perceived person, object, or event—such as contrast, intensity, figure–ground separation, size, motion, and repetition or novelty—are also important in the perceptual process. For example, one mainframe computer among six PCs or one man among six women will be perceived differently than one of six mainframe computers or one of six men—where there is less contrast. Intensity can vary in terms of brightness, color, depth, sound, and the like. A bright red sports car stands out from a group of gray sedans; whispering or shouting stands out from ordinary conversation. This concept is known as figure–ground separation, and it depends on which image is perceived as the background and which as the figure. For an illustration, look at Figure 5.3. What do you see? Faces or a vase?

In the matter of size, very small or very large people tend to be perceived differently and more readily from average-sized people. Similarly, in terms of motion, moving objects are perceived differently from stationary objects. And, of course, advertisers hope that ad repetition or frequency will positively influence people's perception of a product. Television advertising blitzes for new models of personal computers are a case in point. Finally, the novelty of a situation affects its perception. A purple-haired teenager is perceived differently from a blond or a brunette, for example.

Stages of the Perceptual Process

So far we have discussed key factors influencing the perceptual process. Now we'll look at the stages involved in processing the information that ultimately determines a person's perception and reaction, as shown in Figure 5.4. The infor-

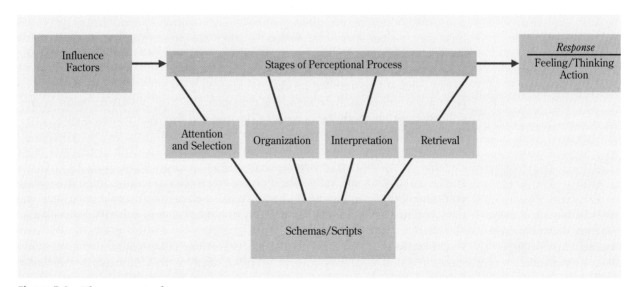

Figure 5.4   The perceptual process.

Research Insight
Perceived Victimization and Workplace Aggression and Conflict

A sample of nearly 500 employed men between ages 32 and 36 responded to questions concerning victimization rates based on having been involved in workplace aggression and conflict. These men also completed a personality inventory and provided information on past antisocial behavior and alcohol abuse. Such variables as stress reaction and aggression, along with past antisocial behavior and alcohol abuse, were found to be moderated by perceptions of being victimized by others—the perceptions strengthened the relationships between workplace aggression and other risk factors.

In other words, measures of past antisocial behavior and alcohol abuse were related to three of the Big Five personality variables—neuroticism, agreeableness, and conscientiousness—and these relationships were strengthened when moderated by perceived victimization.

Reference: Victor Jockin, Richard D. Arvey, and Matt McGue, "Perceived Victimization Moderates Self-Reports of Workplace Aggression and Conflict," *Journal of Applied Psychology* 866) (2001):1262–1269.

mation-processing stages are divided into information attention and selection, organization of information, information interpretation, and information retrieval.

Attention and Selection   Our senses are constantly bombarded with so much information that if we don't screen it, we quickly become incapacitated with information overload. *Selective screening* lets in only a tiny proportion of all the information available. Some of the selectivity comes from controlled processing—consciously deciding what information to pay attention to and what to ignore. In this case, the perceivers are aware that they are processing information. Think about the last time you were at a noisy restaurant and screened out all the sounds but those of the person with whom you were talking.

In contrast to controlled processing, screening can also take place without the perceiver's conscious awareness. For example, you may drive a car without consciously thinking about the process of driving; you may be thinking about a problem you are having with your coursework instead. In driving the car, you are affected by information from the world around you, such as traffic lights and other cars, but you don't pay conscious attention to that information. Such selectivity of attention and automatic information processing works well most of the time when you drive, but if a nonroutine event occurs, such as an animal darting onto the road, you may have an accident unless you quickly shift to controlled processing.

Schemas are cognitive frameworks that represent organized knowledge about a given concept or stimulus developed through experience.

Organization   Even though selective screening takes place in the attention stage, it is still necessary to find ways to organize the information efficiently. **Schemas** help us do this. Schemas are cognitive frameworks that represent organized knowledge about a given concept or stimulus developed through expe-

Leaders on Leadership

SYLVESTER CROOM: LONG TIME COMING

One of the last remaining college sports taboos was busted when Sylvester Croom became the first African-American hired as a football coach in the Southeastern Conference (SEC). Even

so, many people say Mississippi State hired a coach, not a color. People are arguing that too much time has passed to yammer on about color. In the South, where a coach's prestige sometimes exceeds that of a governor, the first SEC hire had to be someone about whom there was no question, someone who simply could not be denied.

Croom played for the legendary Bear Bryant at Alabama and was elected captain of the team, won outside honors, and

was signed, as a pro, by the New Orleans Saints. He was almost hired as head coach at Alabama. As a leader, Croom remembers Bryant saying, "Go where they want you." There has been virtually no backlash on his hiring, and players want to play for him because he is above reproach and emphasizes discipline, conditioning, and passing—and because he played for Coach Bryant. He indeed fits their "good leader" prototype. Such is Croom's leadership image.

Question: What characteristics would you include in your own prototype of a good leader?

rience.[5] A *self schema* contains information about a person's own appearance, behavior, and personality. For instance, a person with a decisiveness schema tends to perceive himself or herself in terms of that aspect, especially in circumstances calling for leadership.

Person schemas refer to the way individuals sort others into categories, such as types or groups, in terms of similar perceived features. The term *"prototype,"* or *"stereotype,"* is often used to represent these categories; it is an abstract set of features commonly associated with members of that category. Once the prototype is formed, it is stored in long-term memory; it is retrieved when it is needed for a comparison of how well a person matches the prototype's features. For instance, you may have a "good worker" prototype in mind, which includes hard work, intelligence, punctuality, articulateness, and decisiveness; that prototype is used as a measure against which to compare a given worker. Stereotypes, as discussed in Chapter 4, may be regarded as prototypes based on such demographic characteristics as gender, age, able-bodiedness, and racial and ethnic groups. The chapter opener, for example, refers to a J. R. Ewing stereotype, of *Dallas* fame, based on numerous demographic and behavioral characteristics. The current advertising campaign is a wide-ranging attempt to change that stereotype.

A *script schema* is defined as a knowledge framework that describes the appropriate sequence of events in a given situation.[6] For example, an experienced manager would use a script schema to think about the appropriate steps in-

Communists Hip Again in Russia

Not long ago 18,000 Russians joined the Communist party, which for70 years had ruled the former Soviet Union. Eighty percent of the new members were under 40, and nationwide some half-million Russians identified themselves as Communists.

Young Russians saw joining the party as a way to protest current conditions; they had negative perceptions of Vladimir Putin, the current president of Russia, and young voters claimed that only the Communists could shake up a moribund Russia.

volved in running a meeting. Finally, *person-in-situation schemas* combine schemas built around persons (self and person schemas) and events (script schemas).[7] Thus, a manager might organize his or her perceived information in a meeting around a decisiveness schema for both himself or herself and a key participant in the meeting. Here, a script schema would provide the steps and their sequence in the meeting; the manager would push through the steps decisively and would call on the selected participants periodically throughout the meeting to respond decisively. Note that, although this approach might facilitate organization of important information, the perceptions of those attending might not be completely accurate because the decisiveness element of the person-in-situation schema did not allow the attendees enough time for open discussion.

As you can see in Figure 5.4, schemas are not important just in the organization stage; they also affect other stages in the perception process. Furthermore, schemas rely heavily on automatic processing to free people up to use controlled processing as necessary. Finally, as we will show, the perceptual factors described earlier as well as the distortions to be discussed shortly, influence schemas in various ways.

Interpretation   Once your attention has been drawn to certain stimuli and you have grouped or organized this information, the next step is to uncover the reasons behind the actions. That is, even if your attention is called to the same information and you organize it in the same way your friend does, you may interpret it differently or make different attributions about the reasons behind what you have perceived. For example, as a manager, you might attribute compliments from a friendly subordinate to his being an eager worker, whereas your friend might interpret the behavior as insincere flattery.

Retrieval   So far, we have discussed the stages of the perceptual process as if they all occurred at the same time. However, to do so ignores the important component of memory. Each of the previous stages forms part of that memory and contributes to the stimuli or information stored there. The information stored in our memory must be retrieved if it is to be used. This leads us to the retrieval stage of the perceptual process summarized in Figure 5.4.

All of us at times can't retrieve information stored in our memory. More commonly, our memory decays, so that only some of the information is retrieved. Schemas play an important role in this area. They make it difficult for people to remember things not included in them. For example, based on your prototype about the traits comprising a "high-performing employee" (hard work, punctuality, intelligence, articulateness, and decisiveness), you may overestimate these traits and underestimate others when you are evaluating the performance of a subordinate whom you generally consider good. Thus, you may overestimate the person's decisiveness since it is a key part of your high-performance prototype.

Indeed, people are as likely to recall nonexistent traits as they are to recall those that are really there. Furthermore, once formed, prototypes may be difficult to change and tend to last a long time.[8] Obviously, this distortion can cause major problems in terms of performance appraisals and promotions, not to mention numerous other interactions on and off the job. By the same token, such prototypes allow you to "chunk" information and reduce overload. Thus, prototypes are a double-edged sword.

Response to the Perceptual Process

Throughout this chapter, we have shown how the perceptual process influences numerous OB responses. Figure 5.4 classifies such responses into thoughts and feelings and actions. For example, in countries such as Mexico, bosses routinely greet their secretaries with a kiss, and that is expected behavior. In contrast, in this country your thoughts and feelings might be quite different about such behavior. You might very well perceive this as a form of sexual harassment. As you cover the other OB topics in the book, you also should be alert to the importance of perceptual responses covering thoughts, feelings, and actions.

Common Perceptual Distortions

Figure 5.5 shows some common kinds of distortions that can make the perceptual process inaccurate and affect the response. These are stereotypes and prototypes, halo effects, selective perception, projection, contrast effects, and self-fulfilling prophecy.

Stereotypes or Prototypes

Earlier, when discussing person schemas, we described stereotypes, or prototypes, as useful ways of combining information in order to deal with information overload. At the same time, we pointed out how stereotypes can cause inaccuracies in retrieving information, along with some further problems. In particular, stereotypes obscure individual differences; that is, they can prevent managers from getting to know people as individuals and from accurately assessing their needs, preferences, and abilities. We compared these stereotypes with research results and showed the errors that can occur when stereotypes are relied on for decision making. Nevertheless, stereotypes continue to exist at the board of directors level in organizations. A survey of 133 *Fortune* 500 firms showed that female directors were favored for membership on only the relatively peripheral public affairs committee in these organizations. Males were favored for membership on the more important compensation, executive, and finance committees,

Presidential Candidate Defines Himself

In the summer of 2004, millions of voters knew little about presidential candidate John Kerry. He was in the process of emphasizing aggressive advertising and contrasting himself with the incumbent president, George W. Bush. He had to be very competitive in the race to remove a sitting president.

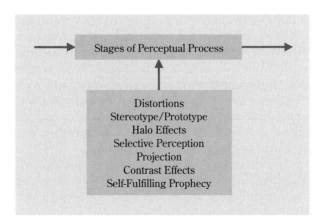

Figure 5.5 Distortions occurring in perceptual process stages.

Stages of Perceptual Process

Distortions
Stereotype/Prototype
Halo Effects
Selective Perception
Projection
Contrast Effects
Self-Fulfilling Prophecy

even when the females were equally or more experienced than their male counterparts.[9]

Here, we reiterate our previous message: both managers and employees need to be sensitive to stereotypes; they must also attempt to overcome them and recognize that an increasingly diverse workforce can be a truly competitive advantage, as we showed in Chapter 4.

Halo Effects

A halo effect occurs when one attribute of a person or situation is used to develop an overall impression of the person or situation.

A **halo effect** occurs when one attribute of a person or situation is used to develop an overall impression of the individual or situation. Like stereotypes, these distortions are more likely to occur in the organization stage of perception. Halo effects are common in our everyday lives. When meeting a new person, for example, a pleasant smile can lead to a positive first impression of an overall "warm" and "honest" person. The result of a halo effect is the same as that associated with a stereotype, however: individual differences are obscured.

Halo effects are particularly important in the performance appraisal process because they can influence a manager's evaluations of subordinates' work performance. For example, people with good attendance records tend to be viewed as intelligent and responsible; those with poor attendance records are considered poor performers. Such conclusions may or may not be valid. It is the manager's job to try to get true impressions rather than allowing halo effects to result in biased and erroneous evaluations.

Selective Perception

Selective perception is the tendency to single out for attention those aspects of a situation or person that reinforce or emerge and are consistent with existing beliefs, values, and needs.

Selective perception is the tendency to single out those aspects of a situation, person, or object that are consistent with one's needs, values, or attitudes. Its strongest impact occurs in the attention stage of the perceptual process. This perceptual distortion was identified in a classic research study involving executives in a manufacturing company.[10] When asked to identify the key problem in a comprehensive business policy case, each executive selected problems consistent with his or her functional area work assignments. For example, most marketing executives viewed the key problem area as sales, whereas production people tended to see the problem as one of production and organization. These differing viewpoints would affect how the executive would approach the problem; they might also create difficulties once these people tried to work together to improve things.

More recently, 121 middle- and upper-level managers attending an executive development program expressed broader views in conjunction with an emphasis on their own function. For example, a chief financial officer indicated an awareness of the importance of manufacturing, and an assistant marketing manager recognized the importance of accounting and finance along with each of their own functions.[11] Thus, this more current research demonstrated very little perceptual selectivity. The researchers were not, however, able to state definitively what accounted for the differing results.

These results suggest that selective perception is more important at some times than at others. Managers should be aware of this characteristic and test whether or not situations, events, or individuals are being selectively perceived. The easiest way to do this is to gather additional opinions from other people.

When these opinions contradict a manager's own, an effort should be made to check the original impression.

Projection

Projection is the assignment of one's personal attributes to other individuals; it is especially likely to occur in the interpretation stage of perception. A classic projection error is illustrated by managers who assume that the needs of their subordinates and their own coincide. Suppose, for example, that you enjoy responsibility and achievement in your work. Suppose, too, that you are the newly appointed manager of a group whose jobs seem dull and routine. You may move quickly to expand these jobs to help the workers achieve increased satisfaction from more challenging tasks because you want them to experience things that you, personally, value in work. But this may not be a good decision. If you project your needs onto the subordinates, individual differences are lost. Instead of designing the subordinates' jobs to best fit their needs, you have designed their jobs to best fit your needs. The problem is that the subordinates may be quite satisfied and productive doing jobs that seem dull and routine to you. Projection can be controlled through a high degree of self-awareness and empathy—the ability to view a situation as others see it.

■■■ **Projection** is the assignment of personal attributes to other individuals.

ETHICS AND SOCIAL RESPONSIBILITY

IVAN SEIDENBERG,
VERIZON'S BORN IMPRESSION MANAGER

Ivan Seidenberg talks about Verizon, not himself. However, he is the role model, the leader, and the family head of what has become the largest local phone service and wireless provider in America. It is also one of the most philanthropic corporations in the country. Employees are strongly encouraged to volunteer for causes that appeal to them personally. He also insists that Verizon actively recruit minority employees and support minority-owned businesses. He emphasizes "the right thing to do" for the company and for himself.

　All of the above actions have, of course, enhanced the perception of Verizon and strengthened its image. Seidenberg's underlying substance has reinforced these.

Question: In what way does projection enter into this example?

Contrast Effects

Earlier, when discussing the perceived, we mentioned how a bright red sports car would stand out from a group of gray sedans because of its contrast. Here, we show the perceptual distortion that can occur when, say, a person gives a talk following a strong speaker or is interviewed for a job following a series of mediocre applicants. We can expect a **contrast effect** to occur when an individual's characteristics are contrasted with those of others recently encountered who rank higher or lower on the same characteristics. Clearly, both managers

■■■ **Contrast effects** occur when an individual's characteristics are contrasted with those of others recently encountered, who rank higher or lower on the same characteristics.

and employees need to be aware of the possible perceptual distortion the contrast effect may create in many work settings.

Self-Fulfilling Prophecies

■■■ **A self-fulfilling prophecy** is the tendency to create or find in another situation or individual that which one has expected to find.

A final perceptual distortion that we consider is the **self-fulfilling prophecy**—the tendency to create or find in another situation or individual that which you expected to find in the first place. A self-fulfilling prophecy is sometimes referred to as the "Pygmalion effect," named for a mythical Greek sculptor who created a statue of his ideal mate and then made her come to life.[12] His prophecy came true! Through self-fulfilling prophecy, you also may create in the work situation that which you expect to find.

Self-fulfilling prophecies can have both positive and negative results for you as a manager. Suppose you assume that your subordinates prefer to satisfy most of their needs outside the work setting and want only minimal involvement with their jobs. Consequently, you are likely to provide simple, highly structured jobs designed to require little involvement. Can you predict what response the subordinates would have to this situation? Their most likely response would be to show the lack of commitment you assumed they would have in the first place. Thus, your initial expectations are confirmed as a self-fulfilling prophecy.

Self-fulfilling prophecies can have a positive side, however (see The Effective Manager 5.1). Students introduced to their teachers as "intellectual bloomers" do better on achievement tests than do their counterparts who lack such a positive introduction. A particularly interesting example of the self-fulfilling prophecy is that of Israeli tank crews. One set of tank commanders was told that according to test data some members of their assigned crews had exceptional abilities but others were only average. In reality, the crew members were assigned randomly, so that the two test groups were equal in ability. Later, the commanders reported that the so-called exceptional crew members performed better than the "average" members. As the study revealed, however, the commanders had paid more attention to and praised the crew members for whom they had the higher expectations.[13] The self-fulfilling effects in these cases argue strongly for managers to adopt positive and optimistic approaches to people at work.

> **THE EFFECTIVE MANAGER 5.1**
> ### Creating Positive Self-Fulfilling Prophecies for Employees
>
> - Create a warmer interpersonal climate between your subordinates and you.
> - Give more performance feedback to subordinates—make it as positive as possible, given their actual performance.
> - Spend more time helping subordinates learn job skills.
> - Provide more opportunities for subordinates to ask questions.

Managing Perceptions

To be successful, managers must understand the perceptual process, the stages involved, and the impact the perceptual process can have on their own and others' responses. They must also be aware of what roles the perceiver, the setting, and the perceived have in the perceptual process. Particularly important with regard to the perceived is the concept of impression management—for both managers and others.

Impression Management

Impression management is a person's systematic attempt to behave in ways that will create and maintain desired impressions in the eyes of others. First impressions are especially important and influence how people respond to one another. Impression management is influenced by such activities as associating with the "right people," doing favors to gain approval, flattering others to favorably impress them, taking credit for a favorable event, apologizing for a negative event while seeking a pardon, agreeing with the opinions of others, downplaying the severity of a negative event, and doing favors for others.[14] Successful managers learn how to use these activities to enhance their own images, and they are sensitive to their use by their subordinates and others in their organizations. In this context, job titles are particularly important.

CULTURES AND THE GLOBAL WORKFORCE

BRITS AND THE CAPED CRUSADER

As we consider the global workforce, we discover a caped crusader residing in London's multifarious culture. He calls himself Angle-Grinder Man (after the noisy, security-boot-destroying circular saw he wields) and trawls London dressed in a homemade superhero outfit, which includes gold lamé underpants and cape. His self-appointed mission is to remove security boots from individuals' illegally parked cars. In many cases, he wheels up in his vehicle, leaps out, cuts, and leaves almost as quickly as he came. For each of these incidents, he can truly say, "My work here is done."

As you can imagine, he has attracted a host of admirers who indeed perceive him as a caped crusader or even a superhero. Of course, Scotland Yard does not, and has threatened both Angle-Grinder Man and the vehicle owners with charges of criminal damage. And of course, we do not recommend his escapades for our readers!

Question: In what ways would perception and impression management help explain Angle-Grinder Man's behavior?

Distortion Management

During the attention and selection stage, managers should be alert to balancing automatic and controlled information processing. Most of their responsibilities, such as performance assessment and clear communication, will involve controlled processing, which will take time away from other job responsibilities. Along with more controlled processing, managers need to be concerned about increasing the frequency of observations and about getting representative information rather than simply responding to the most recent information about a subordinate or a production order, for instance. Some organizations, including 911 systems, have responded to the need for representative and more accurate information by utilizing current technology. In addition, managers should not fail to seek out disconfirming information that will help provide a balance to their typical perception of information.

The various kinds of schemas and prototypes and stereotypes are particularly important at the information organizing stage. Managers should strive to broaden their schemas or should even replace them with more accurate or complete ones.

At the interpretation stage, managers need to be especially attuned to the impact of attribution on information; we discuss this concept further in the next section. At the retrieval stage, managers should be sensitive to the fallibility of memory. They should recognize the tendency to overrely on schemas, especially prototypes or stereotypes that may bias information storage and retrieval.

Throughout the entire perception process, managers should be sensitive to the information distortions caused by halo effects, selective perception, projection, contrast effects, and self-fulfilling prophecies, in addition to the distortions caused by stereotypes and prototypes.

Attribution Theory

Attribution theory is the attempt to understand the cause of an event, assess responsibility for outcomes of the event, and assess the personal qualities of the people involved.

Earlier in the chapter we mentioned attribution theory in the context of perceptual interpretation. **Attribution theory** aids in this interpretation by focusing on how people attempt to (1) understand the causes of a certain event, (2) assess responsibility for the outcomes of the event, and (3) evaluate the personal qualities of the people involved in the event.[15] In applying attribution theory, we are especially concerned with whether one's behavior has been internally or externally caused. Internal causes are believed to be under an individual's control—you believe Jake's performance is poor because he is lazy. External causes are seen as coming from outside a person—you believe Kellie's performance is poor because her machine is old.

The Importance of Attributions

Attributions can have far-reaching effects. For example, over their lifetimes, obese women don't accumulate as much net worth as slender women. Even after controlling for such things as health and marital status, women pay a heavy economic penalty for fat. However, the same is not true for obese men. Attributions concerning fat men are that they are wealthy and successful, whereas attributions concerning fat women are that they have "let themselves go." For obese women, internal attributional causes seem to be operating to their detriment.[16]

According to attribution theory, three factors influence this internal or external determination: distinctiveness, consensus, and consistency. *Distinctiveness* considers how consistent a person's behavior is across different situations. If Jake's performance is low, regardless of the machine on which he is working, we tend to give the poor performance an internal attribution; if the poor performance is unusual, we tend to assign an external cause to explain it.

Consensus takes into account how likely all those facing a similar situation are to respond in the same way. If all the people using machinery like Kellie's perform poorly, we tend to give her performance an external attribution. If other employees do not perform poorly, we attribute her performance to internal causation.

Consistency concerns whether an individual responds the same way across time. If Jake has a batch of low-performance figures, we tend to give the poor performance an internal attribution. In contrast, if Jake's low performance is an isolated incident, we attribute it to an external cause.

Attribution Errors

In addition to these three influences, two errors have an impact on internal versus external determination—the *fundamental attribution error* and the *self-serving bias*.[17] Figure 5.6 provides data from a group of health care managers. When supervisors were asked to identify, or attribute, causes of poor performance among their subordinates, the supervisors more often chose the individual's internal deficiencies—lack of ability and effort—rather than external deficiencies in the situation—lack of support. This demonstrates the **fundamental attribution error**—the tendency to underestimate the influence of situational factors and to overestimate the influence of personal factors in evaluating someone else's behavior. When asked to identify causes of their own poor performance, however, the supervisors overwhelmingly cited lack of support—an external, or situational, deficiency. This indicates the **self-serving bias**—the tendency to deny personal responsibility for performance problems but to accept personal responsibility for performance success.

To summarize, we tend to overemphasize other people's internal personal factors in their behavior and to underemphasize external factors in other people's behavior. In contrast, we tend to attribute our own success to our own internal factors and to attribute our failure to external factors.

The managerial implications of attribution theory can be traced back to the fact that perceptions influence responses. For example, a manager who feels that subordinates are not performing well and perceives the reason to be an internal lack of effort is likely to respond with attempts to "motivate" the subordinates to work harder; the possibility of changing external, situational factors that may remove job constraints and provide better organizational support may be largely ignored. This oversight could sacrifice major performance gains. Interestingly, because of the self-serving bias, when they evaluated their own behavior, the supervisors in the earlier study indicated that their performance would benefit from having better support. Thus, the supervisors' own abilities or willingness to work hard were not felt to be at issue.

The **fundamental attribution error** is the tendency to underestimate the influence of situational factors and to overestimate the influence of personal factors in evaluating someone else's behavior.

The **self-serving bias** is the tendency to deny personal responsibility for performance problems but to accept personal responsibility for performance success.

Cause of Poor Performance by Their Subordinates	Most Frequent Attribution	Cause of Poor Performance by Themselves
7	Lack of *ability*	1
12	Lack of *effort*	1
5	Lack of *support*	23

Figure 5.6   **Health care managers' attributions of causes for poor performance.**

Attributions across Cultures

Research on the self-serving bias and fundamental attribution error has been done in cultures outside the United States with unexpected results.[18] In Korea, for example, the self-serving bias was found to be negative; that is, Korean managers attribute workgroup failure to themselves—"I was not a capable leader"—rather than to external causes. In India, the fundamental attribution error overemphasizes external rather than internal causes for failure. Still another interesting cultural twist on the self-serving bias and fundamental attribution error is suggested by an example of a Ghanian woman who was the only female sea captain in the fleet. The difficulty of her becoming a captain is reinforced by Africans' tendency to attribute negative consequences—driving away fish and angering mermaids into creating squalls—to women but apparently not to men. Why these various differences occurred is not clear, but differing cultural values appear to play a role. Finally, there is some evidence that U.S. females may be less likely to emphasize the self-serving bias than males.[19]

Certain cultures, such as that of the United States, tend to overemphasize internal causes and underemphasize external ones. Such overemphasis may result in negative attributions toward employees. These negative attributions, in turn, can lead to disciplinary actions, negative performance evaluations, transfers to other departments, and overreliance on training, rather than focusing on such external causes as lack of workplace support.[20] Employees, too, take their cues from managerial misattributions and, through negative self-fulfilling prophecies, may reinforce managers' original misattributions. Employees and managers alike (see The Effective Manager 5.2) can be taught attributional realignment to help deal with such misattributions.[21]

THE EFFECTIVE MANAGER 5.2

Keys in Managing Perceptions and Attributions

- Be self-aware.
- Seek a wide range of differing information.
- Try to see a situation as others would.
- Be aware of different kinds of schemas.
- Be aware of perceptual distortions.
- Be aware of self and other impression management.
- Be aware of attribution theory implications.

Chapter 5   Study Guide

Summary

What is the perception process?

- Individuals use the perceptual process to pay attention to and to select, organize, interpret, and retrieve information from the world around them.

- The perceptual process involves the perceiver, the setting, and the perceived.

- Responses to the perceptual process involve thinking and feeling and action classifications.

What are common perceptual distortions?

- Stereotypes or prototypes: An abstract set of features commonly associated with members of a given category.

- Halo effects: One attribute of a person or situation is used to develop an overall impression of the person or situation.

- Selective perception: The tendency to single out for attention those aspects of a situation or person that reinforce or emerge and are consistent with existing beliefs, values and needs.

- Projection: Assignments of personal attributes to other individuals.

- Contrast effects: When an individual's characteristics are contrasted with those of others recently encountered who rank higher or lower on the same characteristics.

How can perceptions be managed?

Managing perception involves:

- Impression management of the self and others

- Managing the information attention and selection stages

- Managing the information organizing stage

- Managing the information interpretation stage

- Managing the information storage and retrieval stage

- Being sensitive to effects of the common perceptual distortions

What is attribution theory?

- Attribution theory involves emphasis on the interpretation stage of the perceptual process and consideration of whether individuals' behaviors result primarily from external causes or from causes internal to the individuals.

- Three factors influence an external or internal causal attribution—distinctiveness, consensus, and consistency.

- Two errors influencing an external or internal causal attribution are the fundamental attribution error and self-serving bias.

- Attributions can be managed by recognizing a typical overemphasis on internal causes of behavior and an underemphasis on external causes.

- An overemphasis on internal causes tends to lead to assignments of failure, to employees accompanied by disciplinary actions, negative performance evaluations, and the like.

- An underemphasis on external causes tends to lead to lack of workplace support.

Key Terms

Attribution theory (p. 112)

Contrast effects (p. 109)

Fundamental attribution error (p. 113)

Halo effect (p. 108)

Perception (p. 100)

Projection (p. 109)

Schema (p. 104)

Selective perception (p. 108)

Self-fulfilling prophecy (p. 110)

Self-serving bias (p. 113)

Chapter 6

Motivation Theories

Chapter at a Glance

The long-term success of the many organizations discussed in this book rests squarely on the motivation and behavior of the individuals who are part of them. As you read Chapter 6, *keep in mind these study questions*.

WHAT IS MOTIVATION?

WHAT DO THE CONTENT THEORIES OF MOTIVATION SUGGEST ABOUT INDIVIDUAL NEEDS AND MOTIVATION?

WHAT DO THE PROCESS THEORIES SUGGEST ABOUT INDIVIDUAL MOTIVATION?

WHAT ARE REINFORCEMENT THEORIES, AND HOW ARE THEY LINKED TO MOTIVATION?

REVIEW IN END-OF-CHAPTER STUDY GUIDE

Students attending one school in Tucson, Arizona, are going to be given the chance to earn college money for good grades. A California benefactress is offering every student at Wakefield Middle School the possibility to earn $50 for every A earned in math, reading, science, social studies, and writing. The incentive, developed in August 2003, follows the student through high school.

The money is available only to pay for college and would provide today's sixth graders up to $4300 by high school graduation. Letters from the benefactors explaining the opportunity are available in the Lapan College Club. It is funded as a part of the Lapan Sunshine Foundation, created by Patricia Lapan, whose son is a Tucson cardiologist. She wants to help and to motivate students who might not otherwise qualify for scholarships to succeed in life. "I'm sure it will be successful," Ms. Lapan said of the program. "I just hope it happens in my lifetime because I'd like to see it happen."[1]

Motivation is a key component of today's current organizations. There are numerous approaches to understanding such motivation, as the topics here and throughout this chapter clearly reveal.

> ## "I'm sure it will be successful. I just hope it happens within my lifetime because I'd like to see it happen."

What Is Motivation?

If asked to identify a major concern or problem at work, a manager is very likely to cite a "motivational" need to do something that will encourage people to work harder to do "what I want." Formally defined, **motivation** refers to the individual forces that account for the direction, level, and persistence of a person's effort expended at work. *Direction* refers to an individual's choice when presented with a number of possible alternatives (e.g., whether to exert effort toward product quality or toward product quantity). *Level* refers to the amount of effort a person puts forth (e.g., a lot or a little). *Persistence* refers to the length of time a person sticks with a given action (e.g., to try to achieve product quality or give up when it is found difficult to attain).

Motivation refers to forces within an individual that account for the level, direction, and persistence of effort expended at work.

Content, Process, and Reinforcement Theories

The theories of motivation can be divided into three broad categories.[2] **Content theories** focus primarily on individual needs—the physiological or psychological deficiencies that we feel a compulsion to reduce or eliminate. These theories suggest that the manager's job is to create a work environment that responds positively to individual needs. They help to explain how poor performance, undesirable behaviors, low satisfaction, and the like can be caused by "blocked"

Content theories profile different needs that may motivate individual behavior.

needs or needs that are not satisfied on the job. **Process theories** focus on the thought or cognitive processes that take place within the minds of people and that influence their behavior. Whereas a content approach may identify job security as an important need for an individual, a process approach probes further to identify why the person behaves in particular ways relative to available rewards and work opportunities. **Reinforcement theories** emphasize the means through which the process of controlling an individual's behavior by manipulating its consequences takes place. They focus on the observable rather than what is inside an employee's head. Thus, reinforcement views place a premium on observing individuals to see which work-related outcomes are highly valued. By altering when, where, how, and why some types of rewards are given, the manager can change the apparent motivation of employees by providing a systematic set of consequences to shape behavior. Although each type of theory contributes to our understanding of motivation, none offers a complete explanation. Therefore, we invite you to use the insights from each of the theories to mix and match the motivational approach most appropriate for a given situation.

> ■ **Process theories** seek to understand the thought processes that determine behavior.
>
> ■ **Reinforcement theories** emphasize the means through which the process of controlling an individual's behavior by manipulating its consequences takes place.

Motivation Across Cultures

Before we examine the motivation theories in detail, an important caveat is in order. Motivation is a key concern in firms across the globe. However, North American theories (and these are the only ones discussed in this chapter) are subject to cultural limitations.[3] The determinants of motivation and the best ways to deal with it are likely to vary considerably across Asia, South America, Eastern Europe, and Africa. As we pointed out in Chapter 3, individual values and attitudes—both important aspects of motivation—have strong cultural foundations. What proves "motivational" as a reward in one culture, for example, might not work in another. We should be sensitive to these issues and avoid being parochial or ethnocentric by assuming that people in all cultures are motivated by the same things in the same ways.[4]

CULTURES AND THE GLOBAL WORKFORCE

INNOVATION AND ITS OWN EBAY

There is an Internet startup named InnoCentive. Firms such as P&G are now farming out chemical synthesis and other problems to a global network of scientific freelancers. The InnoCentive CEO calls this the democratization of science—scientific merit is much more important than where one lives or went to school. Recently, Eli Lilly, the pharmaceutical giant, posted a chemical synthesis problem that a Lilly scientist estimated might take a couple of months to solve. A potential solution from Kazakhstan came in within 72 hours.

    To carry this out, "search" firms put problems online anonymously with a deadline and a promised reward (about $5000 to $100,000). InnoCentive operates much like eBay does for objects. The executive who thought up InnoCentive argues, "There is a whole world of smart people out there."

Question: In what ways might such developments as InnoCentive influence motivation?

Content Theories of Motivation

Content theories, as noted earlier, suggest that motivation results from the individual's attempts to satisfy needs. Four of the better-known content theories have been proposed by Abraham Maslow, Clayton Alderfer, David McClelland, and Frederick Herzberg. Each of these scholars offers a slightly different view of the needs individuals may bring with them to work.

Hierarchy of Needs Theory

Abraham Maslow's **hierarchy of needs theory**, as shown in Figure 6.1, identifies five distinct levels of individual needs: from self-actualization and esteem at the top, to social, safety, and physiological at the bottom.[5] Maslow assumes that some needs are more important than others and must be satisfied before the other needs can serve as motivators. For example, physiological needs must be satisfied before safety needs are activated, safety needs must be satisfied before social needs are activated, and so on.

Maslow's view is quite popular in U.S. firms because it appears to be easily implemented. Unfortunately, however, research evidence fails to support the existence of a precise five-step hierarchy of needs. The needs are more likely to operate in a flexible hierarchy. Some research suggests that **higher-order needs** (esteem and self-actualization) tend to become more important than **lower-order needs**

■■ Maslow's **hierarchy of needs theory** offers a pyramid of physiological, safety, social, esteem, and self-actualization needs.

■■ **Higher-order needs** in Maslow's hierarchy are esteem and self-actualization.

■■ **Lower-order needs** in Maslow's hierarchy are physiological, safety, and social.

Figure 6.1 Higher-order and lower-order needs in Maslow's hierarchy of needs.

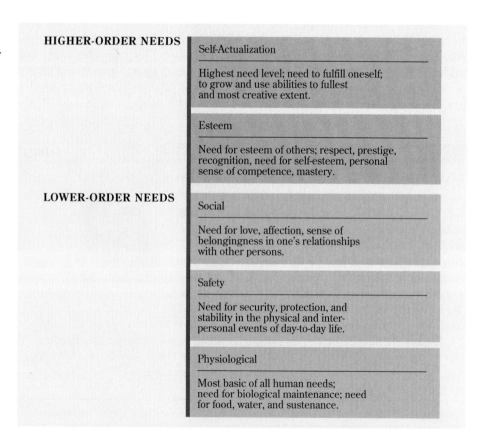

HIGHER-ORDER NEEDS

Self-Actualization

Highest need level; need to fulfill oneself; to grow and use abilities to fullest and most creative extent.

Esteem

Need for esteem of others; respect, prestige, recognition, need for self-esteem, personal sense of competence, mastery.

LOWER-ORDER NEEDS

Social

Need for love, affection, sense of belongingness in one's relationships with other persons.

Safety

Need for security, protection, and stability in the physical and inter-personal events of day-to-day life.

Physiological

Most basic of all human needs; need for biological maintenance; need for food, water, and sustenance.

(psychological, safety, and social) as individuals move up the corporate ladder.[6] Other studies report that needs vary according to a person's career stage, the size of the organization, and even geographic location.[7] There is also no consistent evidence that the satisfaction of a need at one level decreases its importance and increases the importance of the next-higher need.[8] Finally, when the hierarchy of needs is examined across cultures, values such as those discussed in Chapter 2 become important. For instance, social needs tend to dominate in more collectivist societies, such as Mexico and Pakistan.[9]

ERG Theory

Clayton Alderfer's **ERG theory** is also based on needs but differs from Maslow's theory in three basic respects.[10] First, the theory collapses Maslow's five needs categories into three: **existence needs**—desire for physiological and material well-being; **relatedness needs**—desire for satisfying interpersonal relationships; and **growth needs**—desire for continued personal growth and development. Second, whereas Maslow's theory argues that individuals progress up the needs hierarchy, ERG theory emphasizes a unique *frustration-regression* component. An already satisfied lower-level need can become activated when a higher-level need cannot be satisfied. Thus, if a person is continually frustrated in his or her attempts to satisfy growth needs, relatedness needs can again surface as key motivators. Third, unlike Maslow's theory, ERG theory contends that more than one need may be activated at the same time.

Even though more research is needed to shed more light on its validity, the supporting evidence for ERG theory is encouraging.[11] In particular, the theory's allowance for regression back to lower-level needs is a valuable contribution to our thinking. It may help to explain why in some settings, for example, workers' complaints focus on wages, benefits, and working conditions—things relating to existence needs. Although these needs are important, their importance may be exaggerated because the workers' jobs cannot otherwise satisfy relatedness and growth needs. ERG theory thus offers a more flexible approach to understanding human needs than does Maslow's strict hierarchy.

Acquired Needs Theory

In the late 1940s, psychologist David I. McClelland and his co-workers began experimenting with the Thematic Apperception Test (TAT) as a way of measuring human needs.[12] The TAT is a projective technique that asks people to view pictures and write stories about what they see. In one case, McClelland showed three executives a photograph of a man sitting down and looking at family photos arranged on his work desk. One executive wrote of an engineer who was daydreaming about a family outing scheduled for the next day. Another described a designer who had picked up an idea for a new gadget from remarks made by his family. The third described an engineer who was intently working on a bridge-stress problem that he seemed sure to solve because of his confident look.[13] McClelland identified three themes in these TAT stories, with each corresponding to an underlying need that he believes is important for understanding individual behavior. These needs are (1) **need for achievement (nAch)**—the desire to do something better or more efficiently, to solve problems, or to master complex tasks; (2) **need for affiliation (nAff)**—the desire to establish and maintain

---

■ Alderfer's **ERG theory** identifies existence, relatedness, and growth needs.

■ **Existence needs** are desires for physiological and material well-being.

■ **Relatedness needs** are desires for satisfying interpersonal relationships.

■ **Growth needs** are desires for continued personal growth and development.

■ **Need for achievement (nAch)** is the desire to do better, solve problems, or master complex tasks.

■ **Need for affiliation (nAff)** is the desire for friendly and warm relations with others.

■■■ **Need for power (nPower)** is the desire to control others and influence their behavior.

Lee Evans, a football wide receiver, almost left the University of Wisconsin after his junior season. He had been a dominating Big Ten player and now seemed ready for the pros. However, he was motivated to stay at Wisconsin and fine-tune. He then suffered a knee injury and two surgeries and stayed an extra season. "I never regretted the fact I stayed," he said. His motivation enabled him to complete his degree; break Wisconsin records in catches, yards, and touchdowns; and become number two in Big Ten history in career receiving yards.

■■■ Herzberg's **two-factor theory** identifies job context as the source of job dissatisfaction and job content as the source of job satisfaction.

■■■ **Hygiene factors** in the job context—the work setting—are sources of job dissatisfaction.

■■■ **Motivator factors** in the job content—the tasks people actually do—are sources of job satisfaction.

friendly and warm relations with others; and (3) **need for power (nPower)**—the desire to control others, to influence their behavior, or to be responsible for others.

McClelland posits that these three needs are acquired over time, as a result of life experiences. He encourages managers to learn how to identify the presence of nAch, nAff, and nPower in themselves and in others and to create work environments that are responsive to the respective need profiles.

The theory is particularly useful because each need can be linked with a set of work preferences. Someone with a high need for achievement will prefer individual responsibilities, challenging goals, and performance feedback. Someone with a high need affiliation is drawn to interpersonal relationships and opportunities for communication. Someone with a high need for power seeks influence over others and likes attention and recognition. If these needs are truly acquired, it may be possible to acquaint people with the need profiles required to succeed in various types of jobs. For instance, McClelland found that the combination of a moderate to high need for power and a lower need for affiliation is linked with success as a senior executive. High nPower creates the willingness to have influence or impact on others; lower nAff allows the manager to make difficult decisions without undue worry over being disliked.[14]

Research lends considerable insight into nAch in particular and includes some especially interesting applications in developing nations. For example, McClelland trained businesspeople in Kakinda, India, to think, talk, and act like high achievers by having them write stories about achievement and participate in a business game that encouraged achievement. The businesspeople also met with successful entrepreneurs and learned how to set challenging goals for their own businesses. Over a two-year period following these activities, the participants from the Kakinda study engaged in activities that created twice as many new jobs as those who hadn't received the training.[15]

Two-Factor Theory

Frederick Herzberg took a different approach to examining motivation. He simply asked workers to report the times they felt exceptionally good about their jobs and the times they felt exceptionally bad about them.[16] As shown in Figure 6.2, Herzberg and his associates noted that the respondents identified different things when they felt good or bad about their jobs. From this study they developed the **two-factor theory**, also known as the motivator-hygiene theory, which portrays different factors as primary causes of job satisfaction and job dissatisfaction.

According to this theory, **hygiene factors** are sources of job dissatisfaction. These factors are associated with the job context or work setting; that is, they relate more to the environment in which people work than to the nature of the work itself. Among the hygiene factors shown on the left in Figure 6.2, perhaps the most surprising is salary. Herzberg found that a low salary makes people dissatisfied but that paying them more does not necessarily satisfy or motivate them. In the two-factor theory, job satisfaction and job dissatisfaction are totally separate dimensions. Therefore, improving a hygiene factor, such as working conditions, will not make people satisfied with their work; it will only prevent them from being dissatisfied.

To improve job satisfaction, the theory directs attention to an entirely different set of factors—the **motivator factors**, shown on the right in Figure 6.2. These fac-

Hygiene factors in job context affect job *dis*satisfaction	Motivator factors in job content affect job satisfaction
Organizational policies	Achievement
Quality of supervision	Recognition
Working conditions	Work itself
Base wage or salary	Responsibility
Relationships with peers	Advancement
Relationships with subordinates	Growth
Status	
Security	

High Job *Dis*satisfaction 0 Job Satisfaction High

Figure 6.2 Sources of dissatisfaction and satisfaction in Herzberg's two-factor theory.

tors are related to job content—what people actually do in their work. Adding these satisfiers or motivators to people's jobs is Herzberg's link to performance. These factors include sense of achievement, recognition, and responsibility.

According to Herzberg, when these opportunities are not available, low job satisfaction causes a lack of motivation and performance suffers. He suggests the technique of job enrichment as a way of building satisfiers into job content. This topic is given special attention in Chapter 8. For now, the notion is well summarized in this statement by Herzberg: "If you want people to do a good job, give them a good job to do."[17]

OB scholars continue to debate the merits of the two-factor theory and its applications.[18] Many are unable to confirm the theory. Many criticize it as being method bound. This is a serious criticism, for the scientific approach requires that theories be verifiable under different research methods. Furthermore, this theory, just like the other content theories, fails to account for individual differences, to link motivation and needs to both satisfaction and performance, and to consider cultural and professional differences.[19]

The content theories remain popular in management circles because of their simplicity and the apparent direct linkage from needs to behavior. At the same time, none of the theories links needs directly to the motivated behavior desired by the manager. Rather, managers just misinterpret the theories and often inappropriately assume that they know the needs of their subordinates. Thus, we advise extreme care in simplistic application of content theories.

Process Theories

The various content theories emphasize the "what" aspects of motivation. That is, they tend to look for ways to improve motivation by dealing with activated or deprived needs. They do not delve formally into the thought processes through which people choose one action over another in the workplace. *Process theories* focus on thought processes. Although there are many process theories, we will concentrate on equity and expectancy theory.

Joint Appearances and Motivation

The University Wind Ensemble, a select concert band of Southern Illinois University at Carbondale, traveled to England during a recent May. It was the first time a group from the university's music school had ever toured outside the country. It joined forces with the White Russian Army Band as well as being part of a massed-band festival at the British Royal Military School of Music. Many of the students appeared to be motivated by the trip, and the trip and motivation were related to the joint appearances with other bands.

Research Insight
When and How Does Positive or Negative Feedback Affect Motivation?

When people fail, they sometimes give up and sometimes try harder. Likewise, when individuals succeed, they sometimes rest on their laurels and sometimes increase their efforts. One research stream suggests that failure motivates more than does success. Another stream, based on aspiration levels and self-efficacy notions, suggests that individuals try harder and raise their goals after success.

Two experiments were conducted—one on workers from different occupations, the other with MBA students—to examine the question of when and how positive (negative) feedback increases or decreases motivation. It was found that high levels of motivation were induced either by failure to meet obligations or by success in fulfilling a desire.

> **FEEDBACK AND MOTIVATION**
>
> High levels of motivation were induced either by failure to meet obligation *or* by success in fulfilling a desire.

Reference: Dina Van-Dijk and Avraham N. Kluger, "Feedback Sign Effect on Motivation: Is It Moderated by Regulatory Focus?" *Applied Psychology: An International Review* 53(1) (2004):113–135.

Equity Theory

Adams's **equity theory** posits that people will act to eliminate any felt inequity in the rewards received for their work in comparison with others.

Equity theory is based on the phenomenon of social comparison and is best applied to the workplace through the writing of J. Stacy Adams.[20] Adams argues that when people gauge the fairness of their work outcomes relative to others, any perceived inequity is a motivating state of mind. Perceived inequity occurs when someone believes that the rewards received for their work contributions compare unfavorably to the rewards other people appear to have received for their work. When such perceived inequity exists, the theory states that people will be motivated to act in ways that remove the discomfort and restore a sense of felt equity.

Felt negative inequity exists when an individual feels that he or she has received relatively less than others have in proportion to work inputs. *Felt positive inequity* exists when an individual feels that he or she has received relatively more than others have. When either feeling exists, the individual will likely engage in one or more of the following behaviors to restore a sense of equity.

How to restore perceived equity

- Change work inputs (e.g., reduce performance efforts).
- Change the outcomes (rewards) received (e.g., ask for a raise).
- Leave the situation (e.g., quit).
- Change the comparison points (e.g., compare self to a different co-worker).
- Psychologically distort the comparisons (e.g., rationalize that the inequity is only temporary and will be resolved in the future).
- Take actions to change the inputs or outputs of the comparison person (e.g., get a co-worker to accept more work).

The equity comparison intervenes between the allocation of rewards and the ultimate impact on the recipients. What may seem fair and equitable to a group leader, for example, might be perceived as unfair and inequitable by a team member after comparisons are made with other teammates. Furthermore, such feelings of inequity are determined solely by the individual's interpretation of the situation. It is not the reward-giver's intentions that count; it is how the recipient perceives the reward that will determine actual motivational outcomes. The Effective Manager 6.1 offers ideas for coping with equity comparisons.

Research indicates that people who feel they are overpaid (perceived positive inequity) increase the quantity or quality of their work, whereas those who feel they are underpaid (perceived negative inequity) decrease the quantity or quality of their work.[21] The research is most conclusive with respect to felt negative inequity. It appears that people are less comfortable when they are underrewarded than when they are overrewarded. Such results, however, are particularly tied to individualistic cultures in which self-interest tends to govern social comparisons. In more collectivist cultures, such as those of many Asian countries, the concern often runs more for equality than equity. This allows for solidarity with the group and helps to maintain harmony in social relationships.[22]

> **THE EFFECTIVE MANAGER 6.1**
>
> ## Steps for Managing the Equity Process
>
> - Recognize that equity comparisons are inevitable in the workplace.
> - Anticipate felt negative inequities when rewards are given.
> - Communicate clear evaluations of any rewards given.
> - Communicate an appraisal of performance on which the reward is based.
> - Communicate comparison points appropriate in the situation.

Expectancy Theory

Victor Vroom's **expectancy theory** posits that motivation is a result of a rational calculation.[23] A person is motivated to the degree that he or she believes that (1) effort will yield acceptable performance, (2) performance will be rewarded, and (3) the value of the rewards is highly positive. The interactive combination of all three influences motivation. (See Figure 6.3.) Thus, some key concepts are defined in terms of probabilities.

- The probability assigned by an individual that work effort will be followed by a given level of achieved task performance is called **expectancy**. Expectancy would equal 0 if the person felt it were impossible to achieve the given performance level; it would equal 1 if a person were 100 percent certain that the performance could be achieved.
- **Instrumentality** is the probability assigned by the individual that a given level of achieved task performance will lead to various work outcomes. Instrumentality also varies from 0 to 1.*
- **Valence** is the value attached by the individual to various work outcomes. Valences form a scale from –1 (very undesirable outcome) to +1 (very desirable outcome). Vroom posits that motivation (M), expectancy (E), instrumentality (I), and valence (V) are related to one another by the equation: $M = (E) \times (I) \times (V)$. This multiplier effect means that the motivational appeal of a given

■ Vroom's **expectancy theory** argues that work motivation is determined by individual beliefs regarding effort/performance relationships and work outcomes.

■ **Expectancy** is the probability that work effort will be followed by performance accomplishment.

■ **Instrumentality** is the probability that performance will lead to various work outcomes.

■ **Valence** is the value to the individual of various work outcomes.

---

* Strictly speaking, Vroom's treatment of instrumentality would allow it to vary from –1 to +1. We use the probability definition here and the 0 to +1 range for pedagogical purposes; it is consistent with the instrumentality notion.

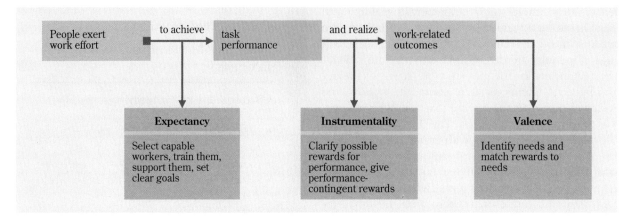

Figure 6.3   Key terms and managerial implications of Vroom's expectancy theory.

work path is sharply reduced whenever any one or more of these factors approaches the value of zero. Conversely, for a given reward to have a high and positive motivational impact as a work outcome, the expectancy, instrumentality, and valence associated with the reward all must be high and positive.

Suppose that a manager is wondering whether or not the prospect of earning a merit raise will be motivational to an employee. Expectancy theory predicts that motivation to work hard to earn the merit pay will be low if *expectancy* is low—a person feels that he or she cannot achieve the necessary performance level. Motivation will also be low if *instrumentality* is low—the person is not confident a high level of task performance will result in a high merit pay raise. Motivation will also be low if *valence* is low—the person places little value on a merit pay increase. And motivation will be low if any combination of these exists. Thus, the multiplier effect requires managers to act to maximize expectancy, instrumentality, and valence when seeking to create high levels of work motivation. A zero at any location on the right side of the expectancy equation will result in zero motivation.

Expectancy logic argues that a manager must try to intervene actively in work situations to maximize work expectancies, instrumentalities, and valences that support organizational objectives.[24] To influence expectancies, managers should select people with proper abilities, train them well, support them with needed resources, and identify clear performance goals. To influence instrumentality, managers should clarify performance–reward relationships and confirm these relationships when rewards are actually given for performance accomplishments. To influence valences, managers should identify the needs that are important to each individual and then try to adjust available rewards to match these needs.

Extrinsic rewards are given to the individual by some other person in the work setting.

Intrinsic rewards are received by the individual directly through task performance.

A great deal of research on expectancy theory has been conducted, and review articles are available.[25] Although the theory has received substantial support, specific details, such as the operation of the multiplier effect, remain subject to some question. One of the more popular modifications of Vroom's original version of the theory distinguishes between work outcomes for calculating valence.[26] Researchers have separated **extrinsic rewards**—positively valued work outcomes given to the individual by some other person—from intrinsic rewards (see The Effective Manager 6.2). **Intrinsic rewards** are positively valued work outcomes that the individual receives directly as a result of task performance. A feeling of achievement after accomplishing a particularly challenging task is an example.

Expectancy theory does not specify exactly which rewards will motivate particular groups of workers. In this sense, the theory allows for the fact that the rewards and their link with performance are likely to be seen as quite different in different cultures. It helps to explain some apparently counterintuitive findings. For example, a pay raise motivated one group of Mexican workers to work fewer hours. They wanted a certain amount of money in order to enjoy things other than work rather than just more money. A Japanese sales representative's promotion to manager of a U.S. company adversely affected his performance. His superiors did not realize that the promotion embarrassed him and distanced him from his colleagues.[27]

THE EFFECTIVE MANAGER 6.2

Work Guidelines for Allocating Extrinsic Rewards

1. Clearly identify the desired behaviors.
2. Maintain an inventory of rewards that have the potential to serve as positive reinforcers.
3. Recognize individual differences in the rewards that will have positive value for each person.
4. Let each person know exactly what must be done to receive a desirable reward. Set clear target antecedents and give performance feedback.
5. Allocate rewards contingently and immediately upon the appearance of the desired behaviors.
6. Allocate rewards wisely in terms of scheduling the delivery of positive reinforcement.

ETHICS AND SOCIAL RESPONSIBILITY

PASTORAL GUIDEBOOKS AND JOBLESS AID

The Rev. Anthony Spearman, a pastor at Moore's Chapel AME Church in Salisbury, North Carolina, recently received a copy of a guidebook aimed at helping pastors handle a job loss among their congregants. He had previously been unprepared to guide his parishioners in applying for such jobless aid as retraining, unemployment insurance, and the like. He and countless other pastors have found the guidebook to be invaluable in today's economy.

Question: What content and/or process motivational effects might this guidebook have on both the pastor and the congregants?

Reinforcement

In OB, reinforcement has a very specific meaning that has its origin in some classic studies in psychology.[28] **Reinforcement** is the administration of a consequence as a result of a behavior. Managing reinforcement properly can change the direction, level, and persistence of an individual's behavior. To understand this idea, we need to review some of the concepts of conditioning and reinforcement you learned in your basic psychology course. We will then move on to applications.

Classical and Operant Conditioning

Recall that Ivan Pavlov studied classical conditioning. **Classical conditioning** is a form of learning through association that involves the manipulation of stimuli

Reinforcement is the administration of a consequence as a result of behavior.

Classical conditioning is a form of learning through association that involves the manipulation of stimuli to influence behavior.

to influence behavior. The Russian psychologist "taught" dogs to salivate at the sound of a bell by ringing the bell when feeding the dogs. The sight of the food naturally caused the dogs to salivate. Eventually, the dogs "learned" to associate the bell ringing with the presentation of meat and to salivate at the ringing of the bell alone. Such "learning" through association is so common in organizations that it is often ignored until it causes considerable confusion. Take a look at Figure 6.4. The key is to understand a stimulus and a conditioned stimulus. A **stimulus** is something that incites action and draws forth a response (the meat for the dogs). The trick is to associate one neutral potential stimulus (the bell ringing) with another initial stimulus that already affects behavior (the meat). The once-neutral stimulus is called a *conditioned stimulus* when it affects behavior in the same way as the initial stimulus. In Figure 6.4, the boss's smiling becomes a conditioned stimulus because of its linkage to his criticisms.

▧ A **stimulus** is something that incites action.

Operant conditioning, popularized by B. F. Skinner, is an extension of the classical case to much more practical affairs.[29] It includes more than just a stimulus and a response behavior. **Operant conditioning** is the process of controlling behavior by manipulating its consequences. Classical and operant conditioning differ in two important ways. First, control in operant conditioning is via manipulation of consequences. Second, operant conditioning calls for examining antecedents, behavior, and consequences. The *antecedent* is the condition leading up to or "cueing" behavior. For example, in Figure 6.4, an agreement between the boss and the employee to work overtime as needed is an antecedent. If the employee works overtime, this would be the *behavior*, while the *consequence* would be the boss's praise.

▧ **Operant conditioning** is the process of controlling behavior by manipulating, or "operating" on, its consequences.

A boss who wants a behavior to be repeated, such as working overtime, must manipulate the consequences. The basis for manipulating consequences is E. L. Thorndike's law of effect.[30] The **law of effect** is simple but powerful: behavior that results in a pleasant outcome is likely to be repeated, while behavior that results in an unpleasant outcome is not likely to be repeated. The implications of this law are rather straightforward. If, as a supervisor, you want more of a behavior, you must make the consequences for the individual positive.

▧ The **law of effect** is the observation that behavior that results in a pleasing outcome is likely to be repeated; behavior that results in an unpleasant outcome is not likely to be repeated.

Note that the emphasis is on consequences that can be manipulated rather than on consequences inherent in the behavior itself. OB research often emphasizes specific types of rewards that are considered by the reinforcement perspective to influ-

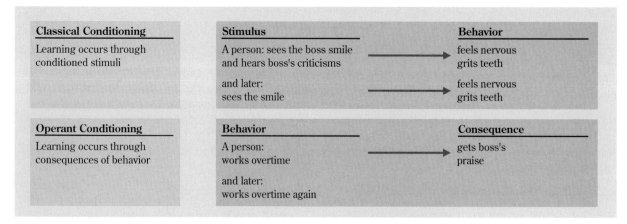

Figure 6.4   **Differences between classical and operant conditioning approaches for a boss and subordinate.**

Contrived Rewards: Some Direct Cost		Natural Rewards: No Direct Cost	
refreshments	promotion	smiles	recognition
piped-in music	trips	greetings	feedback
nice offices	company car	compliments	asking advice
cash bonuses	paid insurance	special jobs	
merit pay increases	stock options		
profit sharing	gifts		
office parties	sport tickets		

Figure 6.5 **A sample of extrinsic rewards allocated by managers.**

ence individual behavior. *Extrinsic rewards* are positively valued work outcomes that are given to the individual by some other person. They are important external reinforcers or environmental consequences that can substantially influence a person's work behaviors through the law of effect. Figure 6.5 presents a sample of extrinsic rewards that managers can allocate to their subordinates.[31] Some of these rewards are contrived, or planned, rewards that have direct costs and budgetary implications. Examples are pay increases and cash bonuses. A second category includes natural rewards that have no cost other than the manager's personal time and efforts. Examples are verbal praise and recognition in the workplace.

Reinforcement Strategies

We now bring the notions of classical conditioning, operant conditioning, reinforcement, and extrinsic rewards together to show how the direction, level, and persistence of individual behavior can be changed. This combination is called **OB Mod** after its longer title of **organizational behavior modification**. OB Mod is the systematic reinforcement of desirable work behavior and the nonreinforcement or punishment of unwanted work behavior. OB Mod includes four basic reinforcement strategies: positive reinforcement, negative reinforcement (or avoidance), punishment, and extinction.[32]

Positive Reinforcement B. F. Skinner and his followers advocate **positive reinforcement**—the administration of positive consequences that tend to increase the likelihood of repeating the desirable behavior in similar settings. For example, a Texas Instruments manager nods to a subordinate to express approval after she makes a useful comment during a sales meeting. Obviously, the boss wants more useful comments. Later, the subordinate makes another useful comment, just as the boss hoped she would.

To begin using a strategy of positive reinforcement, we need to be aware that positive reinforcers and rewards are not necessarily the same. Recognition, for example, is both a reward and a potential positive reinforcer. Recognition becomes a positive reinforcer only if a person's performance later improves. Sometimes, rewards turn out not to be positive reinforcers. For example, a supervisor at Boeing might praise a subordinate in front of other group members for finding errors in a report. If the group members then give the worker the silent treatment, however, the worker may stop looking for errors in the future. In this case, the supervisor's "reward" does not serve as a positive reinforcer.

To have maximum reinforcement value, a reward must be delivered only if the desired behavior is exhibited. That is, the reward must be contingent on the

Organizational behavior modification (OB Mod) is the systematic reinforcement of desirable work behavior and the nonreinforcement or punishment of unwanted work behavior.

Positive reinforcement is the administration of positive consequences that tend to increase the likelihood of repeating the behavior in similar settings.

■■■ The **law of contingent reinforcement** is the view that, for a reward to have maximum reinforcing value, it must be delivered only if the desired behavior is exhibited.

■■■ The **law of immediate reinforcement** states that the more immediate the delivery of a reward after the occurrence of a desirable behavior, the greater the reinforcing effect on behavior.

■■■ **Shaping** is the creation of a new behavior by the positive reinforcement of successive approximations to the desired behavior.

■■■ **Continuous reinforcement** is a reinforcement schedule that administers a reward each time a desired behavior occurs.

■■■ **Intermittent reinforcement** is a reinforcement schedule that rewards behavior only periodically.

desired behavior. This principle is known as the **law of contingent reinforcement**. In the previous Texas Instruments example, the supervisor's praise was contingent on the subordinate's making constructive comments. Finally, the reward must be given as soon as possible after the desired behavior. This is known as the **law of immediate reinforcement**.[33] If the TI boss waited for the annual performance review to praise the subordinate for providing constructive comments, the law of immediate reinforcement would be violated.

Now that we have presented the general concepts, it is time to address two important issues of implementation. First, what do you do if the behavior approximates what you want but is not exactly on target? Second, is it necessary to provide reinforcement each and every time? These are issues of shaping and scheduling, respectively.

Shaping   If the desired behavior is specific in nature and is difficult to achieve, a pattern of positive reinforcement, called shaping, can be used. **Shaping** is the creation of a new behavior by the positive reinforcement of successive approximations leading to the desired behavior. For example, new machine operators in the Ford Motor casting operation in Ohio must learn a complex series of tasks in pouring molten metal into the casting in order to avoid gaps, overfills, or cracks.[34] The molds are filled in a three-step process, with each step progressively more difficult than its predecessor. Astute master craftspersons first show neophytes how to pour the first step and give praise based on what they did right. As the apprentices gain experience, they are given praise only when all of the elements of the first step are completed successfully. Once the apprentices have mastered the first step, they progress to the second. Reinforcement is given only when the entire first step and an aspect of the second step are completed successfully. Over time, apprentices learn all three steps and are given contingent positive rewards immediately for a complete casting that has no cracks or gaps. In this way, behavior is shaped gradually rather than changed all at once.

Scheduling Positive Reinforcement   Positive reinforcement can be given according to either continuous or intermittent schedules. **Continuous reinforcement** administers a reward each time a desired behavior occurs. **Intermittent reinforcement** rewards behavior only periodically. These alternatives are important because the two schedules may have very different impacts on behavior. In general, continuous reinforcement elicits a desired behavior more quickly than does intermittent reinforcement. Thus, in the initial training of the apprentice casters, continuous reinforcement would be important. At the same time, continuous reinforcement is more costly in the consumption of rewards and is more easily extinguished when reinforcement is no longer present. In contrast, behavior acquired under intermittent reinforcement lasts longer upon the discontinuance of reinforcement than does behavior acquired under continuous reinforcement. In other words, it is more resistant to extinction. Thus, as the apprentices master an aspect of the pouring, the schedule is switched from continuous to intermittent reinforcement.

As shown in Figure 6.6, intermittent reinforcement can be given according to fixed or variable schedules. *Variable schedules* typically result in more consistent patterns of desired behavior than do fixed reinforcement schedules. *Fixed-interval schedules* provide rewards at the first appearance of a behavior after a given time has elapsed. *Fixed-ratio schedules* result in a reward each time a certain number of the behaviors have occurred. A *variable-interval schedule* rewards behavior at random times, while a *variable-ratio schedule* rewards behavior after a random number

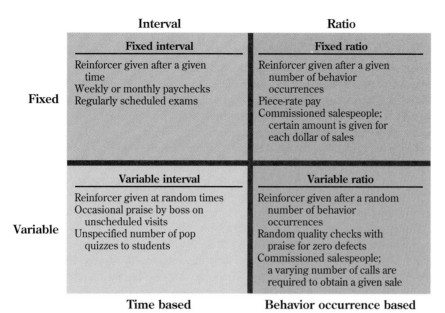

	Interval	Ratio
Fixed	**Fixed interval** Reinforcer given after a given time Weekly or monthly paychecks Regularly scheduled exams	**Fixed ratio** Reinforcer given after a given number of behavior occurrences Piece-rate pay Commissioned salespeople; certain amount is given for each dollar of sales
Variable	**Variable interval** Reinforcer given at random times Occasional praise by boss on unscheduled visits Unspecified number of pop quizzes to students	**Variable ratio** Reinforcer given after a random number of behavior occurrences Random quality checks with praise for zero defects Commissioned salespeople; a varying number of calls are required to obtain a given sale
	Time based	**Behavior occurrence based**

Figure 6.6 Four types of intermittent reinforcement schedules.

of occurrences. For example, as the apprentices perfect their technique for a stage of pouring castings, the astute masters switch to a variable-ratio reinforcement.

Let's look at an example from Drankenfeld Colors, Washington, Pennsylvania, with 250 employees. The absentee rate of these employees was very low, and in a recent year 44 percent of the employees had perfect attendance records. The firm wanted to use positive reinforcement to showcase perfect attendance, even though attendance was already so positive. Consequently, it gave monetary awards of $50 for perfect attendance at 6 and 12 months, with a $25 bonus for a full year of perfect attendance. In addition, the firm entered employees with perfect attendance into a sweepstakes drawing at special award banquets. The winners received an all-expense-paid trip for two to a resort. Perfect attendance increased from 44 percent to 62 percent in the program's first year.[35]

Now, let's consider what kind of reinforcement scheduling was used in this program. A strong argument can be made that a fixed-ratio schedule was used, in conjunction with a variable-ratio schedule. The first schedule rewarded attendance behaviors occurring within 6 months and 12 months, or the specific number of workday attendance behaviors occurring within these periods. Thus, for each period during which a perfect number of attendance days occurred, a person received an award—a fixed-ratio schedule one.

The second schedule focuses on eligibility for the drawing. It is a variable ratio schedule because a random number of perfect attendance days must pass before a specific employee receives a trip. Maintaining perfect attendance to qualify for the drawing is similar to playing a slot machine. In this variable-ratio system, players keep putting coins in the machines because they don't have any idea when they will hit the jackpot.[36] Lotteries similar to Drankenfeld's have been used by firms as different as new-car dealerships and New York Life Insurance.[37]

Negative Reinforcement (Avoidance) A second reinforcement strategy used in OB Mod is **negative reinforcement** or avoidance—the withdrawal of negative consequences, which tends to increase the likelihood of repeating the desirable behavior

■ **Negative reinforcement** is the withdrawal of negative consequences, which tends to increase the likelihood of repeating the behavior in a similar setting; it is also known as avoidance.

Dhyana Ziegler

Dhyana Ziegler has been provided strong positive reinforcement recently for her work in making technology part of a global society. She is Assistant Vice President for Instructional Technology at Florida A&M University. She hosts and co-produces a nationally syndicated radio program, *Delta SEE Connection*, that features African-Americans in science, engineering, and math. She has also co-authored two books and produced several television documentaries.

Punishment is the administration of negative consequences that tend to reduce the likelihood of repeating the behavior in similar settings.

Extinction is the withdrawal of the reinforcing consequences for a given behavior.

in similar settings. For example, a manager at McDonald's regularly nags a worker about his poor performance and then stops nagging when the worker does not fall behind one day. We need to focus on two aspects here: the negative consequences followed by the withdrawal of these consequences when desirable behavior occurs. The term "negative reinforcement" comes from this withdrawal of the negative consequences. This strategy is also sometimes called *avoidance* because its intent is for the person to avoid the negative consequence by performing the desired behavior. For instance, we stop at a red light to avoid a traffic ticket, or a worker who prefers the day shift is allowed to return to that shift if she performs well on the night shift.

Punishment   A third OB Mod strategy is punishment. Unlike positive reinforcement and negative reinforcement, punishment is intended not to encourage positive behavior but to discourage negative behavior. Formally defined, **punishment** is the administration of negative consequences or the withdrawal of positive consequences that tend to reduce the likelihood of repeating the behavior in similar settings. The first type of punishment is illustrated by a Burger King manager who assigns a tardy worker to an unpleasant job, such as cleaning the restrooms. An example of withdrawing positive consequences is a Burger King manager who docks the employee's pay when she is tardy.

Some scholarly work illustrates the importance of punishment by showing that punishment administered for poor performance leads to enhanced performance without a significant effect on satisfaction. However, punishment seen by workers as arbitrary and capricious leads to very low satisfaction as well as low performance.[38] Thus, punishment can be handled poorly, or it can be handled well. Of course, the manager's challenge is to know when to use this strategy and how to use it correctly.

Finally, punishment may be offset by positive reinforcement received from another source. It is possible for a worker to be reinforced by peers at the same time that the worker is receiving punishment from the manager. Sometimes the positive value of such peer support is so great that the individual chooses to put up with the punishment. Thus, the undesirable behavior continues. As many times as an experienced worker may be verbally reprimanded by a supervisor for playing jokes on new employees, for example, the "grins" offered by other workers may well justify continuation of the jokes in the future.

Does all of this mean that punishment should never be administered? Of course not. The important things to remember are to administer punishment selectively and then to do it right.

Extinction   The final OB Mod reinforcement strategy is **extinction**—the withdrawal of the reinforcing consequences for a given behavior. For example, Jack is often late for work, and his co-workers cover for him (positive reinforcement). The manager instructs Jack's co-workers to stop covering for him, withdrawing the reinforcing consequences. The manager has deliberately used extinction to get rid of an undesirable behavior. This strategy decreases the frequency of or weakens the behavior. The behavior is not "unlearned"; it simply is not exhibited. Since the behavior is no longer reinforced, it will reappear if reinforced again. Whereas positive reinforcement seeks to establish and maintain desirable work behavior, extinction is intended to weaken and eliminate undesirable behavior.

Summary of Reinforcement Strategies   Figure 6.7 summarizes and illustrates the use of each OB Mod strategy. They are all designed to direct work behavior toward practices desired by management. Both positive and negative reinforcement are used to strengthen the desirable behavior of improving work quality when it occurs. Punishment is used to weaken the undesirable behavior of high error rates and involves either administering negative consequences or withdrawing positive consequences. Similarly, extinction is used deliberately to weaken the undesirable behavior of high error rates when it occurs. Note also, however, that extinction is used inadvertently to weaken the desirable behavior of low error rates. Finally, these strategies may be used in combination as well as independently.

Ethics and Reinforcement

The effective use of reinforcement strategies can help manage human behavior at work. Testimony to this effect is found in the application of these strategies in many large firms, such as General Electric and B. F. Goodrich, and even in small firms, such as Mid-America Building Maintenance. Mid-America, a janitorial services firm in Wichita, Kansas, provides an incentive program to employees who work 90 consecutive workdays without an absence.[39] Reinforcement strategies are also supported by the growing number of consulting firms that specialize in reinforcement techniques.

Managerial use of these approaches is not without criticism, however. For example, some reports on the "success" of specific programs involve isolated cases that have been analyzed without the benefit of scientific research designs. It is hard to conclude definitively whether the observed results were caused by reinforcement dynamics. In fact, one critic argues that the improved perfor-

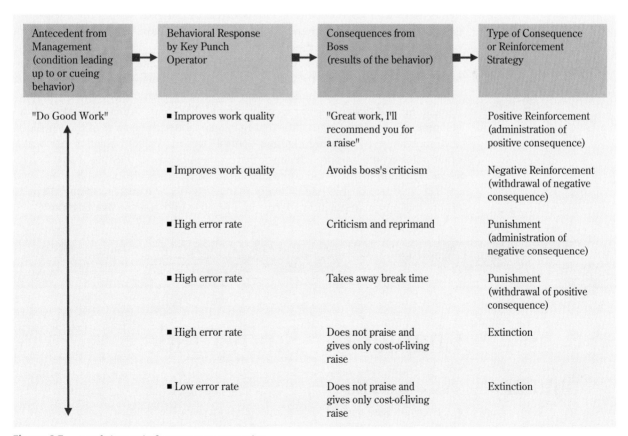

Figure 6.7   Applying reinforcement strategies.

Leaders on Leadership

AUTO RETAILING, WHERE "RETAIL IS DETAIL"

Mike Maroone is President/COO of the largest auto retailer in the world—AutoNation, with $20 billion in sales and over 370 outlets. His leadership philosophy involves moving AutoNation to the next level from good to great. A key objective is to successfully remove the "glass ceiling" of managers related to owners, whereby one can only become manager if related to the owner, and to group dealerships (new and used) in singles markets. He argues that compet-

itive compensation and the potential for career advancement, as well as "retail is detail" training, bring the best and brightest people to AutoNation.

Mike's and AutoNation's leadership philosophy involves four pillars: (1) to promote operational excellence—demonstrate associates' excellence throughout; (2) leverage—demonstrate a reason for a business to be $20 billion or

more in size; (3) productivity—ranking every store within a brand and holding monthly meetings concerning the ranking; and (4) use of a common brand name in markets, and emphasizing advantages of scale and information systems to deal with customers.

His final word: "You are going to spend a large part of your life doing something...you must love it."

Question: How might you interpret Maroone's motivational ideas in terms of content, process, and reinforcement motivation theories?

---

mance may well have occurred only because of the goal setting involved—that is, because specific performance goals were clarified, and workers were individually held accountable for their accomplishment.[40]

Another major criticism rests with the potential value dilemmas associated with using reinforcement to influence human behavior at work. For example, some critics maintain that the systematic use of reinforcement strategies leads to a demeaning and dehumanizing view of people that stunts human growth and development.[41] A related criticism is that managers abuse the power of their position and knowledge by exerting external control over individual behavior. Advocates of the reinforcement approach attack the problem head on: they agree that behavior modification involves the control of behavior, but they also argue that behavior control is an irrevocable part of every manager's job. The real question is how to ensure that any manipulation is done in a positive and constructive fashion.[42]

Chapter 6   Study Guide

Summary

What is motivation?

- Motivation is an internal force that accounts for the level, direction, and persistence of effort expended at work.

- Content theories—including the work of Maslow, Alderfer, McClelland, and Herzberg—focus on locating individual needs that influence behavior in the workplace.

- Process theories, such as equity and expectancy theory, examine the thought processes that affect decisions about alternative courses of action by people at work.

- Reinforcement theories emphasize the means through which the process of controlling an individual's behavior by manipulating its consequences takes place. They focus on observable aspects rather than what is inside an employee's head.

- One should be sensitive to the fact that motivation is important to firms across the globe; however, specific aspects may vary across different cultures.

What do the content theories suggest about individual needs and motivation?

- Maslow's hierarchy of needs theory views human needs as activated in a five-step hierarchy ranging from physiological (lowest), to safety, to social, to esteem, to self-actualization (highest).

- Alderfer's ERG theory collapses the five needs into three: existence, relatedness, and growth; it maintains that more than one need can be activated at a time.

- McClelland's acquired needs theory focuses on the needs for achievement, affiliation, and power, and it views needs as developed over time through experience and training.

- Herzberg's two-factor theory links job satisfaction to motivator factors, such as responsibility and challenge, associated with job content.

- Herzberg's two-factor theory links job dissatisfaction to hygiene factors, such as pay and working conditions, associated with job context.

What do the process theories suggest about individual motivation?

- Equity theory points out that social comparisons take place when people receive rewards and that any felt inequity will motivate them to try to restore a sense of perceived equity.

- When felt inequity is negative—that is, when the individual feels unfairly treated—he or she may decide to work less hard in the future or to quit a job.

- Vroom's expectancy theory describes motivation as a function of an individual's beliefs concerning effort–performance relationships (expectancy), work–outcome relationships (instrumentality), and the desirability of various work outcomes (valence).

- Expectancy theory states that Motivation = Expectancy × Instrumentality × Valence, and argues that managers should make each factor positive in order to ensure high levels of motivation.

What are reinforcement theories, and how are they linked to motivation?

- The foundation of reinforcement is the law of effect, which states that behavior will be repeated or extinguished depending on whether the consequences are positive or negative.

- Positive reinforcement is the administration of positive consequences that tend to increase the likelihood of a person's repeating a behavior in similar settings.

- Positive reinforcement should be contingent and immediate, and it can be scheduled continuously or intermittently, depending on resources and desired outcomes.

- Negative reinforcement (avoidance) is used to encourage desirable behavior through the withdrawal of negative consequences for previously undesirable behavior.

- Punishment is the administration of negative consequences or the withdrawal of positive consequences, which tends to reduce the likelihood of repeating an undesirable behavior in similar settings.

■ Extinction is the withdrawal of reinforcing consequences for a given behavior.

Key Terms

Classical conditioning
(p. 129)
Content theories (p.120)
Continuous reinforcement
(p. 132)
Equity theory (p. 126)
ERG theory (p. 123)
Existence needs (p. 123)
Expectancy (p. 127)
Expectancy theory (p. 127)
Extinction (p. 134)
Extrinsic rewards (p.128)
Growth needs (p. 123)
Hierarchy of needs theory
(p. 122)
Higher-order needs (p. 122)
Hygiene factors (p. 124)
Instrumentality (p. 127)

Intermittent reinforcement
(p. 132)
Intrinsic rewards (p. 128)
Law of contingent
reinforcement (p. 132)
Law of effect (p. 130)
Law of immediate
reinforcement (p.132)
Lower-order needs (p. 122)
Motivation (p. 120)
Motivator factors (p. 124)
Need for achievement
(nAch) (p. 123)
Need for affiliation (nAff)
(p. 123)
Need for power (nPower)
(p. 124)

Negative reinforcement
(p. 133)
Operant conditioning (p 130)
Organizational behavior
modification (OB Mod)
(p. 131)
Positive reinforcement
(p. 131)
Process theories (p. 121)
Punishment (p. 134)
Reinforcement (p. 129)
Reinforcement theories
(p. 121)
Relatedness needs (p. 123)
Shaping (p 132)
Stimulus (p. 130)
Two-factor theory (p. 124)
Valence (p. 127)

Self-Test 6

Multiple Choice

1. Reinforcement emphasizes _____. (a) intrinsic rewards (b) extrinsic rewards (c) the law of diminishing returns (d) social learning
2. OB Mod reinforcement strategies _____. (a) have much carefully controlled research support (b) have been criticized because the observed results may confuse causality (c) are not used much in large firms (d) are useful mostly in large firms
3. Negative reinforcement _____. (a) is similar to punishment (b) seeks to discourage undesirable behavior (c) seeks to encourage desirable behavior (d) is also known as escapism
4. OB Mod emphasizes _____. (a) the systematic reinforcement of desirable work behavior (b) noncontingent rewards (c) noncontingent punishment (d) extinction in preference to positive reinforcement
5. Reinforcement strategies _____. (a) violate ethical guidelines (b) involve the control of behavior (c) work best when they restrict freedom of choice (d) have largely been replaced by computer technology
6. A content theory of motivation is most likely to focus on _____. (a) contingent reinforcement (b) instrumentalities (c) equities (d) individual needs
7. In equity theory, the _____ is a key issue. (a) social comparison of rewards and efforts (b) equality of rewards (c) equality of efforts (d) absolute value of rewards
8. In expectancy theory, _____ is the probability that a given level of performance will lead to a particular work outcome. (a) expectancy (b) instrumentality (c) motivation (d) valence
9. The law of effect argues that _____. (a) behavior that results in a pleasing effect is likely

to be repeated (b) behavior that results in a pleasing effect is *not* likely to be repeated (c) there is no relationship between behavior and effect (d) effect precedes behavior

10. Because motivation is generally considered to be a universal concept, _____. (a) the theories apply equally well in all cultures (b) ability is not important (c) it does not matter which motivation theory one uses (d) U.S. motivation theories work equally well in other cultures

11. Extrinsic rewards _____. (a) are work outcomes received directly from task performance itself (b) are work outcomes administered by someone else in the work setting (c) are typically larger than intrinsic rewards (d) are stronger motivators than intrinsic rewards

12. Reinforcement and process motivation theories _____. (a) are almost the same (b) each emphasize need satisfaction (c) each focus on what is inside an employee's head (d) each offer a useful but incomplete understanding of motivation

13. Expectancy theory posits that _____ (a) motivation is a result of rational calculation (b) work expectancies are irrelevant (c) need satisfaction is critical (d) valence is the probability that a given level of task performance will lead to various work outcomes.

14. Punishment _____. (a) may be offset by positive reinforcement from another source (b) generally is the most effective kind of reinforcement (c) is especially important in today's workplace (d) emphasizes the withdrawal of reinforcing consequences for a given behavior

15. In equity motivation theory, felt negative inequity _____. (a) is not a motivating state (b) is a stronger motivating state than felt positive inequity (c) can be as strong a motivating state as felt positive inequity (d) does not operate as a motivating state

Short Response

16. What is the frustration-regression component in Alderfer's ERG theory?
17. What is the multiplier effect in expectancy theory?
18. Briefly compare and contrast classical conditioning and operant conditioning.
19. Briefly discuss how reinforcement is linked to extrinsic rewards.

Applications Essay

20. While attending a business luncheon, you overhear the following conversation at a nearby table. Person A: "I'll tell you this: if you satisfy your workers' needs, they'll be productive." Person B: "I'm not so sure; if I satisfy their needs, maybe they'll be real good about coming to work but not very good about working really hard while they are there." Which person do you agree with and why?

These learning activities from *The OB Skills Workbook* are suggested for Chapter 6.

OB in Action

CASE	EXPERIENTIAL EXERCISES	SELF-ASSESSMENT
▪ 6. It Isn't Fair	▪ 11. Teamwork and Motivation	▪ 7. Two-Factor Profile
	▪ 12. The Downside of Punishment	

Plus—special learning experiences from *The Jossey-Bass/Pfeiffer Classroom Collection*

Chapter 7

Motivation, Job Design, and Performance

Chapter at a Glance

Chapter 7 moves the previous treatment of motivation into the various job design and technology approaches currently used and extends these into a range of alternative work arrangements, including the virtual office and job outsourcing. As you read Chapter 7, *keep in mind these study questions.*

HOW ARE MOTIVATION, JOB SATISFACTION, AND PERFORMANCE RELATED?
- Job Satisfaction
- Job Satisfaction and Performance
- Integrating the Motivation Theories

WHAT ARE JOB-DESIGN APPROACHES?
- Scientific Management
- Job Enlargement and Job Rotation
- Job Enrichment

WHAT ARE THE KEYS TO DESIGNING MOTIVATING JOBS?
- Job Characteristics Model
- Social Information Processing
- Managerial and Global Implications

HOW ARE TECHNOLOGY AND JOB DESIGN RELATED?
- Automation and Robotics
- Flexible Manufacturing Systems
- Electronic Offices
- Workflow and Process Reengineering

WHAT ALTERNATIVE WORK ARRANGEMENTS ARE USED TODAY?
- Compressed Workweeks
- Flexible Working Hours
- Job Sharing
- Work at Home and the Virtual Office
- Part-Time Work

REVIEW IN END-OF-CHAPTER STUDY GUIDE

At Ford's Kansas City truck and SUV factory, one vehicle a minute is produced, mostly by robots. In a recent year the plant turned out nearly half a million units and brought in about $13 billion in revenue. Kansas City is a flexible factory—with just small changes it can turn out any kind of car Ford makes.

Here, robots steal the show in a clean and quiet plant. Male and female employees in clear protective glasses and standard-issue blue coveralls inhabit the low-lit warehouse. Accompanying these individuals are those on orange tricycles with rickshaw toolboxes on the rear. The people seem to assist the robots. The robots look huge, scary, and like sci-fi birds looking for food. The plant manager, David Savchetz, has a nice office but he is never there; he is on the plant floor.

> "We measure about everything around here except how high the grass grows."

His domain is an 18-acre complex surrounded by room after room of wall charts. Everything is charted, from employee morale to warranty complaints for a particular part. "We measure about everything around here except how high the grass grows," says Savchetz. Thus, every step of every task is carefully detailed. In many cases, employees are grouped together, sometimes for years at a time. Sons follow fathers into the plant, which has very generous pay and fringes. The new tools and robots and computers make for a quieter and cleaner plant, but the magnitude of the factory is still overwhelming. Old-timers like David Savchetz have been impressed by the increased sophistication, competitiveness, and quality of the plant, its jobs, and its employees.[1]

In this chapter we consider not only jobs like the modern automobile assembly plant with its robots and tricycles, but other job designs as well. Throughout we are concerned with motivation, technology, satisfaction, performance, and designs to enhance quality and quantity. We are also concerned with a wide range of alternative work arrangements to those of traditional 9-to-5 work at one location.

How Are Motivation, Job Satisfaction, and Performance Related?

We devoted the previous chapter to motivation. Here, we relate motivation to satisfaction and performance and the latter two to each other, developing an integrated model of motivation. This integrated model of motivation is important to keep in mind, along with technology, when we consider the various job designs and alternative work arrangements.

Job Satisfaction

Formally defined, "job satisfaction" is the degree to which individuals feel positively or negatively about their jobs. It is an attitude or emotional response to one's tasks as well as to the physical and social conditions of the workplace. At first glance, and from the perspective of Herzberg's two-factor theory (Chapter 6), some aspects of job satisfaction should be motivational and lead to positive employment relationships and high levels of individual job performance. But as we will discuss, the issues are more complicated than this conclusion suggests.

On a daily basis, managers must be able to infer the job satisfaction of others by careful observation and interpretation of what they say and do while going about their jobs. Sometimes it is also useful to examine more formally the levels of job satisfaction among groups of workers, especially through formal interviews or questionnaires. Increasingly, other methods are being used as well, such as focus groups and computer-based attitude surveys.[2]

Among the many available job satisfaction questionnaires that have been used over the years, two popular ones are the Minnesota Satisfaction Questionnaire (MSQ) and the Job Descriptive Index (JDI).[3] Both address aspects of satisfaction with which good managers should be concerned for the people reporting to them. For example, the MSQ measures satisfaction with working conditions, chances for advancement, freedom to use one's own judgment, praise for doing a good job, and feelings of accomplishment, among others. The five facets of job satisfaction measured by the JDI are:

- *The work itself*—responsibility, interest, and growth
- *Quality of supervision*—technical help and social support
- *Relationships with co-workers*—social harmony and respect
- *Promotion opportunities*—chances for further advancement
- *Pay*—adequacy of pay and perceived equity vis-à-vis others.

Facets of job satisfaction

Job Satisfaction and Performance

The importance of job satisfaction can be viewed in the context of two decisions people make about their work. The first is the decision to belong—that is, to join and remain a member of an organization. The second is the decision to perform—that is, to work hard in pursuit of high levels of task performance. Not everyone who belongs to an organization performs up to expectations.

The decision to belong concerns an individual's attendance and longevity at work. In this sense, job satisfaction influences *absenteeism*, or the failure of people to go to work. In general, workers who are satisfied with the job itself have more regular attendance and are less likely to be absent for unexplained reasons than are dissatisfied workers. Job satisfaction can also affect *turnover*, or decisions by people to terminate their employment. Simply put, dissatisfied workers are more likely than satisfied workers to quit their jobs.[4]

Alternative Work Arrangements

The USS *Constellation* changed from day to night operations to spread around the airplanes in the crowded Northern Arabian Gulf so the airspace was not so crowded. As a part of an alternative work arrangement, the ship's 5000 sailors and Marines have switched to night duty and now eat breakfast for dinner and dinner for breakfast.

What is the relationship between job satisfaction and performance? There is considerable debate on this issue, with three alternative points of view evident: (1) satisfaction causes performance, (2) performance causes satisfaction, and (3) rewards cause both performance and satisfaction.[5]

Argument: Satisfaction Causes Performance If job satisfaction causes high levels of performance, the message to managers is quite simple: to increase employees' work performance, make them happy. Research, however, indicates that no simple and direct link exists between individual job satisfaction at one point in time and work performance at a later point. This conclusion is widely recognized among OB scholars, even though some evidence suggests that the relationship holds better for professional or higher-level employees than for non-professionals or those at lower job levels. Job satisfaction alone is not a consistent predictor of individual work performance.

Argument: Performance Causes Satisfaction If high levels of performance cause job satisfaction, the message to managers is quite different. Rather than focusing first on peoples' job satisfaction, attention should be given to helping people achieve high performance; job satisfaction would be expected to follow. Research indicates an empirical relationship between individual performance measured at a certain time period and later job satisfaction. A basic model of this relationship, based on the work of Edward E. Lawler and Lyman Porter, maintains that performance accomplishment leads to rewards that, in turn, lead to satisfaction.[6] In this model, rewards are intervening variables; that is, they "link" performance with later satisfaction. In addition, a moderator variable—perceived equity of rewards—further affects the relationship. The moderator indicates that performance will lead to satisfaction only if rewards are perceived as equitable. If an individual feels that his or her performance is unfairly rewarded, the performance-causes-satisfaction argument will not hold.

Argument: Rewards Cause Both Satisfaction and Performance This final argument in the job satisfaction–performance controversy is the most compelling. It suggests that a proper allocation of rewards can positively influence both performance and satisfaction. The key word in the previous sentence is "proper." Research indicates that people who receive high rewards report higher job satisfaction. But research also indicates that performance-contingent rewards influence a person's work performance. In this case, the size and value of the reward vary in proportion to the level of one's performance accomplishment. Large rewards are given for high performance; small or no rewards are given for low performance. And whereas giving a low performer only small rewards initially may lead to dissatisfaction, the expectation is that the individual will make efforts to improve performance in order to obtain greater rewards in the future.

The point is that managers should consider satisfaction and performance as two separate but interrelated work results that are affected by the allocation of rewards. Whereas job satisfaction alone is not a good predictor of work performance, well-managed rewards can have a positive influence on both satisfaction and performance.

Integrating the Motivation Theories

The content, process, and reinforcement motivational approaches, discussed in Chapter 6, deal with one or more aspects of rewards, needs, cognitions, satisfaction, and performance. We have tended to treat each of these separately, and they might be used that way or mixed and matched, as the occasion demands and in whichever way you are comfortable in using them. Now, however, we treat the linkage between satisfaction and performance to help integrate all the views we have discussed.

Figure 7.1 outlines the integrated view. Note that the figure has much in common with Vroom's expectancy theory and the Porter–Lawler framework, both process theories discussed in the previous chapter. In the figure, job performance and satisfaction are separate, but potentially interdependent, work results. Performance is influenced most directly by individual attributes of the kind treated in Chapter 4, such as ability and experience; organizational support, such as resources and technology; and work effort, the point at which an individual's level of motivation comes directly to bear. Individual motivation directly determines work effort, and the key to motivation is the ability to create a work setting that positively responds to individual needs and goals. Whether or not a work setting proves motivational for a given individual depends on the availability of rewards and their perceived value. Note also the importance of contingent rewards, reflecting the law of contingent reinforcement. Recall also the importance of immediacy in rewarding.

The content theories enter the model as the guide to understanding individual attributes and identifying the needs that give motivational value to the possible rewards. When the individual experiences intrinsic rewards for work performance, motivation will be directly and positively affected. Motivation can also occur when job satisfactions result from either extrinsic or intrinsic rewards that are felt to be equitably allocated. When felt negative inequity results, satisfaction will be low and motivation will be reduced. Recall that equity comparison is a key aspect of process theory.

With this reiteration of reinforcement, content, and process theories, you should have a better understanding of motivation. Although it will always be difficult to motivate employees, the knowledge in this chapter should help you reach toward higher performance and satisfaction. Finally, the integrating model rests on cultural assumptions, so that the meaning of the concepts may be culturally specific. The importance of various intrinsic and extrinsic rewards may well differ across cultures, as may the aspects of performance that are highly valued.

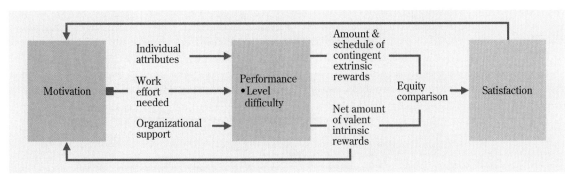

Figure 7.1 An integrated model of individual motivation to work.

Job-Design Approaches

Job design is the process of defining job tasks and the work arrangements to accomplish them.

We now move from our integrated motivation model to job design. Through the process of **job design**, managers plan and specify job tasks and the work arrangements through which they are accomplished. Figure 7.2 shows how alternative job-design approaches differ in the way required tasks are defined and in the amount of intrinsic motivation provided for the worker. The "best" job design is always one that meets organizational requirements for high performance, offers a good fit with individual skills and needs, and provides opportunities for job satisfaction.

Scientific Management

The history of scholarly interest in job design can be traced in part to Frederick Taylor's work with *scientific management* in the early 1900s.[7] Taylor and his contemporaries sought to increase people's efficiency at work. Their approach was to study a job carefully, break it into its smallest components, establish exact time and motion requirements for each task to be done, and then train workers to do these tasks in the same way over and over again. These early efforts were forerunners of current industrial engineering approaches to job design that emphasize efficiency. Such approaches attempt to determine the best processes, methods, workflow layouts, output standards, and person–machine interfaces for various jobs.

Job simplification standardizes tasks and employs people in very routine jobs.

Today the term **job simplification** is used to describe the approach of standardizing work procedures and employing people in clearly defined and highly specialized tasks. The machine-paced automobile assembly line is a classic example of this job-design strategy. Why is it used? Typically, the answer is to increase operating efficiency by reducing the number of skills required to do a job, being able to hire low-cost labor, keeping the needs for job training to a minimum, and emphasizing the accomplishment of repetitive tasks. However, the very nature of such jobs creates potential disadvantages as well. These include loss of efficiency in the face of lower quality, high rates of absenteeism and turnover, and demand for higher wages to compensate for unappealing jobs.

Figure 7.2   A continuum of job-design strategies.

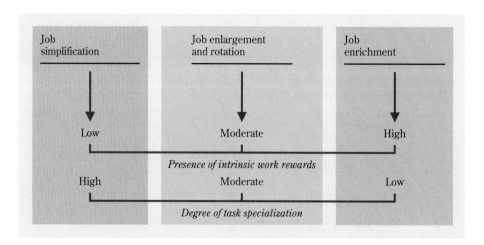

Job Enlargement and Job Rotation

In job simplification the number or variety of different tasks performed is limited. Although this makes the tasks easier to master, the repetitiveness can reduce motivation. Thus, a second set of job-design approaches has been created to add breadth to the variety of tasks performed. **Job enlargement** increases task variety by combining into one job two or more tasks that were previously assigned to separate workers. Sometimes called *horizontal loading*, this approach increases *job breadth* by having the worker perform more and different tasks, but all at the same level of responsibility and challenge. **Job rotation**, another horizontal-loading approach, increases task variety by periodically shifting workers among jobs involving different tasks. Again, the responsibility level of the tasks stays the same. The rotation can be arranged according to almost any time schedule, such as hourly, daily, or weekly schedules. An important benefit of job rotation is training. It allows workers to become more familiar with different tasks and increases the flexibility with which they can be moved from one job to another.

▓▓ **Job enlargement** increases task variety by adding new tasks of similar difficulty to a job.

▓▓ **Job rotation** increases task variety by shifting workers among jobs involving tasks of similar difficulty.

Job Enrichment

Frederick Herzberg's two-factor theory of motivation (described in Chapter 6) suggests that high levels of motivation should not be expected from jobs designed on the basis of simplification, enlargement, or rotation.[8] "Why," asks Herzberg, "should a worker become motivated when one or more 'meaningless' tasks are added to previously existing ones or when work assignments are rotated among equally 'meaningless' tasks?" Instead of pursuing one of these job-design strategies, therefore, Herzberg recommends an alternative approach he calls "job enrichment."

In Herzberg's model, **job enrichment** is the practice of enhancing job content by building into it more motivating factors such as responsibility, achievement, recognition, and personal growth. This job-design strategy differs markedly from strategies previously discussed in that it adds to job content planning and evaluating duties that would otherwise be reserved for managers. These content changes (see The Effective Manager 7.1) involve what Herzberg calls *vertical loading* to increase *job depth*. Enriched jobs, he states, help to satisfy the higher-order needs that people bring with them to work and will therefore increase their motivation to achieve high levels of job performance.

▓▓ **Job enrichment** increases job content by giving workers more responsibility for planning and evaluating duties.

Despite the inherent appeal of Herzberg's ideas, two common questions raise words of caution. *Is job enrichment expensive?* Job enrichment can be very costly, particularly when it requires major changes in workflows, facilities, or technology. *Will workers demand higher pay when moving into enriched jobs?* Herzberg argues that if employees are being paid a truly competitive wage or salary, then the intrinsic rewards of performing enriched tasks will be adequate compensation. Other researchers are more skeptical, advising that pay must be carefully considered.[9]

THE EFFECTIVE MANAGER 7.1

Job Enrichment Advice from Frederick Herzberg

- Allow workers to plan.
- Allow workers to control.
- Maximize job freedom.
- Increase task difficulty.
- Help workers become task experts.
- Provide performance feedback.
- Increase performance accountability.
- Provide complete units of work.

Designing Jobs to Increase Motivation

OB scholars have been reluctant to recommend job enrichment as a universal solution to all job performance and satisfaction problems. The prior questions raise cost and pay concerns. Also, individual differences must be considered in answering the additional question: "Is job enrichment for everyone?" A diagnostic approach developed by Richard Hackman and Greg Oldham offers a broader and contingency-based framework for job design to increase motivation.[10] This model opens up many opportunities to individualize job designs.

Job Characteristics Model

■■■ The **job characteristics model** identifies five core job characteristics of special importance to job design—skill variety, task identity, task significance, autonomy, and feedback.

Core job characteristics

Figure 7.3 presents the **job characteristics model**. It identifies five core job characteristics that are particularly important to job designs. The higher a job scores on each characteristic, the more it is considered to be enriched. The core job characteristics are:

- *Skill variety*—the degree to which a job includes a variety of different activities and involves the use of a number of different skills and talents
- *Task identity*—the degree to which the job requires completion of a "whole" and identifiable piece of work, one that involves doing a job from beginning to end with a visible outcome
- *Task significance*—the degree to which the job is important and involves a meaningful contribution to the organization or society in general
- *Autonomy*—the degree to which the job gives the employee substantial freedom, independence, and discretion in scheduling the work and determining the procedures used in carrying it out

Figure 7.3   Job-design implications of job characteristics theory.

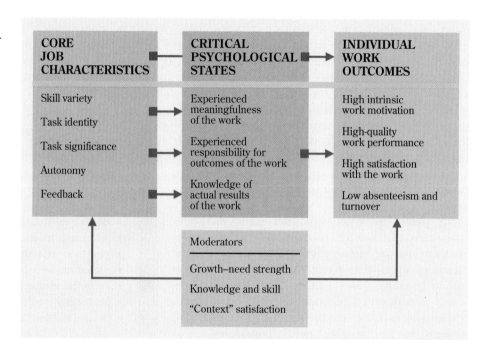

- *Job feedback*—the degree to which carrying out the work activities provides direct and clear information to the employee regarding how well the job has been done.

For those who use this model in an actual work situation, Hackman and Oldham recommend determining the current status of each job on each core characteristic.[11] These characteristics can then be changed systematically to enrich the job and increase its motivational potential. Hackman and his colleagues have developed an instrument called the Job Diagnostic Survey (JDS) for such an assessment (see "OB Skills Workbook" experiential exercise, "Job Design"). Scores on the JDS are then combined to create a **motivating potential score (MPS)**, which indicates the degree to which the job is capable of motivating people.

■■■ The **motivating potential score** describes the extent to which the core characteristics of a job create motivating conditions.

$$MPS = \frac{\text{Skill variety} + \text{Task identity} + \text{Task significance}}{3} \times \text{Autonomy} \times \text{Feedback}$$

A job's MPS can be raised by combining tasks to create larger jobs, opening feedback channels to enable workers to know how well they are doing, establishing client relationships to experience such feedback directly from customers, and employing vertical loading to create more planning and controlling responsibilities. When the core characteristics are enriched in these ways and the MPS for a job is raised as high as possible, they can be expected to positively influence three critical psychological states for the individual: (1) experienced meaningfulness of the work, (2) experienced responsibility for the outcomes of the work, and (3) knowledge of actual results of the work. The positive psychological states, in turn, can be expected to create more positive work outcomes with respect to individual motivation, performance, and satisfaction.

Individual Difference Moderators   The job characteristics model recognizes that the five core job characteristics do not affect all people in the same way. Rather than accept Herzberg's implication that enriched jobs should be good for everyone, this approach allows for individual differences. It accepts the idea that jobs should be designed to arrive at the best match of core characteristics and individual needs and talents. Specifically, the model suggests that enriched jobs will lead to positive outcomes only for those persons who are a good match for them. When the fit between the person and an enriched job is poor, positive outcomes are less likely and problems may well result.

Figure 7.3 highlights three individual difference moderators that can influence individual preferences in how their jobs are designed. The first moderator is *growth-need strength*—the degree to which a person desires the opportunity for self-direction, learning, and personal accomplishment at work. It is similar to Abraham Maslow's esteem and self-actualization needs and Alderfer's growth needs, as discussed in Chapter 6. When applied here, the expectation is that people high in growth-need strengths at work will respond positively to enriched jobs, whereas people low in growth-need strengths will find enriched jobs a source of anxiety. The second moderator is *knowledge and skill*. People whose capabilities fit the demands of enriched jobs are predicted to feel good about them and perform well. Those who are inadequate or who feel inadequate in this regard are likely to experience difficulties. The third moderator is *context satisfaction*, or the extent to which an employee is satisfied with aspects

Blue Man

Three performers are slathered in brilliant blue greasepaint. They never speak. What they do do is things like twirl a canvas while spitting paint on it; thus a work of art is created. Or they might play music by drumming on instruments made from PVC pipe. They make rhythmic noises by chomping on cereal. And all this is great fun. Blue Man has grown its brand without losing focus and seems to have successfully tied together motivation (both performers' and the audiences') and performer job design.

of the work setting such as salary levels, quality of supervision, relationships with co-workers, and working conditions. In general, people more satisfied with job context are more likely than dissatisfied ones to support and do well with job enrichment.

ETHICS AND SOCIAL RESPONSIBILITY

DRIVEN TO HELP OTHERS

There are more than 54 million disabled people in the United States and an additional 76 million Americans over the age of 50. Gary Talbot, 48, is nearly a "twofer," for in 1980 he fell asleep at the wheel of his new Honda, flipped over, and was paralyzed from the waist down. Fast forward to today and you find Talbot and his team changing the automotive landscape. From his own wheelchair, Talbot tests a hoist that can lift a scooter into the back of a mini-van. He does it effortlessly with one hand. "The easier it is for disabled people to get in and out of a vehicle" he says, "the more they'll get out."

Question: Do you think in terms of his current job you can predict his growth-need strength and accompanying knowledge and skill and, if so, how?

Research Results   Considerable research has been done on the job characteristics model in a variety of work settings, including banks, dentist offices, corrections departments, telephone companies, and manufacturing firms, as well as in government agencies. Experts generally agree that the model and its diagnostic approach are useful, but not yet perfect, guides to job design.[12] On average, job characteristics do affect performance but not nearly as much as they do satisfaction. The research also emphasizes the importance of growth-need strength as a moderator of the job design–job performance–job satisfaction relationships. Positive job characteristics affect performance more strongly for high-growth need than low-growth need individuals. The relationship is about the same with job satisfaction. It is also clear that job enrichment can fail when job requirements are increased beyond the level of individual capabilities or interests. Finally, employee perceptions of job characteristics often differ from measures taken by managers and consultants. These perceptions are important and must be considered. After all, they will largely determine whether the workers view a job as high or low in the core characteristics and consequently will affect work outcomes.

Social Information Processing

Gerald Salancik and Jeffrey Pfeffer question whether or not jobs have stable and objective characteristics to which individuals respond predictably and consistently.[13] Instead, they view job design from the perspective of **social information processing theory**. This theory argues that individual needs, task perceptions, and reactions are a result of socially constructed realities. Social information in organizations influences the way people perceive their jobs and respond to them. The same holds true, for example, in the classroom. Suppose

▬ The **social information processing theory** asserts that individual needs and task perceptions result from socially constructed realities.

that several of your friends tell you that the instructor for a course is bad, the content is boring, and the requirements involve too much work. You may then think that the critical characteristics of the class are the instructor, the content, and the workload, and that they are all bad. All of this may substantially influence the way you perceive your instructor and the course and the way you deal with the class—regardless of the actual characteristics.

Research on social information processing indicates that both social information and core characteristics are important. Although social information processing influences task perceptions and attitudes, the job characteristics discussed earlier are also important. Indeed, how someone perceives job characteristics is likely to be influenced by both the objective characteristics themselves and the social information present in the workplace.

Managerial and Global Implications

A question-and-answer approach can again be used to summarize final points and implications worth remembering about job enrichment. *Should everyone's job be enriched?* The answer is clearly "no." The logic of individual differences suggests that not everyone will want an enriched job. Individuals most likely to have positive reactions to job enrichment are those who need achievement, who hold middle-class working values, or who are seeking higher-order growth-need satisfaction at work. Job enrichment also appears to be most advantageous when the job context is positive and when workers have the abilities needed to do the enriched job. Furthermore, costs, technological constraints, and workgroup or union opposition may make it difficult to enrich some jobs.[14] *Can job enrichment apply to groups?* The answer is "yes." The application of job-design strategies at the group level is growing in many types of settings. In Part 3 we discuss creative workgroup designs, including cross-functional work teams and self-managing teams.

A final question extends the job enrichment context globally. *What is the impact of culture on job enrichment?* The answer is "substantial." Research conducted in Belgium, Israel, Japan, the Netherlands, the United States, and Germany found unique aspects of what constitutes work in each country.[15] Work was seen as a social requirement most strongly in Belgium and Japan and least so in Germany. Work was regarded as something done for money in all countries but Belgium. In most cases, however, work was regarded as having both an economic and a societal contribution component. These results, as well as differences in such national cultural dimensions as power distance and individualism, reinforce a contingency approach to job enrichment and further suggest that cultural differences should be given consideration in job design.

Technology and Job Design

The concept of **sociotechnical systems** is used in organizational behavior to indicate the importance of integrating people and technology to create high-performance work systems.[16] As computers and information technologies continue to dominate the modern workplace, this concept is essential in new developments in job designs.

▨ **Sociotechnical systems** integrate people and technology into high-performance work settings.

NUNS, TECHNOLOGY, AND CHOCOLATE

The 50 Cistercian Sisters of Mount Saint Mary Abbey rise every morning at 3:00, pray until nearly 8:00, and then begin their chocolate-making stint to help support their life of "beautiful simplicity." However, paperwork has been swamping them, and members of this eleventh-century convent decided what they needed was a twenty-first-century supply chain. Desktop computers, a server, and an internal network have replaced old, dilapidated equipment. In between prayers, the new equipment, provided with e-mail capacity, handles orders and provides shipping information for United Parcel Service.

Though an abbey isn't a factory and must be approached differently, what the sisters essentially want is efficiency. Now, by reading up on Web marketing and checking advertising on search engines, they have moved into the twenty-first century with a vengeance.

Question: What effect does the motivation for tranquility appear to have on technology, and vice versa?

Automation and Robotics

Automation allows machines to do work previously accomplished by people.

As mentioned earlier, highly simplified jobs often cause problems because they offer little intrinsic motivation for the worker. Such tasks have been defined so narrowly that they lack challenge and lead to boredom when someone has to repeat them over and over again. Given the high technology now available, one way to tackle this problem is through complete **automation**, using a machine to do work previously accomplished by a human. This approach increasingly involves the use of robots, which are becoming ever more versatile and reliable. Also, robot prices are falling as the cost of human labor rises. Japan presently leads the world in robot use; the United States lags far behind, but its robot use is growing rapidly.[17] For example, to lower costs and free up hospital employees for more critical tasks, more and more robots are being used. TUG and HelpMate are two courier robots used to move medicine from the pharmacy to nursing stations throughout large, multi-story hospitals. These robots have sensors so they can "see" and differentiate between a hallway bag and a person standing in its way.[18]

Flexible Manufacturing Systems

Flexible manufacturing systems use adaptive technology and integrated job designs to easily shift production among alternative products.

In **flexible manufacturing systems**, adaptive computer-based technologies and integrated job designs are used to shift work easily and quickly among alternative products. This approach is increasingly common, for example, in companies supporting the automobile industry with machined metal products, such as cylinder heads and gear boxes.[19] A cellular manufacturing system, for example, might contain a number of automated production machines that cut, shape, drill, and fasten together various metal components. The machines can be quickly changed from manufacturing one product to another.[20] Workers in flexible manufacturing cells perform few routine assembly-line tasks. Rather, they ensure that the operations are handled correctly and deal with the changeover from one product configuration to another. They develop expertise across a wide range of functions, and the jobs have great potential for enriched core job characteristics.

Electronic Offices

Electronic office technology was the key when U.S. Healthcare, a large, private practice–based health maintenance organization (HMO), became interested in improving the quality of its health care services. The company installed large electronic bulletin boards that monitored progress toward a range of performance goals, put in robots to deliver the paper mail, and emphasized e-mail and computerized answering services. Essentially, the company tried to automate as many tasks as possible to free people for more challenging work. Similarly, Mutual Benefit Life completely reorganized the way it serviced insurance application forms— once handled by as many as 19 people across five departments. Mutual created a new case manager position responsible for processing applications from their inception until policies were issued. Accompanying this radical change in job design were powerful PC-based workstations designed to assist decision making and connected to a variety of automated subsystems on a mainframe.[21]

Continuing developments in electronic offices offer job enrichment possibilities for those workers equipped to handle the technology. But those jobs can be stressful and difficult for those who do not have the necessary education or skills. One survey showed that even in highly developed countries like those in Europe, 54 percent of workers possessed inadequate skills to operate a computer; the proportion was about one-third in the United States.[22] People who work continuously with computers are also beginning to experience physical ailments associated with repetitive keyboarding and mouse movements. Clearly, the high technologies of the new workplace must be carefully integrated with the human factor.

Workflow and Process Reengineering

Another approach for improving job designs and performance is based on the concept of **process reengineering**—the analysis, streamlining, and reconfiguration of actions and tasks required to reach a work goal.[23] The process design approach systematically breaks processes down into their specific components and subtasks, analyzes each for relevance and simplicity, and then does everything possible to reconfigure the process to eliminate wasted time, effort, and resources. A classic example might be the various steps required to gain approval for a purchase order to buy a new computer. The process reengineering approach looks at every step in the process, from searching for items and vendors to obtaining bids, completing necessary forms, securing required signatures and approvals, actually placing the order, and so on to the point at which the new computer arrives, is checked in, is placed into an equipment inventory, and then is finally delivered to the workplace. In all this, one simple question drives the reengineering approach: What is necessary and what else can be eliminated?

Process reengineering analyzes, streamlines, and reconfigures actions and tasks to achieve work goals.

Alternative Work Arrangements

Alternative ways of scheduling time are becoming increasingly common in the workplace. These arrangements are essentially reshaping the traditional 40-hour week, with 9-to-5 schedules and work done on the premises. Virtually all such plans are designed to influence employee satisfaction and to help employees balance the demands of their work and nonwork lives.[24] They are becoming

Leaders on Leadership

LEADERSHIP IN THE WORLD'S LARGEST UPS DISTRIBUTION CENTER

Mark Susor, whose leadership philosophy is "to always seek perfection but settle for excellence," is a high-ranking engineering manager for the huge UPS distribution system in the Chicago area. It stands hard by a Burlington Northern–Santa Fe railroad loading facility. It sorts some million packages per day and uses four four-hour shifts per working day, with a 3 1/2-hour employee work guarantee. The workforce is well trained and highly motivated and has a long-term, cooperative relationship with the Teamsters union. A management information system provides daily feedback for sorters on productivity, quality, and service. The sorting is highly automated and a gain-sharing program is used.

Susor's leadership philosophy stems from 22 years with UPS. He is a master delegator and believes communication skills are critical for leaders.

Question: In what ways does Susor's leadership philosophy fit the UPS motivation and job-design characteristics?

more and more important in fast-changing societies where demands for "work–life balance" and more "family-friendly" employers are growing ever more apparent.[25] For example, dual-career families with children, part-time students, older workers (retired or near retirement age), and single parents are all candidates for alternative work arrangements.

If there is any doubt regarding the ethical and moral consequences of workplace practices, a study by economists Alan Krueger and Alexandre Mas of the Princeton University Industrial Relations Section deserves attention. They suggest that labor strife at the Bridgestone/Firestone Decatur, Illinois, plant could have contributed to the production of defective tires linked to deaths in a number of Ford Explorer road accidents. This plant, now closed, is shown by the authors to have produced tires more likely to fail during a period of labor–management strife. Managers everywhere should take notice. While circumstantial, this study helps support arguments calling for healthy and positive work environments. Ethical and socially responsible management that pays attention to the human factor, in other words, is important to integrate motivation with appropriate work design.[26]

Compressed Workweeks

■ **A compressed workweek** allows a full-time job to be completed in less than five full workdays.

A **compressed workweek** is any scheduling of work that allows a full-time job to be completed in fewer than the standard five days. The most common form of compressed workweek is the "4/40," or 40 hours of work accomplished in four 10-hour days.

This approach has many possible benefits. For the worker, additional time off is a major feature of this schedule. The individual often appreciates increased leisure time, three-day weekends, free weekdays to pursue personal business, and lower commuting costs. The organization can benefit, too, in terms of lower employee absenteeism and improved recruiting of new employees. But there are also potential disadvantages. Individuals can experience increased fatigue from the extended workday and family adjustment problems. The organization can experience work scheduling problems and customer complaints because of breaks in work coverage. Some organizations may face occasional union opposition and laws requiring payment of overtime for work exceeding eight hours of individual labor in any one day. Overall reactions to compressed workweeks are likely to be most favorable among employees who are allowed to participate in the decision to adopt the new workweek, who have their jobs enriched as a result of the new schedule, and who have strong higher-order needs in Maslow's hierarchy.[27]

Flexible Working Hours

Another innovative work schedule, **flexible working hours**, or flextime, gives individuals a daily choice in the timing of their work commitments. One such schedule requires employees to work four hours of "core" time but leaves them free to choose their remaining four hours of work from among flexible time blocks. One person, for example, may start early and leave early, whereas another may start later and leave later. This flexible work schedule is becoming increasingly popular and is a valuable alternative for structuring work to accommodate individual interests and needs.

■■■ **Flexible working hours** give employees some daily choice in scheduling arrival and departure times from work.

Flextime increases individual autonomy in work scheduling and offers many opportunities and benefits (see The Effective Manager 7.2). It is a way for dual-career couples to handle children's schedules as well as their own; it is a way to meet the demands of caring for elderly parents or ill family members; it is even a way to better attend to such personal affairs as medical and dental appointments, home emergencies, banking needs, and so on. Proponents of this scheduling strategy argue that the discretion it allows workers in scheduling their own hours of work encourages them to develop positive attitudes and to increase commitment to the organization. A majority of American workplaces already have flextime programs, and the number is growing.[28] An Aetna manager, commenting on the firm's flexible working hours program, said: "We're not doing flexible work scheduling to be nice, but because it makes business sense."[29]

> **THE EFFECTIVE MANAGER 7.2**
>
> ## Flextime Benefits
>
> *For organizations:*
> - Less absenteeism, tardiness, turnover
> - More commitment
> - Higher performance
>
> *For workers:*
> - Shorter commuting time
> - More leisure time
> - More job satisfaction
> - Greater sense of responsibility

Job Sharing

In **job sharing**, one full-time job is assigned to two or more persons, who then divide the work according to agreed-upon hours. Often, each person works half a day, but job sharing can also be done on a weekly or monthly basis. Although it is practiced by only a relatively small percentage of employers, human resource experts believe that job sharing is a valuable alternative work arrangement.[30]

■■■ **Job sharing** allows one full-time job to be divided among two or more persons.

Organizations benefit from job sharing when they can attract talented people who would otherwise be unable to work. An example is the qualified teacher who also is a parent. This person may be able to work only half a day. Through job sharing, two such persons can be employed to teach one class. Some job sharers report less burnout and claim that they feel recharged each time they report for work. The tricky part of this arrangement is finding two people who will work well with each other. When middle managers Sue Mannix and Charlotte Schutzman worked together at Bell Atlantic, for example, they faithfully coordinated each other's absences, with Schutzman working Mondays, Tuesdays, and Wednesday mornings and Mannix working the rest of the workweek.[31]

Job sharing should not be confused with a more controversial arrangement called *work sharing*. This occurs when workers agree to cut back on the number of hours they work in order to protect against layoffs. Workers may agree to voluntarily reduce 20 percent of hours worked and pay received, rather than have the employer cut 20 percent of the workforce during difficult economic times. Legal restrictions prohibit this practice in some settings.

Work at Home and the Virtual Office

■■■ **Telecommuting** is work at home or in remote locations and using computer and telecommunications linkages with the office.

High technology is influencing yet another alternative work arrangement that is becoming increasingly visible in many employment sectors ranging from higher education to government and from manufacturing to services. **Telecommuting** is work done at home or in a remote location via use of computers and advanced telecommunications linkages with a central office or other employment locations. At IBM, Canada, an arrangement called *flexiplace* means working most of the time from a home office and coming into IBM corporate offices only for special meetings. In a practice known as *hoteling*, temporary offices are reserved for these workers during the times they visit the main office. Worldwide, some 20 percent of IBM's employees spends two or more days a week working at home or visiting customers.[32]

The notion of telecommuting is more and more associated with the *virtual office*, where the individual works literally "from the road" and while traveling from place to place or customer to customer by car or airplane. In all cases, the worker remains linked electronically with the home office.[33] The number of workers who are telecommuting is growing daily, with organizations like AT&T and Cisco Systems reporting that more than 50 percent of their workers telecommute at least part of the time.[34]

Telecommuting offers the individual the potential advantages of flexibility, the comforts of home, and choice of locations consistent with one's lifestyle. In terms of advantages to the organization, this alternative often produces cost savings and efficiency as well as employee satisfaction. On the negative side, telecommuters sometimes complain of isolation from co-workers, decreased identification with the work team, and technical difficulties with the computer linkages essential to their work arrangement. Yet overall, the practice continues to grow, with more organizations now offering special training in the *virtual management* of telecommuters.

■■■ **Temporary part-time work** is temporary work of fewer hours than the standard week.

Part-Time Work

■■■ **Permanent part-time work** is permanent work of fewer hours than the standard week.

Part-time work has become an increasingly prominent and controversial work arrangement. In **temporary part-time work** an employee is classified as "temporary" and works less than the standard 40-hour workweek. In **permanent part-**

Research Insight
Technology Design and Acceptance and Use of Telecommuter Systems

This was a one-year research study examining the impact of the technology on the acceptance and use of employee telecommuting. In traditional technology, telecommuting employees used a desktop computer system. In this system, one's workspace is represented as a diagram desktop containing folders, documents, and boxes with textualized instructions. While this technology was used for one set of employees, a second virtual reality technology was used for another set of employees. The virtual reality technology provided video images of the workplace, including archived images of the actual office and seamless transmission of audio and visual feed from co-worker chats and planned meeting conferences. In other words, it was designed to reflect a real setting as closely as possible.

Research hypotheses were developed relating to social richness (ability to transmit social cues, change understanding, and resolve differences of opinion), telepresence (conveying a sense of presence), and conveying extrinsic and intrinsic motivation as follows:

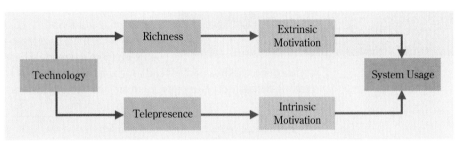

It was found that for a one-year test period, the virtual reality technology was superior—in terms of social richness, telepresence, and motivations—to the traditional system.

Reference: Viswanath Venhatesh and Phillip Johnson, "Telecommuting Technology Implementation: A Within-and-Between Subjects Longitudinal Field Study," *Personnel Psychology* 55(3) (2002):661–687.

time work the person is considered a "permanent" member of the workforce but contributes fewer hours than the standard, typically 40-hour workweek.

Usually, temporary part-timers are easily released and hired as needs dictate. Accordingly, many organizations use part-time work to hold down labor costs and to help smooth out peaks and valleys in the business cycle. Employers may also use part-time work to better manage what may be called "retention quality." These workers are highly skilled individuals committed to their careers who want to continue to develop professionally but who can only work part time. Part-time nurses, among others, fall in this category.[35]

The part-time work schedule can be a benefit to people who want to supplement other jobs or who want something less than a full workweek for a variety of personal reasons. For someone who is holding two jobs, including at least one part time, the added burdens can be stressful and may affect performance in either one or both work settings. Furthermore, part-timers often fail to qualify for fringe benefits, such as health care, life insurance, and pensions, and they may be paid less than their full-time counterparts. Nevertheless, part-time work schedules are of growing practical importance because of the organizational advantages they offer.

GLOBAL RECRUITING CRUCIAL FOR COLLEGIATE TENNIS PLAYERS

In her first year at Texas Tech this season, Cari Groce, head tennis coach, inherited a roster that included seven international players. The men's team has six foreign-born players on its roster. Each player wears a "United We Stand" T-shirt with the flags of the various countries displayed. To play further, most players from foreign countries either turn professional or attend U.S. colleges and universities, such as Texas Tech. It typically takes them at least a month to settle in; there are many differences compared with their home countries. The coaches tend to play a heavier parental role for these students than coaches normally do. Currently, there are not many U.S.-born players at Texas Tech, but Groce predicts Texas will provide many more players in the future.

Question: In terms of motivation and job design, what are some similarities and differences you see between native-born and foreign-born tennis players playing on U.S. college teams?

Chapter 7   Study Guide

Summary

How are motivation, job satisfaction, and performance related?

- Job satisfaction is a work attitude that reflects the degree to which people feel positively or negatively about a job and its various facets.

- Common aspects of job satisfaction relate to pay, working conditions, quality of supervision, co-workers, and the task itself.

- Job satisfaction is empirically related to employee turnover and absenteeism.

- The relationship between job satisfaction and performance is more controversial; current thinking focuses on how rewards influence both satisfaction and performance.

- Reinforcement views emphasize contingent rewards as well as the speed of the rewards.

- The content theories help identify important needs and determine what a person values by way of rewards.

- Equity theory suggests that any rewards must be perceived as equitable in the social context of the workplace.

- Although motivation predicts work efforts, individual performance also depends on job-relevant abilities and organizational support.

What are job-design approaches?

- Job design is the creation of tasks and work settings for specific jobs.

- Job design by scientific management or job simplification standardizes work and employs people in clearly defined and specialized tasks.

- Job enlargement increases task variety by combining two or more tasks previously assigned to separate workers.

- Job rotation increases task variety by periodically rotating workers among jobs involving different tasks.

- Job enrichment builds bigger and more responsible jobs by adding planning and evaluating duties.

What are the keys to designing motivating jobs?

- Job characteristics theory offers a diagnostic approach to job enrichment based on the analysis of five core job characteristics: skill variety, task identity, task significance, autonomy, and feedback.

- Job characteristics theory does not assume that everyone wants an enriched job; it indicates that job enrichment will be more successful for persons with high growth needs, requisite job skills, and context satisfaction.

- The social information processing theory points out that information from co-workers and others in the workplace influences a worker's perceptions and responses to a job.

- Not everyone's job should be enriched; job enrichment can be done for groups as well as individuals; cultural factors may influence job enrichment success.

How are technology and jobs related?

- Well-planned sociotechnical systems integrate people and technology for high performance.

- Robotics and complete automation are increasingly used to replace people to perform jobs that are highly simplified and repetitive.

- Workers in flexible manufacturing cells utilize the latest technology to produce high-quality products with short cycle times.

- The nature of office work is being changed by computer workstation technologies, networks, and various forms of electronic communication.

- Workflow and business process reengineering analyzes all steps in work sequences to streamline activities and tasks, save costs, and improve performance.

What alternative work arrangements are used today?

- Today's complex society is giving rise to a number of alternative work arrangements designed to balance the personal demands on workers with job responsibilities and opportunities.

- The compressed workweek allows a full-time workweek to be completed in less than five days, typically offering four 10-hour days of work and three days free.

- Flexible working hours allow employees some daily choice in timing between work and nonwork activities.

- Job sharing occurs when two or more people divide one full-time job according to agreements among themselves and the employer.

- Telecommuting involves work at home or at a remote location while communicating with the home office as needed via computer and related technologies.

- Part-time work requires less than a 40-hour workweek and can be done on a schedule classifying the worker as temporary or permanent.

Key Terms

Automation (p. 152)
Compressed workweek (p. 154)
Flexible manufacturing systems (p. 152)
Flexible working hours (p. 155)
Job characteristics model (p. 148)

Job design (p. 146)
Job enlargement (p. 147)
Job enrichment (p. 147)
Job rotation (p. 147)
Job sharing (p. 155)
Job simplification (p. 146)
Motivating potential score (MPS) (p. 149)
Permanent part-time work (p. 157)

Process reengineering (p. 153)
Social information processing theory (p. 150)
Sociotechnical systems (p. 151)
Telecommuting (p. 156)
Temporary part-time work (p. 156)

Self-Test 7

Multiple Choice

1. Job simplification is closely associated with _____ as originally developed by Frederick Taylor. (a) vertical loading (b) horizontal loading (c) scientific management (d) self-efficacy

2. Job _____ increases job _____ by combining into one job several tasks of similar difficulty. (a) rotation; depth (b) enlargement; depth (c) rotation; breadth (d) enlargement; breadth

3. In job characteristics theory, _____ indicates the degree to which an individual is able to make decisions affecting his or her work. (a) task variety (b) task identity (c) task significance (d) autonomy

4. The basic logic of sociotechnical systems is that _____. (a) people must be integrated with technology (b) technology is more important than people (c) people are more important than technology (d) technology alienates people

5. Which goals tend to be more motivating? (a) challenging goals (b) easy goals (c) general goals (d) no goals

6. The "4/40" is a type of _____ work arrangement. (a) compressed workweek (b) flextime (c) job sharing (d) permanent part-time

7. The flexible working hours schedule allows workers to choose _____. (a) days of week to work (b) total hours to work per week (c) location of work (d) starting and ending times for workdays

8. Today's society is creating a demand for more jobs that by design _____. (a) are easy to perform (b) minimize the need for employee skills (c) are family-friendly (d) have low-performance goals

9. Two popular job satisfaction questionnaires are _____. (a) the LBDQ and MLQ (b) the MSQ and JDI (c) the PDQ and ISQ (d) the SAT and JCI

10. Whereas job satisfaction alone is not a good predictor of work performance,

_____. (a) poorly managed rewards are important (b) well-managed rewards are important (c) rewards along with job satisfaction are important (d) work performance is not related to a combination of satisfaction and rewards

11. Social information processing argues that _____. (a) jobs have stable and predictable characteristics with stable responses (b) class characteristics operate differently from job characteristics (c) social information in organizations influences the way people perceive and respond to their jobs (d) women process job perceptions differently than men

12. Cultural differences _____. (a) make little difference in response to job enrichment (b) have a strong bearing on job enrichment responses (c) are more important now than before in job enrichment responses (d) were more important in the past in terms of job enrichment responses

13. Flexible manufacturing systems _____. (a) are especially useful for health care organizations (b) break components down very specifically to reconfigure processes (c) are emphasized by Frederick Taylor (d) emphasize what is necessary and what can be eliminated

14. Telecommuting _____. (a) is similar to part-time work (b) involves flexible manufacturing (c) involves job sharing (d) is one kind of virtual office setup

15. For job enrichment, _____. (a) everyone's job should be enriched (b) no one's job should be enriched (c) jobs should also be enlarged (d) not everyone's job should be enriched

Short Response

16. How can you create job enrichment by building job depth?

17. What role does growth-need strength play in job characteristics theory?

18. How can a manager increase employee commitment to stated task goals?

19. What is the difference between temporary part-time and permanent part-time work?

Applications Essay

20. You have just been called in as a consultant to recommend a program to create a motivational work setting in a department which sells men's and women's clothing. Use relevant job design and technology ideas from this chapter. Make any necessary assumptions and discuss your recommendations.

These learning activities from *The OB Skills Workbook* are suggested for Chapter 7.

OB in Action

CASE	EXPERIENTIAL EXERCISES	SELF-ASSESSMENT
■ 8. I'm Not in Kansas Anymore	■ 13. Tinkertoys ■ 14. Job Design Preferences ■ 15. My Fantasy Job ■ 16. Motivation by Job Enrichment	■ 8. Are You Cosmopolitan?

Plus—special learning experiences from *The Jossey-Bass/Pfeiffer Classroom Collection*

Chapter 8

Performance Management and Rewards

Chapter at a Glance

Chapter 8 covers setting goals, appraising and rewarding performance, and human resource development. As you read Chapter 8, *keep in mind these study questions*.

WHAT IS GOAL SETTING?
- Goal Setting Theory
- Goal-Setting Guidelines
- Goal Setting and MBO

WHAT IS PERFORMANCE APPRAISAL?
- Purposes of Performance Appraisal
- Who Does the Performance Appraisal?
- Performance Appraisal Dimensions and Standards
- Performance Appraisal Methods
- Measurement Errors in Performance Appraisal
- Improving Performance Appraisals
- Group Evaluation

WHAT ARE COMPENSATION AND REWARDS?
- Pay as an Extrinsic Reward
- Creative Pay Practices

WHAT ARE HUMAN RESOURCE DEVELOPMENT AND PERSON–JOB FIT?
- Staffing
- Recruitment
- Selection
- Socialization
- Training
- Career Planning and Development

REVIEW IN END-OF-CHAPTER STUDY GUIDE

While America has been at war, a new generation of Marines is in the process of being created in San Diego. Today is judgment day for the 41 recruits of Platoon 3074. Each gets a ceremonial Altoid and blast of Nautica Competition men's cologne—this is the closest to a party these Marines have seen in four weeks of boot camp. This is the first big test—the initial drill evaluation. How well can the men march in formation and demonstrate precise rifle movements? More importantly, how well do they fit the mold of a Marine?

What comes next is learning to fight and kill—combat. "Instant obedience to orders—that's what we're shooting for," the drill sergeant tells the platoon. "You mess up, you mess up," he says, "but don't lose your bearing. That's a sign of weakness." For the drill instructors, bearing is everything.

Forty-eight hours later, all six platoons of Kilo Company come together on a large field. Their guidons (flags with the platoon's identifying number) flutter in the wind except for one. Platoon 3074 finished last in the drill evaluation and has been forced to "furl its guidon." Also, the recruits of 3074

> "You mess up, you mess up, but don't lose your bearing. That's a sign of weakness."

wear their trousers "unbloused," not tucked into their boots, as do the others. Now all the recruits head for the "Confidence Course" with its eleven obstacles that must be climbed or dealt with in some fashion. After an hour, all the recruits gather in front of the "Slide for Life." Here, one must climb a 30-foot diving tower and then crawl, head first, down a 45-foot cable stretched across the length of a swimming pool. Failure means a fall into the icy water. Most make it; some do not and receive scoffs from the drill instructor.

And so it goes, through martial arts, where recruits without a weapon learn to kill a man. This is "controlled aggression" and follows warm-up chants of "kill, kill, kill." For most, this training involves the most intense activities they have ever encountered. Mail from outside helps and is a way of reconnecting with love, tenderness, and fear.[1] All this and more involves the making of a Marine. It illustrates person–job fit, socialization, and training—all of which accompany the goal setting, performance appraisal, and compensation and rewards topics that are covered in this chapter.

Goal Setting

Goals are important aspects of any performance management and reward system. Without proper goals, employees may suffer a direction problem. Some years ago, for example, a Minnesota Vikings' defensive end gathered up an opponent's fumble. Then, with obvious effort and delight, he ran the ball into the wrong end zone. Clearly, the athlete did not lack motivation. Unfortunately, however, he failed to channel his energies toward the right goal. Similar problems are found in many work settings. They can be eliminated, or at least reduced, by the proper setting and clarification of task goals.

Goal-Setting Theory

Goal setting is the process of developing, negotiating, and formalizing the targets or objectives that a person is responsible for accomplishing.[2] Over a number of years, Edwin Locke and his associates have developed a comprehensive framework linking goals to performance, as shown in Figure 8.1. The model uses elements of expectancy theory from Chapter 6 to help clarify the implications of goal setting for performance while taking into account certain moderating conditions, such as ability and task complexity.

Goal-Setting Guidelines

Research on goal setting is now quite extensive. Indeed, more research has been done on goal setting than on any other theory related to work motivation.[3] Nearly 400 studies have been conducted in several countries, including Australia, England, Germany, Japan, and the United States.[4] The basic precepts of goal-setting theory remain a most important source of advice for managing human behavior in the work setting.

Managerially speaking, the implications of the Locke and Latham model and related goal-setting research can be summarized as follows.[5] First, *difficult goals are more likely to lead to higher performance than are less difficult ones.* However, if the goals are seen as too difficult or impossible, the relationship with performance no longer holds. For example, you will likely perform better as a fi-

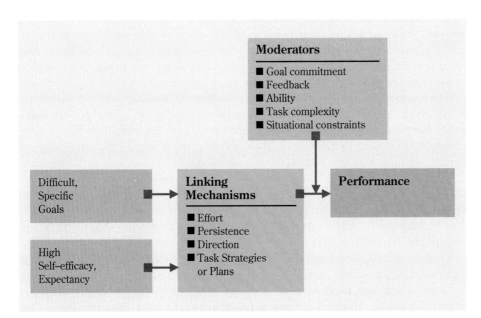

Figure 8.1   Essentials of the Locke and Latham goal-setting framework.

Leaders on Leadership

PUBLISHING CEO BREAKS BARRIERS

Carol Anne Decker wanted to be a television sports commentator when she was in college. However, she shifted gears and is now founder and CEO of her own magazine, *Western Interiors and Design*, for which she broke the gender barrier. Starting with a travel company, she then became the first woman in advertising sales to be employed in the travel/trade publishing industry as a sales executive with *Travel Agent* magazine. She then moved through a series of jobs to co-found *Personal Investor* magazine and did some magazine consulting.

As a part of all this, she became heavily involved in turning an old mansion near Manhattan into a showcase, which, in turn, set the stage for her founding her own magazine based on a sophisticated business plan and raising millions of dollars. She leads some 40 people. She is known as an innovative visionary who likes to mountain climb. She is..."always pushing forward and upward."

Question: How does her career illustrate goal-setting theory?

nancial services agent if you have a goal of selling six annuities a week than if you have a goal of three. However, if your goal is fifteen annuities a week, you may consider that as impossible to achieve, and your performance may well be lower than what it would be with a more realistic goal.

Second, *specific goals are more likely to lead to higher performance than are no goals or vague or very general ones.* All too often people work with very general goals such as the encouragement to "do your best." Research indicates that more specific goals, such as selling six computers a day, are much more motivational than a simple "do your best" goal.

Third, *task feedback, or knowledge of results, is likely to motivate people toward higher performance by encouraging the setting of higher performance goals.* Feedback lets people know where they stand and whether they are on course or off course in their efforts. For example, think about how eager you are to find out how well you did on an examination.

Fourth, *goals are most likely to lead to higher performance when people have the abilities and the feelings of self-efficacy required to accomplish them.* The individual must be able to accomplish the goals and feel confident in those abilities. To take the financial services example again, you may be able to do what's required to sell six annuities a week and feel confident that you can. If your goal is fifteen, however, you may believe that your abilities are insufficient to the task and thus lack the confidence to work hard enough to accomplish it.

Fifth, *goals are most likely to motivate people toward higher performance when they are accepted and there is commitment to them.* Participating in the goal-setting process helps build such acceptance and commitment. It helps create "ownership" of the goals. However, Locke and Latham report that goals assigned by someone else can be equally effective. The assigners are likely to be authority figures, and that can have an impact. The assignment also implies that the subordinate can actually reach the goal. Moreover, assigned goals often are a challenge and help define the standards people use to attain self-satisfaction with their performance. According to Locke and Latham, assigned goals most often lead to poor performance when they are curtly or inadequately explained.

Goal Setting and MBO

When we speak of goal setting and its potential to influence individual performance at work, the concept of *management by objectives (MBO)* immediately comes to mind. The essence of MBO is a process of joint goal setting between a supervisor and a subordinate.[6] It involves managers working with their subordinates to establish performance goals and plans that are consistent with higher-level work unit and organizational objectives. When this process is followed throughout an organization, MBO helps clarify the hierarchy of objectives as a series of well-defined means–end chains.

Figure 8.2 shows a comprehensive view of MBO. The concept is consistent with the notion of goal setting and its associated principles discussed above. Notice how joint supervisor–subordinate discussions are designed to extend participation from the point of establishing initial goals to the point of evaluating results in terms of goal attainment. In addition to these goal-setting steps, a successful MBO system calls for careful implementation. Not only must workers have the freedom to carry out the required tasks, managers should be prepared to actively support their efforts to achieve the agreed-upon goals.

Although a fair amount of research based on case studies of MBO success is available, few rigorously controlled studies have been done. What there is reports mixed results.[7] In general, and as an application of goal-setting theory, MBO has much to offer. But it is by no means easy to start and keep going. Many firms have started and dropped the approach because of difficulties experienced early on. Among the specific problems it creates are too much paper-

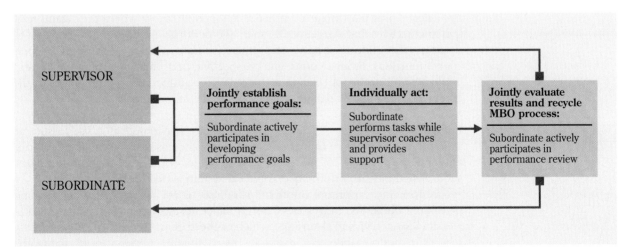

Figure 8.2   How the management by objectives process works.

work documenting goals and accomplishments and too much emphasis on goal-oriented rewards and punishments, top-down goals, goals that are easily stated in objective terms, and individual instead of group goals. MBO also may need to be implemented organizationwide if it is to work well.

Performance Appraisal

Yet another critical performance management function, performance appraisal, helps both the manager and subordinate maintain the organization–job–employee characteristics match, discussed later in this chapter. Formally defined, **performance appraisal** is a process of systematically evaluating performance and providing feedback on which performance adjustments can be made.[8] If the desired level of performance exceeds actual levels, a performance variance requiring special attention exists. For example, if you have a sales quota of 20 CD-ROM drives per month—the desired performance—and you sell only 2 CD-ROM drives per month—your actual performance—your performance variance of 18 CD-ROMS will require the attention of the sales manager.

▓▓▓ A **performance appraisal** is a process of systematically evaluating performance and providing feedback on which performance adjustments can be made.

Purposes of Performance Appraisal

Any performance appraisal system is central to an organization's human resource management activities. Performance appraisals are intended to:

Purposes of performance appraisal

- Define the specific job criteria against which performance will be measured.
- Measure past job performance accurately.
- Justify the rewards given to individuals and/or groups, thereby discriminating between high and low performance.
- Define the development experiences the ratee needs to enhance performance in the current job and to prepare for future responsibilities.

These four functions describe two general purposes served by good performance appraisal systems: evaluation, and feedback and development. From an evaluative perspective, performance appraisal lets people know where they stand relative to objectives and standards. As such, the performance appraisal is an input to decisions that allocate rewards and otherwise administer the organization's personnel functions. From a counseling perspective, performance appraisal facilitates implementing decisions relating to planning for and gaining commitment to the continued training and personal development of subordinates.

Evaluative Decisions   Evaluative decisions are concerned with such issues as promotions, transfers, terminations, and salary increases. When these decisions are made on the basis of performance criteria, as opposed to some other basis, such as seniority, a performance appraisal system is necessary.

Performance appraisal information is also useful for making selection and placement decisions. In this case, performance results are matched against individual characteristics to determine which of these characteristics are most closely related to performance. For example, management checks various individual characteristics, such as education, mathematical ability, verbal ability, mechanical ability, and achievement motivation, to see how closely they are related to performance.

Individuals who score well on those characteristics found to be closely tied to performance for a given job are considered for that position. In addition, if specific aspects of a ratee's performance are found to be inadequate, the performance appraisal process may lead to remedial training. Finally, appraisals form the basis of any performance-contingent reward system (i.e., any system that ties rewards, such as pay, to an individual's or group's performance).

Feedback and Development Decisions   Performance appraisals also can be used to let ratees know where they stand in terms of the organization's expectations and performance objectives. Performance appraisal feedback should involve a detailed discussion of the ratee's job-related strengths and weaknesses. This feedback can then be used for developmental purposes. In terms of the expectancy motivation approach discussed in Chapter 6, feedback can help clarify the ratees' sense of both instrumentality—it can help them better understand what kinds of rewards they will receive if they perform well—and expectancy—it lets them know what actions they need to take to reach that level of performance. Performance appraisal feedback also can be used as a basis for individual coaching or training by the manager to help a subordinate overcome performance deficiencies. Surveys typically indicate that around two-thirds of the sampled firms use performance appraisals for developmental purposes.

Who Does the Performance Appraisal?

Performance appraisals traditionally have been conducted by an individual's immediate superior,[9] the presumption being that since the immediate superior is responsible for the subordinate's performance, the superior should do the appraisal. In many cases, however, others may be able to better perform at least some aspects of the appraisal. For example, peers are closest to the action, and their appraisals can be especially valuable when they are obtained from several peers. Immediate subordinates also can provide insightful evaluations as long as the ratings remain anonymous.

To obtain as much appraisal information as possible, as many as one-quarter of U.S. organizations are now using not only the evaluations of bosses, peers, and subordinates, but also self-ratings, customer ratings, and ratings by others with whom the ratee deals outside the immediate work unit. Such a comprehensive approach is called **360-degree evaluation**. The number of appraisals typically ranges from 5 to 10 per person under evaluation. Firms such as Alcoa and UPS now use 360-degree evaluations. They are made to order for the new, flatter, team-oriented organizations emphasizing total quality or high-performance management, whereby input from many sources is crucial. Computer technology can now facilitate the collection and analysis of some or all of these 360-degree evaluations.[10]

One example involves the use of self- and superior ratings in an innovative way. The subordinate rates himself or herself on the importance of a given job function to the subordinate's performance and on how well the subordinate thinks he or she is performing the function. The supervisor performs a similar evaluation of the employee. A computer program then highlights those areas on which there is the most disagreement. Only the associate gets the printout and

360-degree evaluation is a comprehensive approach that uses self-ratings, customer ratings, and ratings by others outside the work unit.

Manning Plans More Improvement

Peyton Manning has a $98 million contract after having the best season of his career. Even so, Manning the perfectionist has set forth the following specific goals for the coming season: improving his completion percentage, keeping his interceptions in single digits, and making a Super Bowl run before his team (the Indianapolis Colts) has to deal next year with re-signing four key players.

may choose to discuss these areas with the supervisor. Both the timing and the specific content of such a meeting are at the discretion of the subordinate.[11]

Performance Appraisal Dimensions and Standards

In addition to performance outcomes, the behaviors or activities that result in these outcomes are frequently important to performance appraisal as well.

Output Measures   A number of production and sales jobs provide ready measures of *work output*. For example, a final-stage assembler may have a goal of 15 completed computer monitors per hour. The number of monitors is easily measurable, and the organization can set standards concerning how many computer monitors should be completed per hour. Here, the performance dimension of interest is a quantitative one: 15 completed computer monitors per hour. However, the organization also may introduce a *quality* dimension. The individual may be evaluated in terms not only of the number of monitors per hour but also the number of units that pass a *quality control inspection* per hour. Now, both quantity and quality are important, and the individual cannot trade one for the other. Assembling 20 monitors per hour will not do if only 10 pass inspection, nor will having a larger proportion of monitors pass inspection if only 10 monitors are assembled per hour.

In addition, management may be interested in other performance dimensions, such as downtime of the equipment used for assembling. In this case, the assembler would be evaluated in terms of quantity and quality of assembly output and equipment downtime. Management could thereby ensure not only that a desirable product is being assembled at a desirable rate but also that the employee is careful with the equipment.

Activity Measures   In the preceding example, the output measures were straightforward, as was the measure of equipment downtime. Often, however, output measures may be a function of group efforts, or they may be extremely difficult to measure, or they may take so long to accomplish that they can't be readily determined for a given individual during a given time period. For example, it may be very difficult to determine the output of a research scientist attempting to advance new knowledge. In such a case, activity or behavioral measures may be called for, rather than output measures. The research scientist may be appraised in terms of his or her approach to problems, his or her interactions with other scientists, and the like.

Activity measures are typically obtained from the evaluator's observation and rating. In contrast, output measures are often obtained directly from written records or documents, such as production records. The difficulty of obtaining output measures may be one reason for using activity measures. Activity measures are also typically more useful for employee feedback and development than are output measures alone. For example, a salesperson may sell 20 insurance policies a month when the quota is 25. However, activities such as number of sales calls per day or number of community volunteer events attended per week (where some potential clients are likely to be found) can provide more specific information than simply the percentage of monthly quota output measures. Where jobs lend themselves to systematic analysis, important activities can be inferred from the job analysis.

Research Insight
Negative Affectivity Affects Reactions to Formal Appraisal Feedback

Negative affectivity (NA) is a personality factor that represents people's predispositions to experience aversive emotional states. People high in NA tend to focus on the negative side of others and are less satisfied with themselves as well as with their lives.

A study of 329 bank tellers was conducted in a large, international bank. The tellers were provided performance appraisal feedback and a 10-item scale was used to measure NA. Essentially, NA was found to moderate the link between favorable appraisal feedback and job attitudes for the tellers, such that:

- Among the higher-rated performers, attitudes were improved one month after the performers were notified of favorable results (time 2).

- Improved attitudes persisted for six months after the performance appraisal (time 3) among low-NA tellers but not among high NA tellers.

- Among lower-rated performers, mean levels of attitudes did not significantly change during the study.

In summary, NA was found to moderate the attitudinal effects of positive performance feedback on worker reactions.

Reference:: Simon S. K. Lam, Michelle S. M. Yik, and John Schaubroeck, "Responses to Formal Performance Appraisal Feedback: The Role of Negative Affectivity," *Journal of Applied Psychology* 87(1) (2002):192–201.

Performance Appraisal Methods

Performance appraisal methods can be divided into two general categories: comparative methods and absolute methods.[12]

Comparative methods of performance appraisal seek to identify one's relative standing among those being rated, that is, comparative methods can establish that Bill is better than Mary, who is better than Leslie, or who is better than Tom on a performance dimension. Comparative methods can indicate that one person is better than another on a given dimension, but not *how much better*. These methods also fail to indicate whether the person receiving the better rating is "good enough" in an absolute sense. It may well be that Bill is merely the best of a bad lot. Three comparative performance appraisal methods are (1) ranking, (2) paired comparison, and (3) forced distribution.

In contrast, absolute methods of performance appraisal specify precise measurement standards. For example, tardiness might be evaluated on a scale ranging from "never tardy" to "always tardy." Four of the more common absolute rating procedures are (1) graphic rating scales, (2) critical incident diaries, (3) behaviorally anchored rating scales, and (4) management by objectives. The comparative methods are less likely than absolute measures to be used in more collectivist-oriented cultures because of their emphasis on the group.

Ranking   **Ranking** is the simplest of all the comparative techniques. It consists of merely rank ordering each individual from best to worst on each performance dimension being considered. For example, in evaluating work quality, I compare

Ranking is a comparative technique of performance appraisal that involves rank ordering of each individual from best to worst on each performance dimension.

Smith, Jones, and Brown. I then rank Brown number 1, Smith number 2, and Jones number 3. The ranking method, though relatively simple to use, can become burdensome when there are many people to consider.

Paired comparison is a comparative method of performance appraisal whereby each person is directly compared with every other person.

Paired Comparison   In a **paired comparison** method, each person is directly compared with every other person being rated. The frequency of endorsement across all pairs determines one's final ranking. Every possible paired comparison within a group of ratees is considered, as shown below (italics indicate the person rated better in each pair):

Bill vs. Mary	*Mary* vs. Leslie	*Leslie* vs. Tom
Bill vs. Leslie	*Mary* vs. Tom	
Bill vs. Tom		

Number of times Bill is better	=	3
Number of times Mary is better	=	2
Number of times Leslie is better	=	1
Number of times Tom is better	=	0

The best performer in this example is Bill, followed by Mary, then Leslie, and, last of all, Tom. When there are many people to compare, the paired comparison approach can be even more tedious than the ranking method.

Forced distribution is a method of performance appraisal that uses a small number of performance categories, such as "very good," "good," "adequate," and "very poor" and forces a certain proportion of people into each.

Forced Distribution   **Forced distribution** uses a small number of performance categories, such as "very good," "good," "adequate," "poor," and "very poor." Each rater is instructed to rate a specific proportion of employees in each of these categories. For example, 10 percent of employees must be rated very good, 20 percent must be rated good, and so on. This method *forces* the rater to use all of the categories and to avoid rating everyone as outstanding, poor, average, or the like. It can be a problem if most of the people are truly superior performers or if most of the people perform about the same.

A **graphic rating scale** is a scale that lists a variety of dimensions thought to be related to high-performance outcomes in a given job and that the individual is expected to exhibit.

Graphic Rating Scales   **Graphic rating scales** list a variety of dimensions that are thought to be related to high-performance outcomes in a given job and that the individual is accordingly expected to exhibit, such as cooperation, initiative, and attendance. The scales allow the manager to assign the individual scores on each dimension. An example is shown in Figure 8.3. These ratings are sometimes given point values and combined into numerical ratings of performance.

The primary appeal of graphic rating scales is their ease of use. In addition, they are efficient in the use of time and other resources, and they can be applied to a wide range of jobs. Unfortunately, because of generality, they may not be linked to job analysis or to other specific aspects of a given job. This difficulty can be dealt with by ensuring that only relevant dimensions of work based on sound job analysis procedures are rated. However, there is a trade-off: the more the scales are linked to job analyses, the less general they are when comparing people on different jobs.

A **critical incident diary** is a method of performance appraisal that records incidents of unusual success or failure in a given performance aspect.

Critical Incident Diary   Supervisors may use **critical incident diaries** to record incidents of each subordinate's behavior that led to either unusual success or failure in a given performance aspect. These incidents are typically recorded in a diary-type log that is kept daily or weekly under predesignated dimensions. In a sales job, for example, following up sales calls and communicat-

Employee: _Jayne Burroughs_   Supervisor: _Dr. Cutter_
Department: _Pathology_   Date: _11-28-02_

Work Quantity		Work Quality		Cooperation	
1. Far below average	—	1. Far below average	—	1. Far below average	—
2. Below average	✓	2. Below average	—	2. Below average	✓
3. Average	—	3. Average	✓	3. Average	—
4. Above average	—	4. Above average	—	4. Above average	—
5. Far above average	—	5. Far above average	—	5. Far above average	—

Employee: _John Watson_   Supervisor: _Dr. Cutter_
Department: _Pathology_   Date: _12-24-02_

Work Quantity		Work Quality		Cooperation	
1. Far below average	—	1. Far below average	—	1. Far below average	—
2. Below average	—	2. Below average	—	2. Below average	—
3. Average	✓	3. Average	—	3. Average	—
4. Above average	—	4. Above average	✓	4. Above average	—
5. Far above average	—	5. Far above average	—	5. Far above average	✓

Figure 8.3   Sixth-month performance reviews for Burroughs and Watson.

ing necessary customer information might be two of the dimensions recorded in a critical incident diary. Descriptive paragraphs can then be used to summarize each salesperson's performance for each dimension as it is observed.

This approach is excellent for employee development and feedback. Since the method consists of qualitative statements rather than quantitative information, however, it is difficult to use for evaluative decisions. To provide for such information, the critical incident technique is sometimes combined with one of the other methods.

Behaviorally Anchored Rating Scales   The **behaviorally anchored rating scale (BARS)** is a performance appraisal approach that has received increasing attention. The procedure for developing this type of scale starts with the careful collection of descriptions of observable job behaviors. These descriptions are typically provided by managers and personnel specialists and include both superior and inferior performance. Once a large sample of behavioral descriptions is collected, each behavior is evaluated to determine the extent to which it describes good versus bad performance. The final step is to develop a rating scale in which the anchors are specific critical behaviors, each reflecting a different degree of performance effectiveness. An example of a BARS is shown in Figure 8.4 for a retail department manager. Note the specificity of the behaviors and the scale values for each. Similar behaviorally anchored scales would be developed for other dimensions of the job.

▬ A **behaviorally anchored rating scale (BARS)** is a performance appraisal approach that describes observable job behaviors, each of which is evaluated to determine good versus bad performance.

Supervising Sales Personnel

Gives sales personnel a clear idea of their job duties and responsibilities; exercises tact and consideration in working with subordinates; handles work scheduling efficiently and equitably; supplements formal training with his or her own "coaching"; keeps informed of what the salespeople are doing on the job; and follows company policy in agreements with subordinates.

Effective   9   Could be expected to conduct full day's sales clinic with two new sales personnel and thereby develop them into top salespeople in the department.

8   Could be expected to give his or her sales personnel confidence and strong sense of responsibility by delegating many important tasks.

7   Could be expected never to fail to conduct weekly training meetings with his or her people at a scheduled hour and to convey to them exactly what is expected.

6   Could be expected to exhibit courtesy and respect toward his or her sales personnel.

5   Could be expected to remind sales personnel to wait on customers instead of conversing with one another.

4   Could be expected to be rather critical of store standards in front of his or her own people, thereby risking their development of poor attitudes.

3   Could be expected to tell an individual to come in anyway even though he or she called in to say he or she was ill.

2   Could be expected to go back on a promise to an individual who he or she had told could transfer back into previous department if he or she did not like the new one.

Ineffective   1   Could be expected to make promises to an individual about his or her salary being based on department sales even when he or she knew such a practice was against company policy.

Figure 8.4   Example of a behaviorally anchored rating scale dimension.

As you can see, the BARS approach is detailed and complex. It requires lots of time and effort to develop. But the BARS also provides specific behaviors that are useful for counseling and feedback, combined with quantitative scales that are useful for evaluative comparative purposes. Initial results of the use of BARS suggested that they were less susceptible to common rating errors than were more traditional scales. More recent evidence suggests that the scales may not be as superior as originally thought, especially if an equivalent amount of developmental effort is put into other types of measures.[13] A somewhat simpler variation of behaviorally anchored scales is the *Behavioral Observation Scale* (BOS), which uses a 5-point frequency scale (ranging from "almost always" to "almost never") for each separate statement of behavior.

■ **Management by objectives (MBO)** is a process of joint goal setting between a supervisor and a subordinate.

Management by Objectives   Of all the appraisal methods available, **management by objectives (MBO)** is linked most directly to means–ends chains and goal setting, as discussed later in this chapter.[14] When an MBO system is used, subordinates work with their supervisor to establish specific task-related objectives that fall within their domains and serve as means to help accomplish the supervisor's higher-level objectives. Each set of objectives is worked out between a supervisor and a subordinate for a given time period. The establishment of objectives is similar to a job analysis, except that it is directed toward a particular individual in his or her job rather than toward a particular job type alone. The increased discretion of the MBO approach means that each specific person is likely to have a custom-tailored set of work goals while still working within the action context of organizational means–ends chains.

MBO is the most individualized of all the appraisal systems and tends to work well for counseling if the objectives go beyond simply desired outputs and focus on important activities as well. In comparing one employee with another, a key concern is the ease or difficulty of achieving the goals. If one person has an easier set of objectives to meet than another, then comparisons are unfair. Since MBO tends to rely less heavily on ratings than do other appraisal systems, rating errors are less likely to be a problem.

Measurement Errors in Performance Appraisal

To be meaningful, an appraisal system must be both *reliable*—provide consistent results each time it is used—and *valid*—actually measure people on relevant job content. A number of measurement errors can threaten the reliability or validity of performance appraisals.[15] Note the strong tie between these errors and Chapter 5, covering perception and attribution.

Halo Errors A **halo error** results when one person rates another person on several different dimensions and gives a similar rating for each dimension. For example, a sales representative considered to be a "go-getter" and thus rated high on "dynamism" also would be rated high on dependability, tact, and whatever other performance dimensions were used. The rater fails to discriminate between the person's strong and weak points; a "halo" carries over from one dimension to the next. This effect can create a problem when each performance dimension is considered an important and relatively independent aspect of the job. A variation is the *single criterion error*, in which only one of several important performance aspects is considered at all.

Leniency/Strictness Errors Just as some professors are known as "easy A's," some managers tend to give relatively high ratings to virtually everyone under their supervision. This is known as a **leniency error**. Sometimes the opposite occurs; some raters tend to give everyone a low rating. This is called a **strictness error**. The problem in both instances is the inadequate discrimination between good and poor performers. Leniency is likely to be a problem when peers assess one another, especially if they are asked to provide feedback to each other, because it is easier to discuss high ratings than low ones.

Central Tendency Errors **Central tendency errors** occur when managers lump everyone together around the average, or middle, category. This tendency gives the impression that there are no very good or very poor performers on the dimensions being rated. No true performance discrimination is made. Both leniency and central tendency errors are examples of raters who exhibit **low-differentiation errors**. These raters simply restrict themselves to only a small part of the rating scale.

A **halo error** results when one person rates another person on several different dimensions and gives a similar rating for each one.

A **leniency error** is the tendency to give relatively high ratings to virtually everyone.

A **strictness error** occurs when a rater tends to give everyone a low rating.

A **central tendency error** occurs when managers lump everyone together around the average, or middle, category.

A **low-differentiation error** occurs when raters restrict themselves to a small part of the rating scale.

▓▓▓ A **recency error** is a biased rating that develops by allowing the individual's most recent behavior to speak for his or her overall performance on a particular dimension.

▓▓▓ A **personal bias error** occurs when a rater allows specific biases, such as racial, age, or gender, to enter into performance appraisal.

Recency Errors   A different kind of error, known as a **recency error**, occurs when a rater allows recent events to influence a performance rating over earlier events. Take, for example, the case of an employee who is usually on time but shows up one hour late for work the day before his or her performance rating. The employee is rated low on "promptness" because the one incident of tardiness overshadows his or her usual promptness.

Personal Bias Errors   Raters sometimes allow specific biases to enter into performance evaluations. When this happens, **personal bias errors** occur. For example, a rater may intentionally give higher ratings to white employees than to nonwhite employees. In this case, the performance appraisal reflects a racial bias. Bias toward members of other demographic categories—such as age, gender, and disability—also can occur, based on stereotypes the rater may have. Such bias appears to have been widespread at Monarch Paper Company, when a former vice president was demoted to a warehouse-maintenance job for not accepting an early retirement offer. A federal jury judged the firm guilty of age bias.[16] This example shows that raters must reflect carefully on their personal biases and guard against their interference with performance-based ratings of subordinates.

Cultural Bias Errors   Managers must be aware of the cultural backgrounds that they bring with them to the task of performance appraisal. They should be careful to avoid criticizing employees for cultural differences, described in Chapter 3, such as time orientation or ideas of appropriate power distance, unless these differences adversely affect performance on a regular basis.

Improving Performance Appraisals

As is true of most other issues in organizational behavior, managers must recognize certain trade-offs in setting up and implementing any performance appraisal system. In addition to the pros and cons already mentioned for each method, some specific issues to keep in mind in order to reduce errors and improve appraisals include the following:[17]

Steps to improve performance appraisals

1. Train raters so that they understand the evaluation process rationale and can recognize the sources of measurement error.
2. Make sure that raters observe ratees on an ongoing, regular basis and that they do not try to limit all their evaluations to the formally designated evaluation period, for instance, every six months or every year.
3. Do not have the rater rate too many ratees. The ability to identify performance differences drops, and fatigue sets in when the evaluation of large numbers of people is involved.
4. Make sure that the performance dimensions and standards are stated clearly and that the standards are as noncontaminating and nondeficient as possible.
5. Avoid terms such as "average" because different evaluators tend to react differently to the terms.

Remember that appraisal systems cannot be used to discriminate against employees on the basis of age, gender, race, ethnicity, and so on. To help provide a legally defensible system in terms of legislation, the following recommendations are useful.[18]

- Appraisal must be based on an analysis of job requirements as reflected in performance standards.

- Appraisal is appropriate only where performance standards are clearly understood by employees.

- Clearly defined individual dimensions should be used rather than global measures.

- Dimensions should be behaviorally based and supported by observable evidence.

- If rating scales are used, abstract trait names, such as "loyalty," should be avoided unless they can be defined in terms of observable behaviors.

- Rating scale anchors should be brief and logically consistent.

- The system must be validated and psychometrically sound, as must the ratings given by individual evaluators.

- An appeal mechanism must be in place in the event the evaluator and the ratee disagree.

Technological advances now provide various PC programs designed to facilitate the rating process. Specifically, these allow for easier and more comprehensive scale construction, faster feedback, and the additional flexibility called for in today's new workplace.[19]

Legal foundations of performance appraisals

Group Evaluation

As indicated earlier, the growing trend is toward group or team performance evaluations. Such an evaluation is consistent with self-managed teams and high-performance organizations. Frequently, this emphasis is accompanied by a group-based compensation system such as discussed later in this chapter. Traditional individually oriented appraisal systems are no longer appropriate and need to be replaced with a group system such as suggested in The Effective Manager 8.1.

> **THE EFFECTIVE MANAGER 8.1**
> ## Suggestions for a Group Performance Evaluation System
>
> - Link the team's results to organizational goals.
> - Start with the team's customers and the team work process needed to satisfy those needs:
>   Customer requirements
>   Delivery and quality
>   Waste and cycle time
> - Evaluate team and each individual member's performance.
> - Train the team to develop its own measures.

Compensation and Rewards

Accompanying goal setting and performance appraisal is the design and implementation of reward systems. These reward systems emphasize a mix of extrinsic and intrinsic rewards. As we noted in Chapter 6, *extrinsic rewards* are positively valued work outcomes that are given to an individual or group by some other person or source in the work setting. In contrast, *intrinsic rewards* are positively valued work outcomes that the individual receives directly as a result of task performance; they do not require the participation of another person or source. A feeling of achievement after accomplishing a particularly challenging task is an example of an intrinsic reward. Managing intrinsic work rewards presents the additional challenge of designing a work setting so that employees can, in effect, reward themselves for a job well done. Managers can also provide a variety of extrinsic rewards, as described in Chapter 6. Many, such as sincere praise for a job well done, or symbolic tokens of accomplishment such as "employee-of-the-month" awards, involve low cost to the company. In the remainder of this chapter, we emphasize the management of pay as an extrinsic reward.

Pay as an Extrinsic Reward

Pay is an especially complex extrinsic reward. It can help organizations attract and retain highly capable workers, and it can help satisfy and motivate these workers to work hard to achieve high performance. But if there is dissatisfaction with the salary, pay can also lead to strikes, grievances, absenteeism, turnover, and sometimes even poor physical and mental health.

Edward Lawler, a management expert, has contributed greatly to our understanding of pay as an extrinsic reward. His research generally concludes that, for pay to serve as a source of work motivation, high levels of job performance must be viewed as the path through which high pay can be achieved.[20] **Merit pay** is defined as a compensation system that bases an individual's salary or wage increase on a measure of the person's performance accomplishments during a specified time period. That is, merit pay is an attempt to make pay contingent upon performance.

▒ **Merit pay** is a compensation system that bases an individual's salary or wage increase on a measure of the person's performance accomplishments during a specified time period.

Although research supports the logic and theoretical benefits of merit pay, it also indicates that the implementation of merit pay plans is not as universal or as easy as we might expect. In fact, surveys over the past 30 or so years have found that as many as 80 percent of respondents felt that they were not rewarded for a job well done.[21] An effective merit pay system is one approach to dealing with this problem.

To work well, a merit pay plan should be based on realistic and accurate measures of individual work performance and create a belief among employees that the way to achieve high pay is to perform at high levels. In addition, merit pay should clearly discriminate between high and low performers in the amount of pay reward received. Finally, managers should avoid confusing "merit" aspects of a pay increase with "cost-of-living" adjustments.

Merit pay plans are just one attempt to enhance the positive value of pay as a work reward. Some argue that merit pay plans are not consistent with the demands of today's organizations, for they fail to recognize the high degree of task interdependence among employees, as illustrated particularly in today's organizations. Also, as we argued earlier, performance management and reward strategies should be consistent with overall organization strategies. For example, the pay system of a firm with an emphasis on highly skilled individuals in short supply should emphasize employee retention rather than performance.[22]

With these points in mind, let us examine a variety of creative pay practices. These practices are becoming more common in organizations with increasingly diverse workforces and increased emphasis on TQM or similar setups.[23] They include skill-based pay, gain-sharing plans, profit-sharing plans, employee stock ownership plans, lump-sum pay increases, and flexible benefit plans.

▒ **Skill-based pay** is a system that rewards people for acquiring and developing job-relevant skills in number and variety relevant to the organization's need.

Creative Pay Practices

Skill-Based Pay   **Skill-based pay** rewards people for acquiring and developing job-relevant skills. Pay systems of this sort pay people for the mix and depth of skills they possess, not for the particular job assignment they hold. An example is the cross-functional team approach at Monsanto-Benevia, where each team member has developed quality, safety, administrative, maintenance, coaching, and team leadership skills. In most cases, these skills involve high-tech, automated equipment. Workers are paid for this "breadth" of capability and their willingness to use any of the skills needed by the company.

Skill-based pay is one of the fastest-growing pay innovations in the United States. Among the better-known firms using this plan is Polaroid.[24] Besides flexibility, some advantages of skill-based pay are employee cross-training—workers learn to do one another's job; fewer supervisors—workers can provide more of these functions themselves; and more individual control over compensation—workers know in advance what is required to receive a pay raise. One disadvantage is possible higher pay and training costs that are not offset by greater productivity. Another is that of deciding on appropriate monetary values for each skill.[25]

Gain-Sharing Plans   Cash bonuses, or extra pay for performance above standards or expectations, have been common practice in the compensation of managers and executives for a long time. Top managers in some industries earn annual bonuses of 50 percent or more of their base salaries. Attempts to extend such opportunities to all employees are growing in number and importance today. One popular plan is **gain sharing**, which links pay and performance by giving workers the opportunity to share in productivity gains through enhanced earnings.

The Scanlon Plan is probably the oldest and best-known gain-sharing plan. Others you may have heard about are the Lincoln Electric Plan, the Rucker Plan™ or IMPROSHARE™. Gain-sharing plans possess some similarities to profit-sharing plans, but they are not the same. Typically, profit-sharing plans grant individuals or workgroups a specified portion of any economic profits earned by an organization as a whole. Gain-sharing plans involve a specific measurement of productivity combined with a calculation of a bonus designed to offer workers a mutual share of any increase in total organizational productivity.

The intended benefits of gain-sharing plans include increased worker motivation because of the pay-for-performance incentives and a greater sense of personal responsibility for making performance contributions to the organization. Because they can be highly participative in nature, gain-sharing plans also may encourage cooperation and teamwork in the workplace. Although more remains to be learned about gain sharing, the plans are receiving increasing attention from organizations.[26]

Profit-Sharing Plans   **Profit-sharing plans** possess some similarities to gain-sharing plans, but they are not identical. Profit-sharing plans reward employees based on the entire organization's performance. Unlike gain sharing, profit-sharing plans do not attempt to reward employees for productivity gains, and they reflect things, such as economic conditions, over which employees have no control. At the same time, gain-sharing plans generally use a "hard productivity" measure, while profit-sharing plans do not.

Profit sharing also tends to use a mechanistic formula for profit allocation and does not utilize employee participation. Most often, profit-sharing plans fund employee retirement and thus are considered benefits, not incentives.[27]

Gain sharing is a pay system that links pay and performance by giving workers the opportunity to share in productivity gains through increased earnings.

Profit-sharing plans reward employees based on the entire organization's performance.

▦ **ESOPs**, like profit sharing, are based on the total
organization's perfor-
mance—but measured in
terms of stock price.

Employee Stock Ownership Plans (ESOPs) Like profit sharing, **ESOPs** are based
on the total organization's performance—but measured in terms of stock price. The
stock may be given to employees, or employees may purchase it at a price below
market value. Organizations often use ESOPs as a low-cost retirement benefit for employees because they are nontaxable to the organization until the employees redeem
the stock. Of course, like all stock investments, ESOPs involve risk.[28]

▦ **Lump-sum increases**
is a pay system in which
people elect to receive
their wage or salary in-
crease in one or more
lump-sum payments.

Lump-Sum Pay Increases While most pay plans distribute increases as part
of a regular pay check, an interesting alternative is the **lump-sum increase** program, by which individuals can elect to receive an increase in one or more
lump-sum payments. The full increase may be taken at the beginning of the year
and used for some valued purpose, for example, a down payment on a car or a
sizable deposit in a savings account. Or a person may elect to take one-half of
the raise early and get the rest at the start of the winter holiday season. In either
case, the individual should be more motivated because of the larger doses or because it is attached to something highly valued.

A related, but more controversial, development in this area is the lump-sum
payment, which differs from the lump-sum increase. The lump-sum payment is
an attempt by employers to hold labor costs in line while still giving workers
more money, if corporate earnings allow. It involves giving workers a one-time
lump-sum payment, often based on a gain-sharing formula, instead of a yearly
percentage wage or salary increase. In this way, a person's base pay remains
fixed, whereas overall monetary compensation varies according to the bonus
added to this figure by the annual lump-sum payment. American labor unions
typically are resistant to this approach since base pay does not increase and
management determines the size of the bonus. However, surveys generally show
that around two-thirds of the respondents have favorable reactions and think
that the plans have a positive effect on performance.[29]

▦ **Flexible benefit plans**
are pay systems that allow
workers to select benefits
according to their individual needs.

Flexible Benefit Plans An employee's total compensation package includes
not only direct pay but also any fringe benefits that are paid by the organization.
These fringe benefits often add an equivalent of 10 to 40 percent to a person's
salary. It is argued that organizations need to allow for individual differences
when developing such benefit programs. Otherwise, the motivational value of
this indirect form of pay incentive is lost. One approach is to let individuals
choose their total pay package by selecting benefits, up to a certain dollar
amount, from a range of options made available by the organization. These **flexible benefit plans** allow workers to select benefits according to needs. A single
worker, for example, may prefer quite a different combination of insurance and
retirement contributions than would a married person.[30]

Human Resource Development and Person–Job Fit

A key managerial activity involved in performance management and rewards is
human resource development (HR) and person–job fit. Human resource development is the more popular term for what is sometimes called "personnel man-

agement" or "personnel administration." HR starts with **human resource strategic planning**—the process of providing capable and motivated people to carry out the organization's mission and strategy. Key parts of this process are the *staffing function*, which involves the recruitment of employees—generating applicants; *selection*—making hiring decisions for each applicant; and *socialization*—orienting new hires to the organization.[31] These functions, along with *training* and career planning and development, are a critical part of an organization's job requirements–employee characteristics match emphasized so strongly in Chapter 4. Once an HR staffing strategy is in place, managers must continue to assess current HR needs to make sure the organization continues to retain people to meet its strategic objectives.[32]

Staffing

Staffing aspects of the person–job fit begin with an understanding of the positions or jobs for which individuals are needed in the organization. **Job analysis** provides this information; it is the process and procedures used to collect and classify information about tasks the organization needs to complete.[33] Job analysis assists in the understanding of job activities required in a work process and helps define jobs, their interrelationships, and the demographic, aptitude and ability, and personality characteristics needed to do these jobs. The results can be applied to job descriptions, job evaluation and classification, training and career development, performance appraisal, and other HR aspects. Information concerned with the job itself is laid out in the job description. The job description typically contains such information as job duties and responsibilities, equipment and materials used, working conditions and hazards, supervision, work schedules, standards of performance, and relationships to other jobs.

The worker characteristics of job analysis needed to meet the job requirements and specified in the job description are laid out in a job specification. For example, a safety supervisor must have a knowledge of safety regulations. The job requirements and minimum qualifications make up the job specification part of the job analysis.

In addition to other important contributions, the job content and relative importance of different job duties and responsibilities included in job analysis help organizations deal with legal requirements. Such information is useful in defending actions from legal challenges that allege discrimination or unfairness. The generic defense against a charge of discrimination is that the contested decision (hiring, providing a pay raise, termination) was made for job-related reasons, such as provided by job analysis. For example, a firefighter may be required to carry a 180-pound person from a burning building. Job analysis can help a city defend itself against sex discrimination if it can show the relevance of this requirement with a job analysis.[34]

Recruitment   Once job analysis provides the necessary job requirements and employee characteristics, qualified people need to be drawn in to apply for various positions. **Recruitment** is the process of attracting the best-qualified individuals to apply for a given job.[35] It typically involves (1) advertisement of a position vacancy, (2) preliminary contact with potential job candidates, and (3) preliminary screening to obtain a pool of candidates. Home Depot, as an example, essentially follows a variation of these steps in its hiring practices. These

▓▓ **Human resource strategic planning** is the process of providing capable and motivated people to carry out the organization's mission and strategy.

▓▓ **Staffing** involves the recruitment of employees, selection, and socialization.

▓▓ **Job analysis** is the procedure used to collect and classify information about tasks the organization needs to complete.

▓▓ **Recruitment** is the process of attracting the best-qualified individuals to apply for a job.

practices are illustrative of external recruitment, or of attracting individuals from outside the organization. External recruitment involves such sources as general advertisements, often in newspapers, trade journals, or via the Internet; word-of-mouth suggestions from current employees; use of employment agencies; and applicant walk-ins. By contrast, internal recruitment is a process for attracting job applicants from those currently working for the firm. Postings of vacant positions on bulletin boards, in internal memos, and over intranets are frequently used ways to recruit internally.

Most firms tend to use a mix of external and internal recruitment. Some organizations, notably the U.S. armed forces, rely heavily on external recruitment for entry-level positions and then fill higher-level positions entirely from internal promotions. Both approaches have advantages. Internal recruitment is encouraging to current employees, and external recruitment tends to bring in "new blood" and fresh ideas to the firm.

■ **Realistic job previews** provide applicants with an objective description of a job and organization.

Traditionally, firms have attempted to "sell" their organization and jobs to build up the applicant pool. More recently, an approach called a **realistic job preview**, is increasingly being used. In a realistic job preview, applicants are provided with an objective description of the prospective organization and job. Such descriptions have been found to reduce turnover and to better prepare new hires to cope with their jobs.[36]

Selection   After an applicant pool has been recruited, the selection aspect of staffing comes into play. **Selection** involves the series of steps from initial applicant screening to final hiring of the new employee. The selection process involves completing application materials, conducting an interview, completing any necessary tests, doing a background investigation, and deciding to hire or not to hire.

■ **Selection** is the series of steps from initial applicant screening to hiring.

Application Materials   These materials may involve a traditional application form requesting various aspects of background and experience. These forms may be in traditional hard copy or on the Internet. Sometimes résumés (brief summaries of one's background and qualifications) are used in lieu of, or in addition to, other materials. Sometimes tests are included as part of the application materials.

THE EFFECTIVE MANAGER 8.2

Steps to Emphasize in Conducting Hiring Interviews

- Prepare yourself—check applicant's résumé and prepare agenda.
- Initially put applicant at ease—use smalltalk.
- Guard against stereotypes—emphasize applicant as individual.
- Emphasize results-oriented questions—not only what applicant has done but results of these actions.
- Allow for pauses to gather thoughts.
- Bring interview to a natural close.

Employment Interviews   Many of you have experienced employment interviews at one time or another. Interviews are almost invariably used in the selection process (see The Effective Manager 8.2), although they are prone to the kinds of perceptual distortions discussed in Chapter 5, as well as other problems. Nevertheless, they are a mainstay of the selection process, perhaps because they can serve as public relations tools for the organization. At their best, interviews provide rough ideas concerning fit with the job and organization.[37]

Tests   Tests may be administered either before or after the interview. They include cognitive aptitude or ability and personality tests and, increasingly, tests for drug use. Intelligence tests are the most common examples of cognitive tests. Other examples are clerical and mechanical tests. Personality tests evaluate the kinds of personality characteristics discussed in Chapter 4. For example, the California Personality Inventory measures such characteristics as dominance, sociability, and flexibility. Again, whatever kind of test is used must be validated against job requirements so that the organization is not guilty of discrimination.

Performance tests take many forms but often ask candidates to perform tasks that are identical to or at least closely related to what will be required on the job. As technology has become more important, performance tests involving computer skills have become more frequent. Also, a battery of tests is often used to explore a range of job behaviors.

For managerial jobs in particular, but increasingly for other jobs as well, assessment centers are often used. *Assessment centers* provide a firm with a comprehensive view of a candidate by evaluating the candidate's performance across many situations. Such assessments typically involve one to four days of various tests, simulations, role plays, and interviews, all based on dimensions the person occupying the job will need to demonstrate. AT&T has used assessment centers for many years, with considerable effectiveness, spending as much as $1500 per employee in the process.[38] IBM and the FBI are also among the more than 2000 organizations that use assessment centers for managerial selection and promotion.[39] Assessment centers also are utilized by some universities, such as Texas Tech, in training their MBAs.[40]

Background Investigation   Background investigation is yet another step that can be used either early or late in the selection process. Companies providing background audits say requests for their services have jumped sharply in the wake of the World Trade Center disaster. Hospitals, retailers, and firms that own private jets have had especial interest. Two-thirds of employers check on potential hires. Basic-level checks often include a Social Security trace as well as checks of employment history, educational records, criminal records, and driving records.

Typically, a background investigation also involves reference checks. Generally, letters of reference tend to be positively biased and so are not highly related to job performance.[41] Moreover, unless the references, either written or provided over the phone, are very carefully worded, they can lead to lawsuits. References should disclose only information about the job duties the individual in question has been performing. Any personal descriptions should involve only information that can be objectively verified.

Decision to Hire   Based on the previous steps, the organization may choose to make the hiring decision and present a formal job offer. The offer may be made by the potential employee's future boss or by a group of people. At this point, a physical examination may be required if it is shown to be relevant for job performance. For some jobs, negotiations concerning salary or other benefits may occur.

Socialization   Socialization occurs during and after the completion of the staffing process. **Socialization** is the process that adapts employees to the organization's culture. A useful way of considering socialization is in terms of three phases. The first phase is "anticipatory," covering all the learning that occurs before a new mem-

▬ **Socialization** means the process that adapts employees to the organization's culture.

ber joins an organization. This can include such things as realism about the organization and the job and assessing how well the person can meet the required skills and abilities and can have personal needs met by the organization.

The second phase is "encounter," where the new recruit sees what the organization is truly like and where realistic job previews, mentioned earlier, are often employed to speed the process along. Here, some initial shifting of values, skills, and attitudes may occur.

The third phase, "change and acquisition," is where the relatively long-lasting changes take place. Here, new hires master their on-the-job skills, perform their new roles successfully, and adjust to their work group's values and norms. As a part of this process, they also become familiar with their organization's culture, so important that we devote Chapter 19 to it.

At least part of the socialization process is clearly reflected in the familiar "orienting new employees to the firm and the work unit" and is reflected in the second phase—encounter. Orientation can be conducted formally or informally, or it may involve a combination of the two. For complex positions, orientation may take place over an extended period of time. Orientation and, indeed, socialization in general can facilitate the person–job fit by helping to fill in gaps. Also, as previously indicated, socialization can help facilitate an understanding of the organization's culture.[42]

PEOPLE AND TECHNOLOGY

STAFF TREATED LIKE KIDS?

A division manager of a small division of a midsized manufacturing firm is concerned that software is being installed to monitor employees' Internet use, with the aim of cutting down on surfing non-work-related Web sites and affecting their socialization in the current work setting. The manager's subordinates are insulted and accuse top management of "spying on them" and "treating them like children."

An Internet monitoring firm expert asks what might happen if an assembly-line worker in one of the organization's plants kept wandering off to plan his next vacation. He would never get away with it, says the consultant, so why should these people?

Question: What would you do, in terms of performance management and rewards, to deal with this kind of issue?

Training

■■■ **Training** provides the opportunity to acquire and improve job-related skills.

After an employee is selected, it is important that he or she undergo training. **Training** is a set of activities that provides the opportunity to acquire and improve job-related skills.[43] In addition to initial training, training to improve skills is important and might cover such areas as computer skills, diversity, sexual harassment, and implementation of new systems or technology.

Training can be on the job, off the job, or both. *On-the-job training* (OJT) involves job instruction while performing the job in the actual workplace. Internships, apprenticeships, and job rotation are common forms of OJT. Internships are an opportunity for students to gain real-world experience. They are often offered in the summer and may or may not be paid. *Apprenticeships* involve learning a trade from an experienced worker. They are quite common in Europe and relatively uncommon in the United States.

Related coaching or mentoring programs for managerial and professional jobs are quite common in the United States, however. *Job rotation* provides a broad range of experience in different kinds of jobs in a firm. It is often used as part of management training programs, where future managers may spend from a few weeks to much longer in activities such as information processing, computer software, or computer sales. The total program could last up to one or two years, with varying amounts of mentoring.

Off-the-job training commonly involves lectures, videos, and simulations. E-training is becoming more popular. It includes such developments as classes or information modules delivered via computer or the Internet that may be completed at any time or place and group workshops offered through "virtual classroom" distance-learning technology. Lectures convey specific information and work well for problem-solving and technical skills. Videos are particularly good for demonstrating various skills. Simulations, such as experiential exercises, business games, and various computer-based exercises, are particularly useful for teaching interpersonal, leadership, strategic management, and other complex skills such as those required of police officers.

A Canadian airline used a comprehensive combination of on- and off-the-job training to deal with the impact of five mergers and to cope with an extremely dynamic environment. The training was done worldwide and was conducted in combination with American Airlines. Numerous Canadian/U.S. cultural differences had to be worked through in the process.[44]

Career Planning and Development

In addition to employee training for short-term jobs, both the employee and the organization need to be concerned about longer-term **career planning and development**, whereby individuals work with their managers and/or HR experts on career issues.[45]

▰ **Career planning and development** means working with managers and/or HR experts on career issues.

Figure 8.5 offers a basic framework for formal career planning. The five steps in the framework begin with personal assessment and then progress through analysis of opportunities, selection of career objectives, and implemen-

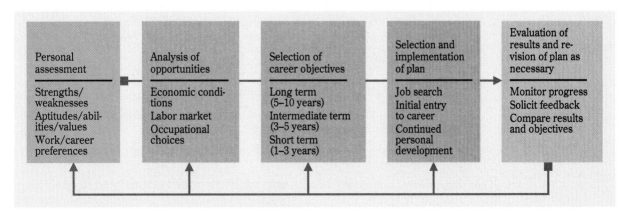

Figure 8.5 **Five-steps in formal career planning.**

tation of strategies, until the final step: evaluation of results. The process is recycled as necessary to allow for constructive revision of the career plan over time. Success in each of these steps entails a good deal of self-awareness and frank assessment. Thus, a successful career begins with sufficient insight to make good decisions about matching personal needs and capabilities with job opportunities over time. The manager's responsibility concerning career planning is twofold: first, planning and managing a personal career; second, assisting subordinates in assuming responsibility for their career planning and development.

Thoughts about careers take on a special relevance in the new workplace. We live and work in a time when the implications of constant change pressure us to continually review and reassess our career progress. Businesses are becoming smaller, employing fewer people, and moving beyond traditional organizational forms. Thus, there is increasing emphasis on horizontal and cross-functional relationships. Technical workers are becoming so important that they are sometimes treated almost like high-level managers in terms of perquisites and rewards. The nature of "work" is changing and will be less bound by 9-to-5 traditions. Continuous learning will be required, and training and electronic education marketplaces will become more and more important.

In this setting, the old notions of a career based within a single organization that takes responsibility for a person's career development are becoming increasingly obsolete. In *The Age of Unreason*, British scholar and consultant Charles Handy argues forcefully that each of us must take charge of our own careers and prepare for inevitable uncertainties and changes by building a "portfolio" of skills.[46] This portfolio needs continuous development: each new job assignment must be well selected and rigorously pursued as a learning opportunity.

▓▓▓ Outsourcing jobs occurs when people outside a firm are contracted to perform selected job activities.

Outsourcing as an Illustration   In our previous edition, **outsourcing jobs**, whereby people outside a firm are contracted to perform selected job activities, was barely mentioned. Now such outsourcing is receiving almost constant attention, especially from the media, and indeed we mentioned it earlier. Obviously, if it is your job that is being contracted out, it is a problem—for you—and it certainly has become a huge political concern at both state and national levels.[47] If we wade through much of the hype on both sides of this issue, the following points become increasingly important:

- One expert estimates the current outsourcing trend will not significantly hurt U.S. employment. Forrester Research estimates about 3.3 million U.S. jobs will move offshore by 2015. However, it is pointed out that even as the U.S. service sector loses about 10 million jobs every year, it creates 12 million new jobs. Therefore, there actually is a net job gain.

- This new means of holding down costs will combat inflation and help customers as well as help U.S. firms remain competitive.

- Outsourcing allows firms to do what they could not afford to do before; for example, follow up on bills as small as $100.

- Outsourcing helps spread wealth from rich nations to poor nations.

Regardless of these arguments, you are likely to be even more in need than before of the portfolio of skills previously mentioned. Therefore, sensitivity and flexibility are increasingly important.

MINORITY LEGAL INTERNSHIP PROGRAM

Charles R. Morgan, an executive VP and general counsel at BellSouth, has implemented a minority legal internship program. BellSouth's Atlanta headquarters hires two first-year minority law students each summer "to give them the experience of working in a corporate law environment." He expects that his interns will work at a law firm the next summer and that their BellSouth time will give them an advantage. The students' agendas also involve pro bono work.

Question: In what ways does this internship encourage person–job fit and career planning and development?

Initial Entry to a Career   The full implications of the new workplace become apparent at the point of initial entry to a career. Choosing a job and a work organization are difficult decisions; our jobs inevitably exert a lot of influence over our lives. Whenever a job change is considered, the best advice is to know yourself and to learn as much as possible about the new job and the organization. This helps to ensure the best person–job–organization match. By working hard to examine personal needs, goals, and capabilities and to gather relevant information, share viewpoints, and otherwise make the recruitment process as realistic as possible, you can help start a new job on the best possible note.

When considering a new job or a possible job change, a "balance sheet" analysis of possible "gains" and "losses" is important. Ask at least two questions. First, "What are my potential gains and losses?" Things to consider in answering this question include salary and fringe benefits, work hours and schedules, travel requirements, use and development of skills and competencies, and opportunities for challenging new job assignments. Second, "What are the potential gains and losses for my significant others?" Here, you should consider income available to meet family responsibilities, time available to be with family and friends, impacts of a geographic move on family and friends, and implications of work stress for nonwork life.

ARRESTING TENOR

The Senegalese artist Youssou N'Dour is noted for his remarkable range and poise. He is also recognized for his prodigious musical intelligence as a writer, bandleader, and producer. He has made *mbalance*—a blend of Senegal's traditional *griot* percussion and praise singing with Afro-Cuban music—famous throughout the world during more than 20 years of recording and touring outside of Senegal with his band, The Super Étoile.

Question: Discuss some key performance management and reward implications of N'Dour's career.

Adult Life Cycle and Career Stages   Chapter 4 showed that as people mature, they pass through an adult life cycle with many different problems and prospects.

As a manager, it is especially important to recognize the effects of this cycle on the people with whom you work. Recall that the previously mentioned life cycle stages popularized by Gail Sheehy were provisional adulthood (ages 18–30), first adulthood (ages 30–45), and second adulthood (ages 45–85+).[48] These are only approximate ages, and there are transitional periods in moving from one stage to the next.

Given the age of change in which we live, the stages and transitions are also much less predictable than in earlier years. Where once a person had one or two careers and a single spouse, now there also can be numerous careers and either no spouse or more than one spouse. In the provisional adult period, people may move back with their parents, stretch out their education, and try many jobs, for example. And where once people retired at age 65, now it is becoming increasingly common to start yet another career at that age.

Career stages are different points of work responsibility and achievement through which people pass during the course of their work lives.

It is useful to link the adult life cycle literature and the **career stages** literature. For those who still follow a traditional career path, we can think of it in terms of: entry and establishment—roughly comparable to the provisional adulthood stage; advancement—the first adulthood stage; and maintenance, withdrawal, and retirement—the second adulthood stage.

Entry and establishment involve on-the-job development of relevant skills and abilities. Individuals also undergo the organizational and professional socialization mentioned earlier. At the same time, progressive organizations actively engage in mentoring new employees.

In the advancement stage, the individual seeks growth and increased responsibility. There may be advancement through internal career paths or external career paths, outside the organization.

A career plateau is a position from which someone is unlikely to move to advance to a higher level of responsibility.

During the maintenance, withdrawal, and retirement stage of second adulthood, individuals may experience continued growth of accomplishments or may encounter career stability. Many people encounter a **career plateau**—they find themselves in a position where they are unlikely to advance to a higher level of responsibility.

At some point during the maintenance career stage, individuals consider withdrawal and ultimate retirement. Now, some prolong this stage well into the second adulthood life cycle stage. Others start planning for an orderly retirement at age 65 or so.

Of course, as we have said, the traditional route above is no longer typical. People may very well have many jobs and more than one career and choose not to retire until they can no longer work. All of these changes reinforce the difficulty of managers building and maintaining commitment to the job and organization and provide many OB challenges.

Chapter 8   Study Guide

Summary

What is goal setting?

- Goal setting is the process of developing, negotiating, and formalizing performance targets or objectives.

- Research supports predictions that the most motivational goals are challenging and specific, allow for feedback on results, and create commitment and acceptance.

- The motivational impact of goals may be affected by individual difference moderators such as ability and self-efficacy.

- Management by objectives is a process of joint goal setting between a supervisor and worker.

- The management by objectives process is a good action framework for applying goal-setting theory on an organizationwide basis.

What is performance appraisal?

- Performance appraisal involves systematically evaluating performance and providing feedback on which performance adjustments can be made.

- Performance appraisals serve the two general purposes of evaluation and feedback and development.

- Performance appraisals traditionally are done by an individual's immediate superior but are moving toward 360-degree evaluations involving the full circle of contacts a person may have in job performance.

- Performance appraisals use either or both output measures and activity measures.

- Performance appraisal methods involve comparative methods and absolute methods.

- There are at least half a dozen rater errors important in performance appraisal.

- There are six steps that can be used to reduce errors and improve performance appraisals.

- Group performance evaluation systems are being increasingly used.

What are compensation and rewards?

- Rewards involve the design and implementation of positively valued work outcomes.

- Reward systems emphasize a mix of extrinsic and intrinsic rewards.

- Pay as an extrinsic reward involves merit pay and creative pay practices.

- Creative pay practices include skill-based pay, gain-sharing plans, lump-sum pay increases, and flexible benefit plans.

What are human resource development and person–job fit?

- HR strategic planning is the process of providing capable and motivated people to carry out the organization's mission and strategy.

- A key part of HR strategic planning, HR staffing involves job analysis, attracting individuals through recruitment, selecting those best qualified through screening and hiring, and socializing employees through initial orientation and follow-up over time. All these together help provide for person–job fit.

- Job analysis assists in understanding necessary job activities and helps define jobs, their interrelationships, and the demographic, aptitude and ability, and personality characteristics for these jobs. Information concerning the job itself appears in the job description. A job specification then merges requirements of the job analysis and job description. The above also help deal with legal requirements.

- Training is a set of activities that provide the opportunity to acquire and improve job-related skills.

- On-the-job training involves job instruction in the workplace and commonly utilizes internships, apprenticeships, and job rotation.

- Off-the-job training takes place off the job and commonly involves lectures, videos, and simulations.

- Career planning and development involves working with managers and HR experts on careers and involves the following: a five-stage planning framework, personal responsibility for developing a portfolio of skills to keep one marketable at any time, a balance sheet approach to evaluating each career opportunity, and recognition of the relationship between life and career stages and transitions.

Key Terms

Behaviorally anchored rating scale (BARS) (p. 173)
Career planning and development (p. 185)
Career plateau (p. 188)
Career stages (p. 188)
Central tendency error (p. 175)
Critical incident diary (p. 172
ESOPs (p. 180)
Flexible benefit plans (p. 180)
Forced distribution (p. 172)
Gain sharing (p. 179)

Graphic rating scales (p. 172)
Halo error (p. 175)
Human resource strategic planning (p. 181)
Job analysis (p. 181)
Leniency error (p. 175)
Low-differentiation error (p. 175)
Lump-sum increases (p. 180)
Management by objectives (MBO) (p. 174)
Merit pay (p. 178)
Outsourcing jobs (p. 186)
Paired comparison (p. 172)

Performance appraisal (p. 168)
Personal bias error (p. 176)
Profit-sharing plans (p. 179)
Ranking (p. 171)
Realistic job preview (p. 182)
Recency error (p. 176)
Recruitment (p. 181)
Selection (p. 182)
Skill-based pay (p. 178)
Socialization (p. 183)
Strictness error (p. 175)
360-degree evaluation (p. 169)
Training (p. 184)

Self-Test 8

Multiple Choice

1. HR staffing consists of all of the following except _____. (a) selection (b) socialization (c) recruitment (d) training

2. Job analysis is _____. (a) the same as job description (b) the same as job specification (c) involved with organizational tasks (d) the same as performance appraisal

3. Training _____. (a) is the same as socialization (b) is another name for career development (c) is a set of activities for improving job-related skills (d) precedes staffing

4. The notions of a career based within a single organization _____. (a) are truer than ever (b) are increasingly obsolete (c) were never really true (d) apply to some industries but not others

5. Performance appraisal and job analysis are _____. (a) similar (b) unrelated (c) related such that the job analysis should be based on the performance appraisal (d) related such that the performance appraisal should be based on the job analysis

6. Performance appraisals have the two general purposes of _____. (a) rewards and punishments (b) evaluation and development decisions (c) rewards and evaluation decisions (d) feedback and job analysis decisions

7. Merit pay _____. (a) rewards people for increased job-related skills (b) is a form of gain sharing (c) is similar to a lump-sum pay increase (d) enhances the positive value of pay as a work reward

8. In a flexible benefit plan, _____. (a) workers select benefits according to needs (b) there are high benefits early in a job and lower ones later (c) there are low benefits early in a job and higher ones later (d) rewards can be split between salary and nonsalary payouts

9. Which goals tend to be more motivating? (a) challenging goals (b) easy goals (c) general goals (d) no goals

10. The MBO process emphasizes _____ as a way of building worker commitment to goal accomplishment. (a) authority (b) joint goal setting (c) infrequent feedback (d) general goals

11. Training can be _____. (a) on or off the job (b) upside or downside (c) vestibule vs. foyer (d) given in lieu of retirement pay

12. Performance appraisals _____. (a) are built around output measures (b) are built around activity measures (c) can be built around either activity or output measures (d) assess job satisfaction

13. Selection _____. (a) follows socialization (b) precedes socialization (c) follows training (d) precedes recruiting

14. Adult and career stages and transitions _____. (a) are identical (b) are unrelated (c) are related (d) are not emphasized much anymore

15. Pay is generally considered _____. (a) an extrinsic reward (b) an intrinsic reward (c) neither an extrinsic or intrinsic reward (d) too high by most people

Short Response

16. Discuss the relationship between an organization's mission and HR strategic planning.

17. Discuss how training and career development relate to the organization–job requirements–individual characteristics match.

18. Discuss the linkage between adult and career stages and transitions.

19. Compare and contrast the evaluative and feedback and development aspects of performance appraisal.

Applications Essay

20. Assume you belong to a student organization on campus. Making any necessary assumptions, discuss, in some detail, how the performance management and reward concepts in this chapter could be applied at the local and/or national level of your student organization.

These learning activities from the *OB Skills Workbook* are suggested for Chapter 8.

OB in Action

CASE	EXPERIENTIAL EXERCISE	SELF-ASSESSMENT
■ 8. I'm Not in Kansas Anymore	■ 17. Annual Pay Raises	■ 8. Are You Cosmopolitan?

Plus—special learning experiences from *The Jossey-Bass/Pfeiffer Classroom Collection*

Chapter 9

How Groups Work

Chapter at a Glance

Groups can bring out the best in performance, creativity, and enthusiasm.
This chapter will help you to understand groups, teams, and how they work.
As you read Chapter 9, *keep in mind these study questions*.

WHAT IS THE NATURE OF GROUPS IN ORGANIZATIONS?

- What Is an Effective Group?
- Synergy and Group Accomplishments
- Formal and Informal Groups

WHAT ARE THE STAGES OF GROUP DEVELOPMENT?

- Forming Stage
- Storming Stage
- Norming Stage
- Performing Stage
- Adjourning Stage

WHAT ARE THE FOUNDATIONS OF GROUP PERFORMANCE?

- Group Inputs
- Group and Intergroup Dynamics
- Group Communication Networks

HOW DO GROUPS MAKE DECISIONS?

- How Groups Make Decisions
- Assets and Liabilities of Group Decision Making
- Groupthink
- How to Improve Group Decisions

REVIEW IN END-OF-CHAPTER STUDY GUIDE

The new workplace places great value on change and adaptation. Organizations are continually under pressure to find new ways of operating in the quest for higher productivity, total quality and service, customer satisfaction, and better quality of working life. Among the many trends and developments we perceive today, none are more important than the attempts being made to tap the full potential of groups more creatively as critical organizational resources.

When you use an Apple computer or see an ad for one of its new products, an i-Pod for example, you should know the story of the original MacIntosh. A team created it. The brainchild of Apple's co-founder Steve Jobs, the MacIntosh team was composed of high-achieving members who were excited and turned on to a highly challenging task. They worked all hours and at an unrelenting pace. Housed in a separate building flying the Jolly Roger, the MacIntosh team combined youthful enthusiasm with great expertise and commitment to an exciting goal. The result was a benchmark computer produced in record time.

Product innovation continues to be a hallmark of Apple Computer, Inc. And that, so to speak, is what groups in organizations should be all about.[1] There is no doubt that an organization's success depends in significant part on the performance of its internal networks of formal and informal groups. Groups are increasingly becoming focal points as organizations seek the advantages of smaller size, flatter structures, cross-functional integration, and more flexible operations. To meet competitive demands in challenging environments, the best organizations mobilize groups and teams in many capacities in the quest to reach their full potential as high-performance systems. Groups in this sense are an important component of the human resources and intellectual capital of organizations.

> "To meet competitive demands... the best organizations mobilize groups and teams."

Groups in Organizations

There is no doubt that groups can be important sources of performance, creativity, and enthusiasm for organizations. But it takes great leadership to achieve these results consistently. The pathways to such success all begin with an understanding of groups in organizations.

What Is an Effective Group?

Groups involve two or more people working together regularly to achieve common goals.

A **group** is a collection of two or more people who work with one another regularly to achieve common goals. In a true group, members (1) are mutually dependent on one another to achieve common goals and (2) interact regularly with one another to pursue those goals over a sustained period of time.[2] Groups are important resources that are good for both organizations and their members. They help organizations to accomplish important tasks. They also help to maintain a high-quality workforce by satisfying needs of their members. Consultant and management scholar Harold J. Leavitt is a well-known advocate for the power and usefulness of groups.[3] He describes "hot groups," ones like the original MacIntosh team, that thrive in conditions of crisis and competition and whose creativity and innovativeness generate extraordinary returns.[4]

An **effective group** is one that achieves high levels of task performance, member satisfaction, and team viability. With regard to *task performance*, an effective group achieves its performance goals—in the standard sense of quantity, quality, and timeliness of work results. For a formal workgroup, such as a manufacturing team, this may mean meeting daily production targets. For a temporary group, such as a new policy task force, this may involve meeting a deadline for submitting a new organizational policy to the company president. With regard to *member satisfaction*, an effective group is one whose members believe that their participation and experiences are positive and meet important personal needs. They are satisfied with their tasks, accomplishments, and interpersonal relationships. With regard to *team viability*, the members of an effective group are sufficiently satisfied to continue working well together on an ongoing basis and/or to look forward to working together again at some future point in time. Such a group has all-important long-term performance potential.

■ **Effective groups** achieve high levels of task performance, member satisfaction, and team viability.

PEOPLE AND TECHNOLOGY

TEAMWORK MAKES GREAT THINGS HAPPEN

The San Diego Zoo is known for showing its animals in natural environments. Animals and plants from a particular region are housed together in cageless enclosures designed to resemble natural settings with appropriate bioclimatic zones. Each bioclimatic zone is managed by its own team, typically consisting of 7 to 10 employees. A typical team is likely to be made up of mammal specialists, bird experts, horticulturists, and maintenance and construction workers. Their jobs blend and merge, making it difficult sometimes to tell who does what. Gone is the "it's-not-my-job" syndrome. If something needs to be done, it is the job of the entire team. In learning to work well together, members let go of traditional practices and develop new skills matched to team concepts.

Question: What work settings are you familiar with that could benefit from a stronger focus on groups and teamwork?

Synergy and Group Accomplishments

When groups are effective, they help organizations accomplish important tasks. In particular, they offer the potential for **synergy**—the creation of a whole that is greater than the sum of its parts. When synergy occurs, groups accomplish more than the total of their members' individual capabilities. Group synergy is necessary for organizations to become competitive and achieve long-term high performance in today's dynamic times.

■ **Synergy** is the creation of a whole greater than the sum of its parts.

The Effective Manager 9.1 lists several benefits that groups can bring to organizations. In three specific situations groups often have performance advantages over individuals acting alone.[5] First, when there is no clear "expert" in a particular task or problem, groups seem to make better judgments than does the average individual alone. Second, groups are typically more successful than individuals when problems are complex, requiring a division of labor and the sharing of information. Third, because of their tendencies to make riskier decisions, groups can be more creative and innovative than individuals.

Groups are important settings where people learn from one another and share job skills and knowledge. The learning environment and the pool of experience within a group can be used to solve difficult and unique problems. This is especially helpful to newcomers, who often need help in their jobs. When group members support and help each other in acquiring and improving job competencies, they may even make up for deficiencies in organizational training systems.

Groups are also important sources of need satisfaction for their members. Opportunities for social interaction within a group can provide individuals with a sense of security in available work assistance and technical advice. Group members can also provide emotional support for one another in times of special crisis or pressure. And the many contributions individuals make to groups can help them experience self-esteem and personal involvement.

Social loafing occurs when people work less hard in groups than they would individually.

At the same time that they have enormous performance potential, however, groups can also have problems. One concern is **social loafing**, also known as the *Ringlemann effect*. It is the tendency of people to work less hard in a group than they would individually.[6] Max Ringlemann, a German psychologist, pinpointed the phenomenon by asking people to pull on a rope as hard as they could, first alone and then in a group.[7] He found that average productivity dropped as more people joined the rope-pulling task. He suggested that people may not work as hard in groups because (1) their individual contributions are less noticeable in the group context and (2) they prefer to see others carry the workload. Some ways for dealing with social loafing or preventing its occurrence include the following:

How to handle social loafing

- Define roles and tasks to maximize individual interests.
- Raise accountability by making individual performance expectations clear and identifiable.
- Tie individual rewards to their performance contributions to the group.

Social facilitation is the tendency for one's behavior to be influenced by the presence of others in a group.

An important aspect of group work is **social facilitation**—the tendency for one's behavior to be influenced by the presence of others in a group or social setting.[8] In general, *social facilitation theory* indicates that working in the presence of others creates an emotional arousal or excitement that stimulates behavior and therefore affects performance. Arousal tends to work positively when one is proficient with the task. Here, the excitement leads to extra effort at doing something that already comes quite naturally. An example is the play of a world-class athlete in front of an enthusiastic hometown crowd. On the other hand, the

Leaders on Leadership

LEADING TAKES SELF-CONFIDENCE AND COMMITMENT TO A VISION

Leadership capability certainly helped Robert L. Johnson found a major television network, Black Entertainment Television; be majority owner of professional sports teams, the Charlotte Bobcats and the Charlotte Sting; and serve on many boards of major corporations and nonprofit organizations. And if you ask him what it takes for an African-American to achieve such success, he is likely to answer that you have to believe in yourself. "I have always recognized that chal-lenge is part of the landscape," says Johnson. "I never give up because I am going to run into racism or I am going to be held back because of lack of access to education, capital, or whatever comes from racism." He started BET with the goal of becoming "the preeminent African-American entertainment media company in the world," and he succeeded.

Question: If leaders bring goals and vision to organizations, what type of vision would stimulate you to commit your time and talents to a potential employer?

effect of social facilitation can be negative when the task is not well learned. You may know this best in the context of public speaking. When asked to speak in front of a class or larger audience, you may well stumble as you try hard in public to talk about an unfamiliar topic.

Formal and Informal Groups

There are many ways in the new workplace for groups to be used to great advantage. A **formal group** is officially designated to serve a specific organizational purpose. An example is the *work unit* headed by a manager and consisting of one or more direct reports. The organization creates such a group to perform a specific task, which typically involves the use of resources to create a product such as a report, decision, service, or commodity. The head of a formal group is responsible for the group's performance accomplishments, but all members contribute the required work. Also, the head of the group plays a key linchpin role that ties it horizontally and vertically with the rest of the organization.[9]

Formal groups may be permanent or temporary. *Permanent workgroups*, or command groups in the vertical structure, often appear on organization charts as departments (e.g., market research department), divisions (e.g., consumer products division), or teams (e.g., product-assembly team). Such groups can vary in size from very small departments or teams of just a few people to large divisions employing a hundred or more people. As permanent workgroups, they are each officially created to perform a specific function on an ongoing basis. They continue to exist until a decision is made to change or reconfigure the organization for some reason.

■ **Formal groups** are officially designated for a specific organizational purpose.

In contrast, *temporary workgroups* are task groups specifically created to solve a problem or perform a defined task. They often disband once the assigned purpose or task has been accomplished. Examples are the many temporary committees and task forces that are important components of any organization.[10] Indeed, today's organizations tend to make more use of *cross-functional teams* or *task forces* for special problem-solving efforts. The president of a company, for example, might convene a task force to examine the possibility of implementing flexible work hours for nonmanagerial employees. Usually, such temporary groups appoint chairpersons or heads who are held accountable for results, much as is the manager of a work unit. Another common form is the *project team* that is formed, often cross-functionally, to complete a specific task with a well-defined end point. Examples include installing a new e-mail system and introducing a new product modification.

Information technology is bringing a new type of group into the workplace. This is the **virtual group**, a group whose members convene and work together electronically via computers.[11] In this electronic age, virtual groups are increasingly common in organizations. Facilitated by ever more functional team-oriented software, or *groupware*, members of virtual groups can do the same things as members of face-to-face groups. They can share information, make decisions, and complete tasks. The important role of virtual groups or teams in the high-performance workplace is discussed in the next chapter.

Informal groups emerge without being officially designated by the organization. They form spontaneously through personal relationships or special interests, not by any specific organizational endorsement. *Friendship groups*, for example, consist of persons with natural affinities for one another. They tend to work together, sit together, take breaks together, and even do things together outside of the workplace. *Interest groups* consist of persons who share common interests. These may be job-related interests, such as an intense desire to learn more about computers, or nonwork interests, such as community service, sports, or religion.

Informal groups often help people get their jobs done. Through their network of interpersonal relationships, they have the potential to speed up the workflow as people assist each other in ways that formal lines of authority fail to provide. They also help individuals satisfy needs that are thwarted or otherwise left unmet in a formal group. In these and related ways, informal groups can provide their members with social satisfactions, security, and a sense of belonging.

■ Members of **virtual groups** work together via computer networks.

■ **Informal groups** are unofficial and emerge to serve special interests.

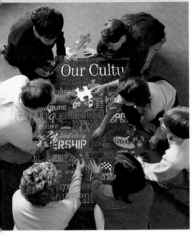

W. L. Gore & Associates

Teams are center stage at this maker of popular GORE-TEX fabrics and other high-tech products. Employees, or associates, engage in creative team-building to help build and maintain the firm's unique corporate culture.

Stages of Group Development

Whether one is part of a formal work unit, a temporary task force, or a virtual team, the group itself passes through a series of life cycle stages.[12] Depending on the stage the group has reached, the leader and members can face very different challenges. Figure 9.1 describes five stages of group development: (1) forming, (2) storming, (3) norming, (4) performing, and (5) adjourning.[13]

Forming Stage

In the *forming stage* of group development, a primary concern is the initial entry of members to a group. During this stage, individuals ask a number of questions as they begin to identify with other group members and with the group itself.

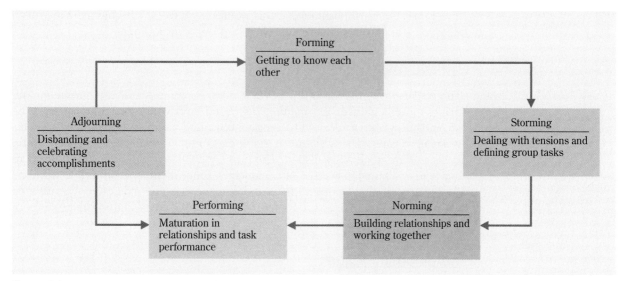

Figure 9.1   Five stages of group development.

Their concerns may include: "What can the group offer me?" "What will I be asked to contribute?" "Can my needs be met at the same time I contribute to the group?" Members are interested in getting to know each other and discovering what is considered acceptable behavior, in determining the real task of the group, and in defining group rules.

Storming Stage

The *storming stage* of group development is a period of high emotionality and tension among the group members. During this stage, hostility and infighting may occur, and the group typically experiences many changes. Coalitions or cliques may form as individuals compete to impose their preferences on the group and to achieve a desired status position. Outside demands, including premature expectations for performance results, may create uncomfortable pressures. In the process, membership expectations tend to be clarified and attention shifts toward obstacles standing in the way of group goals. Individuals begin to understand one another's interpersonal styles, and efforts are made to find ways to accomplish group goals while also satisfying individual needs.

Norming Stage

The *norming stage* of group development, sometimes called initial integration, is the point at which the group really begins to come together as a coordinated unit. The turmoil of the storming stage gives way to a precarious balancing of forces. With the pleasures of a new sense of harmony, group members will strive to maintain positive balance. Holding the group together may become more important to some than successfully working on the group's tasks. Minority viewpoints, deviations from group directions, and criticisms may be discouraged as group members experience a preliminary sense of closeness. Some members may mistakenly perceive this stage as one of ultimate maturity. In fact, a premature sense of accomplishment at this point needs to be carefully managed as a stepping stone to the next-higher level of group development.

Performing Stage

The *performing stage* of group development, sometimes called total integration, marks the emergence of a mature, organized, and well-functioning group. The group is now able to deal with complex tasks and handle internal disagreements in creative ways. The structure is stable, and members are motivated by group goals and are generally satisfied. The primary challenges are continued efforts to improve relationships and performance. Group members should be able to adapt successfully as opportunities and demands change over time. A group that has achieved the level of total integration typically scores high on the criteria of group maturity, shown in Figure 9.2.

Adjourning Stage

A well-integrated group is able to disband, if required, when its work is accomplished. The *adjourning stage* of group development is especially important for the many temporary groups that are increasingly common in the new workplace, including task forces, committees, project teams, and the like. Members of these groups must be able to convene quickly, do their jobs on a tight schedule, and then adjourn—often to reconvene later if needed. Their willingness to disband when the job is done and to work well together in future responsibilities, group or otherwise, is an important long-run test of group success.

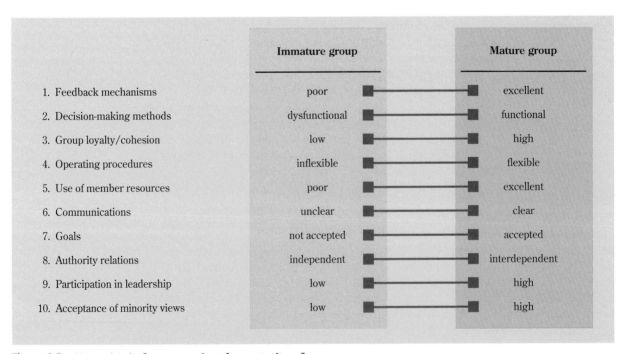

Figure 9.2   Ten criteria for measuring the maturity of a group.

Foundations of Group Performance

To best understand the foundations of group performance, the open-systems model shown in Figure 9.3 is helpful. This figure shows how groups, like organizations, pursue effectiveness by interacting with their environments to transform resource inputs into product outputs.[14]

Group Inputs

The inputs are the initial "givens" in any group situation. They are the foundations for all subsequent action. As a general rule of thumb, one can expect that the stronger the input foundations, the better the chances for long-term group effectiveness. Key group inputs include the nature of the task, goals, rewards, resources, technology, membership diversity, characteristics, and group size.

Tasks   The tasks they are asked to perform can place different demands on groups, with varying implications for group effectiveness. The technical demands of a group's task include its routineness, difficulty, and information requirements. The social demands of a task involve relationships, ego involvement, controversies over ends and means, and the like. Tasks that are complex in technical demands require unique solutions and more information processing; those that are complex in social demands involve difficulties reaching agreement on goals or methods for accomplishing them. Naturally, group effectiveness is harder to achieve when the task is highly complex.[15] To master complexity, group members must apply and distribute their efforts broadly and actively cooperate to achieve desired results. When their efforts lead to success at mastering complex tasks, however, group members tend to experience high levels of satisfaction with the group and its accomplishments.

Goals, Rewards, and Resources   Appropriate goals, well-designed reward systems, and adequate resources are all essential to support long-term performance accomplishments. A group's performance, just like individual perfor-

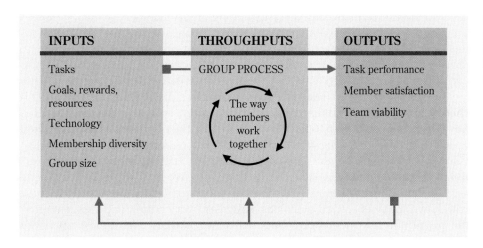

Figure 9.3   The work-group as an open system transforming resource inputs into product outputs.

DaimlerChrysler

New-car models are the result of teamwork. Representatives of engineering, manufacturing, design, finance, marketing, and other areas work in cross-functional teams to bring new products from development to market.

mance, can suffer when goals are unclear, insufficiently challenging, or arbitrarily imposed. It can also suffer if goals and rewards are focused too much on individual-level instead of group-level accomplishments. And it can suffer if adequate budgets, the right facilities, good work methods and procedures, and the best technologies are not available. By contrast, having the right goals, rewards, and resources can be a strong launching pad for group success.

Technology   Technology provides the means to get work accomplished. It is always necessary to have the right technology available for the task at hand. The nature of the workflow technology can also influence the way group members interact with one another while performing their tasks. It is one thing to be part of a group that crafts products to specific customer requests; it is quite another to be part of a group whose members staff one section of a machine-paced assembly line. The former technology permits greater interaction among group members. It will probably create a closer-knit group with a stronger sense of identity than the one formed around one small segment of an assembly line.

Membership Characteristics   To achieve success, a group must have the right skills and competencies available for task performance and problem solving. Although talents alone cannot guarantee desired results, they establish an important baseline of performance potential. It is difficult to overcome the performance limits that result when the input competencies are insufficient to the task at hand.

In *homogeneous groups*, where members are very similar to one another, members may find it very easy to work together. But they may still suffer performance limitations if their collective skills, experiences, and perspectives are not a good match for complex tasks. In *heterogeneous groups*, whose members vary in age, gender, race, ethnicity, experience, culture, and the like, a wide pool of talent and viewpoints is available for problem solving. But this diversity may create difficulties as members try to define problems, share information, and handle interpersonal conflicts. These difficulties may be quite pronounced in the short run or early stages of group development. Once members learn how to work together, however, research confirms that diversity can be turned into enhanced performance potential.[16]

Researchers identify what is called the **diversity–consensus dilemma**. This is the tendency for increasing diversity among group members to make it harder for group members to work together, even though the diversity itself expands the skills and perspectives available for problem solving.[17] The challenge to group effectiveness in a culturally mixed multinational team, for example, is to take advantage of the diversity without suffering process disadvantages.[18]

The blend of personalities is also important in a group or team. The **FIRO-B theory** (with FIRO standing for "fundamental interpersonal orientation") identifies differences in how people relate to one another in groups based on their needs to express and receive feelings of inclusion, control, and affection.[19] Developed by William Schutz, the theory suggests that groups whose members have compatible needs are likely to be more effective than groups whose members are more incompatible. Symptoms of incompatibilities in a group include withdrawn members, open hostilities, struggles over control, and domination of the group by a few members. Schutz states the management implications of the FIRO-B theory this way: "If at the outset we can choose a group of people who

■■■ The **diversity–consensus dilemma** is the tendency for diversity in groups to create process difficulties even as it offers improved potential for problem solving.

■■■ **FIRO-B theory** examines differences in how people relate to one another based on their needs to express and receive feelings of inclusion, control, and affection.

can work together harmoniously, we shall go far toward avoiding situations where a group's efforts are wasted in interpersonal conflicts."[20]

CULTURES AND THE GLOBAL WORKFORCE

MULTICULTURAL DIVERSITY CREATES A HIGH-PERFORMANCE EDGE

With outsourcing a major issue, American companies are looking for the high-performance edge. One source of competitive advantage lies in the country's diversity. Head to head with India, for example, students graduating from American campuses have a better chance to learn about and work with students from other countries and cultures. The same holds true in American high-tech firms, where the likelihood is that talent blends with abilities to speak languages from Mandarin to Russian to Japanese to German, and more. Amar Gupta, professor at MIT, says: "These people can act as bridges to the global economy."

Question: There is little doubt, in theory, that diversity is a potential team asset, but what does it take to turn this potential into real performance advantage?

Another source of diversity within group membership is *status*—a person's relative rank, prestige, or standing in a group. Status within a group can be based on any number of factors, including age, work seniority, occupation, education, performance, or standing in other groups. **Status congruence** occurs when a person's position within the group is equivalent in status to positions held outside of the group. Problems are to be expected when status incongruence is present. In high–power distance cultures such as Malaysia, for example, the chair of a committee is expected to be the highest-ranking member of the group. When present, such status congruity helps members feel comfortable in proceeding with their work. If the senior member is not appointed to head the committee, members are likely to feel uncomfortable and have difficulty working as a group. Similar problems might occur, for example, when a young college graduate is appointed to chair a project group composed of senior and more experienced workers.

Status congruence involves consistency between a person's status within and outside of a group.

Group Size   The size of a group, as measured by the number of its members, can have an impact on group effectiveness. As a group becomes larger, more people are available to divide up the work and accomplish needed tasks. This can boost performance and member satisfaction, but only up to a point. As a group continues to grow in size, communication and coordination problems often set in. Satisfaction may dip, and turnover, absenteeism, and social loafing may increase. Even logistical matters, such as finding time and locations for meetings, become more difficult for larger groups and can hurt performance.[21]

A good size for problem-solving groups is between five and seven members. A group with fewer than five may be too small to adequately share responsibilities. With more than seven, individuals may find it harder to participate and offer ideas. Larger groups are also more prone to possible domination by aggressive members and have tendencies to split into coalitions or subgroups.[22] Groups with an odd number of members find it easier to use majority-vote rules to resolve disagreements. When speed is required, this form of conflict management is useful, and odd-numbered groups may be preferred. But when careful deliberations are required and the emphasis is more on consensus, such as in jury duty or very complex problem solving, even-numbered groups may be more effective unless an irreconcilable deadlock occurs.[23]

Group and Intergroup Dynamics

The effectiveness of any group as an open system (depicted earlier in Figure 9.3) requires more than the correct inputs. It always depends also on how well members work together to utilize these inputs to produce the desired outputs. When we speak about people "working together" in groups, we are dealing with issues of **group dynamics**—the forces operating in groups that affect the way members relate to and work with one another. In the open systems model, group dynamics are the processes through which inputs are transformed into outputs.

■■■ **Group dynamics** are the forces operating in groups that affect the ways members work together.

What Goes On Within Groups   George Homans described a classic model of group dynamics involving two sets of behaviors—required and emergent. In a workgroup, *required behaviors* are those formally defined and expected by the organization.[24] For example, they may include such behaviors as punctuality, respect for customers, and assistance to co-workers. *Emergent behaviors* are those that group members display in addition to what the organization asks of them. They derive not from outside expectations but from personal initiative. Emergent behaviors often include things that people do beyond formal job requirements and that help get the job done in the best ways possible. Rarely can required behaviors be specified so perfectly that they meet all the demands that arise in a work situation. This makes emergent behaviors essential. An example might be someone taking the time to send an e-mail message to an absent member to keep her informed about what happened during a group meeting. The concept of empowerment, often discussed in this book as essential to the high-performance workplace, relies strongly on unlocking this positive aspect of emergent behaviors.

Homans's model of group dynamics also describes member relationships in terms of activities, interactions, and sentiments, all of which have their required and emergent forms. *Activities* are the things people do or the actions they take in groups while working on tasks. *Interactions* are interpersonal communications and contacts. *Sentiments* are the feelings, attitudes, beliefs, or values held by group members. You might think of it this way in the context of a typical student workgroup: members of the group have different attitudes as they interact with one another to accomplish various task- and non-task-related activities.

■■■ **Intergroup dynamics** are relationships between groups cooperating and competing with one another.

What Goes On Between Groups   The term **intergroup dynamics** refers to the dynamics that take place between two or more groups. Organizations ideally operate as cooperative systems in which the various components support one another. In the real world, however, competition and intergroup problems often

Research Insight
Expectations and Newcomer Performance in Groups

As the importance of teams in organizations is increasing, and as more of these teams are temporary and cross-functional types, the problem of managing newcomer socialization into groups becomes increasingly important as well. Gilad Chen and Richard J. Klimoski tested a model of newcomer effectiveness in work teams with a special focus on the performance of knowledge workers. They studied the effects of leaders' expectations on newcomer performance, the effect of newcomers' personal expectations on their performance, and related influences of self-efficacy, work characteristics, and empowerment. Through survey research of some 70 work teams in three IT organizations, Chen and Klimoski found, among other, things that: (1) newcomers' self-effi-

PRACTICAL TIPS FOR NEWCOMER EFFECTIVENESS IN TEAMS

- Expose to early successes.
- Set challenging early goals.
- Model positive role behaviors.
- Assign high-motivation potential tasks.
- Ensure team encouragement and support.

cacy was positively related to their performance expectations, (2) these expectations were positively related to newcomer empowerment, and (3) this empowerment was positively related to newcomer role performance. They conclude that work characteristics, social exchanges, and newcomer empowerment help to explain the effectiveness of newcomers in groups. They suggest that this research should be extended to other types of teams, including management teams and production teams.

Reference: Gilad Chen and Richard J. Klimoski, "The Impact of Expectations on Newcomer Performance in Teams as Mediated by Work Characteristics, Social Exchanges, and Empowerment," *Academy of Management Journal* Vol. 46 (October 2003), pp.591–607.

develop within an organization and have mixed consequences. On the negative side, such as when manufacturing and sales units don't get along, intergroup dynamics may divert energies as members focus more on their animosities toward the other group than on the performance of important tasks.[25] On the positive side, competition among groups can stimulate them to work harder, become more focused on key tasks, develop more internal loyalty and satisfaction, or achieve a higher level of creativity in problem solving. Japanese companies, for example, often use competitive themes to motivate their organizationwide workforces. At Sony, workers once rallied around the slogan: beat Matsushita whatsoever."[26]

Organizations and their managers go to great lengths to avoid the negative and achieve the positive aspects of intergroup dynamics. Groups engaged in destructive competition, for example, can be refocused on a common enemy or a common goal. Direct negotiations can be held among the groups, and members can be trained to work more cooperatively. It is important to avoid win–lose reward systems in which one group must lose something in order for the other to gain. Rewards can be refocused on contributions to the total organization and on how much groups help one another. Also, cooperation tends to increase as interaction between groups increases.

Group Communication Networks

Figure.9.4 depicts three interaction patterns and communication networks that are common within organizations.[27] Having the right interaction pattern and communication network can make a big difference in the way groups function and in the performance results they achieve. Members of *interacting groups* work closely together on tasks in which close coordination of activities takes place. Information flows to everyone. This creates a **decentralized communication network** in which all group members communicate directly and share information with one another. Sometimes these structures are also referred to as all-channel or star communication networks.[28] They work best for groups trying to accomplish complex and nonroutine tasks. They also tend to create high levels of member satisfaction.

■■■ **Decentralized communication networks** link all group members directly with one another.

Members of *coacting groups* work on tasks independently, linked together through some form of central coordination. Groups operating in this fashion divide up the work, and individuals working alone then complete most of it. Each individual's activities are coordinated and results pooled by one person who acts as a central control point. Information flows among the members through the person in charge, who collects and redistributes information and task contributions. This creates a **centralized communication network**, with the central person serving as the "hub." Sometimes these are called wheel or chain communication networks. They work best in groups when tasks are routine and/or easily subdivided. In coacting groups it is usually the central or hub person who ex-

■■■ **Centralized communication networks** link group members through a central control point.

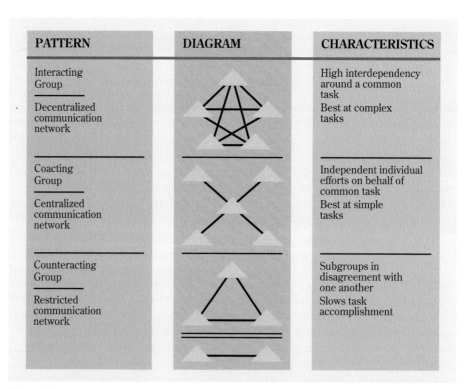

PATTERN	DIAGRAM	CHARACTERISTICS
Interacting Group ———— Decentralized communication network		High interdependency around a common task ———— Best at complex tasks
Coacting Group ———— Centralized communication network		Independent individual efforts on behalf of common task ———— Best at simple tasks
Counteracting Group ———— Restricted communication network		Subgroups in disagreement with one another ———— Slows task accomplishment

Figure 9.4   Interaction patterns and communication networks found in groups.

periences the most satisfaction, since he or she is most involved in and informed about all aspects of the group's work.

Counteracting groups exist when subgroups disagree on some aspect of workplace operations. The subgroups may experience issue-specific disagreements, such as a temporary debate over the best means to achieve a goal, or the disagreements may be of longer-term duration, such as labor–management disputes. In either case, the resulting interaction pattern involves a **restricted communication network** in which polarized subgroups contest one anothers' positions and sometimes maintain antagonistic relations with one another. As would be expected, communication between the counteracting groups is often limited and biased. Problems of destructive competition in the resulting intergroup dynamics are likely.

Restricted communication networks link subgroups that disagree with one another's positions.

Decision Making in Groups

One of the most important activities in any group is decision making, discussed in detail in Chapter 17 as the process of choosing among alternative courses of action. Obviously, the quality and timeliness of decisions made and the processes through which they are arrived at can have an important impact on group effectiveness.

How Groups Make Decisions

Edgar Schein, a noted scholar and consultant, has worked extensively with groups to analyze and improve their decision-making processes.[29] He observes that groups may make decisions through any of the following six methods: lack of response, authority rule, minority rule, majority rule, consensus, or unanimity.

In decision by *lack of response*, one idea after another is suggested without any discussion taking place. When the group finally accepts an idea, all others have been bypassed and discarded by simple lack of response rather than by critical evaluation. In decision by *authority rule*, the chairperson, manager, or leader makes a decision for the group. This can be done with or without discussion and is very time efficient. Whether the decision is a good one or a bad one depends on whether the authority figure has the necessary information and on how well other group members accept this approach. In decision by *minority rule*, two or three people are able to dominate, or "railroad," the group into making a decision with which they agree. This is often done by providing a suggestion and then forcing quick agreement by challenging the group with such statements as: "Does anyone object?… No? Well, let's go ahead then."

One of the most common ways groups make decisions, especially when early signs of disagreement set in, is decision by *majority rule*. Formal voting may take place, or members may be polled to find the majority viewpoint. This method parallels the democratic political system and is often used without awareness of its potential problems. The very process of voting can create coalitions. That is, some people will be "winners" and others will be "losers" when the final vote is tallied. Those in the minority—the "losers"—may feel left out or discarded without having had a fair say. As a result, they may be less enthusiastic about implementing the decision of the "winners." Lingering resentments may impair group effectiveness in the future.

THE EFFECTIVE MANAGER 9.2

Guidelines for Group Consensus

1. Don't argue blindly; consider others' reactions to your points.

2. Don't change your mind just to reach quick agreement.

3. Avoid conflict reductions by voting, coin tossing, and bargaining to avoid conflict.

4. Try to involve everyone in the decision process.

5. Allow disagreements to surface so that information and opinions can be deliberated.

6. Don't focus on winning versus losing; seek alternatives acceptable to all.

7. Discuss assumptions, listen carefully, and encourage participation by everyone.

■■■■ **Consensus** is a group decision that has the expressed support of most members.

Another alternative is decision by *consensus*. Formally defined, **consensus** is a state of affairs whereby discussion leads to one alternative being favored by most members and the other members agreeing to support it. When a consensus is reached, even those who may have opposed the chosen course of action know that they have been listened to and have had a fair chance to influence the outcome. Consensus, as suggested by the guidelines in The Effective Manager 9.2, does not require unanimity. What it does require is the opportunity for any dissenting members to feel that they have been able to speak and that their voices have been heard.[30]

A decision by *unanimity* may be the ideal state of affairs. Here, all group members agree totally on the course of action to be taken. This is a "logically perfect" group decision method that is extremely difficult to attain in actual practice. One reason that groups sometimes turn to authority decisions, majority voting, or even in minority decisions is the difficulty of managing the group process to achieve consensus or unanimity.[31]

Assets and Liabilities of Group Decision Making

The best groups don't limit themselves to just one decision-making method, using it over and over again regardless of circumstances. Instead, they operate in contingency fashion by changing decision methods to best fit the problem and situation at hand. An important leadership skill is helping a group choose the "right" decision method—one providing for a timely and quality decision to which the members are highly committed. The choice among decision methods should be made with a full awareness of these potential assets and liabilities of group decision making.

Potential advantages of group decision making

■■ **Advantages of group decision making**

1. *Information*—more knowledge and expertise is available to solve the problem.

2. *Alternatives*—a greater number of alternatives are examined, avoiding tunnel vision.

3. *Understanding and acceptance*—the final decision is better understood and accepted by all group members.

4. *Commitment*—there is more commitment among all group members to make the final decision work.

Potential disadvantages of group decision making

■■ **Disadvantages of group decision making**

1. *Social pressure to conform*—individuals may feel compelled to go along with the apparent wishes of the group.

2. *Minority domination*—the group's decision may be forced, or "railroaded through," by one individual or a small coalition.

3. *Time delays*—with more people involved in the dialogue and discussion, group decisions usually take longer to make than individual decisions.

Groupthink

An important potential problem when groups make decisions was identified by social psychologist Irving Janis and called **groupthink**—the tendency of members in highly cohesive groups to lose their critical evaluative capabilities.[34] Janis believes that, because highly cohesive groups demand conformity, their members tend to become unwilling to criticize one anothers' ideas and suggestions. Desires to hold the group together and to avoid unpleasant disagreements lead to an overemphasis on agreement and an underemphasis on critical discussion. The possible result is a poor decision. Janis suggests that groupthink played a role in the lack of preparedness of U.S. forces at Pearl Harbor in World War II. It has also been linked to flawed U.S. decision making during the Vietnam War, to events leading up to the space shuttle disasters and, most recently, to failures in American intelligence agencies on the status of weapons of mass destruction in Iraq.

Groupthink is the tendency of cohesive group members to lose their critical evaluative capabilities.

There is no doubt that groupthink is a serious threat to the quality of decision making in groups. Group leaders and members should be alert to the symptoms and be quick to take any necessary action to prevent its occurrence.[35] The Effective Manager 9.3 identifies steps that can be taken to avoid groupthink. For example, President Kennedy chose to absent himself from certain strategy discussions by his cabinet during the Cuban Missile Crisis. Reportedly, this facilitated discussion and helped to improve decision making as the crisis was successfully resolved.

> **THE EFFECTIVE MANAGER 9.3**
> ### How to Avoid Groupthink
>
> - Assign the role of critical evaluator to each group member.
> - Have the leader avoid seeming partial to one course of action.
> - Create subgroups that each work on the same problem.
> - Have group members discuss issues with outsiders and report back.
> - Invite outside experts to observe and react to group processes.
> - Assign someone to be a "devil's advocate" at each meeting.
> - Write alternative scenarios for the intentions of competing groups.
> - Hold "second-chance" meetings after consensus is apparently achieved.

How to Improve Group Decisions

In order to take full advantage of the group as a decision-making resource, care must be taken to manage group dynamics to balance individual contributions and group operations.[36] A particular concern is with the process losses that often occur in free-flowing meetings, such as a committee deliberation or a staff meeting on a specific problem. In these settings the risk of social pressures to conform, domination, time pressures, and even highly emotional debates may detract from the purpose at hand. They are also settings in which special group decision techniques may be used to advantage.[37]

Brainstorming   In **brainstorming**, group members actively generate as many ideas and alternatives as possible, and they do so relatively quickly and without inhibitions. Four rules typically govern the brainstorming process. First, *all criticism is ruled out*. No one is allowed to judge or evaluate any ideas until the idea-generation process has been completed. Second, *"freewheeling" is welcomed*. The emphasis is on creativity and imagination; the wilder or more radical the ideas, the better. Third, *quantity is wanted*. The emphasis is also on the number of ideas; the greater the number, the more likely a superior idea will appear. Fourth, *"piggy-backing" is good*. Everyone is encouraged to suggest how others'

Brainstorming involves generating ideas through "freewheeling" and without criticism.

ideas can be turned into new ideas or how two or more ideas can be joined into still another new idea. Typical results include enthusiasm, involvement, and a free flow of ideas useful in creative problem solving.

ETHICS AND SOCIAL RESPONSIBILITY

TECHNOLOGY, DESIGN, AND COMMITMENT HELP SAVE MANUFACTURING JOBS

It is no secret that communities suffer when they lose jobs as local manufacturers shift operations abroad. New Balance athletic shoes is trying hard to win the battle to keep jobs at home. Owner Jim Davis says, "It's part of the company's culture to design and manufacture here." His strategy involves constant innovation in operations management plus a commitment to people-oriented work practices. Workers at the factory are organized into teams, they swap jobs with one another, and they are trained to do multiple tasks. Working with the latest technologies, they can turn out in 24 minutes shoes that might take three hours in a foreign plant. The corporate Web site says that this commitment to talent and teams helps the firm "to offer creative alternatives to foreign competition."

Question: How can firms best utilize human capital and technology to meet the challenges of foreign competition?

The nominal group technique involves structured rules for generating and prioritizing ideas.

Nominal Group Technique   In any group, there will be times when the opinions of members differ so much that antagonistic arguments will develop during freewheeling discussions. At other times the group will be so large that open discussion and brainstorming are awkward to manage. In such cases, a form of structured group decision making called the **nominal group technique** may be helpful.[38] It puts people in small groups of six to seven members and asks everyone to respond individually and in writing to a "nominal question" such as: "What should be done to improve the effectiveness of this work team?" Everyone is encouraged to list as many alternatives or ideas as they can. Next, participants read aloud their responses to the nominal question in round-robin fashion. The recorder writes each response on large newsprint as it is offered. No criticism is allowed. The recorder asks for any questions that may clarify items on the newsprint. This is again done in round-robin fashion, and no evaluation is allowed. The goal is simply to make sure that everyone present fully understands each response. A structured voting procedure is then used to prioritize responses to the nominal question. The nominal group procedure allows ideas to be evaluated without risking the inhibitions, hostilities, and distortions that may occur in an open meeting.

The Delphi technique involves generating decision-making alternatives through a series of survey questionnaires.

Delphi Technique   The Rand Corporation developed a third group decision approach, the **Delphi technique**, for situations where group members are unable to meet face to face. In this procedure, a series of questionnaires are distributed to a panel of decision makers, who submit initial responses to a decision coordinator. The coordinator summarizes the solutions and sends the summary back to the panel members, along with a follow-up questionnaire. Panel members again send in their responses, and the process is repeated until a consensus is reached and a clear decision emerges.

Computer-Mediated Decision Making   Today's information and computer technologies enable group decision making to take place across great distances with the help of group decision support systems.[39] The growing use of *electronic brainstorming* is one example of the trend toward virtual meetings. Assisted by special software, participants use personal computers to enter ideas at will, either through simultaneous interaction or over a period of time. The software compiles and disseminates the results. Both the nominal group and Delphi techniques also lend themselves to computer mediation. Electronic approaches to group decision making can offer several advantages, including the benefits of anonymity, greater number of ideas generated, efficiency of recording and storing for later use, and ability to handle large groups with geographically dispersed members.

Chapter 9   Study Guide

What is the nature of groups in organizations?

- A group is a collection of people who interact with one another regularly to attain common goals.

- Groups can help organizations by helping their members to improve task performance and experience more satisfaction from their work.

- One way to view organizations is as interlocking networks of groups whose managers serve as leaders in one group and subordinates in another.

- Synergy occurs when groups are able to accomplish more than their members could by acting individually.

- Formal groups are designated by the organization to serve an official purpose; examples are work units, task forces, and committees; informal groups are unofficial and emerge spontaneously because of special interests.

What are the stages of group development?

- Groups pass through various stages in their life cycles, and each stage poses somewhat distinct management problems.

- In the forming stage, groups have problems managing individual entry.

Summary

- In the storming stage, groups have problems managing expectations and status.

- In the norming or initial integration stage, groups have problems managing member relations and task efforts.

- In the performing or total integration stage, groups have problems managing continuous improvement and self-renewal.

- In the adjourning stage, groups have problems managing task completion and the process of disbanding.

What are the foundations of group performance?

- An effective group is one that achieves high levels of task accomplishment and member satisfaction, and achieves viability to perform successfully over the long term.

- As open systems, groups must interact successfully with their environments to obtain resources that are transformed into outputs.

- Group input factors establish the core foundations for effectiveness, including goals, rewards, resources, technology, the task, membership characteristics, and group size.

- Group dynamics are the way members work together to utilize inputs; they are another foundation of group effectiveness.

- Group dynamics are based on the interactions, activities, and sentiments of group members, as well as on the required and emergent ways in which members work together.

- Intergroup dynamics are the forces that operate between two or more groups.

- The disadvantages of intergroup competition can be reduced through management strategies to direct, train, and reinforce groups to pursue cooperative instead of purely competitive actions.

- Groups in organizations work with different interaction patterns and use different communication networks.

- Interacting groups with decentralized networks tend to perform well on complex tasks; coacting groups with centralized networks may do well at simple tasks.

- Restricted communication networks are common in counteracting groups involving subgroup disagreements.

How do groups make decisions?

- Groups can make decisions by lack of response, authority rule, minority rule, majority rule, consensus, and unanimity.

- The potential assets of more group decision making include having more information available and generating more understanding and commitment.

- The potential liabilities of more group decision making include social pressures to conform and greater time requirements.

- Groupthink is the tendency of some groups to lose critical evaluative capabilities.

- Techniques for improving creativity in group decision making include brainstorming, nominal group technique, and the Delphi technique, including computer applications.

Key Terms

Brainstorming (p. 209)
Centralized communication
  network (p. 206)
Consensus (p. 208)
Decentralized communica-
  tion network (p. 206)
Delphi technique (p. 210)
Diversity–consensus
  dilemma (p. 202)

Effective groups (p. 195)
FIRO-B theory (p. 202)
Formal groups (p. 197)
Group dynamics (p. 204)
Groups (p. 194)
Groupthink (p. 209)
Informal groups (p. 198)
Intergroup dynamics
  (p. 204)

Nominal group technique
  (p. 210)
Restricted communication
  network (p. 207)
Social facilitation (p. 196)
Social loafing (p. 196)
Status congruence (p. 203)
Synergy (p. 195)
Virtual groups (p. 198)

Self-Test 9

Multiple Choice

1. The FIRO-B theory addresses _____ in groups. (a) membership compatibili-
ties (b) social loafing (c) dominating members (d) conformity

2. It is during the _____ stage of group development that members begin to really come together as a coordinated unit. (a) storming (b) norming (c) performing
(d) total integration

3. An effective group is defined as one that achieves high levels of task performance,
member satisfaction, and _____. (a) coordination (b) harmony (c) creativity
(d) team viability

4. Task characteristics, reward systems, and group size are all _____ that can
make a difference in group effectiveness. (a) group processes (b) group dynamics
(c) group inputs (d) human resource maintenance factors

5. The best size for a problem-solving group is usually _____ members. (a) no
more than 3 or 4 (b) 5 to 7 (c) 8 to 10 (d) around 12 to 13

6. When two groups are in competition with one another, within each group
_____ may be expected. (a) more in-group loyalty (b) less reliance on the
leader (c) poor task focus (d) more conflict

7. A coacting group is most likely to use a(n) _____ communication network.
(a) interacting (b) decentralized (c) centralized (d) restricted

8. A complex problem is best dealt with by a group using a(n) _____ communication network. (a) all-channel (b) wheel (c) chain (d) linear

9. The tendency of groups to lose their critical evaluative capabilities during decision
making is a phenomenon called _____. (a) groupthink (b) the slippage effect
(c) decision congruence (d) group consensus

10. When a decision requires a high degree of commitment for its implementation, a(n)
_____ decision is generally preferred. (a) authority (b) majority-vote (c)
group consensus (d) railroading

11. What does the Ringlemann effect describe in respect to group behavior? (a) the
tendency of groups to make risky decisions (b) social loafing (c) social facilitation
(d) satisfaction of members' social needs

12. Members of a multinational task force in a large international business should be aware that _____ might initially slow the progress of the group in meeting its task objectives. (a) synergy (b) groupthink (c) the diversity–consensus dilemma (d) intergroup dynamics

13. When a group member engages in social loafing, one of the recommended strategies for dealing with this situation is to _____. (a) forget about it (b) ask another member to force this person to work harder (c) give the person extra rewards and hope he or she will feel guilty (d) better define member roles to improve individual accountability

14. When a person holds a prestigious position outside of a group—for example, is a vice president—but is considered just another member on an employee involvement group that a lower-level supervisor is appointed to head, the person might experience _____. (a) role underload (b) role overload (c) status incongruence (d) the diversity–consensus dilemma

15. If a group is susceptible to groupthink, which of the following strategies is a recommended way to avoid its occurrence? (a) Be sure the leader makes his or her opinions clear. (b) Isolate the group from outside influences. (c) Appoint one member to be a "devil's advocate" at each meeting. (d) Don't let subgroups form to work independently on the problem.

Short Response

16. In what ways are groups good for organizations?

17. What types of formal groups are found in organizations today?

18. What is the difference between required and emergent behaviors in group dynamics?

19. How can intergroup competition be bad for organizations?

Applications Essay

20. Alejandro Puron recently encountered a dilemma in working with his quality circle (QC) team. One of the team members claims that the QC must always be unanimous in its recommendations. "Otherwise," she says, "we will not have a true consensus." Alejandro, the current QC leader, disagrees. He believes that unanimity is desirable but not always necessary to achieve consensus. You are a management consultant specializing in group utilization in organizations. Alejandro calls you for advice. What would you tell him and why?

These learning activities from the *OB Skills Workbook* are suggested for Chapter 9.

OB in Action

CASE	EXPERIENTIAL EXERCISES	SELF-ASSESSMENTS
■ 9. The Forgotten Group Member	■ 17. Annual Pay Raises ■ 18. Serving on the Boundary ■ 19. *Eggs*periental Exercise	■ 9. Group Effectiveness ■ 17. Decision-Making Biases

Plus—special learning experiences from *The Jossey-Bass/Pfeiffer Classroom Collection*

Chapter 10

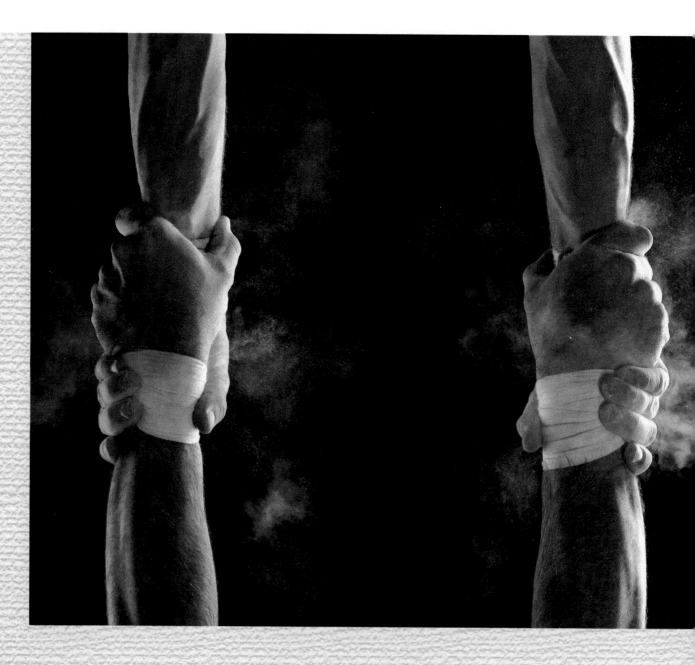

Teamwork and Team Performance

Chapter at a Glance

Teams put creativity to work. This chapter introduces highly motivated and successful teams and teamwork as benchmarks of successful organizations today. As you read Chapter 10, *keep in mind these study questions.*

What's behind innovative organizations? Without a doubt, it takes visionary leadership at the top, the willingness to support entrepreneurship at all levels, and creativity in tapping the new powers of technology. Donald Katz knows this well. He founded Audible.com, the firm that makes it possible for you to listen on demand to an audible digest of issues of *The Wall Street Journal*, programs on NPR, and more. But Katz and others like him know that it takes more than good ideas, risk taking, and technology to build successful, innovative organizations. It takes people, working individually and in teams, to make them possible. Audible.com was brought to life by a team of 35 people working together in atypical ways, including Friday afternoon breaks for darts and refreshments.[1]

"Who needs a boss?" once read the headline of a provocative *Fortune* magazine article. "Not the employees who work in self-managed teams," answered the first paragraph.[2] Since then, the shift of focus from individual jobs to teams and teamwork has been one of the most notable ways in which work is changing today.[3] In most settings, teams and teamwork are considered major, even essential, keys to productivity and improvements in the quality of working life. Even so, success at putting team concepts to work is a major challenge for people used to more traditional ways of working. As more and more jobs are turned over to teams, special problems relating to group dynamics and team building may occur. It is not enough for visionary entrepreneurs, leaders, and managers like Donald Katz to recognize the value of teams and implement creative workgroup designs. They must also carefully nurture and support people and relationships if the groups are to become confident and enduring high-performance teams.

> **"Success at putting team concepts to work is a major challenge."**

Teams and Teamwork

Teams are groups of people who work actively together to achieve a purpose for which they are all accountable.

When we think of the word "teams," a variety of popular sporting teams usually come to mind. Workgroups can also be considered as teams to the extent that they meet the demands of this definition. A **team** is a small group of people with complementary skills who work actively together to achieve a common purpose for which they hold themselves collectively accountable.[4]

Teams are one of the major forces behind today's revolutionary changes in organizations. Management scholar Jay Conger calls the team-based organization the management system of the future, the business world's response to the need for speed in an ever more competitive environment.[5] He cites the example of an American jet engine manufacturer that switched to cross-functional teams instead of traditional functional work units. The firm cut the time required to design and produce new engines by 50 percent. Conger says, "Cross-functional teams are

Leaders on Leadership

LEADERSHIP IN A POST-9/11 WORLD

Rudy Guiliani knows the challenges of leadership firsthand, not just through the responsibilities of his public offices but also in the context of his worst nightmare—dealing with 9/11 as mayor of New York City. This quotation highlights some of the principles that he believes establish true leadership. "A leader is a person of strong beliefs.... A leader is optimistic, solving problems and inspiring hope.... A good leader has a strong sense of ethics and thinks about right and wrong.... A leader undertakes 'relentless preparation' on behalf of his or her organization." According to Guiliani, beliefs and optimism are must-have traits. Relentless preparation is necessary in order to deal with the unanticipated. This all builds on a foundation of courage, teamwork, and communication. He says that leaders should always be able to answer the question: "What is important to me?" And finally, he says: "Ask of yourself, 'Do you love people?' Ultimately it is human beings who perform; you have to love them."

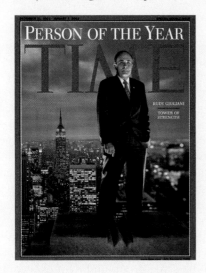

Question: What do you think: Does it take a unique person and special leadership qualities to excel in times of crisis?

speed machines."[6] Clearly, we need to know more about such teams and the processes of teamwork in organizations.

Types of Teams

A major challenge in any organization is to turn the formal groups discussed in the last chapter into true high-performance teams that function well in any of the following settings.[7] First, there are *teams that recommend things*. Established to study specific problems and recommend solutions to them, these teams typically work with a target completion date and disband once their purpose has been fulfilled. They are temporary groups including task forces, ad hoc committees, project teams, and the like. Members of these teams must be able to learn quickly how to work well together, accomplish the assigned task, and make good action recommendations for follow-up work by other people.

Second, there are *teams that run things*. Such management teams consist of people with the formal responsibility for leading other groups. These teams may exist at all levels of responsibility, from the individual work unit composed of a team leader and team members to the top-management team composed of a CEO and other senior executives. Teams can add value to work processes at any level and offer special opportunities for dealing with complex problems and uncertain situations. Key issues addressed by top-management teams include, for example, identifying overall organizational purposes, goals, and values; crafting strategies; and persuading others to support them.[8]

Third, there are *teams that make or do things*. These are functional groups and work units that perform ongoing tasks, such as marketing or manufacturing. Members of these teams must have good long-term working relationships with one another, solid operating systems, and the external support needed to achieve effectiveness over a sustained period of time. They also need energy to keep up the pace and meet the day-to-day challenges of sustained high performance.

The Nature of Teamwork

Teamwork occurs when group members work together in ways that utilize their skills well to accomplish a purpose.

All teams need members who believe in team goals and are motivated to work with others actively to accomplish important tasks—whether those tasks involve recommending things, making or doing things, or running things. Indeed, an essential criterion of a true team is that the members feel "collectively accountable" for what they accomplish.[9] This sense of collective accountability sets the stage for real **teamwork**, with team members actively working together in such a way that all their respective skills are well utilized to achieve a common purpose.[10] A commitment to teamwork is found in the willingness of every member to "listen and respond constructively to views expressed by others, give others the benefit of the doubt, provide support, and recognize the interests and achievements of others."[11] Although such teamwork is essential for any high-performance team, developing and sustaining it are challenging leadership tasks (see The Effective Manager 10.1). The fact is that it takes a lot more work to build a well-functioning team than simply assigning members to the same group and then expecting them to do a great job.[12]

High-performance teams have special characteristics that allow them to excel at teamwork and achieve special performance advantages. First, high-performance teams have strong core values that help guide their attitudes and behaviors in directions consistent with the team's purpose. Such values act as an internal control system for a group or team that can substitute for outside direction and supervisory attention. Second, high-performance teams turn a general sense of purpose into specific performance objectives. Whereas a shared sense of purpose gives general direction to a team, commitment to specific performance results makes this purpose truly meaningful. Specific objectives—such as reducing the time of getting the product to market by half—provide a clear focus for solving problems and resolving conflicts. They also set standards for measuring results and obtaining performance feedback. And they help group members understand the need for collective versus purely individual efforts. Third, members of high-performance teams have the right mix of skills, including technical skills, problem-solving and decision-making skills, and interpersonal skills. Finally, high-performance teams possess creativity. In the new workplace, teams must use their creativity

---

THE EFFECTIVE MANAGER 10.1

How to Create a High-Performing Team

- Communicate high-performance standards.
- Set the tone in the first team meeting.
- Create a sense of urgency.
- Make sure members have the right skills.
- Establish clear rules for team behavior.
- As a leader, model expected behaviors.
- Find ways to create early "successes."
- Continually introduce new information.
- Have members spend time together.
- Give positive feedback.
- Reward high performance.

to assist organizations in continuous improvement of operations and in continuous development of new products, services, and markets.

ETHICS AND SOCIAL RESPONSIBILITY

**LASER MONKS TEAM PURSUES
E-BUSINESS WITH A SOCIAL PURPOSE**

It's not all prayers and meditation for monks at the Cistercian Abbey of Our Lady of Spring Bank in Sparta, Wisconsin. They also spend considerable time online supporting their business of selling refilled printer cartridges. Their group goal is to raise funds to support a variety of social causes and projects, including a special camp for children with HIV and a computer school for street children in Vietnam. The Reverend Bernard McCoy says they are like the "little Davids that came along to play in the Goliath

world." And all the while, the monks are true to ideals that focus on prayer and work. The monks strive to make "quality products" and "do good work with the extra income." In just two years, the monks reached $500,000 in annual sales; the team goal is now to at least quadruple that.

Question: What ideas can you generate for a group to use e-business opportunities to raise funds for community-improvement projects?

Diversity and Team Performance

In order to create and maintain high-performance teams, all of the various elements of group effectiveness discussed in Chapter 9 must be addressed and successfully managed. And as previously noted, membership diversity is an important group input.[13] When teams are relatively *homogeneous*—that is, when members are similar in respect to such things as age, gender, race, experience, ethnicity, and culture—there are certain potential benefits for group dynamics. It will probably be easy for members to quickly build social relationships and engage in the interactions needed for teamwork. On the other hand, a homogeneous membership may limit the group in terms of ideas, viewpoints, and creativity.

When teams are more *heterogeneous*—with members diverse in demography, experiences, lifestyles, cultures, and more—they also have potential benefits. Membership diversity offers a rich pool of information, talent, and varied perspectives that can help improve team problem solving and increase creativity. These assets are especially valuable to teams working on complex and very demanding tasks, but they must be tapped for the team to realize the performance benefits. Research indicates that team diversity can be a source of performance difficulties, especially early in the team's life or stage of development. Problems may occur as interpersonal stresses and conflicts that emerge from the heterogeneity. Working through these dynamics can slow group development and impede relationship building, information sharing, and problem solving.[14] But once such difficulties are resolved, heterogeneous teams are well positioned to take full advantage of the performance advantages of membership diversity.[15] Al-

Charles Schwab & Co.

The financial services giant Charles Schwab & Co. works hard to improve team performance. In meetings, someone serves as "observer" and completes a Plus/Delta list of what went right and wrong. The lists are used companywide to create agendas for change.

though it may take a bit more time and effort to create teamwork from foundations of diversity, longer-term gains in creativity and performance can make it all worthwhile. Unlocking the full potential of teams and teamwork rich in diversity is one of the great advantages of high-performance organizations.

Team Building

Teamwork doesn't always happen naturally in a group. It must be nurtured and supported; it is something that team members and leaders must continuously work hard to achieve. In the sports world, for example, coaches and managers focus on teamwork when building new teams at the start of each season. And as you are aware, even experienced teams often run into problems as a season progresses. Members slack off or become disgruntled; some have performance "slumps"; some are traded to other teams. Even world-champion teams have losing streaks, and the most talented players can lose motivation at times, quibble among themselves, and end up contributing little to team success. When these things happen, the owners, managers, and players are apt to examine their problems, take corrective action to rebuild the team, and restore the teamwork needed to achieve high-performance results.[16]

Workgroups and teams have similar difficulties. When newly formed, they must master challenges as members come together and begin the process of growing and working together as they pass though the various stages of group development. Even when they are mature, most work teams encounter problems of insufficient teamwork at different points in time. This is why a process known as **team building** is so important. This is a sequence of planned activities designed to gather and analyze data on the functioning of a group and to initiate changes designed to improve teamwork and increase group effectiveness.[17] When done well and at the right times, team building is a good way to deal with teamwork difficulties when they occur or to help prevent them from developing in the first place.

■■■ **Team building** is a collaborative way to gather and analyze data to improve teamwork.

How Team Building Works

The action steps and process of continuous improvement highlighted in Figure 10.1 are typical of most team-building approaches. The process begins when someone notices that a problem exists or may develop with team effectiveness. Members then work together to gather data relating to the problem, analyze these data, plan for improvements, and implement the action plans. The entire team-building process is highly collaborative. Everyone is expected to participate actively as group operations are evaluated and decisions are made on what needs to be done to improve the team's functioning in the future. This process can and should become an ongoing part of any team's work agenda. It is an approach to continuous improvement that can be very beneficial to long-term effectiveness.

Team building is participatory, and it is data based. Whether the data are gathered by questionnaire, interview, nominal group meeting, or other creative methods, the goal is to get good answers to such questions as: "How well are we doing in terms of task accomplishment?" "How satisfied are we as individual

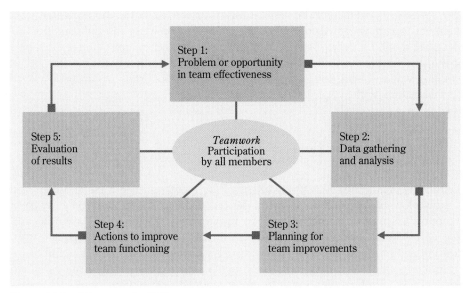

Figure 10.1   The team-building process.

members with the group and the way it operates?" There are a variety of ways for such questions to be asked and answered in a collaborative and motivating manner.

Approaches to Team Building

In the *formal retreat approach*, team building takes place during an off-site "retreat." During this retreat, which may last from one to several days, group members work intensively on a variety of assessment and planning tasks. They are initiated by a review of team functioning using data gathered through survey, interviews, or other means. Formal retreats are often held with the assistance of a consultant, who is either hired from the outside or made available from in-house staff. Team-building retreats offer opportunities for intense and concentrated efforts to examine group accomplishments and operations.

Not all team building is done at a formal retreat or with the assistance of outside consultants. In a *continuous improvement approach*, the manager, team leader, or group members themselves take responsibility for regularly engaging in the team-building process. This method can be as simple as periodic meetings that implement the team-building steps; it can also include self-managed formal retreats. In all cases, the team members commit themselves to continuously monitoring group development and accomplishments and making the day-to-day changes needed to ensure team effectiveness. Such continuous improvement of teamwork is essential to the themes of total quality and total service management so important to organizations today.

The *outdoor experience approach* is an increasingly popular team-building activity that may be done on its own or in combination with other approaches. It places group members in a variety of physically challenging situations that must be mastered through teamwork, not individual work. By having to work together in the face of difficult obstacles, team members are supposed to experience in-

PeopleSoft

PeopleSoft has used videoconferencing technology to help manage the opportunities and problems of explosive growth. One executive says: "It's simply better when you meet someone over video than the phone. It's much more like a live meeting."

creased self-confidence, more respect for others' capabilities, and a greater commitment to teamwork. A popular sponsor of team building through outdoor experience is the Outward Bound Leadership School, but many others exist. For a group that has never done team building before, outdoor experience can be an exciting way to begin; for groups familiar with team building, it can be a way of further enriching the experience.

Improving Team Processes

Like many changes in the new workplace, the increased emphasis on teams and teamwork is a major challenge for people used to more traditional ways of working. As more and more jobs are turned over to teams and as more and more traditional supervisors are asked to function as team leaders, special problems relating to team processes may arise. As teams become more integral to organizations, multiple and shifting memberships can cause complications. Team leaders and members alike must be prepared to deal positively with such issues as introducing new members, handling disagreements on goals and responsibilities, resolving delays and disputes when making decisions, and reducing friction and interpersonal conflicts. Given the complex nature of group dynamics, team building in a sense is never done. Something is always happening that creates the need for further leadership efforts to help improve team processes.

Entry of New Members

Special difficulties are likely to occur when members first get together in a new group or work team, or when new members join an existing one. Problems arise as new members try to understand what is expected of them while dealing with the anxiety and discomfort of a new social setting. New members, for example, may worry about:

**New member
concerns in groups**

> *Participation*—"Will I be allowed to participate?"
> *Goals*—"Do I share the same goals as others?"
> *Control*—"Will I be able to influence what takes place?"
> *Relationships*—"How close do people get?"
> *Processes*—"Are conflicts likely to be upsetting?"

Edgar Schein points out that people may try to cope with individual entry problems in self-serving ways that may hinder group operations.[18] He identifies three behavior profiles that are common in such situations. The *tough battler* is frustrated by a lack of identity in the new group and may act aggressively or reject authority. This person wants answers to the question: "Who am I in this group?" The *friendly helper* is insecure, suffering uncertainties of intimacy and control. This person may show extraordinary support for others, behave in a dependent way, and seek alliances in subgroups or cliques. The friendly helper needs to know whether he or she will be liked. The *objective thinker* is anxious about how personal needs will be met in the group. This person may act in a passive, reflective, and even single-minded manner while struggling with the fit between individual goals and group directions.

Research Insight
National Norms and Ethical Decision Making

For managers in international business, differences in home- and host-country norms can be a source of conflict and tension. Integrative social contracts theory suggests that instead of universalism (consistently applying home-country norms) or relativism (always following local norms), managers can balance local ethical norms with "hypernorms" in ethical decision making. Spicer, Dunfee, and Bailey used ethical scenarios to study the decision intentions of American managers working in the United States and in Russia. Their hypothesis that the influence of national context on ethical decision making would vary between scenarios dealing with local norms and hypernorms was confirmed. Results showed managers in the two samples differing in their ethical evaluations of scenarios involving local norms, such as consideration of

- National context has little effect on ethical attitudes in situations involving hypernorms.
- National context does have an effect on ethical attitudes in situations involving local norms.

stakeholders, bookkeeping and accounting standards, and personal payments and corruption. They showed no differences for hypernorm scenarios involving dangerous health hazards, honoring of promises and formal contracts, and promises of wage payments. The researchers conclude that "expatriate managers distinguish between hypernorm and local norm situations when assessing ethical dilemmas." They call for research to further identify hypernorms and types of local norms. They also admit that their study looks only at "intended" behaviors, not actual ones.

Reference: Andrew Spicer, Thomas W. Dunfee, and Wendy J. Bailey, "Does National Context Matter in Ethical Decision Making? An Empirical Test of Integrative Social Contracts Theory," *Academy of Management Journal* 47(4) Vol. 47 (August 2004), pp 610–620.

Task and Maintenance Leadership

Research in social psychology suggests that the achievement of sustained high performance by groups requires that both "task needs" and "maintenance needs" be met.[19] Even though anyone who is formally appointed as group leader should help fulfill these needs, all members should also contribute helpful activities. This sharing of responsibilities for contributions that move a group forward, called **distributed leadership**, is an important characteristic of any high-performance team.

Figure 10.2 describes group **task activities** as the various things members do that directly contribute to the performance of important group tasks. They include initiating discussion, sharing information, asking information of others, clarifying something that has been said, and summarizing the status of a deliberation.[20] A group will have difficulty accomplishing its objectives when task activities are not well performed. In an effective team, by contrast, members each pitch in to contribute important task leadership as needed.

Maintenance activities support the social and interpersonal relationships among group members. They help a team stay intact and healthy as an ongoing and well-functioning social system. A team member can contribute maintenance leadership by encouraging the participation of others, trying to harmonize dif-

▧ Distributed leadership is the sharing of responsibility for meeting group task and maintenance needs.

▧ Task activities directly contribute to the performance of important tasks.

▧ Maintenance activities support the emotional life of the team as an ongoing social system.

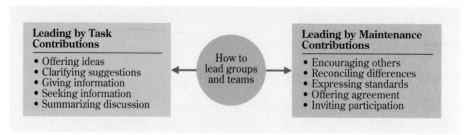

Figure 10.2   Task and maintenance leadership in group team dynamics.

ferences of opinion, praising the contributions of others, and agreeing to go along with a popular course of action. When maintenance leadership is poor, members become dissatisfied with one another, the value of their group membership diminishes, and emotional conflicts may drain energies otherwise needed for task performance. In an effective group, by contrast, maintenance activities help sustain the relationships needed for team members to work well together over time.

In addition to helping meet a group's task and maintenance needs, group members share the additional responsibility of avoiding *disruptive behaviors*—behaviors that harm the group process. Full participation in shared leadership of a team means taking individual responsibility for avoiding the following types of behaviors and helping others do the same:

Disruptive behaviors that harm teams

1. Being overly aggressive toward other members
2. Withdrawing and refusing to cooperate with others
3. Horsing around when there is work to be done
4. Using the group as a forum for self-confession
5. Talking too much about irrelevant matters
6. Trying to compete for attention and recognition

Roles and Role Dynamics

A **role** is a set of expectations for a team member or person in a job.

In groups and teams, new and old members alike need to know what others expect of them and what they can expect from others. A **role** is a set of expectations associated with a job or position on a team. When team members are unclear about their roles or experience conflicting role demands, performance problems can occur. Unfortunately, this is a common problem in groups. But it is also one that can be managed when leaders and members are able to identify role ambiguities and conflicts and to take action to clarify role expectations.

Role ambiguity occurs when someone is uncertain about what is expected of him or her.

Role ambiguity occurs when a person is uncertain about his or her role. To do any job well, people need to know what is expected of them. In new group or team situations, role ambiguities may create problems as members find that their work efforts are wasted or unappreciated by others. Even on mature groups and teams, the failure of members to share expectations and listen to one another may at times create a similar lack of understanding. Being asked to do too much or too little as a team member can also create problems. **Role overload** occurs when too much work is expected of the individual.

Role overload occurs when too much is expected and the individual feels overwhelmed with work; **role underload** occurs when too little is expected and the individual feels underutilized. Members of any group typically benefit from

Role underload occurs when too little work is expected of the individual.

ROLE NEGOTIATION

Issue Diagnosis Form
Messages from   Jim
           to   Diane

If you were to do the following, it would help me to increase my performance:
• Be more receptive to my suggestions for improvement
• Provide help when new software is installed
• Work harder to support my staffing request
• Stop asking for so many detailed progress reports
• Keep providing full information in our weekly meetings
• Keep being available when I need to talk with you

Figure 10.3   A sample role negotiation agreement.

having clear and realistic expectations regarding their expected tasks and responsibilities.

Role conflict occurs when a person is unable to meet the expectations of
others. The individual understands what needs to be done but for some reason
cannot comply. The resulting tension can reduce satisfaction and affect both an
individual's performance and relationships with other group members. There are
four common forms of role conflict. (1) *Intrasender role conflict* occurs when the
same person sends conflicting expectations. (2) *Intersender role conflict* occurs
when different people signal conflicting and mutually exclusive expectations. (3)
Person–role conflict occurs when one's personal values and needs come into
conflict with role expectations. (4) **Interrole conflict** occurs when the expectations of two or more roles held by the same individual become incompatible,
such as the conflict between work and family demands.

> ▰ **Role conflict** occurs when someone is unable to respond to role expectations that conflict with one another.

> **Forms of role conflict**

One way of managing role dynamics in any group or work setting is by *role
negotiation*. This is a process through which individuals negotiate to clarify the
role expectations each holds for the other. Sample results from an actual role negotiation are shown in Figure 10.3. Note the presence of a constructive "give and
take" between the persons negotiating with one another.

Positive Norms

The **norms** of a group or team represent ideas or beliefs about how members
are expected to behave. They can be considered as "rules" or "standards" of conduct.[21] Norms help clarify the expectations associated with a person's membership in a group. They allow members to structure their own behavior and to predict what others will do. They help members gain a common sense of direction,
and they reinforce a desired group or team culture. When someone violates a
group norm, other members typically respond in ways that are aimed at enforcing the norm. These responses may include direct criticisms, reprimands, expul-
sion, and social ostracism.

> ▰ **Norms** are rules or standards for the behavior of group members.

Managers, task force heads, committee chairs, and team leaders should help
their groups adopt positive norms that support organizational goals (see The Ef-

THE EFFECTIVE MANAGER 10.2

Seven Steps to Positive Norms

1. Act as a positive role model.
2. Hold meetings to agree on goals.
3. Select members who can and will perform.
4. Provide support and training for members.
5. Reinforce and reward desired behaviors.
6. Hold meetings for performance feedback.
7. Hold meetings to plan for improvements.

fective Manager 10.2). A key norm in any setting is the *performance norm*, which conveys expectations about how hard group members should work. Other norms are important, too. In order for a task force or a committee to operate effectively, for example, norms regarding attendance at meetings, punctuality, preparedness, criticism, and social behaviors are needed. Groups also commonly have norms regarding how to deal with supervisors, colleagues, and customers, as well as norms establishing guidelines for honesty and ethical behaviors. Norms are often evident in the everyday conversations of people at work. The following examples show the types of norms that operate with positive and negative implications for groups and organizations.[22]

Types of group norms

- *Ethics norms*—"We try to make ethical decisions, and we expect others to do the same" (positive); "Don't worry about inflating your expense account, everyone does it here" (negative).

- *Organizational and personal pride norms*—"It's a tradition around here for people to stand up for the company when others criticize it unfairly" (positive); "In our company, they are always trying to take advantage of us" (negative).

- *High-achievement norms*—"On our team, people always try to work hard" (positive); "There's no point in trying harder on our team, nobody else does" (negative).

- *Support and helpfulness norms*—"People on this committee are good listeners and actively seek out the ideas and opinions of others" (positive); "On this committee it's dog-eat-dog and save your own skin" (negative).

- *Improvement and change norms*—"In our department people are always looking for better ways of doing things" (positive); "Around here, people hang on to the old ways even after they have outlived their usefulness" (negative).

Team Cohesiveness

Cohesiveness is the degree to which members are attracted to a group and motivated to remain a part of it.

The **cohesiveness** of a group or team is the degree to which members are attracted to and motivated to remain part of it.[23] Persons in a highly cohesive group value their membership and strive to maintain positive relationships with other group members. In this sense, cohesive groups and teams are good for their members. In contrast to less cohesive groups, members of highly cohesive ones tend to be more energetic when working on group activities, less likely to be absent, and more likely to be happy about performance success and sad about failures. Cohesive groups generally have low turnover and satisfy a broad range of individual needs, often providing a source of loyalty, security, and esteem for their members.

Cohesiveness tends to be high when group members are similar in age, attitudes, needs, and backgrounds. It also tends to be high in groups of small size, where members respect one another's competencies, agree on common goals, and work on interdependent tasks. Cohesiveness tends to increase when groups are physically isolated from others and when they experience performance success or crisis.

Conformity to Norms   Even though cohesive groups are good for their members, they may or may not be good for the organization. This will depend on the match of cohesiveness with performance norms. Figure 10.4 shows the performance implications of a basic *rule of conformity* in group dynamics: the more cohesive the group, the greater the conformity of members to group norms.

When the performance norms are positive in a highly cohesive workgroup or team, the resulting conformity to the norm should have a positive effect on task performance as well as member satisfaction. This is a best-case situation for everyone. When the performance norms are negative in a highly cohesive group, however, the same power of conformity creates a worst-case situation for the organization. Although team members are highly motivated to support group norms, the organization suffers from poor performance results. In between these two extremes are mixed-case situations in which a lack of cohesion fails to rally strong conformity to the norm. With its strength reduced, the outcome of the norm is somewhat unpredictable and performance will most likely fall on the moderate or low side.

How to Influence Cohesiveness   Team leaders and managers must be aware of the steps they can take to build cohesiveness, such as in a group that has positive norms but suffers from low cohesiveness. They must also be ready to deal with situations when cohesiveness adds to the problems of negative and hard-to-change performance norms. Figure 10.5 shows how group cohesiveness can be increased or decreased by making changes in group goals, membership composition, interactions, size, rewards, competition, location, and duration.

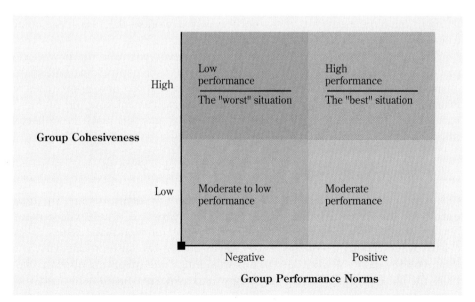

Figure 10.4   How cohesiveness and conformity to norms affect group performance.

How to Decrease Cohesion	TARGETS	How to Increase Cohesion
Create disagreement	Goals	Get agreement
Increase heterogeneity	Membership	Increase homogeneity
Restrict within team	Interactions	Enhance within team
Make team bigger	Size	Make team smaller
Focus within team	Competition	Focus on other teams
Reward individual results	Rewards	Reward team results
Open up to other teams	Location	Isolate from other teams
Disband the team	Duration	Keep team together

Figure 10.5 **Ways to increase and decrease group cohesiveness.**

Teams in the High-Performance Workplace

When it was time to reengineer its order-to-delivery process to eliminate an uncompetitive and costly 26-day cycle time, Hewlett-Packard turned to a team. In just nine months, they slashed the time to eight days, improved service, and cut costs. How did they do it? Team leader Julie Anderson said: "We took things away: no supervisors, no hierarchy, no titles, no job descriptions...the idea was to create a sense of personal ownership." Said a team member: "No individual is going to have the best idea, that's not the way it works—the best ideas come from the collective intelligence of the team."[24]

This isn't an isolated example. Organizations everywhere in the new workplace are finding creative ways of using teams to solve problems and make changes to improve performance. The catchwords of these new approaches to teamwork are empowerment, participation, and involvement, and the setting is increasingly described as an organization that looks and acts much more lateral or horizontal than vertical.[25]

Problem-Solving Teams

▪ Members of **employee involvement teams** meet regularly to examine work-related problems and opportunities.

▪ Members of a **quality circle** meet regularly to find ways for continuous improvement of quality operations.

One way organizations can use teams is in creative problem solving. The term **employee involvement team** applies to a wide variety of teams whose members meet regularly to collectively examine important workplace issues. They discuss ways to enhance quality, better satisfy customers, raise productivity, and improve the quality of work life. In this way, employee involvement teams mobilize the full extent of workers' know-how and gain the commitment needed to fully implement solutions.

A special type of employee involvement group is the **quality circle**, or QC for short. It is a small group of persons who meet periodically (e.g., an hour or so, once a week) to discuss and develop solutions for problems relating to quality, productivity, or cost.[26] QCs are popular in organizations around the world but cannot be seen as panaceas for all of an organization's ills. To be successful, members of QCs should receive special training in group dynamics, information gathering, and problem analysis techniques. Leaders of quality circles should also be trained in participation and team building; QCs work best in organizations that place a clear emphasis on quality in their mission and goals, promote a culture that supports participation and empowerment, encourage trust and willingness to share important information, and develop a "team spirit."

PEOPLE AND TECHNOLOGY

**PEOPLE SKILLS LEAD THE WAY
IN HIGH-TECHNOLOGY PROJECT TEAMS**

Even the best computer programmers are worrying about their jobs these days. But, as always, those with the best people skills have a competitive advantage. When Hal Reed was hired by cMarkets, his new boss and company founder Jon Carson knew he was hiring someone with more than technical skills. Says Carson: "He had great strategic thinking skills; you can't outsource that." Many programmers are realizing that they can help protect their jobs and expand their career opportunities by developing the people skills that lead to success in project management. In other words, it's not just the ability to write programs that counts; it's the ability to lead teams of programmers whose members may be scattered around the world.

Question: What are the special challenges of leading a team project when the members are working virtually from homes in different countries?

Cross-Functional Teams

In today's organizations, teams are essential components in the achievement of more horizontal integration and better lateral relations. The **cross-functional team**, consisting of members representing different functional departments or work units, plays an important role in this regard. Traditionally, many organizations have suffered from what is often called the **functional silos problem**. This problem occurs when members of functional units stay focused on matters internal to their function and minimize their interactions with members dealing with other functions. In this sense, the functional departments or work units create artificial boundaries, or "silos," that discourage rather than encourage more integrative thinking and active coordination with other parts of the organization.

The new emphasis on team-based organizations, discussed often in this book, is designed to help break down this problem and improve lateral communication.[27] Members of cross-functional teams can solve problems with a positive combination of functional expertise and integrative or total systems thinking. They do so with the great advantages of better information and more speed.[28] Boeing, for example, used this concept to great advantage in designing and bringing to market the 777 passenger jet. A complex network of cross-functional teams brought together design engineers, mechanics, pilots, suppliers, and even customers to manage the "design/build" processes.

■ **Cross-functional teams** bring together persons from different functions to work on a common task.

■ The **functional silos problem** occurs when people fail to communicate across functions.

Virtual Teams

▥ A **virtual team** convenes and operates with members linked together electronically via networked computers.

It used to be that teamwork was confined in concept and practice to those circumstances in which members could meet face to face. The advent of new technologies and sophisticated computer programs known as groupware has now changed all that. **Virtual teams**, introduced in the last chapter as ones whose members meet at least part of the time electronically and with computer support, are a fact of life in many organizations today.[29] The real world of work in businesses and other organizations involves a variety of electronic communications that allow people, often separated by vast geographic distances, to work together through computer mediation, often separated by vast geographical space. *Groupware* in a variety of popular forms easily allows for virtual meetings and group decision making in a variety of situations.[30] All of this is further supported by advancements in conferencing and collaboration, including audio, data, and videoconferencing alternatives.

Virtual teams offer a number of potential advantages. They bring cost-effectiveness and speed to teamwork when members cannot easily meet face to face. They also bring the power of the computer to bear on typical team needs for information processing and decision making.[31] When the computer is the "go-between" among virtual team members, however, group dynamics can be different from those of face-to-face settings. Although technology makes communication possible among people separated by great distance, the team members may have very little, if any, direct "personal" contact. Virtual teams may suffer from less social rapport and less direct interaction among members. Whereas computer mediation may have the advantage of focusing interaction and decision making on facts and objective information rather than emotional considerations, it may also increase risks as group decisions are made in a limited social context.

CULTURES AND THE GLOBAL WORKFORCE

VIRTUAL TEAMS HELP ORGANIZATIONS HARNESS TALENT FROM AROUND THE WORLD

Virtual teams are an everyday phenomenon at Texas Instruments, where physical distance doesn't stop people from working together. On any given day you can find computer designers working together from all over the world—linked via computers to pool ideas and create new products. Talented engineers in Bangalore, India, may work with other group members in Japan and Texas to develop a new chip. Employees in Bangalore work on complex chip designs. When the designs are finished, they are sent via computer to Texas for fabrication. They go back to Bangalore for any required "debugging." Says a TI group vice president, "Problems that used to take three years now take a year."

Question: Based on your experience, what special efforts by members are necessary to achieve success for virtual teams?

Just as with any form of teamwork, virtual teams rely on the efforts and contributions of their members as well as organizational support to achieve effectiveness. Teamwork in any form always takes work. The same stages of development, the same input considerations, and the same process requirements are likely to apply in a virtual team as with any team. Where possible, the advantages of face-to-face and virtual teamwork should be combined for maximum benefit. The computer technology should also be appropriate, and team members should be well trained in using it.[32]

Self-Managing Teams

A high-involvement workgroup design that is increasingly well established today is known as the **self-managing team**. These are small groups empowered to make the decisions needed to manage themselves on a day-to-day basis.[33] Although there are different variations of this theme, Figure 10.6 shows that members of a true self-managing work team make decisions on scheduling work, allocating tasks, training for job skills, evaluating performance, selecting new team members, and controlling quality of work. Members are collectively held accountable for the team's overall performance results.

Self-managing teams are empowered to make decisions about planning, doing, and evaluating their daily work.

How Self-Managing Teams Work   Self-managing teams, also called self-directed teams or empowered teams, are permanent and formal elements in the organizational structure. They replace the traditional workgroup headed by a supervisor. What differentiates self-managing teams from the more traditional workgroup is that the team members assume duties otherwise performed by a

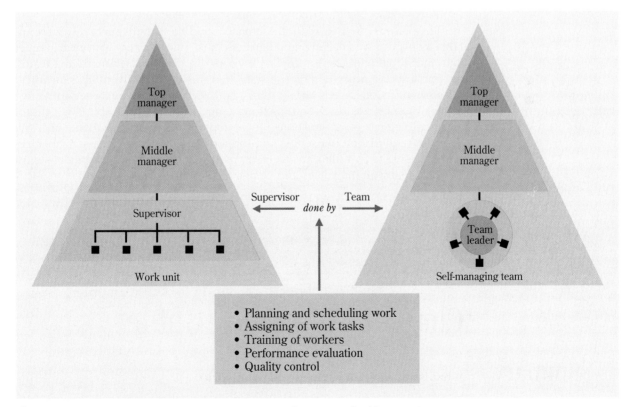

Figure 10.6   **Organizational and management implications of self-managing teams.**

manager or first-line supervisor. The team members, not a supervisor, perform and are collectively accountable for such activities as planning and work scheduling, performance evaluation, and quality control.

A self-managing team should probably include between 5 and 15 members. The teams must be large enough to provide a good mix of skills and resources but small enough to function efficiently. Members must have substantial discretion in determining work pace and in distributing tasks. This is made possible, in part, by **multiskilling**, whereby team members are trained in performing more than one job on the team. In self-managing teams, each person is expected to perform many different jobs—even all of the team's jobs—as needed. The more skills someone masters, the higher the base pay. Team members themselves conduct the job training and certify one another as having mastered the required skills.

Operational Implications of Self-Managing Teams   The expected benefits of self-managing teams include productivity and quality improvements, production flexibility and faster response to technological change, reduced absenteeism and turnover, and improved work attitudes and quality of work life. But these results are not guaranteed. Like all organizational changes, the shift to self-managing teams can encounter difficulties. Structural changes in job classifications and management levels will have consequent implications for supervisors and others used to more traditional ways. Simply put, with a self-managing team you don't need the formal first-line supervisor anymore. The possible extent of this change is shown in Figure 10.6, where the first level of supervisory management in the traditional organization has been eliminated and replaced by self-managing teams. Note also that the supervisor's tasks are reallocated to the team.

For persons used to more traditional work, the new team-based work arrangements can be challenging. Managers must learn to deal with teams rather than individual workers; for any supervisors displaced by self-managing teams, the implications are even more personal and threatening. Given this situation, a question must be asked: Should all organizations operate with self-managing teams? The best answer is "no." Self-managing teams are probably not right for all organizations, work situations, and people. They have great potential, but they also require a proper setting and support. At a minimum, the essence of any self-managing team—high involvement, participation, and empowerment—must be consistent with the values and culture of the organization.

■ **Multiskilling** occurs when team members are trained in skills needed to perform different jobs.

Chapter 10   Study Guide

Summary

What is the nature of teams and teamwork?

- A team is a small group of people working together to achieve a common purpose for which they hold themselves collectively accountable.

- High-performance teams have core values, clear performance objectives, the right mix of skills, and creativity.

- Teamwork occurs when members of a team work together so that their skills are well utilized to accomplish common goals.

What is team building?

- Team building is a data-based approach to analyzing group performance and taking steps to improve it in the future.

- Team building is participative and engages all group members in collaborative problem solving and action.

How does team building improve group performance?

- Individual entry problems are common when new teams are formed and when new members join existing teams.

- Task leadership involves initiating and summarizing, making direct contributions to the group's task agenda; maintenance leadership involves gatekeeping and encouraging, helping to support the social fabric of the group over time.

- Role difficulties occur when expectations for group members are unclear, overwhelming, underwhelming, or conflicting.

- Norms, as rules or standards for what is considered appropriate behavior by group members, can have a significant impact on group processes and outcomes.

- Members of highly cohesive groups value their membership and are very loyal to the group; they also tend to conform to group norms.

How do teams contribute to the high-performance workplace?

- An employee involvement team is one whose members meet regularly to address important work-related problems and opportunities.

- Members of a quality circle, a popular type of employee involvement group, meet regularly to deal with issues of quality improvement in work processes.

- Self-managing teams are small workgroups that operate with empowerment and essentially manage themselves on a day-to-day basis.

- Members of self-managing teams typically plan, complete, and evaluate their own work; train and evaluate one another in job tasks; and share tasks and responsibilities.

- Self-managing teams have structural and management implications for organizations because they largely eliminate first-line supervisors.

Key Terms

Cohesiveness (p. 228)
Cross-functional teams (p. 231)
Distributed leadership (p. 225)
Employee involvement team (p. 230)

Functional silos problem (p. 231)
Maintenance activities (p. 225)
Multiskilling (p. 234)
Norms (p. 227)
Quality circle (p. 230)

Role (p. 226)
Role ambiguity (p. 226)
Role conflict (p. 227)
Role overload (p. 226)
Role underload (p. 226)
Self-managing team (p. 233)

Task activities (p. 225)   Teams (p. 218)   Virtual team (p. 232)
Team building (p. 222)   Teamwork (p. 220)

Self-Test 10

Multiple Choice

1. A group with _____ may experience special difficulty becoming a high-performance team. (a) specific performance objectives (b) high creativity (c) narrow mix of membership skills (d) strong core values

2. The team-building process can best be described as participative, data based and _____. (a) action oriented (b) leader centered (c) process-oriented (d) dysfunctional

3. When a new team member is anxious about questions such as "Will I be able to influence what takes place?" the underlying issue is one of _____. (a) relationships (b) goals (c) processes (d) control

4. A person facing an ethical dilemma involving differences between personal values and the expectations of the team is experiencing _____ conflict. (a) person–role (b) intrasender role (c) intersender role (d) interrole

5. The statement "On our team, people always try to do their best" is an example of a(n) _____ norm. (a) support and helpfulness (b) high-achievement (c) organizational pride (d) organizational improvement

6. Highly cohesive teams tend to _____. (a) be bad for organizations (b) be good for their members (c) have more social loafing among members (d) have greater membership turnover

7. To increase team cohesiveness, one would _____. (a) make the group bigger (b) increase membership diversity (c) isolate the group from others (d) relax performance pressures

8. Self-managing teams _____. (a) reduce the number of different job tasks members need to master (b) largely eliminate the need for a traditional supervisor (c) rely heavily on outside training to maintain job skills (d) add another management layer to overhead costs

9. Which statement about self-managing teams is correct? (a) They can improve performance but not satisfaction. (b) They should have limited decision-making authority. (c) They should operate without any team leaders. (d) They should let members plan their own work schedules.

10. A team member who does a good job at summarizing discussion, offering new ideas, and clarifying points made by others is providing leadership by contributing _____ activities to the group process. (a) required (b) disruptive (c) task (d) maintenance

11. One of the big differences between a group and a real team is that a team _____. (a) has fewer than 7 members (b) uses a designated leader (c) has a sense of collective accountability (d) relies on consensus decision making

12. In the team-building process _____ analyzes and develops action plans in response to data on group functioning. (a) all of the members (b) the team leader (c) higher management (d) an outside consultant

13. When someone is being aggressive, makes inappropriate jokes, or talks about irrele-

vant matters in a group meeting, these are all examples of _____. (a) dysfunctional behaviors (b) maintenance activities (c) task activities (d) role dynamics

14. If you heard from an employee of a local bank that "it's a tradition here for us to stand up and defend the bank when someone criticizes it," you could assume that the bank employees have strong _____ norms. (a) support and helpfulness (b) organizational and personal pride (c) ethical and social responsibility (d) improvement and change

15. What can be predicted when you know that a work group is highly cohesive? (a) high-performance results (b) high member satisfaction (c) positive performance norms (d) status congruity

Short Response

16. Describe the steps in a typical team-building process?

17. How can a team leader help build positive group norms?

18. How do cohesiveness and conformity to norms influence group performance?

19. What are members of self-managing teams typically expected to do?

Applications Essay

20. While surfing the Internet, you encounter this note posted in your favorite discussion group: "Help! I have just been assigned to head a new product design team at my company. The division manager has high expectations for the team and me, but I have been a technical design engineer for four years since graduating from university. I have never 'managed' anyone, let alone led a team. The manager keeps talking about her confidence that I will create a 'high-performance team.' Does anyone out there have any tips to help me master this challenge? Help! [signed] Galahad." As a good citizen of the Internet, you decide to answer. What message will you send out?

OB in Action

These learning activities from *The OB Skills Workbook* are suggested for Chapter 10.

CASE	EXPERIENTIAL EXERCISES	SELF-ASSESSMENTS
■ 10. NASCAR's Racing Teams	■ 20. Scavenger Hunt— Team Building	■ 9. Group Effectiveness
	■ 21. Work Team Dynamics	■ 13. Empowering Others
	■ 22. Identifying Group Norms	
	■ 23. Workgroup Culture	
	■ 24. The Hot Seat	

Plus—special learning experiences from *The Jossey-Bass/Pfeiffer Classroom Collection*

Chapter 11

Leadership

Chapter at a Glance

In the chapters in Part 1, we discussed managers and management functions, roles, activities, and skills. The question to ask now is: How are leaders and leadership linked to all of this? As you read Chapter 11, *keep in mind these study questions*:

WHAT IS LEADERSHIP, AND HOW DOES IT DIFFER FROM MANAGEMENT?

Trait Theories

Behavioral Theories

WHAT ARE SITUATIONAL CONTINGENCY APPROACHES TO LEADERSHIP?

Fiedler's Leadership Contingency Theory

House's Path–Goal Theory of Leadership

Substitutes for Leadership

WHAT ARE ATTRIBUTIONAL APPROACHES TO LEADERSHIP?

Leadership Prototypes

Exaggeration of the Leadership Difference

WHAT ARE SOME EMERGING LEADERSHIP PERSPECTIVES, AND WHY ARE THEY ESPECIALLY IMPORTANT IN TODAY'S ORGANIZATION?

Charismatic Approaches

Transformational Versus Transactional Approaches

Leadership in Self-Managing Work Teams

Emerging Leadership Issues

REVIEW IN END-OF-CHAPTER STUDY GUIDE

How hard it is to keep from being king,
When it's in you and in the situation.
And that is half the trouble with the world,
(Or more than half I'm half inclined to say),
—ROBERT FROST

The Tao gives birth to all actions.
Character raises them, matter shapes
them, circumstances complete them.
—TAO TE CHING
(DAO-DEJING, 51)

As Frost points out, some people feel compelled to lead because there is an inner desire and because situations or circumstances make this possible. Sometimes, however, the results are not favorable. In contrast, the Chinese classic Tao Te Ching suggests that leadership emerges from a state of being that transcends the individual leader and is then shaped by a mixture of his or her character and circumstances.[1] Conversely, Western views assume that leaders derive their influence from a transcendent (superior or supreme) source, such as the U.S. Constitution, the church, or the corporation. When leadership is consistent with the Tao, the interaction between inner impulses and outer conditions emphasizes factors associated with effective leadership. When such circumstances that support leadership emerge, the leaders may lead wisely—and so it is, especially with leadership in virtual and self-managed teams (which, you recall from Chapter 10, call for a special and increasingly important kind of leadership).

As you also recall, virtual teams are made up of people located anywhere throughout the world. They seldom or never meet together and instead use information technologies and much communication to tie together time and space differences. Global virtual teams can pass work from East to West as the earth rotates and maintain the team's effort around the clock. Thus, leadership must be exerted through time and space—it must stretch its boundaries to match the elasticity of work throughout the world.

Taoism is especially relevant for virtual team leadership because of its focus on understanding and managing change—and so it was with ancient Chinese leaders. They used Taoists as advisers. Today, Chinese leaders use Taoist principles. While difficult to define and explain, the Tao can be experienced and realized, and such experience can lead to balance, harmony, and contentment. For us, this might be called "going with the flow": if a leader reaches this state, he or she feels a sense of well-being, mastery, and heightened self-esteem.

These notions and more are covered in this chapter, after we discuss the more basic notions originally emanating from the West—the United States to be exact.

> "Some people feel compelled to lead because there is an inner desire and because circumstances make this possible."

Leadership and Management

We start by considering once again the Part 1 discussion of managers and management functions, roles, activities, and skills. Then we ask, "How are leaders and leadership linked to all this?"

Currently, controversy has arisen over whether leaders are different from managers or whether management is different from leadership and, if so, how. One way of making these differentiations is to argue that the role of *management* is to promote stability or to enable the organization to run smoothly, whereas the role of *leadership* is to promote adaptive or useful changes.[2] Persons in managerial positions could be involved with both management and leadership activities, or they could emphasize one activity at the expense of the other. Both management and leadership are needed, however, and if managers don't assume responsibility for both, then they should ensure that someone else handles the neglected activity.

For our purpose, we treat **leadership** as a special case of interpersonal influence that gets an individual or group to do what the leader or manager wants done. The broader influence notions, of which leadership is a part, are dealt with in Chapter 12. Leadership appears in two forms: (1) *formal leadership*, which is exerted by persons appointed to or elected to positions of formal authority in organizations, and (2) *informal leadership*, which is exerted by persons who become influential because they have special skills that meet the resource needs of others. Although both types are important in organizations, this chapter will emphasize formal leadership.

> **Leadership** is a special case of interpersonal influence that gets an individual or group to do what the leader wants done.

The leadership literature is vast—10,000 or so studies at last count—and consists of numerous approaches.[3] We have grouped these into trait and behavioral theory perspectives, situational contingency perspectives, attributional leadership perspectives, and "new leadership" perspectives—including charismatic approaches, transformational approaches, and leadership of self-directing work teams. These new leadership theories are especially important for high-performance organizations. Within each of these perspectives are several models. While each of these models may be useful to you in a given work setting, we invite you to mix and match them as necessary in your setting, just as we earlier did with the motivational models in Chapter 6. This is a trial-and-error process, but it is a good way to bring together the contributions from each model in a combination that meets your needs as a manager.

Trait Theories

Trait perspectives assume that traits play a central role in differentiating between leaders and nonleaders (leaders must have the "right stuff")[4] or in predicting leader or organizational outcomes. The *great person–trait approach* reflects this leader/nonleader difference and is the earliest approach in studying leadership, having been introduced more than a century ago. What traits differentiated "great persons" from the masses? (For example, how did Catherine the Great differ from her subjects?)[5] Later studies examined both leader/nonleader differences and trait predictions of outcomes. For various reasons, including inadequate theorizing and trait measurement, the studies were not successful enough to provide consistent findings.

> **Trait perspectives** assume that traits play a central role in differentiating between leaders and nonleaders or in predicting leader or organizational outcomes.

More recent work has yielded more promising results. A number of traits have been found that help identify important leadership strengths (see Figure 11.1). As it turns out, most of these traits also tend to predict leadership outcomes.[6]

Leaders tend to be energetic and to operate on an even keel. They crave power not as an end in itself but as a means to achieving a vision or desired goals. Leaders are also very ambitious and have a high need for achievement. At the same time, they have to be emotionally mature enough to recognize their own strengths and weaknesses, and they are oriented toward self-improvement. Furthermore, as shown by The Caring General, to be trusted they must have integrity; without trust, they cannot hope to maintain the loyalty of their followers. Leaders also must not be easily discouraged. They need to stick to a chosen course of action and to push toward goal accomplishment. At the same time, they must be cognitively sharp enough to deal well with the large amount of information they receive. However, they do not need to be brilliant; they just need to show above-average intelligence. In addition, leaders must have a good understanding of their social setting. Finally, they must possess extensive specific knowledge concerning their industry, firm, and job.

ETHICS AND SOCIAL RESPONSIBILITY

THE CARING GENERAL

"When I was 8 years old, I wanted to be an officer in the United States Army. As an officer, your word was your bond. You were judged by your word, not by your skin color." Today, at 50, Brigadier General Robert Crear is commander and division engineer of the Army Corps of Engineers, Southwestern Division, in Dallas. Before that, he had the Vicksburg, Mississippi, command. His major assignment was to help with various Army and community projects. He joined the Rotary, got on the United Way board of directors, and visited older people in the community. Everywhere he went, he "gave back." Vicksburg was, indeed, where he was born and raised. These caring ways carried over to Iraq, where he oversaw extinguishing the oil-field fires set by the Iraqi soldiers in 1991 as the U.S. military stormed the country and then repaired the lines.

Question: How might his Corps of Engineers command experience and training affect his leadership, and how might his leadership affect his command?

Behavioral Theories

■ The **behavioral perspective** assumes that leadership is central to performance and other outcomes.

Like the trait perspective covered above, the **behavioral perspective** assumes that leadership is central to performance and other outcomes. In this case, however, instead of underlying traits, behaviors are considered. Two classic research programs—at the University of Michigan and Ohio State University—provide useful insights into leadership behaviors.

Michigan Studies In the late 1940s, researchers at the University of Michigan introduced a research program on leadership behavior. They sought to identify the leadership pattern that results in effective performance. From interviews of

Energy and adjustment or stress tolerance: Physical vitality and emotional resilience

Prosocial power motivation: A high need for power exercised primarily for the benefit of others

Achievement orientation: Need for achievement, desire to excel, drive to success, willingness to assume responsibility, concern for task objectives

Emotional maturity: Well-adjusted, does not suffer from severe psychological disorders.

Self-confidence: General confidence in self and in the ability to perform the job of a leader

Integrity: Behavior consistent with espoused values; honest, ethical, trustworthy

Perseverance or tenacity: Ability to overcome obstacles; strength of will

Cognitive ability, intelligence, social intelligence: Ability to gather, integrate, and interpret information; intelligence, understanding of social setting

Task-relevant knowledge: Knowledge about the company, industry, and technical aspects

Flexibility: Ability to respond appropriately to changes in the setting

Figure 11.1 Traits with positive implications for successful leadership.

high- and low-performing groups in different organizations, the researchers derived two basic forms of leader behaviors: employee centered and production centered. Employee-centered supervisors are those who place strong emphasis on their subordinates' welfare. In contrast, production-centered supervisors are more concerned with getting the work done. In general, employee-centered supervisors were found to have more productive workgroups than did the production-centered supervisors.[7]

These behaviors may be viewed on a continuum, with employee-centered supervisors at one end and production-centered supervisors at the other. Sometimes, the more general terms *human relations oriented* and *task oriented* are used to describe these alternative leader behaviors.

Ohio State Studies   At about the same time as the Michigan studies, an important leadership research program was started at Ohio State University. A questionnaire was administered in both industrial and military settings to measure subordinates' perceptions of their superiors' leadership behavior. The researchers identified two dimensions similar to those found in the Michigan studies: **consideration** and **initiating structure**.[8] A highly considerate leader is sensitive to people's feelings and, much like the employee-centered leader, tries to make things pleasant for his or her followers. In contrast, a leader high in initiating structure is more concerned with defining task requirements and other aspects of the work agenda; he or she might be seen as similar to a production-centered supervisor. These dimensions are related to what people sometimes refer to as socioemotional and task leadership, respectively.

At first, the Ohio State researchers believed that a leader high in consideration, or socioemotional warmth, would have more highly satisfied or better-performing subordinates. Later results indicated that leaders should be high in both consideration and initiating structure, however. This dual emphasis is reflected in the leadership grid approach.

The Leadership Grid   Robert Blake and Jane Mouton have developed the leadership grid approach, based on extensions of the Ohio State dimensions. Re-

A leader high in **consideration** is sensitive to people's feelings and tries to make things pleasant for the followers.

A leader high in **initiating structure** is concerned with spelling out the task requirements and clarifying other aspects of the work agenda.

eBay CEO Leadership

Meg Whitman, CEO of eBay (the giant firm providing a worldwide market for buyers and sellers), is a stickler for measurement: "If you can't measure it, you can't control it." Understanding management-consultant culture is key to understanding her measure-oriented leadership style: Where do you spend money, where are more people needed, and which projects aren't working? Her major goal is to develop leaders capable of maximizing growth in eBay's weird, almost competition-free world—leaders who realize there's only so much any eBay boss can or should do—to reinforce the company's meteoric rise. Driving the train just right is harder than you think.

sults are plotted on a nine-position grid that places concern for production on the horizontal axis and concern for people on the vertical axis, where 1 is minimum concern and 9 is maximum concern. As an example, those with a 1/9 style—low concern for production and high concern for people—are termed "country club management." They do not emphasize task accomplishment and stress the attitudes, feelings, and social needs of people.

Similarly, leaders with a 1/1 style—low concern for both production and people—are termed "impoverished," while a 5/5 style is labeled "middle of the road." A 9/1 leader—high concern for production and low concern for people—has a "task management" style. Finally, a 9/9 leader, high on both dimensions, is considered to have a "team management" style, ideal in Blake and Mouton's framework.

Graen's Leader–Member Exchange Theory   Another perspective that emphasizes the centrality of leadership to outcomes is Graen's leader–member exchange (LMX) approach. However, in contrast to the perspectives just described, which emphasize the influence of the leader's behavior on follower outcomes, LMX theory focuses on the quality of the working relationship between leaders and followers. The LMX 7 scale assesses the degree to which leaders and followers have mutual respect for one anothers' capabilities, feel a deepening sense of mutual trust, and have a strong sense of obligation to one another. Taken together, these dimensions determine the extent to which followers will be part of the leader's "in-group" or "out-group."[9]

In-group followers tend to function as assistants, lieutenants, or advisers and to have higher-quality personalized exchanges with the leader than do out-group followers. The out-group followers tend to emphasize more formalized job requirements, and a relatively low level of mutual influence exists between leaders and out-group followers. The more personalized in-group exchanges typically involve a leader's emphasis on assignments to interesting tasks, delegation of important responsibilities, information sharing, and participation in the leader's decisions, as well as special benefits, such as personal support and approval and favorable work schedules.

Research suggests that high-quality LMX is associated with increased follower satisfaction and productivity, decreased turnover, increased salaries, and faster promotion rates. These findings are encouraging, and the approach continues to receive increasing emphasis in the literature. Of course, many questions remain, such as: What happens in the event of too much disparity in the treatment of in-group and out-group members? Will out-group members become resentful and sabotage team efforts? In addition, more needs to be learned about how the in-group/out-group exchange starts in the first place and how these relations change over time.[10]

Cross-Cultural Implications   It is important to consider how well the kinds of behavioral dimensions discussed earlier transfer internationally. Some work in the United States, Britain, Hong Kong, and Japan shows that the behaviors must be carried out in different ways in alternative cultures. For instance, British leaders are seen as considerate if they show subordinates how to use equipment, whereas in Japan the highly considerate leader helps subordinates with personal problems.[11] Similarly, LMX theory has been shown to be alive and well in Japan.[12]

Situational Contingency Theories

The trait and behavioral perspectives assume that leadership, by itself, would have a strong impact on outcomes. Another development in leadership thinking has recognized, however, that leader traits and behaviors can act in conjunction with *situational contingencies*—other important aspects of the leadership situation—to predict outcomes.

House and Aditya argue that the effects of traits are enhanced by their relevance to the leader's situational contingencies.[13] For example, achievement motivation should be most effective for challenging tasks that require initiative and require assumption of personal responsibility for success. Leader flexibility should be most predictive in unstable environments or when leaders lead different people over time. Prosocial power motivation is likely to be most important in complex organizations where decision implementation requires lots of persuasion and social influence. "Strong" or "weak" situations also make a difference. An example of a strong situation is a highly formal organization with lots of rules, procedures, and so forth. Here, traits will have less impact than in a weaker, more unstructured situation (e.g., I can't show my dynamism as much when the organization restricts me). Traits sometimes have a direct relationship to outcomes or to leaders versus nonleaders. They may also make themselves felt by influencing leader behaviors (e.g., a leader high in energy engages in directive, take-charge behaviors).[14]

Fiedler's Leadership Contingency Theory

Fred Fiedler's work began the situational contingency era in the mid-1960s.[15] His theory holds that group effectiveness depends on an appropriate match between a leader's style (essentially a trait measure) and the demands of the situation. Specifically, Fiedler considers **situational control**—the extent to which a leader can determine what his or her group is going to do as well as the outcomes of the group's actions and decisions.

Fiedler uses an instrument called the **least preferred co-worker (LPC) scale** to measure a person's leadership style. Respondents are asked to describe the person with whom they have been able to work least well—their least preferred co-worker, or LPC—using a series of adjectives such as the following two:

Unfriendly	__ __ __ __ __ __ __ __	Friendly
	1 2 3 4 5 6 7 8	
Pleasant	__ __ __ __ __ __ __ __	Unpleasant
	1 2 3 4 5 6 7 8	

The **least preferred co-worker (LPC) scale** is a measure of a person's leadership style based on a description of the person with whom respondents have been able to work least well.
Fiedler's three

Fiedler argues that high-LPC leaders (those describing their LPC very positively) have a relationship-motivated style, whereas low-LPC leaders have a task-motivated style. He considers this task or relationship motivation to be a trait that leads to either directive or nondirective behavior, depending on the amount of situational control that the leader has. Here, a task-motivated leader tends to be nondirective in high- and low-control situations and directive in those in between. A relationship-motivated leader tends to be the opposite.

Figure 11.2 shows the task-motivated leader as having greater group effectiveness under high and low situational control and the relationship-motivated leader as having a more effective group in in-between situations. The figure also

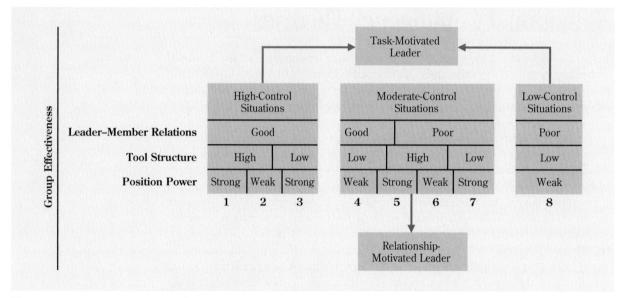

Figure 11.2   Summary of Fiedler's situational variables and their preferred leadership styles.

shows that Fiedler measures the range of control with the following three variables arranged in the situational combinations indicated:

Fiedler's three situational control variables

- *Leader–member relations* (good/poor)—membership support for the leader
- *Task structure* (high/low)—spelling out the leader's task goals, procedures, and guidelines in the group
- *Position power* (strong/weak)—the leader's task expertise and reward or punishment authority

Consider an experienced and well-trained supervisor of a group manufacturing a part for a personal computer. The leader is highly supported by his group members and can grant raises and make hiring and firing decisions. This supervisor has very high situational control and is operating in situation 1 in Figure 11.2. Those leaders operating in situations 2 and 3 would have high situational control, though lower than our production supervisor. For these high-control situations, a task-oriented leader behaving directively would have the most effective group.

Now consider the chair of a student council committee of volunteers (the chair's position power is weak) who are unhappy about this person being the chair and who have the low-structured task of organizing a Parents' Day program to improve university–parent relations. This low-control situation 8 calls for a task-motivated leader who needs to behave directively to keep the group together and focus on the ambiguous task; in fact, the situation demands it. Finally, consider a well-liked academic department chair with tenured faculty. This is a situation 4 moderate-control situation with good leader–member relations, low task structure, and weak position power, calling for a relationship-motivated leader. The leader should emphasize nondirective and considerate relationships with the faculty.

Fiedler's Cognitive Resource Theory   Fiedler eventually moved beyond his contingency theory by developing cognitive resource theory.[16] Cognitive resources are abilities or competencies. According to this approach, whether a leader should use directive or nondirective behavior depends on the following situational contingencies: (1) the leader's or subordinate group members' ability or competency, (2) stress, (3) experience, and (4) group support of the leader. Basically, cognitive resource theory is most useful because it directs us to leader or subordinate group-member ability, an aspect not typically considered in other leadership approaches.

The theory views directiveness as most helpful for performance when the leader is competent, relaxed, and supported. In this case, the group is ready, and directiveness is the clearest means of communication. When the leader feels stressed, he or she is diverted. In this case, experience is more important than ability. If support is low, then the group is less receptive and the leader has less impact. Group-member ability becomes most important when the leader is nondirective and receives strong support from group members. If support is weak, then task difficulty or other factors have more impact than do either the leader or the subordinates.

Evaluation and Application   The roots of Fiedler's contingency approach date back to the 1960s and have elicited both positive and negative reactions. The biggest controversy concerns exactly what Fiedler's LPC instrument measures. Some question Fiedler's behavioral interpretation, whereby the specific behaviors of high- and low-LPC leaders change depending on the amount of situational control. Furthermore, the approach makes the most accurate predictions in situations 1 and 8 and 4 and 5; results are less consistent in the other situations.[17] Tests of cognitive resource theory have shown mixed results.[18]

In terms of application, Fiedler has developed **leader match training**, which Sears, Roebuck and other organizations have used. Leaders are trained to diagnose the situation to match their high and low LPC scores with situational control, as measured by leader–member relations, task structure, and leader position power, following the general ideas shown in Figure 11.2. In cases with no match, the training shows how each of these situational control variables can be changed to obtain a match. Alternatively, another way of getting a match is through leader selection or placement based on LPC scores.[19] For example, a high-LPC leader would be selected for a position with high situational control, as in our earlier example of the manufacturing supervisor. As in the case of Fiedler's contingency theory, a number of studies have been designed to test leader match. Although they are not uniformly supportive, more than a dozen such tests have found increases in group effectiveness following the training.[20]

We conclude that although there are still unanswered questions concerning Fiedler's contingency theory, especially concerning the meaning of LPC, the theory and the leader match program have relatively strong support.[21] The approach and training program are also especially useful in encouraging situational contingency thinking.

House's Path–Goal Theory of Leadership

Another well-known approach to situational contingencies is one developed by Robert House based on the earlier work of others.[22] **House's path–goal theory of leadership** has its roots in the expectancy model of motivation discussed in Chapter 6. The term "path–goal" is used because of its emphasis on how a leader influences subordinates' perceptions of both work goals and personal goals and the links, or paths, found between these two sets of goals.

In **leader match training**, leaders are trained to diagnose the situation to match their high and low LPC scores with situational control.

House's **path–goal theory of leadership** assumes that a leader's key function is to adjust his or her behaviors to complement situational contingencies.

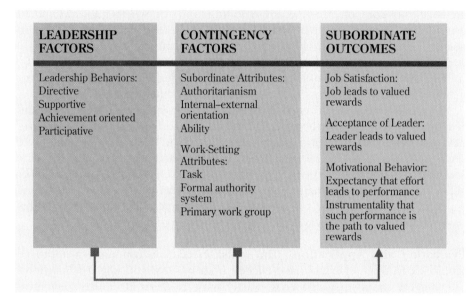

Figure 11.3   Summary of major path–goal relationships in House's leadership approach.

The theory assumes that a leader's key function is to adjust his or her behaviors to complement situational contingencies, such as those found in the work setting. House argues that when the leader is able to compensate for things lacking in the setting, subordinates are likely to be satisfied with the leader. For example, the leader could help remove job ambiguity or show how good performance could lead to more pay. Performance should improve as the paths by which (1) effort leads to performance—expectancy—and (2) performance leads to valued rewards—instrumentality—become clarified.

House's approach is summarized in Figure 11.3. The figure shows four types of leader behavior (directive, supportive, achievement oriented, and participative) and two categories of situational contingency variables (subordinate attributes and work-setting attributes). The leader behaviors are adjusted to complement the situational contingency variables in order to influence subordinate satisfaction, acceptance of the leader, and motivation for task performance.

Directive leadership has to do with spelling out the what and how of subordinates' tasks; it is much like the initiating structure mentioned earlier. **Supportive leadership** focuses on subordinate needs and well-being and promoting a friendly work climate; it is similar to consideration. **Achievement-oriented leadership** emphasizes setting challenging goals, stressing excellence in performance, and showing confidence in the group members' ability to achieve high standards of performance. **Participative leadership** focuses on consulting with subordinates and seeking and taking their suggestions into account before making decisions.

Important subordinate characteristics are *authoritarianism* (close-mindedness, rigidity), *internal–external orientation* (i.e., locus of control), and *ability*. The key work-setting factors are the nature of the subordinates' tasks (task structure), the *formal authority system*, and the *primary workgroup*.

Predictions from Path–Goal Theory   Directive leadership is predicted to have a positive impact on subordinates when the task is ambiguous; it is predicted to have just the opposite effect for clear tasks. In addition, the theory pre-

Directive leadership spells out the what and how of subordinates' tasks.

Supportive leadership focuses on subordinate needs, well-being, and promotion of a friendly work climate.

Achievement-oriented leadership emphasizes setting challenging goals, stressing excellence in performance, and showing confidence in people's ability to achieve high standards of performance.

Participative leadership focuses on consulting with subordinates and seeking and taking their suggestions into account before making decisions.

dicts that when ambiguous tasks are being performed by highly authoritarian and close-minded subordinates, even more directive leadership is called for.

Supportive leadership is predicted to increase the satisfaction of subordinates who work on highly repetitive tasks or on tasks considered to be unpleasant, stressful, or frustrating; the leader's supportive behavior helps compensate for these adverse conditions. For example, many would consider traditional assembly-line auto worker jobs to be highly repetitive, perhaps even unpleasant and frustrating. A supportive supervisor could help make these jobs more pleasant. Achievement-oriented leadership is predicted to encourage subordinates to strive for higher performance standards and to have more confidence in their ability to meet challenging goals. For subordinates in ambiguous, nonrepetitive jobs, achievement-oriented leadership should increase their expectations that effort leads to desired performance.

Participative leadership is predicted to promote satisfaction on nonrepetitive tasks that allow for the ego involvement of subordinates. For example, on a challenging research project, participation allows employees to feel good about dealing with the challenge of the project on their own. On repetitive tasks, openminded or nonauthoritarian subordinates will also be satisfied with a participative leader. On a task where employees screw nuts on bolts hour after hour, for example, those who are nonauthoritarian will appreciate having a leader who allows them to get involved in ways that may help break the monotony.

Evaluation and Application   House's path–goal approach has now been with us for 30 years or so. Early work provided some support for the theory in general and for the particular predictions discussed earlier.[23] However, current assessments by well-known scholars have pointed out that many aspects have not been tested adequately, and there is very little recent research concerning the theory.[24] House himself recently revised and extended path–goal theory into the theory of work unit leadership. It's beyond our scope to discuss details of this new theory, but as a base, the new theory expands the list of leader behaviors beyond those in path–goal theory, including aspects of both traditional and new leadership.[25] It remains to be seen how much research it will generate.

In terms of application, there is enough support for the original path–goal theory to suggest two possibilities. First, training could be used to change leadership behavior to fit the situational contingencies. Second, the leader could be taught to diagnose the situation and to learn how to try to change the contingencies, as in leader match.

Hersey and Blanchard's Situational Leadership Model   Like other situational contingency approaches, the situational leadership model developed by Paul Hersey and Kenneth Blanchard posits that there is no single best way to lead.[26] Hersey and Blanchard focus on the situational contingency of maturity, or "readiness," of followers, in particular. Readiness is the extent to which people have the ability and willingness to accomplish a specific task. Hersey and Blanchard argue that "situational" leadership requires adjusting the leader's emphasis on task behaviors, for instance, giving guidance and direction, and relationship behaviors, for example, providing socioemotional support, according to the readiness of followers to perform their tasks. Figure 11.4 identifies four leadership styles: delegating, participating, selling, and telling. Each emphasizes a different combination of task and relationship behaviors by the leader. The figure also suggests the following situational matches as the best choice of leadership style for followers at each of four readiness levels.

Take Charge Leadership

Recently, because one would not expect it from two such take charge personalities, a very unusual event occurred for the Dallas Cowboys football team— Jerry Jones, the flamboyant owner, hired Bill Parcells, one of the outstanding coaches of our time. Both have huge egos, share power, and are very strong leaders. Jones gets an immediate dose of star power on the field as he turns around "America's Team." Parcells gets to rebuild a once-spectacular team, but a moribund one when he took over.

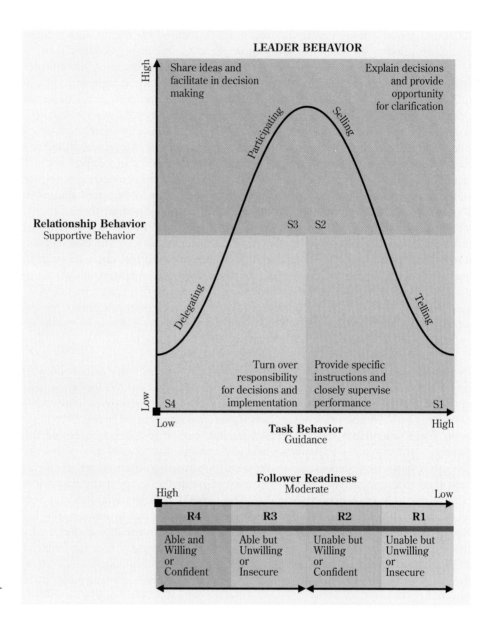

Figure 11.4   Hersey and Blanchard model of situational leadership.

A "telling" style (S1) is best for low follower readiness (R1). The direction provided by this style defines roles for people who are unable and unwilling to take responsibility themselves; it eliminates any insecurity about the task that must be done.

A "selling" style (S2) is best for low to moderate follower readiness (R2). This style offers both task direction and support for people who are unable but willing to take task responsibility; it involves combining a directive approach with explanation and reinforcement in order to maintain enthusiasm.

A "participating" style (S3) is best for moderate to high follower readiness (R3). Able but unwilling followers require supportive behavior in order to increase their motivation; by allowing followers to share in decision making, this style helps enhance the desire to perform a task.

A "delegating" style (S4) is best for high readiness (R4). This style provides little in terms of direction and support for the task at hand; it allows able and willing followers to take responsibility for what needs to be done.

This situational leadership approach requires the leader to develop the capability to diagnose the demands of situations and then to choose and implement the appropriate leadership response. The model gives specific attention to followers and their feelings about the task at hand and suggests that an effective leader focus especially on emerging changes in the level of readiness of the people involved in the work.

In spite of its considerable history and incorporation into training programs by a large number of firms, the situational leadership approach has received very little systematic research attention.[27]

Substitutes for Leadership

In contrast to the previous traditional leadership approaches, the substitutes for leadership theory argues that sometimes hierarchical leadership makes essentially no difference. John Jermier and others contend that certain individual, job, and organizational variables can either serve as substitutes for leadership or neutralize a leader's impact on subordinates.[28] Some examples of these variables are shown in Figure 11.5.

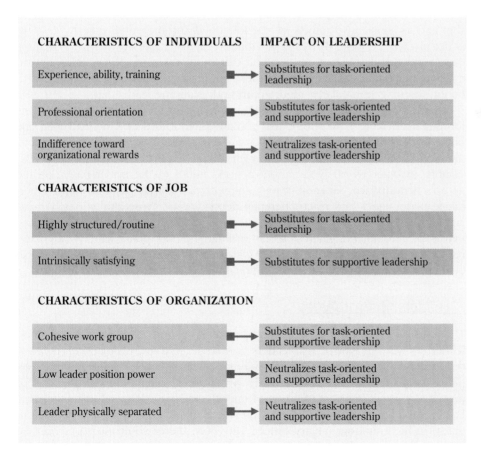

CHARACTERISTICS OF INDIVIDUALS   **IMPACT ON LEADERSHIP**

Experience, ability, training → Substitutes for task-oriented leadership

Professional orientation → Substitutes for task-oriented and supportive leadership

Indifference toward organizational rewards → Neutralizes task-oriented and supportive leadership

CHARACTERISTICS OF JOB

Highly structured/routine → Substitutes for task-oriented leadership

Intrinsically satisfying → Substitutes for supportive leadership

CHARACTERISTICS OF ORGANIZATION

Cohesive work group → Substitutes for task-oriented and supportive leadership

Low leader position power → Neutralizes task-oriented and supportive leadership

Leader physically separated → Neutralizes task-oriented and supportive leadership

Figure 11.5   Some examples of leadership substitutes and neutralizers.

■■■ **Substitutes for leadership** make a leader's influence either unnecessary or redundant in that they replace a leader's influence.

Substitutes for leadership make a leader's influence either unnecessary or redundant in that they replace a leader's influence. For example, in Figure 11.5, it will be unnecessary and perhaps not even possible for a leader to provide the kind of task-oriented direction already available from an experienced, talented, and well-trained subordinate. In contrast, neutralizers prevent a leader from behaving in a certain way or nullify the effects of a leader's actions. If a leader has little formal authority or is physically separated, for example, his or her leadership may be nullified even though task supportiveness may still be needed.

Some research comparing Mexican and U.S. workers, as well as workers in Japan, suggests both similarities and differences between various substitutes in the countries examined. More generally, a review of 17 studies in the United States as well as other countries found mixed results for the substitutes theory. Among other things, the authors argued that the kinds of characteristics and leader behaviors should be broadened and that the approach appeared to be especially important for high-performance work teams.[29] With regard to these work teams, for example, in place of a hierarchical leader specifying standards and ways of achieving goals (task-oriented behaviors), the team might set its own standards and substitute those for the leader's.

Attribution Theory and Leadership

The traditional leadership theories discussed so far have all assumed that leadership and its substantive effects can be identified and measured objectively. This is not always the case, however. Attribution theory addresses this very point—that of individuals trying to understand causes, to assess responsibilities, and to evaluate personal qualities, as all of these are involved with certain events. Attribution theory is particularly important in understanding leadership.

For openers, think about a workgroup or student group that you see as performing really well. Now assume that you are asked to describe the leader on one of the leadership scales discussed earlier in the chapter. If you are like many others, the group's high performance probably encouraged you to describe the leader favorably; in other words, you attributed good things to the leader based on the group's performance. Similarly, leaders themselves make attributions about subordinate performance and react differently depending on those attributions. For example, if leaders attribute an employee's poor performance to lack of effort, they may issue a reprimand, whereas if they attribute the poor performance to an external factor, such as work overload, they will probably try to fix the problem. A great deal of evidence supports these attributional views of subordinates and leaders.[30]

■■■ A **leadership prototype** is an image people have in their minds of what a model leader should look like.

Leadership Prototypes

There is also evidence that people have a mental picture of what makes a "good leader" or ways in which "real leaders" would act in a given situation. The view that people have an image in their minds of what a model leader should look like is sometimes called a **leadership prototype**.[31] These implicit theories or prototypes usually consist of a mix of specific and more general characteristics. For example, a prototype of a bank president would differ in many ways from that of a high-ranking military officer. However, there would probably also be

Research Insight
Implicit Leadership Theories Across Settings and Time

A recent study examined implicit leadership theories (ILTs) or leadership prototypes to determine (1) whether a previously developed implicit leadership scale could be cross-validated in several organizational settings; (2) whether ILTs were context-sensitive, dynamic states rather than static entities, as traditionally assumed; and (3) whether ILTs change across time.

A six-factor structure was found to most accurately represent ILTs in organizational settings. The structure was found to be reasonably consistent across different kinds of groups. Finally, the ILT structure remained stable one year after the first measurement.

The authors conclude that "Viewing leadership as a dynamic interplay between explicit leader behaviors, subordinate leadership schem[as], and leadership outcomes further implies that in-depth understanding of effective leadership necessitates training approaches sensitive to followers' ILTs" (p. 308).

SIX-FACTOR ILT STRUCTURE

- More Sensitivity
- More Intelligence
- More Dedication
- More Dynamic
- Less Tyranny
- Less Masculinity

Reference:: Olga Epitropaki and Robin Martin, "Implicit Leadership Theories in Applied Settings: Factor Structure, Generalizability, and Stability Over Time," *Journal of Applied Psychology* 89(2) (2004):293–310.

some core characteristics reflecting leaders in our society in general—for example, integrity and self-efficacy.

We also would expect differences in prototypes by country and by national culture. Indeed, a major study, termed GLOBE, (the Global Leadership and Organizational Behavior Effectiveness Research Project) involving some 60 countries, empirically examined just this question, among other things. Using the European subset of the GLOBE data, evidence was presented that clusters of European countries with similar cultural values also shared similar patterns of "culturally endorsed leadership theories." A North/West and South/East European cluster emerged based on leadership prototypes. However, France formed a unique cluster on its own.

Key leadership attributes in these countries, except for France, included being inspirational, being visionary, having a performance orientation, being decisive, having integrity, and being a team integrator. Self-centeredness and malevolence were described as impeding leadership throughout Europe, including France. Many other findings were reported, but these capture their flavor.[32]

An earlier, smaller-scope study contrasted typical business leader prototypes between Japan and the United States.[33]

- *Japan:* responsible, educated, trustworthy, intelligent, disciplined
- *United States:* determined, goal oriented, verbally skilled, industrious, persistent

The closer the behavior of a leader is to the implicit theories of his or her followers, the more favorable the leader's relations and key outcomes tend to be.[34] Both of the attributional treatments above emphasize leadership as something that is largely symbolic or resides in the eye of the beholder. This general notion has also carried over to a related set of research directions. Ironically, the first of these directions argues that leadership makes little or no real difference in organizational effectiveness. The second tends to attribute greatly exaggerated importance to leadership and ultimately leads us into charisma and other aspects of the new leadership.

Exaggeration of the Leadership Difference

Jeffrey Pfeffer has looked at what happens when leaders at the top of the organization are changed. Pfeffer is among those contending that even CEOs of large corporations have little leadership impact on profits and effectiveness compared to environmental and industry forces, such as cutbacks in the federal defense budget. Furthermore, these leaders are typically accountable to so many groups of people for the resources they use that their leadership impact is greatly constrained. Pfeffer argues that in light of such forces and constraints, much of the impact a top leader does have is symbolic; leaders and others develop explanations to legitimize the actions they take.[35]

▇▇▇ In the **romance of leadership**, people attribute romantic, almost magical qualities to leadership.

This symbolic treatment of leadership occurs particularly when performance is either extremely high or extremely low or when the situation is such that many people could have been responsible for the performance. James Meindl and his colleagues call this phenomenon the **romance of leadership**, whereby people attribute romantic, almost magical, qualities to leadership.[36] Consider the firing of a baseball manager or football coach whose team doesn't perform well. Neither the owner nor anyone else is really sure why this occurred. But the owner can't fire all the players, so a new team manager is brought in to symbolize "a change in leadership" that is "sure to turn the team around."

Emerging Leadership Perspectives

▇▇▇ The **new leadership** emphasizes charismatic and transformational leadership approaches and various aspects of vision related to them and also includes self-directing work teams.

The focus on leadership attributions and symbolic aspects moves us away from traditional leadership and into the new leadership. The **new leadership** emphasizes charismatic and transformational leadership approaches and various aspects of vision related to them, and we extend the term to include leadership of self-directing work teams. The new leadership is considered especially important in changing and transforming individuals and organizations with a commitment to high performance.[37]

Charismatic Approaches

Robert House and his associates have done a lot of work based on extensions of an earlier charismatic theory House developed. (Do not confuse this with House's path–goal theory or its extension, discussed earlier in the chapter.)[38] Of special interest is the fact that House's theory uses both trait and behavior combinations.

▇▇▇ **Charismatic leaders** are those leaders who, by force of their personal abilities, are capable of having a profound and extraordinary effect on followers.

House's **charismatic leaders** are leaders who, by force of their personal abilities, are capable of having a profound and extraordinary effect on followers. These leaders are high in need for power and have high feelings of self-efficacy and conviction in the moral rightness of their beliefs. That is, the need for power motivates these people to want to be leaders. This need is then reinforced by their conviction of the moral rightness of their beliefs. The feeling of self-efficacy, in turn, makes these people feel that they are capable of being leaders.

These traits then influence such charismatic behaviors as role modeling, image building, articulating goals (focusing on simple and dramatic goals), emphasizing high expectations, showing confidence, and arousing follower motives.

PEOPLE AND TECHNOLOGY

THE AMAZON WAY

Some think Jeff Bezos, Amazon's owner and CEO, is goofy, with his braying honk of a laugh, undignified behavior, and exaggerated gestures. More and more, however, experts are asking, "Is he as goofy as Bill Gates? Is he as goofy as Michael Dell?" For underlying his goofiness lurks leadership that depends on data, makes employees owners through stock options, emphasizes empowerment, thinks long term, insists on data for decisions, compels him to spend time "in the trenches," and bets on technology. All of this takes place in what is now a $20 billion dollar revenue-generator, growing at more than 20 percent a year.

Question: How is it that an apparent goofball can build such a business?

Some of the more interesting and important work based on aspects of House's charismatic theory involves a study of U.S. presidents.[39] The research showed that behavioral charisma was substantially related to presidential performance and that the kind of personality traits in House's theory, along with response to crisis, among other things, predicted behavioral charisma for the sample of presidents. Related work by others also shows that voters who saw Bill Clinton as charismatic followed through by voting for him.[40]

House and his colleagues summarize other work that partially supports the theory. Some of the more interesting related work has shown that negative, or "dark-side," charismatic leaders emphasize personalized power—focus on themselves—whereas positive, or "bright-side," charismatics emphasize socialized power that tends to empower their followers. This helps explain differences between such dark-side leaders as Adolf Hitler and David Koresh, and a bright-side Martin Luther King Jr.[41]

Jay Conger and Rabindra Kanungo have developed a three-stage charismatic leadership model.[42] In the initial stage, the leader critically evaluates the status quo. Deficiencies in the status quo lead to formulations of future goals. Before developing these goals, the leader assesses available resources and constraints that stand in the way of the goals. The leader also assesses follower abilities, needs, and satisfaction levels. In the second stage, the leader formulates and articulates the goals along with an idealized future vision. Here the leader emphasizes articulation and impression management skills. Then, in the third stage, the leader shows how these goals and the vision can be achieved. The leader emphasizes innovative and unusual means to achieve the vision. Martin Luther King Jr. illustrated these three stages in his nonviolent civil rights approach, changing race relations in this country.

Conger and Kanungo have argued that if leaders use behaviors such as vision articulation, environmental sensitivity, and unconventional behavior, rather than maintaining the status quo, followers will attribute charismatic leadership to

Leaders on Leadership

BUILDING A WORLD-CLASS UNIVERSITY

Most of us know Notre Dame for its football teams. However, while people were not looking, it became a world-class university, moving from a budget of 7 million to half a billion dollars a year. All this evolved over a 35-year period from the vision of Father Theodore Hesburgh, now president emeritus. He started young, and in the days before visions were emphasized as much as they are now, developed one unique to Notre Dame. The vision grew as he grew, and he saw the university better as he became closer to it.

The vision started with his distinction between leadership and management—a manager could run a place very well for 10 years, with no big failures but no greatness either. Thus, Hesburgh's leadership vision to build a great university: Where is the institution to go? What is it to be? For him, this meant raising the budget, the quality of a mediocre faculty, and the academic quality of middle-level students. Also needed was a new, much larger library—the centerpiece of a great university.

Hesburgh believed in strong empowerment of his several VPs and in a strong development office. Ultimately, he prepared a new charter to provide control by a lay board with approval by the state of Indiana, where the university is located.

Question: What charismatic leadership characteristics has Father Hesburgh shown and how do they appear to have influenced Notre Dame?

---

them. Such leaders are also seen as behaving quite differently from those labeled "noncharismatic."[43]

Finally, an especially important question about charismatic leadership is whether it is described in the same way for close-up or at-a-distance leaders. Boas Shamir examined this issue in Israel.[44] He found that descriptions of distant charismatics (e.g., former Israeli prime minister Golda Meir) and close-up charismatics (e.g., a specific teacher) were generally more different than they were similar. Figure 11.6 shows the high points of his findings. Clearly, leaders with whom followers have close contact and those with whom they seldom, if ever, have direct contact are both described as charismatic but possess quite different traits and behaviors.

Transformational Versus Transactional Approaches

Transactional leadership involves leader–follower exchanges necessary for achieving routine performance agreed upon between leaders and followers.

Building on notions originated by James MacGregor Burns, as well as ideas from House's work, Bernard Bass has developed an approach that focuses on both transformational and transactional leadership.[45]

Transactional leadership involves leader–follower exchanges necessary for achieving routine performance agreed upon between leaders and followers. These exchanges involve four dimensions, as shown in The Effective Manager 11.1.

Distant Charismatics Should Demonstrate
- Persistence
- Rhetorical skills
- Courage
- An emphasis on social courage (expressing opinions, not conforming to pressure)
- Ideological orientation

Close-up Charismatics Should Demonstrate
- Sociability
- Expertise
- Humor
- Dynamism, activity
- Physical appearance
- Intelligence
- High standards
- Originality

Both Distant and Close-up Charismatics Should Demonstrate
- Self-confidence
- Honesty
- Authoritativeness
- Sacrifice

Figure 11.6 **Descriptions of characteristics of distant and close-up charismatics.**

Transformational leadership goes beyond this routine accomplishment, however. For Bass, **transformational leadership** occurs when leaders broaden and elevate their followers' interests, when they generate awareness and acceptance of the group's purposes and mission, and when they stir their followers to look beyond their own self-interests to the good of others.

Dimensions of Transformational Leadership Transformational leadership has four dimensions: charisma, inspiration, intellectual stimulation, and individualized consideration. *Charisma* provides vision and a sense of mission, and it instills pride, along with follower respect and trust. For example, Steve Jobs, who founded Apple Computer, showed charisma by emphasizing the importance of creating the Macintosh as a radical new computer. Inspiration communicates high expectations, uses symbols to focus efforts, and expresses important purposes in simple ways. For example, in the movie *Patton*, George C. Scott stood on a stage in front of his troops with a wall-sized American flag in the background and ivory-handled revolvers in holsters at his side. *Intellectual stimulation* promotes intelligence, rationality, and careful problem solving. For instance, your boss encourages you to look at a very difficult problem in a new way. *Individualized consideration* provides personal attention, treats each employee individually, and coaches and advises. For example, your boss drops by and makes remarks reinforcing your worth as a person.

Bass concludes that transformational leadership is likely to be strongest at the top-management level, where there is the greatest opportunity for proposing and communicating a vision. However, it is not *restricted* to the top level; it is found throughout the organization. Furthermore, transformational leadership operates *in combination with* transactional leadership. Transactional leadership is similar to

■■■ **Transformational leadership** occurs when leaders broaden and elevate followers' interests and stir followers to look beyond their own interests to the good of others.

THE EFFECTIVE MANAGER 11.1

Four Dimensions of Transactional Leadership

- *Contingent rewards*—Providing various kinds of rewards in exchange for mutually agreed-upon goal accomplishment
- *Active management by exception*—Watching for deviations from rules and standards and taking corrective action
- *Passive management by exception*—Intervening only if standards are not met
- *Laissez-faire*—Abdicating responsibilities and avoiding decisions

most of the traditional leadership approaches mentioned earlier. Leaders need both transformational and transactional leadership in order to be successful, just as they need to display both leadership and abilities.[46]

Evaluation and Application   Reviews have summarized a large number of studies using Bass's approach. These reviews report significant favorable relationships between Bass's leadership dimensions and various aspects of performance and satisfaction, as well as extra effort, burnout and stress, and predispositions to act as innovation champions on the part of followers. The strongest relationships tend to be associated with charisma or inspirational leadership, although, in most cases, the other dimensions are also important. These findings are consistent with those reported elsewhere.[47] They broaden leadership outcomes beyond those cited in traditional leadership studies.

CULTURES AND THE GLOBAL WORKFORCE

WHERE GOETH TOYOTA?

Toyota is working to make the soul or style of its vehicles as compelling as their value. Two leaders characterize this thrust, with an increasing emphasis on "Americanization." The first is Fiyio Cho, current president and seldom seen without a smile. In 1988, he opened Toyota's first wholly owned U.S. assembly plant in Georgetown, Kentucky. He has placed American and other non-Japanese executives closer to Toyota's centers of power. He strongly emphasizes Americanization. The second is Yoshi Inaba, one of the company's 14 senior managing directors, who says he is strong to push this Americanization. He is a specialist in sales and marketing, earned an MBA from Northwestern, and is widely touted as Toyota's next president.

Toyota's boldest leap has been its hybrid (gasoline/electric) cars. This movement has left American manufacturers in its dust. A smooth Cho–Inaba leadership transition can reinforce this lead and the more rapid transformation of Toyota.

Question: Based on this description, what leadership components appear to be particularly important for the leadership team, and why?

Leadership in Self-Managing Work Teams

We have talked about self-managing work teams many tmes throughout this text—they are certainly one of the emerging perspectives. However, we have not said much about leadership of such teams. That leadership can be from outside the team or from inside the team. Within a team, such leadership can be assigned to one person, rotated across team members, or even shared simultaneously as different needs arise across time.

Outside the team, the leaders can be traditional, formally designated first-level supervisors, or foremen or an outside leader of a self-managing team whose duties tend to be quite different from those of a traditional supervisor. Often these nontraditional leaders are called "coordinators" or "facilitators". A key part of their job is to provide resources to their unit and liaison with other units but without the authority trappings of traditional supervisors. Here, team members tend to carry out traditional managerial/leadership functions internal to the team along with direct performance activities.

The activities or functions vary and could involve a designated team role or even be defined more generally as a process to facilitate team performance ("whatever it takes"). In the latter case, you are likely to see job rotation activities, along with skill-based pay, as discussed in Chapter 7, where workers are paid for the mix and depth of skills they possess as opposed to skills of a given job assignment they might hold.

If we argue that a key contribution to team performance (regardless of who provides it) is to create and maintain conditions for that performance, then the following are important considerations.[48]

Efficient, Goal-Directed Effort   The key here is to coordinate the effort both inside and outside the team. Team leaders can play a crucial role here. It is harder than it looks because you need to coordinate individual efforts with those of the team, and team efforts with those of the organization or major subunit. Among other things, such coordination calls for shared visions and goals and the like.

Adequate Resources   Teams rely on their leaders to obtain enough equipment, supplies, and so on to carry out the team's goals. As mentioned earlier, these are often handled by the outside facilitator and almost always involve internal and external negotiations so the facilitator can then do his or her negotiating outside the team.

Competent, Motivated Performance   Team members also need the appropriate knowledge, skills, abilities, and motivation to perform collective tasks well. Here, leaders may be able to influence team composition so as to enhance collective efficacy and performance. We often see this demonstrated with short-term teams such as task forces. Sometimes student teams are selected with this point in mind.

A Productive, Supportive Climate   Here, we are talking about high levels of cohesiveness, mutual trust, and cooperation among team members. Sometimes these kinds of aspects are part of a team's "interpersonal climate." Team leaders contribute to this climate by role-modeling and supporting relationship that build the high levels indicated above. Team leaders can also work to enhance shared beliefs about team efficacy and collective capability.

Commitment to Continuous Improvement and Adaptation   A really good team should be able to adapt to changing conditions. Again, both internal and external team leaders may play a role.

These conditions often encourage member self-leadership activities, where key leadership aspects are carried out with little or no input from an outside leader—or sometimes even an inside one. Where this happens, we see partial substitutes for hierarchical leadership even though they may be encouraged by a coordinator. Also, these behaviors may or may not be charismatic or transformational. They should work best when reinforced by bright-side charismatic or transformational leaders adding a little something extra from inside or outside the team.[49]

Emerging Leadership Issues

We now examine some charismatic, transformational, and visionary new leadership issues. First: *Can people be trained in new leadership?* According to research

Leadership and Technology

Les Clonch is Vice President of Information Services at Parkland Health System in Dallas. He is responsible for leading the unit charged with providing responsive computer systems to meet the ever-increasing demand for clinical and financial information needed to effectively operate Parkland's large and complex system. Key leadership responsibilities include keeping abreast of rapid technological changes and numerous health care changes due to government regulations, and hiring and retaining good technical people. His leadership emphasizes integrity and positive attitude, results orientation, and dependability.

THE EFFECTIVE MANAGER 11.2

Five Charismatic Skills

- *Sensitivity to most appropriate contexts for charisma*—Emphasis on critical evaluation and problem detection
- *Vision*—Emphasis on creative thinking to learn and think about profound change
- *Communication*—Working with oral and written linguistic aspects
- *Impression management*—Emphasis on modeling, appearance, body language, and verbal skills
- *Empowering*—Emphasis on communicating high-performance expectations, improving participation in decision making, loosening up bureaucratic constraints, setting meaningful goals, and establishing appropriate reward systems

in this area, the answer is yes. Bass and his colleagues have put a lot of work into such training efforts. For example, they have created a workshop where leaders are given initial feedback on their scores on Bass's measures. The leaders then devise improvement programs to strengthen their weaknesses and work with the trainers to develop their leadership skills. Bass as well as Bass and Avolio report findings that demonstrate the beneficial effects of this training. They also report team training and programs tailored to individual firms' needs.[50] Similarly, Conger and Kanungo propose training to develop the kinds of behaviors summarized in their model, as suggested in The Effective Manager 11.2.[51]

Approaches with special emphasis on vision often emphasize training. Kouzas and Posner report results of a week-long training program at AT&T. The program involved training leaders on five dimensions oriented around developing, communicating, and reinforcing a shared vision. According to Kouzas and Posner, leaders showed an average 15 percent increase in these visionary behaviors 10 months after participating in the program.[52] Similarly, Sashkin and Sashkin have developed a leadership approach that emphasizes various aspects of vision and organizational culture change. They discuss a number of ways to train leaders to be more visionary and to enhance the culture change.[53] All of the new leadership training programs involve a heavy hands-on workshop emphasis so that leaders do more than just read about vision.

A second issue involves the question: *Is new leadership always good?* As pointed out earlier, dark-side charismatics, such as Adolf Hitler, can have negative effects on followers. Similarly, new leadership is not always needed. Sometimes emphasis on a vision diverts energy from more important day-to-day activities. It is also important to note that new leadership by itself is not sufficient. New leadership needs to be used in conjunction with traditional leadership. Finally, new leadership is important not only at the top. A number of experts argue that it applies at all levels of organizational leadership.

Chapter 11   Study Guide

Summary

What is leadership, and how does it differ from management?

- Leadership is a special case of interpersonal influence that gets an individual or group to do what the leader wants done.
- Leadership and management differ in that management is designed to promote stability or to make the organization run smoothly, whereas the role of leadership is to promote adaptive change.

- Trait or great person approaches argue that leader traits have a major impact on differentiating between leaders and nonleaders and predicting leadership outcomes.

- Traits are considered relatively innate and hard to change.

- Similar to trait approaches, behavioral theories argue that leader behaviors have a major impact on outcomes.

- The Michigan, Ohio State, and Graen's leader–member exchange (LMX) approaches are particularly important leader behavior theories.

- Leader behavior theories are especially suitable for leadership training.

What are the situational contingency approaches to leadership?

- Leader situational contingency approaches argue that leadership, in combination with various situational contingency variables, can have a major impact on outcomes.

- The effects of traits are enhanced to the extent of their relevance to the situational contingencies faced by the leader.

- Strong or weak situational contingencies influence the impact of leadership traits.

- Fiedler's contingency theory, House's path–goal theory, Hersey and Blanchard's situational leadership theory, and Kerr and Jermier's substitutes for leadership theory are particularly important, specific situational contingency approaches.

- Sometimes, as in the case of the substitutes for leadership approach, the role of situational contingencies replaces that of leadership, so that leadership has little or no impact in itself.

What are attribution approaches to leadership?

- Attribution theory extends traditional leadership approaches by recognizing that substantive effects cannot always be objectively identified and measured.

- Leaders form attributions about why their employees perform well or poorly and respond accordingly.

- Leaders and followers often infer that there is good leadership when their group performs well.

- Leaders and followers often have in mind a good leader prototype; compare the leader against such a prototype; and conclude that the closer the fit, the better the leadership.

- Some contend that leadership makes no real difference and is largely symbolic; others, following the "romance of leadership" notion, embrace this symbolic emphasis and attribute almost magical qualities to leadership.

What are emerging leadership perspectives, and why are they especially important in today's organizations?

- Some emerging leadership perspectives consist of charismatic, transformation, and visionary leadership as well as leadership of self-directing work teams.

- Charismatic, transformational, and visionary attributions help move followers to achieve goals that transcend their own self-interests and help transform the organization.

- Particularly important emerging leadership approaches are Bass's transformational theory and House's and Conger and Kanungo's charismatic theories.

- Transformational approaches are broader than charismatic ones and often include charisma as one of their dimensions.

- Leadership in high-performance work teams, particularly involved in today's organizations, often changes the external leadership role by making it a facilitative one so as to encourage team members to lead themselves.

- Behaviors of team coordinators are assumed to work best when reinforced by leaders who provide empowerment and stress various aspects of the new leadership.
- The new leadership, in general, is important because it goes beyond traditional leadership in facilitating change in the increasingly fast-moving workplace.

Key Terms

Achievement-oriented leadership (p. 248)
Behavioral perspective (p. 242)
Charismatic leaders (p. 254)
Consideration (p. 243)
Directive leadership (p. 248)
Initiating structure (p. 243)
Leader match training (p. 247)

Leadership (p. 241)
Leadership prototype (p. 252)
Least preferred co-worker (LPC) scale (p. 245)
New leadership (p. 254)
Participative leadership (p. 248)
Path–goal theory of leadership (p. 247)
Romance of leadership (p. 254)

Situational control (p. 245)
Substitutes for leadership (p. 252)
Supportive leadership (p. 248)
Trait perspectives (p. 241)
Transactional leadership (p. 256)
Transformational leadership (p. 257)

Self-Test 11

Multiple Choice

1. "Leadership is central, and other variables are less important" best describes _____ theories. (a) trait and behavioral (b) attribution (c) situational contingency (d) substitutes for leadership
2. Leader trait and behavioral approaches assume that traits and behaviors are _____. (a) equally important with other variables (b) more important than other variables (c) caused by other variables (d) symbolic of leadership
3. In comparing leadership and management, _____. (a) leadership promotes stability and management promotes change (b) leadership promotes change and management promotes stability (c) leaders are born but managers are developed (d) the two are pretty much the same.
4. The earliest theory of leadership stated that individuals become leaders because of _____. (a) the behavior of those they lead (b) the traits they possess (c) the particular situation in which they find themselves (d) being very tall
5. Which leadership theory argues that a leader's key function is to act in ways that complement the work setting? (a) trait (b) behavioral (c) path–goal (d) multiple influence
6. A leadership prototype _____. (a) is useful primarily for selection and training (b) uses LPC as an important component (c) depicts the image of a model leader (d) emphasizes leadership skills
7. Conger and Kanungo's model emphasizes all of the following except _____. (a) active management by exception (b) vision articulation (c) environmental sensitivity (d) unconventional behavior
8. For situational leadership theory, _____. (a) management is substituted for leadership (b) position power is very important (c) there is considerable empirical support (d) maturity or readiness of followers is emphasized
9. Transformational leadership _____. (a) is similar to transactional leadership

(b) is particularly useful in combination with transactional leadership (c) is not related to charismatic leadership (d) has been studied for more than 100 years

10. In terms of the importance of leadership, it has been argued that _____. (a) leadership makes little or no difference (b) only charismatic leadership is important (c) charismatic leadership is more important than transformational leadership (d) leadership is important only in a situational contingencies context

11. In the romance of leadership, _____. (a) supervisors are encouraged to lead each other to the altar (b) leaders are encouraged to marry each other (c) leaders are given credit for difficult-to-explain happenings (d) leadership substitutes for traditional romantic actions

12. Attributional theory _____. (a) is one important leadership direction (b) is no longer popular in studying leadership (c) helps explain Fiedler's model (d) helps explain situational leadership

13. Close-up and at-a-distance charismatic leaders _____. (a) use the same behaviors (b) exhibit a number of different behaviors (c) are hard to distinguish (d) have similar impacts on individual performance

14. In terms of charismatic or transformational leadership, _____. (a) people can be trained (b) these characteristics are inborn (c) neither is as important as transactional leadership (d) both tend to become managerial in orientation

15. Leadership traits _____. (a) are largely passé (b) are excellent substitutes for behaviors (c) are now being combined with behaviors (d) are too rigid to be used in analyzing leadership

Short Response

16. Define "leadership" and contrast it with "management."

17. Discuss the role of leader trait and behavior approaches in leadership.

18. Discuss the role of situational contingency approaches in leadership.

19. Compare and contrast traditional leadership and the new leadership.

Applications Essay

20. You have just been called in as a consultant to analyze the role of leadership in the Jerry Jones and Bill Parcells situation described on page 249. Suggest ways to develop it further. Making any necessary assumptions, discuss how you would handle this assignment.

These learning activities from *The OB Skills Workbook* are suggested for Chapter 11.

OB in Action

CASE	EXPERIENTIAL EXERCISES	SELF-ASSESSMENTS
▪ 11. Perot Systems: Can a High-Performance Company Have a Human Side?	▪ 25. Interview a Leader ▪ 26. Leadership Skills Inventories ▪ 27. Leadership and Participation in Decision Making	▪ 12. Least Preferred Co-Worker Scale ▪ 13. Leadership Style ▪ 14. "TI" Leadership Style

Plus—special learning experiences from *The Jossey-Bass/Pfeiffer Classroom Collection*

Chapter 12

Power and Politics

Chapter at a Glance

Since individuals join organizations for their own reasons to meet their own goals, they vie for their own interests in a hierarchical setting. Thus, analyses of power and politics are a key to understanding the behavior of individuals within organizations. As you read Chapter 12, *keep in mind these study questions:*

WHAT ARE POWER AND INFLUENCE IN AN ORGANIZATION?

HOW ARE POWER, OBEDIENCE, AND FORMAL AUTHORITY INTERTWINED IN AN ORGANIZATION?

WHAT IS EMPOWERMENT?

WHAT IS ORGANIZATIONAL POLITICS?

REVIEW IN END-OF-CHAPTER STUDY GUIDE

Edward J. Zore is the sixteenth president of Northwestern Mutual. Northwestern Mutual is the largest direct provider of individual life insurance, with assets of more than $1 billion.[1] It is the only company that has been ranked at the top of its industry on the list of most admired companies in America every year since the survey began. Zore does not "maximize stockholder wealth." The customers actually own the firm because it is a mutual. In a mutual, no stock options go to the executives. Instead, dividend proceeds are given back to the customers. It is refreshing in an era of questionable executive actions to hear one of our leading mangers say, "Our mutuality is about fairness. It's about upholding strong principles. It's about delivering value through our dividend. It's about taking the long-term view and looking beyond next quarter's earnings. It's about avoiding conflict between the interests of shareholders and customers. It's about serving you today and tomorrow."

> " Our mutuality is about fairness.... It's about avoiding conflict between the interests of shareholders and customers."

Power and Influence

Edward J. Zore obviously does not have a problem with a conflict of interest between owners and customers (they are the same). Yet, as head of the largest individual life insurance provider, he must still deal effectively with questions of power and politics. Most managers find there are never enough resources—money, people, time, or authority—to get things done. They see a power gap.[2] As discussed throughout this chapter, power and politics have two sides. On the one hand, power and politics represent the seamy side of management, since organizations are not democracies composed of individuals with equal influence. On the other hand, power and politics are important organizational tools that managers must use to get the job done. Yet it is possible to isolate many instances where individual and organizational interests are compatible.[3]

In OB, **power** is defined as the ability to get someone to do something you want done or the ability to make things happen in the way you want them to. In Chapter 11 we examined leadership as a key power mechanism to make things happen. Now it is time to discuss other ways. The essence of power is control over the behavior of others.[4] While power is the force you use to make things happen in an intended way, **influence** is what you have when you exercise power, and it is expressed by others' behavioral response to your exercise of power. Managers derive power from both organizational and individual sources. These sources are called *position power* and *personal power*, respectively.[5]

Power is the ability to get someone else to do something you want done or the ability to make things happen or get things done the way you want.

Influence is a behavioral response to the exercise of power.

Position Power

In the modern firm, one important source of power available to a manager stems solely from his or her position in the organization. Specifically, position power stems from roots associated with the position. There are six important aspects of position power: reward, coercive, legitimate, process, information, and representative power.

Reward power is the extent to which a manager can use extrinsic and intrinsic rewards to control other people. Examples of such rewards include money, promotions, compliments, or enriched jobs. Although all managers have some access to rewards, success in accessing and utilizing rewards to achieve influence varies according to the skills of the manager.

Power can also be founded on punishment instead of reward. For example, a manager may threaten to withhold a pay raise or to transfer, demote, or even recommend the firing of a subordinate who does not act as desired. Such **coercive power** is the extent to which a manager can deny desired rewards or administer punishments to control other people. The availability of coercive power also varies from one organization and manager to another. The presence of unions and organizational policies on employee treatment can weaken this power base considerably.

The third base of position power is **legitimate power**, or formal hierarchical authority. It stems from the extent to which a manager can use subordinates' internalized values or beliefs that the "boss" has a "right of command" to control their behavior. For example, the boss may have the formal authority to approve or deny such employee requests as job transfers, equipment purchases, personal time off, or overtime work. Legitimate power represents a special kind of power a manager has because subordinates believe it is legitimate for a person occupying the managerial position as their boss to have the right to command. If this legitimacy is lost, authority will not be accepted by subordinates.

Process power is the control over methods of production and analysis. The source of this power is the placing of the individual in a position to influence how inputs are transformed into outputs for the firm, a department in the firm, or even a small group. Firms often establish process specialists who work with managers to ensure that production is accomplished efficiently and effectively. Closely related to this is control of the analytical processes used to make choices. For example, many organizations have individuals with specialties in financial analysis. They may review proposals from other parts of the firm for investments. Their power derives not from the calculation itself, but from the assignment to determine the analytical procedures used to judge the proposals. Process power may be separated from legitimate hierarchical power simply because of the complexity of the firm's operations. A manager may have the formal hierarchical authority to decide but may be required to use the analytical schemes of others and/or to consult on effective implementation with process specialists. As you can tell, the issue of position power can get quite complex very quickly in sophisticated operations. This leads us to another related aspect of position power—the role of access to and control of information.

Information power is the access to and/or the control of information. It is one of the most important aspects of legitimacy. The "right to know" and use information can be, and often is, conferred on a position holder. Thus, information power may complement legitimate hierarchical power. Information power may also be granted to specialists and managers who are in the middle of the information systems of the firm. For example, the chief information officer of the firm may not only control all the computers, but may also have access to almost any information desired. Managers jealously guard the formal "right to know," be-

Reward power is the extent to which a manager can use extrinsic and intrinsic rewards to control other people.

Coercive power is the extent to which a manager can deny desired rewards or administer punishment to control other people.

Legitimate power or formal authority is the extent to which a manager can use the "right of command" to control other people.

Process power is the control over methods of production and analysis.

Information power is the access to and/or the control of information.

cause it means they are in a position to influence events, not merely react to them. For example, most chief executive officers believe they have the right to know about everything in "their" firm. Deeper in the organization, managers often protect information from others based on the notion that outsiders would not understand it. For instance, engineering drawings are not typically allowed outside of the engineering department. In other instances, information is to be protected from outsiders. Marketing plans may be labeled "top secret." In most instances the nominal reason for controlling information is to protect the firm. The real reason is often to allow information holders to increase their power.

Representative power is the formal right conferred by the firm to speak as a representative for a potentially important group composed of individuals across departments or outside the firm. In most complex organizations there are a wide variety of different constituencies that may have an important impact on their firm's operations and/or its success. They include such groups as investors, customers, alliance partners, and, of course, unions. Astute executives often hire individuals to act as representatives of and to these constituencies to ensure that their influence is felt but does not dominate. So, for instance, investor relations managers are expected to deal with the mundane inquiries of small investors, anticipate the questions of financial analysts, and represent the sentiment of investors to senior management. To continue the example, the investor relations manager may be asked to anticipate the questions of investors and guide the type of responses senior management may make. The influence of the investor relations manager is in part based on the assignment to represent the interests of this important group.

■■■ **Representative power** is the formal right conferred by the firm to speak for and to a potentially important group.

ETHICS AND SOCIAL RESPONSIBILITY

THE IMPORTANCE OF ETHICS AT TEXAS INSTRUMENTS

On its Web site, the company states, "Our reputation at TI depends upon all of the decisions we make and all the actions we take personally each day. Our values define how we will evaluate our decisions and actions." TI backs this up with a business-card-sized minipamphlet with the TI ethics quick test:

Is the action legal?
Does it comply with our values?
If you do it, will you feel bad?
How will it look in the newspaper?
If you know it's wrong, don't do it.
If you're not sure, ask.
Keep asking until you get an answer.

Question: How applicable is the quick test for all firms?

Finally, it is important to stress the unstated underpinning of legitimacy in most organizations. This is an implicit moral and technical order. As we will note later in this chapter, from the crib to the school to work to retirement, individuals in our society are taught to obey "higher authority." In U.S. firms, "higher authority" means those close to the top of the corporate pyramid. In other societies, "higher authority" does not have a bureaucratic or organizational reference but consists of those with moral authority such as tribal chiefs, religious leaders, and the like. In firms, the legitimacy of those at the top increasingly derives from their positions as representatives for various constituencies. This is a technical or instrumental role. Many senior executives also evoke ethics and social causes in their role as authority figures, and many firms, such as Texas Instruments, recognize that ethics is important as a foundation for its power.

Personal Power

Personal power resides in the individual and is independent of that individual's position. Personal power is important in many well-managed firms. Three bases of personal power are expertise, rational persuasion, and reference.

Expert power is the ability to control another person's behavior through the possession of knowledge, experience, or judgment that the other person does not have but needs. A subordinate obeys a supervisor possessing expert power because the boss ordinarily knows more about what is to be done or how it is to be done than does the subordinate. Expert power is relative, not absolute.

Rational persuasion is the ability to control another's behavior because, through the individual's efforts, the person accepts the desirability of an offered goal and a reasonable way of achieving it. Much of what a supervisor does day to day involves rational persuasion up, down, and across the organization.

Rational persuasion involves both explaining the desirability of expected outcomes and showing how specific actions will achieve these outcomes. Relational persuasion rests on trust. The Effective Manager 12.1 shows some basics in building trust.

Referent power is the ability to control another's behavior because the person wants to identify with the power source. In this case, a subordinate obeys the boss because he or she wants to behave, perceive, or believe as the boss does. This obedience may occur, for example, because the subordinate likes the boss personally and therefore tries to do things the way the boss wants them done. In a sense, the subordinate attempts to avoid doing anything that would interfere with the pleasing boss–subordinate relationship. A person's referent power can be enhanced when the individual taps into the moral order or shows a clearer long-term path to a morally desirable end. In common language, individuals with the ability to tap into these more esoteric aspects of corporate life have "charisma" and "the vision thing." Followership is not based on what the subordinate will get for specific actions or specific levels of performance, but on what the individual represents—a path toward a loftier future.

> **■ Expert power** is the ability to control another's behavior because of the possession of knowledge, experience, or judgment that the other person does not have but needs.

> **■ Rational persuasion** is the ability to control another's behavior because, through the individual's efforts, the person accepts the desirability of an offered goal and a reasonable way of achieving it.

> **■ Referent power** is the ability to control another's behavior because of the individual's desire to identify with the power source.

THE EFFECTIVE MANAGER 12.1

Developing Trust

One key to ethically developing power is to build trust. To build trust, a manager should, at a minimum:

- Always honor implied and explicit social contracts.
- Seek to prevent, avoid, and rectify harm to others.
- Respect the unique needs of others.

Building Influence

A considerable portion of any manager's time is directed toward what is called power-oriented behavior. Power-oriented behavior is action directed primarily at developing or using relationships in which other people are to some degree will-

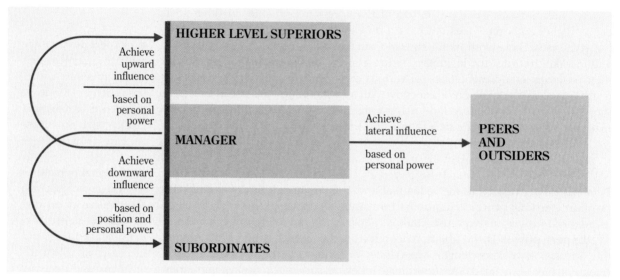

Figure 12.1   **Three dimensions of managerial power and influence.**

ing to defer to one's wishes.[6] Figure 12.1 shows three basic dimensions of power and influence with which a manager will become involved in this regard: downward, upward, and lateral. Also shown in the figure are some preliminary ideas for achieving success along each of these dimensions.

The effective manager is one who succeeds in building and maintaining high levels of both position and personal power over time. Only then is sufficient power of the right types available when the manager needs to exercise influence on downward, lateral, and upward dimensions.

Building Position Power   Position power can be enhanced when managers are able to demonstrate to others that their work units are highly relevant to organizational goals and are able to respond to urgent organizational needs. To increase centrality and criticality in the organization, managers may seek to acquire a more central role in the workflow by having information filtered through them, making at least part of their job responsibilities unique, expanding their network of communication contacts, and occupying an office convenient to main traffic flows.

Managers may also attempt to increase the relevance of their tasks and those of their unit to the organization. There are many ways to do this. Executives may attempt to become an internal coordinator within the firm or external representative. They may suggest their subordinates take on these roles, particularly when the firm is downsizing. When the firm is in a dynamic setting of changing technology, the executive may also move to provide unique services and information to other units. This is particularly effective if the executive moves his or her unit into becoming involved with decisions central to the organization's top-priority goals. To expand their position, managers may also delegate routine activities, expand the task variety and novelty for subordinates, initiate new ideas, and get involved in new projects. We will have more to say about this matter when discussing empowerment.

CULTURES AND THE GLOBAL WORKFORCE

RECOGNIZING A MANAGER'S ABILITY TO CAPITALIZE ON MAJOR OPPORTUNITIES

Avocent is a global supplier of KVM (keyboard, video, and mouse) switching and network appliances. These products provide IT managers with access to control of multiple servers and network data center devices. KVM switching systems provide access and control of multiple racks of servers from a single console, as well as control from remote locations. These switches eliminate extra keyboards, monitors, and mice and allow businesses to save critical space in their data centers. Avocent's KVM solutions are distributed by the world's largest server manufacturers and installed in *Fortune* 100 companies around the world.

When Stephen F. Thornton, CEO, announced the promotion of Doyle C. Weeks to the newly created position of Executive Vice President, Group Operations and Business Development, he cited Doyle's critical role in "directing our international expansion." Unsaid, but recognized by both market analysts and key individuals within the firm, was the five-year average growth of 42 percent for the company, much of it outside the United States.

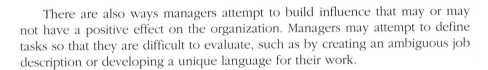

Question: Had Doyle Weeks focused only on domestic operations, do you think he would have been promoted?

There are also ways managers attempt to build influence that may or may not have a positive effect on the organization. Managers may attempt to define tasks so that they are difficult to evaluate, such as by creating an ambiguous job description or developing a unique language for their work.

Building Personal Power Personal power arises from the personal characteristics of the manager rather than from the location and other characteristics of his or her position in the organization's hierarchy of authority.

Three personal characteristics—expertise, political savvy, and likability—have special potential for enhancing personal power in an organization. The most obvious is *building expertise.* Additional expertise may be gained by advanced training and education, participation in professional associations, and involvement in the early stages of projects.

A somewhat less obvious way to increase personal power is to learn *political savvy*—better ways to negotiate, persuade individuals, and understand the goals and means they are most willing to accept. The novice believes that most individuals are very much the same, see the same goals, and will accept much the same paths toward these goals. The more astute individual recognizes important individual differences.

A manager's reference power is increased by characteristics that enhance his or her *likability* and create personal attraction in relationships with other people. These include pleasant personality characteristics, agreeable behavior patterns, and attractive personal appearance. The demonstration of sincere hard work on behalf of task performance can also increase personal power by enhancing both expertise and reference. A person who is perceived to try hard may be expected to know more about the job and thus be sought out for advice. A person who tries hard is also likely to be respected for the attempt and may even be depended on by others to maintain that effort.

Using Information and Influence Techniques   From a purely analytical standpoint, most sources of power can be traced to position power or personal power. However, many of the influential actions and behaviors are combinations of position and personal power.

Increasing Visibility and Control over Information   Most managers attempt to increase the visibility of their job performance by (1) expanding the number of contacts they have with senior people, (2) making oral presentations of written work, (3) participating in problem-solving task forces, (4) sending out notices of accomplishment, and (5) generally seeking additional opportunities to increase personal name recognition. Most managers also recognize that, between superiors and subordinates, access to or control over information is an important element. A boss may appear to expand his or her expert power over a subordinate by not allowing the individual access to critical information. Although the denial may appear to enhance the boss's expert power, it may reduce the subordinate's effectiveness. In a similar manner, a supervisor may also control access to key organizational decision makers. An individual's ability to contact key persons informally can offset some of this disadvantage. Furthermore, astute senior executives routinely develop "back channels" to lower-level individuals deep within the firm to offset the tendency of bosses to control information and access.

Expert power is often relational and embedded within the organizational context. Many important decisions are made outside formal channels and are substantially influenced by key individuals with the requisite knowledge. By developing and using coalitions and networks, an individual may build on his or her expert power. Through coalitions and networks, an individual may alter the flow of information and the context for analysis. By developing coalitions and networks, executives also expand their access to information and their opportunities for participation.

Controlling Decision Premises   Executives also attempt to control, or at least influence, decision premises. A decision premise is a basis for defining the problem and for selecting among alternatives. By defining a problem in a manner that fits the executive's expertise, it is natural for that executive to be in charge of solving it. Thus, the executive subtly shifts his or her position power.

Executives who want to increase their power often make their goals and needs clear and bargain effectively to show that their preferred goals and needs are best. They do not show their power base directly but instead provide clear "rational persuasion" for their preferences. So the astute executive does not threaten or attempt to invoke sanctions to build power. Instead, he or she combines personal power with the position of the unit to enhance total power. As the organizational context changes, different personal sources of power may become more important alone and in combination with the individual's position power. So there is an art to building power.

Perfecting Influence Techniques   Using position and personal power well to achieve the desired influence over other people is a challenge for most managers. Practically speaking, there are many useful ways of exercising relational influence. The most common techniques involve the following:[7]

Reason	Using facts and data to support a logical argument.	
Friendliness	Using flattery, goodwill, and favorable impressions.	
Coalition	Using relationships with other people for support.	
Bargaining	Using the exchange of benefits as a basis for negotiation.	
Assertiveness	Using a direct and forceful personal approach.	
Higher authority	Gaining higher-level support for one's requests.	
Sanctions	Using organizationally derived rewards and punishments.	

Techniques for exercising relational influence

Research on these strategies suggests that reason is the most popular technique overall.[8] In addition, friendliness, assertiveness, bargaining, and higher authority are used more frequently to influence subordinates than to influence supervisors. This pattern of influence attempts is consistent with our earlier contention that downward influence generally includes mobilization of both position and personal power sources, whereas upward influence is more likely to draw on personal power.

Little research is available on the subject of upward influence in organizations. This is unfortunate, since truly effective managers are able to influence their bosses as well as their subordinates. One study reports that both supervisors and subordinates view reason, or the logical presentation of ideas, as the most frequently used strategy of upward influence.[9] When queried on reasons for success and failure, however, the two groups show both similarities and differences in their viewpoints. The perceived causes of success in upward influence are similar for both supervisors and subordinates and involve the favorable content of the influence attempt, a favorable manner of its presentation, and the competence of the subordinate.[10] The two groups disagree on the causes of failure, however. Subordinates attribute failure in upward influence to the close-mindedness of the supervisor, unfavorable content of the influence attempt, and unfavorable interpersonal relationships with the supervisor. In contrast, supervisors attribute failure to the unfavorable content of the attempt, the unfavorable manner in which it was presented, and the subordinate's lack of competence.

Power, Formal Authority, and Obedience

As we have shown, power is the potential to control the behavior of others, and formal authority is the potential to exert such control through the legitimacy of a managerial position. But why should subordinates respond to a manager's authority, or "right to command," in the first place? Furthermore, given that subordinates are willing to obey, what determines the limits of obedience?

Obedience

The mythology of American independence and unbridled individualism is so strong we need to spend some time explaining how most of us are really quite obedient. So we turn to the seminal studies of Stanley Milgram on obedience.[11] Milgram designed experiments to determine the extent to which people obey the commands of an authority figure, even if they believe they are endangering the life of another person. Subjects, ranging in age from 20 to 50 and representing a diverse set of occupations (engineers, salespeople, schoolteachers, laborers, and others), were paid a nominal fee for participation in the project.

The subjects were falsely told that the purpose of the study was to determine the effects of punishment on learning. The subjects were to be the "teachers." The "learner" was a confederate of Milgram's, who was strapped to a chair in an adjoining room with an electrode attached to his wrist. The "experimenter," another confederate of Milgram's, was dressed in a laboratory coat. Appearing impassive and somewhat stern, the experimenter instructed the teacher to read a series of word pairs to the learner and then to reread the first word along with four other terms. The learner was supposed to indicate which of the four terms was in the original pair by pressing a switch that caused a light to flash on a response panel in front of the teacher.

The teacher was instructed to administer a shock to the learner each time a wrong answer was given. This shock was to be increased one level of intensity each time the learner made a mistake. The teacher controlled switches that ostensibly administered shocks ranging from 15 to 450 volts. In reality, there was no electric current in the apparatus, but the learners purposely "erred" often and responded to each level of "shock" in progressively distressing ways. If a teacher (subject) proved unwilling to administer a shock, the experimenter used the following sequential prods to get him or her to perform as requested. (1) "Please continue" or "Please go on"; (2) "The experiment requires that you continue"; (3) "It is absolutely essential that you continue"; and (4) "You have no choice, you must go on." Only when the teacher refused to go on after the fourth prod would the experiment be stopped. When would you expect the teachers to refuse to go on?

Milgram asked some of his students and colleagues the same question. Most felt that few, if any, of the subjects would go beyond the "very strong shock" level. Actually, 26 subjects (65 percent) continued to the end of the experiment and shocked the learners to the maximum. None stopped before 300 volts, the point at which the learner pounded on the wall. The remaining 14 subjects refused to obey the experimenter at various intermediate points.

Most people are surprised by these results, as was Milgram. The question is why other people would have a tendency to accept or comply with authoritative commands under such extreme conditions. Milgram conducted further experiments to try to answer this question. The subjects' tendencies toward compliance were somewhat reduced (1) when experimentation took place in a rundown office (rather than a university lab), (2) when the victim was closer, (3) when the experimenter was farther away, and (4) when the subject could observe other subjects. However, the level of compliance was still much higher than most of us would expect. In short, there is the tendency for individuals to comply and be obedient—to switch off and merely do exactly what they are told to do.

Acceptance of Authority

Direct defiance within organizational settings is quite rare, as is the individual who institutes new and different ways to get the job done. If the tendency to follow instructions is great and defiance is rare, then why do so many organizations appear to drift into apparent chaos?

The answer to this question can be found in work by the famous management writer Chester Barnard.[12] Barnard's argument focused on the "consent of the governed" rather than on the rights derived from ownership. He argued that subordinates accepted or followed a directive from the boss only under special circumstances.

All four of these circumstances must be met: (1) the subordinate can and must understand the directive; (2) the subordinate must feel mentally and physically capable of carrying out the directive; (3) the subordinate must believe that the directive is not inconsistent with the purpose of the organization; and (4) the subordinate must believe that the directive is not inconsistent with his or her personal interests.

These four conditions are very carefully stated. For instance, to accept and follow an order, the subordinate does not need to understand how the proposed action will help the organization. He or she only needs to believe that the requested action is not inconsistent with the purpose of the firm. The astute manager will not take these guidelines for granted. In giving directives, the astute manager recognizes that the acceptance of the request is not assured.

Zone of Indifference

Most people seek a balance between what they put into an organization (contributions) and what they get from an organization in return (inducements). Within the boundaries of the psychological contract, therefore, employees will agree to do many things in and for the organization because they think they should. In exchange for certain inducements, subordinates recognize the authority of the organization and its managers to direct their behavior in certain ways. Based on his acceptance view of authority, Chester Barnard calls this area in which directions are obeyed the "zone of indifference."[13]

A **zone of indifference** is the range of authoritative requests to which a subordinate is willing to respond without subjecting the directives to critical evaluation or judgment. Directives falling within the zone are obeyed. Requests or orders falling outside the zone of indifference are not considered legitimate under terms of the psychological contract. Such "extraordinary" directives may or may not be obeyed. This link between the zone of indifference and the psychological contract is shown in Figure 12.2.

A **zone of indifference** is the range of authoritative requests to which a subordinate is willing to respond without subjecting the directives to critical evaluation or judgment.

Figure 12.2   Hypothetical psychological contract for a secretary.

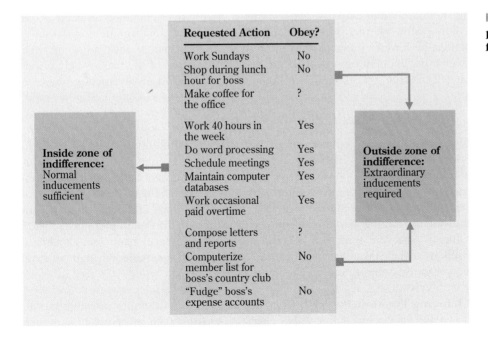

Requested Action	Obey?
Work Sundays	No
Shop during lunch hour for boss	No
Make coffee for the office	?
Work 40 hours in the week	Yes
Do word processing	Yes
Schedule meetings	Yes
Maintain computer databases	Yes
Work occasional paid overtime	Yes
Compose letters and reports	?
Computerize member list for boss's country club	No
"Fudge" boss's expense accounts	No

Inside zone of indifference: Normal inducements sufficient

Outside zone of indifference: Extraordinary inducements required

The zone of indifference is not fixed. There may be times when a boss would like a subordinate to do things falling outside the zone. In this case, the manager must enlarge the zone to accommodate additional behaviors. In these attempts, a manager most likely will have to use more incentives than pure position power. In some instances, no power base may be capable of accomplishing the desired result. Consider your own zone of indifference and tendency to obey. When will you say "No" to your boss? When should you be willing to say "No"? At times, the situation may involve ethical dilemmas, where you may be asked to do things that are illegal, unethical, or both.

Research on ethical managerial behavior shows that supervisors can become sources of pressure for subordinates to do such things as support incorrect viewpoints, sign false documents, overlook the supervisor's wrongdoing, and do business with the supervisor's friends.[14] Most of us will occasionally face such ethical dilemmas during our careers. Some firms, such as Texas Instruments, are very clear about ethical boundaries. Others are more vague. For now, we must simply remember that saying "No" or "refusing to keep quiet" can be difficult and potentially costly.

Empowerment

Empowerment is the process by which managers help others to acquire and use the power needed to make decisions affecting themselves and their work.

Empowerment is the process by which managers help others to acquire and use the power needed to make decisions affecting themselves and their work. More than ever before, managers in progressive organizations are expected to be good at (and highly comfortable with) empowering the people with whom they work. Rather than considering power to be something to be held only at higher levels in the traditional "pyramid" of organizations, this view considers power to be something that can be shared by everyone working in flatter and more collegial structures.

The concept of empowerment is part of the sweeping change being witnessed in today's corporations. Corporate staff is being cut back; layers of management are being eliminated; the number of employees is being reduced as the volume of work increases. What is left is a leaner and trimmer organization staffed by fewer managers who must share more power as they go about their daily tasks. Indeed, empowerment is a key foundation of the increasingly popular self-managing work teams and other creative worker involvement groups.

Keys to Empowerment

One of the bases for empowerment is a radically different view of power itself. So far, our discussion has focused on power that is exerted over other individuals. In this traditional view, power is relational in terms of individuals. In contrast, the concept of empowerment emphasizes the ability to make things happen. Power is still relational, but in terms of problems and opportunities, not individuals. Cutting through all the corporate rhetoric on empowerment is quite difficult, since the term has become quite fashionable in management circles. Each individual empowerment attempt needs to be examined in light of how power in the organization will be changed.

Changing Position Power When an organization attempts to move power down the hierarchy, it must also alter the existing pattern of position power.

Changing this pattern raises some important questions. Can "empowered" individuals give rewards and sanctions based on task accomplishment? Has their new right to act been legitimized with formal authority? All too often, attempts at empowerment disrupt well-established patterns of position power and threaten middle- and lower-level managers. As one supervisor said, "All this empowerment stuff sounds great for top management. They don't have to run around trying to get the necessary clearances to implement the suggestions from my group. They never gave me the authority to make the changes, only the new job of asking for permission."

Expanding the Zone of Indifference   When embarking on an empowerment program, management needs to recognize the current zone of indifference and systematically move to expand it. All too often, management assumes that its directive for empowerment will be followed because management sees empowerment as a better way to manage. Management needs to show precisely how empowerment will benefit the individuals involved and provide the inducement needed to expand the zone of indifference.

Power as an Expanding Pie

Along with empowerment, employees need to be trained to expand their power and their new influence potential. This is the most difficult task for managers and a difficult challenge for employees, for it often changes the dynamic between supervisors and subordinates. The key is to change the concept of power within the organization from a view that stresses power over others to one that emphasizes the use of power to get things done. Under the new definition of power, all employees can be more powerful.

A clearer definition of roles and responsibilities may help managers empower others. For instance, senior managers may choose to concentrate on long-term, large-scale adjustments to a variety of challenging and strategic forces in the external environment. If top management tends to concentrate on the long term and downplay quarterly mileposts, others throughout the organization must be ready and willing to make critical operating decisions to maintain current profitability. By providing opportunities for creative problem solving coupled with the discretion to act, real empowerment increases the total power available in an organization. In other words, the top levels don't have to give up power in order for the lower levels to gain it. Note that senior managers must give up the illusion of control—the false belief that they can direct the actions of employees five or six levels of management below them.

The same basic arguments hold true in any manager–subordinate relationship. Empowerment means that all managers need to emphasize different ways of exercising influence. Appeals to higher authority and sanctions need to be replaced by appeals to reason. Friendliness must replace coercion, and bargaining must replace orders for compliance.

Given the all too familiar history of an emphasis on coercion and compliance within firms, special support may be needed for individuals so that they become comfortable in developing their own power over events and activities. What executives fear, and all too often find, is that employees passively resist empowerment by seeking directives they can obey or reject. The fault lies with the executives and the middle managers who need to rethink what they mean by power and rethink their use of traditional position and personal power sources. The key is to lead, not push; reward, not sanction; build, not destroy; and expand, not shrink. To expand the zone of indifference also calls for expanding the inducements for thinking and acting, not just for obeying.

Organizational Politics

Any study of power and influence inevitably leads to the subject of "politics." For many, this word may conjure up thoughts of illicit deals, favors, and special personal relationships. Perhaps this image of shrewd, often dishonest, practices of obtaining one's way is reinforced by Machiavelli's classic fifteenth-century work *The Prince*, which outlines how to obtain and hold power via political action. It is important, however, to adopt a perspective that allows politics in organizations to function in a much broader capacity.[15]

The Traditions of Organizational Politics

There are two quite different traditions in the analysis of organizational politics. One tradition builds on Machiavelli's philosophy and defines *politics in terms of self-interest* and the use of nonsanctioned means. In this tradition, **organizational politics** may be formally defined as the management of influence to obtain ends not sanctioned by the organization or to obtain sanctioned ends through nonsanctioned influence means.[16] Managers are often considered political when they seek their own goals or use means that are not currently authorized by the organization or that push legal limits. Where there is uncertainty or ambiguity, it is often extremely difficult to tell whether a manager is being political in this self-serving sense.[17] For instance, was John Meriwether a great innovator when he established Long Term Capital Management (LTCM) as a hedge fund to bet on interest rate spreads?[18] At one time, the firm included 2 Nobel laureates and some 25 PhDs. Or was he the consummate insider when he got the U.S. Federal Reserve to orchestrate a bailout when it looked like he would either go broke or lose control to a rich investor? Or, as often happens in the world of corporate politics, could both of these statements be partially true?

The second tradition treats politics as a necessary function resulting from differences in the self-interests of individuals. Here, *organizational politics* is viewed as the art of creative compromise among competing interests. In the case of John Meriwether and LTCM, when it went bankrupt the country's financial leaders were concerned that it could cause a panic in the global financial markets and hurt everyone. So the Federal Reserve stepped in. That Meriwether did not lose everything was merely a by-product of saving the whole financial system. In a heterogeneous society, individuals will disagree as to whose self-interests are most valuable and whose concerns should therefore be bounded by collective interests. Politics arises because individuals need to develop compromises, avoid confrontation, and live together. The same holds true in organizations, where individuals join, work, and stay together because their self-interests are served. Furthermore, it is important to remember that the goals of the organization and the acceptable means of achieving them are established by organizationally powerful individuals in negotiation with others. Thus, organiza-

■ **Organizational politics** is the management of influence to obtain ends not sanctioned by the organization or to obtain sanctioned ends through nonsanctioned means and the art of creative compromise among competing interests.

tional politics is also the use of power to develop socially acceptable ends and means that balance individual and collective interests.

Political Interpretation   The two different traditions of organizational politics are reflected in the ways executives describe their effects on managers and their organizations. In one survey, some 53 percent of those interviewed indicated that organizational politics enhanced the achievement of organizational goals and survival.[19] Yet some 44 percent suggested that it distracted individuals from organizational goals. In this same survey, 60 percent of respondents suggested that organizational politics was good for career advancement; 39 percent reported that it led to a loss of power, position, and credibility.

Organizational politics is not automatically good or bad. It can serve a number of important functions, including overcoming personnel inadequacies, coping with change, and substituting for formal authority. As shown in The Effective Manager 12.2, political skill has even been linked to lower executive stress.

Even in the best-managed firms, mismatches arise among managers who are learning, burned out, lacking in needed training and skills, overqualified, or lacking the resources needed to accomplish their assigned duties. Organizational politics provides a mechanism for circumventing these inadequacies and getting the job done. Organizational politics can facilitate adaptation to changes in the environment and technology of an organization.

Organizational politics can help identify problems and move ambitious, problem-solving managers into the breach. It is quicker than restructuring. It allows the firm to meet unanticipated problems with people and resources quickly, before small headaches become major problems. Finally, when a person's formal authority breaks down or fails to apply to a particular situation, political actions can be used to prevent a loss of influence. Managers may use political behavior to maintain operations and to achieve task continuity in circumstances where the failure of formal authority may otherwise cause problems.

Political Forecasting   Managers may gain a better understanding of political behavior to forecast future actions by placing themselves in the positions of other persons involved in critical decisions or events. Each action and decision can be seen as having benefits for and costs to all parties concerned. Where the costs exceed the benefits, the manager may act to protect his or her position.

Figure 12.3 shows a sample payoff table for two managers, Lee and Leslie, in a problem situation involving a decision as to whether or not to allocate resources to a special project. If both managers authorize the resources, the project gets completed on time and their company keeps a valuable client. Unfortunately, if they do this, both Lee and Leslie overspend their budgets. Taken on its own, a budget overrun would be bad for the managers' performance records. Assume that the overruns are acceptable only if the client is kept. Thus, if both managers act, both they and the company win, as depicted in the upper-left

---

THE EFFECTIVE MANAGER 12.2

Political Skill as an Antidote for Stress

Ever wonder why executives under tremendous daily stress don't burn out? Some argue it is their political skill that saves them. Which specific political skills? Think of these:

- The ability to use practical intelligence (as opposed to analytical or creative intelligence)
- The ability to be calculating and shrewd about social connections
- The ability to inspire trust and confidence
- The ability to deal with individuals having a wide variety of backgrounds, styles, and personalities

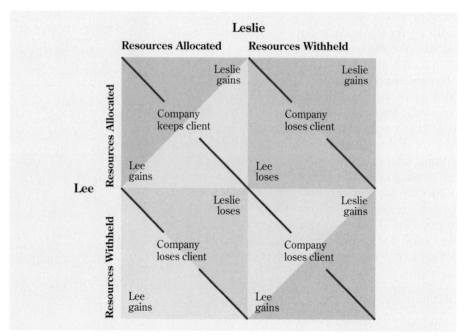

Figure 12.3   **Political payoff matrix for the allocation of resources on a sample project.**

block of the figure. Obviously, this is the most desirable outcome for all parties concerned.

Assume that Leslie acts, but Lee does not. In this case, the company loses the client, Leslie overspends the budget in a futile effort, but Lee ends up within budget. While the company and Leslie lose, Lee wins. This scenario is illustrated in the lower-left block of the figure. The upper-right block shows the reverse situation, where Lee acts but Leslie does not. In this case, Leslie wins, while the company and Lee lose. Finally, if both Lee and Leslie fail to act, each stays within the budget and therefore gains, but the company loses the client.

The company clearly wants both Lee and Leslie to act. But will they? Would you take the risk of overspending the budget, knowing that your colleague may refuse? The question of trust is critical here, but building trust among co-managers and other workers takes time and can be difficult. The involvement of higher-level managers may be needed to set the stage better. Yet in many organizations both Lee and Leslie would fail to act because the "climate" or "culture" too often encourages people to maximize their self-interest at minimal risk.

Subunit Power   To be effective in political action, managers should also understand the politics of subunit relations.[20] Line units are typically more powerful than are staff groups, and units toward the top of the hierarchy are often more powerful than are those toward the bottom. More subtle relationships are found among units at or near the same level in a firm.

Political action links managers more formally to one another as representatives of their work units. Five of the more typical lateral, intergroup relations in which you may engage as a manager are workflow, service, advisory, auditing,

Leaders on Leadership

CO-CEOS WORK AT SMUCKERS

Family businesses often disintegrate when there are several family rivals for the top spot. J. M.

Smucker Company was founded in 1897 when J. M. started selling apple butter from the back of a horse-drawn wagon in Ohio. Now Smuckers is more than just jam, jellies, and preserves. It is also about peanut butter, ice cream toppings, shortening, and the two who hold the position of chief executive officer. It is still headquartered in Orrville, Ohio, and it has been a family-run business for four generations. Timothy P. Smucker and Richard K. Smucker solved the problem of

who would run the family business—they would. Instead of trying to pick one person to be the all-powerful chief executive officer, they have divided the duties. Timothy is chairman and co-CEO, while Richard is president, co-CEO, and chief financial officer. These executives believe that their unique arrangement actually helps minimize organizational politics and promotes Smuckers' basic values of quality, people ethics, growth, and independence.

Question: Why must there be only one individual at the top of a corporation?

---

and approval.[21] Workflow linkages involve contacts with units that precede or follow in a sequential production chain. Service ties involve contacts with units established to help with problems. For instance, an assembly-line manager may develop a service link by asking the maintenance manager to fix an important piece of equipment on a priority basis. In contrast, advisory connections involve formal staff units having special expertise, such as a manager seeking the advice of the personnel department on evaluating subordinates. Auditing linkages involve units that have the right to evaluate the actions of others after action has been taken, whereas approval linkages involve units whose approval must be obtained before action may be taken. In general, units gain power as more of their relations with others are of the approval and auditing types. Workflow relations are more powerful than are advisory associations, and both are more powerful than are service relations.

Politics and Corporate Strategy   While much of the strategy literature has been preoccupied with the economic and organizational aspects of strategy, there is growing awareness of the importance of political strategy. Three aspects have received considerable recent attention. First is the absence of a political strategy in some corporations, mainly Silicon Valley and software firms. It can be argued, for example, that Microsoft's antitrust problems were in part due to an unwillingness of Bill Gates and Steven Ballmer to consider the political ramifications of their attempts to block competitors by coercing computer manufacturers.

In contrast, consider the approach of John Chambers, CEO of Cisco Systems. Cisco has over 80 percent of the high-speed server market, clearly almost a monopolistic position. He met with U.S. Justice Department officials to preempt government action. He assured regulators his firm was not acting like Microsoft. It just had the patents and a superior technology.[22] In general, U.S. firms are admonished to reject passive reaction to government policy or even passive anticipation. Instead they are advised to engage in the public political process by becoming politically active firms that can co-evolve with key parts of their setting.[23]

PEOPLE AND TECHNOLOGY

IGNORING THE POLITICAL ASPECTS OF STRATEGY COMES AT A BIG COST

Bill Gates (founder) and Steven A. Ballmer (now CEO) paid little attention to the political side of Microsoft's strategy. As the twentieth century closed, however, the U.S. government sued, claiming that the software giant was a monopolist. With 95 percent of new computers using Windows, the suit claimed Microsoft used its power to unfairly eliminate competitors and potential competitors. Microsoft bundled something called a browser into its Windows operating system and required computer makers to incorporate its new system into virtually all of their machines. A federal judge ordered massive payments by the firm, a cessation of coercive practices, and a breakup of the firm.

Microsoft, however, negotiated a settlement. Without pleading guilty, Microsoft agreed to stop coercive practices, it made some elements of Windows more open to rival developers, and it agreed to spend over a billion dollars on computers and software to be sent to deserving U.S. public schools.

Question: What do you think the public reaction would be if Bill Gates and Steven Ballmer became much more politically active?

A second aspect of a corporate political strategy is turning the government from a regulator of the industry to a protector. Immediately after the events of 9/11, a wounded airline industry collectively sought government help with an immediate financial bailout in the billions of dollars. On a more routine basis, U.S. steel companies have sought protection from foreign competition for over 40 years. Here, the industry's largest firms dominated the politics surrounding trade protection. They sought and generally received protection when U.S. demand was weakest. They used a variety of tactics ranging from political contributions to information campaigns to establish an agenda favoring their position.[24]

Of course, a third and most critical aspect of a corporate political strategy is when and how to get involved in the public policy processes. There are no easy answers. Smaller firms with less governmental regulation of their industry may be willing to take a so-called transactional approach. They become involved in specific issues with specific public policy officials who deal with a given issue. Larger firms in more regulated settings should not wait for the agenda to be formed. Instead they should be more relationally oriented. That is, they should monitor the environment, help shape emerging issues, and build solid relationships with a broad spectrum of policymakers. While firms may do this alone, most seek allies and build coalitions of firms to shape and guide the process of issue development.

As the economy continues to globalize and firms move across national boundaries, the development and implementation of an effective political strategy have become both more important and more difficult.[25] For example, U.S. regulators were willing to allow General Electric to buy a firm called Honeywell. Unfortunately for General Electric, European Union representatives were not, and the proposed merger fell through. While Microsoft has apparently resolved its U.S. antitrust problems, the European Union has yet to rule.

The Politics of Self-Protection

While organizational politics may be helpful to the organization as a whole, it is probably more commonly known and better understood in terms of self-protection.[26] Whether or not management likes it, all employees recognize that in any organization they must watch out for themselves first. In too many organizations, if the employee doesn't protect himself or herself, no one else will.

Individuals can employ three common strategies to protect themselves. They can (1) avoid action and risk taking, (2) redirect accountability and responsibility, or (3) defend their turf.

Avoidance   Avoidance is quite common in controversial areas where the employee must risk being wrong or where actions may yield a sanction. Perhaps the most common reaction is to "work to the rules." That is, employees are protected when they adhere strictly to all the rules, policies, and procedures and do not allow deviations or exceptions. Perhaps one of the most frustrating but effective techniques is to "play dumb." We all do this at some time or another. When was the last time you said, "Officer, I didn't know the speed limit was 35. I couldn't have been going 52."

Although working to the rules and playing dumb are common techniques, experienced employees often practice somewhat more subtle techniques of self-protection. These include depersonalization and stalling. Depersonalization involves treating individuals, such as customers, clients, or subordinates, as numbers, things, or objects. Senior managers don't fire long-term employees; the organization is merely "downsized" or "delayered." Routine stalling involves slowing down the pace of work to expand the task so that the individuals look as if they are working hard. With creative stalling, the employees may spend the time supporting the organization's ideology, position, or program and delaying implementation of changes they consider undesirable.

Redirecting Responsibility   Politically sensitive individuals will always protect themselves from accepting blame for the negative consequences of their actions. Again, a variety of well-worn techniques may be used for redirecting responsibility. "Passing the buck" is a common method employees and managers use. The trick here is to define the task in such a way that it becomes someone else's formal responsibility. The ingenious ways in which individuals can redefine an issue to avoid action and transfer responsibility are often amazing.

Both employees and managers may avoid responsibility by buffing, or rigorous documentation. Here, individuals take action only when all the paperwork is in place and it is clear that they are merely following procedure. Closely related

Little Caesars

Marian Ilitch, co-founder of Little Caesars Pizza, has helped put her stamp on the corporate philosophy of Little Caesars by making it one of the best places for working women. The firm also has a long and distinguished record of supporting local charities and is headquartered in downtown Detroit. Marian recently made a million-dollar contribution to establish a hospice in Detroit.

to rigorous documentation is the "blind memo," which explains an objection to an action implemented by the individual. Here, the required action is taken, but the blind memo is prepared should the action come into question. Politicians are particularly good at this technique. They will meet with a lobbyist and then send a memo to the files confirming the meeting. Any relationship between what was discussed in the meeting and the memo is accidental.

As the last example suggests, a convenient method some managers use to avoid responsibility is merely to rewrite history. If a program is successful, the manager claims to have been an early supporter. If a program fails, the manager was the one who expressed serious reservations in the first place. Whereas a memo in the files is often nice to have to show one's early support or objections, some executives don't bother with such niceties. They merely start a meeting by recapping what has happened in such a way that makes them look good.

For the really devious, there are three other techniques for redirecting responsibility. One technique is to blame the problem on someone or some group that has difficulty defending itself. Fired employees, outsiders, and opponents are often targets of such scapegoating. Closely related to scapegoating is blaming the problem on uncontrollable events. The really astute manager goes far beyond the old "the-dog-ate-my-homework" routine. A perennial favorite is, "Given the unexpected severe decline in the overall economy, firm profitability was only somewhat below reasonable expectations." Meaning, the firm lost a bundle.

Should these techniques fail, there is always another possibility: facing apparent defeat, the manager can escalate commitment to a losing cause of action. That is, when all appears lost, assert your confidence in the original action, blame the problems on not spending enough money to implement the plan fully, and embark on actions that call for increased effort. The hope is that you will be promoted, have a new job with another firm, or be retired by the time the negative consequences are recognized.

Defending Turf Defending turf is a time-honored tradition in most large organizations. As noted earlier in the chapter, managers seeking to improve their power attempt to expand the jobs their groups perform. Defending turf also results from the coalitional nature of organizations. That is, the organization may be seen as a collection of competing interests held by various departments and groups. As each group attempts to expand its influence, it starts to encroach on the activities of other groups. Turf protection is common in organizations and runs from the very lowest position to the executive suite.

Politics and Governance

From the time of the 1890s robber barons such as Jay Gould, Americans have been fascinated with the politics of the chief executive suite. Recent accounts of alleged and proven criminal actions emanating from the executive suites of WorldCom, Enron , Global Crossings, and Tyco have brought the media spotlight to penetrate the mysterious veil shrouding politics at the top of organizations.[27]An analytical view of executive suite dynamics may lift some of the mystery.

Agency theory suggests that public corporations can function effectively even though their managers are self-interested and do not automatically bear the full consequences of their managerial actions.

Agency Theory An essential power problem in today's modern corporation arises from the separation of owners and managers. A body of work called

agency theory suggests that public corporations can function effectively even though their managers are self-interested and do not automatically bear the full consequences of their managerial actions. The theory argues that (1) all the interests of society are served by protecting stockholder interests, (2) stockholders have a clear interest in greater returns, and (3) managers are self-interested and unwilling to sacrifice these self-interests for others (particularly stockholders) and thus must be controlled. The term *agency theory* stems from the notion that managers are "agents" of the owners.[28]

So what types of controls should be instituted? There are several types. One type of control involves making sure that what is good for stockholders is good for management. Incentives in the pay plan for executives may be adjusted to align the interests of management and stockholders. For example, executives may get most of their pay based on the stock price of the firm via stock options. A second type of control involves the establishment of a strong, independent board of directors, since the board is to represent the stockholders. While this may sound unusual, it is not uncommon for a CEO to pick a majority of the board members and to place many top managers on the board. A third way is for stockholders with a large stake in the firm to take an active role on the board. For instance, mutual fund managers have been encouraged to become more active in monitoring management. And there is, of course, the so-called market for corporate control. For instance, poorly performing executives can be replaced by outsiders.[29] The problem with the simple application of all of these control mechanisms is that they do not appear to work very well even for the stockholders and clearly, some suggest, not for others either.[30]

The recent storm of controversy over CEO pay illustrates using a simple application of agency theory to control executives. Traditionally, U.S. CEOs made about 30 times the pay of the average worker. This was similar to CEO pay scales in Europe and Japan.[31] Today many U.S. CEOs are making 600 times the average pay of workers. How did they get so rich? Executive compensation specialists have derived plans that link executive pay to short-term increases in the firm's stock price. As one might expect, executives have become so interested in short-term stock price increases they may have downplayed other goals and other interests.[32] When a CEO downsizes, outsources jobs abroad, embarks on a merger campaign, or cuts such benefits as worker health care, short-term profits may jump dramatically and lift the stock price. Although the long-term health of the firm may be put in jeopardy, few U.S. CEOs seem able to resist the temptation. It is little wonder that there is renewed interest in how U.S. firms are governed. Rather than proposing some quick fix based on a limited theory of the firm, we suggest you come to a better understand of some different views on the politics of the executive suite. By taking a broader view, you can better understand politics in the modern corporation.

Resource Dependencies   Executive behavior can sometimes be explained in terms of resource dependencies—the firm's need for resources that are controlled by others.[33] Essentially, the resource dependence of an organization increases as (1) needed resources become more scarce, (2) outsiders have more control over needed resources, and (3) there are fewer substitutes for a particular type of resource controlled by a limited number of outsiders. Thus, one political role of the chief executive is to develop workable compromises among the competing resource dependencies facing the organization—compromises that

Research Insight
When CEO Stock Options Are Under Water

To align the interests of stockholders and the CEO, many advocates of agency theory suggest that CEOs should be given stock options. Here is how they work. If the current stock price is $100, the board of directors might reward the CEO with 10,000 options to buy the stock at $110, hoping that the CEO will be such a great leader that the stock price will rise well above $110. This is an option to buy, and no one would exercise an option to buy at $110 when the price is $100. In the colorful language of stock options, when the option "strike price" is less than the current price, the option is under water. Well, what happens if the stock price drops to, say, $50? The gap is huge. Will the board change the option price? Recent research by Pollock, Fischer, and Wade suggests that the board might cut the CEO a better deal. The chances that the CEO will benefit increase when (1) there is a larger gap between the option price and the current price and (2) the CEO is also chairperson of the board of directors. These results could be expected. What was not expected was the following: the greater the number of board members selected by the CEO and the more staggered their terms, the less likely the board is to give the CEO a favorable revaluation. Why? Pollock, Fischer, and Wade speculate that giving the CEO a revised set of options is such a visible action that it would be broadcast to investors and the public. A weaker board dominated by the CEO could be afraid of loosing legitimacy. By not revaluating the options, the board is sending a signal that they are not as weak as they appear. Like many other studies regarding power and politics, there are many surprises. The bottom line? The authors conclude that stock options are not a good way to align CEO and stockholder interests.

Reference: T. G. Pollock, H. M. Fischer, and J. B. Wade. "The Role of Power and Politics in the Repricing of Executive Options." *Academy of Management Journal* 45(6) (2002): 1172–1183.

enhance the executive's power. To create such compromises, executives need to diagnose the relative power of outsiders and to craft strategies that respond differently to various external resource suppliers.

For larger organizations, many strategies may center on altering the firm's degree of resource dependence. Through mergers and acquisitions, a firm may bring key resources within its control. By changing the "rules of the game," a firm may also find protection from particularly powerful outsiders. For instance, before being absorbed by another firm, Netscape sought relief from the onslaught of Microsoft by appealing to the U.S. government. Markets may also be protected by trade barriers, or labor unions may be put in check by "right to work" laws. Yet there are limits on the ability of even our largest and most powerful organizations to control all important external contingencies.

International competition has narrowed the range of options for chief executives; they can no longer ignore the rest of the world. Some may need to fundamentally redefine how they expect to conduct business. For instance, once U.S. firms could go it alone without the assistance of foreign corporations. Now, chief executives are increasingly leading them in the direction of more joint ventures and strategic alliances with foreign partners from around the globe. Such "combinations" provide access to scarce resources and technologies among partners, as well as new markets and shared production costs.

Organizational Governance   With some knowledge of agency theory and re-source dependencies it is much easier to understand the notion of organizational governance. **Organizational governance** refers to the pattern of authority, in-fluence, and acceptable managerial behavior established at the top of the organi-zation. This system establishes what is important, how issues will be defined, who should and should not be involved in key choices, and the boundaries for acceptable implementation.

> ▬ **Organizational gover-nance** is the pattern of au-thority, influence, and ac-ceptable managerial behavior established at the top of the organization.

Students of organizational governance suggest that a "dominant coalition" comprised of powerful organizational actors is a key to understanding a firm's governance.[34] Although one expects many top officers within the organization to be members of this coalition, the dominant coalition occasionally includes out-siders with access to key resources. Thus, analysis of organizational governance builds on the resource dependence perspective by highlighting the effective control of key resources by members of a dominant coalition. It also recognizes the relative power of key constituencies, such as the power of stockholders stressed in agency theory.

This view of the executive suite recognizes that the daily practice of organi-zational governance is the development and resolution of issues. Through the governance system, the dominant coalition attempts to define reality. By accept-ing or rejecting proposals from subordinates, by directing questions toward the interests of powerful outsiders, and by selecting individuals who appear to es-pouse particular values and qualities, the pattern of governance is slowly estab-lished within the organization. Furthermore, this pattern rests, at least in part, on very political foundations.

While organizational governance was an internal and a rather private matter in the past, it is now becoming more public and openly controversial. Some ar-gue that senior managers don't represent shareholder interests well enough, as we noted in the discussion of agency theory. Others are concerned that they give too little attention to broader constituencies. The question of downsizing il-lustrates the point.

It has been estimated that the *Fortune* 500 corporations have cut some 8 mil-lion positions over the last 15 years of downsizing.[35] Managers and employees of these firms once felt confident that the management philosophy of their firm in-cluded their interests. In the new millennium, only a few employees seem to share this confidence. For instance, Boeing announced record production, near-record profits, and a merger with McDonnell-Douglas at the same time that it eliminated some 20,000 engineers from its home Seattle operations. After the tragedy of 9/11, it announced another round of cuts, expected to be in the vicin-ity of 30,000. Boeing eliminated almost all of the engineers hired in the last four years. As one critic caustically noted, "They ate their young to get executive bonuses." Obviously, Boeing is not a high-performance organization.

Politics, Organizational Governance, and Ethics   Public concerns about U.S. corporations, especially those organizations with high-risk technologies such as chemical processing, medical technology, and integrated oil refineries, appear on the rise.

Imbalanced organizational governance by some U.S. corporations may limit their ability to manage global operations effectively. Although U.S. senior man-agers may blame such externalities as unfavorable trade laws for their inability to compete against Japanese or other Asian competitors, their critics suggest that it's just a lack of global operating savvy that limits the corporations these managers are supposed to be leading. Organizational governance is too closely tied to the short-term interests of stockholders and the pay of the CEO.

On a more positive note, there are bright spots suggesting that the governance of U.S. firms is extending well beyond the limited interests of the owners to include employees and the communities in which the firms are located. Cavanagh, Moberg, and Velasquez argue that organizational governance should have an ethical base.[36] They suggest that from the CEO to the lowest employee, a person's behavior must satisfy the following criteria to be considered ethical. First, the behavior must result in optimizing the satisfaction of people both inside and outside the organization to produce the greatest good for the greatest number of people. Second, the behavior must respect the rights of all affected parties, including the human rights of free consent, free speech, freedom of conscience, privacy, and due process. Third, the behavior must respect the rules of justice by treating people equitably and fairly, as opposed to arbitrarily.

There may be times when a behavior is unable to fulfill these criteria but can still be considered ethical in the given situation. This special case must satisfy the criterion of overwhelming factors, in which the special nature of the situation results in (1) conflicts among criteria (e.g., a behavior results in some good and some bad being done), (2) conflicts within criteria (e.g., a behavior uses questionable means to achieve a positive end), or (3) incapacity to employ the criteria (e.g., a person's behavior is based on inaccurate or incomplete information).

Choosing to be ethical often involves considerable personal sacrifice, and, at all corporate levels, it involves avoiding common rationalizations. CEOs and employees alike may justify unethical actions by suggesting that (1) the behavior is not really illegal and so could be moral; (2) the action appears to be in the firm's best interests; (3) the action is unlikely ever to be detected; and (4) it appears that the action demonstrates loyalty to the boss, the firm, or short-term stockholder interests. Whereas these rationalizations may appear compelling at the moment of action, each deserves close scrutiny if the firm's organizational governance system is to avoid being dominated by the more unsavory side of organizational politics.

Chapter 12   Study Guide

Summary

What are power and influence in an organization?

- Power is the ability to get someone else to do what you want him or her to do.

- Power vested in managerial positions derives from three sources: rewards, punishments, and legitimacy (formal authority).

- Influence is what you have when you exercise power.

- Position power is formal authority is based on the manager's position in the hierarchy.

- Personal power is based on one's expertise and referent capabilities.

- Managers can pursue various ways of acquiring both position and personal power.

- They can also become skilled at using various techniques—such as reason, friendliness, ingratiation, and bargaining—to influence superiors, peers, and subordinates.

How are power, obedience and formal authority intertwined in an organization?

- Individuals are socialized to accept power (the potential to control the behavior of others) and formal authority (the potential to exert such control through the legitimacy of a managerial position).

- The Milgram experiments illustrate that people have a tendency to obey directives coming from others who appear powerful and authoritative.

- Power and authority work only if the individual "accepts" them as legitimate.

- The zone of indifference defines the boundaries within which people in organizations let others influence their behavior.

What is empowerment?

- Empowerment is the process through which managers help others acquire and use the power needed to make decisions that affect themselves and their work.

- Clear delegation of authority, integrated planning, and the involvement of senior management are all important to implementing empowerment.

- Empowerment emphasizes power as the ability to get things done rather than the ability to get others to do what you want.

What is organizational politics?

- Politics involves the use of power to obtain ends not officially sanctioned and the use of power to find ways of balancing individual and collective interests in otherwise difficult circumstances.

- For the manager, politics often occurs in decision situations where the interests of another manager or individual must be reconciled with one's own.

- For managers, politics also involves subunits that jockey for power and advantageous positions vis-à-vis one another.

- Politics can also be used strategically.

- The politics of self-protection involves efforts to avoid accountability, redirect responsibility, and defend one's turf.

- While some suggest that executives are agents of the owners, politics also comes into play as resource dependencies with external environmental elements that must be strategically managed.

- Organizational governance is the pattern of authority, influence, and acceptable managerial behavior established at the top of the organization.

- CEOs and managers can develop an ethical organizational governance system that is free from rationalizations.

Key Terms

Agency theory (p. 285)
Coercive power (p. 267)
Empowerment (p. 276)
Expert power (p. 269)
Influence (p. 266)
Information power (p. 267)
Legitimate power (p. 267)

Organizational governance (p. 287)
Organizational politics (p. 278)
Power (p. 266)
Process power (p. 267)
Rational persuasion (p. 269)

Referent power (p. 269)
Representative power (p. 268)
Reward power (p. 267)
Zone of indifference (p. 275)

Self-Test 12

Multiple Choice

1. Three bases of position power are _____. (a) reward, expertise, and coercive power (b) legitimate, experience, and judgment power (c) knowledge, experience, and judgment power (d) reward, coercive, and knowledge power

2. _____ is the ability to control another's behavior because, through the individual's efforts, the person accepts the desirability of an offered goal and a reasonable way of achieving it. (a) Rational persuasion (b) Legitimate power (c) Coercive power (d) Charismatic power

3. A worker who behaves in a certain manner to ensure an effective boss–subordinate relationship shows _____ power. (a) expert (b) reward (c) approval (d) referent

4. One guideline for implementing a successful empowerment strategy is that _____. (a) delegation of authority should be left ambiguous and open to individual interpretation (b) planning should be separated according to the level of empowerment (c) it can be assumed that any empowering directives from management will be automatically followed (d) the authority delegated to lower levels should be clear and precise

5. The major lesson of the Milgram experiments is that _____. (a) Americans are very independent and unwilling to obey (b) individuals are willing to obey as long as it does not hurt another person (c) individuals will obey an authority figure even if it does appear to hurt someone else (d) individuals will always obey an authority figure

6. The range of authoritative requests to which a subordinate is willing to respond without subjecting the directives to critical evaluation or judgment is called the _____. (a) psychological contract (b) zone of indifference (c) Milgram experiments (d) functional level of organizational politics

7. The three basic power relationships to ensure success are _____. (a) upward, downward, and lateral (b) upward, downward, and oblique (c) downward, lateral, and oblique (d) downward, lateral, and external

8. In which dimension of power and influence would a manager find the use of both position power and personal power most advantageous? (a) upward (b) lateral (c) downward (d) workflow

9. Reason, coalition, bargaining, and assertiveness are strategies for _____. (a) enhancing personal power (b) enhancing position power (c) exercising referent power (d) exercising influence

10. Negotiating the interpretation of a union contract is an example of _____. (a) organizational politics (b) lateral relations (c) an approval relationship (d) an auditing linkage

11. _____ is the ability to control another's behavior because of the possession of

knowledge, experience, or judgment that the other person does not have but needs.
(a) Coercive power (b) Expert power (c) Information power (d) Representative power

12. A _____ is the range of authoritative requests to which a subordinate is willing to respond without subjecting the directives to critical evaluation or judgment. (a) A zone of indifference (b) Legitimate authority (c) Power (d) Politics

13. The process by which managers help others to acquire and use the power needed to make decisions affecting themselves and their work is called _____.
(a) politics (b) managerial philosophy (c) authority (d) empowerment

14. The pattern of authority, influence, and acceptable managerial behavior established at the top of the organization is called _____. (a) organizational governance (b) agency linkage (c) power (d) politics

15. _____suggests that public corporations can function effectively even though their managers are self-interested and do not automatically bear the full consequences of their managerial actions. (a) Power theory (b) Managerial philosophy (c) Virtual theory (d) Agency theory

Short Response

16. Explain how the various bases of position and personal power do or do not apply to the classroom relationship between instructor and student. What sources of power do students have over their instructors?

17. Identify and explain at least three guidelines for the acquisition of (a) position power and (b) personal power by managers.

18. Identify and explain at least four strategies of managerial influence. Give examples of how each strategy may or may not work when exercising influence (a) downward and (b) upward in organizations.

19. Define *organizational politics* and give an example of how it operates in both functional and dysfunctional ways.

Applications Essay

20. What explanations for mergers and acquisitions would you offer if it were found that they rarely produce positive financial gains for the shareholders?

These learning activities from the *OB Skills Workbook* are suggested for Chapter 12.

OB in Action

CASE	EXPERIENTIAL EXERCISES	SELF-ASSESSMENTS
▪ 12. Power or Empowerment at GM?	▪ 25. Interview a Leader ▪ 28. My Best Manager: Revisited ▪ 42. Power Circles	▪ 13. Empowering Others ▪ 14. Machiavellianism ▪ 18. Conflict Management Styles

Plus—special learning experiences from The Jossey-Bass/Pfeiffer Classroom Collection

Chapter 13

Information and Communication

Chapter at a Glance

Communication is the glue that holds organizations together. This chapter examines the process of communication in organizations, with special attention to effective communication in today's complex social context. As you read Chapter 13, *keep in mind these study questions*.

WHAT IS THE NATURE OF COMMUNICATION IN ORGANIZATIONS?

WHAT ARE THE ESSENTIALS OF INTERPERSONAL COMMUNICATION?

WHAT ARE THE BARRIERS TO EFFECTIVE COMMUNICATION?

WHAT ARE CURRENT ISSUES IN ORGANIZATIONAL COMMUNICATION?

REVIEW IN END-OF-CHAPTER STUDY GUIDE

Scott G. McNealy, CEO of Sun Microsystems, Inc., is well known for his unique vision of a high-tech future based on computer networking. "The PC is just a blip," he says. "Fifty years from now, people are going to look back and say: 'Did you really have a computer on your desk? How weird.'" He harnesses computing power at Sun to drive a comprehensive organizational communication program that includes e-mail questionnaires or polls to gather information on employee perceptions of such things as "performance inhibitors" that make it hard for them to do a good job. At Sun, top management recognizes that information and communication are keys to continued organizational development.[1]

Everyone knows that communication is vital to an organization. But it takes hard work and true commitment to create the type of information-rich environment that delivers real and sustainable competitive advantage. Technology alone won't do it; people must be fully engaged with the great powers of information and communication that it makes available. Great organizations are built on an extraordinary willingness of managers to communicate and to build communication-rich organizational cultures. These cultures are built on trust that encourages and facilitates a free flow of ideas and suggestions up and down the hierarchy, as well as among peers and colleagues. Unfortunately, this type of communication-rich culture is notably absent in too many workplaces. Respondents to a survey by the American Management Association, for example, gave their managers only a 63 percent success rating in respect to "communicating information and direction." Respondents in another survey rated their managers' skills in "listening and asking questions" at an average of only 3.36 on a 5-point scale.[2] Obviously, there is a lot yet to be accomplished in respect to managerial and workplace communication!

> "Great organizations are built on an extraordinary willingness of managers to communicate."

The Nature of Communication

Have you ever stopped to consider just how great an impact information technology has had on our communication practices? One can safely estimate that today more than a billion voice-mail messages will be exchanged and about 4 trillion e-mails will be sent annually, more than 100 million Internet users will come online each year, and Internet traffic will double as fast as every 100 days.[3] The figures are amazing, and the implications are clear. The appetite for information is growing by leaps and bounds, and the future of organizations is increasingly linked to their abilities to harness information and information technology for competitive advantage. At the center of all this stand the great demands and opportunities of the process we know as "communication."

The Communication Process

It is useful to think of **communication** as a process of sending and receiving messages with attached meanings. The key elements in the communication process are illustrated in Figure 13.1. They include a *source*, which encodes an intended meaning into a message, and a *receiver*, which decodes the message into a perceived meaning. The receiver may or may not give *feedback* to the source. Although this process may appear to be very elementary, it is not quite as simple as it looks. **Noise** is the term used to describe any disturbance that disrupts it and interferes with the transference of messages within the communication process.

The information source is a person or group trying to communicate with someone else. The source seeks to communicate, in part, to change the attitudes, knowledge, or behavior of the receiver. A team leader, for example, may want to communicate with a division manager in order to explain why the team needs more time or resources to finish an assigned project. This involves *encoding*—the process of translating an idea or thought into a message consisting of verbal, written, or nonverbal symbols (such as gestures), or some combination of them. Messages are transmitted through various **communication channels**, such as face-to-face meetings, e-mail and online discussions, written letters or memoranda, and telephone communications or voice mail, among others. The choice of channel can have an important impact on the communication process. Some people are better at using certain channels over others, and specific channels better handle some messages. In the case of the team leader communicating with the division manager, for example, it can make quite a difference whether the message is sent face to face, in a written memo, by voice mail, or by e-mail.

The communication process is not completed just because a message is sent. The receiver is the individual or group of individuals to whom a message is directed. In order for meaning to be assigned to any received message, its contents must be interpreted through *decoding*. This process of translation is complicated

■ **Communication** is the process of sending and receiving symbols with attached meanings.

■ **Noise** is anything that interferes with the effectiveness of communication.

■ **Communication channels** are the pathways through which messages are communicated.

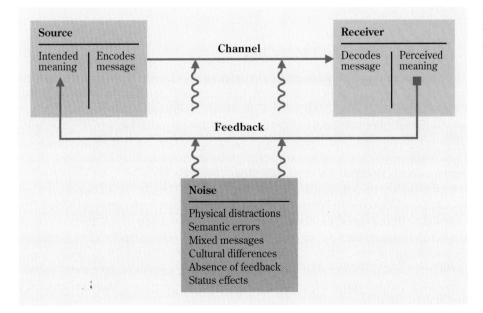

Figure 13.1   The communication process and possible sources of "noise."

Leaders on Leadership

LEADING AND LEARNING GO HAND IN HAND

Entrepreneurship for Richard Branson started early, when he launched a student magazine. From there, he moved on to start Virgin Records and has since become the brains and drive behind the multibillion-dollar global conglomerate Virgin Group. Named England's best business leader by his peers, Branson believes in starting companies—Virgin Airlines, Virgin Mobile, Virgin Cola, and more—rather than buying them. "We start from scratch each time as a way of making sure it's really ours," he says. Change is part of the Virgin culture, focused on satisfaction, creativity, irreverence, and fun. Branson's leadership fits the image, packaged with an ever-present smile, open-necked shirt, and eye toward the future. "I love to learn things I know little about," he says.

Question: How can a leader turn a personal love for learning into an organization-wide commitment to change and innovation?

by many factors, including the knowledge and experience of the receiver and his or her relationship with the sender. A message may also be interpreted with the added influence of other points of view, such as those offered by friends, co-workers, or organizational superiors. Ultimately, the decoding may result in the receiver interpreting a message in a way that is different from that originally intended by the source.

Feedback and Communication

■■■ **Feedback** communicates how one feels about something another person has done or said.

Most receivers are well aware of the potential gap between the intended message of the source and the perceived meaning assigned to it by the recipient. One way in which these gaps are identified is **feedback**, the process through which the receiver communicates with the sender by returning another message. The exchange of information through feedback can be very helpful in improving the communication process, and the popular advice to always "keep the feedback channels open" is good to remember.

■■■ **360-degree feedback** provides performance feedback from peers, co-workers, and direct reports as well as the supervisor.

In practice, giving "feedback" is often associated with one or more persons communicating an evaluation of what another person has said or done. The practice of **360-degree feedback**, in which not only a supervisor but also one's peers, co-workers, and direct reports provide feedback on performance, was introduced in Chapter 7. This is an increasingly popular approach to performance reviews that adds further challenge to feedback processes. Like any feedback situation, all parties must engage in the 360-degree feedback situation carefully and with interpersonal skill.[4]

As pointed out in The Effective Manager 13.1, there is an art to giving feedback so that the receiver accepts it and uses it constructively. Words that are intended to be polite and helpful can easily end up being perceived as unpleasant and even hostile. This risk is particularly evident in the performance appraisal process. A manager or team leader must be able to do more than just complete a written appraisal to document another person's performance for the record. To serve the person's developmental needs, feedback regarding the results of the appraisal—both the praise and the criticism—must be well communicated.

> **THE EFFECTIVE MANAGER 13.1**
> ## How to Give Constructive Feedback
>
> - Give it directly and in a spirit of mutual trust.
> - Be specific, not general; use clear examples.
> - Give it when receiver is most ready to accept.
> - Be accurate; check its validity with others.
> - Focus on things the receiver can control.
> - Limit how much receiver gets at one time.

Communication Channels

Information flows in organizations through both formal and informal channels of communication. **Formal channels** follow the chain of command established by an organization's hierarchy of authority. For example, an organization chart indicates the proper routing for official messages passing from one level or part of the hierarchy to another. Because formal channels are recognized as authoritative, it is typical for communication of policies, procedures, and other official announcements to adhere to them. On the other hand, much "networking" takes place through the use of **informal channels** that do not adhere to the organization's hierarchy of authority.[5] They coexist with the formal channels but frequently diverge from them by skipping levels in the hierarchy or cutting across vertical chains of command. Informal channels help to create open communications in organizations and ensure that the right people are in contact with one another.[6]

> **Formal channels** follow the official chain of command.

One familiar informal channel is the **grapevine**, or network of friendships and acquaintances through which rumors and other unofficial information are passed from person to person. Grapevines have the advantage of being able to transmit information quickly and efficiently. Grapevines also help fulfill the needs of people involved in them. Being part of a grapevine can provide a sense of security from "being in the know" when important things are going on. It also provides social satisfaction as information is exchanged interpersonally. The primary disadvantage of grapevines occurs when they transmit incorrect or untimely information. Rumors can be very dysfunctional, to both people and organizations. One of the best ways to avoid them is to make sure that key persons in a grapevine get the right information to begin with.

> **Informal channels** do not follow the chain of command.

Today, more than ever before, computer technology plays a major role in how information is shared and utilized in organizations. Research in the area of *channel richness*, the capacity of a channel to convey information effectively, lends insight into how various channel alternatives may be used depending on the type of message to be conveyed.[7] In general, the richest channels are face to face. Next are telephone, video conferences, e-mail, written memos, and letters. The leanest channels are posted notices and bulletins. When messages get more complex and open ended, richer channels are necessary to achieve effective communication; leaner channels work well for more routine and straightforward messages, such as announcing the location of a previously scheduled meeting.

> A **grapevine** transfers information through networks of friendships and acquaintances.

Communication Directions and Flows

**Organizational com-
munication** is the process
by which information is exchanged in the organiza-
tional setting.

Communication among members of an organization, as well as between them and external customers, suppliers, distributors, alliance partners, and a host of outsiders, provides vital information for the enterprise. **Organizational communication** is the specific process through which information moves and is exchanged throughout an organization.[8] Information flows through both the formal and informal channels just described, and it flows downward, upward, and laterally.

As shown in Figure 13.2, *downward communication* follows the chain of command top to bottom. One of its major functions is to achieve influence through information. Lower-level personnel need to know what higher levels are doing and to be regularly reminded of key policies, strategies, objectives, and technical developments. Of special importance is feedback and information on performance results. Sharing such information helps minimize the spread of rumors and inaccuracies regarding higher-level intentions. It also helps create a sense of security and involvement among receivers, who feel they know the whole story. Unfortunately, a lack of adequate downward communication is often cited as a management failure. On the issue of corporate downsizing, for example, one sample showed that 64 percent of employees did not believe what management said, 61 percent felt uninformed about company plans, and 54 percent complained that decisions were not well explained.[9]

The flow of messages from lower to higher levels is *upward communication*. As shown in Figure 13.2, it serves several purposes. Upward communication keeps higher levels informed about what lower level workers are doing, what their problems are, what suggestions they have for improvements, and how they feel about the organization and their jobs. The employee surveys used by Sun Microsystems and mentioned in the chapter opener are examples. But, as you should recall, status effects can potentially interfere with the effectiveness of upward communication.

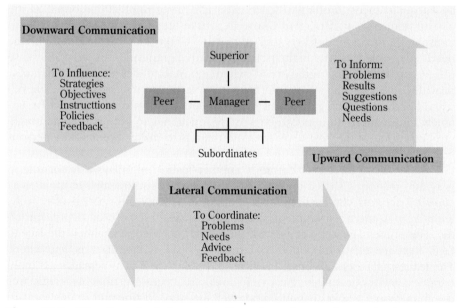

Figure 13.2   Directions for information flows in and around organizations.

The importance of *lateral communication* in the new workplace has been a recurrent theme in this book. Today's customer-sensitive organizations need timely and accurate feedback and product information. To serve customer needs, they must get the right information—and get it fast enough—into the hands of workers. Furthermore, inside the organization, people must be willing and able to communicate across departmental or functional boundaries and to listen to one another's needs as "internal customers." New organization designs are emphasizing lateral communication in the form of cross-departmental committees, teams, or task forces and the matrix organization. Among the developments is growing attention to *organizational ecology*—the study of how building design may influence communication and productivity by improving lateral communications.

Essentials of Interpersonal Communication

Monsanto

"Box buddies" at Monsanto's headquarters in St. Louis, Missouri, improve communication, creativity, and speed with scientists and functional specialists working in adjoining cubicles. Says one: "We can look at problems from different perspectives."

Organizations today, with their emphasis on horizontal structures and functional integration, are information rich and increasingly high-tech. But even with the support provided by continuing developments in information technology, it is important to remember that people still drive organizational systems and performance. People who are willing and able to work together well and commit their mutual talents and energies to the tasks at hand are the foundations of any high-performance organization. And to create this foundation, people must excel in the processes of interpersonal communication.

Effective and Efficient Communication

When people communicate with one another, at least two important things are at issue. One is the accuracy of the communication—an issue of effectiveness; the other is its cost—an issue of efficiency. **Effective communication** occurs when the intended meaning of the source and the perceived meaning of the receiver are virtually the same.[10] Although this should be the goal in any communication, it is not always achieved. Even now, we worry about whether or not you are interpreting these written words exactly as we intend. Our confidence would be higher if we were face to face in class together and you could ask clarifying questions. Opportunities to offer feedback and ask questions are important ways of increasing the effectiveness of communication.

Efficient communication occurs at minimum cost in terms of resources expended. Time, for example, is an important resource. Picture your instructor taking the time to communicate individually with each student in your class about the course subject matter. It would be virtually impossible to do so. Even if it were possible, it would be very costly in terms of time. People at work often choose not to visit one another personally to communicate messages. Instead, they rely on the efficiency of written memos, posted bulletins, group meetings, e-mail, or voice mail.

As efficient as these forms of communication may be, they are not always effective. A change in policy posted by efficient e-mail may save time for the sender, but it may not achieve the desired interpretations and responses. Similarly, an effective communication may not be efficient. For a business manager to visit each employee and explain a new change in procedures may guarantee

■ **Effective communication** is when the intended meaning equals the perceived meaning.

■ **Efficient communication** is low cost in its use of resources.

that everyone understands the change, but it may also be prohibitively expensive in terms of the required time expenditure.

Nonverbal Communication

We all know that people communicate in ways other than the spoken or written word. Indeed, **nonverbal communication** that takes place through facial expressions, body position, eye contact, and other physical gestures is important both to understand and to master. It is basically the act of speaking without using words. *Kinesics*, the study of gestures and body postures, has achieved a rightful place in communication theory and research.[11] The nonverbal side to communication can often hold the key to what someone is really thinking or meaning. It can also affect the impressions we make on others. Interviewers, for example, tend to respond more favorably to job candidates whose nonverbal cues, such as eye contact and erect posture, are positive than to those displaying negative nonverbal cues, such as looking down or slouching. The art of impression management during interviews and in other situations requires careful attention to both verbal and nonverbal aspects of communication, including one's dress, timeliness, and demeanor.

Nonverbal communication can also take place through the physical arrangement of space, such as that found in various office layouts. *Proxemics*, the study of the way space is utilized, is important to communication.[12] Figure 13.3 shows three different office arrangements and the messages they may communicate to visitors. Check the diagrams against the furniture arrangement in your office or that of your instructor or a person with whom you are familiar. What are you/they saying to visitors by the choice of furniture placement?[13]

Active Listening

The ability to listen well is a distinct asset to anyone whose job involves a large proportion of time spent "communicating" with other people. After all, there are always two sides to the communication process: (1) sending a message, or

"I am the boss!"   "I am the boss, but let's talk."   "Forget I'm the boss, let's talk."

Figure 13.3   Furniture placement and nonverbal communication in the office.

"telling," and (2) receiving a message, or "listening." Unfortunately, too many people emphasize the telling and neglect the listening.[14]

Everyone in the new workplace should develop good skills in **active listening**—the ability to help the source of a message say what he or she really means. The concept comes from the work of counselors and therapists, who are trained to help people express themselves and talk about things that are important to them.[15] Take a moment to more thoroughly consider the guidelines for active listening shown in The Effective Manager 13.2. Then read the conversations below. One involves active listening on the part of the branch manager; the other does not. How would you feel as the group leader in each case?[16]

> **THE EFFECTIVE MANAGER 13.2**
> ## Guidelines for Active Listening
>
> **1.** *Listen for content*—try to hear exactly what is being said.
> **2.** *Listen for feelings*—try to identify how the source feels about things.
> **3.** *Respond to feelings*—let the source know that his or her feelings are recognized.
> **4.** *Note all cues*—be sensitive to both verbal and nonverbal expressions.
> **5.** *Reflect back*—repeat in your own words what you think you are hearing.

▓ **Active listening** encourages people to say what they really mean.

Example 1

Group leader: Hey, Sal, I don't get this work order. We can't handle this today. What do they think we are?

Branch manager: But that's the order. So get it out as soon as you can. We're under terrific pressure this week.

Group leader: Don't they know we're behind schedule already because of that software problem?

Branch manager: Look, I don't decide what goes on upstairs. I just have to see that the work gets out, and that's what I'm going to do.

Group leader: The team won't like this.

Branch manager: That's something you'll have to work out with them, not me.

Example 2

Group leader: Hey, Kelley, I don't get this work order. We can't handle this today. What do they think we are?

Branch manager: Sounds like you're pretty sore about it.

Group leader: I sure am. We're just about getting back to schedule while fighting that software breakdown. Now this comes along.

Branch manager: As if you didn't have enough work to do?

Group leader: Right, I don't know how to tell the team about this. They're under a real strain today. Seems like everything we do around here is rush, rush, rush.

Branch manager: I guess you feel like it's unfair to load anything more on them.

Group leader: Well, yes. But I know there must be plenty of pressure on everybody up the line. If that's the way it is, I'll get the word to them.

Branch manager: Thanks. If you'll give it a try, I'll do my best to hold with the schedule in the future.

The branch manager in Example 2 possesses active listening skills. She responded to the group leader's communication in a way that increased the flow of information. The manager learned more about the situation. The group leader felt better after having been able to really say what she thought—and after being heard!

Research Insight
Workplace Identities and Office Décor

Research conducted by Kimbery D. Elsbach offers insight on how office décor can influence co-workers' perceptions of the office-holder's workplace identity—defined as "an individual's central and enduring status and distinctiveness categorizations in the workplace." Using a qualitative research design, Elsbach interviewed two samples of employees in corporate offices. She questioned them on how they interpreted variations in permanent office décor—things like furniture, photos, artifact decorations, art, personal mementos and neatness. Findings showed that these types of "physical identity markers" are used to "cue and/or affirm a person's workplace identity." Also, physical markers independent of the per-

SAMPLE OFFICE DÉCOR IDENTITY MARKERS

Family photos—say family oriented, balanced, not work focused

Hobby photos, artifacts—say ambitious, outgoing, well rounded

Conversation pieces—say funny, off-beat, approachable

Awards, diplomas—say hard-working, successful, pretentious

Professional products—say "company person", functional expert

son—such as the apparent quality or expensiveness of office furniture, were found to relate more to perceived workplace status than distinctiveness. The results help to confirm that such physical markers—office décor and things like personal dress—act along with behavioral markers as important influences on the ways people acquire identities at work. In respect to practical implications, Elsbacher points out that employees working in certain settings may want to choose office décors that communicate a desired workplace identity.

Reference: Kimberly D. Elsbach, "Interpreting Workplace Identities: The Role of Office Décor," *Journal of Organizational Behavior*, Vol. 25 (2004), pp. 99-128.

Cross-Cultural Communication

People must always exercise caution when they are involved in cross-cultural communication—whether between persons of different geographic or ethnic groupings within one country, or between persons of different national cultures. A common problem is *ethnocentrism*, first defined in Chapter 3 as the tendency to believe one's culture and its values are superior to those of others. It is often accompanied by an unwillingness to try to understand alternative points of view and to take the values they represent seriously. This mind-set can easily create communication problems among people of diverse backgrounds.

The difficulties with cross-cultural communication are perhaps most obvious in respect to language differences. Advertising messages, for example, may work well in one country but encounter difficulty when translated into the language of another. Problems accompanied the introduction of Ford's European model, the "Ka," in Japan. (In Japanese, *ka* means "mosquito.") Gestures may also be used quite differently in the various cultures of the world. For example, crossed legs are quite acceptable in the United Kingdom but are rude in Saudi Arabia if the sole of the foot is directed toward someone. Pointing at someone to get their attention may be acceptable in Canada, but in Asia it is considered inappropriate.[17]

International business experts advise that one of the best ways to gain understanding of cultural differences is to learn at least some of the language of the country that one is dealing with. Says one global manager: "Speaking and understanding the local language gives you more insight; you can avoid misunderstandings." A former American member of the board of a German multinational says: "Language proficiency gives a [non-German] board member a better grasp of what is going on...not just the facts and figures but also texture and nuance."[18] Although the prospect of learning another language may sound daunting, The Effective Manager 13.3 points out that it can be well worth the effort.[19]

THE EFFECTIVE MANAGER 13.3

Why Build Foreign-Language Skills?

- Increase your self-confidence as a traveler.
- Show respect to local hosts.
- Build relationships with locals.
- Earn the trust and respect of locals.
- Gain insights into local culture.
- Prepare for emergencies.
- Find greater pleasure in day-to-day interactions.
- Experience less frustration with local ways.

Communication Barriers

In all interpersonal communication, it is important to understand the sources of noise that can easily cause problems in the communication process. As shown earlier in Figure 13.1, potential noise comes from the cultural differences just discussed, as well as physical distractions, semantic problems, mixed messages, absence of feedback, and status effects.

ETHICS AND SOCIAL RESPONSIBILITY

AVOIDING STEREOTYPES RESPECTS DIVERSITY IN WORK-RELATED VALUES

Aging is something that may be difficult for most of us to understand until we are well into the cycle. And it isn't just a personal issue; it's a work-related one as well. In others and in ourselves, it is helpful to recognize how work values may vary with age. In a Society for Human Resource Management survey, these differences were noted. For those 35 and younger, communication and work–life balance top the list; 36- to 55-year-olds emphasize job security and benefits; those 56 and older focus on benefits and communication.

Question: What is the significance of differences in work-related values—for people at work and for their managers?

Physical Distractions

Any number of physical distractions can interfere with the effectiveness of a communication attempt. Some of these distractions are evident in the following conversation between an employee, George, and his manager.[20]

Okay, George, let's hear your problem (phone rings, boss picks it up, promises to deliver the report, "just as soon as I can get it done"). Uh, now, where were we—

Springfield ReManufacturing Corp.

Outsiders visit this Missouri-based company to learn about "open book management." Employee-owners are trained to understand financial data that is shared with them. Given the numbers and their implications, people work better and with greater satisfaction.

oh, you're having a problem with marketing. They (the manager's secretary brings in some papers that need immediate signatures; he scribbles his name and the secretary leaves)…you say they're not cooperative? I tell you what, George, why don't you (phone rings again, lunch partner drops by)…uh, take a stab at handling it yourself. I've got to go now.

Besides what may have been poor intentions in the first place, George's manager allowed physical distractions to create information overload. As a result, the communication with George suffered. Setting priorities and planning can eliminate this mistake. If George has something to say, his manager should set aside adequate time for the meeting. In addition, interruptions such as telephone calls, drop-in visitors, and the like should be prevented. At a minimum, George's manager could start by closing the door to the office and instructing his secretary not to disturb them.

Semantic Problems

Semantic barriers to communication involve a poor choice or use of words and mixed messages. The following illustrations of the "bafflegab" that once tried to pass as actual "executive communication" are a case in point.[21]

> *A.* "We solicit any recommendations that you wish to make, and you may be assured that any such recommendations will be given our careful consideration."
>
> *B.* "Consumer elements are continuing to stress the fundamental necessity of a stabilization of the price structure at a lower level than exists at the present time."

One has to wonder why these messages weren't stated more simply as: (*A*) "Send us your recommendations; they will be carefully considered" and (*B*) "Consumers want lower prices." When in doubt regarding the clarity of your written or spoken messages, the popular **KISS principle** of communication is always worth remembering: "Keep it short and simple."

▪▪▪ The **KISS principle** stands for "keep it short and simple."

Mixed Messages

▪▪▪ **Mixed messages** occur when words say one thing while nonverbal cues say something else.

Mixed messages occur when a person's words communicate one thing while his or her actions or body language communicate quite another. They are important to spot since nonverbal signals can add important insight into what is really being said in face-to-face communication.[22] For instance, someone may voice a cautious "yes" during a business meeting at the same time that her facial expression shows stress and she begins to lean back in her chair. The body language in this case may suggest the existence of important reservations, even though the words indicate agreement.

Absence of Feedback

One-way communication flows from sender to receiver only, as in the case of a written memo or a voice-mail message. There is no direct and immediate feedback from the recipient. Two-way communication, by contrast, goes from sender to receiver and back again. It is characterized by the normal interactive conversations in our daily experiences. Research indicates that two-way communication is more accurate and effective than is one-way communication, even though it is also more costly and time consuming. Because of their efficiency, however, one-way forms of communication—memos, letters, e-mail, voice mail, and the like—are frequently used in work settings. One-way messages are easy for the sender but often frustrating for the receiver, who may be left unsure of just what the sender means or wants done.

CULTURES AND THE GLOBAL WORKFORCE

CHINESE EXECUTIVES LEARN TO COMMUNICATE WESTERN STYLE

It used to be that when Chen XI Guo received e-mail inquiries from abroad regarding his factory's products, he would send back price lists and delivery schedules. This form of communication bothered Jack Ma, a Chinese entrepreneur whose company specializes in linking Western firms with Chinese manufacturers. He started a special training program to help his local clients better understand basic business and international trade protocols—Western style. Executives like Mr. Ma learn how to build better client relationships through communication that is more personal, even though still mostly electronic. They are also advised on how to make their Web sites more appealing and functional for Western customers.

Question: What should you know about communicating electronically with persons from different cultures?

Status Effects

Status differences in organizations create potential communication barriers between persons of higher and lower ranks. On the one hand, given the authority of their positions, managers may be inclined to do a lot of "telling" but not much "listening." On the other hand, we know that communication is frequently biased when flowing upward in organizational hierarchies.[23] Subordinates may filter information and tell their superiors only what they think the boss wants to hear. Whether the reason is a fear of retribution for bringing bad news, an unwillingness to identify personal mistakes, or just a general desire to please, the result is the same: the higher-level decision maker may end up taking the wrong actions because of biased and inaccurate information supplied from below. This is sometimes called the **mum effect** in reference to tendencies to sometimes keep "mum" from a desire to be polite and a reluctance to transmit bad news.[24]

The **mum effect** occurs when people are reluctant to communicate bad news.

To avoid such problems, managers and group leaders must develop trust in their working relationships with subordinates and team members, and take advantage of all opportunities for face-to-face communications. Management by wandering around, or **MBWA**, is now popularly acclaimed as one way to achieve this trust.[25] It simply means getting out of the office and talking to people regularly as they do their jobs. Managers who spend time walking around can greatly reduce the perceived "distance" between themselves and their subordinates. It helps to create an atmosphere of open and free-flowing communication between the ranks. As a result, more and better information is available for decision making, and the relevance of decisions to the needs of operating workers increases.

MBWA involves getting out of the office to directly communicate with others.

Issues in Organizational Communication

One of the greatest changes in organizations and in everyday life in recent years has been the great explosion in new communication technologies. We have moved from the world of the telephone, mail, photocopying, and face-to-face meetings into one of voice mail, e-mail, instant messaging, online discussions and chats, video conferencing and computer-mediated conferencing, and ever-expanding use of intranets and Web portals. Indeed, the ability to participate effectively in all aspects of the electronic office and workspace is well established as an essential career skill. The pace and extensiveness of these changes along with the ever-present dynamics of social context mean that everyone must keep themselves up to date with the issues and challenges of communication in organizations.

Electronic Communication

The impact of the new technologies is discussed throughout this book with respect to job design and the growth of telecommuting, organizational design and the growth of network organizations, and teamwork and the availability of software for electronic meetings and decision making, among many other applications. Advances in information technology are allowing organizations to (1) distribute information much faster than before; (2) make more information available than ever before; (3) allow broader and more immediate access to this information; (4) encourage participation in the sharing and use of information; and (5) integrate systems and functions, and use information to link with environments in unprecedented ways.

The potential disadvantages of electronic communications must also be recognized. To begin, the technologies are largely impersonal; people interact with machines, not with one another. Electronics also removes nonverbal communications from the situation—aspects that may otherwise add important context to an interaction. In addition, the electronic medium can influence the emotional aspects of communication. Some argue, for example, that it is far easier to be blunt, overly critical, and insensitive when conveying messages electronically rather than face to face. The term "flaming" is sometimes used to describe rudeness in electronic communication. In this sense, the use of computer mediation may make people less inhibited and more impatient in what they say.

Another risk of the new communication technologies is information overload. In some cases, too much information may find its way into the communication networks and e-mail systems and basically overload the systems—both organizational and individual. Individual users may have difficulty sorting the useful from the trivial and may become impatient while doing so. Even the IT giant Intel experiences e-mail problems. Says one employees: "We're so wrapped up in sending e-mail to each other, we don't have time to be dealing with the outside." Intel

---

THE EFFECTIVE MANAGER 13.4

How to Streamline Your E-Mail

- Read items once.
- Take action immediately to answer, move to folders, or delete.
- Regularly purge folders of outdated messages.
- Send group mail and use "reply to all" only when really necessary.
- Get off distribution lists that don't offer value to your work.
- Send short messages in the subject line, avoiding a full-text message.
- Put large files on Web sites, instead of sending as attachments.

offers training in e-mail processing as a way of helping employees gain the advantages and avoid the disadvantages of electronic messaging. The Effective Manager 13.4 lists several suggested guidelines.[26]

In all this, one point remains undeniable: new communication technologies will continue to keep changing the nature of work and of office work in particular. The once-conventional office is fast giving way to new forms such as telecommuting and the use of electronic networks. Workers in the future will benefit as new technologies allow them to spend more time out of the traditional office and more time working with customers on terms that best fit individual needs.

Virtual Workspaces

There is hardly any need to remind anyone that today's organizations are moving more and more into the world of the electronic office. One of the most significant current developments is the use of work-sharing software tools to create **virtual workspaces**. These are online sites that allow users to share information, documents, calendars, and discussions continuously and on demand. They are increasingly central to organizational designs that emphasize networking and intense lateral communication, including that among members separated from one another by time and distance. For example, at EMC Corporation, a virtual workspace allows members of account teams around the United States to share plans, calendars, project drafts, and designs.[27] Continuing developments in software support are greatly expanding the opportunities for virtual workspaces and their applications. Among the newer possibilities are online polling of virtual team members, project management planning support, and automatic document feeds to authorized users. A major advantage of the new technologies is that everyone involved always has access to the latest versions of documents, calendars, and other materials.[28] Such collaboration efficiencies are significant in the context of the performance demands faced by today's organizations and their members.

> ▧ **Virtual workspaces** allow users to continuously share information, documents, calendars, and discussions.

Workplace Privacy

Among the controversies in organizational communication today is the issue of privacy. An example is eavesdropping by employers on employee use of electronic messaging in corporate facilities. A study by the American Management Association found that electronic monitoring of employee performance increased by more than 45 percent in a year's time. You may be surprised to learn that the most frequently reported things bosses watch are number of telephone calls and time spent on telephone calls (39 percent), e-mail messages (27 percent), computer files (21 percent), telephone conversations (11 percent), and voice-mail messages (6 percent).[29]

Progressive organizations are developing internal policies regarding the privacy of employee communications, and the issue is gaining attention from legislators. A state law in Illinois now makes it legal for bosses to listen in on employees' telephone calls. But the law leaves the boundaries of appropriateness unclear. Such eavesdropping is common in some service areas such as airline reservations, where union concerns are sometimes expressed in the context of "Big brother is watching you!" The privacy issue is likely to remain controversial as communication technologies continue to make it easier for employers to electronically monitor the performance and communications of their workers.

American Express

Kenneth Chenault is not only one of the few African-Americans to head one of the world's large multinational corporations. Junior managers know him for an open office door, engaging personality, and his role as mentor.

DO YOU KNOW WHEN YOUR EMPLOYER IS WATCHING YOU?

In our wonderful new world of technology, a new force has appeared with a dramatic impact on the workplace—continuous performance monitoring by computers. At Jet-Blue Airways, home-based reservations agents are monitored by computers that check when they answer calls, how long they talk, and who hangs up first. Although this information is used for training as well as control, some worry about the invasion of new technologies. Software can now count keystrokes on computers, log Web sites visited, track software applications used, and more. A Cigna Corp. manager says that her firm uses the technology responsibly, saying: "The philosophy around what we've built is positive reinforcement."

Question: What do you believe is the line between legitimate performance measurement and the invasion of privacy?

Communication and Social Context

There are many issues affecting communication in the complex social context of organizations today. One of continuing interest is the study of male and female communication styles. In *Talking 9 to 5*, Deborah Tannen argues that men and women learn or are socialized into different styles and as a result often end up having difficulties communicating with one another.[30] She sees women as more oriented toward relationship building in communication, for example, while men are more prone to seek status through communications.[31] Because people tend to surround themselves with those whose communication styles fit with their own, a further implication is that either women or men may dominate communications in situations where they are in the majority.[32]

More and more people are asking a question related to the prior discussion: "Are women better communicators than men?" A study by the consulting firm Lawrence A. Pfaff and Associates suggests they may well be.[33] The survey shows that supervisors rank female managers higher than male managers on communication, approachability, evaluations, and empowering others; the subordinates also rank women higher on these same items. A possible explanation is that early socialization and training better prepare women for the skills involved in communication and may make them more sensitive in interpersonal relationships. In contrast, men may be more socialized in ways that cause communication problems—such as aggression, competitiveness, and individualism.[34] In considering such possibilities, however, it is important to avoid gender stereotyping and to focus instead on the point of ultimate importance—how communication in organizations can be made most effective.[35]

Also, our society also values the political correctness of communications in the workplace. The vocabulary of work is changing, and people are ever more on guard not to let their choice of words offend another individual or group. The references to "people of color," the "physically challenged," and "seniors," and others like them might have been phrased quite differently in the past. And, importantly, they may be different again in the future. People in organizations are aware of such issues, and many employers offer training to help their members understand and best deal with the importance of language that supports norms and cultures of inclusion, tolerance, and sensitivity to individual differences.

Chapter 13 Study Guide

Summary

What is the nature of communication in organizations?

- Communication is the process of sending and receiving messages with attached meanings.
- The communication process involves encoding an intended meaning into a message, sending the message through a channel, and receiving and decoding the message into perceived meaning.
- Noise is anything that interferes with the communication process.
- Feedback is a return message from the original recipient back to the sender.
- To be constructive, feedback must be direct, specific, and given at an appropriate time.
- Organizational communication is the specific process through which information moves and is exchanged within an organization.
- Organizations depend on complex flows of information—upward, downward, and laterally—to operate effectively.

What are the essentials of interpersonal communication?

- Communication is effective when both sender and receiver interpret a message in the same way.
- Communication is efficient when messages are transferred at a low cost.
- Nonverbal communication occurs through facial expressions, body position, eye contact, and other physical gestures.
- Active listening encourages a free and complete flow of communication from the sender to the receiver; it is nonjudgmental and encouraging.
- Communication in organizations uses a variety of formal and informal channels; the richness of the channel, or its capacity to convey information, must be adequate for the message.

What are the barriers to effective communication?

- The possible barriers to communication include physical distractions, semantic problems, and cultural differences.
- Mixed messages that give confused or conflicting verbal and nonverbal cues may interfere with communications.
- The absence of feedback can make it difficult to know whether or not an intended message has been accurately received.
- Status effects in organizations may result in restricted and filtered information exchanges between subordinates and their superiors.

What are current issues in organizational communication?

- As new electronic communication technologies change the workplace, the emphasis on electronic communications and virtual workspaces brings many performance advantages.
- Potential disadvantages in a world of information technology include the loss of emotion and personality in the communication process.
- Researchers are interested in possible differences in communication styles between men and women and in the relative effectiveness of these styles for conditions in the new workplace.
- Current issues in organizational communication also include those of privacy and political correctness in workplace communications.

Key Terms

Active listening (p. 301)
Communication (p. 295)
Communication channels (p. 295)
Effective communication (p. 299)
Efficient communication (p. 299)

Feedback (p. 296)
Formal channels (p. 297)
Grapevine (p. 297)
Informal channels (p. 297)
KISS principle (p. 304)
MBWA (p. 305)
Mixed messages (p. 304)
Mum effect (p. 305)

Noise (p. 295)
Nonverbal communication (p. 300)
Organizational communication (p. 298)
360-degree feedback (p. 296)
Virtual workspaces (p. 307)

Self-Test 13

Multiple Choice

1. In _____ communication the cost is low, whereas in _____ communication the intended message is fully received. (a) effective; electronic (b) efficient; open (c) electronic; open (d) efficient; effective

2. When you give criticism to someone, the communication will be most effective when the criticism is _____. (a) general and nonspecific (b) given when the sender feels the need (c) tied to things the recipient can do something about (d) given all at once to get everything over with

3. Which communication is the best choice for sending a complex message? (a) face to face (b) written memorandum (c) e-mail (d) telephone call

4. When someone's words convey one meaning and their body posture conveys something else, a(n) _____ is occurring. (a) ethnocentric message (b) mixed message (c) semantic problem (d) status effect

5. Management by wandering around is a technique that can help to overcome the limitations of _____ in the communication process. (a) status effects (b) semantics (c) physical distractions (d) proxemics

6. Which of the following communication methods has more two-way characteristics? (a) e-mail (b) written letter (c) voice mail (d) instant messaging

7. In _____, a variety of persons that one works with, including peers and supervisor as well as direct reports, are involved in the process of communication. (a) 360-degree feedback (b) mixed messages (c) the Mum effect (d) a grapevine

8. Although new electronic communication technologies have the advantage of handling large amounts of information, they may also make communication among organizational members _____. (a) less accessible (b) less immediate (c) more informal (d) less personal

9. The study of gestures and body postures for their impact on communication is an issue of _____. (a) kinesics (b) proxemics (c) semantics (d) informal channels

10. In _____ communication the sender is likely to be most comfortable, whereas in _____ communication the receiver is likely to feel most informed. (a) one-way; two-way (b) top-down; bottom-up (c) bottom-up; top-down (d) two-way; one-way

11 A manager who spends a lot of time out of her office, walking around as well as talking with and listening to other people, could be described as using _____. (a) the KISS principle (b) MBWA (c) MBO (d) the grapevine

12. _____help to improve horizontal linkages and the more intense lateral communication characteristic of the new workplaces. (a) Status effects (b) Ethnocentrism (c) Virtual workspaces (d) Nonverbal communication

13. If someone is interested in proxemics as a means of improving communication with others, that person would likely pay a lot of attention to his or her _____. (a) office layout (b) status (c) active listening skills (d) 360-degree feedback

14. Among the rules for active listening is _____. (a) remain silent and communicate only nonverbally (b) confront emotions (c) don't let feelings become part of the process (d) reflect back what you think you are hearing

15. The impact of social context on communication among people in organizations is represented in concerns for _____. (a) the political correctness of one's vocabulary (b) skill in the use of computer technology (c) privacy and electronic performance monitoring (d) flaming in an e-mail message

Short Response

16. Why is channel richness a useful concept for managers?

17. What place do informal communication channels have in organizations today?

18. Why are communications between lower and higher organizational levels sometimes filtered?

19. Is there a gender difference in communication styles?

Applications Essay

20. "People in this organization don't talk to one another anymore. Everything is e-mail, e-mail, e-mail. If you are mad at someone, you can just say it and then hide behind your computer." With these words, Wesley expressed his frustrations with Delta General's operations. Xiaomei echoed his concerns, responding, "I agree, but surely the managing director should be able to improve organizational communication without losing the advantages of e-mail." As a consultant overhearing this conversation, how would you suggest the managing director respond to Xiaomei's challenge?

These learning activities from *The OB Skills Workbook* are suggested for Chapter 13.

OB in Action

CASE	EXPERIENTIAL EXERCISES	SELF-ASSESSMENTS
▪ 13. The Poorly Informed Walrus	▪ 29. Active Listening ▪ 30. Upward Appraisal	▪ 12. "TT" Leadership Style ▪ 13. Empowering Others

Plus—special learning experiences from The Jossey-Bass/Pfeiffer Classroom Collection

Chapter 14

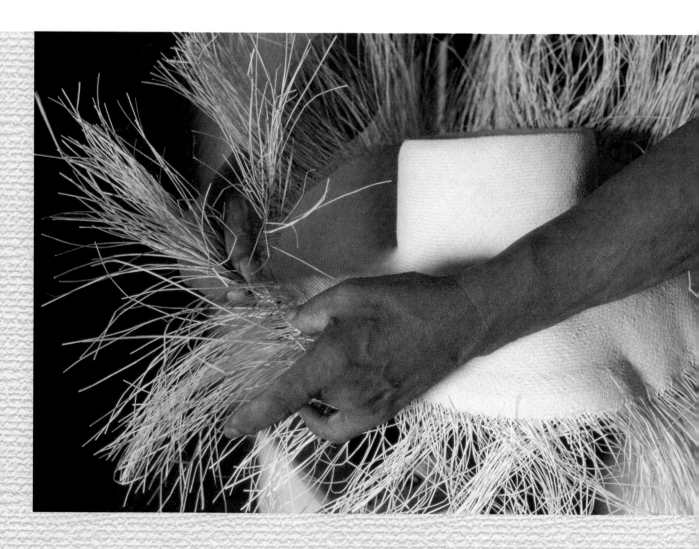

Decision Making

Chapter at a Glance

Organizations depend for their success on day-to-day decisions made by their members. The quality of these decisions influences both the long-term performance of an organization and its day-to-day "character"—in the eyes of employees, customers, and society at large. This chapter examines the many aspects of decision making in organizations. As you read Chapter 14, *keep in mind these study questions*.

WHAT IS THE DECISION-MAKING PROCESS IN ORGANIZATIONS?

- Decision Environments
- Types of Decisions

WHAT ARE THE USEFUL DECISION-MAKING MODELS?

- Classical and Behavioral Decision Theory
- The Garbage Can Model
- Decision-Making Realities

HOW DO INTUITION, JUDGMENT, AND CREATIVITY AFFECT DECISION MAKING?

- Judgmental Heuristics
- Creativity

HOW DO YOU MANAGE THE DECISION-MAKING PROCESS?

- Choosing Problems to Address
- Deciding Who Should Participate
- Knowing When to Quit

WHAT ARE SOME OF THE CURRENT ISSUES IN DECISION MAKING?

- Information Technology and Decision Making
- Cultural Factors and Decision Making
- Ethical Issues and Decision Making

REVIEW IN END-OF-CHAPTER STUDY GUIDE

Today's challenging environments demand ever more rigor and creativity in the decision-making process. Consider the challenge to the managing partner at Plante Moran, William M. Hermann. In the aftermath of the accounting scandals at Arthur Andersen, firms that do both consulting and accounting are under new scrutiny. Fortunately for Bill Hermann, this consulting and accounting firm is unique, with an even more unique track record of accomplishment. While it is comparatively small when compared to the industry giants and it confines its practice to the middle of America (both in terms of location and size of its clients), it is very highly respected. It leads accounting firms in the proportion of female partners. It minimizes ranks and status within the firm. And it is ranked one of America's best places to work. Their principle of decision making illustrates their uniqueness: "It is our intent to maintain timely yet thorough decision-making processes, with decisions made at the most appropriate level. We will strive to be effective by keeping a balance between participation and efficiency."

This principle is but one of 15 guiding principles designed to help all staff associates and partners understand that this professional service firm believes it cannot long exist on what it was but only on what it aspires to be. It must meet today's challenges with sound creative decisions with real potential for the client.[1]

> **"It is our intent to maintain timely yet thorough decision-making processes, with decisions made at the most appropriate level. We will strive to be effective by keeping a balance between participation and efficiency"**

The Decision-Making Process

Within an organization, managers must provide for decision making that encourages the free flow of new ideas and supports the efforts of people who want to make their ideas work. And just as with organizations themselves, the success of our individual careers depends on the quality of the decisions we make regarding our jobs and employment situations.

Decision making is choosing a course of action to deal with a problem.

Formally defined, **decision making** is the process of choosing a course of action for dealing with a problem or opportunity.[2] The five basic steps involved in systematic decision making are:

Five steps in decision making

1. Recognize and define the problem or opportunity.
2. Identify and analyze alternative courses of action, and estimate their effects on the problem or opportunity.
3. Choose a preferred course of action.

4. Implement the preferred course of action.
5. Evaluate the results and follow up as necessary.

We must also recognize that in settings where substantial change and many new technologies prevail, this step-by-step approach may not be followed. Occasionally, a nontraditional sequence works and yields superior performance over the traditional view. We also think it is important to consider the ethical consequences of decision making. To understand when and where to use the traditional or novel decision techniques calls for a further understanding of decision environments and the types of decisions to be made.

Decision Environments

Problem-solving and opportunity-seeking decisions in organizations are typically made under three different conditions or environments: certainty, risk, and uncertainty.[3] **Certain environments** exist when information is sufficient to predict the results of each alternative in advance of implementation. When a person invests money in a savings account, for example, absolute certainty exists about the interest that will be earned on that money in a given period of time. Certainty is an ideal condition for managerial problem solving and decision making. The challenge is simply to locate the alternative offering the best or ideal solution. Unfortunately, certainty is the exception instead of the rule in decision environments.

Risk environments exist when decision makers lack complete certainty regarding the outcomes of various courses of action but are aware of the probabilities associated with their occurrence. A probability, in turn, is the degree of likelihood of an event's occurrence. Probabilities can be assigned through objective statistical procedures or through personal intuition. For instance, managers can make statistical estimates of quality rejects in production runs, or a senior production manager can make similar estimates based on past experience. Risk is a common decision environment in today's organizations.

Uncertain environments exist when managers have so little information on hand that they cannot even assign probabilities to various alternatives and their possible outcomes. This is the most difficult of the three decision environments. Uncertainty forces decision makers to rely heavily on individual and group creativity to succeed in problem solving. It requires unique, novel, and often totally innovative alternatives to existing patterns of behavior. Responses to uncertainty are often heavily influenced by intuition, educated guesses, and hunches. Furthermore, an uncertain decision environment may also be characterized as a rapidly changing organizational setting in terms of (1) external conditions, (2) the information technology requirements called for to analyze and make decisions, and (3) the personnel influencing problem and choice definitions. This has been called an **organized anarchy**, a firm or division in a firm in a transition characterized by very rapid change and lack of a legitimate hierarchy and collegiality. Although this was once a very unique setting, many high-tech firms and those with expanding global operations share many of the characteristics of an organized anarchy. For instance, KPMG, one of the world's largest and most prestigious consulting firms, has a large practice in what they call enterprise risk management to help firms identify risks and manage them.[4]

Regardless of where they operate or the dominant culture of the managers, KPMG consultants known they must go far beyond the traditional risk mitigation

Certain environments provide full information on the expected results for decision-making alternatives.

Risk environments provide probabilities regarding expected results for decision-making alternatives.

Uncertain environments provide no information to predict expected results for decision-making alternatives.

Organized anarchy is a firm or division in a firm in a transition characterized by very rapid change and lack of a legitimate hierarchy.

notion of using controls to limit the exposure of a firm. They systematically ask managers to separately identify: (1) strategic risks (threats to overall business success); (2) operational risks (threats inherent in the technologies used to reach business success); and (3) reputation risks (threats to a brand or to the firm's reputation). While they also note the importance of threats from regulatory sources, they pay special attention to financial threats, challenges to information systems, and new initiatives from competitors, in addition to change in the competitive setting (e.g., recession, disasters). They want firms to focus on critical risks, develop a strategy for dealing with these critical risks, and define specific responsibilities for dealing with the identified risks. They coach executives to know their risk tolerances and move toward viewing risks in the context of the firm's strategy. This allows leaders to recognize the risk environment in which they operate and incorporate this into their decision-making process. Further, by a systematic process, firms can more clearly identify which aspects of their environment and operations are risky and which are truly uncertain.

Types of Decisions

The many routine and nonroutine problems in the modern workplace call for different types of decisions. Routine problems arise on a regular basis and can be addressed through standard responses, called **programmed decisions**. These decisions simply implement solutions that have already been determined by past experience as appropriate for the problem at hand. Examples of programmed decisions are reordering inventory automatically when stock falls below a predetermined level and issuing a written reprimand to someone who violates a certain personnel procedure.

Routine operations are at the heart of many corporations, and they are finding that when they or their customers face programmed decisions, they can utilize new Web-based technologies to get speedier and better decisions. For example, REI (Recreational Equipment, Inc.) tied their Web site to inventory-monitoring systems to quickly offer discounts on overstocked items.

Programmed decisions are determined by past experience as appropriate for a problem at hand.

PEOPLE AND TECHNOLOGY

LINKING THE INTERNET TO AN INVENTORY SYSTEM

When you think REI and technology, you are probably envisioning the latest in tents, mountain gear, or ice axes. REI is the largest consumer cooperative, selling quality outdoor recreation gear. REI currently has two e-commerce sites: REI.com and REI-OUTLET.com. Rather than just do the conventional Web development, REI integrated their online sites into their inventory system that serves their stores and mail-order customers. They are also using a routine purchasing sequence to help them chart what to buy and how much of an item to stock.

Question: How often have you used the Internet to buy versus just shop?

Nonroutine problems are unique and new, having never been encountered before. Because standard responses are not available, these circumstances call for creative problem solving. These **nonprogrammed decisions** are specifically crafted or tailored to the situation at hand. Higher-level managers generally spend a greater proportion of their decision-making time on nonroutine problems. An example is a senior marketing manager who has to respond to the introduction of a new product by a foreign competitor. Although past experience may help deal with this competitive threat, the immediate decision requires a creative solution based on the unique characteristics of the present market situation.

For firms in or characterized by "organized anarchy," we also suggest there is a third class of decisions called associative choices. **Associative choices** are decisions that can be loosely linked to nagging continual problems but that were not specifically developed to solve the problem. Given the chaotic nature of the setting, the necessity of taking action as opposed to waiting, and the ability of employees to make nearly any "decision" work, a stream of associative choices may be used to improve the setting, even though the problems are not solved.

■ **Nonprogrammed decisions** are created to deal uniquely with a problem at hand.

■ **Associative choices** are decisions that can be loosely linked to nagging continual problems but that were not specifically developed to solve the problem.

Decision-Making Models

The field of organizational behavior has historically emphasized two alternative approaches to decision making—classical and behavioral (Figure 14.1).[5] **Classical decision theory** models view the manager as acting in a world of complete certainty. **Behavioral decision theory** models accept the notion of bounded rationality and suggest that people act only in terms of what they perceive about a given situation.

■ **Classical decision theory** views decision makers as acting in a world of complete certainty.

■ **Behavioral decision theory** views decision makers as acting only in terms of what they perceive about a given situation.

Classical and Behavioral Decision Theory

Ideally, the manager faces a clearly defined problem, knows all possible action alternatives and their consequences, and then chooses the alternative that offers the best, or "optimum," solution to the problem. This optimizing style is an ideal

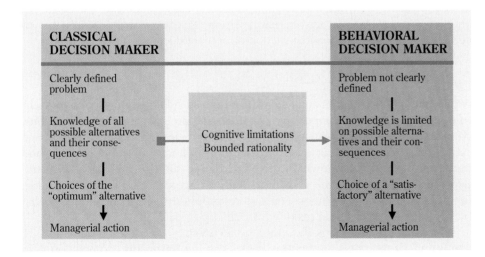

Figure 14.1 Decision making viewed from the classical and behavioral perspectives.

way to make decisions. This classical approach is normative and prescriptive, and it is often used as a model for how managers should make decisions.

Behavioral scientists are cautious about applying classical decision theory to many decision situations. They recognize that the human mind is a wonderful creation, capable of infinite achievements. But they also recognize that human beings have cognitive limitations that restrict their information-processing capabilities. Information deficiencies and overload compromise the ability of decision makers to achieve complete certainty and otherwise operate according to the classical model. Human decision makers also operate with bounded rationality.[6] Bounded rationality is a shorthand term suggesting that, while individuals are reasoned and logical, humans have their limits. Individuals interpret and make sense of things within the context of their personal situation. They engage in decision making "within the box" of a simplified view of a more complex reality. This makes it difficult to realize the ideal of classical decision making. As a result, the classical model does not give a full and accurate description of how most decisions are made in organizations.[7]

Classical decision theory does not appear to fit today's chaotic world of globalizing high-tech organizations, yet it would be a mistake to dismiss it and the types of progress that can be made with classical models. Classical models can be used toward the bottom of many firms. For instance, even the most high-tech firm faces many clearly defined problems with known alternatives where firms have already selected an optimal solution. That a firm's managers don't know the answer may make it appear nonclassical when, in fact, it should not be.

As noted above, behavioral decision theory models accept the notion of bounded rationality and suggest that people act only in terms of what they perceive about a given situation. Because these perceptions are frequently imperfect, most organizational decision making does not take place in a world of complete certainty. Rather, the behavioral decision maker is viewed as acting most often under uncertain conditions and with limited information. Organizational decision makers face problems that are often ambiguous, and they have only partial knowledge of the available action alternatives and their consequences. This leads to a phenomenon that Herbert Simon has described as **satisficing**— decision makers choose the first alternative that appears to give an acceptable or a satisfactory resolution of the problem. As Simon states: "Most human decision making, whether individual or organizational, is concerned with the discovery and selection of satisfactory alternatives; only in exceptional cases is it concerned with the discovery and selection of optimal decisions."[8]

> ▦ **Satisficing** is choosing the first alternative that appears to give an acceptable or satisfactory resolution of the problem.

The Garbage Can Model

> ▦ **Garbage can model** views the main components of the choice process—problems, solutions, participants, and choice situations—as all mixed up together in the garbage can of the organization.

A third view of decision making stems from the so-called **garbage can model**.[9] In this view, the main components of the choice process—problems, solutions, participants, and choice situations—are all mixed up together in the "garbage can" of the organization. In many organizations where the setting is stable and the technology is well known and fixed, tradition, strategy, and the administrative structure help order the contents of the garbage can. Specific problems can be matched to specific solutions, an orderly process can be maintained, and the behavioral view of decision making may be appropriate.

But when the setting is dynamic, the technology is changing, demands are conflicting, or the goals are unclear, things can get mixed up. More action than

Leaders on Leadership

GUARANTEED ACCESS TO A DECISION MAKER

Downey Bridgwater is president of Sterling Bank. You have probably never heard of this Houston-based financial institution that thrives on serving local owner-operated businesses. Sterling has grown from its initial start in 1974 to become one of the largest locally owned banks in Texas. It now holds assets of more that $3 billion. Downey Bridgwater, together with the chairman, George Martinez, decided that to compete effectively, Sterling would need to offer services that its owner-operators appreciated. The key, they felt, was to decentralize decision making so that clients could get fast, accurate, high-quality service. Now, their owner-operator clients can talk directly with a decision maker at one of their 30 branches. Downey Bridgwater also feels it is critical to develop and reinforce a decision-making environment characterized by respect, courtesy, and understanding both among employees and with clients.

Question: If Sterling continues to expand, can it easily maintain it's emphasis on decentralized decision making?

thinking can take place. Solutions emerge as "potential capabilities"—capabilities independent of problems or opportunities. Solutions often emerge not to solve specific problems but as lessons learned from the experience of other organizations. These new solutions/capabilities may be in the form of new employees, new technical experts, consultants, or reports on best practices. Many solutions might well be implemented even if they cannot be tied to a specific problem. Solutions may also be implemented when no other solution has solved a persistent, chronic problem. Although implemented solutions change the organization, they are unlikely to solve specific problems.

The garbage can model highlights an important feature of decision making in many large organizations. Choice making and implementation may be done by quite different individuals. Often, the job of subordinates is to make the decisions of senior managers work. They must interpret the intentions of their bosses as well as solve local problems. Implementation becomes an opportunity to instill many changes related to the choice of more senior executives. So what is chosen gets implemented along with many other changes. The link between choice and implementation may become even weaker when senior managers are vague or do not vigorously follow up on implementation. The net result from those actually implementing the decision is the appearance that what was chosen does not exactly match what is implemented.

There is a final aspect of the garbage can view. Many problems go unsolved. That is, all organizations have chronic, persistent deficiencies that never seem to get much better. In a garbage can view, this is because decision makers cannot agree to match these problems with solutions, make a choice, and implement it on a timely and consistent basis; nor do they know how to resolve chronic problems. It is only when a problem and a solution "bump into one another" under a decision maker willing to implement a choice that problems, solutions, and choice come together as expected under other views. Thus, one key job challenge for the astute manager is to make the appropriate linkages among problems and solutions.

Decision-Making Realities

All three of these models highlight specific features of the complex choice processes managers must engage in as professionals. A key difference between a manager's ability to make an optimum decision in the classical style and the manager's tendency to make a satisfying decision in the behavioral style is the availability of information. The organizational realities of bounded rationality and cognitive limitations affect the way people define problems, identify action alternatives, and choose preferred courses of action. By necessity, most decision making in organizations involves more than the linear and step-by-step rational choice that models often suggest. The process may not be as chaotic as the garbage can model; yet it is often not as rational as even a behavioral view suggests. In real organizations, decisions must be made under risk and uncertainty. Decisions must be made to solve nonroutine problems. And decisions must be made under the pressures of time and information limitations. Finally, we hope decisions will be made on an ethical foundation.

ETHICS AND SOCIAL RESPONSIBILITY

LINKING ETHICS AND THE ENVIRONMENT

Pella is one of the world's leading manufacturers of premium-quality windows and doors. Gary Christensen, president and CEO, links ethics and environmental responsibility, and he attempts to infuse them into all aspects of the firm's operations. For instance, Pella makes many of its windows from new-growth pine, recycled aluminum, and even some recycled glass. While it is cheaper not to use these materials, Christensen sees that emphasizing recycling is the best choice for Pella.

Question: If Pella were to maximize short-term profits, would it engage in extensive recycling?

Intuition, Judgment, and Creativity

Choices always bear the unique imprint of the individuals who make them, the politics within the organization, and the challenges facing its decision makers. In reality, intuition, judgment, and creativity are as critical as understanding how decisions can be made.

A key element in decision making under risk and uncertainty is intuition. **Intuition** is the ability to know or recognize quickly and readily the possibilities of

Intuition is the ability to know or recognize quickly the possibilities of a situation.

a given situation.[10] Intuition adds elements of personality and spontaneity to decision making. As a result, it offers potential for creativity and innovation.

In an earlier time, scholars carried on a vigorous debate regarding how managers should plan and make decisions.[11] On one side of the issue were those who believed that planning could be accomplished in a systematic step-by-step fashion. On the other side were those who believed that the very nature of managerial work made this hard to achieve in actual practice. We now know that managers favor verbal communication. Thus, they are more likely to gather data and to make decisions in a relational or interactive way than in a systematic step-by-step fashion.[12] Managers often deal with impressions. Thus, they are more likely to synthesize than to analyze data as they search for the "big picture" in order to redefine problems and link problems with a variety of solutions. Managers work fast, do a variety of things, and are frequently interrupted. Thus, they do not have a lot of quiet time alone to think, plan, or make decisions systematically (see The Effective Manager 14.1).

> **THE EFFECTIVE MANAGER 14.1**
> ## Ways to Improve Intuition
>
> Relaxation Techniques
> - Drop the problem for a while.
> - Spend some quiet time by yourself.
> - Try to clear your mind.
>
> Mental Exercises
> - Use images to guide your thinking.
> - Let ideas run freely without a specific goal.

Are managers correct when they favor the more intuitive and less systematic approach? The more chaotic environments and technologies of many of today's organizations press for this emphasis on intuition. Unfortunately, many business firms are better at implementing the common solutions of others than uniquely solving their own problems. Since managers do work in chaotic settings, this reality should be accepted and decision makers should be confident in using their intuitive skills. However, they should combine analytical and intuitive approaches to create new and novel solutions to complex problems.

Judgmental Heuristics

Judgment, or the use of one's intellect, is important in all aspects of decision making. When we question the ethics of a decision, for example, we are questioning the "judgment" of the person making it. Research shows that people are prone to mistakes using biases that often interfere with the quality of decision making.[13] These can be traced to the use of **heuristics**—simplifying strategies or "rules of thumb" used to make decisions. Heuristics serve a useful purpose in making it easier to deal with uncertainty and limited information in problem situations. But they can also lead to systematic errors that affect the quality, and perhaps the ethical implications, of any decisions made. It is helpful to understand the common judgmental heuristics of availability, representativeness, and anchoring and adjustment.[14]

▨ **Heuristics** are simplifying strategies or "rules of thumb" used to make decisions.

The Availability Heuristic The **availability heuristic** involves assessing a current event based on past occurrences that are easily available in one's memory. An example is the product development specialist who bases a decision not to launch a new product on her recent failure with another product offering. In this case, the existence of a past product failure has negatively, and perhaps inappropriately, biased the decision maker's judgment of how to best handle the new product.

▨ The **availability heuristic** bases a decision on recent events relating to the situation at hand.

■■■ The **representativeness heuristic** bases a decision on similarities between the situation at hand and stereotypes of similar occurrences.

The Representativeness Heuristic   The **representativeness heuristic** involves assessing the likelihood that an event will occur based on its similarity to one's stereotypes of similar occurrences. An example is the team leader who selects a new member not because of any special qualities of the person, but only because the individual comes from a department known to have produced high performers in the past. In this case, it is the individual's current place of employment—not his or her job qualifications—that is the basis for the selection decision.

■■■ The **anchoring and adjustment heuristic** bases a decision on incremental adjustments to an initial value determined by historical precedent or some reference point.

The Anchoring and Adjustment Heuristic   The **anchoring and adjustment heuristic** involves assessing an event by taking an initial value from historical precedent or an outside source, and then incrementally adjusting this value to make a current assessment. An example is the executive who makes salary increase recommendations for key personnel by simply adjusting their current base salaries by a percentage amount. In this case, the existing base salary becomes an "anchor" that drives subsequent salary increases. In some situations this anchor may be inappropriate, such as the case of an individual whose market value has become substantially higher than is reflected by the base salary plus increment.

■■■ The **confirmation trap** is the tendency to seek confirmation for what is already thought to be true and not to search for disconfirming information.

In addition to using the common judgmental heuristics, decision makers are also prone to more general biases in decision making. One bias is the **confirmation trap**, whereby the decision maker seeks confirmation for what is already thought to be true and neglects opportunities to acknowledge or find disconfirming information. A form of selective perception, this bias involves seeking only those cues in a situation that support a preexisting opinion. A second bias is the **hindsight trap**, whereby the decision maker overestimates the degree to which he or she could have predicted an event that has already taken place. One risk of hindsight is that it may foster feelings of inadequacy or insecurity in dealing with future decision situations.

■■■ The **hindsight trap** is a tendency to overestimate the degree to which an event that has already taken place could have been predicted.

Creativity

■■■ **Creativity** generates unique and novel responses to problems.

Creativity in decision making involves the development of unique and novel responses to problems and opportunities. In a dynamic environment full of nonroutine problems, creativity in crafting decisions often determines how well people and organizations do in response to complex challenges.[15]

Earlier, we examined the group as an important resource for improving creativity in decision making. Indeed, making good use of such traditional techniques as brainstorming, nominal groups, and the Delphi method can greatly expand the creative potential of people and organizations. The addition of new computer-based group meeting and decision-making techniques extends this great potential even further.

Stages of Creative Thinking   Creative thinking may unfold in a series of five stages. First is *preparation*.[16] Here people engage in the active learning and day-to-day sensing required to deal successfully with complex environments. The second stage is *concentration*, whereby actual problems are defined and framed so that alternatives can be considered for dealing with them. In the third stage, *incubation*, people look at the problems in diverse ways that permit the consideration of unusual alternatives, avoiding tendencies toward purely linear and systematic problem solving. The fourth stage is *illumination*, in which people respond to flashes of insight and recognize when all pieces to the puzzle suddenly fit into place. The fifth and final stage is *certification*, which proceeds with logical analysis to confirm that good problem-solving decisions have really been made.[17]

All of these stages of creativity need support and encouragement in the organizational environment. However, creative thinking in decision making can be limited by a number of factors. Judgmental heuristics like those just reviewed can limit the search for alternatives. When attractive options are left unconsidered, creativity can be limited. Cultural and environmental blocks can also limit creativity. This occurs when people are discouraged from considering alternatives viewed as inappropriate by cultural standards or inconsistent with prevailing norms.

Fostering Creativity   Perhaps the most important development in creativity research has been the recognition that group and organizational factors play an important role. To foster creativity, several scholars suggest that decision makers (1) diversify teams to include members with different backgrounds, training, and perspectives, (2) encourage analogical reasoning (applying a concept or idea from one domain to another), (3) stress periods of silent reflection, (4) record all ideas so that the same ones are not rediscovered, (5) establish high expectations for creativity, and (6) develop a physical space that encourages fun, divergent ideas.[18] It is important to recognize that when seeking high-quality creative decisions, more ideas can often produce better ones.[19]

CULTURES AND THE GLOBAL WORKFORCE

COMPETING IN THE GLOBAL TELECOM BUSINESS

Nokia, initially a Finnish Corporation, is the world's second-largest mobile phone manufacturer and a leading supplier of digital and fixed networks. Its ability to maintain its leadership position in the fastest-growing telecommunications segments is based squarely on its employees and the way they make decisions. It is not just a Finnish way—it is a Nokia way. The choice-making process is characterized by an emphasis on technology development and goal attainment, not bureaucracy, so that Nokia can quickly apply and refine the newest technologies. The decision-making process is supported by four Nokia values—customer satisfaction, respect for the individual, achievement, and continuous learning. Moreover, Nokia managers recognize that the application and emphasis on these values as well as their incorporation into the decision-making process will vary substantially across different cultures.

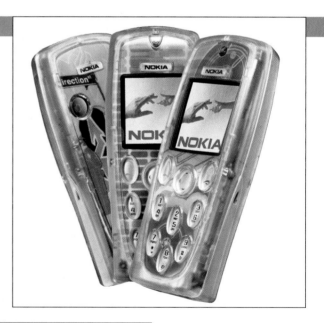

Question: Does Nokia's recognition of a varying emphasis on cultural values help in fostering creative decisions?

There are also a series of studies suggesting that combining individual, group, and organizational conditions fosters creativity.[20] At the individual level, personality and individual cognitive skills (such as linguistic ability and the willingness to engage in divergent thinking as well as intelligence) are important.

Innovation and Decision Making at Jack in the Box

Tired of the same old burger and fries? Check out Jack in the Box® restaurants. Since Robert O. Peterson started the drive-through hamburger chain in 1951, Jack in the Box has been a major innovator in the fast-food business. While its advertising features the company's fictional founder, Jack, and his irreverent commentary on most any topic relevant to the chain's primary audience—young men age 18–34—Jack in the Box constantly explores new food trends, such as ethnic and regional foods aimed at adult tastes. From its award-winning ads to its broad selection of distinctive and innovative food products, the key to the company's success is senior management's support of creative decision making. They let ideas flow, and they encourage employees at all levels of the organization to look at the world in a different way. Internally, this approach is called "Jack's Way"—with employees asking themselves, "What would Jack do in any given situation?"

Further, individual creativity is higher when individuals are motivated by the task itself and derive satisfaction from task accomplishment. Creativity is further enhanced when the decision maker provides opportunities for creativity, eliminates as many constraints as possible, and provides rewards for creative effort.[21]

Above all, recent research suggests that creativity is a process involving the interaction of individuals within their organizational settings.[22] The decision maker can stress engagement in the creative process and counsel individuals to share their ideas with others under a norm of constructive assistance. In this view, creativity is an ebb and flow of engagement among representatives from slightly different portions of the organization.[23] Decision makers should encourage subordinates to recognize ambiguity, contact others with different views, and be prepared to make considerable changes as they attempt to develop new meanings and interpretations of problems and causes as well as solutions. Often this will mean that subordinates will need to seek out individuals who are only loosely connected to their home department.[24] The expansion of creative networks to change the views of individuals appears to be a key to the longer-term development of creativity.[25]

Managing the Decision-Making Process

As suggested by our discussion of creativity, people working at all levels, in all areas, and in all types and sizes of organizations are not supposed to simply make decisions. They must make good decisions—the right decisions in the right way at the right time.[26] Managing the decision-making process involves choices itself. Critical choices include which "problems" to work on, who to involve, and how to involve them as well as when to quit.

Choosing Problems to Address

Most people are too busy and have too many valuable things to do with their time to personally make the decisions on every problem or opportunity that comes their way. The effective manager and team leader knows when to delegate decisions to others, how to set priorities, and when to abstain from acting altogether. When faced with the dilemma of whether or not to deal with a specific problem, asking and answering the following questions can sometimes help.[27]

Is the problem easy to deal with? Small and less significant problems should not get the same time and attention as bigger ones. Even if a mistake is made, the cost of decision error on small problems is also small. Might the problem resolve itself? Putting problems in rank order leaves the less significant for last. Surprisingly, many of these less important problems resolve themselves or are solved by others before you get to them. One less problem to solve leaves decision-making time and energy for other uses. *Is this my decision to make?* Many problems can be handled by other persons. They should be delegated to people who are best prepared to deal with them; ideally, they should be delegated to people whose work they most affect. Finally, *is this a solvable problem within the context of the organization?* The astute decision maker recognizes the difference between problems that realistically can be solved and those that are simply not solvable for all practical purposes.

Paul Nutt, a leading authority on decision making in corporations, argues that half the decisions in organizations fail.[28] Why? The decision tactics managers most often use are those most prone to failure. Managers take too many short-cuts. Too often, they merely copy the choices of others and try to sell these to subordinates. While such copying appears practical and pragmatic, it fails to recognize unanticipated difficulties and delays. No two firms are alike, and subtle adjustments are typically needed to copy another's solution. Subordinates may believe the manager is just using his or her clout—not working for the best interests of all. Related to the overemphasis on immediate action is the tendency for managers to emphasize problems and solutions. The tactics related to success are underutilized. Managers need to focus on the outcomes they want, rather than the problems they see. Above all, managers need to use participation more. Let's take a closer look.

Deciding Who Should Participate

A mistake commonly made by many new managers and team leaders is presuming that they must solve every problem by making every decision themselves.[29] In practice, good organizational decisions are made by individuals acting alone, by individuals consulting with others, and by groups of people working together.

Several scholars argue that who participates and how decisions are to be made should reflect the issues at hand. Further, making a choice is insufficient. It is critical that a choice be followed by effective implementation. Victor Vroom, Phillip Yetton, and Arthur Jago have developed a framework for helping managers choose the decision-making methods most appropriate for various problem situations.[30] Since making choices is complicated, their recommendations, charted in Figure 14.2, also appear complicated to many unfamiliar with decision trees. What these scholars have done is sequentially array the key factors that should guide your participation choices. The most important is the technical quality of the decision. If it is high, the figure starts you in one direction to consider other factors. If it is low, there are fewer factors to consider. Is this figure too complex and unrealistic? No, not really. Selecting the appropriate decision-making method for a problem is critical to effective implementation. Successful and experienced managers often consider the factors in the model. The figure is just a way to display the hard-won lessons of experience.

So what attributes make a difference? As shown in the figure, the attributes are: (1) the required quality of the decision; (2) the commitment needed from subordinates; (3) the amount of information the leader has; (4) the problem structure; (5) commitment probability—the chances subordinates would be committed if you made the choice; (6) goal congruence—the degree to which subordinates share the goals to be achieved by the choice; (7) subordinate conflict; and (8) subordinate information. For example, if the quality requirement is low and subordinates have high goal congruence, the model suggests you would make the choice. The analysis forces you to recognize how time, quality requirements, information availability, and subordinate acceptance issues can affect who should participate and how. It also reminds you that effective decision making can involve individual choices, working with others, and group decisions. The key to effectively managing participation in decision making is first knowing when to use each decision method and then knowing how to implement each of them well.

Chase

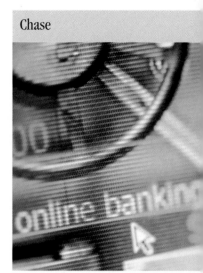

More firms are recognizing the strategic value of information technology and using IT as a basis for global operations. In an annual report, Chase states that the "effective use of information technology is allowing Chase to successfully pursue a consumer services strategy different from that of many competitors. For example, in auto finance, where Chase is the leading bank lender, more than 1,000 car dealerships across the country provide the channel, many tied directly to Chase by computer for instantaneous credit decisions. In mortgage banking, loan officers with laptops are the channel."

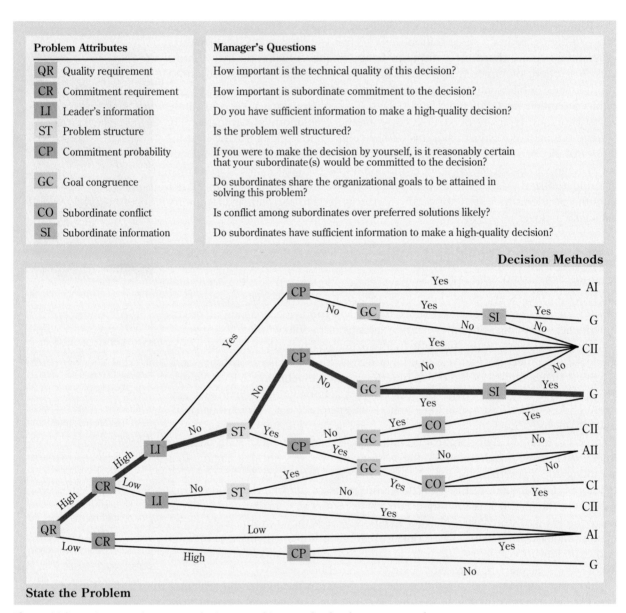

Problem Attributes		Manager's Questions
QR	Quality requirement	How important is the technical quality of this decision?
CR	Commitment requirement	How important is subordinate commitment to the decision?
LI	Leader's information	Do you have sufficient information to make a high-quality decision?
ST	Problem structure	Is the problem well structured?
CP	Commitment probability	If you were to make the decision by yourself, is it reasonably certain that your subordinate(s) would be committed to the decision?
GC	Goal congruence	Do subordinates share the organizational goals to be attained in solving this problem?
CO	Subordinate conflict	Is conflict among subordinates over preferred solutions likely?
SI	Subordinate information	Do subordinates have sufficient information to make a high-quality decision?

Figure 14.2   Selecting alternative decision-making methods: the Vroom and Jago decision process flowchart.

Authority decisions are made by the manager or team leader without involving others using information that he or she possesses.

When individual decisions, also called **authority decisions**, are made, the manager or team leader uses information that he or she possesses and decides what to do without involving others. This decision method often reflects the prerogatives of a person's position of formal authority in the organization. For instance, in deciding a rotation for lunch hours in a retail store, the manager may post a schedule. In **consultative decisions**, by contrast, inputs on the problem are solicited from other persons. Based on this information and its interpretation, the decision maker arrives at a final choice. To continue the example, the manager may tell subordinates that a lunch schedule is needed and ask them when they would like to schedule their lunch and why before making the decision. In other cases, true **group decisions** can be made by both consulting with others and allowing them to help make the final choice. To complete the example, the manager may hold a meeting to get everyone's agreement on a lunch schedule or a system for deciding how to make the schedule. Vroom and his associates further clarify individual, consultative, and group decision options as follows:

- *AI (first variant on the authority decision):* The manager solves the problem or makes the decision alone, using information available at that time.

- *AII (second variant on the authority decision):* The manager obtains the necessary information from subordinate(s) or other group members and then decides on the problem solution. The manager may or may not tell subordinates what the problem is before obtaining the information from them. The subordinates provide the necessary information but do not generate or evaluate alternatives.

- *CI (first variant on the consultative decision):* The manager shares the problem with relevant subordinates or other group members individually, getting their ideas and suggestions without bringing them together as a group. The manager then makes a decision that may or may not reflect the subordinates' input.

- *CII (second variant on the consultative decision):* The manager shares the problem with subordinates or other group members, collectively obtaining their ideas and suggestions. The manager then makes a decision that may or may not reflect the subordinates' input.

- *G (the group or consensus decision):* The manager shares the problem with the subordinates as a total group and engages the group in consensus seeking to arrive at a final decision.

In Figure 14.2 the problem attributes are sequentially depicted and the various combinations of these attributes are linked to a recommendation. Try it by working through Figure 14.2 for an organizational problem with which you are familiar.

Knowing When to Quit

The organization's natural desire to continue on a selected course of action reinforces some natural tendencies among decision makers.[31] Once the agonizing process of making a choice is apparently completed, executives make public commitments to implementation, and implementation begins, managers are often reluctant to change their minds and admit a mistake. Instead of backing off, the tendency is to press on to victory. This is called **escalating commitment**— continuation and renewed efforts on a previously chosen course of action, even though it is not working. Escalating commitment is reflected in the popular adage, "If at first you don't succeed, try, try, again."

In beginning finance courses, students learn about the fallacy of sunk costs. Money committed and spent is gone. The decision to continue is just that—a decision. It needs to be based on what investment is needed and the returns on that investment. This is one of the most difficult aspects of decision making to convey to executives simply because so many of these executives rose to their positions by turning apparently losing courses of action into winners.[32] The ten-

Consultative decisions are made by one individual after seeking input from or consulting with members of a group.

Group decisions are made by all members of the group.

Escalating commitment is the tendency to continue a previously chosen course of action even when feedback suggests that it is failing.

Research Insight
Monitoring Escalation of Commitment

In this chapter we outlined the problem of escalating commitment. Individuals can persist even though it is clear there is a losing course of action. Some individuals escalate commitment to a losing course of action when it is clear to others they should quit. McNamara, Moon, and Bromiley asked whether monitoring by more senior management would help stop escalating commitment in a group of bank loan officers. At first blush their data seems to suggest that monitoring worked. When individual clients were put in higher-risk categories (poorer credit risks), loan offers were monitored more closely on these accounts. Undue overcommitment to these higher-risk individuals was apparently reduced. On closer examination, however, they found that loan officers were reluctant to admit that individual clients with deteriorating credit should be placed in a higher-risk category where the loan officer would be subject to greater monitoring. For this group of clients there was overcommitment. The authors called this reluctance to recategorize "intervention avoidance." They argued that the question of escalation is more complex than traditionally recognized and may involve a host of organizational factors that indirectly influence the tendencies of individuals to make undesirable decision commitments.

Reference: G. McNamara, H. Moon, and P. Bromiley, "Banking on Commitment: Intended and Unintended Consequences of Organizations' Attempt to Attenuate Escalation of Commitment, *Academy of Management Journal* 45 (2002):443–452.

dency to escalate commitments often outweighs the willingness to disengage from them. Decision makers may rationalize negative feedback as a temporary condition, protect their egos by not admitting that the original decision was a mistake, or characterize any negative results as a "learning experience" that can be overcome with added future effort.[33]

The self-discipline required to admit mistakes and change direction, however, is sometimes difficult to achieve. Escalating commitments are a form of decision entrapment that leads people to do things that the facts of a situation do not justify. We should be proactive in spotting "failures" and more open to reversing decisions or dropping plans that do not appear to be working.[34] But again, this is easier said than done. Good decision makers know when to call it quits. They are willing to reverse previous decisions and stop investing time and other resources in unsuccessful courses of action. As the late W. C. Fields is said to have muttered, "If at first you don't succeed, try, try, again. Then quit."

Current Issues in Decision Making

In today's environments, the problems facing organizational decision makers seem to get ever more complex. For example, consider the following workplace trends.[35]

- Business units are becoming smaller in size: they are doing more outsourcing and employing fewer full-time workers.

- New, more flexible and adaptable organizational forms are replacing the traditional pyramid structures.

- Multifunctional understanding is increasingly important as organizations emphasize lateral coordination.

- Workers with both technical knowledge and team skills are becoming increasingly sought after.

- The nature of "work" is in flux as jobs change fast, require continuous learning, and are less bound by the "9-to-5" tradition.

Each of these trends is changing by whom, when, where, and how decision making is accomplished. We face difficult stresses and strains as the quest for higher and higher productivity challenges the needs, talents, and opportunities of people at work. Complexities in the decision-making process include issues of information technology, culture, and ethics.

Information Technology and Decision Making

As we have discussed throughout this book, today's organizations are becoming ever more sophisticated in applying information technologies. Eventually, developments in the field of **artificial intelligence** (AI), the study of how computers can be programmed to think like the human brain, will allow computers to displace many decision makers.[36] Nobel laureate and decision scientist Herbert Simon was convinced that computers will someday be more intelligent than humans.

Artificial intelligence is the study of how computers can be programmed to think like the human brain.

Already, the applications of AI to organizational decision making are significant. We have access to decision-making support from expert systems that reason like human experts and follow "either–or" rules to make deductions. For example, if you call an advertised 800 number to apply for a home equity loan, you will not get a human but a computer program to take all the necessary information and provide confirmation of a loan. On the factory floor, decision support systems schedule machines and people for maximum production efficiencies.

In the very near future, fuzzy logic that reasons beyond either–or choices and neural networks that reason inductively by simulating the brain's parallel-processing capabilities will become operational realities to move beyond simple programmed decisions. Uses for such systems may be found everywhere from hospitals, where they will check on medical diagnoses, to investment houses, where they will analyze potential investment portfolios, to a wide and growing variety of other settings.[37]

Computer support for group decision making, including developments with the Internet and with intranets, has broken the decision-making meeting out of the confines of face-to-face interactions. With the software now available, problems can be defined and decisions can be made through virtual teamwork by people in geographically dispersed locations. We know that group decision software can be especially useful for generating ideas, such as in electronic brainstorming, and for improving the time efficiency of decisions. People working under electronically mediated conditions tend to stay focused on tasks and avoid the interpersonal conflicts and other problems common in face-to-face deliberations. On the negative side, decisions made by "electronic groups" carry some risks of being impersonal and perhaps less compelling in terms of commitments to implementation and follow-through. There is evidence, moreover, that use of computer technology

Creative Decision Making at Fresh Express

Fresh Express was the originator and is the world leader of the packaged salad category. Getting salads to stay fresh in a bag, however, was not an easy process. It took perseverance and creativity. The eventual breakthrough came with the development and patenting of a new breathable film. As it turns out, the principal cause of decay in lettuce is the overabsorption of oxygen and a self-induced rapid rate of decomposition. The scientists eventually created a film that allowed more carbon dioxide to escape and less oxygen to enter; they also injected the bag with nitrogen. The result is a green salad made from thoroughly washed greens that can stay fresh for weeks—inside a bag. No preservatives are used.

for decision making is better accepted by today's college students than by persons who are already advanced in their organizational careers.[38]

What new information technology will not do is deal with the issues raised by the garbage can model. The information technologies promise a more orderly world where the process of choosing conforms more to the traditional models with an extension of the normal boundaries of rationality. For us, what is still on the information technology horizon are the most important decisions that come before the classical and standard approaches. These are predecision choices that are heavily influenced by cultural factors and ethics.

Cultural Factors and Decision Making

Fons Trompenaars notes that culture is "the way in which a group of people solves problems."[39] It is only reasonable to expect that as cultures vary, so too will choices concerning what is to be solved and how. For example, there are historical cultural preferences for solving problems. The approach favored in this chapter emphasizes the North American view stressing decisiveness, speed, and individual selection of alternatives. This view speaks more to choice and less to implementation. Yet the garbage can view suggests that implementation can proceed almost separately from other aspects of decision making.

Other cultures place less emphasis on individual choice than on developing implementations that work. They start with what is workable and better rather than with the classical and behavioral comparison of current conditions with some ideal.[40] If a change can improve the current situation, even if it is not apparently directed toward a problem identified by senior management, subordinate managers may work together to implement it. And then senior management may be informed of the success of the change. To emphasize the importance of smooth implementation over grand decision making, corporations may adopt systems similar to the Japanese *ringi* system. With a ringi system lower-level managers indicate their written approval of proposals prior to formal implementation. Written approval is an issue not of whether the change should be made but whether it is feasible for the group to implement.[41]

The more important role of culture in decision making concerns not how problems are solved but which concerns are elevated to the status of problems solvable within the firm. For instance, the very fact that a procedure is old may make it more suspect in the United States than in France.[42] Far too many of our views may be dictated by Western bureaucratic thinking.[43] Not all cultures are as pluralistic, bluntly competitive, or impersonal as that of the United States. In other parts of the world, personal loyalties may drive decisions, and preserving harmony may be considered more important than achieving a bit more efficiency. In short, problems may be more person centered and socially defined than bureaucratically prescribed.

Ethical Issues and Decision Making

The subject of ethical behavior in the workplace cannot be overemphasized, and it is worth reviewing once again the framework for ethical decision making first introduced in Chapter 1.[44] An *ethical dilemma* was defined as a situation in which a person must decide whether or not to do something that, although personally or organizationally beneficial, may be considered unethical and perhaps illegal.

Often, ethical dilemmas are associated with risk and uncertainty and with nonroutine problem situations. Just how decisions are handled under these circumstances, ones that will inevitably appear during your career, may well be the ultimate test of your personal ethical framework. As a manager you also have the responsibility to integrate ethical decision making into your part of the firm. Check The Effective Manager 14.2 for some help.

When it comes to the ethics of decision making, the criteria individuals use to define problems and the values that underlie these criteria must be considered.[45] Moral conduct is involved in choosing problems, deciding who should be involved, estimating the impacts of alternatives, and selecting an alternative for implementation.

Moral conduct does not arise from after-the-fact embarrassment. As Fineman suggests, "If people are unable to anticipate shame or guilt before they act in particular ways, then moral codes are invalid.... Decisions may involve lying, deceit, fraud, evasion of negligence—disapproved of in many cultures. But ethical monitoring and control go beyond just the pragmatics of harm."[46] In other words, when you are the decision maker, decision making is not just a choice process followed by implementation for the good of the organization. It involves your values and your morality, whether or not you think it should. Thus, effective implemented choices need not only solve a problem or capitalize on choices, but also to match your values and help others. It is little wonder, then, that decision making will likely be the biggest challenge of your organizational career.

> **THE EFFECTIVE MANAGER 14.2**
>
> ## Suggestions for Integrating Ethical Decision Making into a Firm
>
> Infusing ethics into decision making is difficult. Several scholars recommend the following:
>
> - Develop a code of ethics and follow it.
> - Establish procedures for reporting violations.
> - Involve employees in identifying ethical issues.
> - Monitor ethical performance.
> - Reward ethical behavior.
> - Publicize efforts.

Chapter 14 Study Guide

Summary

What is the decision-making process in organizations?

- Decision making is a process of identifying problems and opportunities and choosing among alternative courses of action for dealing successfully with them.

- Organizational decisions are often made in risky and uncertain environments, where situations are ambiguous and information is limited.

- Routine and repetitive problems can be dealt with through programmed decisions; nonroutine or novel problems require nonprogrammed decisions that are crafted to fit the situation at hand.

What are the useful decision-making models?

- Classical, behavioral, and garbage can models are often useful views of decision making.

- According to classical decision theory, optimum decisions are made after carefully analyzing all possible alternatives and their known consequences.

- According to behavioral decision theory, most organizational decisions are made with limited information and by satisficing—choosing the first acceptable or satisfactory solutions to problems.

- According to the garbage can model, the main components of the choice process—problems, solutions, participants, and choice situations—are all mixed up together in the garbage can of the organization.

- The pressures of time and the lack of information are two important decision-making realities.

How do intuition, judgment, and creativity affect decision making?

- Both systematic decision making and intuitive decision making are important in today's complex work environments.

- Intuition is the ability to quickly recognize the action possibilities for resolving a problem situation.

- The use of judgmental heuristics, or simplifying rules of thumb, is common in decision making but can lead to biased results.

- Common heuristics include availability decisions based on recent events, representativeness decisions based on similar events, and anchoring and adjustment decisions based on historical precedents.

- Creativity in finding unique and novel solutions to problems can be enhanced through both individual and group problem-solving strategies.

How do you manage the decision-making process?

- Good managers know that not every problem requires an immediate decision; they also know how and when to delegate decision-making responsibilities.

- A common mistake is for a manager or team leader to make all decisions alone; instead, a full range of individual, consultative, and group decision-making methods should be utilized.

- The Vroom–Yetton–Jago model offers a way of matching problems with appropriate decision methods, based on quality requirements, information availability, and time constraints.

- Tendencies toward escalating commitment, continuing previously chosen courses of action even when they are not working, should be recognized in work settings.

What are some of the current issues in decision making?

- Technology, culture, and ethics are key issues in decision making.

- Technological developments are continuing to change the nature of organizational decision making.

- Culture counts; differences in culture alter by whom, how, when, and why decisions are made.

- Ethics is involved in each stage of the decision-making process, and effective decision making includes individual moral criteria and values.

Key Terms

Anchoring and adjustment heuristic (p. 322)

Artificial intelligence (p. 329)

Associative choices (p. 317)

Authority decisions (p. 326)

Availability heuristic (p. 321)

Behavioral decision theory (p. 317)

Certain environments (p. 315)

Classical decision theory (p. 317)

Confirmation trap (p. 322)

Consultative decisions (p. 326)

Creativity (p. 322)

Decision making (p. 314)

Escalating commitment (p. 327)

Garbage can model (p. 318)

Group decisions (p. 327)

Heuristics (p. 321)

Hindsight trap (p. 322)

Intuition (p. 320)

Nonprogrammed decisions (p. 317)

Organized anarchy (p. 315)

Programmed decisions (p. 316)

Representativeness heuristic (p. 322)

Risk environments (p. 315)

Satisficing (p. 318)

Uncertain environments (p. 315)

Multiple Choice

Self-Test 14

1. After a preferred course of action has been implemented, the next step in the decision-making process is to _____. (a) recycle the process (b) look for additional problems or opportunities (c) evaluate results (d) document the reasons for the decision

2. In which environment does the decision maker deal with probabilities regarding possible courses of action and their consequences? (a) certain (b) risk (c) organized anarchy (d) uncertain

3. In which characterization of the decision environment is associative choice most likely to occur? (a) organized anarchy (b) certainty (c) risk (d) satisficing

4. A manager who must deal with limited information and substantial risk is most likely to make decisions based on _____. (a) optimizing (b) classical decision theory (c) behavioral decision theory (d) escalation

5. A team leader who makes a decision not to launch a new product because the last new product launch failed is falling prey to the _____ heuristic. (a) anchoring (b) availability (c) adjustment (d) representativeness

6. The five steps in the creativity process are preparation, _____, illumination, _____, and verification. (a) extension, evaluation (b) reduction, concentration (c) adaptation, extension (d) concentration, incubation

7. In Vroom's decision-making model, the choice among individual and group decision methods is based on criteria that include quality requirements, availability of informa-

tion, and _____. (a) need for implementation commitments (b) size of the organization (c) number of people involved (d) position power of the leader

8. The saying "If at first you don't succeed, try, try again" is most associated with a decision-making tendency called _____. (a) groupthink (b) the confirmation trap (c) escalating commitment (d) associative choice

9. Among the developments with artificial intelligence, _____ attempt to have computers reason inductively in solving problems. (a) neural networks (b) expert systems (c) fuzzy logics (d) electronic brainstorms

10. Preferences for who makes decisions _____. (a) vary slightly across cultures (b) characterize individualistic cultures (c) are important only in high power distance cultures (d) vary substantially across cultures

11. Decisions that can be loosely linked to nagging continual problems but that were not specifically developed to solve the problem are called (a) program decisions (b) associative choices (c) authority decisions (d) artificial intellegence

12. Which model views the main components of the choice process—problems, solutions, participants, and choice situations—as all mixed up together? (a) the garbage can model (b) the behavioral model (c) the turbulence model (d) the classical model

13. The _____ bases a decision on similarities between the situation at hand and stereotypes of similar occurrences. (a) representativeness heuristic (b) anchoring and adjustment heuristic (c) confirmation trap (d) hindsight trap

14. The _____ bases a decision on incremental adjustments to an initial value determined by historical precedent or some reference point. (a) representativeness heuristic (b) anchoring and adjustment heuristic (c) confirmation trap (d) hindsight trap

15. The _____ is the tendency to seek confirmation for what is already thought to be true and not to search for disconfirming information. (a) representativeness heuristic (b) anchoring and adjustment heuristic (c) confirmation trap (d) hindsight trap

Short Response

16. What are heuristics, and how can they affect individual decision making?

17. What are the main differences among individual, consultative, and group decisions?

18. What is escalating commitment, and why is it important to recognize in decision making?

19. What questions might a manager or team leader ask to help determine which problems to deal with and with what priorities?

Applications Essay

20. Your friends know you are taking OB courses and constantly show you Dilbert cartoons in which managers are implementing decisions that are unrelated to problems. What insight can you share with them to understand Dilbert better?

OB in Action

These learning activities from *The OB Skills Workbook* are suggested for Chapter 14.

CASE	EXPERIENTIAL EXERCISES	SELF-ASSESSMENTS
■ 14. Johnson& Johnson: One Large Company Made of Many	■ 32. Role Analysis Negotiation ■ 33. Lost at Sea ■ 34. Entering the Unknown ■ 36. The Ugli Orange ■ 38. Force-Field Analysis	■ 16. Your Intuitive Ability ■ 17. Decision-Making Bias

Plus—special learning experiences from *The Jossey-Bass/Pfeiffer Classroom Collection*

Chapter 15

Conflict and Negotiation

Chapter at a Glance

Conflict and negotiation are key processes of organizational behavior. Chapter 15 examines both, with specific attention to further developing your interpersonal skills. As you read Chapter 15, *keep in mind these study questions.*

WHAT IS CONFLICT?

HOW CAN CONFLICT BE MANAGED SUCCESSFULLY?

WHAT IS NEGOTIATION?

WHAT ARE THE DIFFERENT STRATEGIES INVOLVED IN NEGOTIATION?

REVIEW IN END-OF-CHAPTER STUDY GUIDE

When Whitney Johns Martin needed investment capital to expand her consulting firm, it was very hard to find. A member of the board for the National Association of Women Business Owners, she took matters into her own hands and founded a venture capital fund, Capital Across America, specifically to serve female-owned businesses. More than 8 million business owners in the United States are women, and they employ one in four American corporate workers. But it is often hard for women to find investment capital.

Men who seemed more comfortable dealing with men managed most of the venture capital funds that Martin dealt with. She believes that women and men have somewhat different approaches to business. According to her, women often underestimate themselves and don't ask for enough during negotiations. Men, by contrast, "shoot for the moon" and ask for more than they typically need. But women have a great capacity to develop extensive networks and relationships with customers, suppliers, and others. These are great resources that can be rallied to help a business in economic difficulties. As a final reminder in dealing with the venture capitalists, Martin tells women to remember the basics when entering the negotiation: "Have an excellent business plan."[1]

Like the case of Whitney Johns, the daily work of people in organizations is intensely based on communication and interpersonal relationships. Everyone, including managers, must have the interpersonal skills to work well with others in order to implement action agendas in situations that are often complicated and stressful.[2] Communication and interpersonal relationships frequently open the door for differences and disagreements that can create difficulties. There is no doubt that success in today's high-performance organizations requires a good understanding of the fundamentals of conflict and negotiation.

> **"Women often underestimate themselves and don't ask for enough during negotiations."**

Conflict in Organizations

Conflict occurs when parties disagree over substantive issues or when emotional antagonisms create friction between them.

Conflict occurs whenever disagreements exist in a social situation over issues of substance or whenever emotional antagonisms create frictions between individuals or groups.[3] Managers and team leaders can spend considerable time dealing with conflict, including conflicts in which the manager or leader is directly involved as one of the principal actors.[4] In other situations, the manager or leader may act as a mediator, or third party, whose job it is to resolve conflicts between other people. In all cases, a manager and team leader must be comfortable with the interpersonal conflict. This includes being able to recognize situations that have the potential for conflict and to deal with these situations in ways that will best serve the needs of both the organization and the people involved.[5]

Types of Conflict

Conflict as it is experienced in the daily workplace involves at least two basic forms. **Substantive conflict** is a fundamental disagreement over ends or goals to be pursued and the means for their accomplishment.[6] A dispute with one's boss over a plan of action to be followed, such as the marketing strategy for a new product, is an example of substantive conflict. When people work together day in and day out, it is only normal that different viewpoints on a variety of substantive workplace issues will arise. At times people will disagree over such things as group and organizational goals, the allocation of resources, the distribution of rewards, policies and procedures, and task assignments. Dealing with such conflicts successfully is an everyday challenge for most managers.

By contrast, **emotional conflict** involves interpersonal difficulties that arise over feelings of anger, mistrust, dislike, fear, resentment, and the like.[7] This conflict is commonly known as a "clash of personalities." Emotional conflicts can drain the energies of people and distract them from important work priorities. They can emerge from a wide variety of settings and are common among coworkers as well as in superior–subordinate relationships. The latter form of emotional conflict is perhaps the most upsetting organizational conflict for any person to experience. Unfortunately, competitive pressures in today's business environment and the resulting emphasis on downsizing and restructuring have created more situations in which the decisions of a "tough" boss can create emotional conflict.

Substantive conflict involves fundamental disagreement over ends or goals to be pursued and the means for their accomplishment.

Emotional conflict involves interpersonal difficulties that arise over feelings of anger, mistrust, dislike, fear, resentment, and the like.

Levels of Conflict

When dealing personally with conflicts in the workplace, the relevant question becomes: "How well prepared are you to encounter and deal successfully with conflicts of various types?" People at work may encounter conflict at the intrapersonal level (conflict among the individual), the interpersonal level (individual-to-individual conflict), the intergroup level (conflict among groups or teams), or the interorganizational level (conflict among organizations).

Some conflicts that affect behavior in organizations involve the individual alone. These **intrapersonal conflicts** often involve actual or perceived pressures from incompatible goals or expectations of the following types: *Approach–approach conflict* occurs when a person must choose between two positive and equally attractive alternatives. An example is when someone has to choose between a valued promotion in the organization or a desirable new job with another firm. *Avoidance–avoidance conflict* occurs when a person must choose between two negative and equally unattractive alternatives. An example is being asked either to accept a job transfer to another town in an undesirable location or to have one's employment with an organization terminated. *Approach–avoidance conflict* occurs when a person must decide to do something that has both positive and negative consequences. An example is being offered a higher-paying job whose responsibilities entail unwanted demands on one's personal time.

Interpersonal conflict occurs between two or more individuals who are in opposition to one another. It may be substantive or emotional or both. Two persons debating each other aggressively on the merits of hiring a job applicant is an example of a substantive interpersonal conflict. Two persons continually in

Intrapersonal conflict occurs within the individual because of actual or perceived pressures from incompatible goals or expectations.

Interpersonal conflict occurs between two or more individuals in opposition to each other.

disagreement over each other's choice of work attire is an example of an emotional interpersonal conflict. One of the places where interpersonal conflict often arises is in the performance evaluation process. When P. J. Smoot became learning and development leader at International Paper's Memphis, Tennessee, office, she realized that the traditional concept of the boss passing judgment on the subordinate just doesn't work. It is difficult to give performance reviews that end up motivating subordinates and improving their performance. Smoot reversed the traditional top-down process and initiated a new program that began the reviews from the bottom up—with the employee's self-evaluation. Smoot focused the manager's job on helping and guiding others to meet agreed-upon performance plans. Her advice: "Listen for understanding and then react honestly and constructively. Focus on the business goals, not the personality."[8]

Intergroup conflict occurs among groups in an organization.

Intergroup conflict that occurs among members of different teams or groups can also have substantive and/or emotional underpinnings. Intergroup conflict is quite common in organizations, and it can make the coordination and integration of task activities very difficult.[9] The classic example is conflict among functional groups or departments, such as marketing and manufacturing, in organizations. The growing use of cross-functional teams and task forces is one way of trying to minimize such conflicts and promote more creative and efficient operations.

CULTURES AND THE GLOBAL WORKFORCE

WORKING TOGETHER ACROSS CULTURES

"Something magical happens," says project engineer, John Thomas, when European and American scientists from Corning's research centers solve problems together. "Europeans are very creative thinkers; they take time to really reflect on a problem to come up with the very best theoretical solution," he states. "Americans are more tactical and practical—we want to get down to developing a working solution as soon as possible." His partner at Fontainebleau in France says: "The French are more focused on ideas and concepts. If we get blocked in the execution of those ideas, we give up. Not the Americans. They pay more attention to details, processes, and time schedules. They make sure they are prepared and have involved everyone in the planning process so that they won't get blocked. But it's best if you mix the two approaches. In the end, you will achieve the best results."

Question: How can members of culturally diverse teams make sure that any conflicts lead to creativity and performance improvements?

Interorganizational conflict occurs between organizations.

Interorganizational conflict is most commonly thought of in terms of the competition and rivalry that characterizes firms operating in the same markets. A good example is the continuing battle between U.S. businesses and their global rivals. But interorganizational conflict is a much broader issue than that represented by market competition alone. Consider, for example, disagreements between unions and the organizations employing their members, between government regulatory agencies and the organizations subject to their surveillance, between organizations and those who supply them with raw materials.

Functional and Dysfunctional Conflict

Conflict in organizations can be upsetting both to the individuals directly in-volved and to others affected by its occurrence. It can be quite uncomfortable, for example, to work in an environment in which two co-workers are continu-ally hostile toward each other. In OB, however, the two sides to conflict shown in Figure 15.1 are recognized—the functional or constructive side, and the dys-functional or destructive side.

Functional conflict, alternatively called *constructive conflict*, results in posi-tive benefits to individuals, the group, or the organization. On the positive side, conflict can bring important problems to the surface so that they can be addressed. It can cause decisions to be considered carefully and perhaps reconsidered to en-sure that the right path of action is being followed. It can increase the amount of information used for decision making. And it can offer opportunities for creativity that can improve individual, team, or organizational performance. Indeed, an ef-fective manager is able to stimulate constructive conflict in situations in which sat-isfaction with the status quo inhibits needed change and development.

Dysfunctional conflict, or *destructive conflict*, works to the disadvantage of an individual or a group. It diverts energies, hurts group cohesion, promotes interpersonal hostilities, and overall creates a negative environment for workers. This occurs, for example, when two employees are unable to work together be-cause of interpersonal differences (a destructive emotional conflict) or when the members of a committee fail to act because they cannot agree on group goals (a destructive substantive conflict). Destructive conflicts of these types can decrease work productivity and job satisfaction and contribute to absenteeism and job turnover. Managers must be alert to destructive conflicts and be quick to take ac-tion to prevent or eliminate them or at least minimize their disadvantages.

■ **Functional conflict** results in positive benefits to the group.

■ **Dysfunctional con-flict** works to the group's or organization's disadvan-tage.

Culture and Conflict

Society today shows many signs of wear and tear in social relationships. We ex-perience difficulties born of racial tensions, homophobia, gender gaps, and more. All trace in some way to tensions among people who are different in some ways from one another. They are also a reminder that culture and cultural differ-ences must be considered for their conflict potential.

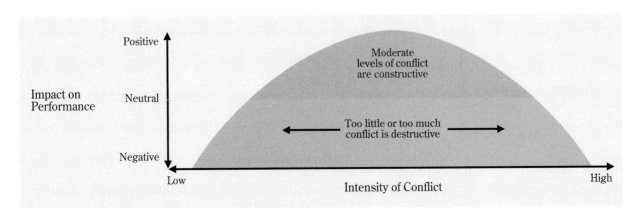

Figure 15.1   **The two faces of conflict: functional conflict and dysfunctional conflict.**

Research Insight
Importance of Cultural Intelligence

As the global economy continues to develop, so, too, does the need for intercultural understanding. In an article by P. Christopher Earley and Randall S. Peterson, the concept of "cultural intelligence," or "CQ," is described as a basis for improving the preparation of managers for international assignments. Stating that "intercultural differences have long been a challenge confronting multinational organizations," Earley and Peterson argue that training for global management requires more than an awareness of alternative cultural values. To be ultimately meaningful, intercultural capabilities must avoid simplistic cultural stereotyping and be designed to truly help people function effectively when working in alternative cultures. They ad-vocate training that emphasizes a model of cultural adaptation and the three CQ facet needs identified in the accompanying figure. Such training focuses on the importance of helping people learn strategies for cultural sense making (metacognitive/cognitive facet), for developing cultural empathy and self-efficacy (motivation facet), and for practicing behaviors that are culturally acceptable (behavior facet). The goal, they say, is to focus training on the "fundamental human capability for adjustment to others."

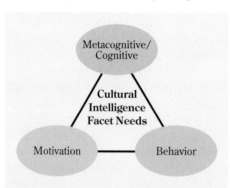

Reference: P. Christopher Earley and Randall S. Peterson, "The Elusive Cultural Chameleon: Cultural Intelligence as a New Approach to Intercultural Training for the Global Manager," *Academy of Management Learning and Education* 3(1) (2004):100–115.

Among the popular dimensions of culture discussed in Chapter 3, for example, substantial differences may be noted in time orientation. When persons from short-term cultures such as the United States try to work with persons from long-term cultures such as Japan, the likelihood of conflict developing is high. The same holds true when individualists work with collectivists and when persons from high–power distance cultures work with those from low–power distance cultures.[10] In each case, individuals who are not able to recognize and respect the impact of culture on behavior may contribute to the emergence of dysfunctional situations. On the other hand, by approaching a cross-cultural work situation with sensitivity and respect, one can find ways to work together without great difficulty and even with the advantages that constructive conflict may offer.

Conflict Management

Conflict resolution occurs when the reasons for a conflict are eliminated.

Conflict can be addressed in many ways, but the important goal is to achieve or set the stage for true **conflict resolution**—a situation in which the underlying reasons for a given destructive conflict are eliminated. The process begins with a good understanding of causes and recognition of the stage to which conflict has developed.

Stages of Conflict

Most conflicts develop in stages, as shown in Figure 15.2. Managers should recognize that unresolved prior conflicts help set the stage for future conflicts of the same or related sort. Rather than trying to deny the existence of conflict or settle on a temporary resolution, it is always best to deal with important conflicts so that they are completely resolved.[11] *Conflict antecedents* establish the conditions from which conflicts are likely to develop. When the antecedent conditions become the basis for substantive or emotional differences between people or groups, the stage of *perceived conflict* exists. Of course, this perception may be held by only one of the conflicting parties. It is important to distinguish between perceived and *felt conflict*. When conflict is felt, it is experienced as tension that motivates the person to take action to reduce feelings of discomfort. For conflict to be resolved, all parties should both perceive it and feel the need to do something about it.

When conflict is expressed openly in behavior, it is said to be manifest. Removing or correcting its antecedents may resolve a state of *manifest conflict*. Conflict can also be suppressed. With suppression, no change in antecedent conditions occurs; the manifest conflict behaviors are controlled. For example, one or both parties may choose to ignore the conflict in their dealings with one another. *Suppression* is a superficial and often temporary form of conflict resolution. Indeed, we have already noted that unresolved and suppressed conflicts fall into this category. Both may continue to fester and cause future conflicts

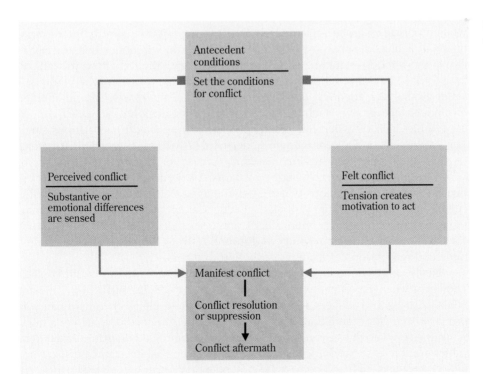

Figure 15.2   The stages of conflict.

Equal Employment Opportunity Commission

The Equal Employment Opportunity Commission (EEOC) handles complaints filed by employees against their employers. As many as one in five companies have faced age discrimination claims. Workers who are 40 years of age or older are protected by the Age Discrimination Act.

over similar issues. In the short run, however, they may represent the best a manager can achieve until antecedent conditions can be changed.

Unresolved substantive conflicts can result in sustained emotional discomfort and escalate into dysfunctional emotional conflict between individuals. In contrast, truly resolved conflicts may establish conditions that reduce the potential for future conflicts or make it easier to deal with them. Thus, any manager should be sensitive to the influence of *conflict aftermath* on future conflict episodes.

Causes of Conflict

The process of dealing successfully with conflict begins with recognition of several types of conflict situations. *Vertical conflict* occurs between hierarchical levels. It commonly involves supervisor–subordinate disagreements over resources, goals, deadlines, or performance results. *Horizontal conflict* occurs between persons or groups at the same hierarchical level. These disputes commonly involve goal incompatibilities, resource scarcities, or purely interpersonal factors. A common variation of horizontal conflict is *line–staff conflict*. It often involves disagreements over who has authority and control over certain matters such as personnel selection and termination practices.

Also common to work situations are *role conflicts* that occur when the communication of task expectations proves inadequate or upsetting. As discussed in respect to teamwork in Chapter 9, this often involves unclear communication of work expectations, excessive expectations in the form of job overloads, insufficient expectations in the form of job underloads, and incompatibilities among expectations from different sources.

Workflow interdependencies are breeding grounds for conflicts. Disputes and open disagreements may erupt among people and units who are required to cooperate to meet challenging goals.[12] When interdependence is high—that is, when a person or group must rely on or ask for contributions from one or more others to achieve its goals—conflicts often occur. You will notice this, for example, in a fast-food restaurant, when the people serving the food have to wait too long for it to be delivered from the cooks. Conflict also escalates when individuals or groups lack adequate task direction or goals. *Domain ambiguities* involve misunderstandings over such things as customer jurisdiction or scope of authority. Conflict is likely when individuals or groups are placed in ambiguous situations where it is difficult for them to understand just who is responsible for what.

Actual or perceived *resource scarcity* can foster destructive competition. When resources are scarce, working relationships are likely to suffer. This is especially true in organizations that are experiencing downsizing or financial difficulties. As cutbacks occur, various individuals or groups try to position themselves to gain or retain maximum shares of the shrinking resource pool. They are also likely to try to resist resource redistribution or to employ countermeasures to defend their resources from redistribution to others.

Finally, *power or value asymmetries* in work relationships can create conflict. They exist when interdependent people or groups differ substantially from one another in status and influence or in values. Conflict resulting from asymmetry is prone to occur, for example, when a lower-power person needs the help of a high-power person who does not respond, when people who hold dramatically different values are forced to work together on a task, or when a high-status person is required to interact with and perhaps be dependent on someone of lower status.

Indirect Conflict Management Approaches

Indirect conflict management approaches share the common ground of avoiding direct dealings with personalities. They include reduced interdependence, appeals to common goals, hierarchical referral, and alterations in the use of mythology and scripts.

Reduced Interdependence   When workflow conflicts exist, managers can adjust the level of interdependency among units or individuals.[13] One simple option is *decoupling*, or taking action to eliminate or reduce the required contact between conflicting parties. In some cases, the units' tasks can be adjusted to reduce the number of required points of coordination. The conflicting units can then be separated from one another, and each can be provided separate access to valued resources. Although decoupling may reduce conflict, it may also result in duplication and a poor allocation of valued resources.

   Buffering is another approach that can be used when the inputs of one group are the outputs of another group. The classic buffering technique is to build an inventory, or buffer, between the two groups so that any output slowdown or excess is absorbed by the inventory and does not directly pressure the target group. Although it reduces conflict, this technique is increasingly out of favor because it increases inventory costs. This consequence is contrary to the elements of just-in-time delivery, which is now valued in operations management.

   Conflict management can be facilitated by assigning people to serve as formal linking pins between groups that are prone to conflict.[14] Persons in *linking-pin roles*, such as a project liaison, are expected to understand the operations, members, needs, and norms of their host group. They are supposed to use this knowledge to help their group work better with other groups in order to accomplish mutual tasks. Though expensive, this technique is often used when different specialized groups, such as engineering and sales, must closely coordinate their efforts on complex and long-term projects.

Appeals to Common Goals   An *appeal to common goals* can focus the attention of potentially conflicting parties on one mutually desirable conclusion. By elevating the potential dispute to a common framework wherein the parties recognize their mutual interdependence in achieving common goals, petty disputes can be put in perspective. However, this can be difficult to achieve when prior performance is poor and individuals or groups disagree over how to improve performance. In this negative situation, the manager needs to remember the attribution tendency of individuals to blame poor performance on others or on external conditions. In this case, conflict resolution begins by making sure that the parties take personal responsibility for improving the situation. Wal-Mart, for example, is noted for its emphasis on common goals. The famous cheer ("Who's number one?") and answer ("The customer—always") is a part of the company culture. It is all about keeping the focus, staying on goal, minding the values, and sharing the vision—a lasting legacy of the founder, Sam Walton.[15]

Hierarchical Referral   *Hierarchical referral* makes use of the chain of command for conflict resolution.[16] Here, problems are simply referred up the hierarchy for more senior managers to reconcile. Whereas hierarchical referral can be definitive in a given case, it also has limitations. If conflict is severe and recur-

Josephson Institute on Ethics

The Josephson Institute of Ethics is concerned about employers that push people too hard, asking them to meet unrealistic goals. Impossible performance standards can lead to unethical behavior and cheating as workers try to make their performance look good.

ring, the continual use of hierarchical referral may not result in true conflict resolution. Managers removed from day-to-day affairs may fail to diagnose the real causes of a conflict, and conflict resolution may be superficial. Busy managers may tend to consider most conflicts as results of poor interpersonal relations and may act quickly to replace a person with a perceived "personality" problem.

Altering Scripts and Myths   In some situations, conflict is superficially managed by scripts, or behavioral routines, that become part of the organization's culture.[17] The scripts become rituals that allow the conflicting parties to vent their frustrations and to recognize that they are mutually dependent on one another via the larger corporation. An example is a monthly meeting of "department heads," which is held presumably for purposes of coordination and problem solving but actually becomes just a polite forum for superficial agreement.[18] Managers in such cases know their scripts and accept the difficulty of truly resolving any major conflicts. By sticking with the script, expressing only low-key disagreement, and then quickly acting as if everything has been resolved, for instance, the managers publicly act as if problems are being addressed. Such scripts can be altered to allow and encourage active confrontation of issues and disagreements.

Avoidance involves pretending a conflict does not really exist.

Accommodation, or **smoothing**, involves playing down differences and finding areas of agreement.

Compromise occurs when each party gives up something of value to the other.

Direct Conflict Management Approaches

Figure 15.3 describes the five approaches to conflict management from the perspective of their relative emphasis on cooperativeness and assertiveness in the relationship. Consultants and academics generally agree that true conflict resolution can occur only when the underlying substantive and emotional reasons for the conflict are identified and dealt with through a solution that allows all conflicting parties to "win."[19] This important issue of "Who wins?" can be addressed from the perspective of each conflicting party. See The Effective Manager 15.1 for tips on when to use the various conflict management styles.

Lose–Lose Conflict   *Lose–lose conflict* occurs when nobody really gets what he or she wants. The underlying reasons for the conflict remain unaffected and a similar conflict is likely to occur in the future. Lose–lose conflicts often result when there is little or no assertiveness and conflict management takes the following forms. **Avoidance** is an extreme form of inattention; everyone simply pretends that the conflict does not really exist and hopes that it will go away. **Accommodation**, or **smoothing** as it is sometimes called, involves playing down differences among the conflicting parties and highlighting similarities and areas of agreement. This peaceful coexistence ignores the real essence of a given conflict and often creates frustration and resentment. **Compromise** occurs when each party gives up something of value to the other. As a result of no one getting their full desires, the antecedent conditions for future conflicts are established.

THE EFFECTIVE MANAGER 15.1

When to Use Conflict Management Styles

- Collaboration and problem solving is preferred to gain true conflict resolution when time and cost permit.
- Avoidance may be used when an issue is trivial, when more important issues are pressing, or when people need to cool down temporarily and regain perspective.
- Authoritative command may be used when quick and decisive action is vital or when unpopular actions must be taken.
- Accommodation may be used when issues are more important to others than to yourself or when you want to build "credits" for use in later disagreements.
- Compromise may be used to arrive at temporary settlements of complex issues or to arrive at expedient solutions when time is limited.

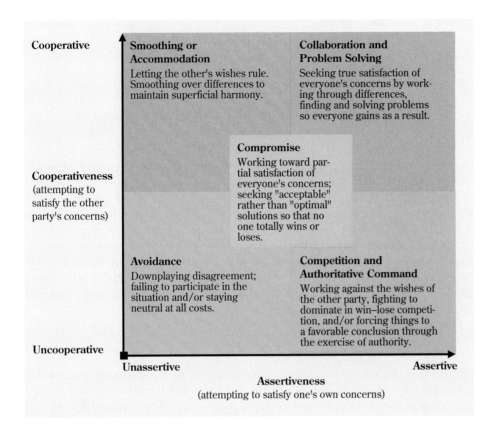

Figure 15.3 **Five ways to manage conflict.**

Win–Lose Conflict In *win–lose conflict*, one party achieves its desires at the expense and to the exclusion of the other party's desires. This is a high-assertiveness and low-cooperativeness situation. It may result from outright **competition** in which one party achieves a victory through force, superior skill, or domination. It may also occur as a result of **authoritative command**, whereby a formal authority simply dictates a solution and specifies what is gained and what is lost by whom. Win–lose strategies fail to address the root causes of the conflict and tend to suppress the desires of at least one of the conflicting parties. As a result, future conflicts over the same issues are likely to occur.

Win–Win Conflict *Win–win conflict* is achieved by a blend of both high cooperativeness and high assertiveness.[20] **Collaboration**, or **problem solving**, involves recognition by all conflicting parties that something is wrong and needs attention. It stresses gathering and evaluating information in solving disputes and making choices. Win–win conditions eliminate the reasons for continuing or resurrecting the conflict since nothing has been avoided or suppressed. All relevant issues are raised and openly discussed. The ultimate test for a win–win solution is whether or not the conflicting parties see that the solution (1) achieves each other's goals, (2) is acceptable to both parties, and (3) establishes a process whereby all parties involved see a responsibility to be open and honest about facts and feelings. When success is achieved, true conflict resolution has occurred.

Although collaboration and problem solving are generally favored, one limitation is the time and energy it requires. It is also important to realize that both

Competition seeks victory by force, superior skill, or domination.

Authoritative command uses formal authority to end conflict.

Collaboration involves recognition that something is wrong and needs attention through problem solving.

Problem solving uses information to resolve disputes.

parties to the conflict need to be assertive and cooperative in order to develop a win–win joint solution. Finally, collaboration and problem solving may not be feasible if the firm's dominant culture does not place a value on cooperation.[21]

Negotiation

Talk about conflict! Picture yourself trying to make a decision in the following situation: You have ordered a new state-of-the-art notebook computer for a staff member in your department. At about the same time, another department ordered a different brand. Your boss indicates that only one brand will be ordered. Of course, you believe the one chosen by your department is the best. Or consider this one: You have been offered a new job in another location and want to take it but are disappointed with the salary. You remember from one of your college courses that compensation and benefits packages can sometimes be modified from the first offer—if the candidate approaches things right.[22] You are concerned about the costs of relocating and would like a sign-on bonus as well as a guarantee of an early salary review.

What Is Negotiation?

■■■ **Negotiation** is the process of making joint decisions when the parties involved have different preferences.

The preceding examples are just a sample of the many situations that involve managers and others in **negotiation**—the process of making joint decisions when the parties involved have different preferences.[23] Negotiation has special significance in work settings, where disagreements are likely to arise over such diverse matters as wage rates, task objectives, performance evaluations, job assignments, work schedules, work locations, and more.

Negotiation Goals and Outcomes

In negotiation, two important goals must be considered: substance and relationship goals. *Substance goals* deal with outcomes that relate to the "content" issues under negotiation. The dollar amount of a wage agreement in a collective-bargaining situation is one example. *Relationship goals* deal with outcomes that relate to how well people involved in the negotiation and any constituencies they may represent are able to work with one another once the process is concluded. An example is the ability of union members and management representatives to work together effectively after a contract dispute has been settled.

Unfortunately, many negotiations result in damaged relationships because the negotiating parties become preoccupied with substance goals and self-interests. In contrast, *effective negotiation* occurs when substance issues are resolved and working relationships are maintained or even improved. It results in recognition of overlapping interests and joint decisions that are "for the better" of all parties. Three criteria for effective negotiation are described in The Effective Manager 15.2.

THE EFFECTIVE MANAGER 15.2

Criteria of an Effective Negotiation

1. *Quality*—The negotiation results offer a "quality" agreement that is wise and satisfactory to all sides.
2. *Harmony*—The negotiation is "harmonious" and fosters rather than inhibits good interpersonal relations.
3. *Efficiency*—The negotiation is "efficient" and no more time consuming or costly than absolutely necessary.

Ethical Aspects of Negotiation

To maintain good working relationships in negotiations, managers and other involved parties should strive for high ethical standards. This goal may be sidetracked by an overemphasis on self-interests. The motivation to behave ethically in negotiations is put to the test by each party's desire to "get more" than the other from the negotiation and/or by a belief that there are insufficient resources to satisfy all parties.[24] After the heat of negotiations dies down, the parties involved often try to rationalize or explain away questionable ethics as unavoidable, harmless, or justified. Such after-the-fact rationalizations may be offset by long-run negative consequences, such as not being able to achieve one's wishes again the next time. At the very least, the unethical party may be the target of revenge tactics by those who were disadvantaged. Furthermore, once some people have behaved unethically in one situation, they may become entrapped by such behavior and prone to display it again in the future.[25]

ETHICS AND SOCIAL RESPONSIBILITY

NEGOTIATING FOR NATURE— FROM BEES TO A NATIONAL PARK

Can a business do good things for society while making profits for its owners? Roxanne Quimby would surely say "yes." She recently negotiated the sale of 80 percent of her founding ownership in Burt's Bees for $177 million. From a backyard beehive to multimillion-dollar corporation, she led the firm with a commitment to sell only environmentally friendly and natural products. From hand creams to lip gloss to children's toothpaste and more, the market has proven the worth of her ideas. Now Quimby is using some of her profits to buy undeveloped land in Maine (16,000 acres so far) with the hope of creating a new national forest. She says the park "would solve three big problems in Maine: conservation, recreation, and the economy." She believes that being a steward for the environment helped create her business success.

Question: What other examples can you find of businesses that include protection and support of our natural environment as a basic part of their missions?

Organizational Settings for Negotiation

Managers and team leaders should be prepared to participate in at least four major action settings for negotiations. In *two-party negotiation*, the manager negotiates directly with one other person. In a *group negotiation*, the manager is part of a team or group whose members are negotiating to arrive at a common decision. In an *intergroup negotiation*, the manager is part of a group that is negotiating with another group to arrive at a decision regarding a problem or situation affecting both. And in a *constituency negotiation*, the manager is involved in negotiation with other persons, with each party representing a broader constituency. A common example of *constituency negotiation* involves representatives of management and labor negotiating a collective-bargaining agreement.

Culture and Negotiation

The existence of cultural differences in time orientation, individualism–collectivism, and power distance can have a substantial impact on negotiation. For example, when American businesses try to negotiate quickly with Chinese counterparts, they often do so with the goal of getting definitive agreements that will govern a working relationship. Culture isn't always on their side. A typical Chinese approach to negotiation might move much more slowly, require the development of good interpersonal relationships prior to reaching any agreement, display reluctance to commit everything to writing, and anticipate that any agreement reached will be subject to modification as future circumstances may require.[26] All this is quite the opposite of the typical expectations of negotiators used to the individualist and short-term American culture.

Negotiation Strategies

Managers and other workers frequently negotiate with one another over access to scarce organizational resources. These resources may be money, time, people, facilities, equipment, and so on. In all such cases, the general approach to or strategy for the negotiation can have a major influence on its outcomes. In **distributive negotiation**, the focus is on "positions" staked out or declared by conflicting parties. Each party is trying to claim certain portions of the available "pie." In **integrative negotiation**, sometimes called *principled negotiation*, the focus is on the "merits" of the issues. Everyone involved tries to enlarge the available pie rather than stake claims to certain portions of it.[27]

■ **Distributive negotiation** focuses on positions staked out or declared by the parties involved, who are each trying to claim certain portions of the available pie.

■ **Integrative negotiation** focuses on the merits of the issues, and the parties involved try to enlarge the available pie rather than stake claims to certain portions of it.

Distributive Negotiation

In distributive bargaining approaches, the participants would each ask the question: "Who is going to get this resource?" This question, and the way in which it frames subsequent behavior, will have a major impact on the negotiation process and outcomes. A case of distributive negotiation usually unfolds in one of two directions, neither of which yields optimal results. *"Hard" distributive negotiation* takes place when each party holds out to get its own way. This leads to competition, whereby each party seeks dominance over the other and tries to maximize self-interests. The hard approach may lead to a win–lose outcome in which one party dominates and gains. Or it can lead to an impasse.

"Soft" distributive negotiation, by contrast, takes place when one party is willing to make concessions to the other to get things over with. In this case, one party tries to find ways to meet the other's desires. A soft approach leads to accommodation, in which one party gives in to the other, or to compromise, in which each party gives up something of value in order to reach agreement. In either case, at least some latent dissatisfaction is likely to develop. Even when the soft approach results in compromise (e.g., splitting the difference between the initial positions equally), dissatisfaction may exist since each party is still deprived of what it originally wanted.

Figure 15.4 introduces the case of the graduating senior negotiating a job offer with a corporate recruiter.[28] The example illustrates the basic elements of classic two-party negotiation in distributive contexts. To begin, look at the situa-

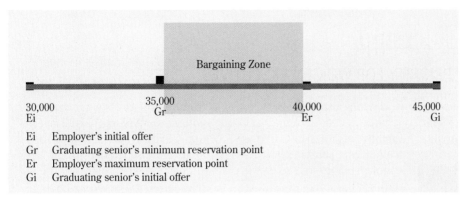

Ei   Employer's initial offer
Gr   Graduating senior's minimum reservation point
Er   Employer's maximum reservation point
Gi   Graduating senior's initial offer

Figure 15.4   An example of the bargaining zone in classic two-party negotiation.

tion from the graduate's perspective. She has told the recruiter that she would like a salary of $45,000; this is her initial offer. But she also has in mind a minimum reservation point of $35,000—the lowest salary that she will accept for this job. Thus, she communicates a salary request of $45,000 but is willing to accept one as low as $35,000. The situation is somewhat reversed from the recruiter's perspective. His initial offer to the graduate is $30,000, and his maximum reservation point is $40,000; this is the most he is prepared to pay.

The **bargaining zone** is defined as the range between one party's minimum reservation point and the other party's maximum reservation point. In Figure 15.4, the bargaining zone is $35,000–$40,000. This is a positive bargaining zone since the reservation points of the two parties overlap. Whenever a positive bargaining zone exists, bargaining has room to unfold. Had the graduate's minimum reservation point been greater than the recruiter's maximum reservation point (for example, $42,000), no room would have existed for bargaining. Classic two-party bargaining always involves the delicate tasks of first discovering the respective reservation points (one's own and the other's) and then working toward an agreement that lies somewhere within the resulting bargaining zone and is acceptable to each party.

■ The **bargaining zone** is the zone between one party's minimum reservation point and the other party's maximum reservation point in a negotiating situation.

Integrative Negotiation

In the integrative approach to negotiation, participants would ask: "How can the resource best be utilized?" Notice that this question is very different from the one described for distributive negotiation. It is much less confrontational, and it permits a broader range of alternatives to be considered in the process. From the outset there is much more of a "win–win" orientation.

At one extreme, integrative negotiation may involve selective avoidance, in which both parties realize that there are more important things on which to focus their time and attention. The time, energy, and effort needed to negotiate may not be worth the rewards. Compromise can also play a role in the integrative approach, but it must have an enduring basis. This is most likely to occur when the compromise involves each party giving up something of perceived lesser personal value to gain something of greater value. For instance, in the classic two-party bargaining case over salary, both the graduate and the recruiter could expand the negotiation to include the starting date of the job. Since it will be a year before the candidate's first vacation, she may be willing to take a little less money if she can start a few weeks later. Finally, integrative negotiation may

Leaders on Leadership

FLEXIBILITY IS A KEY PRIORITY FOR WOMEN EXECUTIVES

For women in the top executive ranks, finding personal flexibility can be an important key to leadership success. Shelly Lazarus is chairman and CEO of the advertising firm Ogilvy & Mather. She started as an account manager and rose through the ranks to senior management, while raising and enjoying three children. Says Lazarus: "You will always passionately love your children, so if you don't have work that is stimulating, rewarding, and involving, you are going to miss every minute that you are away from them." Lazarus has been willing to challenge expectations. Even when executive retreats were scheduled to start on Sunday evenings, she would arrive on Monday morning. She had the personal confidence to inform her bosses that to do her best work she needed Sundays with family. Her advice is that if women show talent and strength and "set their terms with employers," the likelihood is that they will be accommodated.

Question: What lines will you try to draw in balancing your work and career goals with family and personal responsibilities?

involve true collaboration. In this case, the negotiating parties engage in problem solving to arrive at a mutual agreement that maximizes benefits to each.

How to Gain Integrative Agreements

Underlying the integrative or principled approach is negotiation based on the merits of the situation. The foundations for gaining truly integrative agreements include supportive attitudes, constructive behaviors, and good information.[29]

Attitudinal Foundations   There are three attitudinal foundations of integrative agreements. First, each party must approach the negotiation with a *willingness to trust* the other party. This is a reason why ethics and maintaining relationships are so important in negotiations. Second, each party must convey a *willingness to share information* with the other party. Without shared information, effective problem solving is unlikely to occur. Third, each party must show a *willingness to ask concrete questions* of the other party. This further facilitates information sharing.

Behavioral Foundations   During a negotiation, all behavior is important for both its actual impact and the impressions it leaves behind. Accordingly, the following behavioral foundations of integrative agreements must be carefully considered and included in any negotiator's repertoire of skills and capabilities:

Behavioral foundations of integrative agreements

- The ability to separate the people from the problem to avoid allowing emotional considerations to affect the negotiation

- The ability to focus on interests rather than positions
- The ability to avoid making premature judgments
- The ability to keep the acts of alternative creation separate from their evaluation
- The ability to judge possible agreements on an objective set of criteria or standards

Information Foundations   The information foundations of integrative agreements are substantial. They involve each party becoming familiar with the BATNA, or "best alternative to a negotiated agreement." That is, each party must know what he or she will do if an agreement can't be reached. This requires that both negotiating parties identify and understand their personal interests in the situation. They must know what is really important to them in the case at hand, and they must come to understand the relative importance of the other party's interests. As difficult as it may seem, each party must achieve an understanding of what the other party values, even to the point of determining its BATNA.

Common Negotiation Pitfalls

The negotiation process is admittedly complex on cultural and many other grounds. It is further characterized by all the possible confusions of interpersonal and group dynamics that sometimes get volatile. Accordingly, negotiators need to guard against some common negotiation pitfalls.[30]

First is the tendency in negotiation to stake out your position based on the assumption that in order to gain your way, something must be subtracted from the gains of the other party. This *myth of the fixed pie* is a purely distributive approach to negotiation. The whole concept of integrative negotiation is based on the premise that the pie can sometimes be expanded or utilized to the maximum advantage of all parties, not just one.

Second, because parties to negotiations often begin by stating extreme demands, the possibility of *escalating commitment* is high. That is, once demands have been stated, people become committed to them and are reluctant to back down. Concerns for protecting one's ego and saving face may lead to irrational escalation of conflict. Self-discipline is needed to spot this tendency in one's own behavior as well as in others.

Third, negotiators often develop *overconfidence* that their positions are the only correct ones. This can lead them to ignore the other party's needs. In some cases, negotiators completely fail to see merits in the other party's position—merits that an outside observer would be sure to spot. Such overconfidence makes it harder to reach a positive common agreement.

Fourth, communication problems can cause difficulties during a negotiation. It has been said that "negotiation is the process of communicating back and forth for the purpose of reaching a joint decision."[31] This process can break down because of a *telling problem*—the parties don't really talk to each other, at least not in the sense of making themselves truly understood. It can also be damaged by a *hearing problem*—the parties are unable or unwilling to listen well enough to understand what the other is saying. Indeed, positive negotiation is most likely when each party engages in active listening and frequently asks questions to clarify what the other is saying. Each party occasionally needs to "stand in the other party's shoes" and to view the situation from the other's perspective.[32]

Human Resource Management News

The 360-degree performance review is used by a large percentage of top companies, according to the *Human Resource Management News*. The approach helps reduce conflict and create fairness by expanding performance evaluation beyond the views of the boss alone.

PEOPLE AND TECHNOLOGY

LEADER USES TECHNOLOGY IN OPERATIONS MAKEOVER

Robert Nardelli's leadership as CEO of Home Depot began with the challenge of bringing new discipline to a highly entrepreneurial firm with performance problems. "Being an outsider," he says, created the advantage of "not having to stick with the past." For Home Depot this has meant a new culture, stronger organizational controls, a new emphasis on leadership training, investment in new technology, and a continued emphasis on growth. In critiquing Nardelli's approach to bringing new leadership to the top-management team, one observer notes that he led with a commitment to revolution, not evolution.

Question: When a top-management team takes over a struggling or complacent organization, is it better to go fast or go slow with a change agenda?

▓▓ **Alternative dispute resolution** involves a neutral third party who helps others resolve negotiation impasses and disputes.

▓▓ In **arbitration**, a neutral third party acts as judge with the power to issue a decision binding on all parties.

▓▓ In **mediation**, a neutral third party tries to engage the parties in a negotiated solution through persuasion and rational argument.

Third-Party Roles in Negotiation

Negotiation may sometimes be accomplished through the intervention of third parties, such as when stalemates occur and matters appear unresolvable under current circumstances. In a process called **alternative dispute resolution**, a neutral third party works with persons involved in a negotiation to help them resolve impasses and settle disputes. There are two primary forms through which "ADR" is implemented. In **arbitration**, such as the salary arbitration now common in professional sports, the neutral third party acts as a "judge" and has the power to issue a decision that is binding on all parties. This ruling takes place after the arbitrator listens to the positions advanced by the parties involved in a dispute. In **mediation**, the neutral third party tries to engage the parties in a negotiated solution through persuasion and rational argument. This is a common approach in labor–management negotiations, where trained mediators acceptable to each side are called in to help resolve bargaining impasses. Unlike an arbitrator, the mediator is not able to dictate a solution.

Chapter 15   Study Guide

Summary

What is conflict?

- Conflict appears in a social situation as any disagreement over issues of substance or emotional antagonisms that create friction between individuals or groups.
- Conflict can be either emotional—based on personal feelings—or substantive—based on work goals.

- When kept within tolerable limits, conflict can be a source of creativity and performance enhancement; it becomes destructive when these limits are exceeded.

- Conflict situations in organizations occur in vertical and lateral working relations and in line–staff relations.

- Most typically, conflict develops through a series of stages, beginning with antecedent conditions and progressing into manifest conflict.

- Unresolved prior conflicts set the stage for future conflicts of a similar nature.

How can conflict be managed successfully?

- Indirect forms of conflict management include appeals to common goals, hierarchical referral, organizational redesign, and the use of mythology and scripts.

- Direct conflict management proceeds with different combinations of assertiveness and cooperativeness by conflicting parties.

- Win–win conflict resolution is preferred; it is achieved through collaboration and problem solving.

- Win–lose conflict resolution should be avoided; it is associated with competition and authoritative command.

What is negotiation?

- Negotiation occurs whenever two or more people with different preferences must make joint decisions.

- Managers may find themselves involved in various types of negotiation situations, including two-party, group, intergroup, and constituency negotiation.

- Effective negotiation occurs when issues of substance are resolved and human relationships are maintained, or even improved, in the process.

- Ethical conduct is important to successful negotiations.

What are the different strategies involved in negotiation?

- In distributive negotiation, the focus of each party is on staking out positions in the attempt to claim desired portions of a "fixed pie."

- In integrative negotiation, sometimes called principled negotiation, the focus is on determining the merits of the issues and finding ways to satisfy one another's needs.

- The success of the strategies depends on avoiding common negotiating pitfalls and building good communications.

Key Terms

Accommodation, or smoothing (p. 346)
Alternative dispute resolution (p. 354)
Arbitration (p. 354)
Authoritative command (p. 347)
Avoidance (p. 346)

Bargaining zone (p. 351)
Collaboration (p. 347)
Competition (p. 347)
Compromise (p. 346)
Conflict (p. 338)
Conflict resolution (p. 342)
Distributive negotiation (p. 350)

Dysfunctional conflict (p. 341)
Emotional conflict (p. 339)
Functional conflict (p. 341)
Integrative negotiation (p. 350)
Intergroup conflict (p. 340)

Self-Test 15

Multiple Choice

1. A/an _____ conflict occurs in the form of a fundamental disagreement over ends or goals to be pursued and the means for accomplishment. (a) relationship (b) emotional (c) substantive (d) procedural

2. The indirect conflict management approach that uses chain of command for conflict resolution is known as _____. (a) hierarchical referral (b) avoidance (c) smoothing (d) appeal to common goals

3. Conflict that ends up being "functional" for the people and organization involved would most likely be _____. (a) of high intensity (b) of moderate intensity (c) of low intensity (d) nonexistent

4. One of the problems with the suppression of conflicts is that it _____. (a) creates winners and losers (b) is often a temporary solution that sets the stage for future conflict (c) works only with emotional conflicts (d) works only with substantive conflicts

5. When a manager asks people in conflict to remember the mission and purpose of the organization and try to reconcile their differences in that context, she is using a conflict management approach known as _____. (a) reduced interdependence (b) buffering (c) resource expansion (d) appeal to common goals

6. The best time to use accommodation in conflict management is _____. (a) when quick and decisive action is vital (b) when you want to build "credit" for use in later disagreements (c) when people need to cool down and gain perspective (d) when temporary settlement of complex issues is needed

7. Which of the following is an indirect approach to managing conflict? (a) buffering (b) win–lose (c) workflow interdependency (d) power asymmetry

8. A lose–lose conflict is likely when the conflict management approach focuses on _____. (a) linking pin roles (b) altering scripts (c) accommodation (d) problem-solving

9. Which approach to conflict management can be best described as both highly cooperative and highly assertive? (a) competition (b) compromise (c) accommodation (d) collaboration

10. Both_____ goals should be considered in any negotiation. (a) performance and evaluation (b) task and substance (c) substance and relationship (d) task and performance

11. The three criteria for effective negotiation are _____. (a) harmony, efficiency, and quality (b) quality, efficiency, and effectiveness (c) ethical behavior, practicality, and cost-effectiveness (d) quality, practicality and productivity

12. Which of the following statements is true? (a) Principled negotiation leads to accommodation. (b) Hard distributive negotiation leads to collaboration. (c) Soft distributive negotiation leads to accommodation or compromise. (d) Hard distributive negotiation leads to win–win conflicts.

13. Another name for integrative negotiation is _____. (a) arbitration (b) mediation (c) principled negotiation (d) smoothing

14. When a person approaches a negotiation with the assumption that in order for him to gain his way the other party must lose or give up something, which negotiation pitfall is being exhibited? (a) myth of the fixed pie (b) escalating commitment (c) overconfidence (d) hearing problem

15. In the process of alternative dispute resolution known as _____, a neutral third party acts as a "judge" to determine how a conflict will be resolved. (a) mediation (b) arbitration (c) conciliation (d) collaboration

Short Response

16. List and discuss three conflict situations faced by managers.

17. List and discuss the major indirect conflict management approaches.

18. Under what conditions might a manager use avoidance or accommodation?

19. Compare and contrast distributive and integrative negotiation. Which is more desirable? Why?

Applications Essay

20. Discuss the common pitfalls you would expect to encounter in negotiating your salary for your first job, and explain how you would try to best deal with them.

These learning activities from *The OB Skills Workbook* are suggested for Chapter 15.

OB in Action

CASE	EXPERIENTIAL EXERCISES	SELF-ASSESSMENT
■ 15. Faculty Empowerment and the Changing University Environment	■ 35. Vacation Puzzle ■ 36. The Ugli Orange ■ 37. Conflict Dialogues	■ 18. Conflict Management Styles

Plus—special learning experiences from *The Jossey-Bass/Pfeiffer Classroom Collection*

Chapter 16

Change, Innovation, and Stress

Chapter at a Glance

Organizations must change and innovate. Chapter 16 addresses the important issues of change and innovation as well as the role of stress in the modern workplace. As you read Chapter 16, *keep in mind these study questions.*

WHAT IS ORGANIZATIONAL CHANGE?

WHAT CHANGE STRATEGIES ARE USED IN ORGANIZATIONS?

HOW IS RESISTANCE TO CHANGE BEST MANAGED?

HOW DO ORGANIZATIONS INNOVATE?

HOW DOES STRESS AFFECT PEOPLE IN CHANGE

REVIEW IN END-OF-CHAPTER STUDY GUIDE

A common theme throughout this book has been the importance of respecting and valuing people, their diversity, and the talents they bring to organizations.[1] The best managers help build high-performance work settings rich in opportunities for both task accomplishment and personal satisfaction. Even as organizations are pressured by competition and environmental challenges to continuously change and innovate in order to survive, people and their needs are never taken for granted. Like all of us, you must make good choices about where to work, whom to work for, and under what conditions. The ideal is an organization that masters the challenges of change while still creating a satisfying, healthy, and high-performance workplace for its employees.

Not too long ago an article in the *Harvard Business Review* opened with this sentence: "The new economy has ushered in great business opportunities—and great turmoil.[2] Not since the Industrial Revolution have the stakes of dealing with change been so high." The terms "turmoil" and "turbulence" are now often used to describe the current environment of business and management. The forces of globalization are full of problems and opportunities; the new economy is constantly springing surprises on even the most experienced business executives. And always standing at the heart of any successful response to the challenges of change are the people who make organizations work. This is what makes the insights of organizational behavior so essential to change leadership.

Flexibility, competency, and commitment are the rules of the day. People in the new workplace must be comfortable dealing with adaptation and continuous change. Amid the calls for greater productivity, willingness to learn from the successes of others, total quality, and continuous improvement, everyone is being called upon to achieve success while pursuing change and innovation and experiencing inevitable stress. In the words of management consultant Tom Peters: "The turbulent marketplace demands that we make innovation a way of life for everyone. We must learn—individually and as organizations—to welcome change and innovation as vigorously as we have fought it in the past."[3]

> "The turbulent marketplace demands that we make innovation a way of life...."

Change in Organizations

▨ Transformational change radically shifts the fundamental character of an organization.

"Change" is the watchword of the day for many, if not most, organizations. Some of this change may be described as *radical change*, or frame-breaking change.[4] This is **transformational change**, which results in a major overhaul of the organization or its component systems. Organizations experiencing transformational change undergo significant shifts in basic characteristics, including the overall pur-

Leaders on Leadership

HOW LEADERS CREATE TRANSFORMATIONS

When Carly Fiorina took over as CEO of Hewlett-Packard, she faced the problem of leading a company known for a strong organizational culture but also facing major competitive pressures in a changing global economy. In her words, it was a company that was "so in love with its past" that "it had forgotten to build its future." But she saw HP's problems as opportunities for strategic change leadership. With confidence and hard work, she challenged old ways of thinking, dealt with resistance to change, and brought a new vision to the firm. Fiorina believes that leaders have a responsibility to "see things before everyone else sees them." In reflecting back on her decision to pursue a controversial merger with Compaq, she says: "I would do it again if I had to. We did it because tech was changing. If you're not leading, you're losing." And when it comes to leadership, she believes the key is "unlocking the potential of others and helping others achieve more than they think is possible."

Question: How effective are the change leadership styles of top managers at firms and organizations that you are familiar with?

pose/mission, underlying values and beliefs, and supporting strategies and structures.[5] In today's business environments, transformational changes are often initiated by a critical event, such as a new CEO, a new ownership brought about by merger or takeover, or a dramatic failure in operating results. When it occurs in the life cycle of an organization, such radical change is intense and all encompassing.

Another common form of organizational change is *incremental change,* or frame-bending change. This type of change, being part of an organization's natural evolution, is frequent and less traumatic. Typical incremental changes include the introduction of new products, new technologies, and new systems and processes. Although the nature of the organization remains relatively the same, incremental change builds on the existing ways of operating to enhance or extend them in new directions. The capability of improving continuously through incremental change is an important asset in today's demanding environments.

The success of both radical and incremental change in organizations depends in part on **change agents** who lead and support the change processes. These are individuals and groups who take responsibility for changing the existing behavior patterns of another person or social system. Although change agents are sometimes hired as consultants from outside the organization, any manager or leader in today's dynamic times is expected to act in the capacity of change agent. Indeed, this responsibility is increasingly defined even more specifically as essential to the leadership role. Simply put, being an effective change agent means being a great "change leader."

Change agents are people who take action to change the behavior of people and systems.

Planned and Unplanned Change

Unplanned change occurs spontaneously and without a change agent's direction.

Not all change in organizations is the result of a change agent's direction. **Unplanned changes** occur spontaneously or randomly. They may be disruptive, such as a wildcat strike that ends in a plant closure, or beneficial, such as an interpersonal conflict that results in a new procedure designed to smooth the flow of work between two departments. When the forces of unplanned change begin to appear, the appropriate goal is to act quickly to minimize any negative consequences and maximize any possible benefits. In many cases, unplanned changes can be turned into good advantage.

Planned change is intentional and occurs with a change agent's direction.

A performance gap is a discrepancy between the desired and actual state of affairs.

In contrast, **planned change** is the result of specific efforts by a change agent. It is a direct response to someone's perception of a **performance gap**—a discrepancy between the desired and actual state of affairs. Performance gaps may represent problems to be resolved or opportunities to be explored. Most planned changes may be regarded as efforts intended to deal with performance gaps in ways that benefit an organization and its members. The processes of continuous improvement require constant vigilance to spot performance gaps—both problems and opportunities—and to take action to resolve them.

Forces and Targets for Change

The forces for change driving organizations of all types and sizes are ever present in and around today's dynamic work settings. They are found in the *organization–environment relationship*, with mergers, strategic alliances, and divestitures among the examples of organizational attempts to redefine their relationships with challenging social and political environments. They are found in the *organizational life cycle*, with changes in culture and structure among the examples of how organizations must adapt as they evolve from birth through growth and toward maturity. They are found in the *political nature of organizations*, with changes in internal control structures, including benefits and reward systems that attempt to deal with shifting political currents.

CULTURES AND THE GLOBAL WORKFORCE

LACK OF CONTROL COSTLY IN COMPLEX INTERNATIONAL OPERATIONS

Lucent Corporation is taking steps to improve control and coordination of its international operations. Asia and especially China have been important growth areas for the firm, but expansion has come at a cost. The firm announced that it had fired two top executives in its China operations because of possible violations of the U.S. Foreign Corrupt Practices Act. The act prohibits officials of U.S. firms from paying bribes in foreign countries. According to Lucent, "internal control deficiencies" contributed to the problem with its operations in China, and those control systems will need to change.

Question: In what ways can conflicting values create problems in international business?

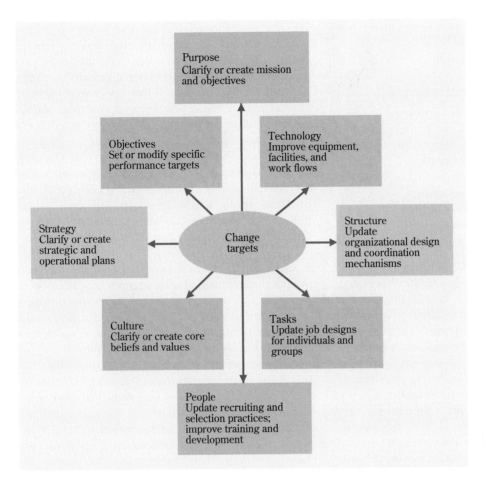

Figure 16.1 **Organizational targets for planned change.**

Planned change based on any of these forces can be internally directed toward a wide variety of organizational components, most of which have already been discussed in this book. As shown in Figure 16.1, these targets include organizational purpose, strategy, structure, and people, as well as objectives, culture, tasks, and technology. When considering these targets, however, it must be recognized that they are highly intertwined in the workplace. Changes in any one are likely to require or involve changes in others. For example, a change in the basic *tasks*—what it is that people do—is almost inevitably accompanied by a change in *technology*—the way in which tasks are accomplished. Changes in tasks and technology usually require alterations in *structures*, including changes in the patterns of authority and communication as well as in the roles of workers. These technological and structural changes can, in turn, necessitate changes in the knowledge, skills, and behaviors of *people*—the members of the organization.[6] In all cases, of course, tendencies to accept easy-to-implement, but questionable, "quick fixes" to problems should be avoided.

Phases of Planned Change

Researchers suggest that the failure rate of organizational change attempts is as high as 70 percent.[7] The challenges of transformational change are especially large, as

THE EFFECTIVE MANAGER 16.1

Why Transformational Efforts Fail

1. No sense of urgency
2. No powerful guiding coalition
3. No compelling vision
4. Failure to communicate the vision
5. Failure to empower others to act
6. Failure to celebrate short-term wins
7. Failure to build on accomplishments
8. Failure to institutionalize results

The Effective Manager 16.1 suggests.[8] One way to approach the task of improving the success rate of change initiatives is by understanding the underlying processes of social change in organizations. Psychologist Kurt Lewin recommends that any change effort be viewed in three phases—unfreezing, changing, and refreezing—all of which must be well handled for a change to be successful.[9] He also suggests that we may become easily preoccupied with the changing phase and neglect the importance of the unfreezing and refreezing stages. Although the continuous nature of change means that these phases will often overlap in today's organizations, Lewin's understanding of the challenges of the change process remain very helpful.

■■■ **Unfreezing** is the stage at which a situation is prepared for change.

Unfreezing   In Lewin's model, **unfreezing** is the managerial responsibility of preparing a situation for change. It involves disconfirming existing attitudes and behaviors to create a felt need for something new. Environmental pressures, declining performance, recognition of a problem, or awareness that someone else has found a better way, among other things, facilitate the unfreezing stage. But many changes are never tried, or they fail simply because situations are not properly unfrozen to begin with.

Large systems seem particularly susceptible to what is sometimes called the *boiled frog phenomenon*.[10] This refers to the notion that a live frog will immediately jump out when placed in a pan of hot water. When placed in cold water that is then heated very slowly, however, the frog will stay in the water until the water boils the frog to death. Organizations, too, can fall victim to similar circumstances. When managers fail to monitor their environments, recognize important trends, or sense the need to change, their organizations may slowly suffer and lose their competitive edge. Although the signals that change may be needed are available, they aren't noticed or given any special attention—until it is too late. In contrast, people who are always on the alert and understand the importance of "unfreezing" in the change process lead the best organizations.

■■■ **Changing** is the stage in which specific actions are taken to create change.

Changing   The **changing** stage involves taking action to modify a situation by changing things, such as the people, tasks, structure, or technology of the organization. Lewin believes that many change agents are prone to an activity trap. They bypass the unfreezing stage and start changing things prematurely or too quickly. Although their intentions may be correct, the situation has not been properly prepared for change. This often leads to failure. Changing something is difficult enough in any situation, let alone having to do so without the proper foundations.

■■■ **Refreezing** is the stage in which changes are reinforced and stabilized.

Refreezing   The final stage in the planned change process is **refreezing**. Designed to maintain the momentum of a change and eventually institutionalize it as part of the normal routine, refreezing secures the full benefits of long-lasting change. Refreezing involves positively reinforcing desired outcomes and providing extra support when difficulties are encountered. It involves evaluating progress and results, and assessing the costs and benefits of the change. And it allows for modifications to be made in the change to increase its success over time. When all of this is not done and refreezing is neglected, changes are often abandoned after a short time or incompletely implemented.

Planned Change Strategies

Managers and other change agents use various means for mobilizing power, exerting influence over others, and getting people to support planned change efforts. As described in Figure 16.2, each of these strategies builds from the various bases of social power discussed in Chapter 12. Note in particular that each power source has somewhat different implications for the planned change process.[11]

Force–Coercion

A **force–coercion strategy** uses authority, rewards, or punishments as primary inducements to change. That is, the change agent acts unilaterally to "command" change through the formal authority of his or her position, to induce change via an offer of special rewards, or to bring about change via threats of punishment. People respond to this strategy mainly out of the fear of being punished if they do not comply with a change directive or out of the desire to gain a reward if they do. Compliance is usually temporary and continues only as long as the change agent and his or her legitimate authority are visible or as long as the opportunities for rewards and punishments remain obvious. Your actions as a change agent using the force–coercion strategy might match the following profile.

> You believe that people who run things are basically motivated by self-interest and by what the situation offers in terms of potential personal gains or losses. Since you feel that people change only in response to such motives, you try to find out where their vested interests lie and then put the pressure on. If you have formal authority, you use it. If not, you resort to whatever possible rewards and punishments you have access to and do not hesitate to threaten others with these weapons. Once you find a weakness, you exploit it and are always wise to work "politically" by building supporting alliances wherever possible.[12]

■ A **force–coercion strategy** uses authority, rewards, and punishments to create change.

Rational Persuasion

Change agents using a **rational persuasion strategy** attempt to bring about change through the use of special knowledge, empirical support, or rational arguments. This strategy assumes that rational people will be guided by reason

■ A **rational persuasion strategy** uses facts, special knowledge, and rational argument to create change.

Power base	Change strategy	Change agent behavior	Predicted outcomes
Rewards Punishments Legitimacy	Force–coercion	Unilateral action; "command"	Temporary compliance
Expertise	Rational persuasion	Rational persuasion; expert testimony; demonstration projects	Long-term internalization
Reference	Shared powers	Empowerment; participative decisions	Long-term internalization

Figure 16.2 Power bases, change strategies, and predicted change outcomes.

Research Insight
Leadership and the Intricacies of Radical Change

Leaders and researchers have long been interested in learning more about the processes of organizational change. One area of special interest is the pace, sequencing, and nature of "radical change." Amis, Slack, and Hinings review the literature on change and note the importance of learning more about these issues in change leadership. They report an extensive study of changes in 36 Canadian Olympic NSOs over a 12-year period, one they describe as "probably the most turbulent in the history of Canadian amateur sport." The researchers found a pattern in the organizations that were most successful in their change transformations. The successful NSOs intermixed periods of change activity with ones of consol-

LESSONS OF RADICAL CHANGE

- Be cautious in trying to change rapidly
- Spend time building relationships among key change stakeholders
- Give priority to changing key elements first
- Be alert that resistance might be high in the most sensitive change areas

idation, where trust and working relationships were developed in support of change. These NSOs also followed a sequence that initiated change with a focus on "high-impact" organizational components, thus signaling to everyone its importance. They point out some of the difficulties of conducting research over such a long period of time with a set of organizations. They also call for more research to further investigate why and how pace, sequencing, and linearity affect the success of organizational changes.

Reference: John Amis, Trevor Slack, and C. R. Hinings, "The Pace, Sequence, and Linearity of Radical Change," *Academy of Management Journal* 47(1) (2004):15–40.

and self-interest in deciding whether or not to support a change. Expert power is mobilized to convince others that the change will leave them better off than before. It is sometimes referred to as an empirical-rational strategy of planned change. When successful, this strategy results in a longer-lasting, more naturalized change than does force–coercion. As a change agent taking the rational persuasion approach to a change situation, you might behave as follows.

> You believe that people are inherently rational and are guided by reason in their actions and decision making. Once a specific course of action is demonstrated to be in a person's self-interest, you assume that reason and rationality will cause the person to adopt it. Thus, you approach change with the objective of communicating—through information and facts—the essential "desirability" of change from the perspective of the person whose behavior you seek to influence. If this logic is effectively communicated, you are sure of the person's adopting the proposed change.[13]

Shared Power

■ A **shared-power strategy** uses participatory methods and emphasizes common values to create change.

A **shared-power strategy** actively and sincerely involves the people who will be affected by a change in planning and making key decisions relating to this change. Sometimes called a normative-reeducative approach, this strategy tries to develop directions and support for change through involvement and empowerment. It builds essential foundations, such as personal values, group norms, and shared goals, so that support for a proposed change emerges naturally. Managers using normative-reeducative approaches draw on the power of personal reference and also share power by allowing others to participate in planning and implementing the change. Given this high level of involvement, the strategy is likely to result in a longer-lasting and internalized change. As a change agent who shares power and adopts a normative-reeducative approach to change, you are likely to fit this profile.

> You believe that people have complex motivations. You feel that people behave as they do as a result of sociocultural norms and commitments to these norms. You also recognize that changes in these orientations involve changes in attitudes, values, skills, and significant relationships, not just changes in knowledge, information, or intellectual rationales for action and practice. Thus, when seeking to change others, you are sensitive to the supporting or inhibiting effects of group pressures and norms. In working with people, you try to find out their side of things and to identify their feelings and expectations.[14]

Resistance to Change

In organizations, **resistance to change** is any attitude or behavior that indicates unwillingness to make or support a desired change. Change agents often view any such resistance as something that must be "overcome" in order for change to be successful. This is not always the case, however. It is helpful to view resistance to change as feedback that the change agent can use to facilitate gaining change objectives.[15] The essence of this constructive approach to resistance is to recognize that when people resist change, they are defending something important that appears to be threatened by the change attempt.

Why People Resist Change

People have many reasons to resist change—fear of the unknown, insecurity, lack of a felt need to change, threat to vested interests, contrasting interpretations, and lack of resources, among other possibilities. A work team's members, for example, may resist the introduction of advanced workstation computers because they have never used the operating system and are apprehensive. They may wonder whether the new computers will eventually be used as justification for "getting rid" of some of them, or they may believe that they have been doing their jobs just fine and do not need the new computers to improve things. These and other viewpoints often create resistance to even the best and most well-intended planned changes. See The Effective Manager 16.2 for a reminder on the common reasons why people tend to resist change.

Resistance to the Change Itself Sometimes a change agent experiences resistance to the change itself. People may reject a change because they believe it is not worth their time, effort, or attention. To minimize

Lonnie Johnson

Lonnie Johnson, former NASA engineer, holds the patent for the Super Soaker water gun along with Larami Limited. After discovering that a special pump he developed was perfect for squirt guns, Johnson built a prototype and eventually took it to Larami. The rest is histoy, with more than 250 million sold to date.

■ **Resistance to change** is an attitude or behavior that shows unwillingness to make or support a change.

THE EFFECTIVE MANAGER 16.2

Eight Reasons for Resisting Change

1. Fear of the unknown
2. Lack of good information
3. Fear of loss of security
4. No reasons to change
5. Fear of loss of power
6. Lack of resources
7. Bad timing
8. Habit

resistance in such cases, the change agent should make sure that everyone who may be affected by a change knows specifically how it satisfies the following criteria:[16]

- *Benefit*—The change should have a clear relative advantage for the people being asked to change; it should be perceived as "a better way."
- *Compatibility*—The change should be as compatible as possible with the existing values and experiences of the people being asked to change.
- *Complexity*—The change should be no more complex than necessary; it must be as easy as possible for people to understand and use.
- *Triability*—The change should be something that people can try on a step-by-step basis and make adjustments as things progress.

Resistance to the Change Strategy   Change agents must also be prepared to deal with resistance to the change strategy. Someone who attempts to bring about change via force–coercion, for example, may create resistance among individuals who resent management by "command" or the use of threatened punishment. People may resist a rational persuasion strategy in which the data are suspect or the expertise of advocates is not clear. They may resist a shared-power strategy that appears manipulative and insincere.

Resistance to the Change Agent   Resistance to the change agent is directed at the person implementing the change and often involves personality and other differences. Change agents who are isolated and aloof from other persons in the change situation, who appear self-serving, or who have a high emotional involvement in the changes are especially prone to such problems. Research also indicates that change agents who differ from other persons in the change situation on such dimensions as age, education, and socioeconomic factors may encounter greater resistance to change.[17]

How to Deal with Resistance

An informed change agent has many options available for dealing positively with resistance to change, in any of its forms.[18] The first approach is through *education and communication*. The objective is to educate people about a change before it is implemented and to help them understand the logic of the change. Education and communication seem to work best when resistance is based on inaccurate or incomplete information. A second way is the use of *participation and involvement*. With the goal of allowing others to help design and implement the changes, this approach asks people to contribute ideas and advice or to work on task forces or committees that may be leading the change. This is especially useful when the change agent does not have all the information needed to successfully handle a problem situation.

Facilitation and support help to deal with resistance by providing help—both emotional and material—for people experiencing the hardships of change. A manager using this approach actively listens to problems and complaints, provides training in the new ways, and helps others to overcome performance pressures. Facilitation and support are highly recommended when people are frustrated by work constraints and difficulties encountered in the change process. A *negotiation and agreement* approach offers incentives to actual or potential change resistors.

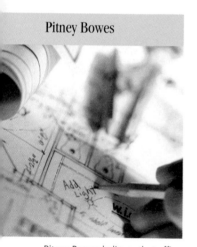

Pitney Bowes

Pitney Bowes believes that office space design facilitates innovation. A company executive once called the park-like setting of one division an "idea factory" with the goal of creativity with "no straight lines" and "no linear thinking."

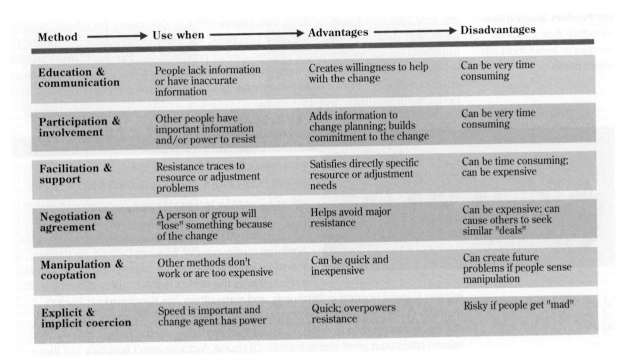

Method ⟶	Use when ⟶	Advantages ⟶	Disadvantages
Education & communication	People lack information or have inaccurate information	Creates willingness to help with the change	Can be very time consuming
Participation & involvement	Other people have important information and/or power to resist	Adds information to change planning; builds commitment to the change	Can be very time consuming
Facilitation & support	Resistance traces to resource or adjustment problems	Satisfies directly specific resource or adjustment needs	Can be time consuming; can be expensive
Negotiation & agreement	A person or group will "lose" something because of the change	Helps avoid major resistance	Can be expensive; can cause others to seek similar "deals"
Manipulation & cooptation	Other methods don't work or are too expensive	Can be quick and inexpensive	Can create future problems if people sense manipulation
Explicit & implicit coercion	Speed is important and change agent has power	Quick; overpowers resistance	Risky if people get "mad"

Figure 16.3   Methods for dealing with resistance to change.

Trade-offs are arranged to provide special benefits in exchange for assurances that the change will not be blocked. It is most useful when dealing with a person or group that will lose something of value as a result of the planned change.

Manipulation and cooptation make use of covert attempts to influence others, selectively providing information and consciously structuring events so that the desired change occurs. In some cases, leaders of the resistance may be "bought off" with special side deals to gain their support. Manipulation and cooptation are common when other tactics do not work or are too expensive. Finally, *explicit or implicit coercion* employs the force of authority to get people to accept change. Often, resistors are threatened with a variety of undesirable consequences if they do not go along as planned. This may be done, for example, in crisis situations when speed is of the essence.

Figure 16.3 summarizes additional insights into how and when each of these methods may be used to deal with resistance to change. Regardless of the chosen strategy, it is always best to remember that the presence of resistance typically suggests that something can be done to achieve a better fit among the change, the situation, and the people affected. A good change agent deals with resistance to change by listening to feedback and acting accordingly.

Innovation in Organizations

The best organizations don't stagnate; they innovate.[19] And they are able to innovate on an ongoing basis—they value and expect "innovation," and it becomes a normal part of everyday operations. **Innovation** is the process of creat-

Innovation is the process of creating new ideas and putting them into practice.

stressors can be traced directly to what people experience in the workplace, whereas others derive from nonwork and personal factors.

Work Stressors   Without doubt, work can be stressful, and job demands can disrupt one's work–life balance. A study of two-career couples, for example, found some 43 percent of men and 34 percent of women reporting that they worked more hours than they wanted to.[24] We know that **work stressors** can arise from many sources—from excessively high or low task demands, role conflicts or ambiguities, poor interpersonal relations, or career progress that is either too slow or too fast. A list of common stressors includes the following:

- *Task demands*—being asked to do too much or being asked to do too little
- *Role ambiguities*—not knowing what one is expected to do or how work performance is evaluated
- *Role conflicts*—feeling unable to satisfy multiple, possibly conflicting, performance expectations
- *Ethical dilemmas*—being asked to do things that violate the law or personal values
- *Interpersonal problems*—experiencing bad relationships or working with others with whom one does not get along
- *Career developments*—moving too fast and feeling stretched; moving too slowly and feeling stuck in a plateau.
- *Physical setting*—being bothered by noise, lack of privacy, pollution, or other unpleasant working conditions.

Life Stressors   A less obvious, though important, source of stress for people at work is the *spillover effect* that results when forces in their personal lives "spill over" to affect them at work. Such **life stressors** as family events (e.g., the birth of a new child), economic difficulties (e.g., the sudden loss of a big investment), and personal affairs (e.g., a separation or divorce) can all be extremely stressful. Since it is often difficult to completely separate work and nonwork lives, life stressors can affect the way people feel and behave on their jobs as well as in their personal lives.

Another set of stressors includes personal factors, such as individual needs, capabilities, and personality. Stress can reach a destructive state more quickly, for example, when experienced by highly emotional people or by those with low self-esteem. People who perceive a good fit between job requirements and personal skills seem to have a higher tolerance for stress than do those who feel less competent as a result of a person–job mismatch.[25] Basic aspects of personality are also important. The achievement orientation, impatience, and perfectionism of individuals with Type A personalities, for example, often create stress for them in work settings that others find relatively stress-free.[26]

Stress and Performance

Even though we tend to view and discuss stress from a negative perspective, it isn't always a negative influence on our lives. Indeed, there are two faces to stress—one positive and one negative.[27] **Constructive stress**, or *eustress*, acts in a positive way. It occurs at moderate stress levels by prompting increased work effort, stimulating creativity, and encouraging greater diligence. You may know such stress as the tension that causes you to study hard before exams, pay attention, and complete as-

Work stressors are the things that arise at work to create stress.

Possible work-related stressors

Life stressors are things that arise in our personal lives to create stress.

Constructive stress has a positive impact on both attitudes and performance.

signments on time in a difficult class. **Destructive stress**, or *distress*, is dysfunctional for both the individual and the organization. One form is the **job burnout** that shows itself as loss of interest in and satisfaction with a job due to stressful working conditions. When a person is "burned out," he or she feels exhausted, emotionally and physically, and thus unable to deal positively with work responsibilities and opportunities. Even more extreme reactions sometimes appear in news reports of persons who attack others and commit crimes in what is known as "desk rage" and "workplace rage." Too much stress can overload and break down a person's physical and mental systems, resulting in absenteeism, turnover, errors, accidents, dissatisfaction, reduced performance, unethical behavior, and even illness. Stanford scholar and consultant Jeffrey Pfeffer, for example, criticizes organizations that suffer from such excessive practices for creating toxic workplaces.[28] A toxic company implicitly says to its employees: "We're going to put you in an environment where you have to work in a style and at a pace that is not sustainable. We want you to come in here and burn yourself out. Then you can leave."[29]

> ▨ **Destructive stress** has a negative impact on both attitudes and performance.

> ▨ **Job burnout** shows itself as loss of interest in and satisfaction with a job due to stressful working conditions.

ETHICS AND SOCIAL RESPONSIBILITY

FOR ONE ENTREPRENEUR, DESPERATION LED TO INSPIRATION

Taking his family on a trip up California's coast was an eye-opener for Gary Hirschfield, president and CEO of an organic dairy farm—fast food was everywhere, but it didn't include the natural and organic foods he cherished. The stress of that trip led to inspiration and the creation of O'Naturals, a fast-food alternative. Stop in and you'll get fresh organic foods served without Styrofoam containers and with no option for accompanying plastic toys. Hirschfield says that America doesn't need another fast-food option, but it wants one. He believes that his firm and others like it will build on changing consumer tastes and help bring needed change to a traditional industry. In this case, social responsibility and solid business performance go hand-in-hand.

Question: What other examples can you come up with of businesses and industries that need similar innovation from customers who simply want more than traditional products?

Stress and Health

As is well known, stress can impact a person's health. It is a potential source of both anxiety and frustration, which can harm the body's physiological and psychological well-being over time.[30] Health problems associated with stress include heart attacks, strokes, hypertension, migraine headache, ulcers, substance abuse, overeating, depression, and muscle aches. As noted in The Effective Manager 16.3, managers and team leaders should be alert to signs of excessive stress in themselves and their co-workers.

THE EFFECTIVE MANAGER 16.3

Signs of Excessive Stress

- Change in eating habits
- Change in alcohol consumption or smoking
- Unhealthy feelings—aches and pains, upset stomach
- Restlessness, inability to concentrate, sleeping problems
- Tense, uptight, fidgety, nervous feelings
- Disoriented, overwhelmed, depressed, irritable feelings

Key symptoms to look for are changes from normal patterns—changes from regular attendance to absenteeism, from punctuality to tardiness, from diligent work to careless work, from a positive attitude to a negative attitude, from openness to change to resistance to change, or from cooperation to hostility.

Stress Management

Stress prevention is the best first-line strategy in the battle against stress. It involves taking action to keep stress from reaching destructive levels in the first place. Work and life stressors must be recognized before one can take action to prevent their occurrence or to minimize their adverse impacts. Persons with Type A personalities, for example, may exercise self-discipline; supervisors of Type A employees may try to model a lower-key, more relaxed approach to work. Family problems may be partially relieved by a change of work schedule; simply knowing that your supervisor understands your situation may also help to reduce the anxiety caused by pressing family concerns.

Once stress has reached a destructive point, special techniques of **stress management** can be implemented. This process begins with the recognition of stress symptoms and continues with actions to maintain a positive performance edge. The term wellness is increasingly used these days. **Personal wellness** involves the pursuit of one's job and career goals with the support of a personal health promotion program. The concept recognizes individual responsibility to enhance and maintain wellness through a disciplined approach to physical and mental health. It requires attention to such factors as smoking, weight, diet, alcohol use, and physical fitness. Organizations can benefit from commitments to support personal wellness. A University of Michigan study indicates that firms have saved up to $600 per year per employee by helping them to cut the risk of significant health problems.[31] Arnold Coleman, CEO of Healthy Outlook Worldwide, a health fitness consulting firm, states: "If I can save companies 5 to 20 percent a year in medical costs, they'll listen. In the end you have a well company and that's where the word 'wellness' comes from."[32]

On the organizational side, there is more and more emphasis today on **employee assistance programs** designed to provide help for employees who are experiencing personal problems and the stress associated with them. Common examples include special referrals on situations involving spousal abuse, substance abuse, financial difficulties, and legal problems. In such cases, the employer is trying to at least make sure that the employee with a personal problem has access to information and advice on how to get the guidance and perhaps even treatment needed to best deal with it. Organizations that build positive work environments and make significant investments in their employees are best positioned to realize the benefits of their full talents and work potential. As Pfeffer says: "All that separates you from your competitors are the skills, knowledge, commitment, and abilities of the people who work for you. Organizations that treat people right will get high returns."[33] That, in essence, is what the study of organizational behavior is all about.

Stress prevention involves minimizing the potential for stress to occur.

Stress management takes an active approach to dealing with stress that is influencing behavior.

Personal wellness involves maintaining physical and mental health to better deal with stress when it occurs.

Employee assistance programs provide help for employees who are experiencing stressful personal problems.

Chapter 16   Study Guide

Summary

What is organizational change?

- Planned change takes place because change agents—individuals and groups—make it happen to resolve performance problems or realize performance opportunities.
- Transformational change radically shifts fundamental aspects of organizations such as purpose and mission, beliefs and values, strategies, and structures.
- Organizational targets for planned change include purpose, strategy, culture, structure, people, tasks, and technology.
- The planned change process requires attention to the three phases—unfreezing, changing, and refreezing.

What change strategies are used in organizations?

- Change strategies are the means change agents use to bring about desired change in people and systems.
- Force–coercion change strategies use position power to bring about change through direct command or through rewards and punishments.
- Rational persuasion change strategies use logical arguments and appeals to knowledge and facts to convince people to change.
- Shared-power change strategies involve other persons in planning and implementing change.

How is resistance to change best managed?

- Resistance to change should be expected and not feared; it is a source of feedback that can be used to improve a change effort.
- People usually resist change because they are defending something of value; they may focus their resistance on the change itself, the change strategy, or the change agent as a person.
- Strategies for dealing with resistance to change include education and communication, participation and involvement, facilitation and support, negotiation and agreement, manipulation and cooptation, and explicit or implicit coercion.

How do organizations innovate?

- Innovation is the process of creating new ideas and then implementing them in practical applications.
- Product innovations result in improved goods or services; process innovations result in improved work methods and operations.
- Steps in the innovation process normally include idea generation, initial experimentation, feasibility determination, and final application.
- Common features of highly innovative organizations include supportive strategies, cultures, structures, staffing, and senior leadership.

How does stress affect people in change environments?

- Stress emerges when people experience tensions caused by extraordinary demands, constraints, or opportunities in their jobs.

- Work-related stressors arise from such things as excessive task demands, interpersonal problems, unclear roles, ethical dilemmas, and career disappointments.
- Nonwork stress can spill over to affect people at work; nonwork stressors may be traced to family situations, economic difficulties, and personal problems.
- Personal stressors derive from personality type, needs, and values; they can influence how stressful different situations become for different people.
- Stress can be managed by prevention—such as making adjustments in work and nonwork factors; it can also be dealt with through personal wellness—taking steps to maintain a healthy body and mind capable of better withstanding stressful situations.

Key Terms

Change agents (p. 361)
Changing (p. 364)
Constructive stress (p. 372)
Destructive stress (p. 373)
Employee assistance programs (p. 374)
Force–coercion strategy (p. 365)
Innovation (p. 369)
Job burnout (p. 373)
Life stressors (p. 372)
Performance gap (p. 362)

Personal wellness (p. 374)
Planned change (p. 362)
Process innovations (p. 370)
Product innovations (p. 370)
Rational persuasion strategy (p. 365)
Refreezing (p. 364)
Resistance to change (p. 367)

Shared-power strategy (p. 366)
Stress (p. 371)
Stress management (p. 374)
Stressors (p. 371)
Stress prevention (p. 374)
Transformational change (p. 360)
Unfreezing (p. 364)
Unplanned change (p. 362)
Work stressors (p. 372)

Self-Test 16

Multiple Choice

1. Performance gaps that create potential change situations include the existence of both problems to be resolved and _____. (a) costs to be avoided (b) people to be terminated (c) problems already resolved (d) opportunities to be explored

2. The presence or absence of a felt need for change is a critical issue in Lewin's _____ phase of planned change. (a) reflective (b) evaluative (c) unfreezing (d) changing

3. Which change strategy relies mainly on empirical data and expert power? (a) force–coercion (b) rational persuasion (c) shared power (d) authoritative command

4. Which change strategy is limited in effectiveness because it tends to create only temporary compliance? (a) force–coercion (b) rational persuasion (c) shared power (d) normative reeducation

5. A good change agent _____ resistance to change in order to best achieve change objectives. (a) eliminates (b) ignores (c) listens to (d) retreats from

6. According to the criterion of _____, a good change is clearly perceived as a better way of doing things. (a) benefit (b) triability (c) complexity (d) compatibility

7. Providing training to those being required to use a new computer technology is an example of managing resistance to change by _____. (a) participation and involvement (b) facilitation and support (c) negotiation and agreement (d) education and communication

8. After idea creation has occurred in the innovation process, the next step is _____. (a) feasibility determination (b) invention (c) initial experimentation (d) final application

9. In a highly innovative organization one would expect to find _____. (a) clear

punishments for failure (b) emphasis on centralization (c) top management support for initiative and creativity (d) intolerance for new ways of doing things

10. Task demands and ethical dilemmas are examples of _____ stressors, while a Type A personality is a _____ stressor. (a) work-related; personal (b) work-related; nonwork (c) nonpersonal; personal (d) real; imagined

11. Stress that comes from not knowing or understanding what you are expected to do is caused by the stressor of _____. (a) role conflict (b) task demands (c) interpersonal problems (d) role ambiguity

12. A typical example of a life stressor is _____. (a) fast-moving career (b) lack of private office space (c) problems in a marriage or relationship (d) being asked to work long hours

13. Things like "desk rage" or "workplace rage" are possible indicators of _____ caused by excessive stress. (a) ethical dilemmas (b) job burnout (c) Type A personality (d) Type B personality

14. The notion of _____ describes how stress experienced at work can influence one's non-work life. (a) role ambiguity (b) stress prevention (c) spill-over effect (d) toxic workplace

15. Which is an example of stress management by the personal wellness strategy? (a) role negotiation (b) empowerment (c) regular physical exercise (d) flexible hours

Short Response

16. What should a manager do when forces for unplanned change appear?

17. What internal and external forces push for change in organizations?

18. What does the "boiled frog phenomenon" tell us about organizational change?

19. How might stress influence individual performance?

Applications Essay

20. When Jorge Maldanado became general manager of the local civic recreation center, he realized that many changes would be necessary to make the facility a true community resource. Having the benefit of a new bond issue, the center had the funds for new equipment and expanded programming. All he needed to do now was get the staff committed to new initiatives. Unfortunately, his first efforts to raise performance have been met with considerable resistance to change. A typical staff comment is, "Why do all these extras? Everything is fine as it is." How can Jorge use the strategies for dealing with resistance to change, as discussed in the chapter, to move the change process along?

These learning activities from *The OB Skills Workbook* are suggested for Chapter 16.

OB in Action

CASE	EXPERIENTIAL EXERCISES	SELF-ASSESSMENTS
■ 16. The New Vice President	■ 32. Role Analysis Negotiation	■ 19. Your Personality Type
	■ 38. Force-Field Analysis	■ 20. Time Management Profile

Plus—special learning experiences from *The Jossey-Bass/Pfeiffer Classroom Collection*

Chapter 17

Organizing for Performance

Chapter at a Glance

In Chapter 1 we said that organizations are collections of people working to-gether to achieve common goals. In this chapter we discuss the goals of or-ganizations and how firms can use the basic attributes of organizations to reach toward accomplishment.[1] As you read Chapter 17, *keep in mind these study questions*.

WHAT IS STRATEGY AND HOW IS IT LINKED TO DIFFERENT TYPES OF ORGANIZATIONAL GOALS?

WHAT ARE THE BASIC ATTRIBUTES OF ORGANIZATIONS?

HOW IS WORK ORGANIZED AND COORDINATED?

WHAT ARE BUREAUCRACIES AND WHAT ARE THE COMMON STRUCTURES?

REVIEW IN END-OF-CHAPTER STUDY GUIDE

If you can't be the biggest, how about being Fifth Third? Fifth Third Bankcorp may be a strange name, and it is not the largest commercial bank in the United States, but it has a record of 29 consecutive years of increasing profits.[2] It now has a loan and lease portfolio of almost $50 billion, with 21,000 employees and 5.5 million customers served in more than 900 branches. George A Schaefer Jr. is the president, CEO, and chief architect of this super-regional bank. George Schaefer has implemented the fundamentals of sound organization as the bank has grown so dramatically from its small Cincinnati base of operations to a dominant pres-ence in much of the Midwest and South. As Fifth Third acquired other banks, they were allowed to maintain considerable autonomy. Each of 16 affiliate banks has its own president and chief executive. Schaefer delegates extensively and is often reported to have said, "These people know their markets." Because Schaefer does not like bureaucracy and red tape, operations are divided into retail banking, commercial banking, investment advisory services, and electronic payment processing. By continually stressing the basics, George Schaefer expects to see a higher profit growth for the thirtieth consecutive year and beyond.

> ## "These people know their markets"

Strategy and Goals of Organizations

The notion that organizations have goals is very familiar to us simply because our world is one of organizations. Most of us are born, go to school, work, and retire in organizations. Without organizations and their limited, goal-directed behavior, modern societies would simply cease to function. We would need to revert to older forms of social organization based on royalty, clans, and tribes. Organizational goals are so pervasive we rarely give them more than passing notice. George A. Schaefer Jr. of Fifth Third Bankcorp knows the goals of his firm. He knows the type of social contribution it makes, whom it serves, and the myriad ways of improving its performance. He is aware that his organization's goals are multifaceted and conflict with one another. He is also aware that corporate goals are common to individuals within the firm only to the extent that an individual's interests can be partially served by the organization. And he understands that the pattern of goals selected and emphasized can help to motivate members and gain support from outsiders. He also understands that strategy and goals are closely linked. Specifically, the strategy of the firm starts with selecting some goals over others.

What Is Strategy?

Strategy is the process of positioning the organization in the competitive environment and implementing actions to compete successfully. It is a pattern in a stream of decisions.[3] Choosing the types of contributions the firm intends to make to the larger society, precisely whom it will serve, and exactly what it will provide to others are conventional ways in which firms begin to make the pattern of decisions and corresponding implementations that define its strategy. The strategy process is ongoing. It should involve individuals at all levels of the firm to ensure that there is a recognizable, consistent pattern—yielding a superior capability over rivals—up and down the firm and across all of its activities.

This recognizable pattern can be unique to a firm and involves many facets. In the following sections we will also show how choices concerning the goals of the firm and the way in which it organizes to accomplish them are an important part of the overall positioning of the organization. In this chapter we will emphasize a static view of structure in terms of both patterning and placement. In Chapter 18 we will stress the more dynamic aspects of both strategy and structure.

No firm can be all things to all people. By selecting goals, firms also define who they are and what they will try to become. The choice of goals involves the type of contribution the firm makes to the larger society and the types of outputs it seeks. Managers decide how to link conditions considered desirable for enhanced survival prospects with its societal and output desires. From these apparently elementary choices, executives can work with subordinates to develop ways of accomplishing the chosen targets. As the opening suggests, the goals of the firm should be consistent with the way in which it is organized, as is the case for Fifth Third Bankcorp.

> ■ **Strategy** is the process of positioning the organization in the competitive environment and implementing actions to compete successfully.

Organizations and Society

Organizations do not operate in a social vacuum but reflect the needs and desires of the societies in which they operate. **Societal goals** reflect an organization's intended contributions to the broader society.[4] Organizations normally serve a specific societal function or an enduring need of the society. Astute top-level managers build on the professed societal contribution of the organization by relating specific organizational tasks and activities to higher purposes. By contributing to the larger society, organizations gain legitimacy, a social right to operate, and more discretion for their nonsocietal goals and operating practices. By claiming to provide specific types of societal contributions, an organization can also make legitimate claims on resources, individuals, markets, and products. For instance, wouldn't you want more money to work for a tobacco firm than a health food store? Tobacco firms are also very heavily taxed and under increasing pressure for regulation simply because their societal contribution is highly questionable.

Often, the social contribution of the firm is a part of its mission statement. **Mission statements** are simply written statements of organizational purpose. Weaving a mission statement together with an emphasis on implementation to provide direction and motivation is an executive order of the first magnitude. A good mission statement says whom the firm will serve and how it will go about accomplishing its societal purpose.[5] A mission statement is often the first visible

> ■ **Societal goals** are goals reflecting the intended contributions of an organization to the broader society.

> ■ **Mission statements** are written statements of organizational purpose.

outcome in developing a strategy. It may be several paragraphs long or as simple as that of Stericycle's. Normally a sound mission statement, such as Sericycle's, incorporates both social responsibility and ethics.

ETHICS AND SOCIAL RESPONSIBILITY

ETHICS AND SOCIAL RESPONSIBILITY BEGIN WITH A MISSION STATEMENT

Founded in 1989, Stericycle is now the largest provider of regulated medical waste management services in the United States. It provides medical waste collection, transportation, treatment, and disposal to over a quarter of a million customers. Its mission statement is quite simple: To be the leading company dedicated to the environmentally responsible management of medical waste for the health care community. At Stericycle, executives have established a pattern among the firm's intended actions and service to the larger society.

Question: Would you also call this mission statement a strategic vision?

We would expect to see the mission statement of a political party linked to generating and allocating power for the betterment of citizens. Mission statements for universities often profess to both develop and disseminate knowledge. Since churches intend to instill values and protect the spiritual well-being of all, many do not have mission statements. Courts are expected to integrate the interests and activities of citizens. Finally, business firms are expected to provide economic sustenance and material well-being to society. Organizations that can more effectively translate the positive character of their societal contribution into a favorable image have an advantage over firms that neglect this sense of purpose.

Executives who link their firm to a desirable mission can lay claim to important motivational tools that are based on a shared sense of noble purpose. Some executives and consultants talk of a "strategic vision" that links highly desirable and socially appealing goals to the contributions a firm intends to make. In one study, some 99 percent of the polled executives believed they had a strategic vision and could effectively state this vision in only one sentence. The visions of these executives were generally positive, future oriented, and designed to communicate the pattern of contributions the firm intended to make.[6]

Output Goals of Organizations

Organizations need to refine their societal contributions in order to target their efforts toward a particular group.[7] In the United States, for example, it is generally expected that the primary beneficiary of business firms is the stockholder. Interestingly, in Japan, employees are much more important, and stockholders are considered as important as banks and other financial institutions. Although each organization may have a primary beneficiary, its mission statement may also recognize the interests of many other parties. Thus, business mission statements often include service to customers, the organization's obligations to employees, and its intention to support the community.

As managers consider how they will accomplish their firm's mission, many begin with a very clear statement of which business they are in.[8] This statement can form the basis for long-term planning and may help prevent huge organizations from diverting too many resources to peripheral areas. For some corporations, answering the question of which business they are in may yield a more detailed statement concerning their products and services. These product and service goals provide an important basis for judging the firm. **Output goals** define the type of business an organization is in and provide some substance to the more general aspects of mission statements. For instance, Fifth Third's output goals would center on retail banking, commercial banking, investment advisory services, and electronic payment processing. These are businesses Fifth Third has chosen.

Output goals are the goals that define the type of business an organization is in.

Systems Goals of Organizations

Fewer than 10 percent of the businesses founded in a typical year can be expected to survive to their twentieth birthday.[9] The survival rate for public organizations is not much better. Even in organizations for which survival is not an immediate problem, managers seek specific types of conditions within their firms that minimize the risk of demise and promote survival. These conditions are positively stated as systems goals.

Systems goals are concerned with the conditions within the organization that are expected to increase the organization's survival potential. The list of systems goals is almost endless, since each manager and researcher links today's conditions to tomorrow's existence in a different way. For many organizations, however, the list includes growth, productivity, stability, harmony, flexibility, prestige, and human resource maintenance. In some businesses, analysts consider market share and current profitability important systems goals. Other recent studies suggest that innovation and quality are also considered important.[10] In a very practical sense, systems goals represent short-term organizational characteristics that higher-level managers wish to promote. Systems goals must often be balanced against one another. For instance, a productivity and efficiency drive, if taken too far, may reduce the flexibility of an organization.

Systems goals are goals concerned with conditions within the organization that are expected to increase its survival potential.

Different parts of the organization are often asked to pursue different types of systems goals. For example, higher-level managers may expect to see their production operations strive for efficiency while pressing for innovation from their R&D lab and promoting stability in their financial affairs.

The relative importance of different systems goals can vary substantially across various types of organizations. Although we may expect the University of British Columbia or the University of New South Wales to emphasize prestige and innovation, few expect such businesses as Pepsi or Coke to subordinate growth and profitability to prestige.

Systems goals are important to firms because they provide a road map that helps them link together various units of their organization to assure survival. Well-defined systems goals are practical and easy to understand; they focus the manager's attention on what needs to be done. Accurately stated systems goals also offer managers flexibility in devising ways to meet important targets. They can be used to balance the demands, constraints, and opportunities facing the firm. In addition, they can form a basis for dividing the work of the firm—a basis for developing a formal structure.

HIGH TOUCH GETS EFFECTIVE HIGH TECH

It does not get any higher tech than biotechnology, and Amgen is the world largest biotechnology company. But being high tech does not mean subordinating the employees to the technology. Rather it means just the opposite. Effective high-tech managers often view the development and treatment of employees as an important system goal. As Kevin Scharer, Amgen's chairman and CEO says, "We have long been convinced that investing in our staff and nurturing a patient-focused values-based work environment is a key part of our ongoing success." To back this up, Amgen offers a stock option program, fitness centers, and opportunities for career development in addition to the more traditional health and retirement benefits offered across many firms. Oh yes, if you work at the corporate headquarters in Thousand Oaks, California, you have access to child care, car rental services, message services, and even a weekly farmers' market.

Question: What do you think Amgen expects in return for these additional benefits?

Basic Attributes of Organizations

Since the work of Alfred Chandler in the 1960s, OB scholars have known that successful organizations develop a structure consistent with the pattern of goals and the strategy established by senior management.[11] That is, decisions regarding what to accomplish must be matched with decisions on an appropriate way of organizing to reach these goals. The formal structure shows the planned configuration of positions, job duties, and the lines of authority among different parts of the enterprise. The configuration selected provides the organization with specific strengths to reach toward some goals more than others. Traditionally, the formal structure of the firm has also been called the division of labor. Some still use this terminology to isolate decisions concerning formal structure from choices regarding the division of markets and/or technology. We will deal with environmental and technology issues in the next chapter after discussing the structure as a foundation for managerial action. Here we emphasize that the formal structure outlines the jobs to be done, the person(s) (in terms of position) who are to perform specific activities, and the ways in which the total tasks of the organization are to be accomplished. In other words, the formal structure is the skeleton of the firm.

Hierarchy

In larger organizations, there is a clear separation of authority and duties by hierarchical rank. That is, firms are vertically specialized. This separation represents **vertical specialization**, a hierarchical division of labor that distributes formal authority and establishes where and how critical decisions are to be made. This division creates a hierarchy of authority—an arrangement of work positions in order of increasing authority.

■ **Vertical specialization** is a hierarchical division of labor that distributes formal authority.

In the United States, the distribution of formal authority is evident in the responsibilities typical of managers. Top managers or senior executives plan the overall strategy of the organization and plot its long-term future.[12] They also act as final judges for internal disputes and certify promotions, reorganizations, and the like.

Middle managers guide the daily operations of the organization, help formulate policy, and translate top-management decisions into more specific guidelines for action. Lower-level managers supervise the actions of subordinates to ensure implementation of the strategies authorized by top management and compliance with the related policies established by middle management. Managers in Japan often have different responsibilities than their counterparts in the typical U.S. firm. Japanese top managers do not develop and decide the overall strategy of the firm. Instead, they manage a process involving middle managers. The process involves extensive dialogue about actions the firm needs to take. Lower-level managers are also expected to act as advocates for the ideas and suggestions of their subordinates. The strategy of the firm emerges from dialogue and discussion, and implementation proceeds according to the ideas and suggestions of lower managers and nonmanagers.

In many European firms, the senior managers are highly trained in the core of their business. For example, it is not unusual for the head of a manufacturing firm to have a PhD in engineering. Thus, many European executives become more centrally involved in plotting the technical future of their firm. In contrast, few U.S. or Japanese executives have the necessary technical background to tackle this responsibility. Despite the differences in managerial responsibilities across Japan, Europe, and North America, all organizations have vertical specialization.

The Organization Chart   **Organization charts** are diagrams that depict the formal structures of organizations. A typical chart shows the various positions, the position holders, and the lines of authority that link them to one another. Figure 17.1 presents a partial organization chart for a large university. The total chart allows university employees to locate their positions in the structure and to

■■■ **Organization charts** are diagrams that depict the formal structures of organizations.

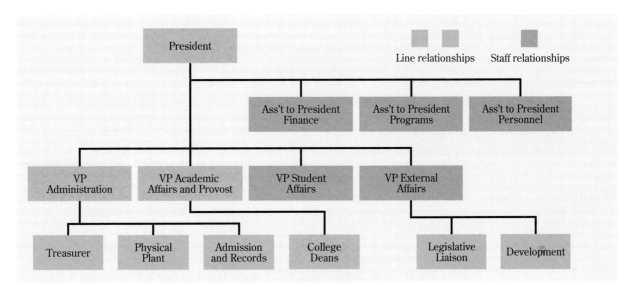

Figure 17.1   **A partial organization chart for a state university.**

identify the lines of authority linking them with others in the organization. For instance, in this figure, the treasurer reports to the vice president of administration, who, in turn, reports to the president of the university.

While an organization chart may clearly indicate who reports to whom, it is also important to recognize that it does not show how work is done, who exercises the most power over specific issues, or how the firm will respond to its environment. An organization chart is just a beginning way to start understanding how a firm organizes its work. In firms facing constant change, the formal chart may be quickly out of date. However, organization charts can be important to the extent that they accurately represent the "chain of command."

The chain of command is a listing of who reports to whom up and down the firm, showing how executives, managers, and supervisors are hierarchically connected. Traditional management theory suggests that each individual should have one boss and each unit one leader. Under these circumstances, there is a "unity of command." Unity of command is considered necessary to avoid confusion, to assign accountability to specific individuals, and to provide clear channels of communication up and down the organization. Under traditional management, with unity of command, the number of individuals a manager can directly supervise is obviously limited.

Span of control refers to the number of individuals reporting to a supervisor.

The number of individuals reporting to a supervisor is called the **span of control**. Narrower spans of control are expected when tasks are complex, when subordinates are inexperienced or poorly trained, or when tasks call for team effort. Unfortunately, narrow spans of control yield many organizational levels. The excessive number of levels is not only expensive, but it also makes the organization unresponsive to necessary change. Communications in such firms often become less effective because they are successively screened and modified so that subtle but important changes get ignored. Furthermore, with many levels, managers are removed from the action and become isolated.

New information technologies, discussed in the next chapter, now allow organizations to broaden the span of control, flatten their formal structures, and still maintain control of complex operations.[13] At Nucor, for instance, senior managers pioneered the development of "minimills" for making steel and developed what they call "lean" management. At the same time, management has expanded the span of control with extensive employee education and training backed by sophisticated information systems. The result: Nucor has four levels of management from the bottom to the top.

Line units are work-groups that conduct the major business of the organization.

Staff units are groups that assist the line units by performing specialized services to the organization.

Line and Staff Units   A very useful way to examine the vertical division of labor is to separate line and staff units. **Line units** and personnel conduct the major business of the organization. The production and marketing functions are two examples. In contrast, **staff units** and personnel assist the line units by providing specialized expertise and services, such as accounting and public relations. For example, the Vice President of Administration in a university (see Figure 17.1) heads a staff unit, as does the Vice President of Student Affairs. All academic departments are line units, since they constitute the basic production function of the university.

Two additional useful distinctions are often made in firms regarding line and staff. One distinction is the nature of the relationship of a unit in the chain of command. A staff department, such as the office of the VP for External Affairs in Figure 17.1, may be divided into subordinate units, such as Legislative Liaison and Development (again, see Figure 17.1). Although all units reporting to a higher-level staff unit are considered staff from an organizational perspective, some subordinate staff units are charged with conducting the major business of the higher unit—they have a line relationship up the chain of command. In Figure 17.1, both Legislative Liaison and Development are staff units with a line relationship to the unit immediately above them in the chain of command—the VP for External Affairs. Why the apparent confusion? It is a matter of history, with the notion of line and staff originally coming from the military, with its emphasis on command. In a military sense, the VP for External Affairs is the commander of this staff effort—the individual responsible for this activity and the one held accountable.

A second useful distinction to be made for both line and staff units concerns the amount and types of contacts each maintains with outsiders to the organization. Some units are mainly internal in orientation; others are more external in focus. In general, internal line units (e.g., production) focus on transforming raw materials and information into products and services, whereas external line units (e.g., marketing) focus on maintaining linkages to suppliers, distributors, and customers. Internal staff units (e.g., accounting) assist the line units in performing their function. Normally, they specialize in specific technical or financial areas. External staff units (e.g., public relations) also assist the line units, but the focus of their actions is on linking the firm to its environment and buffering internal operations. To recapitulate, the Legislative Liaison unit is external staff with a line relationship to the office of the VP for External Affairs.

Staff, particularly internal staff, contribute indirectly to corporate goals by using their specialized knowledge and talents. Traditionally, someone is needed to keep the books, hire and train the personnel, and conduct the research and development. Figure 17.2 shows how the placement of staff alters the appearance of the firm. Staff units can be assigned predominantly to senior-, middle-, or lower-level managers. When staff are assigned predominantly to senior management, the capability of senior management to develop alternatives and make decisions is expanded. When staff are at the top, senior executives can directly develop information and alternatives and check on the implementation of their decisions. Here, the degree of vertical specialization in the firm is comparatively lower because senior managers plan, decide, and control via their centralized staff. With new information technologies, fewer and fewer firms are placing most staff at the top. They are replacing internal staff with information systems and placing talented individuals farther down the hierarchy. For instance, executives at Owens-Illinois have shifted staff from top management to middle management. When staff are moved to the middle of the organization, middle managers now have the specialized help necessary to expand their role.

Many firms are also beginning to ask whether certain staff should be a permanent part of the organization at all. Some are outsourcing many of their staff functions. Manufacturing firms are spinning off much of their accounting, personnel, and public relations activities to small, specialized firms.[14] Outsourcing by large firms has been a boon for smaller corporations. Figure 17.2 illustrates the use of staff via "contracting out."

One of the foremost trends in management involves using information technology to streamline operations and reduce staff in order to lower costs and raise productivity.[15] One way to facilitate these actions is to provide line managers and employees with information and managerial techniques designed to expand on

Noble Drilling

Noble Drilling is one of the largest offshore drilling contractors in the world and a diversified service provider for the global oil and gas industry, with a fleet of some 50 offshore drilling units. The fleet is deployed in the North Sea, Brazil, West Africa, the Middle East, India, and Mexico. To give customers more flexibility, Noble Drilling has designed convertible platforms. The departmental structure to match its diverse range of drilling equipment and services is based on its products and services. With this structure, it can convert some of its fleet to drill in depths over 10,000 feet faster and cheaper than others can build new capability.

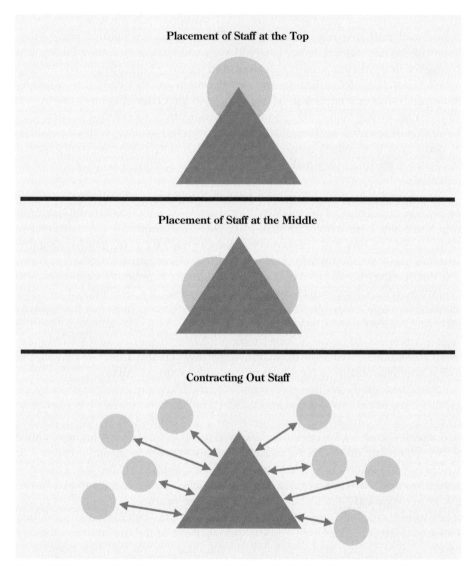

Figure 17.2   How the placement of staff alters the look of an organization.

their analytical and decision-making capabilities—that is, to replace internal staff. For instance, those studying financial management recognize the importance of financial planning models (in detecting problems); financial decision aids, such as capital budgeting models and discounted cash-flow analyses (for selecting among alternatives); and budgets (to monitor progress and ensure that managers stay within financial limits). With computer programs, each of these is now accessible to all levels of management and is no longer restricted to financial staff.[16]

Although a great variety of managerial techniques have been available to managers for decades, only with the widespread use of computers have the costs of these techniques been reduced. Most organizations use a combination of line and staff units, alliances with specialized providers, plus managerial techniques to specialize the division of labor vertically (e.g., to distribute formal authority). The most appropriate pattern of vertical specialization depends on the environment of the organization, its size, its technology, and its goals. For instance, as organizations grow, vertical specialization typically increases just to keep up with the volume of work. We will return to this theme in the next chapter and pay special attention to information technology and its role in changing organizations. For now, let us turn our attention to those issues relating to control of the organization simply because the issue of control should not be separated from the division of labor.

Control

When looking up and down the firm's hierarchy, we see that vertical specialization, with its hierarchical division of labor that distributes formal authority, is only half of the picture. Distributing formal authority calls for control. **Control** is the set of mechanisms used to keep action or outputs within predetermined limits. Control deals with setting standards, measuring results versus standards, and instituting corrective action. We should stress that effective control occurs before action actually begins. For instance, in setting standards, managers need to decide what will be measured and how accomplishment will be determined. In all too many instances, effective control is lost because managers have not considered the data they will need to accurately measure results. Although all organizations need controls, just a few controls may go a long way. Astute managers need to be aware of the danger of too much control in the organization.

Output Controls   Earlier in this chapter, we suggested that systems goals could be used as a road map to tie together the various units of the organization toward achieving a practical objective. Developing targets or standards, measuring results against these targets, and taking corrective action are all steps involved in developing output controls.[17] **Output controls** focus on desired targets and allow managers to use their own methods to reach defined targets. Most modern organizations use output controls as part of an overall method of managing by exception.

Output controls are popular because they promote flexibility and creativity as well as facilitate dialogue concerning corrective action. Reliance on outcome controls separates what is to be accomplished from how it is to be accomplished. Thus, the discussion of goals is separated from the dialogue concerning methods. This separation can facilitate the movement of power down the organization, as senior managers are reassured that individuals at all levels will be working toward the goals senior management believes are important, even as lower-level managers innovate and introduce new ways to accomplish these goals.

Process Controls   Few organizations run on outcome controls alone. Once a solution to a problem is found and successfully implemented, managers do not want the problem to recur, so they institute process controls. **Process controls** attempt to specify the manner in which tasks are accomplished. There are many types of process controls, but three groups have received considerable attention: (1) policies, procedures, and rules; (2) formalization and standardization; and (3) total quality management controls.

Policies, Procedures, and Rules   Most organizations implement a variety of policies, procedures, and rules to help specify how goals are to be accomplished.

Control is the set of mechanisms used to keep actions and outputs within predetermined limits.

Output controls are controls that focus on desired targets and allow managers to use their own methods for reaching defined targets.

Process controls are controls that attempt to specify the manner in which tasks are to be accomplished.

Research Insight
Controlling Alcohol Abuse at Work

In a fascinating study of alcohol abuse by every-day workers, Bacharach, Bamberger, and Sonnen-stuhl investigated the potential for reducing heavy drinking. They studied the role of various factors prior studies had suggested were related to problem drinking on the job. They did not support the notion that worker alienation was a major factor, as some have long suspected. They also found that direct managerial control efforts could boomerang and that job stress was not as major a factor, as one might believe from articles in the popular press. Instead, these researchers found that permissive norms toward drinking held by the firm's employees were the major factor associated with greater abuse. Thus, instead of reducing work stress or enforcing alcohol policies, managers should seek to change the general norms of all workers that suggest on-the-job drinking is OK.

Reference: S. B. Bacharach, P. A. Bamberger, & W. J. Sonnen-stuhl "Driven to Drink: Managerial Control, Work-Related Risk Factors, and Employee Problem Drinking" *Academy of Management Journal* 45(4) (2002):637–659.

Usually, we think of a *policy* as a guideline for action that outlines important objectives and broadly indicates how an activity is to be performed. A policy allows for individual discretion and minor adjustments without direct clearance by a higher level manager. *Procedures* indicate the best method for performing a task, show which aspects of a task are the most important, or outline how an individual is to be rewarded.

Many firms link *rules* and *procedures*. Rules are more specific, rigid, and impersonal than policies. They typically describe in detail how a task or a series of tasks is to be performed, or they indicate what cannot be done. They are designed to apply to all individuals, under specified conditions. For example, most car dealers have detailed instruction manuals for repairing a new car under warranty, and they must follow very strict procedures to obtain reimbursement from the manufacturer for warranty work.

Rules, procedures, and policies are often employed as substitutes for direct managerial supervision. Under the guidance of written rules and procedures, the organization can specifically direct the activities of many individuals. It can ensure virtually identical treatment even across distant work locations. For example, a McDonald's hamburger and fries taste much the same whether they are purchased in Hong Kong, Indianapolis, London, or Toronto simply because the ingredients and the cooking methods follow written rules and procedures.

▨ Formalization is the written documentation of work rules, policies, and procedures.

Formalization and Standardization   **Formalization** refers to the written documentation of rules, procedures, and policies to guide behavior and decision making. Beyond substituting for direct management supervision, formalization is often used to simplify jobs. Written instructions allow individuals with less training to perform comparatively sophisticated tasks. Written procedures may also be available to ensure that a proper sequence of tasks is executed, even if this sequence is performed only occasionally.

Most organizations have developed additional methods for dealing with recurring problems or situations. **Standardization** is the degree to which the range of allowable actions in a job or series of jobs is limited so that actions are performed in a uniform manner. It involves the creation of guidelines so that similar work activities are repeatedly performed in a similar fashion. Such standardized methods may come from years of experience in dealing with typical situations, or they may come from outside training. For instance, if you are late in paying your credit card, the bank will automatically send you a notification and start an internal process of monitoring your account.

> ■ **Standardization** is the degree to which the range of actions in a job or series of jobs is limited.

Total Quality Management   The process controls discussed so far—policies, procedures, rules, formalization, and standardization—represent the lessons of experience within an organization. That is, managers institute these process controls based on past experience, typically one at a time. Often there is no overall philosophy for using control to improve the overall operations of the company. Another way to institute process controls is to establish a total quality management process within the firm.

The late W. Edwards Deming is the modern-day founder of the total quality management movement.[18] When Deming's ideas were not generally accepted in the United States, he found an audience in Japan. Thus, to some managers, Deming's ideas appear in the form of the best Japanese business practices.

The heart of Deming's approach is to institute a process approach to continual improvement based on statistical analyses of the firm's operations. Around this core idea, Deming built a series of 14 points for managers to implement. As you look at these points, note the emphasis on both managers and employees working together using statistical controls to continually improve. Deming's 14 points are:

- Create a consistency of purpose in the company to
  a. innovate.
  b. put resources into research and education.
  c. put resources into maintaining equipment and new production aids.
- Learn a new philosophy of quality to improve every system.
- Require statistical evidence of process control and eliminate financial controls on production.
- Require statistical evidence of control in purchasing parts; this will mean dealing with fewer suppliers.
- Use statistical methods to isolate the sources of trouble.
- Institute modern on-the-job training.
- Improve supervision to develop inspired leaders.
- Drive out fear and instill learning.
- Break down barriers between departments.
- Eliminate numerical goals and slogans.
- Constantly revamp work methods.
- Institute massive training programs for employees in statistical methods.
- Retrain people in new skills.
- Create a structure that will push, every day, on the above 13 points.

Deming's 14 points

All levels of management are to be involved in the quality program. Managers are to improve supervision, train employees, retrain employees in new skills, and create a structure that pushes the quality program. Where the properties of the firm's outcomes are well defined, as in most manufacturing operations, Deming's system, with its emphasis on quality, appears to work well when it is implemented in conjunction with empowerment and participative management.

Centralization and Decentralization

▨ **Centralization** is the degree to which the authority to make decisions is restricted to higher levels of management.

▨ **Decentralization** is the degree to which the authority to make decisions is given to lower levels in an organization's hierarchy.

Different firms use very different mixes of vertical specialization, output controls, process controls, and managerial techniques to allocate the authority or discretion to act.[19] The farther up the hierarchy of authority the discretion to spend money, to hire people, and to make similar decisions is moved, the greater the degree of **centralization**. The more such decisions are delegated, or moved down the hierarchy of authority, the greater the degree of **decentralization**. Greater centralization is often adopted when the firm faces a single major threat to its survival. Thus, it is little wonder that armies tend to be centralized and that firms facing bankruptcy increase centralization.

Generally speaking, greater decentralization provides higher subordinate satisfaction and a quicker response to a diverse series of unrelated problems. Decentralization also assists in the on-the-job training of subordinates for higher-level positions. Decentralization is now a popular approach in many industries. For instance, Union Carbide is pushing responsibility down the chain of command, as are General Motors, Fifth Third Bank, and Hewlett-Packard. In each case, the senior managers hope to improve both performance quality and organizational responsiveness. Closely related to decentralization is the notion of participation. Many people want to be involved in making decisions that affect their work. Participation results when a manager delegates some authority for such decision making to subordinates in order to include them in the choice process. Employees may want a say both in what the unit objectives should be and in how they may be achieved.[20]

Firms such as Intel Corporation, Eli Lilly, Texas Instruments, Ford Motor Company, and Hoffman-LaRoche have also experimented by moving decisions down the chain of command and increasing participation. These firms found that just cutting the number of organizational levels was insufficient. They also needed to alter their controls toward quality, to stress constant improvement, and to change other basic features of the organization. As these firms changed their degree of vertical specialization, they also changed the division of work among units or the firm's horizontal specialization.

Organizing and Coordinating Work

▨ **Horizontal specialization** is a division of labor through the formation of work units or groups within an organization.

Vertical specialization and control are only half the picture. Managers must also divide the total task into separate duties and group similar people and resources together.[21] Organizing work is formally known as horizontal specialization. **Horizontal specialization** is a division of labor that establishes specific work units or groups within an organization. This aspect of the organization is also often discussed under the title of *departmentation*. There are a variety of pure forms of

Leaders on Leadership

THE IMPORTANCE OF BASICS

Jack Gherty is president and CEO of Land O'Lakes and believes strongly in making sure the basics are covered for this $6 billion cooperative. You may know of Land O'Lakes as the butter company. Actually, it is both a producer and consumer cooperative. As a producer cooperative, the owners/farmers have joined together to sell their dairy products such as butter and cheese under the Land O'Lakes brand. As a consumer cooperative, the members buy agricultural supplies (feed, seeds, crop nutrients, and crop protection products) through the cooperative. One of the first things Jack Gherty did as a new CEO was to clarify the mission. Now, the mission statement clearly shows the cooperative's societal contributions and outputs: "We are a market- and customer-driven cooperative committed to optimizing the value of our members' dairy, crop, and livestock production." The cooperative is organized into divisions for (1) dairy operations, (2) feed, (3) seed, and (4) crop nutrients and crop protection products. With its mission statement backed by its basic divisional structure, it is little wonder Jack can say, "The main thrust of what we are trying to do is stay focused on how we add values and service to customers."

---

departmentation. Whenever managers divide tasks and group similar types of skills and resources together, they must also be concerned with how each group's individual efforts will be integrated with others. Integration across the firm is the subject of coordination. As noted below, managers use a mix of personal and impersonal methods of coordination to tie the efforts of departments together.

Traditional Departmental Structures

Since the pattern of departmentation is so visible and important in a firm, managers often refer to their pattern of departmentation as the *departmental structure*. While most firms use a mix of various types of departments, it is important to take a look at the traditional types and what they do and do not provide the firm.

Functional Departments Grouping individuals by skill, knowledge, and action yields a pattern of **functional departmentation**. Recall that Figure 17.1 shows the partial organization chart for a large university in which each department has a technical specialty. Marketing, finance, production, and personnel are important functions in business. In many small firms, this functional pattern dominates. Even large firms use this pattern in technically demanding areas. Figure 17.3 summarizes the advantages of the functional pattern. With all these advantages, it is not surprising that the functional form is extremely popular. It is used in most organizations, particularly toward the bottom of the hierarchy. The

Functional departmentation is grouping individuals by skill, knowledge, and action yields.

Major Advantages and Disadvantages of Functional Specialization	
Advantages	**Disadvantages**
1. Yields very clear task assignments, consistent with an individual's training.	1. May reinforce the narrow training of individuals.
2. Individuals within a department can easily build on one another's knowledge, training, and experience.	2. May yield narrow, boring, and routine jobs.
3. Provides an excellent training ground for new managers.	3. Communication across technical area is complex and difficult.
4. It is easy to explain.	4. "Top-management overload" with too much attention to cross-functional problems.
5. Takes advantage of employee technical quality.	5. Individuals may look up the organizational hierarchy for direction and reinforcement rather than focus attention on products, services, or clients.

Figure 17.3   Major advantages and disadvantages of functional specialization.

extensive use of functional departments also has some disadvantages, which are summarized in Figure 17.3. Organizations that rely heavily on functional specialization may expect the following tendencies to emerge over time: an emphasis on quality from a technical standpoint, rigidity to change, and difficulty in coordinating the actions of different functional areas.

Divisional depart-mentation groups individuals and resources by products, territories, services, clients, or legal entities.

Divisional Departments   In **divisional departmentation**, individuals and resources are grouped by products, territories, services, clients, or legal entities.[22] Figure 17.4 shows a divisional pattern of an organization grouped around products, regions, and customers for three divisions of a conglomerate. This pattern is often used to meet diverse external threats and opportunities. As shown in Figure 17.4, the major advantages of the divisional pattern are its flexibility in meeting external demands, spotting external changes, integrating specialized individuals deep within the organization, and focusing on the delivery of specific products to specific customers. Among its disadvantages are duplication of effort by function, the tendency for divisional goals to be placed above corporate interests, and conflict among divisions. It is also not the structure most desired for training individuals in technical areas, and firms relying on this pattern may fall behind technically to competitors with a functional pattern.

Many larger, geographically dispersed organizations that sell to national and international markets may rely on departmentation by geography. The savings in time, effort, and travel can be substantial, and each territory can adjust to regional differences. Organizations that rely on a few major customers may organize their people and resources by client. Here, the idea is to focus attention on the needs of the individual customer.[23] To the extent that customer needs are unique, departmentation by customer can also reduce confusion and increase synergy. Organizations expanding internationally may also form divisions to meet the demands of complex host-country ownership requirements. For example, NEC, Sony, Nissan, and many other Japanese corporations have developed U.S. divisional subsidiaries to service their customers in the U.S. market. Some huge European-based corporations such as Philips and Nestlé have also adopted a divisional structure in their expansion to the United States. Similarly, most of the internationalized U.S.-based firms, such as IBM, GE, and DuPont, have incorporated the divisional structure as part of their internalization programs.

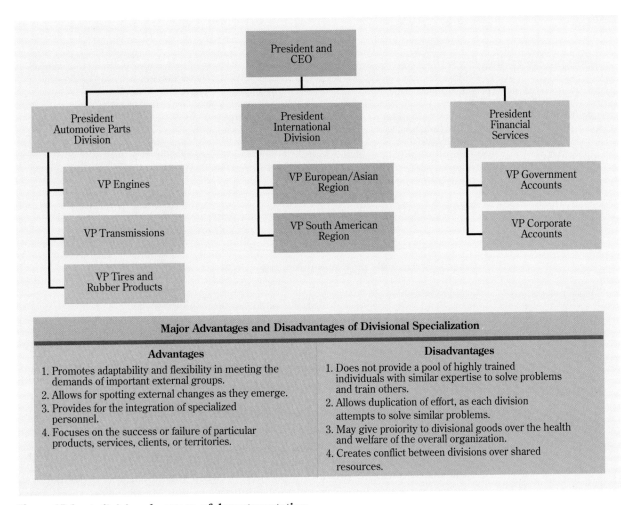

Figure 17.4 A divisional pattern of departmentation.

Matrix Structures Originally from the aerospace industry, a third unique form of departmentation was developed and is now becoming more popular; it is now called the matrix structure.[24] In aerospace efforts, projects are technically very complex, involving hundreds of subcontractors located throughout the world. Precise integration and control are needed across many sophisticated functional specialties and corporations. This is often more than a functional or divisional structure can provide, for many firms do not want to trade the responsiveness of the divisional form for the technical emphasis provided by the functional form. Thus, **matrix departmentation** uses both the functional and divisional forms simultaneously. Figure 17.5 shows the basic matrix arrangement for an aerospace program. Note the functional departments on one side and the project efforts on the other. Workers and supervisors in the middle of the matrix have two bosses—one functional and one project.

The major advantages and disadvantages of the matrix form of departmentation are also summarized in Figure 17.5. The key disadvantage of the matrix method is the loss of unity of command. Individuals can be unsure as to what their jobs are, whom they report to for specific activities, and how various man-

▓▓ **Matrix departmentation** is a combination of functional and divisional patterns wherein an individual is assigned to more than one type of unit.

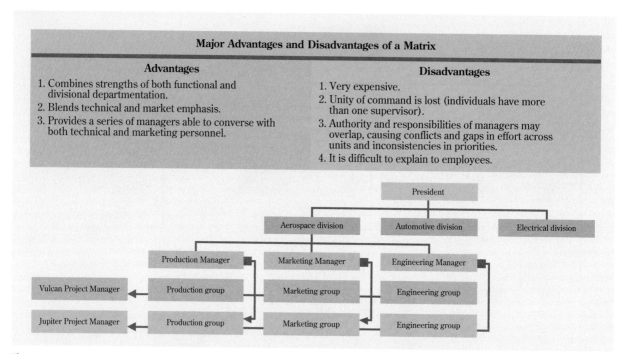

Figure 17.5   A matrix pattern of departmentation in an aerospace division.

agers are to administer the effort. It can also be a very expensive method because it relies on individual managers to coordinate efforts deep within the firm. In Figure 17.5, note that the number of managers in a matrix structure almost doubles compared to either a functional or a divisional structure. Despite these limitations, the matrix structure provides a balance between functional and divisional concerns. Many problems can be resolved at the working level, where the balance among technical, cost, customer, and organizational concerns can be dealt with.

The matrix structure is ideally suited for Pacific Northwest Labs (PNL). PNL is one of the Department of Energy's laboratories for researching new and improved ways to develop energy and clean up the mess from decades of producing nuclear material for bombs. Technical specialists are housed in functional departments while project managers draw talent from these groups to work on myriad new energy and cleanup projects. Some projects may last a few weeks and involve only a handful of technicians while other larger projects may last several years. As the large projects evolve, the project manager can shift the composition of the team to reflect the type of specialized human resources needed at any given stage in a project.

Many organizations also use elements of the matrix structure without officially using the term *matrix*. For example, special project teams, coordinating committees, and task forces can be the beginnings of a matrix. Yet these temporary structures can be used within a predominantly functional or divisional form and without upsetting the unity of command or hiring additional managers.

Which form of departmentation should be used? As the matrix concept suggests, it is possible to departmentalize by two different methods at the same time. Actually, organizations often use a mixture of departmentation forms. It is often desirable to divide the effort (group people and resources) by two methods at the same time in order to balance the advantages and disadvantages of each. In the next chapter we will discuss several mixed forms. These mixed forms help firms use their division of labor to capitalize on environmental opportunities, capture the benefits of larger size, and realize the potential of new technologies in pursuit of its strategy.

CULTURES AND THE GLOBAL WORKFORCE

LINKING SPECIALISTS AROUND THE GLOBE

NBBJ is the world's third-largest architectural practice. To date it has earned more than 300 national and international design awards. NBBJ is a unique multispecialty firm dedicated to providing the highest quality of design and superior client service. NBBJ projects range from the design of corporate offices and buildings to sports and entertainment complexes, to R&D complexes, to senior living systems and even the halls of academia. To meet these diverse challenges, NBBJ uses a matrix structure to draw specialists from its global offices to complete major design projects. In the United States, its specialists may be found in Columbus, Los Angeles, Raleigh, San Francisco, and New York, in addition to staff in its Seattle headquarters. While numerous architectural firms have multiple U.S. offices, NBBJ can also draw on specialized design expertise from their staff in Oslo, Taipei, Tokyo, and London. They use senior contact staff in a local design studio to identify and focus on the specific needs of a client. They matrix across the global locations to supplement a local studio's staff with individuals whose unique skills are needed for a project.

Question: If you were just assigned to a new project at NBBJ, what other information about the structure of the project would you like to know?

Coordination

Whatever is divided up horizontally into departments must also be integrated.[25] **Coordination** is the set of mechanisms that an organization uses to link the actions of their units into a consistent pattern. This linkage includes mechanisms to link managers and staff units, operating units with each other, and divisions with each other. Coordination is needed at all levels of management, not just across a few scattered units. Much of the coordination within a unit is handled by its manager. Smaller organizations may rely on their management hierarchy to provide the necessary consistency and integration. As the organization grows, however, managers become overloaded. The organization then needs to develop more efficient and effective ways of linking work units to one another.

Coordination is the set of mechanisms used in an organization to link the actions of its subunits into a consistent pattern.

Personal Methods of Coordination   Personal methods of coordination produce synergy by promoting dialogue, discussion, innovation, creativity, and learning, both within and across organizational units. Personal methods allow the organization to address the particular needs of distinct units and individuals simultaneously. There is a wide variety of personal methods of coordination.[26] Perhaps the most popular is direct contact between and among organizational members. As new information technologies have moved into practice, the potential for developing and maintaining effective contact networks has expanded. For example, many executives use cell phones, e-mail, and other computer-based links to supplement direct personal communication. Direct personal contact is

THE EFFECTIVE MANAGER 17.1

Adjusting Coordination Efforts

The astute manager should recognize that some individuals and/or units:

1. Have their own views of how best to move toward organizational goals
2. Emphasize immediate problems and quick solutions; others stress underlying problems and longer-term solutions
3. Have their own unique vocabulary and standard way of communicating
4. Have pronounced preferences for formality or informality

also associated with the ever-present "grapevine." Although the grapevine is notoriously inaccurate in its role as the corporate rumor mill, it is often both accurate enough and quick enough that managers cannot ignore it. Instead, managers need to work with and supplement the rumor mill with accurate information.

Managers are also often assigned to numerous committees to improve coordination across departments. Even though committees are generally expensive and have a very poor reputation, they can become an effective personal mechanism for mutual adjustment across unit heads. Committees can be effective in communicating complex qualitative information and in helping managers whose units must work together to adjust schedules, workloads, and work assignments to increase productivity. As more organizations develop flatter structures with greater delegation, they are finding that task forces can be quite useful. Whereas committees tend to be long lasting, task forces are typically formed with a more limited agenda. Individuals from different parts of the organization are assembled into a task force to identify and solve problems that cut across different departments.

No magic is involved in selecting the appropriate mix of personal coordination methods and tailoring them to the individual skills, abilities, and experience of subordinates. Managers need to know the individuals involved, their preferences, and the accepted approaches in different organizational units. Different personal methods can be tailored to match different individuals (see The Effective Manager 17.1). Personal methods are only one important part of coordination. The manager may also establish a series of impersonal mechanisms.

Impersonal Methods of Coordination   Impersonal methods of coordination produce synergy by stressing consistency and standardization so that individual pieces fit together. Impersonal coordination methods are often refinements and extensions of process controls with an emphasis on formalization and standardization. Most larger organizations have written policies and procedures, such as schedules, budgets, and plans that are designed to mesh the operations of several units into a whole by providing predictability and consistency.

Historically, firms used specialized departments to coordinate across units. However, this method is very expensive and often results in considerable rigidity. The most highly developed form of impersonal coordination comes with the adoption of a matrix structure. As noted earlier, this form of departmentation is expressly designed to coordinate the efforts of diverse functional units. Many firms are using cross-functional task forces instead of maintaining a specialized department or implementing a matrix. These task forces are typically formed to solve a particular coordinate problem and then are disbanded upon successful implementation. The task force may call for new procedures, reassignment of tasks, and/or instituting more personal methods to make sure departmental efforts mesh together.

The final example of impersonal coordination mechanisms is undergoing radical change in many modern organizations. Originally, management information systems were developed and designed so that senior managers could coordinate and control the operations of diverse subordinate units. These systems were intended to be computerized substitutes for schedules, budgets, and the like. In some firms, the management information system still operates as a combined process control and impersonal coordination mechanism. In the hands of astute managers, the management information system becomes an electronic network, linking individuals throughout the organization. Using decentralized communication systems, supplemented with the phone, fax machine, and e-mail, once centralized systems have evolved into a supplement to personal coordination.

In the United States there is an aversion to controls because the culture prizes individuality, democracy, and individual free will. Managers often institute controls under the title of coordination. Since some of the techniques used can be deployed for both, many managers suggest that all efforts at control and coordination are for coordination. It is extremely important to separate these two simply because the reactions to controls and coordination are quite different. The underlying logic of control involves setting targets, measuring performance, and taking corrective action to meet goals normally assigned by higher management. Thus, many employees see an increase in controls as a threat based on a presumption that they have been doing something wrong. The logic of coordination is to get unit actions and interactions meshed together into a unified whole. While control involves the vertical exercise of formal authority—involving targets, measures, and corrective action—coordination stresses cooperative problem solving. Most all experienced employees recognize the difference between controls and coordination regardless of what the boss calls it. Increasing controls rarely solves problems of coordination, and emphasizing coordination to solve control issues rarely works.

Bureaucracy and Beyond

In the developed world, most firms are bureaucracies. In OB this term has a very special meaning, beyond its negative connotation (see The Effective Manager 17.2). The famous German sociologist Max Weber suggested that organizations would thrive if they became bureaucracies by emphasizing legal authority, logic, and order.[27] **Bureaucracies** rely on a division of labor, hierarchical control, promotion by merit with career opportunities for employees, and administration by rule.

Weber argued that the rational and logical idea of bureaucracy was superior to building the firm on the basis of charisma or cultural tradition. The "charismatic" ideal-type organization was overreliant on the talents of one individual and would likely fail when the leader left. Too much reliance on cultural traditions blocked innovation, stifled efficiency, and was often unfair. Since the bureaucracy prizes efficiency, order, and logic, Weber hoped that it could also be fair to employees and provide more freedom for individual expression than is allowed when tradition dominates or a dictator rules. Although it is far from perfect, Weber predicted that the bureaucracy, or some variation

Bureaucracy is an ideal form of organization, the characteristics of which were defined by the German sociologist Max Weber.

> **THE EFFECTIVE MANAGER 17.2**
>
> ## The Natural Dysfunctional Tendencies of a Bureaucracy
>
> 1. Overspecialization and failure to mitigate the resulting conflicts of interest
> 2. Overuse of the formal hierarchy and emphasis on adherence to official channels rather than problem solving
> 3. Reification of senior managers as superior performers on all tasks and as rulers of a political system rather than as individuals who should help others reach goals
> 4. Overemphasis on insignificant conformity that limits individual growth
> 5. Treatment of rules as ends in and of themselves rather than as poor mechanisms for control and coordination

of this ideal form, would dominate modern society. And it has. While charismatic leadership and cultural traditions are still important today, it is the rational, legal, and efficiency aspects of the firm that characterize modern corporations.

The notion of a bureaucracy has evolved over time. Figure 17.6 illustrates three popular basic types of bureaucracies: the mechanistic, the organic, and the divisionalized approaches. And it shows how some huge corporations are collections of very different firms called conglomerates. Each is a different mix of the basic elements discussed in this chapter, and each mix yields firms with a slightly different blend of capabilities and natural tendencies. That is, each type of bureaucracy allows the firm to pursue a different type of strategy more effectively. This follows from our discussion that structure should follow strategy.

Mechanistic Structures

Mechanistic type or machine bureaucracy emphasizes vertical specialization and control with impersonal coordination and a heavy reliance on standardization, formalization, rules, policies, and procedures.

The **mechanistic type** emphasizes vertical specialization and control.[28] Organizations of this type stress rules, policies, and procedures; specify techniques for decision making; and emphasize developing well-documented control systems backed by a strong middle management and supported by a centralized staff. There is often extensive use of the functional pattern of departmentation throughout the firm. Henry Mintzberg uses the term *machine bureaucracy* to describe an organization that is entirely structured in this manner.[29]

The mechanistic design results in a management emphasis on routine for efficiency. Firms often used this design in pursuing a strategy of becoming a low-cost leader. Until the implementation of new information systems, most large-scale firms in basic industries were machine bureaucracies. Included in this long list were all the auto firms, banks, insurance companies, steel mills, large retail establishments, and government offices. Efficiency was achieved through extensive vertical and horizontal specialization tied together with elaborate controls and impersonal coordination mechanisms.

There are, however, limits to the benefits of specialization backed by rigid controls. Employees do not like rigid designs, and so motivation becomes a problem. Unions further solidify narrow job descriptions by demanding fixed work rules and regulations to protect employees from the extensive vertical controls. Key employees may leave. In short, using a machine bureaucracy can hinder an organization's capacity to adjust to subtle external changes or new technologies. You are already familiar with this tendency toward stagnation—your high school was probably a machine bureaucracy with the assistant principal as the chief enforcement officer.

Organic Structures

Organic type or professional bureaucracy emphasizes horizontal specialization, extensive use of personal coordination, and loose rules, policies, and procedures.

The **organic type** is much less vertically oriented than its mechanistic counterpart; it emphasizes horizontal specialization. Procedures are minimal, and those that do exist are not as formalized. The organization relies on the judgments of experts and personal means of coordination. When controls are used, they tend to back up professional socialization, training, and individual reinforcement. Staff units tend to be placed toward the middle of the organization. Because this is a popular design in professional firms, Mintzberg calls it a professional bureaucracy.[30]

Your university is probably a professional bureaucracy that looks like a broad, flat pyramid with a large bulge in the center for the professional staff. Power in this

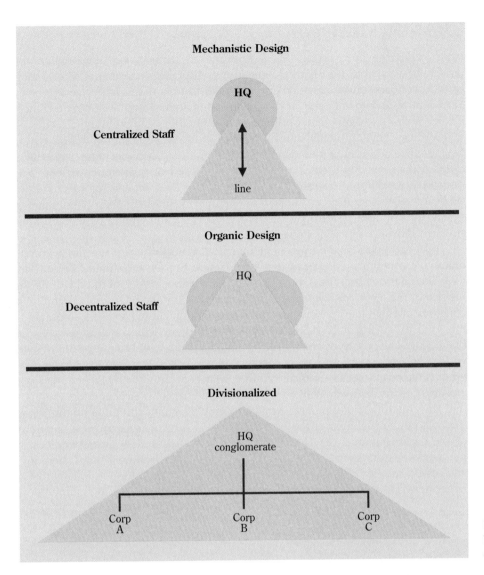

Mechanistic Design

HQ

Centralized Staff

line

Organic Design

HQ

Decentralized Staff

Divisionalized

HQ
conglomerate

Corp
A

Corp
B

Corp
C

Figure 17.6 Different basic overall bureaucratic patterns.

ideal type rests with knowledge. Furthermore, there was often an elaborate staff to "help" the line managers. Often the staff had very little formal power, other than to block action. Control is enhanced by the standardization of professional skills and the adoption of professional routines, standards, and procedures. Other examples of organic types include most hospitals and social service agencies.

Although not as efficient as the machine bureaucracy, the professional bureaucracy is better for problem solving and for serving individual customer needs. Since lateral relations and coordination are emphasized, centralized direction by senior management is less intense. Thus, this type is good at detecting external changes and adjusting to new technologies, but at the sacrifice of responding to central management direction.[31] For instance, many university deans and presidents talk about "herding cats" when it comes to managing faculty and students. Firms using this pattern found it easier to pursue product quality, quick response to customers, and innovation as strategies.

Hybrid Structures

Many very large firms found that neither the mechanistic nor the organic approach was suitable for all their operations. Adopting a machine bureaucracy would overload senior management and yield too many levels of management. Yet adopting an organic type would mean losing control and becoming too inefficient. Senior managers may opt for one of a number of hybrid types.

We have already briefly introduced two of the more common hybrid types. One is an extension of the divisional pattern of departmentation, sometimes called a divisional firm. Here, the firm is composed of quasi-independent divisions so that different divisions can be more or less organic or mechanistic. While the divisions may be treated as separate businesses, they often share a similar mission and systems goals.[32] When adopting this hybrid type, each division can pursue a different strategy.

Conglomerates are firms that own several different unrelated businesses.

A second hybrid is the true conglomerate. A **conglomerate** is a single corporation that contains a number of unrelated businesses. On the surface, these firms look like divisionalized firms, but when the various businesses of the divisions are unrelated, the term *conglomerate* is applied.[33] For instance, General Electric is a conglomerate that has divisions in quite unrelated businesses and industries, ranging from producing light bulbs, to designing and servicing nuclear reactors, to building jet engines, to operating the National Broadcasting Company. Many state and federal entities are also, by necessity, conglomerates. For instance, a state governor is the chief executive officer of those units concerned with higher education, welfare, prisons, highway construction and maintenance, police, and the like.

The conglomerate type also simultaneously illustrates three important points that will be the highlight of the next chapter. (1) All structures are combinations of the basic elements. (2) There is no one best structure—it all depends on a number of factors such as the size of the firm, its environment, its technology, and, of course, its strategy. (3) The firm does not stand alone but is part of a larger network of firms that competes against other networks.

Chapter 17   Study Guide

Summary

What is strategy and how is it linked to different types of organizational goals?

- Strategy and goals are closely intertwined.
- Strategy is a process.
- Strategy is positioning the organization in the competitive environment.
- Strategy is a pattern in a stream of actions.
- Organizations make specific contributions to society and gain legitimacy from these contributions.

- A societal contribution focused on a primary beneficiary may be represented in the firm's mission statement.
- As managers consider how they will accomplish their firm's mission, many begin with a very clear statement of which business they are in.
- Firms often specify output goals by detailing the types of specific products and services they offer.
- Corporations have systems goals to show the conditions managers believe will yield survival and success.
- Growth, productivity, stability, harmony, flexibility, prestige, and human resource maintenance are examples of systems goals.

What are the basic attributes of organizations?

- The formal structure defines the intended configuration of positions, job duties, and lines of authority among different parts of the enterprise.
- The formal structure is also known as the firm's division of labor.
- Vertical specialization is used to allocate formal authority within the organization and may be seen on an organization chart.
- Vertical specialization is the hierarchical division of labor that specifies where formal authority is located.
- Typically, a chain of command exists to link lower-level workers with senior managers.
- The distinction between line and staff units also indicates how authority is distributed, with line units conducting the major business of the firm and staff providing support.
- Managerial techniques, such as decision support and expert computer systems, are used to expand the analytical reach and decision-making capacity of managers to minimize staff.
- Control is the set of mechanisms the organization uses to keep action or outputs within predetermined levels.
- Output controls focus on desired targets and allow managers to use their own methods for reaching these targets.
- Process controls specify the manner in which tasks are to be accomplished through (1) policies, rules, and procedures; (2) formalization and standardization; and (3) total quality management processes.
- Firms are learning that decentralization often provides substantial benefits.
- With centralization, discretion to decide is moved farther up the hierarchy.
- With decentralization, discretion to decide is moved farther down the hierarchy.

How is work organized and coordinated?

- Horizontal specialization is the division of labor that results in various work units and departments in the organization.
- Three main types or patterns of departmentation are observed: functional, divisional, and matrix. Each pattern has a mix of advantages and disadvantages.
- Organizations may successfully use any type, or a mixture, as long as the strengths of the structure match the needs of the organization.
- Coordination is the set of mechanisms an organization uses to link the actions of separate units into a consistent pattern.
- Personal methods of coordination produce synergy by promoting dialogue, discussion, innovation, creativity, and learning.

- Impersonal methods of control produce synergy by stressing consistency and standardization so that individual pieces fit together.

What are bureaucracies and what are the common structures?

- The bureaucracy is an ideal form based on legal authority, logic, and order that provides superior efficiency and effectiveness.
- The mechanistic type emphasizes vertical specialization and control.
- The organic type emphasizes horizontal specialization and coordination.
- Hybrid types are combinations of mechanistic and organic elements and include the divisionalized firm and the conglomorate.

Key Terms

Bureaucracy (p. 399)
Centralization (p. 392)
Conglomerates (p. 402)
Control (p. 389)
Coordination (p. 397)
Decentralization (p. 392)
Divisional departmentation (p. 394)
Formalization (p. 390)
Functional departmentation (p. 393)

Horizontal specialization (p. 392)
Line units (p. 386)
Matrix departmentation (p. 395)
Mechanistic type (p. 400)
Mission statements (p. 381)
Organic type (p. 400)
Organization charts (p. 385)
Output controls (p. 389)

Output goals (p. 383)
Process controls (p. 389)
Societal goals (p. 381)
Span of control (p. 386)
Staff units (p. 386)
Standardization (p. 391)
Strategy (p. 381)
Systems goals (p. 383)
Vertical specialization (p. 384)

Self-Test 17

Multiple Choice

1. The strategy of an organization is _____. (a) a process (b) positioning the organization in the competitive environment (c) consistent implemention actions (d) a pattern in a stream of actions

2. The formal structures of organizations may be shown in a(n) _____. (a) environmental diagram (b) organization chart (c) horizontal diagram (d) matrix depiction

3. A major distinction between line and staff units concerns _____. (a) the amount of resources each is allowed to utilize (b) linkage of their jobs to the goals of the firm (c) the amount of education or training they possess (d) their use of computer information systems

4. The division of labor by grouping people and material resources deals with _____. (a) specialization (b) coordination (c) divisionalization (d) vertical specialization

5. Control involves all but _____. (a) measuring results (b) establishing goals (c) taking corrective action (d) selecting manpower

6. Grouping individuals and resources in the organization around products, services, clients, territories, or legal entities is an example of _____ specialization. (a) divisional (b) functional (c) matrix (d) mixed form

7. Grouping resources into departments by skills, knowledge, and action is the _____ pattern. (a) functional (b) divisional (c) vertical (d) matrix

8. A matrix structure _____. (a) reinforces unity of command (b) is inexpensive (c) is easy to explain to employees (d) gives some employees two bosses

9. _____ is the concern for proper communication, enabling the units to understand one another's activities. (a) Control (b) Coordination (c) Specialization (d) Departmentation

10. Compared to the machine bureaucracy (mechanistic type), the professional bureaucracy (organic type) _____. (a) is more efficient for routine operations (b) has more vertical specialization and control (c) is larger (d) has more horizontal specialization and coordination mechanism

11. Written statements of organizational purpose are called (a) societal contributions (b) output goals (c) mission statements (d) organizational politics

12. _____is the set of mechanisms used to keep actions and outputs within predetermined limits. (a) Coordination (b) Departmentation (c) Control (d) Authority

13. Grouping individuals by skills, knowledge, and action yields _____ departments. (a) divisional (b) functional (c) matrix (d) conglomerate

14. Controls that attempt to specify the manner in which tasks are to be accomplished are called _____. (a) output controls (b) departmental controls (c) process controls (d) managerial controls.

15. The set of mechanisms used in an organization to link the actions of its subunits into a consistent pattern is called _____. (a) coordination (b) control (c) authority (d) mission statements

Short Response

16. Compare and contrast output goals with systems goals.
17. Describe the types of controls that are typically used in organizations.
18. What are the major advantages and disadvantages of functional departmentation?
19. What are the major advantages and disadvantages of matrix departmentation?

Applications Essay

20. Describe some of the side effects of organizational controls in a large mechanistically structured organization, such as the U.S. Postal Service.

These learning activities from *The OB Skills Workbook* are suggested for Chapter 17.

OB in Action

CASE	EXPERIENTIAL EXERCISES	SELF-ASSESSMENTS
■ 8. I'm Not in Kansas Anymore	■ 13. Tinkertoys ■ 39. Organizations Alive ■ 40. Fast-Food Technology ■ 41. Alien Invasion	■ 2. A Twenty-First-Century Manager ■ 21. Organizational Design Preference)

Plus—special learning experiences from *The Jossey-Bass/Pfeiffer Classroom Collection*

Chapter 18

Organizational Design for Strategic Competency

Chapter at a Glance

In this chapter we show how firms can use organizational design options to implement their strategy; respond to the demands of size, technology, and environment; and shape their competitive landscape. As you read Chapter 18, *keep in mind these study questions.*

We all recognize that IBM is a huge, complex technological powerhouse. Its senior executives also recognize that the information revolution is here to stay. IBM continues to back its commitment to this technology by building competencies. In 2001, Louis V. Gerstner, then chairman of the board and chief executive officer at IBM, stated, "We strive to lead in the creation, development and manufacture of the industry's most advanced information technologies, including computer systems, software, networking systems, storage devices and microelectronics.... The Net has emerged as a powerful means for parties of every type to conduct transactions of every type—a place where real work gets done, real competitive advantage is gained and real growth is generated....e-business is a term we coined.... At the new IBM we've always believed that our ability to execute is as important as the strength of the strategies." The new chairman, president, and CEO, Samuel Palmisano, in 2004 reiterated, "We have mobilized the entire IBM company and our expanding network of partners to make our e-business on demand strategy a reality." IBM backs up its intention to be an integrated innovator with a stream of decisions to continue to build the capability to execute. It continues to invest in research capability, in its people, and in the systems needed to deliver world-class products and services for e-business. In 2003, it passed a milestone—3000 patents in only one year.[1]

> **"We have mobilized the entire IBM company...to make our e-business on demand strategy a reality."**

Strategy and Organizational Design

Organizational Design Defined

■ **Organizational design** is the process of choosing and implementing a structural configuration for an organization.

Organizational design is the process of choosing and implementing a structural configuration.[2] It goes beyond just indicating who reports to whom and what types of jobs are contained in each department. The design process takes the basic structural elements discussed in Chapter 17 and molds them to the firm's desires, demands, constraints, and choices. The choice of an appropriate organizational design is contingent upon several factors, including the size of the firm, its operations and information technology, its environment, and, of course, the strategy it selects for growth and survival. For example, IBM's senior management has selected a form of organization for each component of IBM that matches that component's contribution to the whole. The overall organizational design matches the technical challenges facing IBM, allows it to adjust to new developments, and helps it shape its competitive landscape. Above all, the design promotes the development of individual skills and abilities, but different designs stress different skills and abilities. As we discuss each major contingency factor, we will highlight the design option the firm's managers need to consider. These options help the firm build capacity as it reaches toward its goals.

Compare the description of IBM's research labs to a manufacturing operation such as a Ford assembly plant. We all recognize that a Ford assembly plant and an IBM research lab are quite different, but they also have some things in common. Auto assembly plants are organized to emphasize routine and efficient production, while the IBM research lab is loose, experimental, and devoted to innovation. Yet both must also use the most recent and competitive information technologies. For the auto plant it is an information system that supports just-in-time delivery of components. For IBM it is a comprehensive information system to promote learning. The organizational designs of both Ford and IBM are, above all else, established to implement and complement their strategy.

Organizational Design and Strategic Decisions

To show the intricate intertwining of strategy and organizational design, it is important to reiterate and extend the dualistic notion of strategy noted in the previous chapter.[3] Recall that strategy is a positioning of the firm in its environment to provide it with the capability to succeed, and strategy is also a pattern in the stream of decisions. In Chapter 17 we emphasized goals and the basic aspects of structure as important elements in this positioning and in the pattern. Now it is time to emphasize that what the firm intends to do must be backed up by capabilities for implementation in a setting that facilitates success.

Once, executives were told that firms had available a limited number of economically determined generic strategies that were built upon the foundations of such factors as efficiency and innovation. If the firm wanted efficiency, it should adopt the machine bureaucracy (many levels of management backed with extensive controls replete with written procedures). If it wanted innovation, it should adopt a more organic form (fewer levels of management with an emphasis on coordination). Today the corporate world is much more complex, and executives have found much more sophisticated ways of competing.

Today many senior executives are emphasizing the skills and abilities that their firms need not only to compete but also to remain agile and dynamic in a rapidly changing world. The structural configuration or organizational design of the firm should not only facilitate the types of accomplishment desired by senior management but also allow for individuals to experiment, grow, and develop competencies so that the strategy of the firm can evolve. Over time, the firm may develop specific administrative and technical skills as middle- and lower-level managers institute minor adjustments to solve specific problems. As they learn, so can their firms—if the individual learning of employees can be transferred across and up the organization's hierarchy. As the skills of employees and managers develop, they may be recognized by senior management and become a foundation for revisions in the overall strategy of the firm.

With astute senior management, the firm can co-evolve. That is, the firm can adjust to external changes even as it shapes some of the challenges facing it. Co-evolution is a process. One aspect of this process is repositioning the firm in its setting as the setting itself changes. A shift in the environment may call for adjusting the firm's scale of operations. Senior management can also guide the process of positioning and repositioning in the environment. For instance, a firm can introduce

Research Insight
Getting Innovation and Performance

Managers of units inside the organization are almost always searching for more innovation and a higher return on investment than is expected. Wepin Tsai looked at these two performance measures and tested three existing notions found in the current management literature. (1) Did units with a more central position in their corporate network perform better? (2) Did units with more capable personnel (more experience with more new products) outperform others? (3) Did both network position and capability make a combined difference? The answer: yes on all three. The big news was that it took both a central position in an extensive network and the capability to use this opportunity to get more innovation and greater-than-expected returns.

Reference: Wepin Tsai, "Knowledge Transfer in Interorganizational Networks: Effects of Network Position and Absorptive Capacity on Business Unit Innovation and Performance," *Academy of Management Journal* 44 (2001):996–1004.

new technologies and products in new markets. It can join with others to compete. However, senior management must also have the internal capabilities if it is to shape its environment. It cannot introduce new products without extensive product development capabilities or rush into a new market it does not understand. Shaping capabilities via the organization's design is a dynamic aspect of co-evolution.

The second aspect of strategy we emphasized was a pattern in the stream of decisions. The IBM example illustrates this consistency of focus backed by efforts to develop employees. The organizational design can reinforce a focus and provide a setting for the continual development of employee skills. As the environment, strategy, and technology shift, we will see shifts in design and the resulting capabilities. To continue the IBM example, it was once known as *Big Blue*—a button-down, white-shirt, blue-tie-and-black-shoe, second-to-market imitator with the bulk of its business centered on mainframe computers. IBM is now on the move in an entirely different way. Via innovation, it is now a major hub in e-commerce and is on the cutting edge as an integrator across systems, equipment, and service. To remain successful, IBM will continue to rely on the willingness of employees to take chances, refine their skills, and work together creatively.

In Chapter 17 we discussed how the basic elements of the structure emphasize various types of skills (e.g., a stress on market knowledge when organizing by product or an emphasis on deep technical skills when organizing by function). Now it is time to see how an interplay of forces helps mold and shape the behavior in organizations and the development of competencies through a firm's organizational design. Even with co-evolution, managers must maintain a recognizable pattern of choices in the design that leads to accomplishing a broadly shared view of where the firm is going.

Size and Organizational Design

The organizational design of the firm needs to be attuned to its size. For many reasons, large organizations cannot just be bigger versions of their smaller counterparts. As the number of individuals in a firm increases arithmetically, the number of possible interconnections among them increases geometrically. In other words, the direct interpersonal contact among all members in an organization must be managed. The design of small firms is directly influenced by their core operations technology, whereas larger firms have many core operations technologies in a wide variety of much more specialized units. In short, larger organizations are often more complex than smaller firms. While all larger firms are bureaucracies, smaller firms need not be. In larger firms, additional complexity calls for a more sophisticated organizational design.

The **simple design** is a configuration involving one or two ways of specializing individuals and units. That is, vertical specialization and control typically emphasize levels of supervision without elaborate formal mechanisms (e.g., rule books, policy manuals), and the majority of the control resides in the manager. Thus, the simple design tends to minimize bureaucratic aspects and rest more heavily on the leadership of the manager.

The simple design is appropriate for many small firms, such as family businesses, retail stores, and small manufacturing firms.[4] The strengths of the simple design are simplicity, flexibility, and responsiveness to the desires of a central manager—in many cases, the owner. Because a simple design relies heavily on the manager's personal leadership, however, this configuration is only as effective as is the senior manager.

> **Simple design** is a configuration involving one or two ways of specializing individuals and units.

PEOPLE AND TECHNOLOGY

KEY PEOPLE OFTEN KEEP A SMALL FIRM GOING

B&A Travel is a comparatively small travel agency owned by Helen Druse. Reporting to Helen is a part-time staff member—Jane Bloom–for accounting and finance. The operations arm is headed by Joan Wiland. Joan supervises eight travel agents and keeps a dedicated computer system operating. Whereas each of the lead travel agents specializes in a geographical area, all but Sue Connely and Bart Merve take client requests for all types of trips. Sue is in charge of  three major business accounts, and Bart heads a tour operation. Both of these agents report directly to Helen. Coordination is achieved through their dedicated intranet connections. Joan uses weekly meetings and a lot of personal contact by Helen and Joan to coordinate everyone. Control is enhanced by the computerized reservation system they all use. Helen makes sure each agent has a monthly sales target, and she routinely chats with important clients about their level of service. Helen realizes that developing participation from even the newest associate is an important tool in maintaining a "fun" atmosphere. However, now Joan is pregnant and is considering a move to part-time work.

Question: What should you know about the partial loss of key personnel in small organizations?

Operations Technology and Organizational Design

Although the design for an organization should reflect its size, it must also be adjusted to fit technological opportunities and requirements.[5] That is, successful organizations are said to arrange their internal structures to meet the dictates of

■■ Operations technology is the combination of resources, knowledge, and techniques that creates a product or service output for an organization.

■■ Information technology is the combination of machines, artifacts, procedures, and systems used to gather, store, analyze, and disseminate information for translating it into knowledge.

their dominant "technologies" or workflows and, more recently, information technology opportunities.[6] **Operations technology** is the combination of resources, knowledge, and techniques that creates a product or service output for an organization.[7] **Information technology** is the combination of machines, artifacts, procedures, and systems used to gather, store, analyze, and disseminate information for translating it into knowledge.[8]

For over 30 years, researchers in OB have charted the links between operations technology and organizational design. For operations technology, two common classifications have received considerable attention: Thompson's and Woodward's classifications.

Thompson's View of Technology   James D. Thompson classified technologies based on the degree to which the technology could be specified and the degree of interdependence among the work activities with categories called intensive, mediating, and long linked.[9] Under *intensive technology*, there is uncertainty as to how to produce desired outcomes. A group of specialists must be brought together interactively to use a variety of techniques to solve problems. Examples are found in a hospital emergency room or an R&D laboratory. Coordination and knowledge exchange are of critical importance with this kind of technology.

Mediating technology links parties that want to become interdependent. For example, banks link creditors and depositors and store money and information to facilitate such exchanges. Whereas all depositors and creditors are indirectly interdependent, the reliance is pooled through the bank. The degree of coordination among the individual tasks with pooled technology is substantially reduced, and information management becomes more important than coordinated knowledge application.

Under *long-linked technology*, also called mass production or industrial technology, the way to produce the desired outcomes is known. The task is broken down into a number of sequential steps. A classic example is the automobile assembly line. Control is critical, and coordination is restricted to making the sequential linkages work in harmony.

Woodward's View of Technology   Joan Woodward also divides technology into three categories: small-batch, mass production, and continuous-process manufacturing.[10] In units of *small-batch production*, a variety of custom products are tailor-made to fit customer specifications, such as tailor-made suits. The machinery and equipment used are generally not very elaborate, but considerable craftsmanship is often needed. In *mass production*, the organization produces one or a few products through an assembly-line system. The work of one group is highly dependent on that of another, the equipment is typically sophisticated, and the workers are given very detailed instructions. Automobiles and refrigerators are produced in this way. Organizations using *continuous-process technology* produce a few products using considerable automation. Classic examples are automated chemical plants and oil refineries. Millennium Chemicals' operations are a good example of what Woodward called continuous-process manufacturing. As the Ethics and Social Responsibility box suggests, innovative firms such as Millennium Chemicals are infusing ethics into day-to-day operations and making ethics a part of a recognizable pattern we have called *strategy*.

ETHICS AS A PART OF DESIGN AND STRATEGY

Millennium Chemicals is a major international chemical company providing commodity, industrial, and specialty chemicals on five continents. Its goal is to develop safe, scientific solutions for customers not only in the form of chemical products but also in terms of problem-solving expertise, relevant information, and customer-tailored scientific services. It is committed to building trust with all stakeholders, contributing to environmental protection, and maximizing health and safety in the workplace. Its ethical commitment to customers, the environment, and employees is seen not as an addition to its desire to create shareholder wealth but as an integral part of its overall strategy of excellence.

Question: Do you believe that a company integrating ethics into its strategy and design can provide great returns to stockholders as well?

From her studies, Woodward concluded that the combination of structure and technology is critical to the success of organizations. When technology and organizational design were properly matched, a firm was more successful. Specifically, successful small-batch and continuous-process plants had flexible structures with small workgroups at the bottom; more rigidly structured plants were less successful. In contrast, successful mass production operations were rigidly structured and had large workgroups at the bottom. Since Woodward's studies, this technological imperative has been supported by various other investigations. Yet today we recognize that operations technology is just one factor involved in the success of an organization.[11]

Adhocracy as a Design Option

The influence of operations technology is most clearly seen in small organizations and in specific departments within large ones. In some instances, managers and employees simply do not know the appropriate way to service a client or to produce a particular product. This is the extreme of Thompson's intensive type of technology, and it may be found in some small-batch processes where a team of individuals must develop a unique product for a particular client.

Mintzberg suggests that at these technological extremes, the adhocracy may be an appropriate design.[12] An **adhocracy** is characterized by few rules, policies, and procedures; substantial decentralization; shared decision making among members; extreme horizontal specialization (as each member of the unit may be a distinct specialist); few levels of management; and virtually no formal controls.

The adhocracy is particularly useful when an aspect of the firm's operations technology presents two sticky problems: (1) the tasks facing the firm vary considerably and provide many exceptions, as in a management consulting firm, or (2) problems are difficult to define and resolve.[13] The adhocracy places a premium on professionalism and coordination in problem solving.[14] Large firms

Adhocracy is an organizational structure that emphasizes shared, decentralized decision making; extreme horizontal specialization; few levels of management; the virtual absence of formal controls; and few rules, policies, and procedures.

may use temporary task forces, form special committees, and even contract consulting firms to provide the creative problem identification and problem solving that the adhocracy promotes. For instance, Microsoft creates new autonomous departments to encourage talented employees to develop new software programs. Allied Chemical and 3M also set up quasi-autonomous groups to work through new ideas.

Information Technology and Organizational Design

Why IT Makes a Difference

Information technology (IT), the Web, and the computer are not only virtually inseparable but have fundamentally changed the organizational design of firms to capture new competencies.[15] While some suggest that IT refers only to computer-based systems used in the management of the enterprise, we take a broader view.[16] With substantial collateral advances in telecommunication options, advances in the computer as a machine are much less profound than how information technology is transforming how firms manage.

It is important to understand just what IT does from an organizational standpoint—not from the view of the personal computer (PC) user.[17] From an organizational standpoint, IT can be used, among other things, as a partial substitute for some operations as well as some process controls and impersonal methods of coordination. It can also be used as a strategic capability as well as a capability for transforming information to knowledge for learning.

Old bureaucracies prospered and dominated other organizational forms in part because they provided more efficient production through specialization and their approach to dealing with information. Where the organization used mediating technology or long-linked technology, the machine bureaucracy ran rampant. In these firms rules, policies, and procedures, as well as many other process controls, could be rigidly enforced based on very scant information.[18] Such was the case, for example, for the U.S. Postal Service; postal clerks even had rules telling them how to hold their hands when sorting mail.

In many organizations, the initial implementation of IT would displace the most routine, highly specified, and repetitive jobs.[19] The clerical tasks in bookkeeping, writing checks for payroll, and keeping track of sales were some of the first targets of computerization. Here IT was often initiated in the form of a large centralized mainframe computer. For instance, mainframe computers were still the major business for IBM well into the 1990s. Initial implementation did not alter the fundamental character or design of the organization. To continue the example of the post office, initial computerization focused mainly on replacing the hand tracking of mail. Then IT was infused into automated reading machines to help sort mail. This called for implementation of the ZIP code.

A second wave of substitution replaced process controls and informal coordination mechanisms. Rules, policies, and procedures could be replaced with a decision support system (DSS). In the case of a DSS, repetitive routine choices could be programmed into a computer-based system. For instance, if you applied for a credit card, a computer program would check your credit history and other financial information. If your application passed several preset tests, you would be issued a credit card. If your application failed any of the tests, it would either be rejected or sent to an individual for further analysis.

The second wave of implementation brought some marginal changes in organizational design. Specifically, the firm often needed fewer levels of management and fewer internal staff. A small number of firms also recognized that they could outsource some internal staff operations. For instance, in many firms outside units actually do employee payroll.

The emphasis on direct substitution was still the norm in many organizations well into the 1990s, and in smaller firms it continues today. This is much as one would expect with the implementation of a new-to-the-world technology. It takes decades to move from the lab to full implementation, and the first applications are often in the form of substitutes for existing solutions. For instance, autos were once just substitutes for the horse and buggy. Both computer technology and the auto took about 20 years to enter the mass market. However, IT, just as the auto, has transformed our society because it added new capability.

IT as a Strategic Capability

IT has also long been recognized for its potential to add capability.[20] For over 20 years, scholars have talked of using IT to improve the efficiency, speed of responsiveness, and effectiveness of operations. Married to machines, IT became advanced manufacturing technology when computer-aided design (CAD) was combined with computer-aided manufacturing (CAM) to yield the automated manufacturing cell. More complex decision support systems have provided middle- and lower-level managers programs to aid in analyzing complex problems rather than just ratify routine choices. Computer-generated reports now give even senior executives the opportunity to track the individual sales performance of the lowliest salesperson.

Now instead of substituting for existing operations, or process controls, IT provides individuals deep within the organization the information they need to plan, make choices, coordinate with others, and control their own operations.

Although simple substitution could proceed one application at a time, the real impact of adding IT capability could not come until it was broadly available to nearly everyone.[21] To use the auto analogy again, the real impact of the auto was felt only after Henry Ford sold hundreds of thousands of his Model T and new roads were constructed. For IT to have a similar impact on organizational design, the seamless use of computerized information across the organization was needed. The extremely powerful mainframe of the 1970s and 1980s was not up to the task simply because the information individuals required to do their jobs more quickly and better was often unique to them. They now needed a common technology with the capability for uniqueness. And nearly everyone would have to have it and use it in cooperation with others.

IT and Learning

Enter WINTEL—that is, Microsoft Windows in combination with an Intel microprocessing chip. This combination provided a relatively cheap, easy-to-use personal computer with an almost standardized technology that could be individu-

The Monster Reorganizes

TMP Worldwide is now Monster.com in recognition of the technology that is a key to its success. Monster.com is one of the best e-linkages to finding a new job. It recently reorganized its worldwide operations into regions to focus on Europe, Asia, and North America in an attempt to build more direct contacts with local firms and clients.

ally tailored at a comparatively modest cost. WINTEL was the PC equivalent of the tin lizzie—Henry Ford's Model T designed for the masses.

With the adoption of WINTEL, three important changes occurred. First, IT applications for tasks found across many organizations were quickly developed and received broad acceptance. Thus, the era of the spreadsheet and the word-processing program began and displaced the old mainframes. Individuals could develop and transfer information to others with some assurance that the other party could read their output and duplicate their processes. Second, WINTEL expanded to incorporate existing telecommunications systems such as the Internet.[22] Thus, the era of connectivity also emerged. Married to parallel developments in telecommunications, a whole world of electronic commerce, teleconferencing—with combinations of data, pictures, and sound—and cell phones emerged. Third, IT was transformed from a substitute to a mechanism for learning.[23] For example, we now ask you to learn from the Internet connections and Web exercises at the end of each chapter.

Collectively, the impact of IT organizational design was and remains profound. The changes can often occur from the bottom up. New IT systems empower individuals, expanding their jobs and making them both interesting and challenging. The emphasis on narrowly defined jobs replete with process controls imposed by middle management can be transformed to broadly envisioned, interesting jobs based on IT-embedded processes with output controls. More than likely, you will be involved with a "virtual" network of task forces and temporary teams to both define and solve problems. Here the members will be connected only electronically. Recent work on participants of the open-software movement (e.g., the ones refining and developing applications for Linux) suggests you will need to rethink what it means to "manage." Instead of telling others what to do, you will need to treat your colleagues as unpaid volunteers who expect to participate in governing the meetings and who are tied to the effort only by a commitment to identify and solve problems.[24] The Effective Manager 18.1 provides some guidelines to think about managing in a virtual environment.

THE EFFECTIVE MANAGER 18.1

Managing a Virtual Project

When managing a "virtual" project, you should do the following:

1. Establish a set of mutually reinforcing motives for participation, including a share in success.
2. Stress self-governance and make sure there is a manageable number of high-quality contributors.
3. Outline a set of rules that members can adapt to their individual needs.
4. Encourage joint monitoring and sanctions of member behavior.
5. Stress shared values, norms, and behavior.
6. Develop effective work structures and processes via project management software.
7. Emphasize the use of technology for communication and norms about how to use it.

For the production segments of firms using long-linked technology such as in auto assembly plants and canneries, IT can be linked to total quality management (TQM) programs and be embedded in the machinery. Data on operations can be transformed into knowledge of operations and used to systematically improve quality and efficiency. This has also meant that firms have had to rethink their view of employees as brainless robots. To make TQM work with IT, all employees must plan, do, and control. As we discussed when we talked about job enrichment and job design, combining IT and TQM with empowerment and participation is fundamental for success. For instance, in the mid-1990s two computer equipment manufacturers embarked on improvement programs combining IT and TQM. One manufacturer imposed the program on all employees. There was some initial success, but ultimately this program failed. The second combined the IT–TQM program with extensive empowerment and participation. Although implementation was slower, today the combination has produced a constantly improving learning environment.[25]

IT and E-Business

Just as the automobile spawned the mobile society and led to the development of a plethora of auto-related businesses, IT has spawned a whole new series of corporations called e-businesses. It is also transforming aging bricks-and-mortar firms as they incorporate a new type of capability.

As illustrated in our example of IBM, e-business is here to stay.[26] Whether it is business to business (B2B) or business to consumers (B2C), there is a whole new set of dot-com firms with information technology at the core of their operations. One of the more flamboyant entrants to the B2C world is the now-familiar Amazon.com. Opened in 1995 to sell books directly to customers via the Internet, it rapidly expanded to toys and games, health and beauty products, computers and video games, as well as cameras and photography. It is now a virtual general store. After more than six years of losses, Amazon.com posted a nice profit in 2003. It is most interesting to examine the transformation in the design of this firm to illustrate the notion of co-evolution presented earlier. Initially, it was organized as a simple structure. As it grew, it became more complex by adding divisions devoted to each of its separate product areas. To remain flexible and promote growth in both the volume of operations and the capabilities of employees, it did not develop an extensive bureaucracy. There are still very few levels of management. It built separate organizational components based on product categories (divisional structure, as described in Chapter 17) with minimal rules, policies, and procedures. In other words, the organizational design it adopted appeared relatively conventional. What was not conventional was the use of IT for learning about customers and for coordinating and tracking operations. Although its Web site was not the most technically advanced, you could easily order the book you wanted, track the delivery, and feel confident it would arrive as promised. In recent years, Amazon.com has used its IT prowess to develop strategic alliances with bricks-and-mortar firms. It has used IT to change the competitive landscape.

In comparison to Amazon.com, many other new dot-com firms adopted a variation of the adhocracy as their design pattern. The thinking was that e-business was fundamentally different from the old bricks-and-mortar operations. Thus, an entirely new structural configuration was needed to accommodate the development of new e-products and services. The managers of these firms forgot two important liabilities of adhocracy as they grew. First, there are limits on the size of an effective adhocracy. Second, the actual delivery of their products and services did not require continual innovation but rested more on responsiveness to clients and maintaining efficiency. The design did not deliver what they needed. They had great Web sites, but they were grossly inefficient. Many died almost as quickly as they were formed.

IT as a strategic capability is now changing many traditional bricks-and-mortar firms. They too are incorporating e-business into their normal operations. Perhaps IT's most profound effect can be seen in firms that rely on a mediating technology; banks, finance companies, dating services, and employment agencies are some examples. The job of the firm, as we know, is to facilitate exchange by matching types of individuals. In the case of banks, individuals who want to borrow are matched with those who want to lend by placing individual interests into categories. So those who have a savings account are put in a category of precisely that type of savings account and are pooled with others. IT can revolutionize the categorization process that underlies the matching by helping to create much more sophisticated categories and link these categories in novel ways. For example, IT lies behind the multibillion-dollar secondary market for home mortgages. Until recent years, a bank or savings and loan (S&L) provided the funds for the mortgage from its depositors and would hold the mortgage until it was paid off. You would apply to a local bank or S&L for a mortgage. If it granted you a mortgage, you would pay the bank or the S&L that sold it to you. Much the same was the case for student loans. Now, with IT, the bank or S&L can sell the mortgage to others—and normally does—so that it can recoup new funds to sell additional mortgages. It may even sell the right to "service" the loan so that you no longer send your money to the originating bank but to someone else. This change in information technology now allows all types of financial institutions to participate in lending money for mortgages. The job of the old banker or S&L manager has fundamentally changed. Now you can get a mortgage, a credit card, or use the ATM machine without ever contacting an individual.

Some financial firms could not exist without IT, because it is now the base for the industry. Early adopters created whole new segments of the industry with both major contributions to our economy and major new threats. For instance, IT is the foundation for multitrillion-dollar markets in international finance in which exotic new products, nonexistent 20 years ago, are available. In the 1990s few existing financial managers or regulatory agencies had the understanding of IT to develop effective controls for the global derivatives markets. However, a small handful of individuals in Connecticut working for a firm called Long Term Capital used sophisticated IT systems to bet several billion dollars on the interest spread between different kinds of bonds. Although they made several hundred million dollars in the mid-1990s, in 1998 their losses threatened the whole U.S. financial system to the point that the Federal Reserve (a quasi-governmental agency) had to orchestrate a rescue. Of course, IT has not developed in a vacuum, and its effective implementation often rests on others adopting common IT standards and operations. Just because IT presents a potential capability does not automatically mean a firm should adopt it or change its design to facilitate its use. The appropriate design also rests on external factors and the strategy of the firm. We turn to these issues now.

Environment and Organizational Design

An effective organizational design also reflects powerful external forces as well as size and technological factors. Organizations, as open systems, need to receive inputs from the environment and in turn to sell outputs to their environment. Therefore, understanding the environment is important.[27]

The *general environment* is the set of cultural, economic, legal-political, and educational conditions found in the areas in which the organization operates. Much of Chapter 3 dealt with the influences of the general environment, and throughout this book we have shown examples of globalization. The owners, suppliers, distributors, government agencies, and competitors with which an organization must interact to grow and survive constitute its specific environment. A firm typically has much more choice in the composition of its specific environment than its general environment. Although it is often convenient to separate the general and specific environmental influences on the firm, managers need to recognize the combined impact of both. Choosing some businesses, for instance, means entering global competition with advanced technologies.

Environmental Complexity

A basic concern that must be addressed in analyzing the environment of the organization is its complexity. A more complex environment provides an organization with more opportunities and more problems. **Environmental complexity** refers to the magnitude of the problems and opportunities in the organization's environment, as evidenced by three main factors: the degree of richness, the degree of interdependence, and the degree of uncertainty stemming from both the general and the specific environment.

Environmental complexity is the magnitude of the problems and opportunities in the organization's environment as evidenced by the degree of richness, interdependence, and uncertainty.

Environmental Richness Overall, the environment is richer when the economy is growing, when individuals are improving their education, and when those on whom the organization relies are prospering. For businesses, a richer environment means that economic conditions are improving, customers are spending more money, and suppliers (especially banks) are willing to invest in the organization's future. In a rich environment, more organizations survive, even if they have poorly functioning organizational designs. A richer environment is also filled with more opportunities and dynamism—the potential for change. The organizational design must allow the company to recognize these opportunities and capitalize on them.

The opposite of richness is decline. For business firms, a general recession is a good example of a leaner environment. Whereas corporate reactions vary, it is instructive to examine typical responses to decline. In the United States, firms have traditionally reacted to decline first by laying off nonsupervisory workers and then by moving up the organizational ladder as the environment becomes leaner. Firms may downsize without considering all the implications (see The Effective Manager 18.2).

> ### THE EFFECTIVE MANAGER 18.2
> ## Avoiding More Problems with Downsizing
>
> When downsizing, firms should keep in mind that they must do the following:
> 1. Accurately identify the causes of the decline.
> 2. Avoid grandiose attempts to reverse past history.
> 3. Avoid the tendency to increase centralization and rigidity and to reduce participation.
> 4. Target cuts and retrain employees wherever possible.
> 5. Keep employees informed to alleviate fear.
> 6. Systematically work to rebuild morale and emphasize more participation.

Many European firms find it very difficult to cut full-time employees legally when the economy deteriorates. In sustained periods of decline, many firms have therefore turned to national governments for help. Much like U.S.-based firms, European-based firms view changes in organizational design as a last but increasingly necessary resort as they must now compete globally.

Environmental Interdependence The link between external interdependence and organizational design is often subtle and indirect. The organization may coopt powerful outsiders by including them. For instance, many large corporations have financial representatives from banks and insurance companies on their boards of directors. The organization may also adjust its overall design strategy to absorb or buffer the demands of a more powerful external element. Perhaps the most common adjustment is the development of a centralized staff department to handle an important external group. For instance, few large U.S. corporations lack some type of governmental relations group at the top. Where service to a few large customers is considered critical, the organization's departmentation is likely to switch from a functional to a divisionalized form.[28]

Uncertainty and Volatility   Environmental uncertainty and volatility can be particularly damaging to large bureaucracies. In times of change, investments quickly become outmoded and internal operations no longer work as expected. The obvious organizational design response to uncertainty and volatility is to opt for a more organic form. At the extremes, movement toward an adhocracy may be important. However, these pressures may run counter to those that come from large size and operations technology. In these cases, it may be too hard or too time consuming for some organizations to make the design adjustments. Thus, the organization may continue to struggle while adjusting its design just a little bit at a time.

Network Organizations and Alliances

In today's more complex global economy, organizational design must therefore go beyond the traditional boundaries of the firm.[29] Firms must learn to co-evolve by altering their environment. Two ways are becoming more popular—the management of networks and the development of alliances. Many North American firms are learning from their European and Japanese counterparts to develop networks of linkages to key firms they rely on. In Europe, for example, one finds *informal combines* or *cartels*. Here, competitors work cooperatively to share the market in order to decrease uncertainty and improve favorability for all. Except in rare cases, these arrangements are often illegal in the United States.

In Japan, the network of relationships among well-established firms in many industries is called a *keiretsu*. There are two common forms. The first is a bank-centered keiretsu, in which firms are linked to one another directly through cross-ownership and historical ties to one bank. The Mitsubishi group is a good example. In the second type, a vertical *keiretsu*, a key manufacturer is at the hub of a network of supplier firms or distributor firms. The manufacturer typically has both long-term supply contracts with members and cross-ownership ties. These arrangements help isolate Japanese firms from stockholders and provide a mechanism for sharing and developing technology. Toyota is an example of a firm at the center of a vertical *keiretsu*.

A very specialized form of network organization is evolving in U.S.-based firms as well. Here, the central firm specializes in core activities—such as design, assembly, and marketing—and works with a comparatively small number of participating suppliers on a long-term basis for both component development and manufacturing efficiency. The central firm is the hub of a network where others need it more than it needs any other member. While Nike was a leader in the development of these relationships, now it is difficult to find a large U.S. firm that does not outsource extensively. Executives seeking to find cheap sources of foreign labor often justify outsourcing from the U.S. firms.

However, as a design option, managers should be examining how this alternative fits with the firm's strategy and technology as well. For instance, if the firm markets high-quality products matched with service, outsourcing may be inconsistent with the service requirements needed for success. Customers could move to firms that do not outsource service. More extreme variations of this network design are also emerging to meet apparently conflicting environmental, size, and technological demands simultaneously. Firms are spinning off staff functions to reduce their overall size and take advantage of new IT options. With these new environmental challenges and technological opportunities, firms must choose, not just react blindly. With too much outsourcing, the firms become too highly dependent on others and lose the opportunity to be flexible and respond to new opportunities.

Another option is to develop **interfirm alliances**—announced cooperative agreements or joint ventures between two independent firms. Often these agreements involve corporations that are headquartered in different nations. In high-tech areas and businesses dominated by IT, such as robotics, semiconductors, advanced materials (ceramics and carbon fibers), and advanced information systems, a single company often does not have all the knowledge necessary to bring new products to market. Alliances are quite common in such high-technology industries. Via international alliances, high-tech firms seek not only to develop technology but also to ensure that their solutions become standardized across regions of the world.

Developing and effectively managing an alliance is a managerial challenge of the first order. Firms are asked to cooperate rather than compete. The alliance's sponsors normally have different and unique strategies, cultures, and desires for the alliance itself. Both the alliance managers and sponsoring executives must be patient, flexible, and creative in pursuing the goals of the alliance and each sponsor. It is little wonder that many alliances are terminated prematurely.[30]

> **Interfirm alliances** are announced cooperative agreements or joint ventures between two independent firms.

CULTURES AND THE GLOBAL WORKFORCE

SUSTAINING INTERNATIONAL ALLIANCES

There is a myth that all international alliances, particularly in high-tech areas, are short lived. But that is not always the case. The alliance between Warner-Lambert (best known as a U.S.-based pharmaceutical firm) and Japan's Sankyo (one of Japan's most successful pharmaceutical firms) dates to 1902, when Parke-Davis, now a division of Warner-Lambert, selected Sankyo as a distributor for one of its drugs. As Warner-Lambert states in its annual report, "Our relationship has flourished like a great tree." The latest fruit from this relationship is *Rezulin*, a new medication

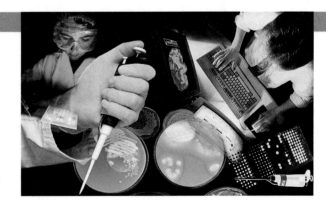

to treat diabetes. First discovered by Sankyo, the drug was developed, perfected, and marketed via the alliance. It is one of the most successful new drugs in the United States. As Maurice Renshaw, president of Parke-Davis, states, "We believe that when our business allies win, we win as well."

Question: What skills would you need to manage an alliance between a U.S. and Japanese firm?

Virtual Organizations

Executives do not just face prospects for growth, more complex operations technology, new IT capabilities, or a more complex environment one at a time. For some firms, all of these internal and external contingencies are changing simultaneously and changing dramatically. Facing dramatic changes across the board, how do firms keep sufficient consistency in the pattern of their actions and yet co-evolve with their environment? That is, what is the design option when everything is changing and changing quickly?

While there is no simple answer, we can start by saying that firms do not do it alone. Some executives have started to develop what are called "virtual organizations."[31] A **virtual organization** is an ever-shifting constellation of firms, with a lead corporation, that pool skills, resources, and experiences to thrive jointly. This ever-changing collection most likely has a relatively stable group of actors (usually independent firms) that normally include customers, competitors, research centers, suppliers, and distributors. There is a lead organization that directs the constellation because this lead firm possesses a critical competence all need. This critical competence may be a key technology or access to customers. Across time, members may come and go, as there are shifts in technology or alterations in environmental conditions. It is also important to stress that key customers are an integral part of a virtual organization. Not only do customers buy but they also participate in the development of new products and technologies. Thus, the virtual organization co-evolves by incorporating many types of firms.

The virtual organization works if it operates by some unique rules and is led in a most untypical way. First, the production system yielding the products and services customers desire needs to be a partner network among independent firms where they are bound together by mutual trust and collective survival. As customer desires change, the proportion of work done by any member firm might change and the membership itself might change. In a similar fashion, the introduction of a new technology could shift the proportion of work among members or call for the introduction of new members. Second, this partner network needs to develop and maintain (1) an advanced information technology (rather than just face-to-face interaction), (2) trust and cross-owning of problems and solutions, and (3) a common shared culture (as discussed in Chapter 19). Developing these characteristics is a very tall order, but the virtual organization can be highly resilient, extremely competent, innovative, and efficient—characteristics that are usually trade-offs. The virtual organization can effectively compete on a global scale in very complex settings using advanced technologies.

The role of the lead firm is also quite unusual and actually makes a network of firms a virtual organization. The lead firm must take responsibility for the whole constellation and coordinate the actions and evolution of autonomous member firms. Executives in the lead firm need to have the vision to see how the network of participants will both effectively compete with a consistent enough pattern action to be recognizable and still rapidly adjust to technological and environmental changes. Executives should not only communicate this vision and inspire individuals in the independent member firms but also treat members as if they were volunteers. To accomplish this across independent firms, the lead corporation and its members also need to rethink how they are internally organized and managed.

Based on a synthesis of successful management experiments by General Electric and its partners, a group of consultants and scholars put together a list of the changes firms need to consider if they are to compete globally in rapidly changing technical settings.[32] They used the buzz words of GE and labeled their package the "boundaryless organization." In essence, the challenge to management is to eliminate barriers vertically, horizontally, externally, and geographically that block desired action. These barriers are the ones noted in this chapter and in Chapter 17. Specifically, an overemphasis on vertical relations can block communication up and down the firm. An overemphasis on functions, product lines, or organizational units blocks effective coordination. Maintaining rigid lines of demarcation between the firm and its partners can isolate it from others. And, of course, natural cultural, national, and geographical borders can limit globally coordinated action. The notion of a boundaryless organization is not to eliminate all boundaries but to make them much more permeable. We think the development of permeable boundaries is a key characteristic of all members of a virtual organization.

This all sounds fine and very esoteric. How is it done? First, executives should systematically (1) examine the culture of the firm (is the culture actually consistent with our strategy?), (2) catalog its competencies (what do we really do best and is this consistent with what we need?), (3) chart how accountability is actually determined (who gets blamed and who gets credit and is this consistent with what we actually want done?), (4) study the organizational design (is the pattern of vertical and horizontal specialization consistent with what we want done and is there effective control and coordination for the whole firm?), (5) assess the actual work processes (have the processes been reengineered and reinvented or are they based on what once worked well?), and (6) evaluate leadership (what type of leadership do we need to succeed and are we helping everyone develop the needed skills)?[33] From this list it is very important to note that the assessment goes well beyond basic organizational characteristics or what is typically called organizational design. It focuses on both organization and people and calls for a comprehensive view that incorporates most every chapter in this book.

Knowing what you have and what you need is just a start. The next phase is to begin a process of improvement. Employees, managers, and executives need to ask how they can improve with others both inside and outside the firm. They need to prioritize before they begin implementation. And once improvements are started, they need to recalibrate to ensure that a new set of boundaries does not emerge. Of course, the notion of a virtual and boundaryless organization is very different from the conditions found in and across most corporations. A movement toward cooperating to compete and removing barriers calls on firms to learn. So we now turn to how firms do this.

Corning's Global Reach via Alliances

Corning is an innovation-driven firm engaged in a variety of advanced materials and technologies. Yet it does not commercialize new products alone. Instead, Corning relies on alliances with more than 50 affiliated companies in 16 countries.

Organizational Learning

Throughout this chapter we have emphasized co-evolution, and we have just described a virtual organization. We have recognized that the firm must not only adapt to its size, technology, and environment but must also shape these forces. It does so through the development of individuals and their skills. In the OB literature, the development of individual skills and capabilities organizationwide is discussed under the topic of organizational learning. **Organizational learning**

Organizational learning is the process of knowledge acquisition, information distribution, information interpretation, and organizational retention.

is the key to successful co-evolution. Organizational learning is the process of knowledge acquisition, information distribution, information interpretation, and organizational retention in adapting successfully to changing circumstances.[34] In simpler terms, organizational learning involves the adjustment of the organization's and individuals' actions based on its experience and that of others. The challenge is doing to learn and learning to do.

How Organizations Acquire Knowledge

Firms obtain information in a variety of ways and at different rates during their histories. Perhaps the most important information is obtained from sources outside the firm at the time of its founding. During the firm's initial years, its managers copy, or mimic, what they believe are the successful practices of others.[35] As they mature, however, firms can also acquire knowledge through experience and systematic search.

▓▓ **Mimicry** is the copying of the successful practices of others.

Mimicry   Mimicry is important to the new firm because (1) it provides workable, if not ideal, solutions to many problems; (2) it reduces the number of decisions that need to be analyzed separately, allowing managers to concentrate on more critical issues; and (3) it establishes legitimacy or acceptance by employees, suppliers, and customers and narrows the choices calling for detailed explanation.

One of the key factors involved in examining mimicry is the extent to which managers attempt to isolate cause–effect relationships. Simply copying others without attempting to understand the issues involved often leads to failure. The literature is filled with examples of firms that have tried to implement quality circles, empowerment, and decentralization simply because others have used them successfully. Too many firms have abandoned these techniques because managers failed to understand why and under what conditions they worked for other firms. When mimicking others, managers need to adjust for the unique circumstances of their corporation.

Experience   A primary way to acquire knowledge is through experience. All organizations and managers can learn in this manner. Besides learning by doing, managers can also systematically embark on structured programs to capture the lessons to be learned from failure and success. For instance, a well-designed research-and-development program allows managers to learn as much through failure as through success.

Learning by doing in an intelligent way is at the heart of many Japanese corporations, with their emphasis on statistical quality control, quality circles, and other such practices. Many firms have discovered that numerous small improvements can cumulatively add up to a major improvement in both quality and efficiency. The major problem with emphasizing learning by doing is the inability to forecast precisely what will change and how it will change. Managers need to believe that improvements can be made, listen to suggestions, and actually implement the changes. It is much more difficult to do than to say, however.

Vicarious Learning   Vicarious learning involves capturing the lessons of others' experiences. At the individual level, managers are building on individualized "social learning" and use it to help transform their potential for organizational improvement.

Individual Social Learning   *Social learning* is learning that is achieved through the reciprocal interactions among people, behavior, and environment. Figure 18.1 illustrates and elaborates on this individualized view of learning drawn from the work of Albert Bandura.[36] According to the figure, the individual uses modeling or vicarious learning to acquire behavior by observing and imitating others. The person then attempts to acquire these behaviors by modeling them through practice. In a work situation, the model may be a manager or co-worker who demonstrates desired behaviors. Mentors or senior workers who befriend younger and more inexperienced protégés can also be important models. Indeed, some have argued that a shortage of mentors for women in senior management has been a major constraint to their progression up the career ladder.[37]

The symbolic processes depicted in Figure 18.1 are also important in social learning. Words and symbols used by managers and others in the workplace can help communicate values, beliefs, and goals and thus serve as guides to the individual's behavior. For example, a "thumbs up" or other signal from the boss lets you know your behavior is appropriate. At the same time, the person's self-control is important in influencing his or her own behavior. Self-efficacy—the person's belief that he or she can perform adequately in a situation—is an important part of such self-control. People with self-efficacy believe that they have the necessary ability for a given job, that they are capable of the effort required, and that no outside events will hinder them from attaining their desired performance level.[38] In contrast, people with low self-efficacy believe that no matter how hard they try, they cannot manage their environment well enough to be successful. For example, if you feel self-efficacious as a student, a low grade on one test is likely to encourage you to study harder, talk to the instructor, or do other things to enable you to do well the next time. In contrast, a person low in self-efficacy would probably drop the course or give up studying. Of course, even people who are high in self-efficacy do not control their environment entirely.

Much of the learning in corporations is less systematic than that depicted in Figure 18.1. Some firms have learned that the process of searching for new information may not always be structured or planned in conjunction with an iden-

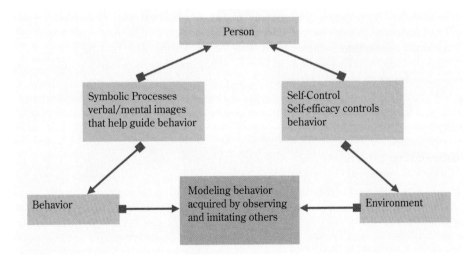

Figure 18.1   Social learning model.

tified problem or opportunity. Managers may embark upon learning in less systematic ways, including scanning, grafting, and contracting out.

Scanning   **Scanning** involves looking outside the firm and bringing back useful solutions. At times, these solutions may be applied to recognized problems. More often, these solutions float around management until they are needed to solve a problem.[39] Astute managers can contribute to organizational learning by scanning external sources, such as competitors, suppliers, industry consultants, customers, and leading firms. For instance, by reverse-engineering the competitor's products (developing the engineering drawings and specifications from the existing product), an organization can quickly match all standard product features. By systematically exploring the proposed developments from suppliers, a firm may become a lead user and be among the first to capitalize on the developments of suppliers.

> ▪ **Scanning** is looking outside the firm and bringing back useful solutions to problems.

Grafting   **Grafting** is the process of acquiring individuals, units, or firms to bring in useful knowledge. Almost all firms seek to hire experienced individuals from other firms simply because experienced individuals may bring with them a whole new series of solutions. For instance, at Dayton-Hudson senior management hired a new vice president for one of its department stores from a leading competitor, Nordstrom's. Dayton-Hudson wanted to know the winning ways of this industry leader.

> ▪ **Grafting** is the process of acquiring individuals, units, and/or firms to bring in useful knowledge to the organization.

The critical problem in grafting is much the same as that in scanning: obtaining the knowledge is not enough; it must be translated into action. A key problem with grafting one unit onto an existing organization is discussed in Chapter 19. That is, there may be a clash of cultures, and instead of getting new solutions, both units may experience substantial conflict. Contracting out, or outsourcing, is the reserve of grafting and involves asking outsiders to perform a particular function. Whereas virtually all organizations contract out, the key question for managers is often what to keep.

Information Distribution, Interpretation, and Retention

Information Distribution   Once information is obtained, managers must establish mechanisms to distribute relevant information to the individuals who may need it. A primary challenge in larger firms is to locate quickly who has the appropriate information and who needs specific types of information. A partial solution is the development of dispersed IT networks that connect related organizational units.

Although data collection is helpful, it is not enough. Data are not information; the information must be interpreted. We will have much more to say about information distribution in Chapter 19.

Information Interpretation   Information within organizations is a collective understanding of the firm's goals and of how the data relate to one of the firm's stated or unstated objectives within the current setting. Unfortunately, the process of developing multiple interpretations is often thwarted by a number of common problems.[40]

Self-Serving Interpretations   Among managers, the ability to interpret events, conditions, and history to their own advantage is almost universal. Managers and employees alike often see what they have seen in the past or see what they want to see. Rarely do they see what is or can be.

Managerial Scripts   A **managerial script** is a series of well-known routines for problem identification and alternative generation and analysis common to managers within a firm.[41] Different organizations have different scripts, often based on what has worked in the past. In a way, the script is a ritual that reflects what the "memory banks" of the corporation hold. Managers become bound by what they have seen. The danger is that they may not be open to what is actually occurring. They may be unable to unlearn.

The script may be elaborate enough to provide an apparently well-tested series of solutions based on the firm's experience. Larger, older firms are rarely structured for learning; rather, they are structured for efficiency. That is, the organizational design emphasizes repetition, volume processing, and routine. In order to learn, the organization needs to be able to unlearn, switch routines to obtain information quickly, and provide various interpretations of events rather than just tap into external archives.

Few managers question a successful script. Consequently, they start solving today's problems with yesterday's solutions. Managers have been trained, both in the classroom and on the job, to initiate corrective action within the historically shared view of the world. That is, managers often initiate small, incremental improvements based on existing solutions instead of creating new approaches to identify the underlying problems.

Common Myths   An **organizational myth** is a commonly held cause–effect relationship or assertion that cannot be empirically supported.[42] Even though myths cannot be substantiated, both managers and workers may base their interpretations of problems and opportunities on the potentially faulty views. Three common myths often block the development of multiple interpretations.

The first common myth is the presumption that there is *a single organizational truth*. This myth is often expressed as, "Although others may be biased, I am able to define problems and develop solutions objectively." We are all subject to bias in varying degrees and in varying ways. The more complex the issue, the stronger the likelihood of many different supportable interpretations.

A second common myth is *the presumption of competence*. Managers at all levels are subject to believing that their part of the firm is OK and just needs minor improvements in implementation. As we have documented throughout this book, such is rarely the case. We are in the middle of a managerial revolution in which all managers need to reassess their general approach to managing organizational behavior.

A third common myth is *the denial of trade-offs*. Most managers believe that their group, unit, or firm can avoid making undesirable trade-offs and simultaneously please nearly every constituency. Whereas the denial of trade-offs is common, it can be a dangerous myth in some firms. For instance, when complex, dangerous technologies are involved, safe operations may come at some sacrifice to efficiency. Yet some firms claim that "an efficient operation is a safe one" and aggressively move to improve efficiency. Although managers are stressing efficiency, they may fail to work on improving safety. The result may be a serious accident.[43]

Information Retention   Organizations contain a variety of mechanisms that can be used to retain useful information.[44] Seven important mechanisms are in-

A managerial script is a series of well-known routines for problem identification and alternative generation and analysis common to managers within a firm.

An organizational myth is a commonly held cause–effect relationship or assertion that cannot be empirically supported.

dividuals, culture, transformation mechanisms, formal structures, physical structures, external archives, and internal information technologies.

Individuals   Individuals are the most important storehouses of information for organizations. Organizations that retain a large and comparatively stable group of experienced individuals are expected to have a higher capacity to acquire, retain, and retrieve information. Collectively, the organizational *culture* is an important repository of the shared experiences of corporate members. The culture often maintains the organizational memory via rich, vivid, and meaningful stories that outlive those who experienced the event.

Transformation Mechanisms   Documents, rule books, written procedures, and even standard but unwritten methods of operation are all *transformation mechanisms* used to store accumulated information. In cases where operations are extremely complex but rarely needed, written sources of information are often invaluable. For example, each nuclear power plant in the United States maintains an extensive library. In the library, one can find the complete engineering drawings for the whole plant as well as the changes made since the plant opened, together with a step-by-step plan for almost every possible accident scenario.

Formal Structure   The organization's *formal structure* and the positions in an organization are less obvious but equally important mechanisms for storing information. When an aircraft lands on the deck of a U.S. Navy aircraft carrier, there are typically dozens of individuals on the deck, apparently watching the aircraft land. Each person on the deck is there for a specific purpose. Each can often trace his or her position to a specific accident that would not have occurred had some individual originally been assigned that position.

Physical Structures   *Physical structures* (or *ecology*, in the language of learning theorists) are potentially important but often neglected mechanisms used to store information. For example, a traditional way of ordering parts and subcomponents in a factory is known as the "two-bin" system. One bin is always kept in reserve. Once an individual opens the reserve bin, he or she automatically orders replacements. In this way, the plant never runs out of components.

External Archives   *External archives* can be tapped to provide valuable information on most larger organizations. Former employees, stock market analysts, suppliers, distributors, and the media can be important sources of valuable information. These external archives are important because they may provide a view of events quite different from that held in the organization.

IT   Finally, the IT system of the organization, its *internal information technology*, can provide a powerful and individually tailored mechanism for storing information. All too often, however, managers are not using their IT systems strategically and are not tapping into them as mechanisms for retention.

Dynamics of Organizational Learning

Throughout the beginning of this century, a common headline running in the business press was: "Major Corporation Downsizes." Whether the corporation was Cisco, General Motors, or Intel, the message appeared to be the same: major

Leaders on Leadership

GOOD LEADING AND GOOD MANAGING

That's how John Chambers, president and CEO of Cisco Systems, ends many of his mes-

sages. Cisco is back from the devastating tech bust and starting to enjoy another benefit cycle. John's strategy for Cisco is as clear as his leadership: " In today's environment, it's all about getting back to the basics in terms of focusing on the areas that a company can influence and control: cash generation, available market share gains, productivity increases, profitabil-

ity, and technology innovation. These factors determine who will survive in this challenging economy." Chambers cut fast and deep after the bust, disposing of some $2 billion in antiquated inventory, and immediately refocused the firm on building for the future. Today Cisco is again highly profitable and growing, thanks to John's leadership and strategic vision.

Question: What else do you need to know about Cisco and John Chambers to understand how he returned his firm to a benefit cycle?

U.S.-based corporations were in trouble. They were finally adjusting to a new competitive reality—on the backs of their workers and managers. As we have noted in this chapter, today the message from these firms is quite different. All are emphasizing competency via individual development and empowerment to learn and to make the needed incremental changes and decisions along the way. All are trying to avoid the past mistakes where they engaged in massive attempts to redirect themselves when it was apparent to all that change was overdue. Some recent work on learning cycles helps explain why many organizations apparently fail to learn, while others appear to improve rapidly.[45]

Deficit Cycles   A **deficit cycle** is a pattern of deteriorating performance that is followed by even further deterioration. Firms that are continually downsizing, such as Boeing Aircraft, are examples of firms in a deficit cycle. The same problems keep recurring, and the firm fails to develop adequate mechanisms for learning. The firm often has problems in one or more phases of the learning process. The past inability to adjust yields more problems and fewer resources available to solve the next wave of problems, and the firm continues to deteriorate.

Major factors associated with deficit cycles are still being uncovered, but three are obvious from current research.[46] One is *organizational inertia*. It is very difficult to change organizations, and the larger the organization, the more inertia it often has. A second is *hubris*. Too few senior executives are willing to challenge their own actions or those of their firms because they see a history of success. They fail to recognize that yesterday's successful innovations are today's outmoded practices. A third is the issue of *detachment*. Executives often believe

> A **deficit cycle** is a pattern of deteriorating performance that is followed by even further deterioration.

lieve they can manage far-flung, diverse operations through analysis of reports and financial records. They lose touch and fail to make the needed unique and special adaptations required of all firms. One consultant has made millions advising executives to focus on improvement and to practice management by walking around the office to avoid detachment. For instance, it is clear Boeing executives lost touch with their major commercial aircraft operations in the Seattle area when they moved their headquarters to Chicago.

Benefit Cycles   Inertia, hubris, and detachment are common maladies, but they are not the automatic fate of all corporations. Firms can successfully co-evolve. As we have repeatedly demonstrated, managers are trying to reinvent their firms each and every day. They hope to initiate a **benefit cycle**—a pattern of successful adjustment followed by further improvements. Cisco and Microsoft are examples of firms experiencing a benefit cycle. In this cycle, the same problems do not keep recurring as the firm develops adequate mechanisms for learning. The firm has few major difficulties with the learning process, and managers continually attempt to improve knowledge acquisition, information distribution, information interpretation, and organizational memory.

Organizations that successfully co-evolve can ride the benefit cycle. Inertia can work for managers if they do not become overconfident, if they can stay directly involved with the key operations of the firm, and if they accurately forecast changes in the environment and technology. However, to keep riding the benefit cycle, managers need to understand their organizations from a cultural perspective. So we turn to this in the next chapter.

A **benefit cycle** is a pattern of successful adjustment followed by further improvements.

Chapter 18   Study Guide

Summary

What is organizational design, and how is it linked to strategy?

- Organizational design is the process of choosing and implementing a structural configuration for an organization.

- Organizational design is a way to implement the positioning of the firm in its environment.

- Organizational design provides a basis for a consistent stream of decisions.

- Strategy and organizational design are interrelated. The organization's design must support the strategy if the firm is to be successful.

- Smaller firms often adopt a simple structure because it works, is cheap, and stresses the influence of the leader.

- Operations technology and organizational design should be interrelated to ensure that the firm produces the desired goods and/or services.

- In highly intensive and small-batch technologies, organizational designs may tend toward adhocracy, a very decentralized form of operation.

What is information technology, and how is it used?

- Information technology is the combination of machines, artifacts, procedures, and systems used to gather, store, analyze, and disseminate information for translating it into knowledge.

- Information technology and organizational design can be interrelated. IT provides an opportunity to change the design by substitution, for learning, and to capture strategic advantages.

- IT has now progressed to the point where it can be a fundamental part of the pattern of decision and the adaptations firms make to the environment.

- Changes can occur from the bottom up so that firms can learn quickly.

- IT and e-business are inseparable, and e-business has become a part of the mix for many firms.

Can the design of the firm co-evolve with the environment?

- In more effective firms, environmental conditions and organizational design are interrelated as the firm is influenced by and influences its setting.

- In analyzing environments, both the general (background conditions) and specific (key actors and organizations) environments are important.

- The more complex the environment, the greater the demands on the organization, and firms should respond with more complex designs, such as the use of interfirm alliances.

- No firm stands alone; it needs to connect with others and develop partners to thrive.

- A virtual organization is an ever-shifting constellation of firms, with a lead corporation, that pool skills, resources, and experiences to thrive jointly.

- A virtual organization is used with extremes in environmental complexity and technological change.

How does a firm learn and continue to learn over time?

- Organizational learning is the process of knowledge acquisition, information distribution, information interpretation, and organizational memory used to adapt successfully to changing circumstances.

- Firms use mimicry, experience, vicarious learning, scanning, and grafting to acquire information.

- Firms establish mechanisms to convert information into knowledge.

- These mechanisms need to avoid self-serving interpretation and an overreliance on scripts and common myths.

- Firms retain information via individuals, transformation mechanisms, formal structure, physical structure, external archives, and their IT system.

- Organizational learning cycles are helpful in understanding organizational behavior because learning is not automatic.

- Noting the presence of a deficit cycle or a benefit cycle helps us understand how some organizations continually decline while others appear to be rising stars.

Key Terms

Adhocracy (p. 413)
Benefit cycle (p. 430)
Deficit cycle (p. 429)
Environmental complexity (p. 419)
Grafting (p. 426)
Information technology (p. 412)

Interfirm alliances (p. 421)
Managerial script (p. 427)
Mimicry (p. 424)
Operations technology (p. 412)
Organizational design (p. 408)

Organizational learning (p. 423)
Organizational myth (p. 427)
Scanning (p. 426)
Simple design (p. 411)
Virtual organization (p. 422)

Self-Test 18

Multiple Choice

1. The design of the organization needs to be adjusted to all but _____. (a) the environment of the firm (b) the strategy of the firm (c) the size of the firm (d) the operations and information technology of the firm

2. _____ is the combination of resources, knowledge, and techniques that creates a product or service output for an organization. (a) Information technology (b) Strategy (c) Organizational learning (c) Operations technology (d) The general environment

3. _____ is the combination of machines, artifacts, procedures, and systems used to gather, store, analyze, and disseminate information for translating it into knowledge. (a) The specific environment (b) Strategy (c) Operations technology (d) Information technology

4. Which of the following is an accurate statement about an adhocracy? (a) The design facilitates information exchange and learning. (b) There are many rules and policies. (c) Use of IT is always minimal. (d) It handles routine problems efficiently.

5. The set of cultural, economic, legal-political, and educational conditions in the areas in which a firm operates is called the _____. (a) task environment (b) specific environment (c) industry of the firm (d) general environment

6. The segment of the environment that refers to the other organizations with which an organization must interact in order to obtain inputs and dispose of outputs is called _____. (a) the general environment (b) the strategic environment (c) the learning environment (d) the specific environment

7. _____ are announced cooperative agreements or joint ventures between two independent firms. (a) Mergers (b) Acquisitions (c) Interfirm alliances (d) Adhocracies

8. The process of knowledge acquisitions, organizational retention, and distribution and interpretation of information is called _____. (a) vicarious learning (b) experience (c) organizational learning (d) an organizational myth

9. Three methods of vicarious learning are _____. (a) scanning, grafting, and contracting out (b) grafting, contracting out, and mimicry (c) scanning, grafting, and mimicry (d) experience, mimicry, and scanning

10. Three important factors that block information interpretation are _____. (a) de-

tachment, scanning, and common myths (b) self-serving interpretations, detachment, and common myths (c) managerial scripts, maladaptive specialization, and common myths (d) common myths, managerial scripts, and self-serving interpretations

11. A(n) organizational structure that emphasizes shared, decentralized decision making; extreme horizontal specialization; few levels of management; the virtual absence of formal controls; and few rules, policies, and procedures is called. (a) bureaucracy (b) professional bureaucracy (c) adhocracy (d) simple structure.

12. The process of knowledge acquisition, information distribution, information interpretation, and organizational retention is called (a) decision making (b) organizational learning (c) organizational design (d) a virtual organization

13. A(n)_____ is a series of well-known routines for problem identification and alternative generation and analysis common to managers within a firm. (a) managerial script (b) deficit cycle (c) benefit cycle (d) organizational myth

14. The process of choosing and implementing a structural configuration for an organization is called _____. (a) virtual organization (b) interfirm alliance (c) strategy (d) organizational design

15. A(n) _____ is a commonly held cause–effect relationship or assertion that cannot be empirically supported. (a) strategy (b) organizational myth (c) virtual organization (d) managerial script

Short Response

16. Explain why a large firm could not use a simple structure.

17. Explain the deployment of IT and its uses in organizations.

18. Describe the effect operations technology has on an organization from both Thompson's and Woodward's points of view.

19. What are the three primary determinants of environmental complexity?

Applications Essay

20. Why would Ford Motors want to shift to a matrix design organization for the design and development of cars and trucks but not do so in its manufacturing and assembly operations?

These learning activities from *The OB Skills Workbook* are suggested for Chapter 18.

OB in Action

CASE	EXPERIENTIAL EXERCISES	SELF-ASSESSMENTS
▪ 18. Mission Management and Trust	▪ 13. Tinkertoys ▪ 39. Organizations Alive! ▪ 41. Alien Invasion	▪ 2. A Twenty-First-Century Manager ▪ 9. Group Effectiveness ▪ 21. Organizational Design Preferences

Plus—special learning experiences from *The Jossey-Bass/Pfeiffer Classroom Collection*

Organizational Culture and Development

Chapter at a Glance

In this chapter we discuss the important topic of organizational culture and describe what it is, how it can be managed, and how a skilled manager can use organizational development to change it. As you read Chapter 19, *keep in mind these study questions*.

WHAT IS ORGANIZATIONAL CULTURE?

- Functions of Organizational Culture
- Dominant Culture, Subcultures, and Counter Cultures
- Valuing Cultural Diversity

HOW DO YOU UNDERSTAND AN ORGANIZATIONAL CULTURE?

- Levels of Cultural Analysis
- Stories, Rites, Rituals and Symbols
- Cultural Rules and Roles
- Shared Values, Meanings, and Organizational Myths
- National Cultural Influences

HOW CAN THE ORGANIZATIONAL CULTURE BE MANAGED?

- Management Philosophy and Strategy
- Building, Reinforcing, and Changing Culture

HOW CAN YOU USE ORGANIZATIONAL DEVELOPMENT TO IMPROVE THE FIRM?

- Underlying Assumptions of OD
- OD Values and Principles
- Action-Research Foundations of OD
- OD Interventions

REVIEW IN END-OF-CHAPTER STUDY GUIDE

Walk into the headquarters of R&R Partners, the Las Vegas–based advertising agency and lobbying firm, and it is immediately obvious that this is a fun place to work.[1] A large sign over the entry courtyard says "Relax, this isn't brain surgery. "The handles to the doors are constructed out of the many advertising awards the agency has received. There is clearly an irreverent attitude at R&R. Yet underneath the fun atmosphere is a strong appreciation for the role that all the employees have in the success of the organization. Billy Vassiliadis, CEO, ensures that the organization's dedication to R&R is reflected in more than just words. R&R provides some of the best health care and child care coverage in the industry and invests in employees with educational reimbursements even for those taking PhD-level courses. In fact, R&R was recently voted one of the top 10 places to work in Nevada. Within R&R there is a creative culture that permeates the entire organization, as everyone is responsible for creating new ideas and campaigns. For instance, when new ideas are needed, everyone at R&R is invited into the agency's "war room" to brainstorm. These brainstorming sessions are called SWARM. In a typical SWARM, an account team would present an issue. Everyone from the CEO to the receptionist is then invited to give his or her ideas.

> ## "Relax, this isn't brain surgery."

Organizational Culture

To be successful in the advertising business, it is critical that companies have fresh and innovative ideas to market clients' goods and services. R&R Partners is a successful ad agency that is responsible for such edgy tag lines to lure tourists to Las Vegas as "What Happens in Vegas Stays in Vegas." To continue its success, R&R relies on its culture to provide the competitive edge.

▪ **Organizational** or **corporate culture** is the system of shared actions, values, and beliefs that develops within an organization and guides the behavior of its members.

Organizational or **corporate culture** is the system of shared actions, values, and beliefs that develops within an organization and guides the behavior of its members.[2] In the business setting, this system is often referred to as the corporate culture. Just as no two individual personalities are the same, no two organizational cultures are identical. Most significantly, management scholars and consultants increasingly believe that cultural differences can have a major impact on the performance of organizations and the quality of work life experienced by their members, as illustrated in the opening example of R&R Partners.

Functions of Organizational Culture

Through their collective experience, members of an organization solve two extremely important survival issues.[3] The first is the question of external adaptation: What precisely needs to be accomplished, and how can it be done? The second is the question of internal integration: How do members resolve the daily problems associated with living and working together?

External Adaptation **External adaptation** involves reaching goals and dealing with outsiders. The issues involved are tasks to be accomplished, methods used to achieve the goals, and methods of coping with success and failure. Through their shared experiences, members may develop common views that help guide their day-to-day activities. Organizational members need to know the real mission of the organization, not just the pronouncements to key constituencies, such as stockholders. Members will naturally develop an understanding of how they contribute to the mission via interaction. This view may emphasize the importance of human resources, the role of employees as cogs in a machine, or a cost to be reduced.

Closely related to the organization's mission and view of its contribution are the questions of responsibility, goals, and methods. For instance, at 3M, employees believe that it is their responsibility to innovate and contribute creatively. They see these responsibilities reflected in achieving the goal of developing new and improved products and processes.

Each collection of individuals in an organization also tends to (1) separate more important from less important external forces; (2) develop ways to measure their accomplishments; and (3) create explanations for why goals are not always met. At Dell, the direct retailer of computers and consumer electronics, managers, for example, have moved away from judging their progress against specific targets to estimating the degree to which they are moving a development process forward. Instead of blaming a poor economy or upper-level managers for the firm's failure to reach a goal, Dell managers have set hard goals that are difficult to reach and have redoubled their efforts to improve participation and commitment.[4]

The final issues in external adaptation deal with two important, but often neglected, aspects of coping with external reality. First, individuals need to develop acceptable ways of telling outsiders just how good they really are. At 3M, for example, employees talk about the quality of their products and the many new, useful products they have brought to the market. Second, individuals must collectively know when to admit defeat. At 3M, the answer is easy for new projects: at the beginning of the development process, members establish "drop" points at which to quit the development effort and redirect it.[5]

In sum, external adaptation involves answering important instrumental or goal-related questions concerning coping with reality: What is the real mission? How do we contribute? What are our goals? How do we reach our goals? What external forces are important? How do we measure results? What do we do if specific targets are not met? How do we tell others how good we are? When do we quit?

Internal Integration The corporate culture also provides answers to the problems of internal integration. **Internal integration** deals with the creation of a collective identity and with finding ways of matching methods of working and living together.

The process of internal integration often begins with the establishment of a unique identity; that is, each collection of individuals and each subculture within the organization develops some type of unique definition of itself. Through dialogue and interaction, members begin to characterize their world. They may see it as malleable or fixed, filled with opportunity or threatening. Real progress toward innovation can begin when group members collectively believe that they

■ **External adaptation** involves reaching goals and dealing with outsiders. Issues involved are tasks to be accomplished, methods used to achieve the goals, and methods of coping with success and failure.

■ **Internal integration** deals with the creation of a collective identity and with ways of working and living together.

can change important parts of the world around them and that what appears to be a threat is actually an opportunity for change.[6]

Three important aspects of working together are (1) deciding who is a member and who is not; (2) developing an informal understanding of acceptable and unacceptable behavior; and (3) separating friends from enemies. These are important questions for managers as well. A key to effective total quality management, for instance, is that subgroups in the organization need to view their immediate supervisors as members of the group. The immediate supervisor is expected to represent the group to friendly higher managers. Of course, should management not be seen as friendly, the process of improving quality could quickly break down.

To work together effectively, individuals need to decide collectively how to allocate power, status, and authority. They need to establish a shared understanding of who will get rewards and sanctions for specific types of actions. Too often, managers fail to recognize these important aspects of internal integration. For example, a manager may fail to explain the basis for a promotion and to show why this reward, the status associated with it, and the power given to the newly promoted individual are consistent with commonly shared beliefs.

Collections of individuals also need to work out acceptable ways to communicate and to develop guidelines for friendships. Although these aspects of internal integration may appear esoteric, they are vital. To function effectively as a team, individuals must recognize that some members will be closer than others; friendships are inevitable. However, the basis for friendships can be inappropriately restricted. At the U.S. Department of the Interior, for example, budget cuts had a beneficial effect. At one time, the political appointees could be found eating together in their own executive dining room. Now, all employees eat at the Interior Department lunchroom, and even the political appointees are making new friends with the career civil servants.

Why do we go from individual saints...

...to groups of scoundrels?

Its the culture! It makes us do things we would not do alone.

Ethics Quality, Inc.

ETHICS AND SOCIAL RESPONSIBILITY

ETHICS IN AN ORGANIZATION'S CULTURE

Ethics Quality Inc. provides a quick test for you to see whether a firm has an ethical culture. Their Web test has 10 items, and the firm will also provide a more comprehensive survey for employees. The 10 items in their yes-or-no format are:

1. Are you proud of your group's ethics?
2. Do the group's ethics work positively for everyone?
3. Is there cooperation in resolving problems and creating opportunities?
4. Is the group improving processes routinely?
5. Do improvements matter and/or last?
6. Is there serious resistance to change?
7. Is there sufficient trust and openness to solve problems?
8. Are there any damaging standards?
9. Does the leadership set good examples and reward good ethics?
10. Are bad ethics risking or hurting business results?

Question: Would these questions be useful in deciding where you took your first job?

Answering these questions of internal integration helps individuals develop a shared identity and a collective commitment. It may well lead to longer-term stability and provide a lens for members to make sense of their part of the world.

In sum, internal integration involves answers to important questions associated with living together. What is our unique identity? How do we view the world? Who is a member? How do we allocate power, status, and authority? How do we communicate? What is the basis for friendship? Answering these questions is important to organizational members because the organization is more than a place to work; it is a place where individuals spend much of their adult life.[7]

Dominant Culture, Subcultures, and Countercultures

Smaller firms often have a single dominant culture with a unitary set of shared actions, values, and beliefs. Most larger organizations contain several subcultures as well as one or more countercultures.[8]

Subcultures **Subcultures** are groups of individuals with a unique pattern of values and a philosophy that is not inconsistent with the organization's dominant values and philosophy.[9] Interestingly, strong subcultures are often found in high-performance task forces, teams, and special project groups in organizations. The culture emerges to bind individuals working intensely together to accomplish a specific task. For example, there are strong subcultures of stress engineers and liaison engineers in the Boeing Renton plant. These highly specialized groups must solve knotty technical issues to ensure that Boeing planes are safe. Though distinct, these groups of engineers share in the dominant values of Boeing.

> **Subcultures** are unique patterns of values and philosophies within a group that are consistent with the dominant culture of the larger organization or social system.

Countercultures In contrast, **countercultures** have a pattern of values and a philosophy that reject the surrounding culture.[10] When Stephen Jobs reentered Apple computer as its CEO, he quickly formed a counterculture within Apple. Over the next 18 months, numerous clashes occurred as the followers of the old CEO (Gil Amelio) fought to maintain their place and the old culture. Jobs won and Apple won. His counterculture became dominant.

> **Countercultures** are the patterns of values and philosophies that outwardly reject those of the larger organization or social system.

Every large organization imports potentially important subcultural groupings when it hires employees from the larger society. In North America, for instance, subcultures and countercultures may naturally form based on ethnic, racial, gender, generational, or locational similarities. In Japanese organizations, subcultures often form based on the date of graduation from a university, gender, or geographic location. In European firms, ethnicity and language play an important part in developing subcultures, as does gender. In many less developed nations, language, education, religion, or family social status are often grounds for forming societally popular subcultures and countercultures.

Within an organization, mergers and acquisitions may produce adjustment problems. Employers and managers of an acquired firm may hold values and assumptions that are quite inconsistent with those of the acquiring firm. This is known as the "clash of corporate cultures."[11] As more firms globalize and use mergers and acquisitions to expand, often they must cope with both importing subcultures and the clash of corporate cultures. For instance, when Daimler Benz said it was merging with Chrysler Corporation, it was billed as a merger of equals. The new combined firm would have a global reach. The corporate culture clash came quickly, however, when Chrysler managers and employees real-

Research Insight
A Culturally Competitive Supply Chain

The link between corporate culture and performance is often quite indirect and complex. Yet researchers generally suggest that there are distinctive aspects of corporate culture that might be
related to performance. Recent research extends
the notion of developing culture to the selection
of firms that you buy from and sell to. We have
repeatedly suggested that firms do not act alone
but in cooperation with others. One way they cooperate is through supply chains or networks of
firms that transform raw materials into finished
products. Are there elements of corporate culture
that separate more from less effective supply

chains? This was the question asked by Hult,
Ketchen, and Nichols. The short answer: yes.
When all members of a supply chain emphasize
the cultural aspects of entrepreneurship, innovativeness, and learning, the whole supply chain is
rated higher on cultural competitiveness. As cultural competitiveness increases, the time it takes
from the start of a purchasing process to completion is substantially reduced.

Reference: G. T. Hult, D. J. Ketchen, and E. L. Nichols, "An
Examination of Cultural Competitiveness and Order Fulfillment Cycle Time Within Supply Chains," *Academy of Management Journal* 45 (2002):567–577.

ized that Daimler executives would control the new combination and forge it
around the German partner.

The difficulty with importing groupings from the larger societies lies in the
relevance these subgroups have to the organization as a whole. At the one extreme, senior managers can merely accept these divisions and work within the
confines of the larger culture. There are three primary difficulties with this approach. First, subordinated groups, such as members of a specific religion or ethnic group, are likely to form into a counterculture and to work more diligently to
change their status than to better the firm. Second, the firm may find it extremely
difficult to cope with broader cultural changes. For instance, in the United States
the expected treatment of women, ethnic minorities, and the disabled has
changed dramatically over the last 20 years. Firms that merely accept old customs and prejudices have experienced a greater loss of key personnel and increased communication difficulties, as well as greater interpersonal conflict, than
have their more progressive counterparts. Third, firms that accept and build on
natural divisions from the larger culture may find it extremely difficult to develop
sound international operations. For example, many Japanese firms have had
substantial difficulty adjusting to the equal treatment of women in their U.S. operations.[12]

Valuing Cultural Diversity

Managers can work to eradicate all naturally occurring subcultures and countercultures. Firms are groping to develop what Taylor Cox calls the multicultural organization. The multicultural organization is a firm that values diversity but systematically works to block the transfer of societally based subcultures into the
fabric of the organization.[13] Because Cox focuses on some problems unique to

the United States, his prescription for change may not apply to organizations located in other countries with much more homogeneous populations.

Cox suggests a five-step program for developing the multicultural organization. First, the organization should develop pluralism with the objective of multibased socialization. To accomplish this objective, members of different naturally occurring groups need to school one another to increase knowledge and information and to eliminate stereotyping. Second, the firm should fully integrate its structure so that there is no direct relationship between a naturally occurring group and any particular job—for instance, there are no distinct male or female jobs. Third, the firm must integrate the informal networks by eliminating barriers and increasing participation. That is, it must break down existing societally based informal groups. Fourth, the organization should break the linkage between naturally occurring group identity and the identity of the firm. In other words, the firm should not be just for the young, old, men, women, and so on. Fifth, the organization must actively work to eliminate interpersonal conflict based on either the group identity or the natural backlash of the largest societally based grouping.

The key problems associated with fully implementing Cox's program are separating the firm from the larger culture in which it must operate and eliminating some societally based groupings that are relevant for achieving the firm's goals. For instance, the U.S. military is barred from fully implementing Cox's recommendations simply because it is not currently legal to put women into all combat roles. The issue of generational groupings provides another example. Implementing Cox's recommendations would call for 20-year-olds to be represented proportionally in the senior-management ranks; most corporations want and need the judgment honed by experience. However, astute senior managers are recognizing that they may be out of touch with younger employees. For example, Robert Hausman, chairman of Coventry Industries of Boca Raton, Florida, routinely meets young employees once a month over pizza.[14]

Dame Anita Roddick and the Body Shop

While Dame Anita Roddick started the first Body Shop out of economic necessity, she has always felt that business has the power to do good. The Body Shop's mission opens with, "To dedicate our business to the pursuit of social and environmental change." She believes that good business is about putting forth solutions, not just opposition. And her solutions have revolutionized the cosmetics products of the Body Shop. Little wonder the Body Shop has such a unique culture.

Understanding Organizational Cultures

Not all aspects of organizational culture are readily apparent. Other aspects are deeply buried in the shared experience of organizational members. It may take years to understand some deeper aspects of the culture. This complexity has led some to examine different levels of analysis ranging from easily observable to deeply hidden.

Levels of Cultural Analysis

There are three important levels of cultural analysis in organizations: observable culture, shared values, and common cultural assumptions.[15] These levels may be envisioned as layers. The deeper one gets, the more difficult it is to discover the culture but the more important an aspect becomes. Figure 19.1 illustrates the observable aspects of culture, shared values, and underlying assumptions.

The first level concerns *observable culture*, or "the way we do things around here." Important parts of an organization's culture emerge from the collective experience of its members. These emergent aspects of the culture help make it

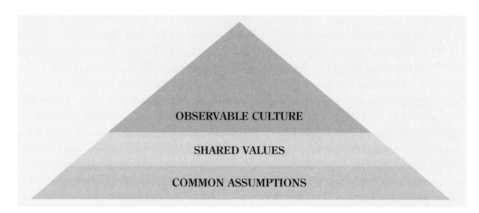

Figure 19.1   Three levels of analysis in studying organizational culture.

unique and may well provide a competitive advantage for the organization. Some of these aspects may be directly observed in day-to-day practices. Others may have to be discovered—for example, by asking members to tell stories of important incidents in the history of the organization. We often learn about the unique aspects of the organizational culture through descriptions of specific events.[16] By observing employee actions, listening to stories, and asking members to interpret what is going on, one can begin to understand the organization's culture. The observable culture includes the unique stories, ceremonies, and corporate rituals that make up the history of the firm or a group within the firm.

PEOPLE AND TECHNOLOGY

PEOPLE, NOT TECHNOLOGY, GOT THE COMPANY RESTARTED

When the terrorists plunged their captured airliners into the World Trade Center on September 11, 2001, the aftermath brought out the best in many survivors. The employees at Cantor Fitzgerald are but one example. Cantor Fitzgerald is a financial services firm. Its eSpeed arm operates a computerized global private network for the buying and selling of financial and nonfinancial products. Cantor Fitzgerald's main offices were on floors 101–105 of the World Trade Center's north tower. After the collapse, some 700 of their 1,000 employees were never found. In the aftermath, Howard Lutnick, chairman of eSpeed and the senior surviving executive of Cantor, could not believe the response of the survivors. Immediately after the tragedy, Cantor and eSpeed employees demanded that they return to work. Laboring continuously in borrowed offices, they used backup equipment and systems as well as their offices in Europe and Asia to restart their high-tech operation. Although they lost their headquarters and too many colleagues to even contemplate, Cantor and its eSpeed unit were back operating one of the most sophisticated computer networks in the world by the restart of the stock exchanges on September 17. It was not the technology that allowed the firm to survive; it was dedicated colleagues who refused to surrender.

Question: Why was returning Cantor Fitzgerald to operating status so important for the employees?

The second level of analysis recognizes that *shared values* can play a critical part in linking people together and can provide a powerful motivational mechanism for members of the culture. Many consultants suggest that organizations should develop a "dominant and coherent set of shared values."[17] The term *shared* in cultural analysis implies that the group is a whole. Every member may not agree with the shared values, but they have all been exposed to them and have often been told they are important. At R&R Partners, for example, *creativity* is part of everyone's vocabulary.

At the deepest level of cultural analysis are *common cultural assumptions*; these are the taken-for-granted truths that collections of corporate members share as a result of their joint experience. It is often extremely difficult to isolate these patterns, but doing so helps explain why culture invades every aspect of organizational life.

Stories, Rites, Rituals, and Symbols

To begin understanding a corporate culture, it is often easiest to start with stories. Organizations are rich with stories of winners and losers, successes and failures. Perhaps one of the most important stories concerns the founding of the organization. The founding story often contains the lessons learned from the heroic efforts of an embattled entrepreneur, whose vision may still guide the firm. The story of the founding may be so embellished that it becomes a **saga**— a heroic account of accomplishments.[18] Sagas are important because they are used to tell new members the real mission of the organization, how the organization operates, and how individuals can fit into the company. Rarely is the founding story totally accurate, and it often glosses over some of the more negative aspects of the founders. Such is the case with Monterey Pasta.

> **Sagas** are embellished heroic accounts of the story of the founding of an organization.

On its Web site, Monterey Pasta says of its history, "The Monterey Pasta Company was launched from a 400-square-foot storefront on Lighthouse Avenue in Monterey, California in 1989.... The founders started their small fresh pasta company in response to the public's growing interest in healthy gourmet foods. Customers were increasingly excited about fresh pasta given its superior quality and nutritional value, as well as ease of preparation.... The company soon accepted its first major grocery account.... In 1993, the company completed its first public offering." The Web site fails to mention two other interesting aspects of the firm. First, as of 2001, it was one of the 30 fastest-growing small firms on the West Coast. Second, it does not mention the founders or some early mistakes. For example, an unsuccessful venture into the restaurant business in the mid-1990s provided a significant distraction, and substantial losses were incurred before the company was refocused on its successful retail business. But why ruin a good founding story?

If you have job experience, you may well have heard stories concerning the following questions: How will the boss react to a mistake? Can someone move from the bottom to the top of the company? What will get me fired? These are common story topics in many organizations.[19] Often, the stories provide valuable hidden information about who is more equal than others, whether jobs are secure, and how things are really controlled. In essence, the stories begin to suggest how organizational members view the world and live together.

> **Rites** are standardized and recurring activities used at special times to influence the behaviors and understanding of organizational members.

Some of the most obvious aspects of organizational culture are rites and rituals.[20] **Rites** are standardized and recurring activities that are used at special times to influence the behaviors and understanding of organizational members; **rituals**

> **Rituals** are systems of rites.

are systems of rites. It is common, for example, for Japanese workers and managers to start their workdays together with group exercises and singing of the "company song." Separately, the exercises and song are rites. Together, they form part of a ritual. In other settings, such as Mary Kay Cosmetics, scheduled ceremonies reminiscent of the Miss America pageant (a ritual) are used regularly to spotlight positive work achievements and reinforce high-performance expectations with awards, including gold and diamond pins and fur stoles.

Rituals and rites may be unique to particular groups within the organization. Subcultures often arise from the type of technology deployed by the unit, the specific function being performed, and the specific collection of specialists in the unit. The boundaries of the subculture may well be maintained by a unique language. Often, the language of a subculture, and its rituals and rites, emerge from the group as a form of jargon. In some cases, the special language starts to move outside the firm and begins to enter the larger society. For instance, look at Microsoft Word's specialized language, with such words as *hyperlink frames* and *autoformat*. It's a good thing they also provide a Help button defining each.

Another observable aspect of corporate culture centers on the symbols found in organizations. A **cultural symbol** is any object, act, or event that serves to transmit cultural meaning. Good examples are the corporate uniforms worn by UPS and Federal Express delivery personnel. Although many such symbols are quite visible, their importance and meaning may not be.

> ▨ A **cultural symbol** is any object, act, or event that serves to transmit cultural meaning.

Cultural Rules and Roles

Organizational culture often specifies when various types of actions are appropriate and where individual members stand in the social system. These cultural rules and roles are part of the normative controls of the organization and emerge from its daily routines.[21] For instance, the timing, presentation, and methods of communicating authoritative directives are often quite specific to each organization. In one firm, meetings may be forums for dialogue and discussion, where managers set agendas and then let others offer new ideas, critically examine alternatives, and fully participate. The example of a SWARM at R&R Partners in the opening illustrates one form of cultural rules and roles. In another firm, the "rules" may be quite different. The manager could go into the meeting with fixed expectations. Private conservations prior to the meeting might be the place for any new ideas or critical examination. Here, the meeting is a forum for letting others know what is being done and for passing out orders on what to do in the future.

Shared Values, Meanings, and Organizational Myths

To describe more fully the culture of an organization, it is necessary to go deeper than the observable aspects. To many researchers and managers, shared common values lie at the very heart of organizational culture.

Shared Values   Shared values help turn routine activities into valuable and important actions, tie the corporation to the important values of society, and possibly provide a very distinctive source of competitive advantage. In organizations, what works for one person is often taught to new members as the correct way to think and feel. Important values are then attributed to these solutions to everyday problems. By linking values and actions, the organization taps into some of the strongest and deepest realms of the individual. The tasks a person performs are given not only meaning but value: what one does is not only workable but correct, right, and important.

Some successful organizations share some common cultural characteristics.[22] Organizations with "strong cultures" possess a broadly and deeply shared value system. Unique, shared values can provide a strong corporate identity, enhance collective commitment, provide a stable social system, and reduce the need for formal and bureaucratic controls. A strong culture can be a double-edged sword, however. A strong culture and value system can reinforce a singular view of the organization and its environment. If dramatic changes are needed, it may be very difficult to change the organization. General Motors may have a "strong" culture, for example, but the firm faces enormous difficulty in its attempts to adapt its ways to a dynamic and highly competitive environment.

In many corporate cultures, one finds a series of common assumptions known to most everyone in the corporation: "We are different." "We are better at...." "We have unrecognized talents." Cisco Systems provides an excellent example. Senior managers often share common assumptions, such as "We are good stewards"/"We are competent managers"/"We are practical innovators." Like values, such assumptions become reflected in the organizational culture. The Effective Manager 19.1 discusses assumptions and other elements of a strong organizational culture.

> **THE EFFECTIVE MANAGER 19.1**
>
> **Elements of Strong Corporate Cultures**
>
> - A widely shared real understanding of what the firm stands for, often embodied in slogans
> - A concern for individuals over rules, policies, procedures, and adherence to job duties
> - A recognition of heroes whose actions illustrate the company's shared philosophy and concerns
> - A belief in ritual and ceremony as important to members and to building a common identity
> - A well-understood sense of the informal rules and expectations so that employees and managers understand what is expected of them
> - A belief that what employees and managers do is important and that it is important to share information and ideas

Shared Meanings   When observing the actions within a firm, it is important to keep in mind the three levels of analysis we mentioned earlier. What you see as an outside observer may not be what organizational members experience because members may link actions to values and unstated assumptions. For instance, in the aftermath of 9/11 many saw crane operators moving wreckage from an 18-acre pile of rubble into waiting trucks. Farther up the worksite, many saw steelworkers cutting beams while police seemed to stand around talking to a few firemen. If you probe the values and assumptions about what these individuals are doing, however, you get an entirely different picture. They were not just hauling away the remnants of the twin towers at the World Trade Center complex. They were rebuilding America. These workers had infused a larger shared meaning—or sense of broader purpose—into their tasks. Through interaction with one another, and as reinforced by the rest of their organizations and the larger society, their work had deeper meaning. In this deeper sense, organizational culture is a "shared" set of meanings and perceptions. In most corporations these shared meanings and perceptions may not be as dramatic as those shared at Ground Zero, yet in most firms employees create and learn a deeper aspect of their culture.[23]

Organizational Myths   In many firms, the management philosophy is supported by a series of organizational myths. **Organizational myths** are unproven and often unstated beliefs that are accepted uncritically. In a study of safety in

An **organizational myth** is an unproven and often unstated belief that is accepted uncritically.

nuclear power plants, senior managers were asked whether they felt there was a trade-off between safety and efficiency. The response was clear: a safe plant is an efficient plant. Yet most of these executives had seen data showing that measures of safety and efficiency were quite independent. To admit there was a trade-off raised the issue of making choices between efficiency and safety. All wanted to believe that to do one was to promote the other.[24]

Whereas some may scoff at these organizational myths and want to see rational, hard-nosed analysis replace mythology, each firm needs a series of managerial myths.[25] Myths allow executives to redefine impossible problems into more manageable components. Myths can facilitate experimentation and creativity, and they allow managers to govern. For instance, senior executives are not just decision makers or rational allocators of resources. All organization members hope these individuals will also be fair, just, and compassionate.

National Cultural Influences

Widely held common assumptions may often be traced to the larger culture of the corporation's host society.[26] The difference between Sony's corporate emphasis on group achievements and Zenith's emphasis on individual engineering excellence, for example, can be traced to the Japanese emphasis on collective action versus the U.S. emphasis on individualism.

CULTURES AND THE GLOBAL WORKFORCE

FORGING ONE COMMON CORPORATE CULTURE

As owner Fred Fernandez looked on, Gloria Johnson pulled the soot-covered leather coat from its sealed container. Was there any question that the blackened coat could not be saved and restored? Not really. A long visit in the Venus Cleaners' Ozone Room, and two cleanings later the coat looked like new. This is no ordinary cleaners. Fred Fernandez has welded a diverse staff of immigrants and long-time Detroit residents into a cohesive, highly skilled, dedicated group. They believe they can clean most anything, and often they do. Although just a small business, Venus is the largest fire restoration cleaning facility in the state. Insurance companies throughout southeast Michigan bring in clothes from fires and natural disasters for its unique services. Customers return because of the quality. And employees stay because Fred knows how to forge a common corporate culture from individuals born and raised in different countries.

Question. How would you create a common culture for a nationally diverse collection of employees?

National cultural values may also become embedded in the expectations of important organizational constituencies and in generally accepted solutions to problems. When moving across national cultures, managers need to be sensitive to national cultural differences so that their actions do not violate common assumptions in the underlying national culture. In Japan and Western Europe, for example, executives are expected to work cooperatively with government officials on an informal basis. Informal business–government relations that are perfectly acceptable in these countries are considered influence peddling in the United States.

Inappropriate actions that violate common assumptions drawn from national culture can have an important impact on performance and may alienate organizational members, even if managers have the best intentions. To improve morale at General Electric's new French subsidiary, Chi. Generale de Radiologie, American managers invited all the European managers to a "get-acquainted" meeting near Paris. The Americans gave out colorful T-shirts with the GE slogan, "Go for One," a typical maneuver in many American training programs. The French resented the T-shirts. One outspoken individual said, "It was like Hitler was back, forcing us to wear uniforms. It was humiliating."

Managing Organizational Culture

Good managers are able to reinforce and support an existing strong culture; good managers are also able to help build resilient cultures in situations where they are absent. Two broad strategies for managing the corporate culture have received considerable attention in the OB literature. One strategy calls for managers to help modify observable culture, shared values, and common assumptions directly. Normally the focus is on altering how the firm deals with issues of external adaptation. A second strategy involves the use of organizational development techniques to modify specific elements of the culture. Here the questions of both external adaptation and internal integration are addressed. First, we turn to reinforcing a strong culture and building resilience.

Management Philosophy and Strategy

The process of managing organizational culture calls for a clear understanding of the organizational subculture at the top and a firm recognition of what can and cannot be changed. The first step in managing an organizational culture is for management to recognize its own subculture. Key aspects of the top-management subculture are often referred to in the OB literature by the term *management philosophy*. A **management philosophy** links key goal-related strategic issues with key collaboration issues and comes up with a series of general ways by which the firm will manage its affairs.[27] A well-developed management philosophy is important because it links strategy to a more basic understanding of how the firm is to operate. Specifically, it (1) establishes generally understood boundaries for all members of the firm, (2) provides a consistent way of approaching new and novel situations, and (3) helps hold individuals together by assuring them of a known path toward success. In other words, it is the way in which top management addresses the questions of external adaptation. For instance, Cisco Systems has a clearly identified management philosophy linking the strategic concerns of growth, profitability, and customer service with observable aspects of culture and selected desired underlying values. In the case of Cisco Systems' growth and profitability, customer service is linked to (1) empowering employees to generate the best ideas quickly and to implement them successfully, (2) hiring the best people because it's the ideas and intellectual assets

Herman Miller

Herman Miller, the Zeeland, Michigan–based furniture manufacturer, consistently gains high marks from those rating corporate citizenship. Known for its employee-friendly culture, the company is over 15 percent employee owned. Its strong emphasis on continuous cultural development is well stated on its Web site: "Our employees share a commitment to innovation and uncompromising participative management, and environmental stewardship."

Management philosophy is a philosophy that links key goal-related issues with key collaboration issues to come up with general ways by which the firm will manage its affairs.

Leaders on Leadership

WAMULLIANS AT THE UN-BANK

Kerry Killinger is chairman, president, and CEO of Washington Mutual. Under his leadership since the early 1990s, this consumer-oriented bank has grown from a sleepy retail bank in Seattle to a national powerhouse by emphasizing service to retail bank customers. Instead of servicing corporations or corporate investors, WaMu stressed checking accounts, mortgages, and the like with ordinary people. With rapid growth accompanied by several acquisitions, Kerry is working hard to make the corporate culture of WaMu consistent with its new branch banks. These un-banks look more like a fashion store than a bank—there are no teller windows or even cash drawers, since all the money is distributed via a cash machine. Most have a place for kids to play. In a whole series of "brand rallies," Kerry and key managers run trivia games, don silly hats, and talk about developing a fun place to work that really serves customers. Kerry wants all to know what it means to be a Wamullian—service, friendliness, and efficiency are stressed along with the less serious business of learning how to work together in a fun atmosphere.

Question: What else would you like to know about Kerry Killinger and how he is managing WaMu's culture?

of these colleagues that drive success, and (3) developing and disseminating information to compete in the world of ideas. While elements of a management philosophy may be formally documented in a corporate plan or statement of business philosophy, it is the well-understood fundamentals these written documents signify that form the heart of a well-developed management philosophy.

Building, Reinforcing, and Changing Culture

Managers can modify the visible aspects of culture, such as the language, stories, rites, rituals, and sagas. They can change the lessons to be drawn from common stories and even encourage individuals to see the reality they see. Because of their positions, senior managers can interpret situations in new ways and can adjust the meanings attached to important corporate events. They can create new rites and rituals. This takes time and enormous energy, but the long-run benefits can also be great.

Top managers, in particular, can set the tone for a culture and for cultural change. Managers at Aetna Life and Casualty Insurance built on its humanistic traditions to provide basic skills to highly motivated but underqualified individuals. Even in the highly cost-competitive steel industry, Chairperson F. Kenneth Iverson of Nucor built on basic entrepreneurial values in U.S. society to reduce the number of management levels by half. And at Procter & Gamble, Richard Nicolosi evoked the shared values for greater participation in decision making dramatically to improve creativity and innovation.

Each of these examples illustrates how managers can help foster a culture that provides answers to important questions concerning external adaptation and internal integration. Recent work on the linkages between corporate culture and financial performance reaffirms the importance of an emphasis on helping employees adjust to the environment. It also suggests that this emphasis alone is not sufficient. Neither is an emphasis solely on stockholders or customers associated with long-term economic performance. Instead, managers must work to emphasize all three issues simultaneously. This emphasis on customers, stockholders, and employees comes at a cost of emphasizing management. Large offices, multimillion-dollar salaries, golden parachutes (protections for executives if the firm is bought by others), as well as the executive plane, dining room, and country club are out.

Early research on culture and cultural change often emphasized direct attempts to alter the values and assumptions of individuals by resocializing them—that is, trying to change their hearts so that their minds and actions would follow.[28] The goal was to establish a clear, consistent organizationwide consensus. More recent work suggests that this unified approach of working through values may not be either possible or desirable.[29]

Trying to change people's values from the top down without also changing how the organization operates and recognizing the importance of individuals does not work very well. Take another look at the example of Cisco Systems. Here managers realize that maintaining a dynamic, change-oriented culture is a mix of managerial actions, decisions about technology, and initiatives from all employees. The values are not set and imposed from someone on high. The shared values emerge, and they are not identical across all of Cisco's operating sites. For instance, subtle but important differences emerge across their operations in Silicon Valley, the North Carolina operation, and the Australian setting.

It is also a mistake for managers to attempt to revitalize an organization by dictating major changes and ignoring shared values. Although things may change a bit on the surface, a deeper look often shows whole departments resisting change and many key people unwilling to learn new ways. Such responses may indicate that the managers responsible are insensitive to the effects of their proposed changes on shared values. They fail to ask whether the changes are contrary to the important values of participants within the firm, a challenge to historically important corporatewide assumptions, and inconsistent with important common assumptions derived from the national culture, outside the firm. Note the example of Stephen Jobs at Apple earlier in this chapter. He did not make all the changes. Rather, he worked with others to make changes in strategy, structure, products, and marketing and to build on deep-seated common assumptions that long-term employees shared. The Effective Manager 19.2 provides some key characteristics managers should foster in Internet companies.

THE EFFECTIVE MANAGER 19.2

Fostering an Effective Internet Culture

To cope with the constant rapid changes in e-business, some recommend developing an Internet culture. Key distinguishing characteristics of such a culture include the following:

- Embracing open communication in all forms and in all possible media
- Emphasizing constant learning and individual development
- Stressing leadership that reinforces courage and risk taking

Organizational Development

Organizational development (OD) is the application of behavioral science knowledge in a long-range effort to improve an organization's ability to cope with change in its external environment and increase its problem-solving capabilities.

To keep the culture fresh and competitive, the challenge today is to engage in a process of continuous self-assessment and planned change in order to stay abreast of problems and opportunities in a complex and demanding environment. **Organizational development (OD)** is a comprehensive approach to planned change that is designed to improve the overall effectiveness of organizations. Formally defined, OD is the application of behavioral science knowledge in a long-range effort to improve an organization's ability to cope with change in its external environment and to increase its internal problem-solving capabilities.[30] It is designed to work on issues of both external adaptation and internal integration.

Organizational development is used to improve performance in organizations of many types, sizes, and settings. It includes a set of tools with which any manager who is concerned about achieving and maintaining high levels of productivity will want to be familiar. Because of its comprehensive nature and scientific foundations, OD was frequently implemented with the aid of an external consultant. As OD techniques have been combined with a better understanding of organizational culture, its basic concepts can and should be used routinely by all managers.

Importantly, OD seeks to achieve change in such a way that the organization's members become more active and confident in taking similar steps to maintain the culture and longer-run organizational effectiveness. A large part of any OD program's success in this regard rests with its assumptions, values, and action research foundations.

Underlying Assumptions of OD

The organizational development foundations for achieving change are rooted in underlying assumptions about individuals, groups, and organizations. *At the individual level*, OD is guided by principles that reflect an underlying respect for people and their capabilities. It assumes that individual needs for growth and development are most likely to be satisfied in a supportive and challenging work environment. It also assumes that most people are capable of taking responsibility for their own actions and of making positive contributions to organizational performance.

At the group level, OD is guided by principles that reflect a belief that groups can be good for both people and organizations. It assumes that groups help their members satisfy important individual needs and can also be helpful in supporting organizational objectives. And it assumes that effective groups can be created by people working in collaboration to meet individual and organizational needs.

At the organizational level, OD is guided by principles that show a respect for the complexity of an organization as a system of interdependent parts. It assumes that changes in one part of the organization will affect other parts as well. And it assumes that organizational structures and jobs can be designed to meet the needs of individuals and groups as well as those of the organization.

OD Values and Principles

Organizational development offers a systematic approach to planned change in organizations that addresses two main goals: outcome goals (mainly issues of external adaptation) and process goals (mainly issues of internal integration). Outcome goals include achieving improvements in task performance by improving external adaptation capabilities. In OD, these goals focus on what is actually accomplished through individual and group efforts. Process goals include achieving improvements in such things as communication, interaction, and decision making among an organization's members. These goals focus on how well people work together, and they stress improving internal integration.

In pursuit of these goals, OD is intended to help organizations and their members by (1) creating an open problem-solving climate throughout an organization, (2) supplementing formal authority with that of knowledge and competence, (3) moving decision making to points where relevant information is available, (4) building trust and maximizing collaboration among individuals and groups, (5) increasing the sense of organizational "ownership" among members, and (6) allowing people to exercise self-direction and self-control at work.[31] Thus, using OD implicitly involves these values. That is, organization development is designed to improve the contributions of individual members in achieving the organizational goals, and it seeks to do so in ways that respect the organization's members as mature adults who need and deserve high-quality experiences in their working lives.

Action-Research Foundations of OD

Organizational development practitioners refer to **action research** as the process of systematically collecting data on an organization, feeding it back to the members for action planning, and evaluating results by collecting and reflecting on more data after the planned actions have been taken. This is a data-based and collaborative approach to problem solving and organizational assessment. When used in the OD process, action research helps identify action directions that may enhance an organization's effectiveness. In a typical action-research sequence depicted in Figure 19.2, the sequence is initiated when someone senses a performance gap and decides to analyze the situation systematically for the problems and opportunities it represents. The process continues through the following steps: data gathering, data feedback, data analysis, and action planning. It continues to the point at which action is taken and results are evaluated. The evaluation or reassessment stage may or may not generate another performance gap. If it does, the action-research cycle begins anew.

Figure 19.3 identifies one set of frameworks that can assist OD practitioners in accomplishing the required diagnoses. These foundations apply the open-systems framework and OB concepts with which you are already familiar from earlier parts of this book. At the organizational level, the figure indicates that effectiveness must be understood with respect to forces in the external environment and major organizational aspects, such as strategy, technology, structure, culture, and management systems. At the group level, effectiveness is viewed in a context of forces in the internal environment of the organization and major group aspects, such as tasks, membership, norms, cohesiveness, and group processes.

> **Action research** is the process of systematically collecting data on an organization, feeding it back for action planning, and evaluating results by collecting and reflecting on more data.

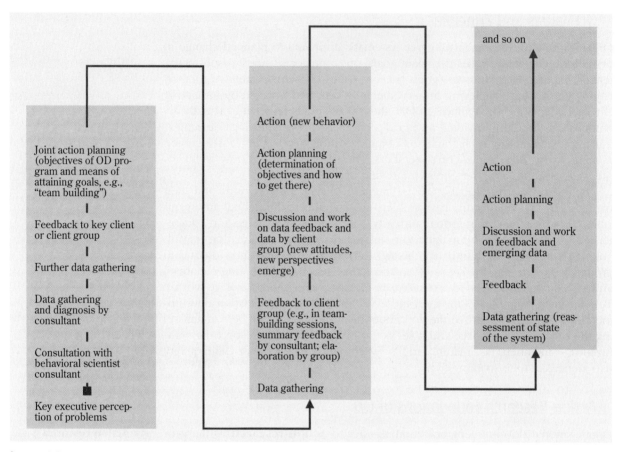

Figure 19.2   An action-research model for organizational development.

At the individual level, effectiveness is considered in relationship to the internal environment of the workgroup and individual aspects, such as tasks, goals, needs, and interpersonal relationships.

OD Interventions

The action-research process should engage members of an organization in activities designed to accomplish the required diagnoses and to develop and implement plans for constructive change. Action research, data collection, and the diagnostic foundations should come together through the choice and use of OD "interventions." **Organizational development interventions** are activities initiated by the consultant to facilitate planned change and to assist the client system in developing its own problem-solving capabilities. With less formality, many of these techniques are also now being used by managers to help them understand and improve their own operations. Major OD interventions can be categorized with respect to their major impact at the organizational, group, and individual levels of action.[32]

Organizationwide Interventions   An effective organization is one that achieves its major performance objectives while maintaining a high quality of

Organizational development interventions are activities initiated to support planned change and improve work effectiveness.

Figure 19.3   Diagnostic foundations of organizational development and OD techniques: concerns for individual, group, and organizational effectiveness.

work life for its members. OD interventions designed for systemwide application include the following.

Survey feedback begins with the collection of data via questionnaire responses from organization members or a representative sample of such responses. The data are then presented, or fed back, to the members. They subsequently engage in a collaborative process to interpret the data and to develop action plans in response.

Confrontation meetings are designed to help determine quickly how an organization may be improved and to take initial actions to better the situation.[33] The intervention involves a one-day meeting conducted by an OD facilitator for a representative sample of organizational members, including top management. In a structured format, the consultant asks participants to make individual lists of what they feel can be done to improve things. Then, through a series of small-group work sessions and sharing of results, these ideas are refined into a tentative set of actions that top management then endorses for immediate implementation. The major trick here is to get senior managers to propose changing their part of the firm. Confrontation meetings fail if all the proposed changes call for adjustments by subordinates without any alterations by the top managers.

Structural redesign involves realigning the structure of the organization or major subsystems to improve performance. It includes examining the best fit among structure, technology, and environment. In today's highly dynamic envi-

Survey feedback begins with the collection of data via questionnaires from organization members or a representative sample of them.

A **confrontation meeting** helps determine how an organization may be improved and start action toward improvement.

Structural redesign involves realigning the structure of the organization or major subsystem in order to improve performance.

ronments, in light of the increasing involvement of organizations in international operations and with rapid changes in information technology, a structure can easily become out of date. Thus, structural redesign is an important OD intervention that can be used to help maintain the best fit between organizational structures and situational demands.

Collateral organization is designed to make creative problem solving possible by pulling a representative set of members out of the formal organization structure to engage in periodic small-group problem-solving sessions.[34] These collateral, or "parallel," structures are temporary and exist only to supplement the activities of the formal structure.

Collateral organization involves a representative set of members in periodic small-group, problem-solving sessions.

Group and Intergroup Interventions   OD interventions at the group level are designed to improve group effectiveness. The major interventions at this level are team building, process consultation, and intergroup team building.

Team building involves a manager or consultant engaging the members of a group in a series of activities designed to help them examine how the group functions and how it may function better. Like survey feedback at the organizational level, team building involves some form of data collection and feedback. The key elements, however, are a collaborative assessment of the data by all members of the group and the achievement of consensus regarding what may be done to improve group effectiveness. Team building is often done at "retreats" or off-site meetings, where group members spend two to three days working intensely together on this reflection–analysis–planning process.

Team building is designed to gather and analyze data on the functioning of a group and implement changes to increase its operating effectiveness.

Process consultation involves structured activities that are facilitated by an OD practitioner and are designed to improve group functioning. Process consultation has a more specific focus than does team building, however: its attention is directed toward the key "processes" through which members of a group work with one another. The process consultant is concerned with helping a group function better on such things as norms, cohesiveness, decision-making methods, communication, conflict, and task and maintenance activities.

Process consultation helps a group improve on such things as norms, cohesiveness, decision-making methods, communication, conflict, and task and maintenance activities.

Intergroup team building is a special form of team building. It is designed to help two or more groups improve their working relationships with one another and, it is hoped, to experience improved group effectiveness as a result. Here, the OD practitioner engages the groups or their representatives in activities that increase awareness of how each group perceives the other. Given this understanding, collaborative problem solving can improve coordination between the groups and encourage more mutual support of one another as important components in the total organization.

Intergroup team building helps groups improve their working relationships with one another and experience improved group effectiveness.

Individual Interventions   Task performance and job satisfaction are important concerns with respect to improving individual effectiveness in the workplace. OD interventions at this level of attention range from those that address personal issues to those that deal more with specific job and career considerations. Individual-level OD interventions include the following.

Role negotiation is a means of clarifying what individuals expect to give and receive of one another in their working relationship. Because roles and personnel change over time, role negotiation can be an important way to maintain task understandings among individuals in an organization. This kind of understanding is quite easily accomplished by helping people who work together clarify what they need from one another to do their jobs well.

Role negotiation is a process through which individuals clarify expectations about what each should be giving and receiving as group members.

Job redesign is the process of creating long-term congruence between individual goals and organizational career opportunities. A good example is the Hackman and Oldham diagnostic approach to job enrichment discussed in Chapter 8.[35] Recall that this approach involves (1) analyzing the core characteristics of a job or group of jobs, (2) analyzing the needs and capabilities of workers in those jobs, and (3) taking action to adjust the core job characteristics either to enrich or to simplify the jobs to best match individual preferences.

Career planning takes the form of structured opportunities for individuals to work with their managers or staff experts from the personnel or human resources department on career issues. They may map career goals, assess personal development needs, and actively plan short-term and long-term career moves. Increasingly, career planning is becoming a major part of the support that highly progressive organizations provide for their members.

OD and Continuous Co-Evolution   Today, a new wave of successful high-tech firms exemplify the use of organizational development assumptions, values, and techniques without using the term *OD*. It is not that such firms as Herman Miller, Cisco, or R&R Partners are trying to force change on their employees. Rather, the managers in these systems take a very practical approach to managing culture. They realize that both external adaptation and internal integration are important for a variety of subcultures within their firms. They use OD intervention techniques to improve both. They do not dictate values or set common assumptions in isolation but with their fellow employees. They are working with others to help nurture and guide the continual evolution of organizational culture from day to day. Further, they work with their partners in the larger organizational network to disseminate these modern management practices. Leading firms such as Cisco help make the environment for all more hospitable.

■ **Job redesign** creates long-term congruence between individual goals and organizational career opportunities.

■ **Career planning** is structured opportunities for individuals to work with their managers on career issues.

Chapter 19   Study Guide

Summary

What is organizational culture?

- Organizational or corporate culture is the system of shared actions, values, and beliefs that develops within an organization and guides the behavior of its members.

- The functions of the corporate culture include responding to both external adaptation and internal integration issues.

- Most organizations contain a variety of subcultures, and a few have countercultures that can become the source of potentially harmful conflicts.

How do you understand an organizational culture?

- A detailed understanding of the functions and manifestations of culture is needed.

- Organizational cultures may be analyzed in terms of observable actions, shared values, and common assumptions (the taken-for-granted truths).

- Observable aspects of culture include the stories, rites, rituals, and symbols that are shared by organization members.

- Cultural rules and roles specify when various types of actions are appropriate and where individual members stand in the social system.

- Shared meanings and understandings help everyone know how to act and expect others to act in various circumstances.

- Common assumptions are the taken-for-granted truths that are shared by collections of corporate members.

- The corporate culture also reflects the values and implicit assumptions of the larger national culture.

How can the organizational culture be managed?

- Executives may manage many aspects of the observable culture directly.

- Nurturing shared values among the membership is a major challenge for executives.

- Adjusting actions to common understandings limits the decision scope of even the CEO.

How can you use organizational development to improve the firm?

- All managers may use organizational development (OD) techniques in their attempts to manage, nurture, and guide cultural change.

- OD is a special application of knowledge gained from behavioral science to create a comprehensive effort to improve organizational effectiveness.

- With a strong commitment to collaborative efforts and human values, OD utilizes basic behavioral science principles with respect to individuals, groups, and organizations.

- OD has two main goals: outcome goals (mainly issues of external adaptation) and process goals (mainly issues of internal integration).

- Organizational development practitioners refer to action research as the process of systematically collecting data on an organization, groups, and individuals.

- Organizationwide interventions include survey feedback, confrontation meetings, structural redesign, and collateral organization.

- Group and intergroup interventions include team building, process consultation, and intergroup team building.

- Individual interventions include role negotiation, job redesign, and career planning.

Key Terms

Action research (p. 451)	Confrontation meeting (p. 453)	External adaptation (p. 437)
Career planning (p. 455)		
Collateral organization (p. 454)	Countercultures (p. 439)	Intergroup team building (p. 454)
	Cultural symbol (p. 444)	

Internal integration (p. 437)
Job redesign (p. 455)
Management philosophy
   (p. 447)
Organizational or corporate
   culture (p. 436)
Organizational development
   (OD) (p. 450)

Organizational development
   interventions (p. 452)
Organizational myth
   (p. 445)
Process consultation
   (p. 454)
Rites (p. 443)

Rituals (p. 443)
Role negotiation (p. 454)
Sagas (p. 443)
Structural redesign (p. 453)
Subcultures (p. 439)
Survey feedback (p. 453)
Team building (p. 454)

Multiple Choice

Self-Test 19

1. Culture concerns all of the following except _____. (a) the collective concepts shared by members of a firm (b) acquired capabilities (c) the personality of the
   leader (d) the beliefs of members

2. The three levels of cultural analysis highlighted in the text concern _____.
   (a) observable culture, shared values, and common assumptions (b) stories, rites, and
   rituals (c) symbols, myths, and stories (d) manifest culture, latent culture, and observable artifacts

3. External adaptation concerns _____. (a) the unproven beliefs of senior executives (b) the process of coping with outside forces (c) the vision of the founder
   (d) the processes working together

4. Internal integration concerns _____. (a) the process of deciding the collective
   identity and how members will live together (b) the totality of the daily life of members as they see and describe it (c) expressed unproven beliefs that are accepted uncritically and used to justify current actions (d) groups of individuals with a pattern of
   values that rejects those of the larger society

5. When Japanese workers start each day with the company song, this is an example of
   a(n) _____. (a) symbol (b) myth (c) underlying assumption (d) ritual

6. _____ is a sense of broader purpose that workers infuse into their tasks as a
   result of interaction with one another. (a) A rite (b) A cultural symbol (c) A foundation myth (d) A shared meaning

7. The story of a corporate turnaround attributed to the efforts of a visionary manager is
   an example of _____. (a) a saga (b) a foundation myth (c) internal integration
   (d) a latent cultural artifact

8. OD is designed primarily to improve _____. (a) the overall effectiveness of an
   organization (b) intergroup relations (c) synergy (d) the planned change process

9. The three stages in the OD process are _____. (a) data collection, intervention, and evaluation (b) diagnosis, intervention, and reinforcement (c) diagnosis, intervention, and evaluation (d) planning, implementing, and evaluating

10. OD is planned change plus _____. (a) evaluation (b) intervention (c) ability
    for self-renewal (d) reinforcement

11. A_____ is any object, act, or event that serves to transmit cultural mean-
    ing. (a) managerial philosophy (b) cultural symbol (c) ritual (d) saga

12. A _____ links key goal-related issues with key collaboration issues to

come up with general ways by which the firm will manage its affairs. (a) managerial philosophy (b) cultural symbol (c) ritual (d) saga

13. _____is the application of behavioral science knowledge in a long-range effort to improve an organization's ability to cope with change in its external environment and increase its problem-solving capabilities. (a) Process improvement (b) Organizational intervention (c) A benefit cycle (d) Organizational development (OD)

14. The patterns of values and philosophies that outwardly reject those of the larger organization or social system are called_____. (a) sagas (b) organizational development (c) rituals (d) countercultures

15. _____ involves realigning the structure of the organization or a major subsystem in order to improve performance. (a) Structural redesign (b) Organizational intervention (c) Process intervention (d) Career counseling

Short Response

16. Describe the five steps Taylor Cox suggests need to be developed to help generate a multicultural organization or pluralistic company culture.

17. List the three aspects that help individuals and groups work together effectively and illustrate them through practical examples.

18. Give an example of how cultural rules and roles affect the atmosphere in a college classroom. Provide specific examples from your own perspective.

19. What are the major elements of a strong corporate culture?

Applications Essay

20. Discuss the process of OD and provide an overview of its diagnostic foundations in a small business such as Venus Cleaners.

OB in Action

These learning activities from *The OB Skills Workbook* are suggested for Chapter 19.

CASE	EXPERIENTIAL EXERCISES	SELF-ASSESSMENTS
▪ 19. Motorola: Seeking Direction	▪ 9. How We View Differences	▪ 8. Are You Cosmopolitan?
	▪ 23. Workgroup Culture	▪ 9. Group Effectiveness
	▪ 40. Fast-Food Technology	▪ 22. Which Culture Fits You?
	▪ 41. Alien Invasion	

Plus—special learning experiences from *The Jossey-Bass/Pfeiffer Classroom Collection*

Primer Research Foundations of Organizational Behavior

While we realize you are most interested in applications, we hope you will take a minute to examine some of the foundations for the theory and research that should underlie applications. Almost anyone who can write well has some commentary about OB. Many are quick to make recommendations for immediate application. Many apparently successful executives without any specialized training seem willing to write about OB and give their advice. There are also many consulting firms willing to give managers helpful hints in exchange for large fees. In the babble you may find it difficult to decide what to believe and what to dismiss. As an educated individual, you should be willing to ask some fundamental questions before you attempt to make improvements based on the mere suggestions of others.

OB is an applied social science that combines basic theory and applications. If you are an engineer, you apply basic physics. You know the laws of physics. You know that applications inconsistent with the laws of physics will fail. As an engineer you will not normally get involved in researching physics or writing about it. Physics is an ancient academic discipline with very specialized theories, language, and standards of proof. For example, there is no perpetual motion machine, even though many have bought variations of it. Well, OB is not physics and management is not the application of a well-developed academic discipline. There are no "laws" of OB. There are many theories.

Theory in OB

Throughout this book we have discussed many theories. In a very broad sense, a theory is simply a story of what to look for, how the things you are looking at are related, and why the pieces do or do not fit together into some meaningful tale. The purpose of a theory is to explain and predict. The better the theory, the better the explanation and prediction. More formally stated, a **theory** is a set of systematically interrelated concepts and hypotheses that are advanced to explain and predict phenomena.[1]

In OB some scholars also incorporate an applications aspect. That is, a good theory also can be applied with confidence. John Miner is one of those who has outlined some bases for judging theory in OB.[2] These include:

1. It should aid in understanding, permit prediction, and facilitate influence.
2. There should be clear boundaries for application.
3. It should direct efforts toward important, high-priority items.

> A **theory** is a set of systematically interrelated concepts, definitions, and hypotheses that are advanced to explain and predict phenomena.

4. It should produce generalizable results beyond a single setting.
5. It should be tested using clearly defined concepts and operational measures.
6. It should be both internally consistent and consistent with studies derived from it.
7. It should be stated in understandable terms.

Now that is a very tall order for any theory, and we know of no theory in OB that passes muster on all accounts. Clearly some are better than others. Some theories are pretty good at explanation but lousy at prediction, while others do a reasonable job of prediction but do not facilitate influence. For example, if circumstances are highly similar, predicting an individual will repeat a behavior is a sound bet. Unfortunately, this prediction is rarely supported by a theory explaining why the individual acted in a given manner in the first place. As a manager, even if you know that an individual will repeat a behavior, you also need to know how to change it. And so it goes.

The bottom line is that theory and research go together. The theory tells one what to look for, and the research tells what was found. What was found also tells us what to look for again. It is important to realize that we may not see what we do not conceptualize. But it is equally important to note that for an acceptable theory others must understand, see, and verify what we see and understand. Among OB researchers this process of seeing, understanding, and verifying is generally accomplished through the scientific method.

The Scientific Method

> ▰ The **scientific method** is a key part of the OB research foundations, which involves four steps: the research question or problem, hypothesis generation or formulation, the research design, and data gathering, analysis, and interpretation.

A key part of OB research foundations is the **scientific method**, which involves four steps. First, a *research question* or *problem* is specified. Then one or more *hypotheses* or explanations of what the research parties expect to find are formulated. These may come from many sources, including previous experience and careful review of the literature covering the problem area. The next step is the creation of a *research design*—an overall plan or strategy for conducting the research to test the hypothesis(es). Finally, *data gathering, analysis*, and *interpretation* are carried out.[3]

The Vocabulary of Research

The previous discussion conveyed a quick summary of the scientific method. It's important to go beyond that summation and further develop a number of aspects of the scientific method. Before doing that, we consider the vocabulary of research. Knowing that vocabulary can help you feel comfortable with several terms used in OB research as well as help in our later discussion.[4]

> ▰ A **variable** is a measure used to describe a real-world phenomenon.

Variable   A **variable** is a measure used to describe a real-world phenomenon. For example, a researcher may count the number of parts produced by workers in a week's time as a measure of the workers' individual productivity.

> ▰ A **hypothesis** is a tentative explanation about the relationship between two or more variables.

Hypothesis   Building on our earlier use of the term, we can define a **hypothesis** as a tentative explanation about the relationship between two or more variables. For example, OB researchers have hypothesized that an increase in supervisory participation will increase productivity. Hypotheses are "predictive" statements. Once supported through empirical research, a hypothesis can be a source of direct action implications. Confirmation of the above hypothesis would lead to the following implication: If you want to increase individual productivity in a work unit, increase the level of supervisory participation.

Dependent Variable   The **dependent variable** is the event or occurrence expressed in a hypothesis that indicates what the researcher is interested in explaining. In the previous example, individual performance was the dependent variable of interest. OB researchers often try to determine what factors appear to predict increases in performance.

Independent Variable   An **independent variable** is the event or occurrence that is presumed by a hypothesis to affect one or more other events or occurrences as dependent variables. In the example of individual performance, supervisory participation is the independent variable.

Intervening Variable   An **intervening variable** is an event or occurrence that provides the linkage through which an independent variable is presumed to affect a dependent variable. It has been hypothesized, for instance, that participative supervisory practices "independent variable" improve worker satisfaction "intervening variable" and therefore increase performance "dependent variable".

Moderator Variable   A **moderator variable** is an event or occurrence that, when systematically varied, changes the relationship between an independent variable and a dependent variable. The relationship between these two variables differs depending on the level—for instance, high/low, young/old, male/female—of the moderator variable. To illustrate, consider again the previous example of the individual performance hypothesis that participative supervision leads to increased productivity. It may well be that this relationship holds true only when the employees feel that their participation is real and legitimate—a moderator variable. Likewise, it may be that participative supervision leads to increased performance for Canadian workers but not those from Brazil—here, country is a moderator variable.

Validity   **Validity** is concerned with the degree of confidence one can have in the results of a research study. It is focused on limiting research errors so that results are accurate and usable.[5] There are two key types of validity: internal and external. *Internal validity* is the degree to which the results of a study can be relied upon to be correct. It is strongest when alternative interpretations of the study's findings can be ruled out.[6] To illustrate, if performance improves with more participative supervisory practices, these results have a higher degree of internal validity if we can rule out the effects of differences in old and new machines.

External validity is the degree to which the study's results can be generalized across the entire population of people, settings, and other similar conditions.[7] We cannot have external validity unless we first have internal validity; that is, we must have confidence that the results are caused by what the study says they are before we can generalize to a broader context.

A **dependent variable** is the event or occurrence expressed in a hypothesis that indicates what the researcher is interested in explaining.

An **independent variable** is the event or occurrence that is presumed by a hypothesis to affect one or more other events or occurrences as dependent variables.

An **intervening variable** is an event or occurrence that provides the linkage through which an independent variable is presumed to affect a dependent variable.

A **moderator variable** is an event or occurrence that, when systematically varied, changes the relationship between an independent variable and a dependent variable.

Validity is the degree of confidence one can have in the results of a research study.

Reliability is the consistency and stability of a score from a measurement scale.

Causality is the assumption that change in the independent variable has caused change in the dependent variable.

Reliability   **Reliability** is the consistency and stability of a score from a measurement scale. There must be reliability for there to be validity or accuracy. Think of shooting at a bull's-eye. If the shots land all over the target, there is neither reliability (consistency) nor validity (accuracy). If the shots are clustered close together but outside the outer ring of the target, they are reliable but not valid. If they are grouped together within the bull's-eye, they are both reliable and valid.[8]

Causality   **Causality** is the assumption that change in the independent variable caused change in the dependent variable. This assumption is very difficult to prove in OB research. Three types of evidence are necessary to demonstrate causality: (1) the variables must show a linkage or association; (2) one variable must precede the other in time; and (3) there must be an absence of other causal factors. [9] For example, say we note that participation and performance increase together—there is an association. If we can then show that an increase in participation has preceded an increase in performance and that other factors, such as new machinery, haven't been responsible for the increased performance, we can say that participation probably has caused performance.

Research Designs

A **research design** is an overall plan or strategy for conducting research to test a hypothesis.

A **laboratory experiment** is conducted in an artificial setting in which the researcher intervenes and manipulates one or more independent variables in a highly controlled situation.

As noted earlier, a **research design** is an overall plan or strategy for conducting the research to test the hypothesis(es). Four of the most popular research designs are laboratory experiments, field experiments, case studies, and field surveys.[10]

Laboratory Experiments

Laboratory experiments are conducted in an artificial setting in which the researcher intervenes and manipulates one or more independent variables in a highly controlled situation. Although there is a high degree of control, which, in turn, encourages internal validity, since these studies are done in an artificial setting, they may suffer from a lack of external validity.

To illustrate, assume we are interested in the impact of three different incentive systems on employee absenteeism: (1) a lottery with a monetary reward; (2) a lottery with a compensatory time-off reward; and (3) a lottery with a large prize, such as a car. The researcher randomly selects individuals in an organization to come to an office to take part in the study. This randomization is important because it means that variables that are not measured are randomly distributed across the subjects so that unknown variables shouldn't be causing whatever is found. However, often it is not possible to obtain subjects randomly in organizations since they may be needed elsewhere by management.

The researcher is next able to select randomly select each worker to one of the three incentive systems as well as a control group with no incentive system. The employees report to work in their new work stations under highly artificial but controlled conditions, and their absenteeism is measured both at the beginning and end of the experiment. Statistical comparisons are made across each group, considering before and after measures.

Ultimately, the researcher develops hypotheses about the effects of each of the lottery treatments on absenteeism. Given support for these hypotheses, the researcher could feel with a high degree of confidence that a given incentive condition caused less absenteeism than did the others since randomized subjects, pre- and posttest measures, and a comparison with a control group were used. However, since the work stations were artificial and the lottery conditions were highly simplified to provide control, external validity could be questioned. Ideally, the researcher would conduct a follow-up study with another design to check for external validity.

Field Experiments

Field experiments are research studies that are conducted in a realistic setting. Here, the researcher intervenes and manipulates one or more independent variables and controls the situation as carefully as the situation permits.

Applying the same research question as before, the researcher obtains management permission to assign one incentive treatment to each of three similar organizational departments, similar in terms of the various characteristics of people. A fourth control department keeps the current payment plan. The rest of the experiment is similar to the laboratory study except that the lottery treatments are more realistic but also less controlled. Also, it may be particularly difficult to obtain random assignment in this case since it may disrupt day-to-day work schedules, and so on. When random assignment is not possible, the other manipulations may still be possible. An experimental research design without any randomization is called a *quasi-experimental design* and does not control for unmeasured variables as well as a randomized design.

> A **field experiment** is a research study that is conducted in a realistic setting, whereby the researcher intervenes and manipulates one or more independent variables and controls the situation as carefully as the situation permits.

Case Studies

Case studies are in-depth analyses of one or a small number of settings. Case studies often are used when little is known about a phenomenon and the researcher wants to examine relevant concepts intensely and thoroughly. They can sometimes be used to help develop theory that can then be tested with one of the other research designs. Returning to the participation and performance example, one might look at one or more organizations and intensely study organizational success or failure in designing or implementing participation. You might look for differences in how employees and managers define participation. This information could provide insights to be investigated further with additional case studies or other research designs.

A major strength of case studies is their realism and the richness of data and insights they can provide. Some disadvantages are their lack of control by the researcher, the difficulty of interpreting the results because of their richness, and the large amount of time and cost that may be involved.

> A **case study** is an in-depth analysis of one or a small number of settings.

Field Surveys

Field surveys typically depend on the use of some form of questionnaire for the primary purpose of describing and/or predicting some phenomenon. Typically, they utilize a sample drawn from some large population. A key objective of field surveys is to look for relationships between or among variables. Two major advantages are their ability to examine and describe large populations quickly and inexpensively and their flexibility. They can be used to do many kinds of OB re-

> A **field survey** is a research design that relies on the use of some form of questionnaire for the primary purpose of describing and/or predicting some phenomenon.

search, such as testing hypotheses and theories and evaluating programs. Field surveys assume that the researcher has enough knowledge of the problem area to know the kinds of questions to ask; sometimes, earlier case studies help provide this knowledge.

A key disadvantage of field surveys is the lack of control. The researcher does not manipulate variables; even such things as who completes the surveys and their timing may not be under the researcher's control. Another disadvantage is the lack of depth of the standardized responses; thus, sometimes the data obtained are superficial.

Data Gathering, Analysis, and Interpretation

Once the research design has been established, we are ready for data gathering, analysis, and interpretation-the final step in the scientific method. Four common OB data-gathering approaches are interviews, observation, questionnaires, and nonreactive measures.[11]

Interviews

An **interview** involves face-to-face, telephone, or computer-assisted interactions to ask respondents questions of interest.

Interviews involve face-to-face, telephone, or computer-assisted interactions to ask respondents questions of interest. Structured interviews ask the respondents the same questions in the same sequence. Unstructured interviews are more spontaneous and do not require the same format. Often a mixture of structured and unstructured formats is used. Interviews allow for in-depth responses and probing. They are generally time consuming, however, and require increasing amounts of training and skill, depending on their depth and amount of structure.

Observation

Observation involves watching an event, object, or person and recording what is seen.

Observation involves watching an event, object, or person and recording what is seen. Sometimes, the observer is separate from the participants and events and functions as an outside researcher. In other cases, the observer participates in the events as a member of a work unit. In the latter case, observations are summarized in some kind of diary or log. Sometimes, the observer is hidden and records observations behind one-way glass or by using hidden cameras and the like.

Two advantages of observation are that (1) behavior is observed as it occurs rather than being obtained by asking people after the fact, and (2) the observer can often obtain data that subjects can't or won't provide themselves. A couple of disadvantages are cost and the possible fallibility of observers, who sometimes do not provide complete and accurate data.

Questionnaires

Questionnaires ask respondents for their opinions, attitudes, perceptions, and/or descriptions of work-related matters.

Questionnaires ask respondents for their opinions, attitudes, perceptions, and/or descriptions of work-related matters. They are usually based on previously developed instruments. Typically, a respondent completes the questionnaire and returns it to the researcher. Questions may be open ended, or they may be structured with true-false or multiple-choice responses.

Advantages of questionnaires include the relatively low cost and the fact that the anonymity that often accompanies them may lead to more open and truthful responses. Some disadvantages are the low response rates, which may threaten the generalizability of the results, and the lack of depth of the responses.

Nonreactive Measures

Nonreactive measures are used to obtain data without disturbing the setting being studied. Sometimes, these are termed *unobtrusive measures* since they are designed not to intrude in a research situation. Nonreactive measures can focus on such things as physical traces, archives, and hidden observation. A kind of physical trace occurred when John Fry at 3M distributed test batches of Post-it Notes to 3M employees and discovered that they were using them at higher rates than 3M's leading adhesive product—Scotch Tape.[12] Archives are records that an organization keeps as a part of its day-to-day activities, for example, minutes and daily production counts.

A major advantage of nonreactive measures is that they don't disturb the research setting and so avoid the reaction of a respondent to a researcher. One possible disadvantage is their indirectness; incorrect inferences may be drawn from nonreactive measures. They work best in combination with more direct measures.

Nonreactive measures are used to obtain data without disturbing the setting.

Data Analysis and Interpretation

Once the data have been gathered, they need to be *analyzed*. The most common means of analysis involves some kind of statistical approach, ranging from simple counting and categorizing to sophisticated multivariate statistical techniques.[13] It's beyond our scope to discuss this area beyond simply emphasizing its importance. However, various statistical tests are often used to examine support for hypotheses, to check for the reliability of various data-gathering approaches, and to provide information on causality and many other aspects of analysis.

After systematic analysis has been performed, the researcher *interprets* the results and prepares a report.[14] Sometimes, the report is used in-house by management; other times, the results are reported at various conferences and published in journals. Ultimately, many of the results in the OB area appear in textbooks like this one.

Ethical Considerations in Research

Given our emphasis on ethical considerations throughout this book, it is appropriate to end our discussion of OB research with a look at its ethical considerations. These ethical considerations involve rights of four broad parties involved in research in general and in OB research in particular: society, subjects, clients, and researchers.[15]

In terms of *societal rights*—those of the broadest of the parties involved in OB research—three key areas exist: the right to be informed, the right to expect objective results, and the right to privacy or to be left alone. Subjects of research also have rights: the right to choose (to participate or not), to safety, and to be informed. The rights of the client involve two primary concerns: the right to expect high-quality research and the right of confidentiality. Finally, two rights of the researcher stand out: the right to expect ethical client behavior and the right to expect ethical subject behavior.

All of these rights need to be communicated and adhered to by all parties. Indeed, various organizations conducting research are increasingly endorsing codes of ethics to codify such rights. Two particular organizations that have codes of ethics for research covering OB and related areas are the American Psychological Association and the Academy of Management.

THE OB S KILLS WORKBOOK

**Featuring
The Jossey-Bass/Pfeiffer
Classroom Collection**

Pfeiffer
An Imprint of WILEY

JOSSEY-BASS
An Imprint of WILEY
Now you know.

SUGGESTED APPLICATIONS OF WORKBOOK MATERIALS

I. The Jossey-Bass/Pfeiffer Classroom Collection

Student Leadership Practices Inventory by Kouzes and Posner

Activity	Suggested Part	Overview
1. Student Leadership Practices Inventory—Student Workbook	All	This workbook includes a worksheet to help interpret feedback and plan improvement in each leadership practice assessed, sections on how to compare scores with the normative sample and how to share feedback with constituents, and more than 140 actual steps your students can take to get results.
2. Student Leadership Practices Inventory—Self	All	This 30-item inventory will help students evaluate their performance and effectiveness as a leader. Results from the simple scoring process help students prepare plans for personal leadership development.
3. Student Leadership Practices Inventory—Observer	All	This version of the LPI is used by others to assess the individual's leadership tendencies, thus allowing for comparison with self-perceptions.

Experiential Exercises from The Pfeiffer Annual: Training

Activity	Suggested Part	Overview
1. Sweet Tooth: Bonding Strangers into a Team	Parts 1, 3, 4	Perception, teamwork, decision making, communication
2. Interrogatories: Identifying Issues and Needs	Parts 1, 3, 4	Current issues, group dynamics, communication
3. Decode: Working with Different Instructions	Parts 3, 4	Decision making, leadership, conflict, teamwork
4. Choices: Learning Effective Conflict Management Strategies	Parts 1, 2, 3, 4, 5	Conflict, negotiation, communication, decision making
5. Internal/External Motivators: Encouraging Creativity	Parts 2, 4, 5	Creativity, motivation, job design, decision making
6. Quick Hitter: Fostering the Creative Spirit	Parts 4, 5	Creativity, decision making, communication

II. Cases for Critical Thinking

Case	Suggested Chapter	Cross-References and Integration
See companion Web site for online versions of many cases: www.wiley.com/schermerhorn		
1. Drexler's Bar-B-Que	1 Introducing Organizational Behavior	organizational structure; design and culture; organizational change and innovation; decision making; leadership
2. The Panera Bread Case–Not by Bread Alone	2 Current Issues in Organizational Behavior	human resource management; organizational cultures; innovation; information technology; leadership

Case	Suggested Chapter	Cross-References and Integration
3. *Crossing Borders*	3 Organizational Behavior Across Cultures	diversity and individual differences; perception and attribution; performance management; job design; communication; conflict decision making
4. *Never on a Sunday*	4 Diversity and Individual Differences	ethics and diversity; organizational structure, design, and culture; decision making; organizational change
5. *MagRec, Inc.*	5 Perception and Attribution	ethics and diversity; organizational structure, design, and culture; decision making; organizational change
6. *It Isn't Fair*	6 Motivation Theories	perception and attribution; performance management and rewards; communication; ethics and decision making
7. *Perfect Pizzeria*	7 Motivation and Job Design	organizational cultures; globalization; communication; decision making
8. *I'm Not in Kansas Anymore*	8 Performance Management and Rewards	organizational design; motivation; performance management and rewards
9. *The Forgotten Group Member*	9 How Groups Work	teamwork; motivation; diversity and individual differences; perception and attribution; performance management and rewards; communication; conflict; leadership
10. *NASCAR's Racing Teams*	10 Teamwork and Team Performance	organizational cultures; leadership; motivation and reinforcement; communication
11. *Perot Systems: Can a High-Performance Company Have a Human Side?*	11 Leadership	organizational cultures; group dynamics and teamwork; motivation and reinforcement
12. *Power or Empowerment at GM?*	12 Power and Politics	communication; conflict; decision making; organizational change; job design
13. *The Poorly Informed Walrus*	13 Information and Communication	diversity and individual differences; perception and attribution
14. *Johnson & Johnson: One Large Company Made of Many*	14 Decision Making	organizational structure; organizational cultures; change and innovation; group dynamics and teamwork; diversity and individual differences
15. *Faculty Empowerment and the Changing University Environment*	15 Conflict and Negotiation	change, innovation and stress; job designs; communication; power and politics
16. *The New Vice President*	16 Change, Stress, and Innovation	leadership; performance management and rewards; diversity and individual differences; communication; conflict and negotiation; power and influence
17. *First Community Financial*	17 Organizing for Performance	organizational structure, designs and culture; performance management and rewards
18. *Mission Management and Trust*	18 Organizational Design for Strategic Competency	organizational structure, designs and culture; performance management and rewards
19. *Motorola: Seeking Direction*	19 Organizational Culture and Development	innovation; conflict and negotiation; leadership; change and stress

III. Cross-Functional Integrative Case

Case	Overview
Trilogy Software: High-Performance Company of the Future?	Cross-functional integrative case on the launch and development of a highly innovative software company—focus on high-performance organizations, competitive environment, innovation, talented workforce, motivation and rewards, organizational culture, technology and change

See companion Web site for online version: www.wiley.com/college/schermerhorn

IV. Experiential Exercises

Exercise	Suggested Chapter	Cross-References and Integration
1. *My Best Manager*	1 Introducing Organizational Behavior	leadership
2. *Graffiti Needs Assessment*	1 Introducing Organizational Behavior	human resource management; communication
3. *My Best Job*	2 Current Issues in Organizational Behavior	motivation; job design; organizational cultures
4. *What Do You Value in Work?*	2 Current Issues in Organizational Behavior	diversity and individual differences; performance management and rewards; motivation; job design; decision making
5. *My Asset Base*	2 Current Issues in Organizational Behavior	perception and attribution; diversity and individual differences; groups and teamwork; decision making
6. *Expatriate Assignments*	3 Organizational Behavior Across Cultures	perception and attribution; diversity and individual differences; decision making
7. *Cultural Cues*	3 Organizational Behavior Across Cultures	perception and attribution; diversity and individual differences; decision making; communication; conflict; groups and teamwork
8. *Prejudice in Our Lives*	4 Diversity and Individual Differences	perception and attribution; decision making; conflict; groups and teamwork
9. *How We View Differences*	5 Perception and Attribution	culture; international; diversity and individual differences; decision making; communication; conflict; groups and teamwork
10. *Alligator River Story*	5 Perception and Attribution	diversity and individual differences; decision making; communication; conflict; groups and teamwork
11. *Teamwork and Motivation*	6 Motivation Theories	performance management and rewards; groups and teamwork
12. *The Downside of Punishment*	6 Motivation Theories	motivation; perception and attribution; performance management and rewards
13. *Tinkertoys*	7 Motivation and Job Design	organizational structure; design and culture; groups and teamwork
14. *Job Design Preferences*	7 Motivation and Job Design	motivation; job design; organizational design; change
15. *My Fantasy Job*	7 Motivation and Job Design	motivation; individual differences; organizational design; change
16. *Motivation by Job Enrichment*	7 Motivation and Job Design	motivation; job design; perception; diversity and individual differences; change

Exercise	Suggested Chapter	Cross-References and Integration
17. *Annual Pay Raises*	8 Performance Management and Rewards	motivation; learning and reinforcement; perception and attribution; decision making; groups and teamwork
18. *Serving on the Boundary*	9 How Groups Work	intergroup dynamics; group dynamics; roles; communication; conflict; stress
19. *Eggsperiential Exercise*	9 How Groups Work	group dynamics and teamwork; diversity and individual differences; communication
20. *Scavenger Hunt—Team Building*	10 Teamwork and Team Performance	groups; leadership; diversity and individual differences; communication; leadership
21. *Work Team Dynamics*	10 Teamwork and Team Performance	groups; motivation; decision making; conflict; communication
22. *Identifying Group Norms*	10 Teamwork and Team Performance	groups; communication; perception and attribution
23. *Workgroup Culture*	10 Teamwork and Team Performance	groups; communication; perception and attribution; job design; organizational culture
24. *The Hot Seat*	10 Teamwork and Team Performance	groups; communication; conflict and negotiation; power and politics
25. *Interview a Leader*	11 Leadership	performance management and rewards; group and teamwork; new workplace; organizational change and stress
26. *Leadership Skills Inventories*	11 Leadership	individual differences; perception and attribution; decision making
27. *Leadership and Participation in Decision Making*	11 Leadership	decision making; communication; motivation; groups; teamwork
28. *My Best Manager: Revisited*	12 Power and Politics	diversity and individual differences; perception and attribution
29. *Active Listening*	13 Information and Communication	group dynamics and teamwork; perception and attribution
30. *Upward Appraisal*	13 Information and Communication	perception and attribution; performance management and rewards
31. *360-Degree Feedback*	14 Decision Making	communication; perception and attribution; performance management and rewards
32. *Role Analysis Negotiation*	14 Decision Making	communication; group dynamics and teamwork; perception and attribution; communication; decision making
33. *Lost at Sea*	14 Decision Making	communication; group dynamics and teamwork; conflict and negotiation
34. *Entering the Unknown*	14 Decision Making	communication; group dynamics and teamwork; perception and attribution
35. *Vacation Puzzle*	15 Conflict and Negotiation	conflict and negotiation; communication; power; leadership
36. *The Ugli Orange*	15 Conflict and Negotiation	communication; decision making
37. *Conflict Dialogues*	15 Conflict and Negotiation	conflict; communication; feedback; perception; stress

Exercise	Suggested Chapter	Cross-References and Integration
38. *Force-Field Analysis*	16 Change, Stress, and Innovation	decision making; organization structures, designs, cultures
39. *Organizations Alive!*	17 Organizing for Performance	organizational design and culture; performance management and rewards
40. *Fast-Food Technology*	18 Organizational Design for Strategic Competency	organizational design; organizational culture; job design
41. *Alien Invasion*	19 Organizational Culture and Development	organizational structure and design; international; diversity and individual differences; perception and attribution
42. *Power Circles Exercise*	16 Change, Stress, and Innovation	influence; power; leadership; change management

V. Self-Assessment Inventories

Assessment	Suggested Chapter	Cross-References and Integration
See companion Web site for online versions of many cases: www.wiley.com/college/schermerhorn		
1. *Managerial Assumptions*	1 Introducing Organizational Behavior	leadership
2. *A Twenty-First-Century Manager*	1 Introducing Organizational Behavior 2 Current Issues in Organizational Behavior	leadership; decision making; globalization
3. *Turbulence Tolerance Test*	1 Introducing Organizational Behavior 2 Current Issues in Organizational Behavior	perception; individual differences; organizational change and stress
4. *Global Readiness Index*	3 Organizational Behavior Across Cultures	diversity, culture, leading, perception, management skills, career readiness
5. *Personal Values*	4 Diversity and Individual Differences	perception; diversity and individual differences; leadership
6. *Intolerance for Ambiguity*	5 Perception and Attribution	perception; leadership
7. *Two-Factor Profile*	6 Motivation Theories	job design; perception; culture; human resource management
8. *Are You Cosmopolitan?*	7 Motivation and Job Design 8 Performance Management and Rewards	diversity and individual differences; organizational culture
9. *Group Effectiveness*	9 How Groups Work 10 Teamwork and Team Performance	organizational designs and cultures; leadership
10. *Least Preferred Coworker Scale*	11 Leadership	diversity and individual differences; perception; group dynamics and teamwork
11. *Leadership Style*	11 Leadership	diversity and individual differences; perception; group dynamics and teamwork
12. *"TT" Leadership Style*	11 Leadership 13 Information and Communication	diversity and individual differences; perception; group dynamics and teamwork

Assessment	Suggested Chapter	Cross-References and Integration
13. *Empowering Others*	12 Power and Politics 13 Information and Communication	leadership; perception and attribution
14. *Machiavellianism*	12 Power and Politics	leadership; diversity and individual differences
15. *Personal Power Profile*	12 Power and Politics	leadership; diversity and individual differences
16. *Your Intuitive Ability*	14 Decision Making	diversity and individual differences
17. *Decision-Making Biases*	14 Decision Making	teams and teamwork, communication, perception
18. *Conflict Management Styles*	15 Conflict and Negotiation	diversity and individual differences; communication
19. *Your Personality Type*	16 Change, Stress, and Innovation	diversity and individual differences; job design
20. *Time Management Profile*	16 Change, Stress, and Innovation	diversity and individual differences
21. *Organizational Design Preference*	17 Organizing for Performance 18 Organizational Design for Strategic Competency	job design; diversity and individual differences
22. *Which Culture Fits You?*	19 Organizational Culture and Development	perception; diversity and individual differences

ossey-Bass/Pfeiffer
lassroom Collection

Pfeiffer
An Imprint of WILEY

JOSSEY-BASS®
An Imprint of WILEY
Now you know.

STUDENT LEADERSHIP PRACTICES INVENTORY
STUDENT WORKBOOK

James M. Kouzes
Barry Z. Posner, Ph.D.
Jossey-Bass Publishers • San Francisco

Printed in the United States of America.

Jossey-Bass books and products are available through most bookstores. To contact Jossey-Bass directly, call (888) 378-2537, fax to (800) 605-2665, or visit our website at www.josseybass.com.

Substantial discounts on bulk quantities of Jossey-Bass books are available to corporations, professional associations, and other organizations. For details and discount information, contact the special sales department at Jossey-Bass.

Printing 10 9 8 7 6 5 4 3 2

This book is printed on acid-free, recycled stock that meets or exceeds the minimum GPO and EPA requirements for recycled paper.

CONTENTS

People WHO BECOME
leaders
DON'T *always* **seek**
THE **challenges**
THEY **face.**
CHALLENGES
also SEEK **leaders.**

1
Leadership: What People Do When They're Leading

"*Leadership is everyone's business.*" That's the conclusion we have come to after nearly two decades of research into the behaviors and actions of people who are making a difference in their organizations, clubs, teams, classes, schools, campuses, communities, and even in their families. We found that leadership is an observable, learnable set of practices. Contrary to some myths, it is not a mystical and ethereal process that cannot be understood by ordinary people. Given the opportunity for feedback and practice, those with the desire and persistence to lead—to make a difference—can substantially improve their ability to do so.

The *Leadership Practices Inventory* (LPI) is part of an extensive research project into the everyday actions and behaviors of people, at all levels and across a variety of settings, as they are leading. Through our research we identified five practices that are common to all leadership experiences. In col-laboration with others, we extended our findings to student leaders and to school and college environments and created the student version of the LPI.[1] The LPI is a tool, not a test, designed to assess your current leadership skills. It will identify your areas of strength as well as areas of leadership that need to be further developed.

The *Student LPI* helps you discover the extent to which you (in your role as a leader of a student group or organization) engage in the following five leadership practices:

Challenging the Process. Leaders are pioneers—people who seek out new opportunities and are willing to change the status quo. They innovate, experiment, and explore ways to improve the organization. They treat mistakes as learning experiences. Leaders also stay prepared to meet whatever challenges may confront them. *Challenging the Process* involves

- Searching for opportunities
- Experimenting and taking risks

As an example of Challenging the Process, one student related how innovative thinking helped him win a student class election: "I challenged the process in more than one way. First, I wanted people to understand that elections are not necessarily popularity contests, so I campaigned on the issues and did not promise things that could not possibly be done. Second, I challenged the incumbent positions. They thought they would win easily because they were incumbents, but I showed them that no one has an inherent right to a position."

---

[1]For more information on our original work, see *The Leadership Challenge: How to Keep Getting Extraordinary Things Done in Organizations* (Jossey-Bass Publishers).

Challenging the Process for a student serving as treasurer of her sorority meant examining and abandoning some of her leadership beliefs: "I used to believe, 'if you want to do something right, do it yourself.' I found out the hard way that this is impossible to do.... One day I was ready to just give up the position because I could no longer handle all of the work. My adviser noticed that I was overwhelmed, and she turned to me and said three magic words: 'Use your committee.' The best piece of advice I would pass along about being an effective leader is that it is okay to experiment with letting others do the work."

Inspiring a Shared Vision. Leaders look toward and beyond the horizon. They envision the future with a positive and hopeful outlook. Leaders are expressive and attract other people to their organization and teams through their genuineness. They communicate and show others how their interests can be met through commitment to a common purpose. *Inspiring a Shared Vision* involves

- Envisioning an uplifting future
- Enlisting others in a common vision

Describing his experience as president of his high school class, one student wrote, "It was our vision to get the class united and to be able to win the spirit trophy.... I told my officers that we could do anything we set our minds on. Believe in yourself and believe in your ability to accomplish things."

Enabling Others to Act. Leaders infuse people with energy and confidence, developing relationships based on mutual trust. They stress collaborative goals. They actively involve others in planning, giving them discretion to make their own decisions. Leaders ensure that people feel strong and capable. *Enabling Others to Act* involves

- Fostering collaboration
- Strengthening people

It is not necessary to be in a traditional leadership position to put these principles into practice. Here is an example from a student who led his team as a team member, not from a traditional position of power. "I helped my team members feel strong and capable by encouraging everyone to practice with the same amount of intensity that they played games with. Our practices improved throughout the year and by the end of the year had reached the point I was striving for: complete involvement among all players, helping each other to perform at our very best during practice times."

Modeling the Way. Leaders are clear about their personal values and beliefs. They keep people and projects on course by behaving consistently with these values and modeling how they expect others to act. Leaders also plan projects and break them down into achievable steps, creating opportunities for small wins. By focusing on key priorities, they make it easier for others to achieve goals. *Modeling the Way* involves

- Setting the example
- Achieving small wins

Working in a business environment taught one student the importance of Modeling the Way. She writes, "I proved I was serious because I was the first one on the job and the last one to leave. I came prepared to work and make the tools available to my crew. I worked alongside them and in no way portrayed an attitude of superiority. Instead, we were in this together."

Encouraging the Heart. Leaders encourage people to persist in their efforts by linking recognition with accomplishments and visibly recognizing contributions to the common vision. They express pride in the achievements of the group or organization, letting others know that their efforts are appreciated. Leaders also find ways to celebrate milestones. They nurture a team spirit, which enables people to sustain continued efforts. *Encouraging the Heart* involves

- Recognizing individual contributions
- Celebrating team accomplishments

While organizing and running a day camp, one student recognized volunteers and celebrated accomplishments through her actions. She explains, "We had a pizza party with the children on the last day of the day camp. Later, the volunteers were sent thank you notes and 'valuable volunteer awards' personally signed by the day campers. The pizza party, thank you notes, and awards served to encourage the hearts of the volunteers in the hopes that they might return for next year's day camp."

Somewhere,
sometime,
THE *leader within*
EACH OF US
MAY get
THE CALL
to STEP forward.

2
Questions Frequently Asked About the *Student LPI*

Question 1: What are the right answers?

Answer: There are no universal right answers when it comes to leadership. The research indicates that the more frequently you are perceived as engaging in the behavior and actions identified in the *Student LPI,* the more likely it is that you will be perceived as an effective leader. The higher your scores on the Student LPI-Observer, the more others perceive you as (1) having personal credibility, (2) being effective in running meetings, (3) successfully representing your organization or group to nonmembers, (4) generating a sense of enthusiasm and cooperation, and (5) having a high-performing team. In addition, findings show a strong and positive relationship between the extent to which people report their leaders engaging in this set of five leadership practices and how motivated, committed, and productive they feel.

Question 2: How reliable and valid is the Student LPI?

Answer: The question of reliability can be answered in two ways. First, the *Student LPI* has shown sound psychometric properties. The scale for each leadership practice is internally reliable, meaning that the statements within each practice are highly correlated with one another. Second, results of multivariate analyses indicate that the statements within each leadership practice are more highly correlated (or associated) with one another than they are between the five leadership practices.

In terms of validity (or, "So what difference do the scores make?"), the *Student LPI* has good face validity and predictive validity. This means, first, that the results make sense to people. Second, scores on the *Student LPI* significantly differentiate high-performing leaders from their less successful counterparts. Whether measured by the leader, his or her peers, or student personnel administrators, those student leaders who engage more frequently, rather than less frequently, in the five leadership practices are more effective.

Question 3: Should my perceptions of my leadership practices be consistent with the ratings other people give me?

Answer: Research indicates that trust in the leader is essential if other people (for example, fellow members of a group, team, or organization) are going to follow that person over time. People must experience the leader as believable, credible, and trustworthy. Trust—whether in a leader or any other person—is developed through consistency in behavior. Trust is further established when words and deeds are congruent.

This does not mean, however, that you will always be perceived in exactly the same way by every person in every situation. Some people may not see you as often as others do, and therefore they may rate you differently on the same behavior. Some people simply may not know you as well as others do. Also, you may appropriately behave differently in different situations, such as in a crisis versus during more stable times. Others may have different expectations of you, and still others may perceive the rating descriptions (such as "once in a while" or "fairly often") differently.

Therefore, the key issue is not whether your self-ratings and the ratings from others are exactly the same, but whether people perceive consistency between what you say you do and what you actually do. The only way you can know the answer to this question is to solicit feedback. The Student LPI-Observer has been designed for this purpose.

Research indicates that people tend to see themselves more positively than others do. The Student LPI-Self norms are consistent with this general trend; scores on the Student LPI-Self tend to be somewhat higher than scores on the Student LPI-Observer. *Student LPI* scores also tend to be higher than LPI scores of experienced managers and executives in the private and public sector.

Question 4: Can I change my leadership practices?

Answer: It is certainly possible—even for experienced people—to learn new skills. You will increase your chances of changing your behavior if you receive feedback on what level you have achieved with a particular skill, observe a positive model of that skill, set some improvement goals for yourself, practice the skill, ask for updated feedback on your performance, and then set new goals. The practices that are assessed with the *Student LPI* fall into the category of learnable skills.

But some things can be changed only if there is a strong and genuine inner desire to make a difference. For example, enthusiasm for a cause is unlikely to be developed through education or job assignments; it must come from within.

Use the information from the *Student LPI* to better understand how you currently behave as a leader, both from your own perspective and from the perspective of others. Note where there are consistencies and inconsistencies. Understand which leadership behaviors and practices you feel comfortable engaging in and those you feel uncomfortable with. Determine which leadership behaviors and practices you can improve on, and take steps to improve your leadership skills and confidence in leading other people and groups. The following sections will help you to become more effective in leadership.

> **Perhaps** NONE OF
> us knows
> OUR *true strength*
> UNTIL **challenged**
> TO **bring**
> *it* **forth.**

3
Recording Your Scores

On pages W-6 through W-9 are grids for recording your *Student LPI* scores. The first grid (Challenging the Process) is for recording scores for items 1, 6, 11, 16, 21, and 26 from the Student LPI-Self and Student LPI-Observer. These are the items that relate to behaviors involved in Challenging the Process, such as searching for opportunities, experimenting, and taking risks. An abbreviated form of each item is printed beside the grid as a handy reference.

In the first column, which is headed "Self-Rating," write the scores that you gave yourself. If others were asked to complete the Student LPI-Observer and if the forms were returned to you, enter their scores in the columns (A, B, C, D, E, and so on) under the heading "Observers' Ratings." Simply transfer the numbers from page W-14 of each Student LPI-Observer to your scoring grids, using one column for each observer. For example, enter the first observer's scores in column A, the second observer's scores in column B, and so on. The grids provide space for the scores of as many as ten observers.

After all scores have been entered for Challenging the Process, total each column in the row marked "Totals." Then add all the totals for observers; do not include the "self" total. Write this grand total in the space marked "Total of All Observers' Scores." To obtain the average, divide the grand total by the number of people who completed the Student LPI-Observer. Write this average in the blank provided. The sample grid shows how the grid would look with scores for self and five observers entered.

Sample Grid with Scores from Self and Five Observers

	SELF-RATING	OBSERVERS' RATINGS										
		A	B	C	D	E	F	G	H	I	J	
1. Seeks challenge	5	4	2	4	4	2						
6. Keeps current	4	4	3	4	4	3						
11. Initiates experiment	3	3	2	2	2	1						
16. Looks for ways to improve	4	3	2	3	5	3						
21. Asks "What can we learn?"	2	3	2	3	3	2						TOTAL OF ALL OBSERVERS' SCORES
26. Lets others take risks	5	3	3	2	3	2						
TOTALS	23	20	14	18	21	13						86

TOTAL SELF-RATING: _____23_____   AVERAGE OF ALL OBSERVERS: _____17.2_____

The other four grids should be completed in the same manner.

The second grid (Inspiring a Shared Vision) is for recording scores to the items that pertain to envisioning the future and enlisting the support of others. These include items 2, 7, 12, 17, 22, and 27.

The third grid (Enabling Others to Act) pertains to items 3, 8, 13, 18, 23, and 28, which involve fostering collaboration and strengthening others.

The fourth grid (Modeling the Way) pertains to items about setting an example and planning small wins.

These include items 4, 9, 14, 19, 24, and 29.

The fifth grid (Encouraging the Heart) pertains to items about recognizing contributions and celebrating accomplishments. These are items 5, 10, 15, 20, 25, and 30.

Grids for Recording *Student LPI* Scores

Scores should be recorded on the following grids in accordance with the instructions on page W-13. As you look at individual scores, remember the rating system that was used:

"1" means that you *rarely or seldom* engage in the behavior.

"2" means that you engage in the behavior *once in a while*.

"3" means that you *sometimes* engage in the behavior.

"4" means that you engage in the behavior *fairly often*.

"5" means that you engage in the behavior *very frequently*.

After you have recorded all your scores and calculated the totals and averages, turn to page W-17 and read the section on interpreting scores.

Challenging the Process

	SELF-RATING	OBSERVERS' RATINGS									
		A	B	C	D	E	F	G	H	I	J
1. Seeks challenge											
6. Keeps current											
11. Initiates experiment											
16. Looks for ways to improve											
21. Asks "What can we learn?"											
26. Lets others take risks											
TOTALS											

TOTAL OF ALL OBSERVERS' SCORES

TOTAL SELF-RATING: _____   AVERAGE OF ALL OBSERVERS: _____

Inspiring a Shared Vision

	SELF-RATING	OBSERVERS' RATINGS									
		A	B	C	D	E	F	G	H	I	J
2. Describes ideal capabilities											
7. Looks ahead and communicates future											
12. Upbeat and positive communicator											
17. Finds common ground											
22. Communicates purpose and meaning											
27. Enthusiastic about possibilities											
TOTALS											

TOTAL OF ALL OBSERVERS' SCORES

TOTAL SELF-RATING: _____   AVERAGE OF ALL OBSERVERS: _____

Enabling Others to Act

	SELF-RATING	OBSERVERS' RATINGS									
		A	B	C	D	E	F	G	H	I	J
3. Includes others in planning											
8. Treats others with respect											
13. Supports decisions of others											
18. Fosters cooperative relationships											
23. Provides freedom and choice											
28. Lets others lead											
TOTALS											

TOTAL OF ALL OBSERVERS' SCORES

TOTAL SELF-RATING: _____   AVERAGE OF ALL OBSERVERS: _____

Modeling the Way

	SELF-RATING	OBSERVERS' RATINGS									
		A	B	C	D	E	F	G	H	I	J
4. Shares beliefs about leading											
9. Breaks projects into steps											
14. Sets personal example											
19. Talks about guiding values											
24. Follows through on promises											
29. Sets clear goals and plans											
TOTALS											

TOTAL OF ALL OBSERVERS' SCORES

TOTAL SELF-RATING: _____   AVERAGE OF ALL OBSERVERS: _____

• •

Encouraging the Heart

	SELF-RATING	OBSERVERS' RATINGS									
		A	B	C	D	E	F	G	H	I	J
5. Encourages other people											
10. Recognizes people's contributions											
15. Praises people for job well done											
20. Gives support and appreciation											
25. Finds ways to publicly celebrate											
30. Tells others about group's good work											
TOTALS											

TOTAL OF ALL OBSERVERS' SCORES

TOTAL SELF-RATING: _____

AVERAGE OF ALL OBSERVERS: _____

> THE unique ROLE
> OF leaders
> IS TO *take us*
> TO places
> WE'VE never
> *been* before.

4

Interpreting Your Scores

This section will help you to interpret your scores by looking at them in several ways and making notes to yourself about what you can do to become a more effective leader.

Ranking Your Ratings

Refer to the previous chapter, "Recording Your Scores." On each grid, look at your scores in the blanks marked "Total Self-Rating."

Each of these totals represents your responses to six statements about one of the five leadership practices. Each of your totals can range from a low of 6 to a high of 30.

In the blanks that follow, write "1" to the left of the leadership practice with the highest total self-rating, "2" by the next-highest total self-rating, and so on. This ranking represents the leadership practices with which you feel most comfortable, second-most comfortable, and so on. The practice you identify with a "5" is the practice with which you feel least comfortable.

Again refer to the previous chapter, but this time look at your scores in the blanks marked "Average of All Observers." The number in each blank is the average score given to you by the people you asked to complete the Student LPI-Observer. Like each of your total self-ratings, this number can range from 6 to 30.

In the blanks that follow, write "1" to the right of the leadership practice with the highest score, "2" by the next-highest score, and so on. This ranking represents the leadership practices that others feel you use most often, second-most often, and so on.

Self		Observers
_____	Challenging the Process	_____
_____	Inspiring a Shared Vision	_____
_____	Enabling Others to Act	_____
_____	Modeling the Way	_____
_____	Encouraging the Heart	_____

Comparing Your Self-Ratings to Observers' Ratings

To compare your Student LPI-Self and Student LPI-Observer assessments, refer to the "Chart for Graphing Your Scores" on the next page. On the chart, designate your scores on the five leadership practices (Challenging, Inspiring,

Enabling, Modeling, and Encouraging) by marking each of these points with a capital "S" (for "Self"). Connect the five resulting "S scores" with a *solid line* and label the end of this line "Self" (see sample chart below).

If other people provided input through the Student LPI-Observer,

designate the average observer scores (see the blanks labeled "Average of All Observers" on the scoring grids) by marking each of the points with a capital "O" (for "Observer"). Then connect the five resulting "O scores" with a *dashed line* and label the end of this line "Observer" (see sample chart). Completing this process will provide you with a graphic representation (one solid and one dashed line) illustrating the relationship between your self-perception and the observations of other people.

Chart for Graphing Your Scores

Percentile	Challenging the Process	Inspiring a Shared Vision	Enabling Others to Act	Modeling the Way	Encouraging the Heart
100%	30 29 28	30 29	30	30 29 28	30
	27	28	29		29
90%	26	27		27	
	25	26	28	26	28
80%		25		25	27
	24		S		
70%					26
	23	S	26	24	
60%		23			S
	22		O	23	O
50%		22	25		24
				S	
40%	S	21			23
		20	24		
30%	20			21	22
		19	23	20	21
20%	19 O	18	22	19	20
	18	17	21		19
10%	17	16 15	20	18	18
	16 15	14	19 18	17 16	17 16

Chart for Graphing Your Scores

Percentile	Challenging the Process	Inspiring a Shared Vision	Enabling Others to Act	Modeling the Way	Encouraging the Heart
100%	30 29 28	30 29	30	30 29 28	30
	27	28	29	27	29
90%	26	27			28
	25	26	28	26	
80%					27
	24	25	27	25	
70%					26
	23	24	26	24	
60%		23			25
	22			23	
50%		22	25		24
	21			22	
40%		21	24		23
30%	20	20		21	22
		19	23	20	21
20%	19	18	22	19	20
	18	17	21	18	19
10%	17	16 15	20	17	18
	16 15	14	19 18	16	17 16

Percentile Scores

Look again at the "Chart for Graphing Your Scores." The column to the far left represents the Student LPI-Self percentile rankings for more than 1,200 student leaders. A percentile ranking is determined by the percentage of people who score at or below a given number. For example, if your total self-rating for "Challenging" is at the 60th percentile line on the "Chart for Graphing Your Scores," this means that you assessed yourself higher than 60 percent of all people who have completed the *Student LPI;* you would be in the top 40 percent in this leadership practice. Studies indicate that a "high" score is one at or above the 70th percentile, a "low" score is one at or below the 30th percentile, and a score that falls between those ranges is considered "moderate."

Using these criteria, circle the "H" (for "High"), the "M" (for "Moderate"), or the "L" (for "Low") for each leadership practice on the "Range of Scores" table below. Compared to other student leaders around the country, where do your leadership practices tend to fall? (Given a "normal distribution," it is expected that most people's scores will fall within the moderate range.)

Range of Scores

In my perception				In others' perception			
Practice	**Rating**			**Practice**	**Rating**		
Challenging the Process	H	M	L	Challenging the Process	H	M	L
Inspiring a Shared Vision	H	M	L	Inspiring a Shared Vision	H	M	L
Enabling Others to Act	H	M	L	Enabling Others to Act	H	M	L
Modeling the Way	H	M	L	Modeling the Way	H	M	L
Encouraging the Heart	H	M	L	Encouraging the Heart	H	M	L

Exploring Specific Leadership Behaviors

Looking at your scoring grids, review each of the thirty items on the *Student LPI* by practice. One or two of the six behaviors within each leadership practice may be higher or lower than the rest. If so, on which specific items is there variation? What do these differences suggest? On which specific items are there agreement? Please write your thoughts in the following space.

Challenging the Process

_____

_____

_____

_____

_____

_____

_____

Inspiring a Shared Vision

_____

_____

_____

_____

_____

_____

Enabling Others to Act

_____

_____

_____

_____

_____

_____

Modeling the Way

_____

_____

_____

Encouraging the Heart

_____

_____

_____

_____

_____

_____

**Comparing Observers'
Responses to One Another**

Study the Student LPI-Observer
scores for each of the five leadership
practices. Do some respondents'
scores differ significantly from others? If so, are the differences local-
ized in the scores of one or two people? On which leadership practices
do the respondents agree? On which
practices do they disagree? If you
try to behave basically the same
with all the people who assessed
you, how do you explain the difference in ratings? Please write your
thoughts in the following space.

_____

_____

_____

_____

_____

_____

_____

_____

_____

_____

_____

_____

_____

Wanting TO LEAD AND
believing THAT
YOU *can lead* ARE THE
departure POINTS
ON THE PATH TO **leadership.**
LEADERSHIP IS AN ART—
A *performing* **art**—
AND THE **instrument**
IS THE **self.**

5

Summary and Action-Planning Worksheets

ake a few moments to summarize your *Student LPI* feedback by completing the following Strengths and Opportunities Summary Worksheet. Refer
to the "Chart for Graphing Your Scores," the "Range of Scores" table, and
any notes you have made.

After the summary worksheet you
will find some suggestions for getting started on meeting the leadership challenge. With these suggestions in mind, review your *Student
LPI* feedback and decide on the actions you will take to become an
even more effective leader. Then
complete the Action-Planning
Worksheet to spell out the steps you
will take. (One Action-Planning
Worksheet is included in this workbook, but you may want to develop
action plans for several practices or
behaviors. You could make copies of
the blank form before you fill it in or
just use a separate sheet of paper for
each leadership practice in which
you plan to improve.)

**Strengths and Opportunities
Summary Worksheet**

Strengths

Which of the leadership practices
and behaviors are you most comfortable with? Why? Can you do more?

_____

_____

_____

_____

_____

_____

_____

Areas for Improvement

What can you do to use a practice more frequently? What will it take to feel more comfortable?

_____

_____

_____

_____

_____

_____

Following are ten suggestions for getting started on meeting the leadership challenge.

Prescriptions for Meeting the Leadership Challenge

Challenge the Process
- Fix something
- Adopt the "great ideas" of others

Inspire a Shared Vision
- Let others know how you feel
- Recount your "personal best"

Enable Others to Act
- Always say "we"
- Make heroes of other people

Model the Way
- Lead by example
- Create opportunities for small wins

Encourage the Heart
- Write "thank you" notes
- Celebrate, and link your celebrations to your organization's values

Action-Planning Worksheet

1. What would you like to be better able to do?

_____

_____

_____

_____

_____

_____

_____

_____

_____

2. What specific actions will you take?

_____

_____

_____

_____

_____

_____

_____

_____

_____

3. What is the first action you will take? Who will be involved? When will you begin?

Action _____

_____

People Involved

_____

_____

_____

_____

Target Date _____

4. Complete this sentence: "I will know I have improved in this leadership skill when . . ."

_____

_____

_____

_____

5. When will you review your progress? _____

About the Authors

James M. Kouzes is chairman of TPG/Learning Systems, which makes leadership work through practical, performance-oriented learning programs. In 1993 *The Wall Street Journal* cited Jim as one of the twelve most requested "nonuniversity executive-education providers" to U.S. companies. His list of past and present clients includes AT&T, Boeing, Boy Scouts of America, Charles Schwab, Ciba-Geigy, Dell Computer, First Bank System, Honeywell, Johnson & Johnson, Levi Strauss & Co., Motorola, Pacific Bell, Stanford University, Xerox Corporation, and the YMCA.

Barry Z. Posner, Ph.D., is dean of the Leavey School of Business, Santa Clara University, and professor of organizational behavior. He has received several outstanding teaching and leadership awards, has published more than eighty research and practitioner-oriented articles, and currently is on the editorial review boards for *The Journal of Management Education, The Journal of Management Inquiry,* and *The Journal of Business Ethics.* Barry also serves on the board of directors for Public Allies and for The Center for Excellence in Non-Profits. His clients have ranged from retailers to firms in health care, high technology, financial services, manufacturing, and community service agencies.

Kouzes and Posner are coauthors of several best-selling and award-winning leadership books. *The Leadership Challenge: How to Keep Getting Extraordinary Things Done in Organizations* (2nd ed., 1995), with over 800,000 copies in print, has been reprinted into fifteen foreign languages, featured in three video programs, and received a Critic's Choice award from the nation's newspaper book review editors. *Credibility: How Leaders Gain and Lose It, Why People Demand It* (1993) was chosen by *Industry Week* as one of the five best management books of the year. Their latest book is *Encouraging the Heart: A Leader's Guide to Rewarding and Recognizing Others* (1998).

STUDENT LEADERSHIP PRACTICES INVENTORY — SELF

Your Name: _____

Instructions

On the next two pages are thirty statements describing various leadership behaviors. Please read each statement carefully. Then rate *yourself* in terms of *how frequently* you engage in the behavior described. *This is not a test* (there are no right or wrong answers).

Consider each statement in the context of the student organization (for example, club, team, chapter, group, unit, hall, program, project) with which you are most involved. The rating scale provides five choices:

(1) If you RARELY or SELDOM do what is described in the statement, circle the number one (1).
(2) If you do what is described ONCE IN A WHILE, circle the number two (2).
(3) If you SOMETIMES do what is described, circle the number three (3).
(4) If you do what is described FAIRLY OFTEN, circle the number four (4).
(5) If you do what is described VERY FREQUENTLY or ALMOST ALWAYS, circle the number five (5).

Please respond to every statement.

In selecting the response, be realistic about the extent to which you *actually* engage in the behavior. Do *not* answer in terms of how you would like to see yourself or in terms of what you should be doing. Answer in terms of how you *typically* behave. The usefulness of the feedback from this inventory will depend on how honest you are with yourself about how frequently you actually engage in each of these behaviors.

For example, the first statement is "I look for opportunities that challenge my skills and abilities." If you believe you do this "once in a while," circle the number 2. If you believe you look for challenging opportunities "fairly often," circle the number 4.

When you have responded to all thirty statements, please turn to the response sheet on the back page and transfer your responses as instructed. Thank you.

STUDENT LEADERSHIP PRACTICES INVENTORY-SELF

How frequently do you typically engage in the following behaviors and actions? *Circle* the number that applies to each statement.

1 SELDOM OR RARELY	2 ONCE IN A WHILE	3 SOMETIMES	4 FAIRLY OFTEN	5 VERY FREQUENTLY

1. I look for opportunities that challenge my skills and abilities.	1	2	3	4	5
2. I describe to others in our organization what we should be capable of accomplishing.	1	2	3	4	5
3. I include others in planning the activities and programs of our organization.	1	2	3	4	5
4. I share my beliefs about how things can be run most effectively within our organization.	1	2	3	4	5
5. I encourage others as they work on activities and programs in our organization.	1	2	3	4	5
6. I keep current on events and activities that might affect our organization.	1	2	3	4	5
7. I look ahead and communicate about what I believe will affect us in the future.	1	2	3	4	5
8. I treat others with dignity and respect.	1	2	3	4	5
9. I break our organization's projects down into manageable steps.	1	2	3	4	5
10. I make sure that people in our organization are recognized for their contributions.	1	2	3	4	5
11. I take initiative in experimenting with the way we do things in our organization.	1	2	3	4	5
12. I am upbeat and positive when talking about what our organization is doing.	1	2	3	4	5
13. I support the decisions that other people in our organization make on their own.	1	2	3	4	5
14. I set a personal example of what I expect from other people.	1	2	3	4	5
15. I praise people for a job well done.	1	2	3	4	5
16. I look for ways to improve whatever project or task I am involved in.	1	2	3	4	5
17. I talk with others about how their own interests can be met by working toward a common goal.	1	2	3	4	5
18. I foster cooperative rather than competitive relationships among people I work with.	1	2	3	4	5
19. I talk about the values and principles that guide my actions.	1	2	3	4	5
20. I give people in our organization support and express appreciation for their contributions.	1	2	3	4	5
21. I ask, "What can we learn from this experience?" when things do not go as we expected.	1	2	3	4	5
22. I speak with conviction about the higher purpose and meaning of what we are doing.	1	2	3	4	5
23. I give others a great deal of freedom and choice in deciding how to do their work.	1	2	3	4	5
24. I follow through on the promises and commitments I make in this organization.	1	2	3	4	5
25. I find ways for us to celebrate our accomplishments publicly.	1	2	3	4	5
26. I let others experiment and take risks even when outcomes are uncertain.	1	2	3	4	5
27. I show my enthusiasm and excitement about what our organization is doing.	1	2	3	4	5
28. I provide opportunities for others to take on leadership responsibilities.	1	2	3	4	5
29. I make sure that we set goals and make specific plans for the projects we undertake.	1	2	3	4	5
30. I make it a point to tell others about the good work done by our organization.	1	2	3	4	5

Transferring the Scores

After you have responded to the thirty statements on the previous two pages, please transfer your responses to the blanks below. This will make it easier to record and score your responses. Notice that the numbers of the statements are listed *horizontally.* Make sure that the number you assigned to each statement is transferred to the appropriate blank. Fill in a response for every item.

1. _____   2. _____   3. _____   4. _____   5. _____

6. _____   7. _____   8. _____   9. _____   10. _____

11. _____   12. _____   13. _____   14. _____   15. _____

16. _____   17. _____   18. _____   19. _____   20. _____

21. _____   22. _____   23. _____   24. _____   25. _____

26. _____   27. _____   28. _____   29. _____   30. _____

Further Instructions

Please write your name here: _____

Please bring this form with you to the workshop (seminar or class) or return this form to:

_____

_____

_____

_____

If you are interested in feedback from other people, ask them to complete the Student LPI-Observer, which provides you with perspectives on your leadership behaviors as perceived by others.

Printed in the United States of America.

Jossey-Bass Publishers
350 Sansome Street
San Francisco, California 94104
(888) 378-2537
Fax (800) 605-2665

www.josseybass.com

Printing 10 9 8 7 6 5 4 3

This instrument is printed on acid-free, recycled stock that meets or exceeds the minimum GPO and EPA requirements for recycled paper.

ISBN: 0-7879-4426-2

STUDENT LEADERSHIP PRACTICES INVENTORY—OBSERVER

Name of Leader:_____

Instructions

On the next two pages are thirty descriptive statements about various leadership behaviors. Please read each statement carefully. Then rate *the person who asked you to complete this form* in terms of *how frequently* he or she typically engages in the described behavior. *This is not a test* (there are no right or wrong answers).

Consider each statement in the context of the student organization (for example, club, team, chapter, group, unit, hall, program, project) with which that person is most involved or with which you have had the greatest opportunity to observe him or her. The rating scale provides five choices:

(1) If this person RARELY or SELDOM does what is described in the statement, circle the number one (1).
(2) If this person does what is described ONCE IN A WHILE, circle the number two (2).
(3) If this person SOMETIMES does what is described, circle the number three (3).
(4) If this person does what is described FAIRLY OFTEN, circle the number four (4).
(5) If this person does what is described VERY FREQUENTLY or ALMOST ALWAYS, circle the number five (5).

Please respond to every statement.

In selecting the response, be realistic about the extent to which this person *actually* engages in the behavior. Do *not* answer in terms of how you would like to see this person behaving or in terms of what this person should be doing. Answer in terms of how he or she *typically behaves*. The usefulness of the feedback from this inventory will depend on how honest you are about how frequently you observe this person actually engaging in each of these behaviors.

For example, the first statement is, "He or she looks for opportunities that challenge his or her skills and abilities." If you believe this person does this "once in a while," circle the number 2. If you believe he or she looks for challenging opportunities "fairly often," circle the number 4.

When you have responded to all thirty statements, please turn to the response sheet on the back page and transfer your responses as instructed. Thank you.

STUDENT LEADERSHIP PRACTICES INVENTORY—OBSERVER

How frequently does this person typically engage in the following behaviors and actions? *Circle* the number that applies to each statement:

1 SELDOM OR RARELY	2 ONCE IN A WHILE	3 SOMETIMES	4 FAIRLY OFTEN	5 VERY FREQUENTLY

He or She:

1. looks for opportunities that challenge his or her skills and abilities.	1	2	3	4	5
2. describes to others in our organization what we should be capable of accomplishing.	1	2	3	4	5
3. includes others in planning the activities and programs of our organization.	1	2	3	4	5
4. shares his or her beliefs about how things can be run most effectively within our organization.	1	2	3	4	5
5. encourages others as they work on activities and programs in our organization.	1	2	3	4	5
6. keeps current on events and activities that might affect our organization.	1	2	3	4	5
7. looks ahead and communicates about what he or she believes will affect us in the future.	1	2	3	4	5
8. treats others with dignity and respect.	1	2	3	4	5
9. breaks our organization's projects down into manageable steps.	1	2	3	4	5
10. makes sure that people in our organization are recognized for their contributions.	1	2	3	4	5
11. takes initiative in experimenting with the way we do things in our organization.	1	2	3	4	5
12. is upbeat and positive when talking about what our organization is doing.	1	2	3	4	5
13. supports the decisions that other people in our organization make on their own.	1	2	3	4	5
14. sets a personal example of what he or she expects from other people.	1	2	3	4	5
15. praises people for a job well done.	1	2	3	4	5
16. looks for ways to improve whatever project or task he or she is involved in.	1	2	3	4	5
17. talks with others about how their own interests can be met by working toward a common goal.	1	2	3	4	5
18. fosters cooperative rather than competitive relationships among people he or she works with.	1	2	3	4	5
19. talks about the values and principles that guide his or her actions.	1	2	3	4	5
20. gives people in our organization support and expresses appreciation for their contributions.	1	2	3	4	5
21. asks "What can we learn from this experience?" when things do not go as we expected.	1	2	3	4	5
22. speaks with conviction about the higher purpose and meaning of what we are doing.	1	2	3	4	5
23. gives others a great deal of freedom and choice in deciding how to do their work.	1	2	3	4	5
24. follows through on the promises and commitments he or she makes in this organization.	1	2	3	4	5
25. finds ways for us to celebrate our accomplishments publicly.	1	2	3	4	5
26. lets others experiment and take risks even when outcomes are uncertain.	1	2	3	4	5
27. shows his or her enthusiasm and excitement about what our organization is doing.	1	2	3	4	5
28. provides opportunities for others to take on leadership responsibilities.	1	2	3	4	5
29. makes sure that we set goals and make specific plans for the projects we undertake.	1	2	3	4	5
30. makes it a point to tell others about the good work done by our organization.	1	2	3	4	5

Transferring the Scores

After you have responded to the thirty statements on the previous two pages, please transfer your responses to the blanks below. This will make it easier to record and score your responses. Notice that the numbers of the statements are listed *horizontally.* Make sure that the number you assigned to each statement is transferred to the appropriate blank. Fill in a response for every item.

1. _____	2. _____	3. _____	4. _____	5. _____
6. _____	7. _____	8. _____	9. _____	10. _____
11. _____	12. _____	13. _____	14. _____	15. _____
16. _____	17. _____	18. _____	19. _____	20. _____
21. _____	22. _____	23. _____	24. _____	25. _____
26. _____	27. _____	28. _____	29. _____	30. _____

Further Instructions

The above scores are for (name of person): _____

Please bring this form with you to the workshop (seminar or class) or return this form to:

_____

_____

_____

_____

ISBN: 0-7879-4427-0

Printed in the United States of America.

Jossey-Bass Publishers
350 Sansome Street
San Francisco, California 94104
(888) 378-2537
Fax (800) 605-2665

www.josseybass.com

Printing 10 9 8 7 6 5 4 3 2 1

This instrument is printed on acid-free, recycled stock that meets or exceeds the minimum GPO and EPA requirements for recycled paper.

EXPERIENTIAL EXERCISES FROM THE PFEIFFER ANNUAL: TRAINING

1. Sweet Tooth: Bonding Strangers into a Team

R.A. Black, *The 2002 Annual: Volume 1, Training* © *2002* Jossey-Bass/Pfeiffer, A Wiley Imprint

EXPERIENTIAL EXERCISES FROM THE PFEIFFER ANNUAL: TRAINING

2. Interrogatories: Identifying Issues and Needs

C. Holton, *The 2002 Annual: Volume 1, Training* © *2002* Jossey-Bass/Pfeiffer, A Wiley Imprint

EXPERIENTIAL EXERCISES FROM THE PFEIFFER ANNUAL: TRAINING

3. Decode: Working with Different Instructions

S. Thiagarajan, *The 2003 Annual: Volume 1, Training* © *2003* Jossey-Bass/Pfeiffer, A Wiley Imprint

EXPERIENTIAL EXERCISES FROM THE PFEIFFER ANNUAL: TRAINING

4. Choices: Learning Effective Conflict Management Strategies

C. Kormanski, Sr. and C. Kormanski, Jr., *The 2003 Annual: Volume 1, Training* © *2003* Jossey-Bass/Pfeiffer, A Wiley Imprint

EXPERIENTIAL EXERCISES FROM THE PFEIFFER ANNUAL: TRAINING

5. Internal/External Motivators: Encouraging Creativity

E.A. Smith, *The 2003 Annual: Volume 1, Training* © *2003* Jossey-Bass/Pfeiffer, A Wiley Imprint

EXPERIENTIAL EXERCISES FROM THE PFEIFFER ANNUAL: TRAINING

6. Quick Hitter: Fostering the Creative Spirit

M.G. Hernandez and T.T. Coronas, *The 2003 Annual: Volume 1, Training* © *2003* Jossey-Bass/Pfeiffer, A Wiley Imprint

SWEET TOOTH: BONDING STRANGERS INTO A TEAM

Process Procedure:

The general idea is just to relax, have fun, and get to know one another while completing a task. Form groups of five. All groups in the room will be competing to see which one can first complete the items below with the name of a candy bar or sweet treat. The team that completes the most items correctly first will win a prize.

1. Pee Wee . . ., baseball player.
2. Dried up cows.
3. Kids' game minus toes.
4. Not bad and more than some.
5. Explosion in the sky.
6. Polka. . . .
7. Rhymes with Bert's, dirts, hurts.
8. Happy place to drink.
9. Drowning prevention device.
10. Belongs to a mechanic from Mayberry's cousin.
11. They're not "lesses"; they're. . . .
12. Two names for a purring pet.
13. Takes 114 licks to get to the center of these.
14. Sounds like asteroids.
15. A military weapon.
16. A young flavoring.
17. Top of mountains in winter.
18. To catch fish you need to. . . .
19. Sounds like riddles and fiddles.

Source: Robert Allan Black, The 2002 Annual Volume 1, Training/© 2002 John Wiley & Sons, Inc.

Questions for discussion:
- What lessons about effective teamwork can be learned from this activity?
- What caused each subgroup to be successful?
- What might be learned about effective teamwork from what happened during this activity.
- What might be done next time to increase the chances of success?

Variation
- Have the individual subgroups create their own lists of clues for the names of candies/candy bars/sweets. Collect the lists and make a grand list using one or two from each group's contribution. Then hold a competition among the total group.

INTERROGATORIES: IDENTIFYING ISSUES AND NEEDS

Procedure:

This activity is an opportunity to discover what issues and questions people have brought to the class. The instructor will select from the topic list below. Once a topic is raised, participants should ask any questions they have related to that topic. No one is to *answer* a question at this time. The goal is to come up with as many questions as possible in the time allowed. Feel free to build on a question already asked, or share a completely different question.

Interrogatories Starter Topic List

- Class requirements
- Coaching
- Communication
- Customers
- Instant messaging
- Job demands
- Leadership
- Management
- Meetings
- Mission
- Performance Appraisal
- Personality
- Priorities
- Project priorities
- Quality
- Rules
- Service
- Social activities
- Success
- Task uncertainty
- Teamwork
- Time
- Training
- Values
- Work styles

Questions for discussion:
- How did you feel about this process?
- What common themes did you hear?
- What questions would you most like to have answered?

Source: Cher Holton, The 2002 Annual: Volume 1, Training/© 2002 John Wiley & Sons, Inc.

DECODE: WORKING WITH DIFFERENT INSTRUCTIONS

Procedure:

1. You are probably familiar with codes and cryptograms from your childhood days. In a cryptogram, each letter in the message is replaced by another letter of the alphabet. For example, LET THE GAMES BEGIN! May become this cryptogram:

YZF FOZ JUKZH CZJVQ!

In the cryptogram Y replaces L, Z replaces E, F replaces T, and so on. Notice that the same letter substitutions are used throughout this cryptogram: Every E in the sentence is replaced by a Z, and every T is replaced by an F.

Here's some information to help you solve cryptograms:

Letter Frequency

The most commonly used letters of the English language are *e, t, a, i, o, n, s, h,* and *r.*

The letters that are most commonly found at the beginning of words are *t, a, o, d,* and *w.*

The letters that are most commonly found at the end of words are *e, s, d,* and *t.*

Word Frequency

One-letter words are either *a* or *I.*

The most common two-letter words are *to, of, in, it, is, as, at, be, we, he, so, on, an, or, do, if, up, by,* and *my.*

The most common three-letter words are *the, and, are, for, not, but, had, has, was, all, any, one, man, out, you, his, her,* and *can.*

The most common four-letter words are *that, with, have, this, will, your, from, they, want, been, good, much, some,* and *very.*

2. The goal of the activity is to learn to work together more effectively in teams. Form into groups of four to seven members each. Have members briefly share their knowledge of solving cryptogram puzzles.

3. In this exercise all groups will be asked to solve the same cryptogram. If a team correctly and completely solves the cryptogram within two minutes, it will earn two hundred points. If it takes more than two minutes but fewer than three minutes, the team will earn fifty points.

4. Before working on the cryptogram, each participant will receive an Instruction Sheet with hints on how to solve cryptograms. Participants can study this sheet for two minutes only. (The sheet will be collected after 2 minutes.) They may not mark up the Instruction Sheet but they may take notes on an index card or a blank piece of paper. The Instruction Sheets will be taken back after two minutes.

5. At any time a group can send one of its members to ask for help from the instructor. The instructor will decode any *one* of the words in the cryptogram selected by the group member.

6. After the points are tallied, the Instructor will lead class discussion.

DECODE CRYPTOGRAM

ISV'B   JZZXYH BPJB BPH SVQE

⎯⎯⎯⎯⎯ ⎯⎯⎯⎯⎯⎯ ⎯⎯⎯⎯ ⎯⎯⎯ ,

UJE BS UCV CZ BS FSYTHBH.

⎯⎯⎯⎯⎯ ⎯⎯ ⎯⎯⎯ ⎯⎯ ⎯⎯ ⎯⎯⎯⎯⎯⎯.

ZSYHBCYHZ BPH AHZB UJE BS

⎯⎯⎯⎯⎯⎯⎯⎯ ⎯⎯⎯ ⎯⎯⎯⎯ ⎯⎯⎯ ⎯⎯

UCV CZ BS FSSTHWJBH UCBP

⎯⎯⎯ ⎯⎯ ⎯⎯ ⎯⎯⎯⎯⎯⎯⎯⎯ ⎯⎯⎯⎯

SBPHWZ—Z. BPCJMJWJOJV

⎯⎯⎯⎯⎯⎯—⎯. ⎯⎯⎯⎯⎯⎯⎯⎯⎯⎯

Source: Sivasailam "Thiagi" Thiagarajan, *The 2003 Annual: Volume 1, Training/* © 2003 John Wiley & Sons, Inc.

CHOICES: LEARNING EFFECTIVE CONFLICT MANAGEMENT STRATEGIES

Procedure: Form teams of three.

Assume you are a group of top managers who are responsible for an organization of seven departments. Working as a team, choose an appropriate strategy to intervene in the situations below when the conflict must be managed in some way. Your choices are *withdrawal, suppression, integration, compromise,* and *authority.* Refer to the list below for some characteristics of each strategy. Write your team's choice following each situation number. Engage in discussion led by the instructor.

CHOICES: STRATEGIES AND CONTINGENCIES

Withdrawal Strategy

Use When (Advantages)
- Choosing sides is to be avoided
- Critical information is missing
- The issue is outside the group
- Others are competent and delegation is appropriate
- You are powerless

Be Aware (Disadvantages)
- Legitimate action ceases
- Direct information stops
- Failure can be perceived
- Cannot be used in a crisis

Suppression (and Diffusion) Strategy

Use When (Advantages)
- A cooling down period is needed
- The issue is unimportant
- A relationship is important

Be Aware (Disadvantages)
- The issue may intensify
- You may appear weak and ineffective

Integration Strategy

Use When (Advantages)
- Group problem solving is needed
- New alternatives are helpful
- Group commitment is required
- Promoting openness and trust

Be Aware (Disadvantages)
- Group goals must be put first
- More time is required for dialogue
- It doesn't work with rigid, dull people

Compromise Strategy

Use When (Advantages)
- Power is equal
- Resources are limited
- A win-win settlement is desired

Be Aware (Disadvantages)
- Action (a third choice) can be weakened
- Inflation is encouraged
- A third party may be needed for negotiation

Authority Strategy

Use When (Advantages)
- A deadlock persists
- Others are incompetent
- Time is limited (crisis)
- An unpopular decision must be made
- Survival of the organization is critical

Be Aware (Disadvantages)
- Emotions intensify quickly
- Dependency is promoted
- Winners and losers are created

Source: Chuck Kormanski, Sr. and Chuck Kormanski, Jr., *The 2003 Annual: Volume 1, Training/© 2003 John Wiley & Sons, Inc.*

Situation #1

Two employees of the support staff have requested the same two-week vacation period. They are the only two trained to carry out an essential task using a complex computer software program that cannot be mastered quickly. You have encouraged others to learn this process so there is more backup for the position, but heavy workloads have prevented this from occurring.

Situation #2

A sales manager has requested a raise because there are now two salespeople on commission earning higher salaries. The work performance of this individual currently does not merit a raise of the amount requested, mostly due to the person turning in critical reports late and missing a number of days of work. The person's sales group is one of the highest rated in the organization, but this may be the result of having superior individuals assigned to the team, rather than to the effectiveness of the manager.

Situation #3

It has become obvious that the copy machine located in a customer service area is being used for a variety of personal reasons, including reproducing obscene jokes. A few copies have sometimes been found lying on or near the machine at the close of the business day. You have mentioned the matter briefly in the organization's employee newsletter, but recently you have noticed an increase in the activity. Most of the office staff seems to be involved.

Situation #4

Three complaints have filtered upward to you from long-term employees concerning a newly hired individual. This person has a pierced nose and a visible tattoo. The work performance of the individual is adequate and the person does not have to see customers; however, the employees who have complained allege that the professional appearance of the office area has been compromised.

Situation #5

The organization has a flex-time schedule format that requires all employees to work the core hours of 10 a.m. to 3 p.m., Monday through Friday. Two department managers have complained that another department does not always maintain that policy. The manager of the department in question has responded by citing recent layoffs and additional work responsibilities as reasons for making exceptions to policy.

Situation #6

As a result of a recent downsizing, an office in a coveted location is now available. Three individuals have made a request to the department manager for the office. The manager has recommended that the office be given to one of the three. This individual has the highest performance rating, but was aided in obtaining employment with the company by the department manager, who is a good friend of the person's family. Colleagues prefer not to work with this individual, as there is seldom any evidence of teamwork.

Situation #7

Two department managers have requested a budget increase in the areas of travel and computer equipment. Each asks that your group support this request. The CEO, not your group, will make the final decision. You are aware that increasing funds for one department will result in a decrease for others, as the total budget figures for all of these categories are set.

Situation #8

Few of the management staff attended the Fourth of July picnic held at a department manager's country home last year. This particular manager, who has been a loyal team player for the past twenty-one years, has indicated that he/she plans to host the event again this year. Many of you have personally found the event to be boring, with little to do but talk and eat. Already, a few of the other managers have suggested that the event be held at a different location with a new format or else be cancelled.

Situation #9

It has come to your attention that a manager and a subordinate in the same department are having a romantic affair openly in the building. Both are married to other people. They have been taking extended lunch periods, yet both remain beyond quitting time to complete their work. Colleagues have begun to complain that neither is readily available mid-day and that they do not return messages in a timely manner.

Situation #10

Two loyal department managers are concerned that a newly hired manager who is wheelchair-bound has been given too much in the way of accommodations beyond what is required by the Americans with Disabilities Act. They have requested similar changes to make their own work lives easier. Specifically, they cite office size and location on the building's main floor as points of contention.

INTERNAL/EXTERNAL MOTIVATORS: ENCOURAGING CREATIVITY

Procedure:

1. This interactive, experience-based activity is designed to increase participants' awareness of creativity and creative processes. Begin by thinking of
   a job that you now hold or have held. Then complete Questions 1 and 2
   from the Internal/External Motivators Questionnaire (see below).
2. Form into groups. Share your questionnaire results and make a list of responses to Question 1.
3. Discuss and compare rankings of major work activities listed for Question
   2. Make a list with at least two responses from each participant.
4. Individually record your answers to Questions 3 and 4 below. Then share
   and again list member responses within your group.

5. Individually, compare your responses to Questions 1 and 2 with your responses to Questions 3 and 4. Then answer Question 5. Again, share with
   the group and make a group list of answers to Question 5 to the recorder,
   who is to record these answers on the flip chart. (Ten minutes.)

Questions for Discussion:

- What was the most important part of this activity for you?
- What have you learned about motivation?
- What impact will having done this activity have for you back in the work-
  place?
- How will what you have learned change your leadership style or future par-
  ticipation in a group?
- What will you do differently based on what you have learned?

INTRINSIC/EXTRINSIC MOTIVATORS QUESTIONNAIRE

1. How could you do your job in a more creative manner? List some ways in
   the space below:

2. List four or five major work activities or jobs you perform on a regular basis
   in the left-hand boxes on the chart below. Use a seven-point scale that
   ranges from 1 (low) to 7 (high) to rate each work activity on three separate
   dimensions: (a) level of difficulty, (b) potential to motivate you, and (c) opportunity to add value to the organization.

Source: Elizabeth A. Smith, *The 2003 Annual: Volume 1, Training/© 2003 John
Wiley & Sons, Inc.*

Major Work Activity	Level of Difficulty	Potential to Motivate	Opportunity to Add Value
1.			
2.			
3.			
4.			
5.			

3. List five motivators or types of rewards that would encourage you to do your job in a more creative manner.

4. List three motivators or types of rewards from Question 3 above that you believe would *definitely increase your creativity.* Indicate whether these motivators are realistic or unrealistic in terms of your job or work setting. Indicate whether each is intrinsic or extrinsic.

Motivators	Realistic/ Unrealistic	Intrinsic	Extrinsic
1.			
2.			
3.			

5. List three types of work activities you like to perform and the motivators or rewards that would stimulate and reinforce your creativity.

Work Activity	Rewards That Reinforce Creativity
1.	
2.	
3.	

QUICK HITTER: FOSTERING THE CREATIVE SPIRIT

Part A Procedure:

1. Write the Roman numeral nine (IX) on a sheet of paper.
2. Add one line to make six. After you have one response, try for others.

Questions for discussion:

- What does solving this puzzle show us about seeing things differently?
- Why don't some people consider alternatives easily?
- What skills or behaviors would be useful for us to develop our ability to see different points of view?

Part B Procedure:

1. Rent the video or DVD of "Patch Adams." In this video Patch (Robin Williams) is studying to become a doctor, but he does not look, act, or think like a traditional doctor. For Patch, humor is the best medicine. He is always willing to do unusual things to make his patients laugh. Scenes from this video can be revealing to an OB class.
2. Show the first Patch Adams scene (5 minutes)—This is in the psychiatric hospital where Patch has admitted himself after a failed suicide attempt. He meets Arthur in the hospital. Arthur is obsessed with showing people four fingers of his hand and asking them: "How many fingers can you see?" Everybody says four. The scene shows Patch visiting Arthur to find out the solution. Arthur's answer is: "If you only focus on the problem, you will never see the solution. Look further. You have to see what other people do not see."
3. Engage the class in discussion of these questions and more:
   - How does this film clip relate to Part A of this exercise?
   - What restricts our abilities to look beyond what we see?
   - How can we achieve the goal of seeing what others do not see?
4. Show the second Patch Adams scene (5 minutes)—This is when Patch has left the hospital and is studying medicine. Patch and his new friend Truman are having breakfast. Truman is reflecting on the human mind and on the changing of behavioral patterns (the adoption of programmed answers) when a person grows older. Patch proposes to carry out the Hello Experiment. The objective of the experiment is "to change the programmed answer by changing the usual parameters."
5. Engage the class in discussion of these questions and more:
   - What is a programmed answer?
   - What is the link between our programmed answers and our abilities to exhibit creativity?
   - How can we "deprogram" ourselves?
6. Summarize the session with a wrap-up discussion of creativity, including barriers and ways to encourage it.

Source: Mila Gascó Hernández and Teresa Torres Coronas, *The 2003 Annual: Volume 1, Training/© 2003 John Wiley & Sons, Inc.*

• •

CASE 1
Drexler's Bar-B-Que
....

Developed by Forrest F. Aven, Jr., University of Houston—Downtown, and V. Jean Ramsey, Texas Southern University; modified by Hal Babson, Columbus State Community College

Change seems to be a fact of life, yet in Texas some things remain the same—people's love for Texas-style barbecue. As you drive from Houston to Waco, for example, you will see many roadside stands asking you to stop by and sample different forms of bbq or bar-b-q (the tastes vary as much as the spellings, and both are often inspired). In the cities, there are many restaurants, several of them large chains, that compete with smaller, neighborhood businesses for the barbecue portion of individuals' dining-out budgets.

Survival can sometimes depend on the restaurant's ability to identify and capitalize on "windows of opportunity." Small businesses are presumed to be more flexible, having the ability to react more quickly to changes when they occur—but the risk is also greater for them than for large organizations, which can more easily absorb losses. But although there may be differences in scale, an important question for *all* organizations is whether they have the willingness and the ability to take advantage of opportunities as they arise. On February 14, 1995, Drexler's Bar-B-Que, a small "neighborhood" restaurant in Houston, the fourth largest city in the United States, had an opportunity to test whether it had what it took.

Drexler's Bar-B-Que is located at 2020 Dowling Street in an area of Houston called the Third Ward—an economically disadvantaged neighborhood not far from downtown—and has been in the family "almost forever." The more recent history, however, begins in the late 1940s, when a great uncle of the present owners operated the establishment as Burney's BBQ. He died in the late 1950s, and an uncle of the present owners took the restaurant over and, because of a leasing arrangement with another popular barbeque restaurant in Southwest Houston, changed the name of the restaurant to Green's Barbecue. In the 1970s, James Drexler, 12 years old, began working with his uncle and learned the secrets of the old family recipes for the barbecue beef, chicken, and sausage. He learned the business "from the ground up." In 1982, when his uncle died, James and his mother took over the business, ended the leasing arrangement, and, in

View online cases with active links at www.wiley.com/college/schermerhorn.

1985, renamed it Drexler's Bar-B-Que. It continued to be a "family affair" but with increased specialization in tasks as business has grown. James Drexler did all the meat preparation; his mother, Mrs. Eunice Scott, handled the other food preparation (the "standard fare" is potato salad, cole slaw, barbeque beans, and slices of white bread); and his sister, Virginia Scott, managed the "front operations"—customer orders and the cash register. There are only two or three other full-time employees, although sometimes during the summer a couple of nephews work part time.

Drexler's is a family business with strong underlying values. It is in the neighborhood and is *of* the neighborhood. Despite the success of the business and the increased patronage of individuals from other parts of the city (many of whom previously had few occasions to do more than drive through the Third Ward), the Drexlers have never considered moving from their original location. The culture of the organization, and the values underpinning it, have been influenced by the long-time head of the family, Mrs. Scott. Her values of honesty, hard work, and treating people fairly and with respect—and her faith in God—permeated the atmosphere and operations of Drexler's. She would move through the restaurant inquiring about individual needs—equally for long-time customers and new ones—and always with a smile and warm greeting for all. She had always been there every day the restaurant was open and held the same set of high standards for herself as she did for others who worked in the restaurant.

Values also get played out in the way in which Drexler's Bar-B-Que "gives back to" the surrounding African-American community.

Drexler's has, for many years, sponsored a softball team and a local Boy Scout troop. Youths from the neighborhood have opportunities to go camping and visit a local amusement park because the family believes that a business should not just involve itself in the community but has the obligation to aggressively seek out opportunities to help others.

In some ways it would appear that Drexler's is not very flexible or adaptable. The restaurant is always closed at 6:00 P.M. on Sundays and Mondays. The menu has remained the same for many years. Drexler's has always been well known in Houston's African-American community, especially in the southwest portion of the city. Regular customers have frequented the restaurant for many years, and a successful side business of catering social functions has also developed. Business has improved every year. During the early 1990s, the business had grown to a point where the small, somewhat ramshackle restaurant could no longer service the demand—there simply were not enough tables or space. So the decision was made in 1994 to close the business for six months, completely raze the building, and rebuild a new and modern restaurant (with additional space attached for future expansion into related, and unrelated, businesses by other family members). It was a good decision—upon reopening, business doubled. But the biggest test of the restaurant's ability to adapt to changes came on February 14, 1995.

Mrs. Scott had two sons, James and Clyde Drexler. James is the co-owner of the restaurant, and Clyde was an NBA basketball player. In 1994, Clyde Drexler appeared at the restaurant to generate publicity for the reopening. But on February 14,

1995, he was traded from the Portland Trailblazers to the local NBA franchise, the Houston Rockets. Clyde had played his collegiate ball at the local university and was popular in the city of Houston. He and Hakeem Olajuwon, the star of the Rockets team, had played together in college and were part of the team known as the Phi Slamma Jamma. Clyde had been a very successful member of the Portland team; he had been selected to play on several all-star teams, had played for two NBA championships, and was a member of the original Dream Team that sent NBA players to the 1992 Summer Olympics.

The Houston Rockets, the defending NBA champions, were struggling during that winter of 1995. The acquisition of Clyde Drexler was seen as a blockbuster one and a key to helping the team repeat as NBA champions. The city was overjoyed with the idea that a local hero was returning home to assist the team in once more winning the championship.

The initial news of the trade brought many new customers to the restaurant. As the Rockets progressed through the playoffs during the spring of 1995, even more customers came. Some days, the restaurant had to close early because it ran out of food. During the semifinals with San Antonio and the finals with Orlando, there appeared to be as many newspaper articles and television reports originating from the restaurant as from the basketball arena. A radio station staged an event outside the restaurant for fans to earn tickets to the game. A major local newspaper gave the restaurant a favorable review in the food section. Many Rockets fans saw frequenting the restaurant as a way to "connect" to the ball team and came to hug Mrs. Scott or chat with her about her son, Clyde, or both. When the Rockets clinched their second NBA championship, everyone in the city knew about the Rockets, and many now knew of Drexler's Bar-B-Que.

The restaurant has since become the hub of several businesses located side by side. In addition to her two sons, Mrs. Scott had four daughters. Virginia Scott, who is heavily involved in the restaurant, is also co-owner of a beauty salon with another sister, Charlotte Drexler. A bakery is owned and operated by a cousin, Barbara Wiltz. A bookstore with a sports emphasis is leased to a non–family member. In January 1996, a new addition was made to the building, and a significantly expanded catering business was begun. Meanwhile, the restaurant has increased its neighborhood involvement by offering free Thanksgiving and Christmas dinners to neighborhood residents in a neighborhood park.

Although food and customer service continues to be a major draw for customers, by 2002 the major attraction (stressed in all of the restaurant's promotional material) has been the opportunity to meet Clyde Drexler, the family's basketball hero. Clyde now has a coaching position in Colorado, but when the basketball season is over, he is in town and often at the restaurant.

Review Questions

1. Use the open systems model described in this chapter to show how Drexler's Bar-B-Que should operate as a learning organization.
2. How do the "values" of Drexler's Bar-B-Que relate to the ethics and social responsibility issues raised in this chapter?
3. What challenges of organization and managerial leadership face Drexler's in its current movement toward expansion?
4. By 2002 the restaurant was appealing to the local interest in Clyde Drexler. Discuss the pros and cons of that approach. ■

$30 million dollars on sales of $355.9 million.[4] While the Panera Bread Company is clearly a high-performance organization that has created value for many of its stakeholders, it now faces the challenges of sustaining these results.

Company History

In 1993 the Au Bon Pain Co. Inc., a chain of restaurants/bakeries that originated in Boston, had saturated the major United States urban and mall markets. To continue the company's growth strategy, Au Bon Pain issued an IPO. The cash generated from the sale of this stock enabled the chain to expand by purchasing the St. Louis Bread Company for twenty-four million dollars. This new division was composed of twenty stores that were primarily located in suburban midwestern locations and sold San Francisco-style sourdough bread products. So that the chain could expand into new geographical areas, the division was renamed Panera, which in Spanish means breadbox or bread-basket.

In 1995, while the Au Bon Pain division was losing money due to strong competition from the fast food chains and coffee shops like Starbucks, the Panera division was thriving and profitable. In 1999 the Au Bon Pain unit was sold for $73 million. One of the former owners, Roy Shaich, stayed with the new Panera chain as chairman and CEO and returned the corporate headquarters to the St. Louis area. Shaich remains as CEO and still owns more than 16% of Panera's stock. Currently, Panera's revenues come from three sources: 75% from the bakery-cafés; 10% from selling franchises; and 15% from the sale of fresh and frozen dough to the franchisees.[5]

CASE 2
The Panera Bread Case— Not by Bread Alone

Developed by Carol P. Harvey, Assumption College

At a time when traditional fast food chains are experiencing stagnation and posting financial losses, the Panera Bread chain of bakeries and market cafés is growing and thriving. Panera was ranked number sixty-three on the Forbes List of the 200 Best Small Companies for 2003.[1] In 2002, Panera was named as the best performing stock on Standard & Poor's Small Cap 600 Stock Index, ahead of such companies as Oshkosh B'Gosh, Chico's, Winnebago Industries, and The Cheesecake Factory.[2] With 669 stores in thirty-five states, two-thirds of these owned and operated by franchisees, Panera bakes over 70,000 loaves of bread a day[3] and in 2003 had a net income of over

The Industry

Fast food was a low margin, no frills industry until the 1990's when Boston Market (originally Boston Chicken), with its quality food, relatively fast service, higher prices, and nicer restaurant atmosphere became the first of the major successful "quick casual" category of restaurant chains.[6] Although business at traditional fast food chains like McDonald's and Burger King is either declining or growing very slowly , the "quick casual" restaurant category where the Panera Bread Company is the industry leader, is expected to grow 15%-29% per year for the next five years.[7] Opportunities in this market niche are predicted to be strong because the target market is the affluent suburbanites, particularly the baby boomers, who are willing to spend more money for what they perceive to be a healthier, more relaxed dining experience.

Value Creation and Customer Satisfaction

As a retail bakery/café, Panera Bread has taken the concept of "quick casual" dining one step further than its competition. Each location features an earth-toned decor with a fireplace, comfortable couches, and current newspapers available to customers. Patrons order and pay at the counter and then wait for their names to be called to pick up their food. The menu features a wide variety of made-to-order sandwiches prepared with freshly baked artisan breads, desserts, crisp salads, homemade soups, and gourmet beverages.

Unlike the paper and plastic fast-food experience, here food is served in baskets or in china plates and cups, and customers eat with metal silverware. Diners are encouraged to linger or to read. At Panera Bread locations, book club and business meetings are welcomed. There is also a separate bakery counter where customers can purchase breads and pastries to take home. However, CEO Ron Shaich says that Panera bakery-cafes "aren't just about the atmosphere. It isn't just about the food. It is the totality of it. This is where you go everyday to catch your breath and chill out."

Corporate Leadership and Social Responsibility

Panera's corporate management is proactive in terms of marketing and quick to respond to changes in the external business environment. For example, in response to a 4% decrease in bread consumption due to the current popularity of the Atkins and South Beach diets, Panera quickly developed high-quality low-carbohydrate breads and suitable lo-carb menu items. Because of the popularity of technology, many store locations are now equipped with Wi-Fi capability which allows customers with Wi-Fi-enabled laptops or PDA's access to the Internet. During the recent hurricane Charley in Florida, the thirty-four outlets in the state that had this technology experienced a 50% increase in customer traffic. People who were without phone service could do business or contact friends and relatives on their laptops at a Panera cafe.[8]

To support the local community in 2003, Panera donated more than $12 million worth of bread products to non-profit organizations and charities such as the American Cancer Society, Habitat for Humanity, Special Olympics, numerous food pantries, homeless shelters, etc. Through "Operation Dough-Nation" Panera matched over a million dollars of customers' in-store cash contributions.[9] Each store features a prominent Community Bulletin Board that displays thank you notes and awards from the various causes and charities that the company supports in the local area.

Staffing/Human Capital

Although Panera has an aggressive growth strategy that requires the organization to open many stores each year, becoming a franchise owner requires considerable financial investment and business experience. In addition to a net worth of $7.5 million and liquid assets of $3 million, applicants must also have worked as a multi-unit restaurant operator. Unlike most franchises, Panera does not allow an owner to open in only one location. Instead he/she must open fifteen or more bakery-cafes in six years within a defined geographical area.[10]

Managers and assistant managers receive competitive salaries and benefits and have the potential of a quarterly bonus. Job requirements vary by location but include outstanding interpersonal skills, formal education, and work experience in the food service industry. Under these full-time employees work many associates who perform counter service and food preparation duties. These workers, who are the customers' primary contact with Panera Bread, are usually paid slightly above the minimum wage, receive no tips, and preferably have some restaurant or fast food experience. Unless they are full-time employees, they do not receive benefits.

Conclusion

Panera Bread is a rapidly growing American corporation. Up until this point, this five-year-old company has been very profitable and is considered to be one of the most successful ventures in the quick casual restaurant market niche. The organization's future will depend on the company's ability to meet the needs of its stakeholders, by continuing to create a satisfying customer experience, being responsive to changing business environments, and adapting to an increasingly diverse workforce.

Discussion Questions:

1. Referring to Figure 2.1, the upside down pyramid view of organizations and management, which one of these levels could be the most likely to undermine the continued success of this organization?
2. Visit www.panerabread.com and www.panera.com. What conclusions might you draw about

diversity at the Panera Bread Corporation from these websites and from the case? What does this company appear to be missing in terms of diversity? What could diversity add to this organization?
3. Since Panera Bread has an aggressive growth strategy, what are the implications for this organization if the corporate management decides to open restaurant-cafes in other countries?

Field Assignment

If there is a Panera restaurant-cafe in your area, go in **alone** as a customer. Order something and sit and observe both the service and the operation. If you were a consultant, hired by Panera Bread to suggest improvements, what changes would you suggest on the basis of your visit? Why?

CASE 3
Crossing Borders
· ·

Developed by Bernardo M. Ferdman, Alliant International University, and Plácida I. Gallegos, Organizational Constultant, San Diego, CA and The Kaleel Jamison Consulting Group, Inc.

This case study is based on the experiences of Angelica Garza, a woman of Mexican-American heritage who worked for 10 years in the Human Resource (HR) function of a multinational medical products company. This maquiladora plant was in Tijuana, Baja California, a large city directly across the U.S.–Mexican border from San Diego, California. Maquiladoras are manufacturing plants owned by foreign capital in the regions of Mexico bordering the United States, which have been set up to take advantage of favorable laws and cheap labor.

Source: This is an abridged version of a case appearing in the Field Guide of E. E. Kossek and S. Cobel, *Managing Diversity: Human Resource Strategies for Transforming the Workplace* (Oxford, England: Blackwell, 1996).

The Tijuana plant was one of a number of operations for USMed. Six other U.S. facilities were located in the Northeast, the Midwest, and Florida. In addition to her work in the manufacturing plant, where Angelica spent most of her time, she was also responsible for human resources for the small, primarily administrative facility in Chula Vista, on the U.S. side of the border. Eventually, there were 34 Americans—12 on the Mexican side and 22 on the U.S. side—and approximately 1100 Mexican nationals on the payroll.

There was little connection between Angelica and the HR managers at the other USMed plants, either in the United States or abroad. Angelica reported that USMed had no overall policy or strategy for dealing with human resources generally and diversity specifically.

The transition in Mexico was not a smooth one for Angelica. Nothing in her U.S. experience had prepared her for what she encountered in Mexico. Her Anglo colleagues had only vague knowledge about the operation in Tijuana and had little interest in understanding or relating to the Mexican workforce. Given her Hispanic upbringing in the United States, Angelica had some understanding of the culture and values of the Mexican employees. Her Spanish-speaking skills also enabled her to understand and relate to the workers. Although she had some understanding of the workers, however, the assumption on the part of U.S. management that her knowledge and connection to the Mexican workers was seamless was false. There were many aspects of cultural differences between her and the Mexican employees that the Anglo managers were unaware of:

In retrospect now, I can look back and [I'm] just amazed at what I was involved in at the time. I mean, I didn't have a clue. One of the things you find is that [people assume that Mexican Americans are most suited to work with Mexicans.] I guess just because I was of Mexican-American descent, it was like I would just know how to mingle with this total[ly] different culture.

As a result, Angelica experienced a great deal of frustration and misunderstanding. Her attempts to intercede between the management in Mexico and that in the United States often led to her disenfranchisement from her American colleagues, who did not value or appreciate her ideas or suggestions. Further complicating her experience in Mexico was the mixed reactions she engendered from the Mexican nationals. Because of her American status, Angelica was misunderstood and sometimes resented by Mexican employees and, at the same time, she lacked support from the U.S. organization.

I found that the Mexican women who were there [two women in accounting who were Mexican nationals, and had been there for about 5 years] were resentful. My saving grace was that I was an American because the Mexican women there looked at the Americans as being like a step above or whatever. And there was resentment of me coming in and taking away jobs. They perceived it as: They weren't doing a good job and we were coming in and taking responsibilities away from them. So me being a woman coming in, I was scrutinized by the two women who had been there. I couldn't get information from them. They gave me the least information or help they could and would be critical of anything I did once I took it from them.

You know, I look back and it was probably pretty frightening for them [the Mexican nationals] too, because we all came in and we knew what we had to do; [USMed was] very straightforward

about, you know, you fail to do this and you can lose your job and you've got to do that or you could lose your job, so getting them to follow these protocols and these operating procedures was very difficult. Change is difficult anyway but getting them to follow some of those rules [was] real challenging.

Angelica understood the employees' approach to the work as stemming from local conditions and from Mexican cultural styles. The great expansion of maquiladoras brought a number of changes, including new expectations and different cultural styles on the part of the managers. At first, potential employees were unfamiliar with these new expectations; the employers needed to train the workers if they were to meet these expectations. This was happening in the context of the meeting of two cultures. In her role, Angelica saw herself as more American than Mexican, yet also as different from her Anglo colleagues. She saw herself as bringing American training, expectations, and styles:

"Well, see I'm American. I mean I was an American manager, and that's where I was coming from. But I was forced to come up with systems that would eliminate future misunderstandings or problems. Being a Mexican American I thought it would be easier working in Mexico because I had some exposure to the culture, but it was a real culture shock for me. It was a different group of people socioeconomically. A lot of those people came from ranchitos, [from] out in the sticks, where there were no restrooms or showers. There weren't infrastructures in Tijuana at all. It's pretty good now compared to what it was 10 years ago. We used to go to work through people's backyards and dirt roads. Dead dogs were marks for how to get there! And I think now, that if you go to Tijuana now—it's been 10 years of maquiladoras there—you can find more qualified Mexican managers or supervi-

sors or clerical people. [Finding] bilingual secretaries and engineers [was like] getting needles in a haystack back then.

I found myself being the only woman in an old-boy-network environment, and that was pretty tough. And it was also tough working in the Mexican environment. Because the Mexican men that I would deal with would look down on me because I was a woman. Again, my saving grace was because I was an American woman. If I had been a Mexican national woman, then I would have really had probably more problems. [For example] I had to work a lot, real close with the Mexican accounting manager, who was a male. And he would come to me and tell me how I had screwed up my numbers, or you didn't do this right, and stuff like that. I would go over the numbers and it was just a difference in terms of how things were calculated. Specifically, calculating an annual salary. He would do it by using 365 days, when I would do it by 52 weeks and you'd take your daily rate, it was different, it would always be off a little bit. But, I reported them the way the Americans would be expecting to see them.

Review Questions

1. What competencies are appropriate to ensure greater effectiveness of U.S. employees operating in a maquiladora or other non-U.S. organization?

2. What are some of the costs of not understanding diversity? What could the organization have gained by approaching the plant with greater cultural understanding?

3. From the HR perspective, what were the unique challenges that Angelica faced at various points in her work for USMed?

4. Angelica worked in a plant outside the United States. What do her experiences and perspectives tell us that applies to domestic operations? ■

• •

CASE 4
Never on a Sunday

Developed by Anne C. Cowden, California State University, Sacramento

McCoy's Building Supply Centers of San Marcos, Texas, have been in continuous successful operation for almost 70 years in an increasingly competitive retail business. McCoy's is one of the nation's largest family-owned and -managed building-supply companies, with sales topping $400 million. The company serves 10 million customers a year in a regional area currently covering New Mexico, Texas, Oklahoma, Arkansas, Mississippi, and Louisiana in 103 stores employing 1600 employees. McCoy's strategy has been to occupy a niche in the market of small and medium-sized cities. McCoy's was originally a roofing business started by Frank McCoy in 1923; roofing remained the company's primary business until the 1960s, when it began to expand under the management of his son, Emmett McCoy.

McCoy's grounding principle is acquiring and selling the finest-quality products that can be found and providing quality service to customers. As an operations-oriented company, McCoy's has always managed without many layers of management. Managers are asked to concentrate on service-related issues in their stores: get the merchandise on the floor, price it, sell it, and help the customer carry it out. The majority of the administrative workload is handled through headquarters so that store employees can concentrate on customer service. The top management team (Emmett McCoy and his two sons, Brian and Mike, who serve as co-presidents) has established 11 teams of managers drawn from the different regions McCoy's stores cover. The teams meet regularly to discuss new products, better ways for product delivery, and a host of items integral to maintaining customer satisfaction. Team leadership is rotated among the managers.

McCoy's has a workforce of 70 percent full-time and 30 percent part-time employees. McCoy's philosophy values loyal, adaptable, skilled employees as the most essential element of its overall success. To operationalize this philosophy, the company offers extensive on-the-job training. The path to management involves starting at the store level and learning all facets of operations before advancing into a management program. All management trainees are required to relocate to a number of stores. Most promotions come from within. Managers are rarely recruited from the outside. This may begin to change as the business implements more technology requiring greater reliance on college-educated personnel.

Permeating all that McCoy's does is a strong religious belief, including a strong commitment to community. In 1961 Emmett McCoy decided, in the wake of a devastating hurricane, to offer McCoy's goods to customers at everyday prices rather than charging what the market would bear. This decision helped establish McCoy's long-standing reputation of fair dealing, a source of pride for all employees, and allowed the company to begin its current expansion perspective. In 1989 McCoy's became a drug-free company. McCoy's takes part in the annual National Red Ribbon Campaign, "Choose to Be Drug Free." McCoy's also supports Habitat for Humanity in the United States and has provided support for low-income housing in Mexico.

Many McCoy family members are Evangelical Christians who believe in their faith through letting their "feet do it"—that is, showing their commitment to God through action, not just talk. Although their beliefs and values permeate the company's culture in countless ways, one very concrete way is reflected in the title of this case: Never on a Sunday. Even though Sundays are busy business days for retailers, all 103 McCoy's stores are closed on Sunday.

Review Questions

1. How do the beliefs of the McCoy family form the culture of this company?
2. Can a retailer guided by such strong beliefs compete and survive in the era of gigantic retailers such as Home Depot? If so, how?
3. Is such a strong commitment to social responsibility and ethical standards a help or a hindrance in managing a company?
4. How does a family-owned and -managed company differ from companies managed by outside professionals? ■

MAGREC, Inc.
••••••••••••••••••••••

Developed by Mary McGarry, Empire State College
and Barry R. Armandi, SUNY–Old Westbury

Background

MagRec, Incorporated was started in the late 1960s by Mr. Leed, a brilliant engineer (he has several engineering patents) who was a group manager at Fairchild Republic. The company's product was magnetic recording heads, a crucial device used for reading, writing, and erasing data on tapes and disks. Need for the product and its future potential was great. The computer industry was in its embryonic stage, and MagRec had virtually no serious competition. In fact, almost all magnetic head manufacturers today use methods, techniques, processes, and so on that were developed and pioneered by MagRec.

Like any other startup, MagRec had a humble beginning. It struggled during the early years, facing cash-flow and technical problems. After a slow start, it began growing rapidly. In the mid-1970s it had captured 35 percent of the tape head market, making it the second-largest supplier of MegaComputer computer tape heads in North America. Financially, the company suffered heavily in the early 1980s because of price erosions caused by Far East competition. Unlike all its competitors, the company resisted and never moved its manufacturing operations offshore. By the mid-1980s, the company had accumulated losses to a point of bankruptcy. Finally, plagued by a no-win situation, the company entered a major international joint venture, in which foreign governments agreed to participate as minority owners (20 percent equity). The company received blanket sales orders from Japanese firms (GME, Victor Data, Fijitsu, etc.). Things looked good once again. But . . .

Pat's Dilemma

When Fred Marsh promoted me to Sales Manager, I was in seventh heaven. Now, six months later, I feel I am in hell. This is the first time in my life that I am really on my own. I have been working with other people all my life. I tried my best and what I could not solve, I took upstairs. Now it's different because I am the boss (or am I?). Fred has taught me a lot. He was my mentor and gave me this job when he became vice president. I have always respected him and listened to his judgment. Now thinking back I wonder whether I should have listened to him at all on this problem.

It started one late Friday evening. I had planned to call my West Coast customer, Partco, to discuss certain contract clauses. I wanted to nail this one fast (Partco had just been acquired by Volks, Inc.). Partco was an old customer, in fact, through good and bad it had always stayed with us. It was also a *major* customer. I was about to call Partco when Dinah Coates walked in clutchin*g a file. I had worked with Dinah for three years. She was good. I knew that my call to Partco would have to wait. Dinah had been cleaning out old files and came across a report about design and manufacturing defects in Partco heads. The report had been written nine years ago. The cover memo read as follows:

To: Ken Smith, Director of Marketing
From: Rich Grillo, V.P. Operations
Sub: Partco Head Schedule

This is to inform you that due to pole-depth problems in design, the Partco heads (all 514 in test) have failed. They can't reliably meet the reading requirements.* The problem is basically a design error in calculations. It can be corrected. However, the fix will take at least six months. Meanwhile Ron Scott in production informs me that the entire 5,000 heads (the year's production) have already been pole-slotted, thus they face the same problem.

Ken, I don't have to tell you how serious this is, but how can we OK and ship them to Partco knowing that they'll cause read error problems in the field? My engineering and manufacturing people realize this is the number one priority. By pushing the Systems Tech job back we will be back on track in less than six months. In the interim I can modify Global Widgets heads. This will enable us to at least continue shipping some product to Partco. As a possible alternate I would like to get six Partco drives. Michaels and his team feel that with quick and easy changes in the drives tape path they can get the head to work. If this is true we should be back on track within six to eight weeks.

A separate section of the report reads as follows:

Confidential
(Notes from meeting with Don Updyke and Rich Grillo)

---

*Authors' Note: Error signifies erroneous reading, not an error message. For example, instead of "$200" the head reads "$3005.42."

Solution to Partco heads problem

All Partco heads can be reworked (.8 hrs. ea.—cost insignificant) to solve Partco's read problems by grinding an extra three-thousandths of an inch off the top of the head. This will reduce the overall pole depth to a point where no read errors occur. The heads will fully meet specifications in all respects except one, namely life. Don estimates that due to the reduced chrome layer (used for wear) the heads' useful life will be 2500 hours instead of 6000 hours of actual usage.

Our experience is that no customer keeps accurate records to tell actual usage and life. Moreover, the cost is removed since Partco sells drives to MegaComputer, who sells systems to end-users. The user at the site hardly knows or rarely complains about extra costs such as the replacement of a head 12 to 18 months down the line instead of the normal 2 years. Besides, the service technicians always innovatively believe in and offer plausible explanations—such as the temperature must be higher than average—or they really must be using the computer a lot.

I have directed that the heads be reworked and shipped to Partco. I also instructed John to tell Partco that due to inclement weather this week's shipment will be combined with next week's shipment.

Dinah was flabbergasted. The company planned to sell products deliberately that it knew would not meet life requirements, she said, "risking our reputation as a quality supplier. Partco and others buy our heads thinking they are the best. Didn't we commit fraud through outright misrepresentation?"

Dinah insisted I had to do something. I told her I would look into the matter and get back to her by the end of next week.

Over the weekend I kept thinking about the Partco issue. We had no customer complaints. Partco had always been extremely pleased with our products and technical support. In fact, we were their sole suppliers. MegaComputer had us placed on the preferred, approved ship to stock, vendors list. It was a fact that other vendors were judged against our standards. MegaComputer's Quality Control never saw our product or checked it.

Monday morning I showed the report to Fred. He immediately recollected it and began to explain the situation to me.

MagRec had been under tremendous pressure and was growing rapidly at the time. "That year we had moved into a new 50,000 sq. ft. building and went from 50 or 60 employees to over 300. Our sales were increasing dramatically." Fred was heading Purchasing at the time and every week the requirements for raw materials would change. "We'd started using B.O.A.s (Broad Order Agreements, used as annual purchasing contracts) guaranteeing us the right to increase our numbers by 100 percent each quarter. The goal was to maintain the numbers. If we had lost Partco then, it could have had a domino effect and we could have ended up having no customers left to worry about."

Fred went on to explain that it had only been a short-term problem that was corrected within the year and no one ever knew it existed. He told me to forget it and to move the file into the back storage room. I conceded. I thought of all the possible hassles. The thing was ancient history anyway. Why should I be concerned about it? I wasn't even here when it happened.

The next Friday Dinah asked me what I had found out. I told her Fred's feelings on the matter and that I felt he had some pretty good arguments regarding the matter. Dinah became angry. She said I had changed since my promotion and that I was just as guilty as the crooks who'd cheated the customers by selling low-life heads as long-life heads. I told her to calm down. The decision was made years ago. No one got hurt and the heads weren't defective. They weren't causing any errors.

I felt bad but figured there wasn't much to do. The matter was closed as far as I was concerned, so I returned to my afternoon chores. Little was I to know the matter was not really closed.

That night Fred called me at 10:00. He wanted me to come over to the office right away. I quickly changed, wondering what the emergency was. I walked into Fred's office. The coffee was going. Charlie (Personnel Manager) was there. Rich Grillo (V.P. Operations) was sitting on the far side of Fred's conference table. I instinctively headed there for that was the designated smoking corner.

Ken (Director of Marketing) arrived 15 minutes later. We settled in. Fred began the meeting by thanking everyone for coming. He then told them about the discovery of the Partco file and filled them in on the background. The problem now was that Dinah had called Partco and gotten through to their new vice president, Tim Rand. Rand had called Fred at 8 P.M. at home and said he was personally taking the Red Eye to find out what this was all about. He would be here in the morning.

We spent a grueling night followed by an extremely tense few weeks. Partco had a team of people going through our tests, quality control, and manufacturing records. Our production slipped, and overall morale was affected.

Mr. Leed personally spent a week in California assuring Partco that this would never happen again. Though we weathered the storm, we had certain losses. We were never to be Partco's sole source again. We still retained 60 percent of their business but had to agree to lower prices. The price reduction had a severe impact. Although Partco never disclosed to anyone what the issues were (since both companies had blanket nondisclosure agreements), word got around that Partco was paying a lower price. We were unable to explain to our other customers why Partco was paying this amount. Actually I felt the price word got out through Joe Byrne (an engineer who came to Partco from Systems Tech and told his colleagues back at Systems Tech that Partco really knew how to negotiate prices down). He was unaware, however, of the real issues. Faced with customers who perceived they were being treated inequitably, we experienced problems. Lowering prices meant incurring losses; not lowering them meant losing customers. The next two financial quarters saw sales dollars decline by 40 percent. As the sales manager, I felt pretty rotten presenting my figures to Fred.

With regard to Dinah, I now faced a monumental problem. The internal feeling was she should be avoided at all costs. Because of price erosions, we faced cutbacks. Employees blamed her for production layoffs. The internal friction kept mounting. Dinah's ability to interface effectively with her colleagues and other departments plummeted to a point where normal functioning was impossible.

Fred called me into his office two months after the Partco episode and suggested that I fire Dinah. He told me that he was worried about results. Although he had nothing personally against her, he felt that she must go because she was seriously affecting my department's overall performance. I defended Dinah by stating that the Partco matter would blow over and given time I could smooth things out. I pointed out Dinah's accomplishments and stated I really wanted her

to stay. Fred dropped the issue, but my problem persisted.

Things went from bad to worse. Finally, I decided to try to solve the problem myself. I had known Dinah well for many years and had a good relationship with her before the incident. I took her to lunch to address the issue. Over lunch, I acknowledged the stress the Partco situation had put on her and suggested that she move away for a while to the West Coast, where she could handle that area independently.

Dinah was hurt and asked why I didn't just fire her already. I recounted by accusing her of causing the problem in the first place by going to Partco.

Dinah came back at me, calling me a lackey for having taken her story to Fred and brought his management message back. She said I hadn't even attempted a solution and that I didn't have the guts to stand up for what was right. I was only interested in protecting my backside and keeping Fred happy. As her manager, I should have protected her and taken some of the heat off her back. Dinah refused to transfer or to quit. She told me to go

ahead and fire her, and she walked out.

I sat in a daze as I watched Dinah leave the restaurant. What the hell went wrong? Had Dinah done the morally right thing? Was I right in defending MagRec's position? Should I have taken a stand with Fred? Should I have gone over Fred's head to Mr. Leed? Am I doing the right thing? Should I listen to Fred and fire Dinah? If not, how do I get my department back on track? What am I saying? If Dinah is right, shouldn't I be defending her rather than MagRec?

Review Questions

1. Place yourself in the role of the manager. What should you do now? After considering what happened, would you change any of your behaviors?
2. Do you think Dinah was right? Why or why not? If you were she and you had it to do all over again, would you do anything differently? If so, what and why?
3. Using cognitive dissonance theory, explain the actions of Pat, Dinah, and Fred. ∎

CASE 6
It Isn't Fair
....

Developed by Barry R. Armandi, SUNY–Old Westbury

Mary Jones was in her senior year at Central University and interviewing for jobs. Mary was in the top 1 percent of her class, active in numerous extracurricular activities, and highly respected by her professors. After the interviews, Mary was offered a number of positions with every company with which she interviewed. After much thought, she decided to take the offer from Universal Products, a multinational company. She felt that the salary was superb ($40,000), there were excellent benefits, and there was good potential for promotion.

Mary started work a few weeks after graduation and learned her job assignments and responsibilities thoroughly and quickly. Mary was asked on many occasions to work late because report deadlines were often moved forward. Without hesitation she said "Of course!" even though as an exempt employee she would receive no overtime.

Frequently, she would take work home with her and use her personal computer to do further analyses. At other times, she would come into the office on weekends to monitor the progress of her projects or just to catch up on the ever-growing mountain of correspondence.

On one occasion her manager asked her to take on a difficult assignment. It seemed that the company's Costa Rican manufacturing facility was having production problems. The quality of one of the products was highly questionable, and the reports on the matter were confusing. Mary was asked to be part of a team to investigate the quality and reporting problems. The team stayed in poor accommodations for the entire three weeks they were there. This was because of the plant's location near its resources, which happened to be in the heart of the jungle. Within the three-week period the team had located the source of the quality problem, corrected it, and altered the reporting documents and processes. The head of the team, a quality engineer, wrote a note to Mary's manager stating the following: "Just wanted to inform you of the superb job Mary Jones did down in Costa Rica. Her suggestions and insights into the reporting system were invaluable. Without her help we would have been down there for another three weeks, and I was getting tired of the mosquitoes. Thanks for sending her."

Universal Products, like most companies, has a yearly performance review system. Since Mary had been with the company for a little over one year, it was time for her review. Mary entered her manager's office nervous, since this was her first review ever and she didn't know what to expect. After closing the door and exchanging the usual pleasantries, her manager, Tom, got right to the point.

Tom: Well, Mary, as I told you last week this meeting would be for your annual review. As you are aware, your performance and compensation are tied together. Since the philosophy of the company is to reward those who perform, we take these reviews very sincerely. I have spent a great deal of time thinking about your performance over the past year, but before I begin I would like to know your impressions of the company, your assignments, and me as a manager.

Mary: Honestly, Tom, I have no complaints. The company and my job are everything I was led to believe. I enjoy working here. The staff are all very helpful. I like the team atmosphere, and my job is very challenging. I really feel appreciated and that I'm making a contribution. You have been very helpful and patient with me. You got me involved right from the start and listened to my opinions. You taught me a lot and I'm very grateful. All in all I'm happy being here.

Tom: Great, Mary, I was hoping that's the way you felt because from my vantage point, most of the people you worked with feel the same. But before I give you the qualitative side of the review, allow me to go through the quantitative appraisal first. As you know, the rankings go from 1 (lowest) to 5 (highest). Let's go down each

category and I'll explain my reasoning for each.

Tom starts with category one (Quantity of Work) and ends with category ten (Teamwork). In each of the categories, Tom has either given Mary a 5 or a 4. Indeed, only two categories have a 4 and Tom explains these are normal areas for improvement for most employees.

Tom: As you can see, Mary, I was very happy with your performance. You have received the highest rating I have ever given any of my subordinates. Your attitude, desire, and help are truly appreciated. The other people on the Costa Rican team gave you glowing reports, and speaking with the plant manager, she felt that you helped her understand the reporting system better than anyone else. Since your performance has been stellar, I'm delighted to give you a 10 percent increase effective immediately!

Mary: (mouth agape, and eyes wide) Tom, frankly I'm flabbergasted! I don't know what to say, but thank you very much. I hope I can continue to do as fine a job as I have this last year. Thanks once again.

After exchanging some parting remarks and some more thank-you's, Mary left Tom's office with a smile from ear to ear. She was floating on air! Not only did she feel the performance review process was uplifting, but her review was outstanding and so was her raise. She knew from other employees that the company was only giving out a 5 percent average increase. She figured that if she got that, or perhaps 6 or 7, she would be happy. But to get 10 percent . . . wow!! Imagine . . .

Sue: Hi, Mary! Lost in thought? My, you look great. Looks like you got some great news. What's up?

Susan Stevens was a recent hire, working for Tom. She had graduated from Central University also, but a year after Mary. Sue had excelled while at Central, graduating in the top 1 percent of her class. She had laudatory letters of recommendation from her professors and was into many after-school clubs and activities.

Mary: Oh, hi, Sue! Sorry, but I was just thinking about Universal and the opportunities here.

Sue: Yes, it truly is . . .

Mary: Sue, I just came from my performance review and let me tell you, the process isn't that bad. As a matter of fact I found it quite rewarding, if you get my drift. I got a wonderful review, and can't wait till next year's. What a great company!

Sue: You can say that again! I couldn't believe them hiring me right out of college at such a good salary. Between you and me, Mary, they started me at $45,000. Imagine that? Wow, was I impressed. I just couldn't believe that they would . . . Where are you going, Mary? Mary? What's that you say, "It isn't fair"? What do you mean? Mary? Mary . . .

Review Questions

1. Indicate Mary's attitudes before and after meeting Sue. If there was a change, why?
2. What do you think Mary will do now? Later?
3. What motivation theory applies best to this scenario? Explain. ■

CASE 7
Perfect Pizzeria

Perfect Pizzeria in Southville, in deep southern Illinois, is the second largest franchise of the chain in the United States. The headquarters is located in Phoenix, Arizona. Although the business is prospering, employee and managerial problems exist.

Each operation has one manager, an assistant manager, and from two to five night managers. The managers of each pizzeria work under an area supervisor. There are no systematic criteria for being a manager or becoming a manager trainee. The franchise has no formalized training period for the manager. No college education is required. The managers for whom the case observer worked during a four-year period were relatively

young (ages 24 to 27) and only one had completed college. They came from the ranks of night managers or assistant managers, or both. The night managers were chosen for their ability to perform the duties of the regular employees. The assistant managers worked a two-hour shift during the luncheon period five days a week to gain knowledge about bookkeeping and management. Those becoming managers remained at that level unless they

expressed interest in investing in the business.

The employees were mostly college students, with a few high school students performing the less challenging jobs. Since Perfect Pizzeria was located in an area with few job opportunities, it had a relatively easy task of filling its employee quotas. All the employees, with the exception of the manager, were employed part time and were paid the minimum wage.

The Perfect Pizzeria system is devised so that food and beverage costs and profits are computed according to a percentage. If the percentage of food unsold or damaged in any way is very low, the manager gets a bonus. If the percentage is high, the manager does not receive a bonus; rather, he or she receives only his or her normal salary.

There are many ways in which the percentage can fluctuate. Since the manager cannot be in the store 24 hours a day, some employees make up for their paychecks by helping themselves to the food. When a friend comes in to order a pizza, extra ingredients are put on the friend's pizza. Occasional nibbles by 18 to 20 employees throughout the day at the meal table also raise the percentage figure. An occasional bucket of sauce may be spilled or a pizza accidentally burned.

In the event of an employee mistake, the expense is supposed to come from the individual. Because of peer pressure, the night manager seldom writes up a bill for the erring employee. Instead, the establishment takes the loss and the error goes unnoticed until the end of the month when the inventory is taken. That's when the manager finds out that the percentage is high and that there will be no bonus.

In the present instance, the manager took retaliatory measures. Previously, each employee was entitled to a free pizza, salad, and all the soft drinks he or she could drink for every 6 hours of work. The manager raised this figure from 6 to 12 hours of work. However, the employees had received these 6-hour benefits for a long time. Therefore, they simply took advantage of the situation whenever the manager or the assistant was not in the building. Although the night manager theoretically had complete control of the operation in the evenings, he did not command the respect that the manager or assistant manager did. This was because he received the same pay as the regular employees, he could not reprimand other employees, and he was basically the same age or sometimes even younger than the other employees.

Thus, apathy grew within the pizzeria. There seemed to be a further separation between the manager and his workers, who started out as a closely knit group. The manager made no attempt to alleviate the problem, because he felt it would iron itself out. Either the employees that were dissatisfied would quit or they would be content to put up with the new regulations. As it turned out, there was a rash of employee dismissals. The manager had no problem in filling the vacancies with new workers, but the loss of key personnel was costly to the business.

With the large turnover, the manager found that he had to spend more time in the building, supervising and sometimes taking the place of inexperienced workers. This was in direct violation of the franchise regulation, which stated that a manager would act as a supervisor and at no time take part in the actual food preparation. Employees were not placed under strict supervision with the manager working alongside them. The operation no longer worked smoothly because of differences between the remaining experienced workers and the manager concerning the way in which a particular function should be performed.

Within a two-month period, the manager was again free to go back to his office and leave his subordinates in charge of the entire operation. During this two-month period, the percentage had returned to the previous low level, and the manager received a bonus each month. The manager felt that his problems had been resolved and that conditions would remain the same, since the new personnel had been properly trained.

It didn't take long for the new employees to become influenced by the other employees. Immediately after the manager had returned to his supervisory role, the percentage began to rise. This time the manager took a bolder step. He cut out any benefits that the employees had—no free pizzas, salads, or drinks. With the job market at an even lower ebb than usual, most employees were forced to stay. The appointment of a new area supervisor made it impossible for the manager to "work behind the counter," since the supervisor was centrally located in Southville.

The manager tried still another approach to alleviate the rising percentage problem and maintain his bonus. He placed a notice on the bulletin board, stating that if the percentage remained at a high level, a lie detector test would be given to all employees. All those found guilty of taking or purposefully wasting food or drinks would be immediately terminated. This did not have the desired effect on the employees, because they knew if they were all subjected to the test, all would be found guilty and the manager would have to dismiss all of them. This would leave him in a worse situation than ever.

Even before the following month's percentage was calculated, the manager knew it would be high. He had evidently received information from one of the night managers about the employees' feelings toward the notice. What he did not expect was that the percentage would reach an all-time high. That is the state of affairs at the present time.

Review Questions

1. Consider the situation where the manager changed the time period required to receive free food and drink from 6 to 12 hours of work. Try to apply each of the motivational approaches to explain what happened. Which of the approaches offers the most appropriate explanation? Why?

2. Repeat Question 1 for the situation where the manager worked beside the employees for a time and then later returned to his office.

3. Repeat Question 1 for the situation as it exists at the end of the case.

4. Establish and justify a motivational program based on one or a combination of motivation theories to deal with the situation as it exists at the end of the case. ■

CASE 8
I'm Not in Kansas Anymore

Developed by Anne C. Cowden, California State University, Sacramento

Telecommuting is defined as work done at home or in a remote location using technology as the link. Approximately 7.6 million people currently telecommute. The decision whether to allow employees to telecommute is controversial, owing to the number of managerial-control questions raised by people working and/or managing off site.

For one manager of software projects (based in Los Angeles) who oversees 11 people in a 50-person office based in Dallas, the answer is that telecommuting is very effective, although not without drawbacks. Our manager, a veteran of nine years of telecommuting, is in constant contact with her employees, software technical writers, and quality analysts–testers, through e-mail, with voice mailbox, phone, fax, and, at least once a month, face-to-face visits on site with each employee. One room in her home is fully outfitted as an office, one she can walk away from as a means of separating her personal and professional life. However, she is always connected to those whom she supervises. For example, on a weekend, if an employee has gone in to work, she can answer a question from home by merely walking into her home-based office.

To keep connected with her employees on a physical level, our manager meets individually with each employee on a monthly basis in Dallas. She spends an hour going over the priorities they have listed as activities for the month. Throughout the month, the manager and the employees are in constant contact. Through both physical and electronic communication, our manager is able to get to know her employees well.

As she has noted, meeting with them in person allows her to "see" them over the phone, judging their psychological "space" by voice intonation when there is no physical face to communicate with. Our manager also interacts with other managers and line personnel through telecommuting. For example, she negotiates over the phone what goes into a product, the timeline, the product budget, and all other factors necessary to managing a product effectively.

While our manager likes telecommuting and is able to manage effectively, there are both good points and drawbacks. The advantages include the freedom from commuting every day in full office dress, the complexity and challenge of staying well connected with employees, and the time gained by staying at home. The drawbacks can be the isolation that some initially feel when not having daily physical contact with others. Another drawback may be "workaholism" if one is unable to separate one's life from one's job. Burnout can be a factor if one works all the time.

If you are thinking of telecommuting, our manager would advise the following: get a good headset for talking on the phone; be prepared for the initial feelings of isolation; and keep in daily, close contact with your employees.

Review Questions

1. Is telecommuting the wave of the future, or does top management lose too much control when people are off site?
2. How would you like being a telecommuter, as either a manager or one being managed?
3. Do you think telecommuting is effective for both the employee and the organization? Why or why not?
4. How might you modify telecommuting so as to overcome the problems covered above and maintain an effective team? ■

CASE 9
The Forgotten Group Member

Developed by Franklin Ramsoomair, Wilfred Laurier University

The Organizational Behavior course for the semester appeared to promise the opportunity to learn, enjoy, and practice some of the theories and principles in the textbook and class discussions. Christine Spencer was a devoted, hard-working student who had been maintaining an A– average to date. Although the skills and knowledge she had acquired through her courses were important, she was also very concerned about her grades. She felt that grades were paramount in giving her a competitive edge when looking for a job and, as a third-year student, she realized that she'd soon be doing just that.

Sunday afternoon. Two o'clock. Christine was working on an accounting assignment but didn't seem to be able to concentrate. Her courses were working out very well this semester, all but the OB. Much of the mark in that course was to be applied to the quality of groupwork, and so she felt somewhat out of control. She recollected the events of the past five weeks. Professor Sandra Thiel had divided the class into groups of five people and had given them a major group assignment worth 30 percent of the final grade. The task was to analyze a seven-page case and to come up with a written analysis. In addition, Sandra had asked the groups to present the case in class, with the idea in mind that the rest of the class members would be "members of the board of directors of the company" who would be listening to how the manager and her team dealt with the problem at hand.

Christine was elected "Team Coordinator" at the first group meeting. The other members of the group were Diane, Janet, Steve, and Mike. Diane was quiet and never volunteered suggestions, but when directly asked, she would come up with high-quality ideas. Mike was the clown. Christine remembered that she had suggested that the group should get together before every class to discuss the day's case. Mike had balked, saying "No way!! This is an 8:30 class, and I barely make it on time anyway! Besides, I'll miss my *Happy Harry* show on television!" The group couldn't help but laugh at his indignation. Steve was the businesslike individual, always wanting to ensure that group meetings were guided by

an agenda and noting the tangible results achieved or not achieved at the end of every meeting. Janet was the reliable one who would always have more for the group than was expected of her. Christine saw herself as meticulous and organized and as a person who tried to give her best in whatever she did.

It was now week 5 into the semester, and Christine was deep in thought about the OB assignment. She had called everyone to arrange a meeting for a time that would suit them all but seemed to be running into a roadblock. Mike couldn't make it, saying that he was working that night as a member of the campus security force. In fact, he seemed to miss most meetings and would send in brief notes to Christine, which she was supposed to discuss for him at the group meetings. She wondered how to deal with this. She also remembered the incident last week. Just before class started, Diane, Janet, Steve, and she were joking with one another before class. They were laughing and enjoying themselves before Sandra came in. No one noticed that Mike had slipped in very quietly and had unobtrusively taken his seat.

She recalled the cafeteria incident. Two weeks ago, she had gone to the cafeteria to grab something to eat. She had rushed to her accounting class and had skipped breakfast. When she got her club sandwich and headed to the tables, she saw her OB group and joined them. The discussion was light and enjoyable as it always was when they met informally. Mike had come in. He'd approached their table. "You guys didn't say you were having a group meeting," he blurted. Christine was taken aback.

We just happened to run into each other. Why not join us?"

"Mike looked at them, with a noncommittal glance. "Yeah . . . right," he muttered, and walked away.

Sandra Thiel had frequently told them that if there were problems in the group, the members should make an effort to deal with them first. If the problems could not be resolved, she had said that they should come to her. Mike seemed so distant, despite the apparent camaraderie of the first meeting.

An hour had passed, bringing the time to 3 P.M., and Christine found herself biting the tip of her pencil. The written case analysis was due next week. All the others had done their designated sections, but Mike had just handed in some rough handwritten notes. He had called Christine the week before, telling her that in addition to his course and his job, he was having problems with his girlfriend. Christine empathized with him. Yet, this was a group project! Besides, the final mark would be peer evaluated. This meant that whatever mark Sandra gave them could be lowered or raised, depending on the group's opinion about the value of the contribution of each member. She was definitely worried. She knew that Mike had creative ideas that could help to raise the overall mark. She was also concerned for him. As she listened to the music in the background, she wondered what she should do.

Review Questions

1. How could an understanding of the stages of group development assist Christine in leadership situations such as this one?
2. What should Christine understand about individual membership in groups in order to build group processes that are supportive of her workgroup's performance?
3. Is Christine an effective group leader in this case? Why or why not? ■

CASE 10
NASCAR'S Racing Teams

Developed by David S. Chappell, Ohio University, moditied by Hal Babson, Columbus State Community College.

The most popular team sport, based on total spectator audience, is not basketball, baseball, football, or even soccer: it is stock car racing. The largest stock car racing group in the world is the National Association for Stock Car Auto Racing (NASCAR). The NASCAR Nextel Cup Series (previously identified as the Winston Cup Series), with 41 events at 24 U.S. tracks, kicks off in February at Daytona International Speedway and runs through November with the Ford 400 at Homestead-Miami Speedway in Miami.

NASCAR

NASCAR has become a marketing powerhouse. Not only are over 12 million fans attracted to race tracks, but another 250 million watch races on television. Drivers are involved in cable network shows as well as syndicated radio shows each week. NASCAR's official Web site, at www. nascar.com, ranks among the five most popular sites on the Internet, receiving 35 million hits each week. Companies such as the Coca-Cola Co. take advantage of NASCAR's popularity with merchandise, collectibles, apparel, accessories, toys, and other marketing tie-ins.

The race cars themselves have been described by some as "200 mile-per-hour billboards." As an organized sport, NASCAR is unique in that its drivers are treated like independent contractors rather than employees. As such, they must not only perform but also seek their own sponsors to finance their race teams. Traditional NASCAR spon-

sors include RJR Nabisco, Penzoil-Quaker State, General Motors, M&M/Mars, Lowe's, and Proctor and Gamble. The popularity and success of NASCAR as a marketing tool continues to induce sponsors to enter the arena.

NASCAR enjoys a history of great drivers, including Richard Petty, Cale Yarborough, and Davey Pearson. A legend in the making is emerging in the league: Jeff Gordon. Jeff Gordon heads Hendrick Motorsport's # 24 Dupont Automotive Finishes team. In 2002, Jeff Gordon was not only recognized for his racing achievements but was designated as the 2002 Sports Ethics Fellow.

Jeff Gordon—Racing Sensation

Jeff Gordon, on the Nextel (Winston) Cup racing scene since 1993, has been a sensation ever since he started racing go-carts and quarter-midget cars at the age of 5.

In 1979 and 1981, he was the quarter-midget national champion, and in 1990 he won the 1990 USAC midget championship. He has captured the imagination of race fans around the world, becoming the youngest driver ever to win three NASCAR Nextel Cup overall championships and has over 68 individual race wins in an nine-year span.

Gordon, 33, says his strong family upbringing in California and Indiana and his marriage to former Miss Winston beauty queen Brooke Sealy have made it easy. (However, in March 2002 Brooke filed for divorce from Jeff.) "There's no question Jeff has helped take our sport to the next level as far as image," said Ned Jarrett, a CBS analyst and two-time NASCAR champion during the 1960s. "He's helped raise the level of competition and also helped get the sport places it's never been before." The question becomes: What does Gordon have that others have trouble imitating?

As the driver of a successful race car, Gordon represents the most visible part of an incredibly complex team of individuals—all with a contribution to make on race day. "To build a winning team, you need three major ingredients—people, equipment, and money," stated Don Hawk, who was president of Dale Earnhardt, Inc. "You can't do it with only one, not even with two—you need all three. Look at Gordon. His team has crew chief Ray Evernham and the Rainbow Warriors pit crew—their multicolored uniforms match Gordon's multicolored car, the best in the garage area; they have the fastest and most reliable Chevrolet on the track; and they have great finances from DuPont. You couldn't do what they've done with just a great driver, just a great car, or an open pocketbook. You must have all three elements meshing. I liken a winning racing team to a Rubik's

*Note: The blue underscored words/phrases in this case indicate Internet links provided in the online version. See the *Organizational Behavior, Ninth Edition* Web site at http://www.wiley.com/college/schermerhorn.

Cube: all the pieces must fit and be in the proper place."

The High-Performance TEAM

"Success is a ruthless competitor, for it flatters and nourishes our weaknesses and lulls us into complacency."

The quote above was found in the shop of Gordon's former crew chief, Ray Evernham, recognized by many in NASCAR as the premier crew chief in the business. While Gordon represented the star attraction, many believed that it was Evernham who pulled the whole act together. He was responsible for a group of over 120 technicians and mechanics with an annual budget estimated between $10 and $12 million! And he had strong opinions as to what it takes to consistently finish first: painstaking preparation, egoless teamwork, and thoroughly original strategizing—principles that apply to any high-performance organization.

You win as a team. Evernham believed that teams needed to experiment with new methods and processes. When he assembled his Rainbow Warriors pit crew, none of them had Nextel/Winston Cup experience and none worked on the car in any other capacity. With the use of a pit crew coach, the Rainbow Warriors provide Gordon with an approximately one-second advantage with each pit stop, which, at a speed of 200 miles per hour, equates to 300 feet of race track.

"When you coach and support a superstar like Jeff Gordon, you give him the best equipment possible, you give him the information he needs, and then you get out of the way. But racing is a team sport. Everyone who races pretty much has the same car and the same equipment. What sets us apart is our people. I like to talk about our "team IQ"—because none of us is as smart as all of us.

"I think a lot about people, management, and psychology: Specifically, how can I motivate my guys and make them gel as a team? I surround them with ideas about teamwork. I read every leadership book I can get my hands on. One thing that I took from my reading is the idea of a 'circle of strength.' When the Rainbow Warriors meet, we always put our chairs in a circle. That's a way of saying that we're stronger as a team than we are on our own."

Evernham backed up this belief in team by emphasizing team performance over individual performance. When the car won a race, everyone shared in the prize money. In addition, when Evernham earned money through personal-service activities such as speaking tours and autograph signings, he shared what he earned with the team. "I wouldn't be in a position to earn that income if it weren't for the team. Everyone should feel as if his signature is on the finished product."

The teamwork during a race could even include adversaries—as in other drivers. In an effort to make races competitive for fans, NASCAR uses several methods to make the cars approximately even in performance, thereby enhancing the competitive environment for the audience. To get ahead, racers depend on their friends in the form of cars that help aerodynamically "slingshot" them ahead of the pack. This may take the form of teammates (Jimmie Johnson and Brian Vickers for Hendrick Motorsports) or opponents.

Push for perfection but accept imperfection. High-performance teams are constantly improving, even in small ways. Evernham made use of every opportunity to learn something new. If the car was running well, Evernham would ask Gordon to find something wrong with it. "We always try to make the car perfect. But the car doesn't have to be perfect to win; it just has to be less imperfect than everyone else's car."

Don't strut your stuff. In the past, most crews concentrated on the car and relied on horsepower and driving talent to win the race. Evernham took a larger view that kept the egos in check:

"There aren't many secrets in the Winston Cup, so you've got to protect as much information as you can. We want to have the fastest car on the track, but we don't want everyone else to know how fast we are. We don't show our hand until it's time to race or to qualify.

"We also try to mix things up on race day. We don't want to fall into patterns or to tip off the competition about our next pit stop. Since everyone can hear us on the scanners, we might use a code word to signal whether we're changing two tires or four. Sometimes, when the car is running well, Jeff might get on the radio and complain to me that the steering is tight, even though he's about to pass another driver. And that driver's crew chief will fall for it: 'Yeah, Gordon can't pass you right now, because he's tight.' The driver will leave a little opening and—boom—we're past him."

To win the race, drive by different rules. Evernham attacked each race as different from the last. He was constantly looking for even the smallest advantage that can give his race car and driver the edge. The team practices passing cars in unsuspected areas of the track, when their competition least expects it.

High-performance teams do not happen by chance; rather, they are the result of good recruiting and meticulous attention to learning every detail of the job. With multiple wins in every season since 1994 (despite a tremendous increase in the level of competition), the Gordon recipe for success has resulted in four Nextel Cup championships. Jeff Gordon wins approximately one of every four races he starts, a pace unmatched in modern times. However, on September 29, 1999, Ray Evernham resigned to form his own organization and was replaced with Brian Whitesell.

Whitesell took over as crew chief on an interim basis. With an engineering degree from Virginia Tech, Whitesell was one of the best-educated NASCAR crew chiefs. His brilliance was recognized by the legendary Dale Earnhardt when Jeff Gordon beat him in a race.

However, when Whitesell moved up to being team manager and the co-owner of the racing team along with Gordon, the search was on for a permanent replacement. The selection was Robbie Loomis. During the transition period and until Robbie Loomis became settled in the new position, Gordon went through six months without winning one race.

Robbie Loomis soon played a key role in a significant turnaround. In 2001 Jeff Gordon had a spectacular season: he was in the top 10 for the eighth season, and he ranked seventh in overall wins during his career. As of 2004 Gordon is within 16 victories of matching the record of Darrell Waltrip. Gordon is the only driver to attain over $75 million dollars in winnings.

What can be learned regarding the change in crew chief leadership and Jeff Gordon's continuing leadership? One test of leadership is how a group performs when the leader is not around. Another is how well a leader can turn a situation around. When Jeff Gordon lost his crew chief, Ray Evernham, there was a period of losses while the team was in transition. Nevertheless, the underlying strength of the team was obviously still there in spite of the losses. Jeff Gordon was still there to inspire team members not to give up. The strength was fully utilized as the new team leader was able to grow, develop rapport and confidence with the team, and begin to function as a transformational leader.

Review Questions

1. Evaluate Jeff Gordon's race team on dimensions covered in the text's discussion of characteristics of high-performance teams.

2. Discuss Jeff Gordon's race team on dimensions covered in the text's discussion of methods to increase group cohesiveness.

3. Compare Gordon's race team on the methods of team building. Which one most applies to this situation?

4. What are the potential pros and cons when a successful team leader such as Evernham leaves and is replaced by someone else? ■

CASE 11

Perot Systems: Can a High-Performance Company Have a Human Side?

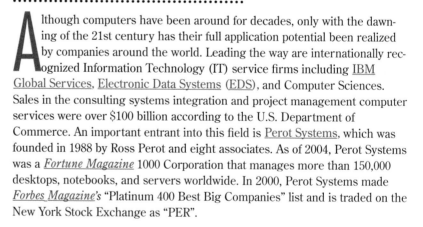

Although computers have been around for decades, only with the dawning of the 21st century has their full application potential been realized by companies around the world. Leading the way are internationally recognized Information Technology (IT) service firms including IBM Global Services, Electronic Data Systems (EDS), and Computer Sciences. Sales in the consulting systems integration and project management computer services were over $100 billion according to the U.S. Department of Commerce. An important entrant into this field is Perot Systems, which was founded in 1988 by Ross Perot and eight associates. As of 2004, Perot Systems was a *Fortune Magazine* 1000 Corporation that manages more than 150,000 desktops, notebooks, and servers worldwide. In 2000, Perot Systems made *Forbes Magazine's* "Platinum 400 Best Big Companies" list and is traded on the New York Stock Exchange as "PER".

A Rich History

Ross Perot is one of the true masters of the American economic free-enterprise system. Born in Texarkana, Texas on June 27, 1930, he has led a life filled with one significant achievement after another. Having lives his whole childhood in Texarkana, he entered the U.S.

Note: The blue underscored words/phrases in this case indicate Internet links provided in the online version. See the *Organizational Behavior, 9/e* site at http://www.wiley.com/college/schermerhorn.

Naval Academy in 1949, where he served as class president and battalion commander, an experience that even to this day motivates him to hire many of his top company officers from ex-military personnel.

Upon his discharge from the Navy, Ross married and began working for IBM's data processing division as a salesman. In 1962, with $1000, he started a one-man data processing company which he called Electronic Data Systems. Drawing on his experience in the military, in addition to recruiting a large number of ex-military personnel, Perot was able to build his firm into the premier data processing company in the U.S.

In 1984 EDS was sold to General Motors for $2.5 billion. GM wanted to greatly increase its use of technology in its manufacturing process and viewed its EDS purchase as an effective way of meeting this goal. As a result of the purchase, Ross Perot became one of the single largest holders of General Motors and a director in the company. However, Perot had great difficulty adjusting to GM's bureaucratic, autocratic management style, and he was eventually bought out of GM in 1986. After waiting the required two-year non-compete period, he started Perot Systems in 1988. Interestingly enough, GM spun EDS off in 1996, as it became obvious that the two entities did not make a good fit.

Throughout his career, Ross Perot has always been a model of citizen volunteerism. In 1969, the U.S, government asked him to determine what action could be taken to assist the prisoners-of-war in Southeast Asia. In recognition for his work, he received the Medal for Distinguished Public Service, the highest civilian award presented by the Department of Defense. In 1992 and again in 1996, Ross Perot ran for president of the United States representing a new third party, the Reform Party, which he founded as an alternative to the Republican and Democratic parties.

Perot's campaign efforts forced him to step down from daily involvement in Perot Systems. That year, Mort Meyerson, who had helped him build EDS into a world-recognized leader in data processing, stepped in to assume the chief executive officer duties. Although he had worked closely with Perot at EDS, Meyerson did not share Perot's desire to recreate EDS's "young, male, military model" corporate climate at Perot Systems. He was convinced that times had changed.

"In purely financial terms, my seven years running EDS had been unbelievably successful. When I left, I was very proud of the people, the company, and our achievements. From the day I started as president in 1979 to the day I left in 1986, EDS never had a single quarter where we lost money. We never even had a quarter where we were flat—every quarter grew like gangbusters. That kind of economic performance made a lot of our people very rich. I used to take enormous pride in the fact that I was instrumental in getting a lot of equity into the hands of the people at EDS.

What I realized after I left was that I had also made a lot of people very unhappy. Our people paid a high price for their economic success. Eighty-hour weeks were the norm. We shifted people from project to project and simply expected them to make the move, no questions asked. We called our assignments "death marches"—without a trace of irony. You were expected to do whatever it took to get the job done. In terms of priorities, work was in first place; family, community, other obligations all came after."

Meyerson's concern was the emphasis on profit at the expense of people. He believed that technology, customers, the market, and what people in organizations wanted from their work had all changed from his previous time at EDS. He asked himself two fundamental questions:

1. To get rich, do you have to be miserable?
2. To be successful, do you have to punish your customers?

Meyerson wanted to move Perot Systems toward a corporate model that recognized that the larger issues in life mattered as much as the demands for profit-and-loss. He was fully aware that at EDS not only had he supported the environment in which profit and loss was the only priority—and one in which non-performers were ridiculed—but he had encouraged it. As president for seven years, he had been largely responsible for the high-performance atmosphere that demanded so much from EDS employees. He tells a story in which an employee named Max missed a day of work due to a snowstorm and how Meyerson himself called the employee at home to question his loyalty to EDS. The employee took the first opportunity he could and left EDS. He was Max Hopper, who later went on to design the highly successful SABRE reservation system for American Airlines.

"None of that happened by accident. I had helped design EDS to operate this way, using the compensation system to motivate people: I tied their pay to profit-and-loss performance. If you ran your project successfully, you were richly rewarded. If you didn't, you weren't. I routinely spent an extraordinary amount of my time on compensation and rewards—roughly 15 percent. I did it because I knew that compensation mattered most.

The system worked; that is, we got exactly what we wanted. We asked people to put financial performance before everything else, and they did. They drove themselves to do whatever was necessary to create those results—even if it meant too much personal sacrifice or doing things that weren't really in the best interests of the customers. Sometimes they did things that produced positive financial results in the short term but weren't in the company's long-term interest. That's a charge you'd usually apply to a CEO—but I've never heard it said about individuals down to the lowest ranks of a company. Yet my pay-for-performance approach effectively encouraged that behavior from my people."

Upon his arrival at Perot Systems, Meyerson inherited a company of 1500 employees and a revenue of $170 million. His initial effort went into meeting with the top 100 leaders in the company. Through these conversations, Meyerson concluded that he had heard "a laundry list of horrifying bad news." He set about to change the company's culture, including a training seminar that over two-thirds of the firm's employees (including Meyerson) attended. Individuals who could not adjust were asked to leave. Meyerson's objective was clear:

"We still tell people we'll give them everything we can in the way of financial rewards. In fact, more than 60 percent of our company is owned by the people who run the company. So if we go public someday, we'll still make a lot of our people very rich.

But we will have done it without having first made them miserable—by offering them another dimension they can't get in most other high performance companies: a human organization. If any of our people has an interest outside the company, we will encourage and support them; if they have needs outside the company, we will recognize them."

Meyerson's other major concern was how EDS had treated customers. He described negotiations as intense, with EDS's desire to win every penny possible from the customer. Not only just to win, but to dominate. At Perot Systems, Meyerson promoted a much closer working relationship with customers and designed the reward system to reflect this newfound cooperation.

Similar to other information technology service firms, Perot Systems concentrates on particular <u>industry groups</u> in order to provide enhanced expertise. These include healthcare, government services, engineering and construction, automotive, transportation and logistics, and telecommunications. Several of the contracts that Perot Systems obtained, for instance in 2004, reflect this new corporate vision.

The change from data processing to systems integration has been motivated by globalization and the need for full supply-chain management. Companies depend on information systems to tie all the functional areas, including marketing, customer support, logistics, service, and operations together into a seamless whole. Rather than develop these competencies on their own, companies are increasingly depending on outside consultants, such as Perot Systems, to provide the expertise to run these complicated systems.

The New Face of Leadership?

Consistent with Mort Meyerson's new attitude toward business was a new emphasis on the shifting face of leadership. He concludes that the new leadership entails three jobs:

1. <u>Make sure that the organization knows itself</u>. Meyerson suggests that the leader's primary purpose is to support and embody certain core principles that define the organization. These values do not have so much to do with business strategy, tactics, or market share; rather they have to do with human relationships and the obligations of the organization to its individual members and its customers.
2. <u>Pick the right people and create an environment where those people can succeed</u>. In this sense, the leader is more coach than executive. This requires collaboration and teamwork among people at every level of the company.

The leader is not viewed as the final authority in decision making; the team represents the source of knowledge.

3. <u>Be accessible to the people in the organization</u>. Meyerson insists that he be in email contact with all employees of the company. He personally answers thousands of email messages every month. No longer is the leader an individual who shows up every six months to deliver a pep rally speech. And the leader must be accessible on issues and concerns that transcend the traditional boundaries of work and the company.

Can a High-Performance Company Have a Human Side?

While Mort Meyerson worked to develop his new view of leadership, Perot Systems struggled to earn a consistent profit. As one of the smaller players in the information technology field, Perot Systems' higher costs and lower net earnings troubled Mr. Perot, so he chose to return to day-to-day operations in late 1997.

Initially announced as interim CEO, Perot evolved into Perot Systems' full-time chief executive office. "He has centralized reviews of spending and new contracts. He has directed every supervisor to attend a leadership training course that reinforces his precepts. He has cut expenses, stepped up recruiting from the military, reinstated mandatory drug testing, and assigned a reading list including his autobiography. He has promoted executives with military backgrounds who have been with him for decades, since his days as commander in chief of Electronic Data Systems. White shirts are in, and, under his current

thinking, same-sex partners' health benefits will be out."

Not everyone was convinced that Mr. Perot could provide the same type of spectacular returns that he did in his EDS heyday. When he stepped aside as Perot Systems' chief, networked personal computers were just beginning to spread. Email addresses (Mr. Perot does not use email; he relies upon face-to-face communication) and Internet access were largely the domain of military personnel and university scientists, and Perot Systems was doing mostly standard corporate work on central computers. "At EDS, he built an organization that was based on command and control," said Allie Young, an analyst at Dataquest, the industry research firm in San Jose, California. "It was 'my way or the highway.' At that time, that type of model worked. Companies wanted that. Today it's very different. Senior executives are involved in the decision making for contracts, very often with the CEO. Information technology is a strategic decision. They don't want anything railroaded by them. They want a business partner."

The IPO

On February 2, 1999, Morgan Stanley Dean Witter conducted Perot Systems' IPO at $16 per share, valuing it at $1.35 billion in the New York Stock Exchange flotation. By mid-afternoon, the price had risen $26—to a value of $42—thereby increasing Perot Systems' value to $3.6 billion. It remained to be seen whether Mr. Perot's leadership style could turn Perot Systems into a major force in the information technology field.

Perhaps recognizing this issue, Mr. Perot turned the reins over to

his son, Ross Perot, Jr. Ross Perot, Jr. was elected President and CEO of Perot Systems in August of 2000. Ross Perot remained as Chairman of the Board of Directors for Perot Systems.

Although Ross Perot, Jr. also came from a military background, having served in the United States Air Force for eight years, he brought a different leadership style into Perot Systems. He is an adventure-oriented individual, as evidenced by the fact that he was the first person to fly around the world in a helicopter. He formulated and established the following statement of values: "Our company is built around tightly-fixed core values which are at the heart of who we are and a climate is fostered to support and instill them in every aspect of our organization. All associates operate in an honest and ethical manner with consistently high standards of integrity in all relationships with clients, governments, the general public and each other."

These values have been instrumental in enabling Perot Systems to have revenues of over $1.5 billion in 2003. In 2004 it was ranked # 46 in the Top 100 Federal Contractors. The *Orlando Sentinel* recognized the change in corporate culture by ranking Perot Systems 3rd in the Top 100 Companies for Working Families. Perot Systems has grown to have more than 14,000 associates worldwide in 2004.

Perhaps the following statements on Perot Systems' website best define the corporate culture: "Our culture encourages initiative and creative approaches to problem solving, yet always within the framework of close teamwork and accountability. Our business and professional ethics set the standard for the industry. Perot Systems has a flexible and dynamic operating structure, enabling our associates to respond to new opportunities and tailor their approach to the issues at hand. We see our company as a web, not a bureaucratic tower."

Review Questions

1. Compare Mr. Meyerson's leadership style versus Mr. Perot's based on the Michigan and Ohio State behavioral theories of leadership.
2. Utilizing Fiedler's Contingency Theory of Leadership, explain how either Meyerson's or Perot's style might be most appropriate based on specific characteristics of the situation at Perot Systems.
3. Evaluate Ross Perot, Jr.'s style of leadership from the viewpoint of transformational leadership.
4. Evaluate the situation at Perot Systems from the point of view of the discussion on New Leadership. ∎

CASE 12
Power or Empowerment at GM?
....

Developed by Aneil Mishra, Pennsylvania State University, Karen Mishra, Pennsylvania State University, and Kim Cameron, Brigham Young University; updated by Hal Babson, Columbus State Community College

Introduction

Effective September 25, 1990, the management of the General Motors (GM) Parma, Ohio, stamping plant finalized another three-year local agreement with the United Auto Workers' Union (UAW), Local 1005. It was the second local agreement they had negotiated together *on time* and *without intervention* from Detroit, since Parma's self-described revolutionary agreement seven years previously. It was revolutionary because Parma's management and union had abandoned their old hostilities and incorporated a team-based approach to work, setting Parma in a new direction. The 1990 agreement formally documented their joint priorities of team-based workgroups, extensive employee training, and a supportive working environment. The assistant personnel director for hourly employment, Bill Marsh, felt that, although this was another positive step in their ongoing relationship with Local 1005, the negotiating process seemed more "traditional" than the previous negotiation in 1987. Bob Lintz, the plant manager, agreed. Unexpectedly, the new Shop Committee chairman, who is Local 1005's prime negotiator, had introduced over 600 demands at the start of Parma's local contract negotiation. Even though management and the union were still able to finalize an agreement quickly, the tension created by the enormous list of demands still lingered. It could destroy the collaborative relationship that had been built over the past decade between management and the union leadership as well as the openness that Bob Lintz had managed to foster between himself and the hourly employees.

Background

In the early 1980s, Parma's corporate parent, GM, conducted a capacity rationalization study that concluded that almost 75 percent of Parma's operations should be either eliminated or transferred to other GM facilities within three years. Despite a one-year lapse in formal relations, and with no contract in effect, Parma's management and Local 1005 responded to this threat to plant survival by conducting a joint effort to bring in new business. This joint effort led to a number of competitive assessments of Parma's operations that identified several noncompetitive work practices. To formally acknowledge this new collaborative relationship, a new labor agreement was drafted and ratified in 1983 by Parma's rank and file that resulted in fewer work classifications and emphasized a team-based approach to managing workgroups.[1]

To implement this agreement, Parma's top management and Local 1005 created the Team Concept Implementation Group (TCIG) to introduce this new Team Concept and spent $40 million on extensive training of the entire workforce in problem solving, group dynamics, and effective communication skills. By 1990, the Team Concept had empowered hourly employees to assume more responsibility in their jobs and to focus on problem-solving and work-related matters and to move beyond status differences exemplified by position titles or neckties.

Roger Montgomery, who had chaired the Shop Committee from 1981 until 1990, felt that he had been able to put aside his past doubts of management's sincerity and work with Bob to create an environment based on teamwork and trust. He credits Bob's sincerity and openness with their ability to respect each other and work together for the good of the plant and its jobs. Roger believed that Bob had to overcome significant obstacles in creating this collaborative relationship at Parma, especially in convincing members of management and supervision. After years of open hostility between management and labor, Roger knew that Bob had supervisors and managers who didn't want to change. After years of fighting for employees by getting doors on bathroom stalls and eliminating hall passes, Roger felt that his union team had achieved greater consensus about the need for change. He felt lucky because even though some of his shop committee might not have agreed with him about every detail, they did support his efforts out of loyalty to him and to his relationship with Bob. Bob Lintz also felt that his managers and Local 1005's leaders had worked hard to overcome decades-long hostilities and build a positive and collaborative relationship.[2]

The Situation

Bob and his managers were concerned about the tension that had been created by the new Shop Committee chairman's large number of demands, especially because the union had made only about 100 demands during the previous contract negotiations. Roger had publicly endorsed this new chairman of the Shop Committee, yet management was not certain that he would continue Roger's strategy of collaboration within the union and between management and the union. With several new individuals in the union leadership, Parma's management also had to consider the possibility that the entire union leadership was actually becoming more adversarial, especially as the two political factions within the union continued to compete for support among members of Local 1005. Relations between hourly and salaried employees on the production floor could also suffer.

The list of demands from the new chairman of the Shop Committee could have resulted from the uncertainty that existed with the announcements of plant closings by GM. Since the mid-1980s, six GM stamping plants had been closed, and Parma's employment level had fallen. These plant closings and pressure from GM were the result of GM losing 10 percentage points of market share in under 10 years and corresponding deterioration in GM's bottom line. By the fall of 1990, GM was losing more than $1100 for every vehicle it produced in North America, in part because of GM's high fixed costs. With over $700 million in sales, Parma is an important plant to GM, but there is no guarantee that it would not be closed if demand for GM's products did not improve. Wall Street was criticizing GM for not being more aggressive in closing plants to remove excess capacity. The corporation was pressuring all of its facilities to reduce expenditures significantly and to eliminate all over time. Parma had made substantial progress in maintaining revenues amid declining demand, but it still needed to make significant improvements in productivity. For example, it still had to better utilize the transfer presses that stamp automotive doors and hoods. These presses were installed during the $600 million modernization in 1983, and in 1990 their uptime stood at 31 percent.

Parma also needed to improve its quality and customer satisfaction. In 1989, Parma began supplying the metal frame for the minivan produced at GM's Tarrytown, New York, facility. Arthur Norelli, general supervisor of Dimensional Control, remembered that in his first encounters with Parma, "I found them initially very defensive, almost adversarial. They were always right until we proved them wrong. If we had a part that wouldn't go together properly, they would say 'Well, you're not putting it together right.'" Another customer, a transmission plant within GM's Powertrain Group, had concerns about Parma's ability to produce quality parts in a timely fashion. In 1988, Parma was Powertrain's worst supplier for transmission components. Bill Hurles, a materials manager within the Powertrain Group, remembered Parma back then as "very dependable and very antagonistic."

In addition to pressures to improve costs, quality, and productivity, there were additional pressures on management from the union to bring stamping work inhouse that had previously been outsourced. As Parma lost its prop shaft production to another GM facility, the union wanted to bring back the production of sheet metal blankings, the first step in the stamping process. Blankings had been outsourced to a supplier, Medina Blanking, Inc., which produced an excellent-quality product and had virtually become another department in Parma because of its highly responsive and capable delivery.

As GM closed plants and continued to downsize, Parma's salaried employees, too, were being significantly affected by efforts to reduce salaried employment and eliminate management layers throughout the organization. With fewer salaried employees, workloads were increasing even as promotional opportunities, compensation, and benefits stagnated. As was the case at most GM facilities, Parma's salaried employees were not unionized. As part of its efforts to cut costs, GM had eliminated the salaried year-end bonus, had sharply reduced merit raises, and was considering other benefit reductions. Profit sharing for both hourly and salaried employees had evaporated as losses in GM's North American operations had mounted to several billion dollars annually.

After 10 years of being a top manager at Parma and assuming responsibility for all of Parma's operations, Bob Lintz continued to fashion a top management team based on trust and openness. He also wanted his managers to be committed to eliminating hostilities that lingered between the stamping and components operations within the plant, as well as between hourly and salaried employees. He was also looking for people who would support his informal and highly participative management style and who would work to increase the level of involvement among Parma's hourly employees. Although the TCIG had formally disbanded, its efforts were still ongoing. The weekly floor board meetings, where union officials and superintendents discussed plant floor issues, were still active and productive. The biweekly joint meeting of Bob and his staff, along with the Shop Committee chairman, the president of Local 1005, and the Shop Committee, were ongoing as well. These groups were representative of the Team Concept at work at Parma.

Conclusion

Even though Bob's management team supported his desire to increase the level of involvement among Parma's hourly employees, Dean Baker commented, "Sometimes I get frustrated, though, because I wish he'd have a little bit more confidence in the management organization."

Parma's lead training coordinator, Pat Camarati, was concerned that many of Parma's managers and supervisors saw the ongoing Team Concept training as more of a disruption than a necessity. Shop Committee member Ray Kopchak believed that, although they had made great strides, the biggest mistake the union and management could make was to assume that their relationship could continue to improve without hard work. Seven years after beginning a new collaborative approach, he still felt that the easiest thing to do was "to go back to the old traditional way. But I don't want to do that, it's not necessary. We've proven that management and the union can work together."

Did Bob Lintz's efforts pay off? In the years following, GM closed many more faclities but the Parma plant continued operations without a significant downsizing. Bob Lintz finally retired, but as of 2002 the plant appeared to be in no imminent danger of closing.

Review Questions

1. How would you describe Parma's environment in terms of its level of uncertainty and complexity?
2. How would you characterize Bob Lintz's approach to communication, decision making, and the exercise of power in creating change at Parma?
3. What were the most critical issues still facing Parma, and what should be done to address them?
4. How can resistance to change be overcome utilizing the existing workforce? ■

CASE 13
The Poorly Informed Walrus

Developed by Barbara McCain, Oklahoma City University

"How's it going down there?" barked the big walrus from his perch on the highest rock near the shore. He waited for the good word.

Down below, the smaller walruses conferred hastily among themselves. Things weren't going well at all, but none of them wanted to break the news to the Old Man. He was the biggest and wisest walrus in the herd, and he knew his business, but he had such a terrible temper that every walrus in the herd was terrified of his ferocious bark.

"What will we tell him?" whispered Basil, the second-ranking walrus. He well remembers how the Old Man had raved and ranted at him the last time the herd had caught less than its quota of herring, and he had no desire to go through that experience again. Nevertheless, the walrus noticed for several weeks that the water level in the nearby Arctic bay had been falling constantly, and it had become necessary to travel much farther to catch the dwindling supply of herring. Someone should tell the Old Man; he would probably know what to do. But who? and how?

Finally Basil spoke up: "Things are going pretty well, Chief," he said. The thought of the receding water line made his heart grow heavy, but he went on: "As a matter of fact, the beach seems to be getting larger."

The Old Man grunted. "Fine, fine," he said. "That will give us a bit more elbow room." He closed his eyes and continued basking in the sun.

The next day brought more trouble. A new herd of walruses moved in down the beach and, with the supply of herring dwindling, this invasion could be dangerous. No one wanted to tell the Old Man, though only he could take the steps necessary to meet this new competition.

Reluctantly, Basil approached the big walrus, who was still sunning himself on the large rock. After some smalltalk, he said, "Oh, by the way, Chief, a new herd of walruses seems to have moved into our territory." The Old Man's eyes snapped open, and he filled his great lungs in preparation for a mighty bellow. But Basil added quickly, "Of course, we don't anticipate any trouble. They don't look like herring eaters to me. More likely interested in minnows. And as you know, we don't bother with minnows ourselves."

The Old Man let out the air with a long sigh. "Good, good," he said. "No point in our getting excited over nothing then, is there?"

Things didn't get any better in the weeks that followed. One day, peering down from the large rock, the Old Man noticed that part of the herd seemed to be missing. Summoning Basil, he grunted peevishly. "What's going on, Basil? Where is everyone?" Poor Basil didn't have the courage to tell the Old Man that many of the younger walruses were leaving every day to join the new herd. Clearing his throat nervously, he said, "Well Chief, we've been tightening up things a bit. You know, getting rid of some of the dead wood. After all, a herd is only as good as the walruses in it."

"Run a tight ship, I always say," the Old Man grunted. "Glad to hear that all is going so well."

Before long, everyone but Basil had left to join the new herd, and Basil realized that the time had

come to tell the Old Man the facts. Terrified but determined, he flopped up to the large rock. "Chief," he said, "I have bad news. The rest of the herd has left you." The old walrus was so astonished that he couldn't even work up a good bellow. "Left me?" he cried. "All of them? But why? How could this happen?"

Basil didn't have the heart to tell him, so he merely shrugged helplessly.

"I can't understand it," the old walrus said. "And just when everything was going so well."

Review Questions

1. What barriers to communication are evident in this fable?
2. What communication "lessons" does this fable offer to those who are serious about careers in the new workplace? ■

CASE 14
Johnson & Johnson: One Large Company Made of Many

Johnson & Johnson is the world's most comprehensive and broadly based manufacturer of health care products, as well as a provider of related services for consumers and pharmaceutical and medical devices of both a consumption and diagnostic manner. With brand names like Tylenol, Band-Aid brands, Reach toothbrushes, Neutrogena skin products, and recently stents, Johnson & Johnson has global recognition. Representative of a conglomerate business model, Johnson & Johnson has more than 200 companies operating in 57 countries employing over 110,000 employees and selling products in more than 175 countries.[1] A constant challenge for such a large, diversified company is to infuse its decision-making process with the entrepreneurial energy of a small start-up firm.

Note: The blue underscored words/phrases in this case indicate Internet links provided in the online version. See the *Organizational Behavior, 9/e* site at http://www.wiley.com/college/schermerhorn.

Johnson & Johnson— Caring

J&J was incorporated in 1887 through the combined efforts of Brothers Robert and Edward Johnson. The brothers pioneered surgical dressings into an industry based on the work of noted English surgeon Sir Joseph Lister. J&J also developed a soft, absorbent cotton and gauze antiseptic dressing that could be mass produced and shipped in quantities to physicians, hospitals, and druggists in the country.[2]

Johnson & Johnson have always had an international focus to its business, beginning in Canada in 1919. It launched a concerted effort at product diversification with the introduction of its Band-Aid brands and Johnson's baby cream. This global idealism has continued to the present day, with over 90 percent of J&J facilities becoming ISO 14001 certified by year-end 2003. J&J received the International Life Award 2003 from the Aging Society. J&J's community responsibility platform supports and partners such diverse programs and organizations as the Nature Conservancy in Peru, World Wildlife Fund in Asia, Women's Wellness in Taiwan, Clean and Healthy Kids in Vietnam, and Preventing Mother-to-Child Transmission of HIV/AIDS in India.[3]

Johnson & Johnson is recognized as a caring company. In 1943, General Robert Wood Johnson wrote the company's credo, a one-page document that outlines J&J's responsibilities to its customers, employees, the community, and shareholders. The credo is available in 36 languages on the J&J website. In his message on the J&J website for investor relations, current Chairman, Board of Directors, and Chief Executive Officer William C. Weldon phrased the Johnson & Johnson credo as "Healthy People, Healthy Planet, and Healthy Future".[4]

Weldon further expresses the credo in the 2003 Sustainability Report for Johnson & Johnson as follows: "Our Ethical Code for the Conduct of Pharmaceutical Medicine is intended to complement Our Credo by providing more specific standards of conduct and behavior for physicians, clinical research scientists and others who are responsible for medical aspects of pharmaceutical research and development. It describes the principles we follow to help ensure the safe use of our products and the best interests of our patients and their families, doctors, nurses and other health care providers".[5]

J&J is well known for its proactive stance of crisis management regarding the cyanide contamination of its Tylenol painkiller. When seven Chicago-area individuals died after taking cyanide-laced Extra Strength Tylenol capsules in 1982, J&J chose to take a very proactive approach to the crisis. It recalled 31 million bottles worth over 100 million dollars from retail stores. From this tragedy, J&J pioneered the tamper-proof, triple-sealed packaging that is now an industry standard. When the situation was repeated in 1986, the company recalled all capsules, vowing never again to offer any Tylenol except in the form of tablets or caplets.[6]

Johnson & Johnson— Challenges

Johnson & Johnson placed fourth in the 2003 *Business Week* ranking of the Nation's Top 50 Best Performing Major Companies. While continuing to discover new products, the health-care giant is relying on other strategies in the face of stiffer competition. These strategies include acquisitions, drug uses, cutting costs, and teamwork.

In acquisitions, J&J has acquired at least 34 companies in the past 5 years and will likely keep shopping.[7] However, like so many other companies, J&J faces a relatively lean profit market. With J&J's share prices down, paying for companies becomes more expensive. It is tougher to use funds for purchasing without diluting earnings. The payoff is that small companies often produce blockbuster products, like the arthritis drug Remicade. In the past, J&J would simply buy new products, but even that is becoming harder.

Finding new uses for existing drugs can be another strategy. This research effort can provide "line extensions" in the product life cycle of maturing drugs, helping to boost revenue growth. On the negative side, any such new uses still require FDA approval.

Cutting costs means cutting labor, never a morale booster. Fear of job loss makes employees lose focus on products and customers. The payoff is that J&J could save $1billion over the next two years.[8] These dollars can be used in research for the development of badly needed new drugs and health-related products. In keeping an "eye" on expenses, the Audit Committee of J&J is made up of solely independent directors with the financial knowledge and experience to provide appropriate oversight.

Teamwork is having workers cross divisional lines to create new products and delivery systems. There is always the problem with cross-functional or product teams of "turf" issues resistance to cooperation. In the past, teamwork at J&J has been very exciting and productive, leading to such products as the coronary stent.

Johnson & Johnson— Organizational Structure

J&J does not view itself as just a pharmaceutical firm; it prefers to think of itself as a health-care organization. It represents a collection of independent entities whose decentralized culture fosters an entrepreneurial spirit. The company is encouraging employees in its famously decentralized realm to cross company lines to spur product development. The aim is to duplicate the success of the Cypher stent, which drew on both device and pharmaceutical divisions within J&J. Other cross-divisional teams are tackling diabetes and stroke.

The Johnson & Johnson Board of Directors is currently made up of

13 individuals, 11 of whom are independent under the standards of the New York Stock Exchange. The independent, non-employee members of the Board meet in executive session, without any members of the J&J management present, after most board meetings.[9]

Not everyone agrees with J&J's conglomerate structure. Some Wall Street analysts complain that Johnson & Johnson should be three separate companies. Of particular concern is the ever-declining roles in sales and profits of the consumer-product lines—falling from 44 percent in 1978 to only 28 percent of revenue in 1998. The J&J stock, rather than trading at the high attractive multiples of the past, fell 3.8% in 2003. J&Js shares trailed many of its rivals.[10]

Decision making requires the application of information, and more importantly, knowledge. "Data, information, and knowledge are points along a continuum of increasing value and human contribution. Data—the signals about human events and activities that we are exposed to each day—has little value in itself, although to its credit it is easy to store and manipulate on computers.

"Information is what data becomes when we as humans interpret and contextualize it. It is also the vehicle we use to express and communicate knowledge in business and in our lives. While information has more value than data, it also has greater ambiguity—as any manager will attest who has ever tried to interpret the terms of a customer's order.

Knowledge is information within people's minds; without a knowing, self-aware person there can be no knowledge. Knowledge is highly valuable, because humans create new ideas, insights, and interpretations and apply these directly to information use and decision making. For managers, knowledge is difficult to "manage" in other people because (being mental) it is invisible and its extraction, sharing, and use depends on human motivation. Companies that prosper with knowledge management will be the ones that realize that it is as much about managing people as about managing information.

Weldon will need to convince shareholders and employees alike that the conglomerate business model of J&J as a source of knowledge is still practical. In 2004, Johnson & Johnson companies worldwide are drafting 2010 goals which will be finalized in 2005. Most insiders agree that the strength of J&J is its diversity; the question becomes how does the company make the most efficient and effective use of this diversity and its associated knowledge base as inputs into its decision making?[11] Until profits from new drugs and devices kick in, the health-care gurus of J&J might do well to keep the Tylenol handy.

Johnson & Johnson— Problem Solving and Decision Making Using FrameworkS

Conceived in 1993 with the assistance of consulting firm McKinsey & Company, FrameworkS involves a series of focused dialogues between operating company executives, specialists, and top management. FrameworkS is an attempt to democratize how strategic choices are made at J&J using employee empowerment.[13]

The first FrameworkS looked at the changing nature of the health care market in the U.S. J&J's executive committee members enlisted senior company executives to explore key topics. After splitting into teams to conduct research, they contacted customers, policy analysts, government officials, and academics regarding the marketplace and their competition. Reconvening

Johnson & Johnson by the Numbers

MEASUREMENTS	2003 DATA	EXAMPLES OF PRODUCTS
Sales (Billions) by Business Segment		
Consumer	$7.4 billion	an increase of 13.2% from 2002
Pharmaceutical	$19.5 billion	an increase of 13.8% from 2002
Medical Devices & Diagnostics	$14.9 billion	an increase of 18.5% from 2002

Professional: Drug coated and coronary stents, surgery and wound-closure products

Pharmaceutical: Products for schizophrenia, infections, and anemia; such products as Procrit and Remicade

Consumer Products: Tylenol, Band-Aids, baby and Neutrogena skin products
Employees
110,600 in 200 companies located in 57 countries
Research and Development Expenses
2001 $3.59 billion dollars
2002 $3.96 billion dollars
2003 $4.70 billion dollars[12]

after several months, they discussed major changes in how medical care is delivered in the United States, from fee-for-service to HMO institutional decision makers. This format and process has caused management at J&J to see things from the customer's perspective, the core values of Johnson & Johnson, and how J&J is organized.[14]

An example of the critical findings of the investigation was that J&J's largest customers, such as hospital networks, government organizations, and managed care plans wanted a single J&J contract to coordinate purchases from J&J's diverse operating companies. As a result, in three months J&J created Health Care Systems, Inc. to support a single point-of-contact supplier to its customers. This was a visible example of organizational use of data, information, and knowledge to create a unique and innovative structure that addresses customer needs while still retaining the J&J culture of autonomous operating companies.

Other examples of innovation at J&J include Glow in the Dark Band-Aids, Reach Toothbrush, and Vistakons disposable contact lenses. The objective is to identify ways J&J can foster more substantial and transformational innovation in products, services, processes, and management. "What's New" is the program that includes a "toolkit" of action lines managers can use to infuse innovation into their organizations.[15] The intent remains at J&J to "exercise core competencies and exorcise corporate rigidities."

Review Questions

1. How is J&J able to demonstrate social responsibility and caring for the global community in its sustainable growth?

2. How does the management of J&J hope that FrameworkS will help with creativity within the organization?
3. How does J&J attempt to infuse ethics into its decision making?
4. After reviewing the recent performance of sales and the responses to the challenges of making a profit, what would you recommend Johnson & Johnson do to sustain its leadership in the health care products industry?

Research Question

1. Using a search engine such as Google or Yahoo, click on to the website of a competitor of Johnson & Johnson. What similarities do you see in meeting the challenges of creating new products, increasing profits, and maintaining a global social responsibility? What differences? How is that company's organizational structure the same or different from J&J? ∎

CASE 15
Faculty Empowerment and the Changing University Environment
∙∙∙

In a typical university, the instructor enjoys a very high level of empowerment and opportunity for creativity in achieving course objectives. Within general limitations of the course description, instructors tend to have a good deal of flexibility in selecting course content, designing instructional activities, and selecting assignments. This allows them to tailor courses in varying ways to do what may seem to work best in a given situation. For example, an instructor teaching a course four times a year may design one section to cover course content in a somewhat different manner or with a slightly different focus due to the unique background and interests of the students. Since not all students learn or can be effectively evaluated in exactly the same way, an instructor normally is able to respond to varying situations by the way in which the text is used, the specific activities assigned, and choice of tests and other means of measuring student performance.

One of the settings in which instructor empowerment has been especially functional is the presence of adult learners (those working full-time and attending school part-time, or returning to school after substantial work experience). Often adult learners have quite different needs than the more traditional student. Course variations that include unique learn-

ing opportunities that tap their work experiences and that accommodate the nature of their work schedules are often necessary. Flexibility and responsiveness by the instructor is also important. A major news event may create intense student interest in a course-related topic, but it might not occur at the specific point in the course in which the topic was scheduled to be covered, and the level of interest might require more time to be allocated to the discussion than was originally planned. Assignment

---

Source: Developed by John Bowen, Columbus State Community College

schedules and requirements are also a challenge when dealing with adult learners. Not all have work schedules such that they have the same amount of work week after week, but instead they may have variations in workloads that may include substantial travel commitments.

Where instructors have a good deal of empowerment, quality of education is maintained through instructor selection and development and through oversight by department heads. The supervision often includes reviews of any changes in course plans, learning activities, exams, assignments, and syllabus. This is facilitated by reviews of student feedback and through personal observation of the instructor conducting a class.

Regardless of the extent to which such quality control measures may or may not work, competition among colleges and universities is beginning to have an impact on faculty empowerment. In the past, schools tended to focus on a given geographic area, certain fields of study, or a particular class of students. Thus, competitive pressures were often relatively minimal. Today competition in the education market is not just local or even national, but is becoming increasingly global. Accelerating the trend is the use of online classes that can enable students in distant locations to take classes over the Internet.

The need to compete for revenues and to contain costs has also produced pressure for universities to operate more like businesses. This has, in some cases, resulted in more standardization of courses and instructional methods, consequently reducing the traditional empowerment of instructors. As an example of what is being done, consider two universities: Upstate University and Downstate University. Upstate and Downstate share two commonalities: (1) each sees their primary target stu-

dent market as the working adult and (2) each is increasing the use of standardization in instructional methods.

Upstate University focuses on the working adult: 82% of its 8200 students are employed and the average age is 32. It still holds traditional face-to-face classes on its main campus and in nearby communities, but its programs now include standardized online courses (including a program for military personnel) in both masters and undergraduate degree programs. It has developed a "Balanced Learning Format" approach involving standardized quality, content, and delivery for its courses—both online and traditional courses.

Downstate University was started to provide a means through which poor but qualified students could work and pay for their education. The school offers both undergraduate and masters degree programs. Enrollment at the main campus is now approximately 2,000 students but it has over 19,000 other students attending around the nation and around the world. Those students attend classes online and at 37 other campuses in 20 states—most of those students are working adults.

Upstate has standardized its courses so that certain specific activities and points are to be covered in each class session. The instructor does not set the assignments (problems, text questions, etc.). Rather, the student taking the course can go online and see what is required for both the instructor and student. The amount of time to be devoted to particular discussion or activities must follow a given script for each class session or at least be within guidelines in which some flexibility may exist. As a result, all instructors covering a given class session will be following the same script—often saying and doing much the same thing. This approach largely limits creativity to the person or persons involved in

developing and modifying the course. Any ideas to change the course would normally have to be approved by that developer. Changes are infrequent, however, perhaps because some instructors might be unwilling to contact the course developer and take the time to argue the need for a change.

Downstate is modifying its courses in ways that are similar to the approach taken at Upstate, although not identical. Standardized test banks are being used. Objective test questions are to be randomly selected from within the test banks and scored by computer, thus reducing subjective evaluation (and any possible favoritism) by individual instructors.

At both Upstate and Downstate, online instruction is playing increasingly important roles. The goal is to assure that all online interaction between students and instructors is proper and consistent with school policies. Online classes are conducted so that any communication must be either at the class website or through use of the school's own e-mail system. Thus, and if desired, the institution can monitor not only what goes on in the "electronic classroom" (the website for the course) but also in what might be comparable to the private chats which traditional students in the past had in the instructor's office. Furthermore, to the extent that a course is online and that all activity is completed using either the course website or the school's e-mail system, protection is provided to both students and instructors. There is always proof available that an assignment was or was not received on time; student complaints or grade challenges are much more verifiable.

From the perspective of administration at both universities, the approach to more standardization ensures uniformity of quality in instructional delivery across settings, students, and instructors. It also provides a benefit in regards to the recruitment of adjunct (part-time) instructors that are increasingly used. Since not all such instructors have the same level of creativity and experience, having a standardized course and common script for all to follow is presumed to help maintain quality of instruction across instructors and course sections. Many instructors—especially those who have taught in the past under empowered conditions, find the new developments at both Upstate and Downstate frustrating. They believe that their prerogatives and talents as professionals are not being fully respected.

Review Questions

1. Would you rather be a student in a class that has been standardized or one in which the instructor has a high degree of empowerment? Why?
2. What issues involving power and politics are involved in moving from a setting that encouraged faculty empowerment to one that required much more standardization of instruction? How would you deal with those issues if you if you were involved in university administration?
3. In the specific case of adult learners and use of multiple instructors, is it possible to reach a compromise between standardization and empowerment so that the benefits of standardization can be obtained while still allowing for the flexibility that comes with empowerment? How can this apply to courses taught online versus face-to-face? ∎

CASE 16
The New Vice President
· ·

[*Note:* Please read only those parts identified by your instructor. Do not read ahead.]

Part A

When the new president at Mid-West U took over, it was only a short time before the incumbent vice president announced his resignation. Unfortunately, there was no one waiting in the wings, and a hiring freeze prevented a national search from commencing.

Many faculty leaders and former administrators suggested that the president appoint Jennifer Treeholm, the Associate Vice President for Academic Affairs, as interim. She was an extremely popular person on campus and had 10 years of experience in the role of associate vice president. She knew everyone and everything about the campus. Jennifer, they assured him, was the natural choice. Besides, Jennifer *deserved* the job. Her devotion to the school was unparalleled, and her energy knew no bounds. The new president, acting on advice from many campus leaders, appointed Jennifer interim vice president for a term of up to three years. He also agreed that she could be a candidate for the permanent position when the hiring freeze was lifted.

Jennifer and her friends were ecstatic. It was high time more women moved into important positions on campus. They went out for dinner to their every-Friday-night watering hole to celebrate and reflect on Jennifer's career.

Except for a brief stint outside of academe, Jennifer's entire career had been at Mid-West U. She started out teaching Introductory History, then, realizing she wanted to get on the tenure track, went back to school and earned her Ph.D. at Metropolitan U while continuing to teach at Mid-West. Upon completion of her degree, she was appointed as an assistant professor and eventually earned the rank of associate based on her popularity and excellent teaching.

Not only was Jennifer well liked, but she devoted her entire life, it seemed, to Mid-West, helping to form the first union, getting grants, writing skits for the faculty club's annual follies, and going out of her way to befriend everyone who needed support.

Eventually, Jennifer was elected president of the Faculty Senate. After serving for two years, she was offered the position of associate vice president. During her 10 years as associate vice president, she handled most of the academic complaints, oversaw several committees, wrote almost all of the letters and reports for the vice president, and was even known to run personal errands for the president. People just knew they could count on Jennifer.

Source: Adapted from Donald D. Bowen, et al., *Experiences in Management and Organizational Behavior*, 4th ed. (New York: Wiley), 1997.

· ·

Review Questions

1. At this point, what are your predictions about Jennifer as the interim vice president?
2. What do you predict will be her management/leadership style?
3. What are her strengths? Her weaknesses? What is the basis for your assessment?

After you have discussed Part A, please read Part B.

Part B

Jennifer's appointment as interim vice president was met with great enthusiasm. Finally, the school was getting someone who was "one of their own," a person who understood the culture, knew the faculty, and could get things done.

It was not long before the campus realized that things were not moving and that Jennifer, despite her long-standing popularity, had difficulty making tough decisions. Her desire to please people and to try to take care of everyone made it difficult for her to choose opposing alternatives. (To make matters worse, she had trouble planning, organizing, and managing her time.)

What was really a problem was that she did not understand her role as the number-two person at the top of the organization. The president expected her to support him and his decisions without question. Over time the president also expected her to implement some of his decisions—to do his dirty work. This became particularly problematic when it involved firing people or saying "no" to old faculty cronies. Jennifer also found herself uncomfortable with the other members of the president's senior staff. Although she was not the only woman (the general counsel, a very bright, analytical woman was part of the group),

Jennifer found the behavior and decision-making style to be different from what she was used to.

Most of the men took their lead from the president and discussed very little in the meetings. Instead, they would try to influence decisions privately. Often a decision arrived in a meeting as a "fait accompli." Jennifer felt excluded and wondered why, as vice president, she felt so powerless.

In time, she and the president spent less and less time together talking and discussing how to move the campus along. Although her relations with the men on the senior staff were cordial, she talked mostly to her female friends.

Jennifer's friends, especially her close-knit group of longtime female colleagues, all assured her that it was because she was "interim." "Just stay out of trouble," they told her. Of course this just added to her hesitancy when it came to making tough choices.

As the president's own image on campus shifted after his "honeymoon year," Jennifer decided to listen to her friends rather than follow the president's lead. After all, her reputation on campus was at stake.

Review Questions

1. What is the major problem facing Jennifer?
2. What would you do if you were in her position?
3. Would a man have the same experience as Jennifer?
4. Are any of your predictions about her management style holding up?

Part C

When the hiring freeze was lifted and Jennifer's position was able to be filled, the president insisted on a national search. Jennifer and her

friends felt this was silly, given that she was going into her third year in the job. Nonetheless, she entered the search process.

After a year-long search, the Search Committee met with the president. The external candidates were not acceptable to the campus. Jennifer, they recommended, should only be appointed on a permanent basis if she agreed to change her management style.

The president mulled over his dilemma, then decided to give Jennifer the benefit of the doubt and the opportunity. He appointed her permanent provost, while making the following private agreement with her.

1. She would organize her office and staff and begin delegating more work to others.
2. She would "play" her number-two position, backing the president and echoing his position on the university's vision statement.
3. She would provide greater direction for the Deans who report to her.

Jennifer agreed to take the position. She was now the university's first female vice president and presided over a council of 11 deans, three of whom were her best female friends. Once again, they sought out their every-Friday-night watering hole for an evening of dinner and celebration.

Review Questions

1. If you were Jennifer, would you have accepted the job?
2. What would you do as the new, permanent, vice president?
3. Will Jennifer change her management style? If so, in what ways?
4. What are your predictions for the future?

Part D

Although people had predicted that things would be better once Jennifer was permanently in the job, things in fact became more problematic. People now expected Jennifer to be able to take decisive action. She did not feel she could.

Every time an issue came up, she would spend weeks, sometimes months, trying to get a sense of the campus. Nothing moved once it hit her office. After a while, people began referring to the vice president's office as "the black hole" where things just went in and disappeared.

Her immediate staff were concerned and frustrated. Not only did she not delegate effectively, but her desire to make things better led her to try to do more and more herself.

The vice president's job also carried social obligations and requests. Here again, she tried to please everyone and often ran from one evening obligation to another, trying to show her support and concern for every constituency on campus. She was exhausted, overwhelmed, and knowing the mandate under which she was appointed, anxious about the president's evaluation of her behavior.

The greatest deterioration occurred within her Dean's Council. Several of the male Deans, weary of waiting for direction from Jennifer regarding where she was taking some of the academic proposals of the president, had started making decisions without Jennifer's approval.

"Loose cannons," was how she described a couple of them. "They don't listen. They just march out there on their own."

One of the big problems with two of the deans was that they just didn't take "no" for an answer when it came from Jennifer. Privately, each conceded that her "no" sounded like a "maybe." She always left room open to renegotiate.

Whatever the problem, and there were several by now, Jennifer's ability to lead was being questioned. Although her popularity was as high as ever, more and more people on campus were expressing their frustrations with what sometimes appeared as mixed signals from her and the president and sometimes was seen as virtually no direction. People wanted priorities. Instead, crisis management reigned.

Review Questions

1. If you were president, what would you do?
2. If you were Jennifer, what would you do?

Conclusion

Jennifer had a few "retreats" with her senior staff. Each time, she committed herself to delegate more, prioritize, and work on time management issues, but within 10 days or so, everything was back to business as usual.

The president decided to hire a person with extensive corporate experience to fill the vacant position of Vice President of Finance and Administration. The new man was an experienced team player who had survived mergers, been fired and bounced back, and had spent years in the number-two position in several companies. Within a few months he had earned the respect of the campus as well as the president and was in fact emerging as the person who really ran the place. Meanwhile, the president concentrated on external affairs and fund-raising.

Jennifer felt relieved. Her role felt clearer. She could devote herself to academic and faculty issues and she was out from under the pressure to play "hatchet man."

As she neared the magic age for early retirement, she began to talk more and more about what she wanted to do next. ■

CASE 17
First Community Financial
· ·

Developed by Marcus Osborn, RSR Partners

First Community Financial is a small business lender that specializes in asset-based lending and factoring for a primarily small-business clientele. First Community's business is generated by high-growth companies in diverse industries, whose capital needs will not be met by traditional banking institutions. First Community Financial will lend in amounts up to $1 million, so its focus is on small business. Since many of the loans that it administers are viewed by many banks as high-risk loans, it is important that the sales staff and loan processors have a solid working relationship. Since the loans and factoring deals that First Community finances are risky, the interest that it charges is at prime plus 6 percent or sometimes higher.

First Community is a credible player in the market because of its history and the human resource policies of the company. The company invests in its employees and works to assure that turnover is low. The goal of this strategy is to develop a consistent, professional team that has more expertise than its competitors.

Whereas Jim Adamany, president and CEO, has a strong history in the industry and is a recognized expert in asset-based lending and factoring, First Community has one of the youngest staff and management teams in the finance industry. In the banking industry, promotions are slow in coming, because many banks employ conservative personnel programs. First Community, however, has recruited young, ambitious people who are specifically looking to grow with the company. As the company grows, so will the responsibility and rewards for these young executives. In his early thirties, for example, Matt Vincent is a vice president; at only 28, Brian Zcray is director of marketing.

Since First Community has a diverse product line, it must compete in distinct markets. Its factoring products compete with small specialized factoring companies. Factoring is a way for businesses to improve their cash flow by selling their invoices at a discount. Factoring clients are traditionally the smallest clients finance companies must serve. Education about the nature of the product is crucial if the company is to be successful since this is often a new approach to financing for many companies. First Community's sales staff is well trained in understanding its product lines and acts as the client's representative as they work through the approval process.

To assure the loans or factoring deals fit within the risk profile of the company, First Community must ask many complex financial questions.

Many small businesses are intimidated by credit officers, so First Community handles all of these inquiries through the business development officers. The business development officers, in turn, must understand the needs of their credit officers, who are attempting to minimize risk to the company while maintaining a friendly rapport with the client. By centralizing the client contract through educated sales representatives, First Community is able to ask the hard financial questions and still keep the clients interested in the process. A potential customer can be easily discouraged by a credit administrator's strong questioning about financial background. Utilizing the business development officers as an intermediary reduces the fear of many applicants about the credit approval process. Thus, a sales focus is maintained throughout the recruitment and loan application process.

Internally at First Community Financial there is a continual pressure between the business development staff and the credit committee. The business development staff is focused on bringing in new clients. Their compensation is in large part dependent on how many deals they can execute for the company. Like sales staff in any industry, they are aggressive and always look for new markets for business. The sales staff sells products from both the finance department and the factoring department, so they must interact with credit officers from each division. In each of these groups are credit administrators specifically responsible for ensuring that potential deals meet the lending criteria of the organization. While the business development officer's orientation is to bring in more and more deals, the credit administrator's primary goal is to limit bad loans.

The pressure develops when business development officers bring

in potential loans that are rejected by the credit administrators. Since the business development officers have some experience understanding the credit risks of their clients, they often understand the policy reasoning for denying or approving a loan. The business development officers have additional concerns that their loans that have potential to be financed are approved because many of the referral sources of the sales staff will only refer deals to companies that are lending. If First Community fails to help many of a bank's referral clients, that source of business may dry up, as bankers refer deals to other lending institutions.

These structural differences are handled by focused attempts at improving communication. As noted before, the First Community staff experiences an extremely low turnover rate. This allows for the development of a cohesive team. With a cohesive staff, the opportunity to maintain frank and open communication helps bridge the different orientations of the sales staff and the administration divisions. A simple philosophy that the opinions of all staff are to be respected is continually implemented.

Since approving a loan is often a policy decision, the sales staff and the loan administrators can have an open forum to discuss whether a loan will be approved. CEO Jim Adamany approves all loans, but since he values the opinions of all of his staff he provides them all an opportunity to communicate. Issues such as the loan history for an applicant's industry, current bank loan policies, and other factors can be openly discussed from multiple perspectives.

Review Questions

1. What coordinative mechanisms does First Community use to manage the potential conflict

between its sales and finance/auditing functions?

2. What qualities should First Community emphasize in hiring new staff to ensure that its functional organizational structure will not yield too many problems?

3. What are the key types of information transfer that First Community needs to emphasize, and how is this transmitted throughout the firm?

4. Why might a small finance company have such a simple structure while a larger firm might find this structure inappropriate? ■

CASE 18
Mission Management and Trust

Developed by Marcus Osborn, RSR Partners

With more than 500 business and political leaders in attendance from across the state of Arizona, CEO Carmen Barmudez of Mission Management and Trust accepted the prestigious ATHENA Award. The ATHENA, which is presented by the Arizona Chamber of Commerce, is annually awarded to companies that have a demonstrated track record in promoting women's issues within their company and the community. The 50-pound bronze statue that was presented to Mission Management and Trust was particularly special for the company's leadership because it was a tangible demonstration of their commitment to the community and to women's issues.

Mission Management and Trust is a small, newly formed company of just eight employees that has already made great headway in an industry that is dominated by giant corporations. Mission Management and Trust opened its doors just two years ago, and it already manages over $45 million in assets. What makes Mission's development even more impressive is that Mission is the first minority- and women-owned trust company in the nation.

The trust management industry provides services to individuals, organizations, and companies who want their assets managed and protected by specialized outside firms. Mission Management provides personal service to its customers at a level of sophistication that is unusual for a firm of its small size. Understanding that the trust management business is highly competitive, Mission developed a unique strategy that highlighted socially conscious policies combined with good business relations.

When the company was formed in 1994, it was created with more than the goal of just making a profit. Founder Carmen Barmudez started Mission with three principal goals in mind. "1. To run a top-quality trust company; 2. To promote within the company and, by example, increase opportunities for women and minorities; and 3. To donate a portion of all revenue to charitable projects supported by clients and staff." As these statements demonstrate, Mission Management and Trust was created with a specific purpose that was focused not just on the business of trust management but on the responsibility of being a good corporate citizen.

Even with these lofty goals, Mission faced the problem of finding clients who not only wanted quality services but were not hindered by some of the potential sacrifices a socially conscious investment company might make. Many investors want a high rate of return for their trusts, and social policy is of a much lesser concern. This was not the market Mission wanted to address, so it had to be selective in developing a client base.

Mission needed to find clients that fit its social philosophy about investing and corporate responsibility. The ideal customers would be individuals and organizations that were committed to socially conscious policies and wanted an investment strategy that reflected this commitment. Mission found a perfect niche in the market with religious institutions. Churches and other civic organizations across the nation have trusts that they use to fund special projects and maintain operating expenses. They need effective service, but in many cases these organizations must be mindful of investing in companies and other projects that do not reflect their ideals. For example, a trust company that invests in companies in the highly profitable liquor and cigarette industries would not be consistent with the philosophy of many religious organizations. Mission services this niche by developing an organization that is structurally designed to make socially conscious decisions.

Mission has already begun to meet one of its principal goals, which is to donate a portion of its profits to charities. By the end of 1994, Mission had already donated $4500 to causes ranging from

Catholic Community Services to the Jewish Community Center scholarship program. These donations not only fulfill a goal of the organization but assist in the socially conscious client recruitment. Mission's target client base will find Mission a much more attractive trust company because of its charity programs. A religious organization can be comforted with the reality that some of the dollars it spends on trust management will be recycled into the causes it promotes itself. The Mission policy makes good social policy, but it also makes good marketing sense. Understanding your clients is crucial to developing a small business, and Mission has mastered this principle.

Mission makes the most of its commitment to charitable causes by keeping its clients informed about the trust's activities and, more importantly, its community activities. *The Mission Bell,* a regular publication of Mission Management and Trust, details news and issues about the trust industry, company activities, and, most importantly, how Mission's social responsibility philosophy is being implemented. The name *Mission Bell* is more consistent with a religious publication than a corporate investing sheet, but it is consistent with its clients' needs. The name of the publication and its content clarifies Mission's role and purpose. For example, the *Mission Bell* summer issue presented articles on new hires, breaking investment news, and an article about how Mission is working with other groups to support socially responsible corporate investing. Thus, the Mission philosophy is clearly defined in its marketing and communication strategies.

To be consistent with the goals of the organizations, Carmen Barmudez collected a small staff of highly experienced individuals whose backgrounds and principles fit Mission's ideals. She frequently comments that the best business decision she ever made was "giving preference to intelligent, talented, compatible people whose main attribute was extensive experience." Mission employees are not just experts in the field of finance but leaders in their communities. These dual qualifications fulfill three important requirements that are crucial for the company's success. With community involvement comes an appreciation of the investment sensitivities that are required by the organizations that Mission services. Second, individuals who are involved in the community have well-developed contacts that can be useful in business recruitment. Finally, socially active employees are committed to the purpose of the organization and help unify the corporate culture within Mission.

Claire B. Moore, vice president of Mission Management and Trust, is a perfect example of how a corporate philosophy has been translated into practical personnel decisions. Claire was recruited because she had extensive banking experience, as demonstrated by her vice president position in Bank of America (Arizona). Her professional qualifications are augmented by her extensive involvement in the community, which includes the University of Arizona Foundation Planned Giving Council, Tucson Symphony, and the Junior League, to name a few.

The Mission case is a clear example of how matching a philosophy with a market can bear solid results. Mission's commitment to its ideals is evident and reflected in all of its business practices. When human resources, investing, marketing, and strategic planning decisions are made with unified goals in mind, the chances are good that a strong, successful corporate culture will develop.

Review Questions

1. How do the mission elements of Mission Management differ from most firms?
2. Does donating to charity before the firm is fully established mean that Mission is not demonstrating financial prudence?
3. Could Mission's unique mission contribute to effective coordination as well as adjustment to the market?
4. Would Mission's unique mission still yield success with more traditional investors? ∎

CASE 19
Motorola: Seeking Direction

Up until the mid 1990s, Motorola Inc., world famous for its Six Sigma quality control program, was an early success story in the computer/electronics age and viewed on Wall Street as an American Icon. Motorola had moved from being a decentralized but integrated, narrowly focused electronics firm at $3 billion sales in 1980 to being a decentralized and disintegrated broad portfolio firm at $30 billion in sales in 2001.[1] Motorola had been one of the world's leading providers of wireless communications, semiconductors, electronic systems, components, and services. Its cellular phone, analog equipment, and pager products were identified among the very best in the mid 1990s. However, increased competition, the Asian economic crisis, and its short-sighted failure to quickly and fully embrace the digital revolution severely tarnished its operating results and image. In the April, 2004 issue of *Business Week,* Motorola ranked 308 of the top 500 companies of the S&P 500, with 3 F grades and 3 D grades out of 8 categories.[2] The question becomes: what can Motorola do to return to its former high-performance ways and what can new CEO Ed Zander do to change the recent record of failures, intracompany turf battles, and oversights?

The Making of Motorola

Motorola Inc. was founded by Paul V. Galvin in 1928. Motorola's long history of technological innovation began in the 1930s with the first car radio. In World War II, the Motorola Handie-Walkie Talkie went to war for the U.S. Army. Under the brand name "Motorola," suggesting "sound in motion" the company name was changed to Motorola, Inc. in 1947.[3] It was the goal of Motorola to provide products that would give people the time and freedom to explore new worlds and handle daily tasks in the most efficient manner.

Motorola has accomplished a number of firsts, including the first rectangular television picture tube, the first practical car radio, and pagers. In 1988, Motorola won the first Malcom Baldrige National Quality Award in recognition of quality in American business.

Beginning in 1987, Motorola began the design of IRIDIUM. The system was a satellite-based, wireless communications network. It consisted of 66 interconnected, low-orbiting satellites that delivered

voice, data, fax, and paging through a hand-held phone. The development of IRIDIUM was intended to provide customers, including business professionals and travelers, with high-quality service at a reasonable rate.

As Motorola continued to expand its worldwide presence in the global marketplace through products and services, the need for talented personnel to uphold these established standards increased. In recognition of this, Motorola demonstrated a high commitment to seeking and developing a broad base of knowledgeable, highly trained employees, as evident through their innovative programs, provided by the establishment of Motorola University, and through the offering of expensive benefit plans to all Motorola associates.

Organizational Culture in Motorola

In the early 1990s, Motorola was recognized as a true high-performance organization with its innovations and socially responsible attitude. Its organizational culture was identified as a source of competitive advantage to the firm and one to be copied. Working in quality teams, members sought to provide the highest level of customer satisfaction, measuring defects in incidents per billion. These teams, however, were not always unified with other teams in the company. Motorola also earmarked more than $100 million a year for training, with everyone in the organization spending at least a week each year in the classroom at Motorola University, courtesy of the company.[4]

Motorola listed its fundamental objectives as total customer satisfaction:" To serve every customer better than our competitors do with

products and services of excellent value and quality and thereby earn continued trust and support".[5] Motorola wishes to accomplish this objective with respect for the individual, a statement it makes clear in its shared beliefs. Somewhere in the 1990s, this philosophy of satisfying customer needs became diluted by organizational egos.

Motorola's People

To treat each employee with dignity, as an individual; to maintain an open atmosphere where direct communication with employees affords the opportunity to contribute to the maximum of their potential and fosters unity of purpose with Motorola; to provide personal opportunities for training and development to ensure the most capable and most effective work force; to respect senior service; to compensate fairly by salary, benefits, and incentives; to promote on the basis of capability; and to practice the commonly accepted policies of equal opportunity and affirmative action.

Integrity and Ethics

To maintain the highest standards of honesty, integrity, and ethics in all aspects of our business—with customers, suppliers, employees, governments, and society at large—and to comply with the laws of each country and community in which we operate.[6]

From a proponent of leadership training to a leader in quality control processes, Motorola has created an internal climate that fostered high standards in a high-performance culture. The firm depended on Total Customer Satisfaction Teams (TCS) to ensure the firm's commitment to quality products and service. These teams were made up of almost 30 percent of Motorola's employees, and a goal of 10 times reduction of defects every two years puts pressure on the teams to constantly devise new ways to develop and deliver their products and services.[7]

However, Organizational culture can sometimes be a two-edged sword. Strong and successful organizational cultures, like Motorola, may contribute to high performance for extended periods of time but may actually result in an inability to adjust when conditions change. It is important to foster a balance between stability and flexibility for change; an objective that is difficult to maintain in a global competition that has no respect for previous accomplishments or industrial icons. For the large firms, like Motorola, success in the short term causes problems with inflexibility toward paradigms of changing situations in the long term.

What Happened to Motorola on the Way to the 21st Century?

In early June 1998, then Motorola CEO Chris Galvin announced that the company would take a $1.95 billion charge and lay off 15,000 employees. Currently, Motorola is down to 88,000 employees from a peak of 147,000. Motorola's semiconductor business, which grew 23 percent in 1995, slowed to a 1 percent growth rate in 1998.[8] In recent years Motorola stock dropped dramatically, with a 52 week high on July 27, 2004 of $20.89, to a low of $9.03, and its share of the cellular phone market had plummeted as Motorola couldn't produce color-screen phones in volume.[9] Samsung came from nowhere to become the number two player by revenue after Nokia in the cell phone industry. Motorola's semiconductor unit had a lock on

PDAs as recently as three years ago, but lost the lead to Intel. In 2003, the company eked out annual profits of $893 million on sales of $27 billion.[10] This profit would have been even less without the revenues from Motorola's chip business. Critics have come to a simple conclusion: Motorola does too many things—and not enough of them well. The company has earned the unenviable reputation of developing killer technology that got stuck in the labs.

Maggie Wilderotter, a former top executive with AT&T Wireless Services, provided insight into Motorola's problems. In the early 1990s, 85 percent of the cell phones sold to subscribers were made by Motorola. Their flip phones, the most advanced at the time, were in hot demand. AT&T decided that the future of cellular was digital, and over the next few years Wilderotter met repeatedly with the managers of Motorola at Motorola's Schaumberg, Illinois headquarters, urging them to develop a digital phone. Motorola kept stalling until the beginning of 1996, not long after AT&T had rolled out its digital network. Motorola unveiled its StarTAC phone: light, beautiful—and "analog". AT&T had no choice but to turn to cellular phone manufacturers Nokia and Ericsson for "digital" handsets. By the end of 1997, fewer than 40 percent of AT&T's wireless cell phones were made by Motorola.[11]

"It was bizarre," says Wilderotter. "We were very forthright with what we wanted. I don't know if they didn't listen or they thought it wasn't going to happen. It is absolutely amazing to me that they lost their way."[12] In 1998, Nokia replaced Motorola as the leading supplier of mobile handsets, a position Motorola had held since the mobile phone industry began.[13]

Much of Nokia's success was based on its digital technology.

Motorola remained the world leader in the U.S. market where digital was slower to take off. When Motorola did provide a digital alternative in its popular Strata model, it retailed for $500, compared to Nokia's 6100 model selling at $200 with twice the battery life.[14]

Inspection of the company's IRIDIUM satellite system uncovered other weaknesses. While the system eliminated "dead cells" by providing complete global coverage, it came with a very expensive price tag. The phones have the look and weight of cell phones years ago along with a thick, ugly, black antenna.[15] Unfortunately, in order to function, the system needed a completely unobstructed view of the sky, with tall buildings and even thick foliage blocking transmissions.

Some of Motorola's troubles were external, including a drop in semiconductor sales due to the Asian economic crisis, increased competition in cellular products, and a decline in pager sales. Motorola tried to meet these challenges by attempting to restructure its operations in combination with cost-cutting measures. The situation illuminated the need for a culture that was both strong and responsive to such external factors. In the quickly changing high-technology field, companies were being forced to make rapid and costly choices among competing technologies. In facing the challenges of rapid technology, including the staying power of new products, Motorola appears laden with a history of 75 years' worth of stuffiness, obscure acronyms, and lack of a unified team approach.

Another concern for many investors and analysts was the presence and performance of Chris Galvin as chief executive officer (CEO) since 1997. Galvin abruptly left the company in September, 2003.

He has since been replaced by new CEO Ed Zander, a loquacious individual of Sun Microsystems fame. Since arriving on the scene, Zander has been traveling worldwide, shaking hands, and getting an "earful" of adverse opinions of Motorola's lack of, or delays of, new electronic products by unhappy customers.[16]

Even before Zander's arrival, by 2002 Motorola made a plunge into digital technology, introducing a broad range of innovative products using digital technology. Zander has, however, begun to articulate a vision of Motorola in terms of its remaining four big end markets: the individual, the home, the auto, and the big organizations, which includes governments.[17] His focus will include collaboration across the company, targeting the mega-large business customers, potentially merging more units within the company, shedding employees, and developing new ways to combine wireless communications and the Net. Since Zander's arrival, Motorola has made impressive performances. On July 20, 2004 the company reported second-quarter sales up a healthy 41% compared to an anemic 2003. The star of these gains was the mobile-phone division, which has boosted revenues 67% to $3.9 billion dollars.[18] Two-way radios have received a big boost from increased spending by local and national government agencies on homeland-security concerns.

Motorola did decide to drop its boom-or-bust chip division. This leaves Motorola with essentially five businesses: cell phones, infrastructure equipment, two-way radio systems, the cable TV division, and one of Motorola's few recent success stories: electronic equipment for automobiles. Plans may be in the making for further mergers of units.

Review Questions

1. Discuss Motorola's relative success at the functions of organizational culture presented in the case.
2. How did Motorola lose its leading position in the electronics technology industry?
3. Discuss the various options managers might use in attempting to change the culture at Motorola.
4. How do you think employees at Motorola will react to the efforts of Ed Zander to bring the company back to a leader? ■

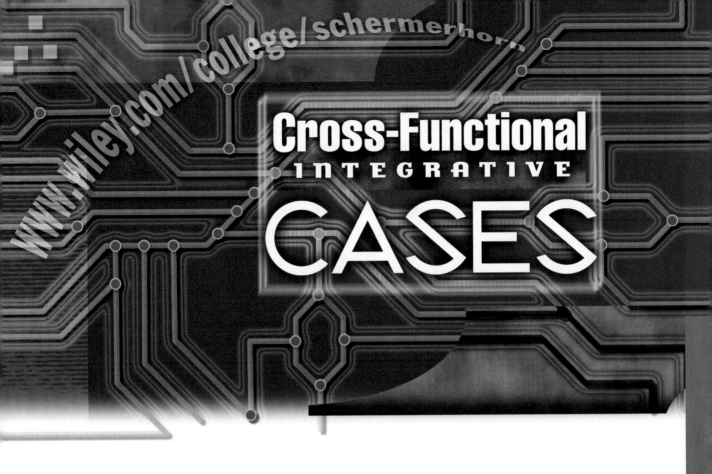

Cross-Functional
INTEGRATIVE
CASES

▶ ## Trilogy Software: High-Performance Company of the Future?

Developed by David S. Chappell, Ohio University

Add Joe Liemandt to the list of successful college dropouts. The Stanford University economics major and part-time computer lab consultant dropped out his senior year in 1989 to form "front-office" software developer Trilogy Software, Inc.[1] When informed by Joe that he was dropping out to start the firm, his father's curt reply: "You're a moron."[2] Today the private firm is valued at over $1 billion and recognized by many as the most successful still-private software start-up in the 1990s. Joe Liemandt's 55 percent ownership of the company works out to over $500 million. The question is: Does Trilogy represent the enterprise of the future?

■ The Social Glues of the Future

Successful twenty-first-century companies recognize the importance of talented people and the tremendous opportunities available to them. These talented individuals' loyalties are not taken lightly. Progressive firms acknowledge that loyalty is a two-way street. Robert Reich, former Secretary of Labor under President Clinton, identifies six "social glues" for the high performance companies of the future:

1. **Money Makes It Mutual.** Rather than competing for money, company founders are enlisting employees

---

Note: View case online with active links at: www.wiley.com/college/schermerhorn.

through the use of stock options. If you want talent to work for your organization with the enthusiasm that comes with ownership, then you have to trade equity for it.

2. **Mission Makes a Difference.** Talented people want to be part of something that they believe in, that involves spiritual goals that energize an organization. A powerful mission is both a magnet and a motivator.

3. **Learning Makes You Grow.** People recognize the importance of intellectual capital in the new economy, and want to join an organization where they will be given every chance to learn continuously.

4. **Fun Makes It Fresh.** Hard work requires that the work be fun, that it support friendship and camaraderie. Hard work must be "harnessed" to shared enjoyment.

5. **Pride Makes It Special.** We all like to be associated with an enterprise that feeds our sense of pride. Membership in these companies confers status—and status is a form of capital.

6. **Balance Makes It Sustainable.** Balance is not just a set of programs to support work and family—rather it is a way of doing business. The choice is moved to the employee, not the firm.

Reich argues that collaboration and mutual advantage are the essence of future organizations. "More fundamentally, companies are experimenting with a new operating system for the employer–employee relationship—one to replace the old set of practices that put employers and employees on opposite sides of the table. The model for the organization of the future aims to create tangible and intangible value that both sides can share and enjoy. It accepts as a core reality—rather than as a pleasant fantasy—the old saw that a company's people are its most important asset. And it builds on that reality to create a way of working that is profoundly human and fundamentally humane."[3]

■ Meet Trilogy Software

From his early youth, Joe Liemandt was steeped in business lore. Working for <u>General Electric</u>, Joe's father Gregory Liemandt's superior was <u>Jack Welch</u>. As a child, Joe played hockey with Mark Welch, Jack's son; spent weekends at the Welches'; and often went on ski trips to Lake Placid with the Welches. Joe Liemandt remains a close friend with the senior Welch, often approaching him for business advice.[4]

Joe Liemandt knew he was going to start a computer software company when he got to college. "I started doing tons of research. I'd sit in the library going

through lists of the top 50 software companies." In addition, he did part-time consulting for computer companies in the surrounding Palo Alto area. The huge teams of programmers—often 50 to 100 people—created such coordination problems that the projects often fell apart. This was a lesson Liemandt would remember in the future.[5]

He quickly recognized that shipments of computer equipment would arrive late and with parts missing or incompatible with his computers. He became aware that while manufacturers' "back-room" operations, including general and administrative expenses, R&D expenses, and manufacturing costs, had been automated through computers, sales and marketing—representing more than 40 percent of their noncapital spending—was not yet computerized.[6] "<u>Sales configuration software</u>" had yet to be born.

"What people usually mean when they say sales force automation is putting a bunch of customer information on a laptop for a sales rep. We didn't see a big return there. We didn't feel that trying to improve the point productivity of salespeople, most of whom did not use computers, was that valuable. The sales rep doesn't need time to manage his contact better. But when he needs a price quote or information from the home office, he needs them instantly."[7]

The problem faced by firms approaching this arena was the complexity involved with a broad product line. Rule-based programming, one promising approach, required too many if/then statements, resulting in unwieldy programs. Constant-based equation models, heavily utilized in optimizing airline passenger yields and in the military, wasn't capable of efficiently handling the large volumes of data required for an effective sales configuration model.[8]

Together with Stanford students <u>John Lynch</u>, <u>Christina Jones</u>, <u>Chris Porch</u>, and <u>Tom Carter</u>, <u>Liemandt</u> applied algebraic algorithms similar to ones used by mathematical economists to construct general equilibrium models of the economy. Forced to move to Austin, Texas, to be near his ailing father, Liemandt was able to attract <u>David Franke</u> to join the fledgling Trilogy. Providing necessary credibility with large corporate clients, Franke was able to land <u>Hewlett-Packard</u> in 1992, which abandoned their own sales configuration software by choosing Trilogy.[9] At this point, Trilogy numbered eight employees. The HP sale was quickly followed by contracts with Boeing, <u>Silicon Graphics</u>, <u>Alcatel</u>, <u>AT&T</u>, and others.

While the initial product was a crude configurator, further refinements led to <u>Selling Chain</u>, a product that went beyond mere sales configuration. Trilogy's Selling

Chain "consists of all the links between a corporation and its customers. These links include the sales team, service department, marketing, advertising, manufacturing, tech support, etc. Every member of the chain has instant access to vital information. Armed with accurate, up-to-date data, salespeople can dramatically reduce costs and shorten the sales cycle."[10] HP was able to cut orders rejected by factories to just 2 percent from up to 40 percent previously. "If you were to pull the plug on the Trilogy system, we simply could not sell any more" says Nick Nebehay, worldwide sales administration manager.[11]

"It takes 12 hours to build a car," says Liemandt. "When the dealer tells you it takes six to eight weeks for delivery, that's all front office administration. For the whole '80s everybody focused on the supply chain, total quality manufacturing, concurrent engineering. They spent all their money on the back office. All the major manufacturers have taken their manufacturing times from six weeks to six days but they haven't done that for the front office. All the return for the next 10 years is going to be in the front office, the selling chain."[12]

Using Trilogy's Selling Chain software, clients load all the options and product specifications they offer into the program. Modules for prices, quotes, financing, catalogs, component compatibility, and all the possible variations are sorted out by computer. According to Trilogy, 2 percent of manufacturers' gross revenues are spent to correct human errors and configuration errors. In 1994, Robert DeBakker, director of order fulfillment for Sequent Computer Systems, purchased Trilogy software and services for $700,000. He claims that the investment saved Sequent over $3 million in the first year.[13]

Reengineering guru Dr. Michael Hammer believes the next big wave of reinvention among American businesses will be for the customer. "Companies are selling more complicated products than ever before. Customers are more demanding. The good news is that after a decade of intensive work in manufacturing and logistics, we've made tremendous progress in order fulfillment. The bad news is that we can't get the order right—the front end is no good." Sales automation for the sake of automation is not the answer. "Automating a mess creates a mess," he declares. "Companies have to rethink the process behind getting the order and placing it."[14]

Hammer identifies three critical benefits to corporations who use sales configuration software: (1) shorter selling cycles, (2) increased customer satisfaction, and (3) higher market share. High-tech firms are on the cutting edge of the selling chain reengineering movement. "Computer companies like IBM and Hewlett-Packard are taking the lead," he contends, "because their products are complex and yet ironically have been commoditized.

They have to differentiate themselves in order to remain competitive." The consumer packaged-goods industry is also taking notice, with companies like Procter & Gamble and Colgate Palmolive attempting to differentiate themselves by improving their front offices.[15]

In all cases and industries, the return on investment for customers installing Selling Chain has been impressive. Recalls Liemandt, "We had a customer who saved $5 million on catalogs alone. Seventy percent of the catalogs they sent out to the field would never get read by anybody. Once they automated the system so a sales rep could print one out locally when he needed it, they saved $5 million."

"One customer, a large distributor, was spending $30 to $40 million a year on their pricing system before we came along. They printed price books and sent them out quarterly, providing their sales reps with weekly updates in the form of paper sheets that had to be inserted into their price books. Forty percent of the time the sales rep was still quoting the wrong price because they missed sheet number 6a."[16]

Boeing provides another excellent example of the value of sales configuration software. A Boeing 747 involves over 6 million parts and a customer can choose from hundreds of options. Every option the customer selects affects the availability of other options and the ultimate price of the plane. Prior to using computers, redesign efforts could take weeks to prepare. Utilizing Trilogy software, a Boeing salesperson can sit down with a customer and configure the 747 on a laptop, complete with price quote in one trip.[17]

■ The Selling Chain at Work

Computer Sales

IBM rolled out Trilogy's Selling Chain to 35,000 members of its worldwide sales force. The program integrates essential information from sales, marketing, and manufacturing that allows salespeople to evaluate customer needs, accurately configure systems, prepare quotes, and create a graphic representation of a product solution.

Automotive Sales

Chrysler uses Selling Chain to allow prospects in shopping malls to create their dream car by selecting features and options at a touch-screen kiosk. Customers can get instant pricing and delivery information, and the kiosk will offer the shopper the option to build a new car or select a near-match available at a nearby dealership.

Retail Sales

Custom Foot shoe stores use Selling Chain to help customers design and order custom-made Italian shoes to their exact specifications. Custom Foot offers more than 10 million shoe options. Selling Chain links stores and corporate offices with factories in Italy. The custom shoes are delivered within two weeks. Jeff Silverman, CEO of Custom Foot, says, "We carry no inventory and there are no middlemen. This is true mass customization at a lower cost."[18]

Although Joe Liemandt's father had made over $30 million by working for the likes of General Electric and UCCEL, a maker of software for mainframes, no family money was used in the start-up. As his mother states, "Outside of slipping him $100 bills in the airport, there was no [family] seed money."[19] Unable to attract venture capital, Liemandt charged over $500,000 on 25 credit cards in the early days. "We bootstrapped ourselves using sweat equity," explained Liemandt.[20]

As Liemandt states, "There are three things venture capitalists look for: an experienced management team—and a bunch of 19- or 20-year-old kids doesn't cut it; a really experienced technical team who's building a product for the second time, which we weren't; or a new hit product. But the last thing you'd ask kids to do is write a mission-critical application for the Fortune 500, which is exactly what we were doing."[21]

They were eventually successful at raising $4 million in their second try with venture financing. "I wanted to sell as little as possible," Liemandt explains, "because I was looking for some help in building the company. I didn't really need the money. One thing about being a successful entrepreneur is that you think you know everything. That's also the downside." He sold under 20 percent to the venture capitalists, who now sit on the board and provide valuable guidance.[22]

■ Want to See That Desk in 3-D?

As far as Jim Hook, director of dealer development at Haworth, Inc., is concerned, designing office space for clients can be as complex as putting together Boeing 747s. Before the first piece of furniture even gets through a customer's door, Haworth's sales force uses computer-visualization software provided by Trilogy to provide a peek at what the customer's offices will look like and the project's cost.

Trilogy, Inc.'s configuration application, which tracks the pricing of thousands of components in Haworth's customizable, build-to-order product line, reduces the number of sales visits required to make a deal from five to two by putting more information into the hands of the sales force. It might take a designer hours to route an electrical wiring layout to a salesperson. But a salesperson can use Trilogy to configure the layout in minutes,

eliminating a lot of the back-and-forth between Haworth and the customer. On a typical $15,000 project, the system also provides pricing estimates within $100.[23]

Haworth's executives hope that the Trilogy application, called the Sales Builder Engine® (one of several modules in a suite called Selling Chain®), will shorten the company's sales cycle, make its huge parts catalog more easily understood, and increase order accuracy. According to Smith, Haworth's senior sales-automation expert, that would be a significant competitive advantage for the 9,000-employee company, which is the world's second-largest seller of office cubicles and had $1.2 billion in sales in 1995. Smith says Haworth spent more than $1 million on the Trilogy software.

Previously, the salesperson and CAD (computer-aided design) operator typically had to go through a CAD mock-up process several times—with the sales representative returning each time to the customer to show the mock-up—to complete an order. Only after the last CAD mock-up is approved is the CAD workstation software used to create a bill of materials that goes to Haworth's factory for manufacturing. With the Trilogy software, Haworth is reengineering its sales by shifting detailed parts-assembly information from the corporate level down to the customer level. (Haworth on Trilogy's Web site)

Trilogy has been quick to embrace the Internet, viewing it as a natural extension of its vision of front-office automation. In 1996, Selling Chain was rewritten in Java to enable it to support e-commerce on the Web. Not content to sit back and enjoy the success, Trilogy continues to innovate, having recently introduced Buying Chain, a low-cost procurement application designed for browser access. Companies using Buying Chain create catalogs of hyperlinks to Web sites of online merchants that have "Buying-Chain-enabled" their sites. One recent convert is Office Depot, allowing its online customers to update their internal product catalogs with Office Depot products.[24]

■ Insanity, Inc.

Does Trilogy represent the company of the future? If so, it exhibits a culture that is refreshing and unique compared to many older companies. With an average age of 27, its employees represent the new importance placed on talent and learning. From POP ("Party on the Patio") to taking the company jet ski out for a spin, the culture looks to cultivate stars. As the company is proud to state, what matters at Trilogy are *results, results, results.*[25]

Trilogy's vision makes it clear that the company sets extreme goals, but it does amazing things to support its employees so they can realize these goals. Trilogy comprehends that the key to fast growth is to recruit the best people, to get them up to speed as quickly as possible, and to turn them loose so that they can make an immediate impact. "At a software company, people are everything," Liemandt says. "You can't build the next great software company—which is what we're trying to do here—unless you're totally committed to that. Of course, the leaders at every company say, 'People are everything.' But they don't act on it."[26]

Thoughts from Joe Liemandt on Nurturing Trilogy's Can-Do Culture

What are your top three challenges?

(1) Hiring the right people, (2) making customers successful, (3) not losing the culture—keeping Trilogy a place where individuals can really shine. I want to make it a place where individuals are constantly challenged, are in over their heads and find ways to get out of it.

How do you recruit the right people?

We look for people who are like us—who have a fiery passion, who really want to make a difference, who are top-notch in their field. We put these people through months of boot camp—we call it Trilogy University—to educate them about the technology and the business. And then we let them loose on the world.

How can companies use technology to improve their sales?

Technology will only have the right impact if it's applied the right way. The focus has got to come from the businesspeople. If the VP of sales wants to drive change in the organization, it's a great tool. The focus we always have is return on investment. If it becomes technology for technology's sake it doesn't bring the return you need.

Who makes the best salesperson?

Our best sales reps make our customers successful by developing and managing a relationship with them. Customers learn to trust that if it's in Trilogy's capability, we will make it work. Developing trust and faith is the number-one thing and this can happen only through proving ourselves over time.

What do you bring to Trilogy as a salesman?

I bring enthusiasm and evangelism. When you talk to me, you get the feeling that we can deliver on our promises. I'm also very content-rich. I've been through so many of these customer experiences that I can customize my presentation to each audience.

What was your most memorable sale?

The best sales were the ones back in '92 when we were still selling the dream. We had something but not enough. I couldn't point to references. All I could say was, "We don't have much to show you but we're so close and you're just going to believe that we can do it. If you have to bet on a system, you will bet on Team Trilogy." It was all personal selling and there was no data to back it up. To an extent I miss it. They'd say, "Who are you? Are you 22 yet? How much money do you want?" In the end, I said, "You've just got to believe me on this."[27]

Trilogy's Hiring Practices

To recruit the talent it so desperately needs, Trilogy utilizes tactics that others refer to as "crazy." The firm aggressively pursues people with the least experience in the job market. It focuses on college campuses and career fairs for every type from computer science to liberal arts majors. The common thread involves young, talented overachievers with entrepreneurial ambition to provide what Jeff Daniel, Trilogy's director of college recruiting, calls "a good technical and cultural fit."[28]

In 1998, the company reviewed 15,000 résumés, conducted 4000 on-campus interviews, flew 850 candidates to Austin for on-site interviews, and ended up hiring a total of 262 college graduates—33 from Carnegie Mellon, 26 from Penn State, 23 from Stanford, 20 from Harvard, 16 from Princeton, 11 from Cornell, and 10 from MIT.[29] Some students have nicknamed Trilogy "The Firm" because its outsized recruiting tactics resemble those of the notorious law firm Bendini, Lambert & Locke in John Grisham's novel.[30] This time-consuming process is expensive, at $13,000 per hire, but the firm is aiming for the "whiz kid" who will develop the next hit software package.[31]

Click here for a look at Trilogy's hiring process

One of Trilogy's most active recruiters is Liemandt himself. One of the youngest members of the Forbes 400 list of the richest Americans, he remains a surprisingly down-to-earth guy—"the most unassuming $600 million man you'll ever meet," claims Daniel. A bachelor, he wears jeans and tennis shoes to work, lives in an apartment without a television, drives a Saturn, dines at Wendy's, and gets his hair trimmed at Supercuts. However, he has accomplished what many of the hotshots drawn to Trilogy only dream of doing: he has taken a great idea and turned it into a successful company.[32]

Trilogy utilizes a sponsor/star approach to developing talent within the organization. Job evaluations rank Trilogians from 1 to 3, with 1 being a "star." In the hiring process, Trilogy doesn't just evaluate its recruits, it also evaluates the evaluators. Employees whose recruits are on their way to becoming stars become "sponsors." There are about 60 sponsors in the company today, and rarely does a candidate get hired without one. In sponsoring a candidate, sponsors are accepting responsibility for his or her performance. "If you hire someone and you're wrong, it's your job to be a mentor and fix the situation."[33]

Testimonial from a Trilogy Employee

Chris Hyams has an AB in History and Theory of Architecture, Princeton University, 1989, Masters in Computer Science (MCS), Rice University, 1996.

I am a developer at Trilogy, working on our core application architecture, the Selling Chain Backbone, primarily focusing on Replication. I initially came to Trilogy because I wanted to work with smart people, solve challenging problems, and generally feel like I had a meaningful and tangible impact on both end users and the company as a whole. I have stayed at Trilogy for the past two and a half years because I have been able to do all of this and more on a regular basis.

A day in my life is both typical of a developer at Trilogy, and at the same time, quite atypical. It is typical in that I spend my time wearing a number of hats: writing code, working with Trilogy consultants helping them customize and deploy our apps, advising other developers integrating to the architectural framework that I work on, interviewing recruits, talking to partners and customers, etc. At the same time, my day is atypical, in that I do this all from my home in Berkeley, CA. I telecommute full-time from my home office, making the trip out to Austin once a month or so.

The point of this is not necessarily that Trilogy lets people live wherever they want; as a rule, they don't. However, Trilogy is one of the rare companies that honestly cares about doing whatever it takes (within reason) to keep people happy. I wanted my two young children to be able to live closer to their grandparents. Trilogy decided that as long as I got my work done, that was cool. Some people like to sleep all day and work all night. Others prefer to work a more normal 9 to 5. Some come to the office only for weekly meetings. Still others sleep on a futon in their office. One thing that I love about Trilogy is that in the end, no one cares how you do your work. What truly matters is how well you do it. Good work is highly regarded, and highly rewarded. This bottom-line kind of attitude is at the same time honest, refreshing, and very effective.

The following example is a sampling of one day in my life at Trilogy—a summary of events from one very real day last week.

- Worked with developers of our Commission product to resolve issues concerning replicating Commission models in a multi-user maintenance environment.
- Made final decisions on what features would go into the next minor release (3.1) of the Backbone and Replicator.
- After a week or so of iterative debugging, finally found and fixed a rare and obscure shared memory allocation bug in the previous (2.1) release of our software.
- Worked with the QA/test team to help automate the running of regression tests for my products after a new build.
- Phone interviewed an industry development candidate on the East Coast.
- Had a conference call with a business unit head and a consultant about the details of the shared memory bug, so they could clearly explain to their customer what the problem was, and how we fixed it.

- Answered a couple dozen assorted e-mail messages on various Trilogy mailing lists, mostly concerning technical details of the Backbone and Replicator architecture.
- Talked on the phone with a half dozen consultants in various cities concerning similar issues.
- Finished up coding a major feature (Schema Replication) of the 3.1 Replicator release.
- Code-read changes to our core database abstraction layer that another developer had implemented.
- Worked with another developer, helping to resolve issues of porting an ActiveX control written in VB to C++.
- Talked with a technical contact at a database company about resolving some of the technical roadblocks to integrating our Backbone with their database.

At Trilogy, we all have a stake in the success of the company as a whole. As a result, we all care not only about our own success, but also about the success of everyone around us. From the list above, it should be clear that I spend a great deal of my time at Trilogy working with and helping other people to succeed. While in some respects this takes away from the time I have to do my work, working with others is 100% aligned with my primary purpose at Trilogy—helping to build the next great Software Company.

More employee testimonials

■ What Trilogy Wants

To improve the evaluation process, Trilogy depends on its best developers and programmers, its best consultants and salespeople. Graham Hesselroth, one of Trilogy's top developers, conducted over 350 interviews in 1998. He's considered one of Trilogy's toughest interviewers in addition to being one of its best judges of talent. He sponsors only a handful of recruits, but those he chooses are almost assured of becoming stars. His approach is direct: "You better blow me away." He reasons that to remain competitive, the company must hire developers and consultants who are better than the ones now on board.[34]

The company pays from $45,000 for recent college graduates up to $90,000 for MBAs. However, it is looking for people that want more than just money from a job. Trilogy views itself as a "movement" and introduces new recruits to mainstream projects immediately upon their arrival. "You don't have to sit around here earning tenure before you can see a customer," says Daniel. "One of our TUers [Trilogy University students], a guy from Harvard, is already working on accounts in France. I go out and tell my recruits, 'A kid your age was here for a month and a half, and now he's in Paris. That's Trilogy.'"[35]

As for work hours, Trilogy believes in flexibility. It makes the most sense that people work when they are most productive, and only you know when that is. Some work from 5 A.M. to 5 P.M., while others don't believe in the cruel and unusual abuse of alarm clocks and never show their faces before lunch time. There is no time clock to punch when you take off to Barton Springs at noon because it's just too gorgeous to be indoors, Lilith Fair tickets are on sale, or you want to take one of the company ski boats out and have lunch at Carlos and Charlie's on the lake. (Excerpt from Trilogy's statement on culture)

■ Trilogy University

Trilogy welcomes its new recruits to Trilogy University (TU), a highly intense, extremely unorthodox orientation program begun in 1995. For three months, Liemandt and seven other Trilogy veterans dedicate almost all their time to training new recruits in Trilogy's corporate boot camp. On the small sign posted in the training facility, someone has written TU's business hours: 8 A.M. to midnight, Monday through Saturday, and noon to 8 P.M. on Sunday. This is not necessarily an exaggeration.[36]

Located in an office building in Northwest Austin, TU sits down the hill from company headquarters (known as "uptown"). But TU is no ordinary training facility. Similar to a computer lab at college, software manuals and compact disks are scattered among IBM ThinkPads. Each section is decorated with bizarre mementos. "The sections are like social units," says Danielle Rios, a section leader. "You bond and learn about Trilogy culture—how we operate, how we talk, how we party, how we work."[37]

TUers wear what they want, and they set their own hours. They eat catered lunches and dinners in the TU conference room, and they snack out in the TU kitchen. Many TUers claim that going through it is like cramming a year of college into the three months they spend at TU. "Here it comes so fast, it's like a fire hose," comments Jamie Sidey, from the University of Pennsylvania. "I had this epiphany recently. A bunch of us were sitting around, and I realized, 'I'm in a room with 14 of the smartest people I've ever met, and we're having this high-level discussion, and none of us thinks it's anything out of the ordinary. This is great!'"[38]

In a game of *Jeopardy!* that you won't see on television, in a packed conference room littered with beer bottles, soda cans, and pizza boxes, a bunch of know-it-alls are shouting answers. They're also objecting to premature buzzer-pressing, to the use of expletives, and, of course, to answers not given in the form of a question. What looks like Alex Trebek's worst nightmare is a dream come true for Joe Liemandt. Liemandt leans back, shakes his head, and laughs. Here it is, 10 P.M. on a Tuesday, and about 200 of his most recent hires are having the time of their lives—while being quizzed not only on the company's products, customers, and employees, but also on its legendary retreats to Las Vegas and Hawaii.[39]

In the second week, the new hires are divided into 80 teams and given three weeks to complete projects ranging from improving an existing Trilogy product to creating new products from scratch. Teams that do well win a two-day trip to Las Vegas. Projecting an overhead that reads, "No Reward for Trying," Liemandt warns, "If you set a hard goal, and don't make it, you don't win points."[40]

Designing a Web advertising campaign for a product Trilogy will soon launch, a team mines the Web for ad rates during the day and brainstorms ideas at a coffee shop into the night. A week into the assignment, Mr. Liemandt asks for a summary. Their best slogan—"Buy Better, Buy Online"—fits nicely with the name of Trilogy's new product offering, called Buying Chain. Three days later, an advertising agency presents its own campaign. Preferring "Buy Better," Mr. Liemandt goes with the team's proposal. "Just like that, he signed off on spending $85,000 on our ideas," team member Victor Karkar remarks.[41]

A primary concept that Joe Liemandt is attempting to convey to his new hires is that of risk. In 1994 Liemandt bet a Trilogy programmer his blue Lexus that the programmer couldn't finish a project in time for a client proposal. The programmer upped the ante: If Liemandt lost, he would have to fork over his Lexus and drive an Aspire, Ford's smallest subcompact car. Lexus-less, Liemandt crammed into the Aspire for over a year.[42]

The purpose behind TU was to re-create the spirit of Trilogy's startup years—indeed, to turn Trilogy into a perpetual startup. Liemandt supports failure in his new recruits, but only up to a point. "They are totally clueless at times," Liemandt explains. "They come up with an idea for a product, and they don't let anything get in their way, even though their basic business plan has this huge hole in it. They expect magic to occur. So I tell them, 'You've got to explain the magic to me.'"[43]

In Las Vegas, Joe Liemandt challenges the TUers to take a $2000 bet on roulette in the belief that the amount is sufficient to convey a sense of pain—and risk. Trilogy puts up the cash, and losers will have $400 a month taken out of their paychecks for five months. Thirty-six recruits agree to bet, enough to fill all the public spots on the wheel. The bettors gather in a special room for highstakes gamblers, while the others stand outside. The colleague holding number 23 wins $72,000. Now part of the exclusive "L2K Club" (for lost $2000) the losers gain a valuable reputation, a T-shirt, and a glass etching of the roulette event and their individual numbers.[44]

The products that have emerged from Trilogy University are impressive. The class of 1995 created Trilogy's Selling Chain software that streamlines the selling process. The class of 1996 moved that product to the

Internet. The class of 1997 developed two major products and five minor ones.[45] TUers are living out their dream, Liemandt explains. "They just came out of school, and they're like, 'I studied a lot. Now I want to work a lot. So don't bore me, and don't spoon-feed me. Give me really hard stuff and lots of responsibility, and I'll go deliver.' And by sheer force of will, they do deliver. They come up the learning curve very quickly."[46]

Because of its phenomenal success, Trilogy itself has become a target for recruiters. Liemandt is not worried about headhunters. "My job is to make this company so compelling that you want to stay. I do that by continuing to hire the best people. The number-one reason that our employees give for not leaving is 'I wouldn't be able to work with these people anymore.' It always comes back to the quality of the people."[47]

■ The "Perpetual" Startup

Liemandt realizes that the configuration software business is too good to be ignored by competitors. A few smaller competitors have sprung up, but the real threat now comes from larger outfits. European software powers—SAP of Germany ($1.9 billion sales) and Baan of the Netherlands ($216 million)—have established themselves in automating back-office operations, as has Oracle Corp. Now all three companies have started to make forays into sales automation.[48] Baan's purchase of Antalys Inc., a provider of sales configuration software, will provide it an ability to package the software with Baan's manufacturing and distribution software in a "suite" of products.[49]

In conversations with Jack Welch, Chairman of General Electric, Welch counsels Liemandt to concentrate on growth. "After talking to Jack, I feel like I'm going half speed," Liemandt reports. "He tells me, 'Don't be such a wuss, Joe.'"[50]

As a result, Trilogy has been aggressive in developing new lines. Trilogy co-founder Christina Jones had a hot concept: use Trilogy's sophisticated software to configure and sell computer systems to individuals, resellers, and small companies over the Internet. Joe Liemandt thought Trilogy should continue to focus on selling software to big corporate accounts. But he made her an offer. If Jones would trade her Trilogy stock back to the company, he'd give her a substantial stake in a new company formed to carry out her Internet idea. "[The Trilogy stock] was all she had," Liemandt says. "But I wanted to make sure she really believed in her idea. I told her it had to be all or nothing."

Jones now owns an estimated 20 percent of newly formed pcOrder.com, Inc., a company that maintains and constantly updates a database with specifications and prices of more than 150,000 products ranging from memory boards and connecting cables to video cards and spreadsheet software made by about 800 hardware and software manufacturers.

Unlike Netscape and most other Internet companies, pcOrder doesn't rely on advertising for the bulk of its revenues. Jones has signed up about 100 computer resellers, which pay $1000 per salesperson per year to use pcOrder's service. These revenues are now running at an annual rate of over $1 million. There are also a half-dozen computer equipment distributors (including two of the largest, MicroAge and Intelligent Electronics) that subscribe to the service and have kicked in about $10 million so far. In addition, pcOrder sells some advertising space on its Web site, and it gets a commission, between 1 percent and 5 percent, on every sale completed over the service. Likely revenues this year: up to $12 million.

The resellers use pcOrder to order systems online rather than by phone or mail. Computer shoppers can use pcOrder's Web site to custom-design and compare computers. By June, Jones expects to have in place encryption technology that will allow individual shoppers to design and buy computers by credit card through pcOrder.

The service is useful to the manufacturers, too, because it gives them immediate feedback on which of their products are in demand. If IBM assembles 500,000 laptop computers with Pentium Pro processors but without CD-ROM drives, and then CD-ROM drives become the rage among consumers, IBM has an inventory problem. By watching the orders flowing across pcOrder, IBM can spot a surge of CD-ROM drive orders early and ramp up its production lines and deliveries accordingly.

Last year Jones hired as her top programmer Carl Samos, who had replaced Marc Andreessen as lead developer of the National Center for Supercomputing Applications' Mosaic, the Internet browser project that spawned Netscape. Samos's name will no doubt help. "It took some blind faith on her part," says Joe Liemandt. "But hey, she'll be liquid first."[51]

On February 26, 1999, pcOrder.com (PCOR) sold 2,200,000 shares at $21 per share in an IPO to an underwriting group led by Goldman Sachs & Co., Credit Suisse First Boston Corporation, and S.G. Cowen Securities Corporation. Shares rose 55 percent on the second day of trading, with share prices stabilizing in a trading range of $21–$92. The offering benefited from the extreme interest in anything with .com in its name.

Jones appreciates the importance of motivating her people. She puts on Friday-afternoon keg parties at pcOrder and keeps a well-stocked kitchen there. The company keeps a 21-foot Sea Ray speedboat for waterski-ing on nearby Lake Austin, and two Kawasaki jet skis. She promises the whole company—190 employees—a Caribbean cruise if all groups meet year-end goals. Recently she gave $5000 bonuses to employees who suc-cessfully recruited a programmer, and entered their names in a raffle for a Porsche Boxster. And a week before the annual pcOrder prom, she hired dance instructors to give lessons in the headquarters lobby. The company even had a tuxedo rental shop come to the office and give individual fittings.[52]

■ A New Computer Selling Model?

Jones's original business plan was to build her own Web site and act as a sales agent for computer makers, taking a commission for each sale. Distributors were horrified; they saw pcOrder as a competitor. Ross Cooley, manager of Compaq's North American operations, persuaded Jones to change the business plan. Instead of setting up her own electronic storefront, pcOrder would provide storefronts for individual manufacturers and dealers. Jones persuaded Cooley to come on board as chairman and chief executive of pcOrder in exchange for a 7 per-cent stake in the fledgling company. After 18 years at IBM and 14 years at Compaq, retirement was looming for Cooley. He welcomed the new challenge.

Building on the concept of Trilogy's Selling Chain, pcOrder may be reshaping the way computers are sold. Dell Computer dominates the direct sales method, but pcOrder is changing things, not through eliminating the middlemen, but by making them more efficient. The technology lets corporate customers go to the Web and choose the features they want—from the speed of a microchip to the hard-disk space—with just a few clicks of the mouse. PC dealers, using Jones's database, can instantly scan 600,000 different parts from 1000 manufac-turers and find out what's in stock and at what price. They then electronically pass the order on to the distribu-tor, which forwards it to the PC maker.[53]

PcOrder's software is a practical outgrowth of artifi-cial intelligence (AI) that allows its software to "recog-nize" which of the thousands of computer parts will work together best. Compaq, HP, and IBM have licensed pcOrder software. So have the three largest U.S. PC dis-tributors, Ingram Micro, Tech Data Corp., and Pinacor, Inc. Despite its momentum, pcOrder is hardly a guaran-teed winner. While the major PC-makers and distributors are on board, only about 5500 salespeople actually use the software; approximately 45,000 remain to be con-vinced that ordering PCs over the Web beats doing busi-ness over phones and faxes.

■ CollegeHire.com

The hiring process at Trilogy has been so successful that the company chose to spin off its acclaimed college recruiting program into a separate company called CollegeHire.com. The new company focuses on helping companies recruit graduates with technical backgrounds. Its chief executive is Jeff Daniel, who led Trilogy's recruiting efforts for the past three years. Trilogy's abili-ty to hire top students from top universities, beating out companies like Microsoft Corp., has attracted attention from businesses and students.

"The college recruiting process is a mess, with a lot of waste and a lot of inefficiency," explains Daniel. "Companies spend a lot of money and end up frustrated when they fail to find the right students. We're going to change the way it works by making it easier for compa-nies and students to connect." CollegeHire takes over the most painful parts of college recruiting for companies: sifting through hundreds of résumés, doing preliminary interviews, and picking out the qualified candidates. If the CollegeHire client hires one of the students, it will pay CollegeHire 22 percent to 33 percent of the first-year base salary. The more students a company wants to hire, the lower its fee.[54]

The service makes particular sense to smaller com-panies and those firms that don't have formal campus recruiting programs get access to IT students. "We don't have the resources to do college recruiting," said Bernadine Wu, a vice president at Jeffries and Co., a bro-kerage in New York. The firm has 1000 employees, 100 IT staffers, and no in-house recruiters. For Jeffries, the costly process of recruiting on college campuses is out of the question, Wu said. "This service is appealing because [CollegeHire.com] would do the legwork for us," she said.[55]

CollegeHire.com has already been implemented at pilot schools in California and Georgia: University of California, Berkeley; California Polytechnic Institute; Harvey Mudd College; Georgia Tech; University of Georgia; and Emory University.[56] With a growing list of high-technology firms, one recent corporate client to join the service is Amazon.com.

■ The Future?

In a hot stock market, numerous investment bankers have approached Liemandt to discuss taking Trilogy pub-lic. Many argue that an initial public offering (IPO) would value Trilogy around $1 billion. Liemandt does not appear to be eager to jump on the IPO craze. "The mar-ket's way overpriced, absolutely," he says. But Liemandt argues, "Making 8 zillion dollars is not the win. If that was it, we'd go public tomorrow and cash out. But if we don't change the way people buy and sell things, then we blew it."[57]

The phenomenal successes of Microsoft and Intel prove that in the computer industry the spoils go to the company that grabs market share early on and keeps it, leaving competitors in the position of always trying to catch up. So it's warp speed ahead for Trilogy to keep its early high market share as the market grows. "It's a land grab," Liemandt says. "Whoever gets the market share and partners first, wins. We've got two years until it [the land grab] is over."[58]

But questions remain. Should Liemandt consider merger with a larger player or purchase smaller players in complementary product lines? One difficulty Trilogy faces is the incompatibility of its products with other, larger firms' product lines. With "product suites" so popular, SAP or Baan might be better positioned to offer a complete package of compatible software for both back-end and front-end situations. Can Trilogy continue to develop new product lines fast enough to stay ahead of the market? Will the spinoffs prove profitable?

If you could sit down with Joe Liemandt for one hour, what would *you* suggest?

Additional Links

What Is it Like to Work at Trilogy Software?
Meet Joe Liemandt
Trilogy History
Trilogy Management Bios
Hoovers on Trilogy Software
Hoovers on the Computer Software Industry
Company Ranking

eXPERIENTIAL eXERCISES

My Best Manager

Procedure

1. Make a list of the attributes that describe the best manager you ever worked for. If you have trouble identifying an actual manager, make a list of attributes you would like the manager in your next job to have.
2. Form a group of four or five persons and share your lists.
3. Create one list that combines all the unique attributes of the "best" managers represented in your group. Make sure that you have all attributes listed, but list each only once. Place a check mark next to those that were reported by two or more members. Have one of your members prepared to present the list in general class discussion.
4. After all groups have finished Step 3, spokespersons should report to the whole class. The instructor will make a running list of the "best" manager attributes as viewed by the class.
5. Feel free to ask questions and discuss the results.

Graffiti Needs Assessment:
Involving Students in the First Class Session

Contributed by Barbara K. Goza, Visiting Associate Professor, University of California at Santa Cruz and Associate Professor, California State Polytechnic University, Pomona. From *Journal of Management Education*, 1993.

Procedure

1. Complete the following sentences with as many endings as possible.
   1. When I first came to this class, I thought . . .
   2. My greatest concern this term is . . .
   3. In 3 years I will be . . .
   4. The greatest challenge facing the world today is . . .
   5. Organizational behavior specialists do . . .
   6. Human resources are . . .
   7. Organizational research is . . .
   8. The most useful question I've been asked is . . .
   9. The most important phenomenon in organizations is . . .
   10. I learn the most when . . .
2. Your instructor will guide you in a class discussion about your responses. Pay careful attention to similarities and differences among various students' answers.

My Best Job

Procedure

1. Make a list of the top five things you expect from your first (or next) full-time job.
2. Exchange lists with a nearby partner. Assign probabilities (or odds) to each goal on your partner's list to indicate how likely you feel it is that the goal can be accomplished. (*Note:* Your instructor may ask that everyone use the same probabilities format.)
3. Discuss your evaluations with your partner. Try to delete superficial goals or modify them to become more substantial. Try to restate any unrealistic goals to make them more realistic. Help your partner do the same.
4. Form a group of four to six persons. Within the group, have everyone share what they now consider to be the most "realistic" goals on their lists. Elect a spokesperson to share a sample of these items with the entire class.
5. Discuss what group members have individually learned from the exercise. Await further class discussion led by your instructor.

What Do You Value in Work?

Procedure

1. The following nine items are from a survey conducted by Nicholas J. Beutell and O. C. Brenner ("Sex Differences in Work Values," *Journal of Vocational Behavior*, Vol.

28, pp. 29–41, 1986). Rank order the nine items in terms of how important (9 = most important) they would be to you in a job.

How important is it to you to have a job that:
____ Is respected by other people?
____ Encourages continued development of knowledge and skills?
____ Provides job security?
____ Provides a feeling of accomplishment?
____ Provides the opportunity to earn a high income?
____ Is intellectually stimulating?
____ Rewards good performance with recognition?
____ Provides comfortable working conditions?
____ Permits advancement to high administrative responsibility?

2. Form into groups as designated by your instructor. Within each group, the *men in the group* will meet to develop a consensus ranking of the items as they think the *women* in the Beutell and Brenner survey ranked them. The reasons for the rankings should be shared and discussed so they are clear to everyone. The *women in the group* should not participate in this ranking task. They should listen to the discussion and be prepared to comment later in class discussion. A spokesperson for the men in the group should share the group's rankings with the class.

3. (*Optional*) Form into groups as designated by your instructor, but with each group consisting entirely of men or women. Each group should meet and decide which of the work values members of the *opposite* sex ranked first in the Beutell and Brenner survey. Do this again for the work value ranked last. The reasons should be discussed, along with reasons that each of the other values probably was not ranked first . . . or last. A spokesperson for each group should share group results with the rest of the class.

————————

Source: Adapted from Roy J. Lewicki, Donald D. Bowen, Douglas T. Hall, and Francine S. Hall, *Experiences in Management and Organizational Behavior,* 3rd ed. (New York: John Wiley & Sons, Inc., 1988), pp. 23–26. Used by permission.

····· **EXERCISE 5** ·······························

My Asset Base

A business has an asset base or set of resources that it uses to produce a good or service of value to others. For a business, these are the assets or resources it uses to achieve results, including capital, land, patented products or processes, buildings and equipment, raw materials, and the human resources or employees, among others.

Each of us has an asset base that supports our ability to accomplish the things we set out to do. We refer to our personal assets as *talents, strengths,* or *abilities.* We probably inherit our talents from our parents, but we acquire many of our abilities and strengths through learning. One thing is certain: we feel very proud of the talents and abilities we have.

Procedure

1. Printed here is a T chart that you are to fill out. On the right-hand side of the T, list four or five of your accomplishments—*things you have done of which you are most proud.* Your accomplishments should only include those things for which you can take credit, those *things for which you are primarily responsible.* If you are proud of the sorority to which you belong, you may be justifiably proud, but don't list it unless you can argue that the sorority's excellence is due primarily to your efforts. However, if you feel that having been invited to join the sorority is a major accomplishment for you, then you may include it.

When you have completed the right-hand side of the chart, fill in the left-hand side by listing *talents, strengths,* and *abilities* that you have that have enabled you to accomplish the outcomes listed on the right-hand side.

My Asset Base

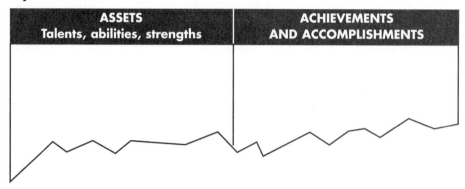

ASSETS Talents, abilities, strengths	ACHIEVEMENTS AND ACCOMPLISHMENTS

2. Share your lists with other team members. As each member takes turn sharing his or her list, pay close attention to your own perceptions and feelings. Notice the effect this has on your attitudes toward the other team members.
3. Discuss these questions in your group:
   (a) How did your attitudes and feelings toward other members of the team change as you pursued the activity? What does this tell you about the process whereby we come to get to know and care about people?
   (b) How did you feel about the instructions the instructor provided? What did you expect to happen? Were your expectations accurate?

Source: Adapted from Donald D. Bowen et al., *Experiences in Management and Organizational Behavior,* 4th ed. (New York: John Wiley & Sons, Inc.), 1997.

• • EXERCISE 6 •

Expatriate Assignments

Contributed by Robert E. Ledman, Morehouse College

This exercise focuses on issues related to workers facing international assignments. It illustrates that those workers face a multitude of issues. It further demonstrates that managers who want employees to realize the maximum benefits of international assignments should be aware of, and prepared to deal with, those issues. Some of the topics that are easily addressed with this exercise include the need for culture and language training for the employees and their families and the impact that international assignments may have on an employee's family and how that may affect an employee's willingness to seek such assignments.

Procedure

1. Form into "families" of four or five. Since many students today have only one parent at home, it is helpful if some groups do not have students to fill both

---

Source: Robert E. Ledman, Gannon University. Presented in the Experiential Exercise Track of the 1996 ABSEL Conference and published in the *Proceedings* of that conference.

parental roles in the exercise. Each student is assigned to play a family member and given a description of that person. Descriptions of family members are given below.

2. Enter into a 20-minute discussion to explore how a proposed overseas assignment will affect the family members. Your goal is to try to reach a decision about whether the assignment should be taken. You must also decide whether the entire family or only the family member being offered the assignment will relocate. The assignment is for a minimum of two years, with possible annual extensions resulting in a total of four years, and your family, or the member offered the assignment, will be provided, at company expense, one trip back to the states each year for a maximum period of 15 days. The member offered the assignment will not receive any additional housing or cost-of-living supplements described in the role assignment if he or she chooses to go overseas alone and can expect his or her living expenses to exceed substantially the living allowance being provided by the company. In your discussion, address the following questions:

(a) What are the most important concerns your family has about relocating to a foreign country?

(b) What information should you seek about the proposed host country to be able to make a more informed decision?

(c) What can the member offered the assignment do to make the transition easier if he or she goes overseas alone? If the whole family relocates?

(d) What should the member offered the assignment do to ensure that this proposed assignment will not create unnecessary stress for him or her and the rest of the family?

(e) What lessons for managers of expatriate assignees are presented by the situation in this exercise?

Try to reach some "family" consensus. If a consensus is not possible, however, resolve any differences in the manner you think the family in the role descriptions would ultimately resolve any differences.

3. Share your answers with the rest of the class. Explain the rationale for your answers and answer questions from the remainder of the class.

4. (*Optional*) After each group has reported on a given question, the instructor may query the class about how their answers are consistent, or inconsistent, with common practice of managers as described in the available literature.

Descriptions of Family Members
Person Being Offered Overseas Assignment

This person is a middle- to upper-level executive who is on a fast track to senior management. He or she has been offered the opportunity to manage an overseas operation, with the assurance of a promotion to a vice presidency upon return to the states. The company will pay all relocation expenses, including selling costs for the family home and the costs associated with finding a new home upon return. The employer will also provide language training for the employee and cultural awareness training for the entire family. The employee will receive a living allowance equal to 20 percent of his or her salary. This should be adequate to provide the family a comparable standard of living to that which is possible on the employee's current salary.

Spouse of the Person Offered an Overseas Assignment (Optional)

This person is also a professional with highly transferable skills and experience for the domestic market. It is unknown how easily he or she may be able to find employment in the foreign country. This person's income, though less than his or her spouse's, is necessary if the couple is to continue paying for their child's college tuition and to prepare for the next child to enter college in two years. This person has spent 15 years developing a career, including completing a degree at night.

Oldest Child

This child is a second-semester junior in college and is on track to graduate in 16 months. Transferring at this time would probably mean adding at least one semester to complete the degree. He or she has been dating the same person for over a year; they have talked about getting married immediately after graduation, although they are not yet formally engaged.

Middle Child

This child is a junior in high school. He or she has already begun visiting college campuses in preparation for applying in the fall. This child is involved in a number of school activities; he or she is photographer for the yearbook and plays a varsity sport. This child has a learning disability for which services are being provided by the school system.

Youngest Child

This child is a middle school student, age 13. He or she is actively involved in Scouting and takes piano lessons. This child has a history of medical conditions that have required regular visits to the family physician and specialists. This child has several very close friends who have attended the same school for several years.

Cultural Cues

Contributed by Susan Rawson Zacur and W. Alan Randolph, University of Baltimore

Introduction

In the business context, culture involves shared beliefs and expectations that govern the behavior of people. In this exercise, *foreign culture* refers to a set of beliefs and expectations different from those of the participant's home culture (which has been invented by the participants).

Procedure

1. (10–15 minutes) Divide into two groups, each with color-coded badges. For example, the blue group could receive blue Post-it notes and the yellow group could receive yellow Post-it notes. Print your first name in bold letters on the badge and wear it throughout the exercise.

    Work with your group members to invent your own cultural cues. Think about the kinds of behaviors and words that will signify to all members that they belong together in one culture. For each category provided below, identify and record at least one important attribute for your culture.

Cultural Cues:	Your Culture:
Facial expression:	_____
Eye contact (note: you must have some eye contact in order to observe others):	_____
Handshake:	_____
Body language (note: must be evident while standing):	_____
Key words or phrases:	_____

   Once you have identified desirable cultural aspects for your group, practice them. It is best to stand with your group and to engage one another in conversations involving two or three people at a time. Your aim in talking with one another is to learn as much as possible about each other—hobbies, interests, where you live, what your family is like, what courses you are taking, and so on, all the while practicing the behaviors and words identified above. It is not necessary for participants to answer questions of a personal nature truthfully. Invention is permissible because the conversation is only a means to the end of cultural observation. Your aim at this point is to become comfortable with the indicators of your particular culture. Practice until the indicators are second nature to you.

2. Now assume that you work for a business that has decided to explore the potential for doing business with companies in a different culture. You are to learn as much as possible about another culture. To do so, you will send from one to three representatives from your group on a "business trip" to the other culture. These representatives must, insofar as possible, behave in a manner that is consistent with your culture. At the same time, each representative must endeavor to learn as much as possible about the

Source: Adapted by Susan Rawson Zacur and W. Alan Randolph from *Journal of Management Education,* Vol. 17, No. 4 (November 1993), pp. 510–516.

people in the other culture, while keeping eyes and ears open to cultural attributes that will be useful in future negotiations with foreign businesses. (*Note:* At no time will it be considered ethical behavior for the representative to ask direct questions about the foreign culture's attributes. These must be gleaned from firsthand experience.)

While your representatives are away, you will receive one or more exchange visitors from the other culture, who will engage in conversation as they attempt to learn more about your organizational culture. You must strictly adhere to the cultural aspects of your own culture while you converse with the visitors.

3. (5–10 minutes) All travelers return to your home cultures. As a group, discuss and record what you have learned about the foreign culture based on the exchange of visitors. This information will serve as the basis for orienting the next representatives who will make a business trip.

4. (5–10 minutes) Select one to three different group members to make another trip to the other culture to check out the assumptions your group has made about the other culture. This "checking out" process will consist of actually practicing the other culture's cues to see whether they work.

5. (5–10 minutes) Once the traveler(s) have returned and reported on findings, as a group, prepare to report to the class what you have learned about the other culture.

EXERCISE 8

Prejudice in Our Lives

Contributed by Susan Schor of Pace University and Annie McKee of The Wharton School, University of Pennsylvania with the assistance of Ariel Fishman of The Wharton School

Procedure

1. As a large class group, generate a list of groups that tend to be targets of prejudice and stereotypes in our culture—such groups can be based on gender, race, ethnicity, sexual orientation, region, religion, and so on. After generating a list, either as a class or in small groups, identify a few common positive and negative stereotypes associated with each group. Also consider relationships or patterns that exist between some of the lists. Discuss the implications for groups that have stereotypes that are valued in organizations versus groups whose stereotypes are viewed negatively in organizations.

2. As an individual, think about the lists you have now generated, and list those groups with which you identify. Write about an experience in which you were stereotyped as a member of a group. Ask yourself the following questions and write down your thoughts:

   (a) What group do I identify with?
   (b) What was the stereotype?
   (c) What happened? When and where did the incident occur? Who said what to whom?
   (d) What were my reactions? How did I feel? What did I think? What did I do?

   (e) What were the consequences? How did the incident affect myself and others?

3. Now, in small groups, discuss your experiences. Briefly describe the incident and focus on how the incident made you feel. Select one incident from the ones shared in your group to role-play for the class. Then, as a class, discuss your reactions to each role play. Identify the prejudice or stereotype portrayed, the feelings the situation evoked, and the consequences that might result from such a situation.

4. Think about the prejudices and stereotypes you hold about other people. Ask yourself, "What groups do I feel prejudice toward? What stereotypes do I hold about members of each of these groups?" How may such a prejudice have developed—did a family member or close friend or television influence you to stereotype a particular group in a certain way?

5. Now try to identify implications of prejudice in the workplace. How do prejudice and stereotypes affect workers, managers, relationships between people, and the organization as a whole? Consider how you might want to change erroneous beliefs as well as how you would encourage other people to change their own erroneous beliefs.

How We View Differences

Contributed by Barbara Walker

Introduction

Clearly, the workplace of the future will be much more diverse than it is today: more women, more people of color, more international representation, more diverse lifestyles and ability profiles, and the like. Managing a diverse workforce and working across a range of differences is quickly becoming a "core competency" for effective managers.

Furthermore, it is also becoming clear that diversity in a work team can significantly enhance the creativity and quality of the team's output. In today's turbulent business environment, utilizing employee diversity will give the manager and the organization a competitive edge in tapping all of the available human resources more effectively. This exercise is an initial step in the examination of how we work with people whom we see as different from us. It is fairly simple, straightforward, and safe, but its implications are profound.

Procedure

1. Read the following:

Imagine that you are traveling in a rental car in a city you have never visited before. You have a one-hour drive on an uncrowded highway before you reach your destination. You decide that you would like to spend the time listening to some of your favorite kind of music on the car radio.

The rental car has four selection buttons available, each with a preset station that plays a different type of music. One plays *country music,* one plays *rock,* one plays *classical,* and one plays *jazz.* Which type of music would you choose to listen to for the next hour as you drive along? (Assume you want to relax and just stick with one station; you don't want to bother switching around between stations.)

Source: Exercise developed by Barbara Walker, a pioneer on work on valuing differences. Adapted for this volume by Douglas T. Hall. Used by permission of Barbara Walker.

2. Form into groups based on the type of music that you have chosen. All who have chosen country will meet in an area designated by the instructor. Those who chose rock will meet in another area, and so on. In your groups, answer the following question. Appoint one member to be the spokesperson to report your answers back to the total group.

Question

For each of the other groups, what words would you use to describe people who like to listen to that type of music?

3. Have each spokesperson report the responses of her or his group to the question in Step 2. Follow with class discussion of these additional questions:
   (a) What do you think is the purpose or value of this exercise?
   (b) What did you notice about the words used to describe the other groups? Were there any *surprises* in this exercise for you?
   (c) Upon what sorts of data do you think these images were based?
   (d) What term do we normally use to describe these generalized perceptions of another group?
   (e) What could some of the consequences be?
   (f) How do the perceptual processes here relate to other kinds of intergroup differences, such as race, gender, culture, ability, ethnicity, health, age, nationality, and so on?
   (g) What does this exercise suggest about the ease with which intergroup stereotypes form?
   (h) What might be ways an organization might facilitate the valuing and utilizing of differences between people?

Alligator River Story

Source: From Sidney B. Simon, Howard Kirschenbaum, and Leland Howe, *Values Clarification, The Handbook,* rev. ed., copyright © 1991, Values Press, P.O. Box 450, Sunderland, MA. 01375. Send for a list of other strategy books from Value Press.

The Alligator River Story

There lived a woman named Abigail who was in love with a man named Gregory. Gregory lived on the shore of a river. Abigail lived on the opposite shore of the same river. The river that separated the two lovers was teeming with dangerous alligators. Abigail wanted to cross the river to be with Gregory. Unfortunately, the bridge had been washed out by a heavy flood the previous week. So she went to ask Sinbad, a riverboat captain, to take her across. He said he would be glad to if she would consent to go to bed with him prior to the voyage. She promptly refused and went to a friend named Ivan to explain her plight. Ivan did not want to get involved at all in the situation. Abigail felt her only alternative was to accept Sinbad's terms. Sinbad fulfilled his promise to Abigail and delivered her into the arms of Gregory.

When Abigail told Gregory about her amorous escapade in order to cross the river, Gregory cast her aside with disdain. Heartsick and rejected, Abigail turned to Slug with her tail of woe. Slug, feeling compassion for Abigail, sought out Gregory and beat him brutally. Abigail was overjoyed at the sight of Gregory getting his due. As the sun set on the horizon, people heard Abigail laughing at Gregory.

Procedure

1. Read "The Alligator River Story."

2. After reading the story, rank the five characters in the story beginning with the one whom you consider the most offensive and end with the one whom you consider the least objectionable. That is, the character who seems to be the most reprehensible to you should be entered first in the list following the story, then the second most reprehensible, and so on, with the least reprehensible or objectionable being entered fifth. Of course, you will have your own reasons as to why you rank them in the order that you do. Very briefly note these too.

3. Form groups as assigned by your instructor (at least four persons per group with gender mixed).

4. Each group should:
   (a) Elect a spokesperson for the group
   (b) Compare how the group members have ranked the characters
   (c) Examine the reasons used by each of the members for their rankings
   (d) Seek consensus on a final group ranking

5. Following your group discussions, you will be asked to share your outcomes and reasons for agreement or nonagreement. A general class discussion will then be held.

Teamwork and Motivation

Contributed by Dr. Barbara McCain, Oklahoma City University

Procedure

1. Read this situation.
You are the *owner* of a small manufacturing corporation. Your company manufactures widgets—a commodity. Your widget is a clone of nationally known widgets. Your widget, "WooWoo," is less expensive and more readily available than the nationally known brand. Presently, the sales are high. However, there are many rejects, which increases your cost and delays the delivery. You have 50 employees in the following departments: sales, assembly, technology, and administration.

2. In groups, discuss methods to motivate all of the employees in the organization—rank order them in terms of preference.

3. Design an organization motivation plan that encourages high job satisfaction, low turnover, high productivity, and high-quality work.

4. Is there anything special you can do about the minimum-wage service worker? How do you motivate this individual? On what motivation theory do you base your decision?

5. Report to the class your motivation plan. Record your ideas on the board and allow all groups to build on the first plan. Discuss additions and corrections as the discussion proceeds.

Worksheet

Individual Worker	Team Member
Talks	
Me oriented	
Department focused	
Competitive	
Logical	
Written messages	
Image	
Secrecy	
Short-term sighted	
Immediate results	
Critical	
Tenure	

Directions: Fill in the right-hand column with descriptive terms. These terms should suggest a change in behavior from individual work to teamwork.

•• **EXERCISE 12** •

The Downside of Punishment

Contributed by Dr. Barbara McCain, Oklahoma City University

Procedure

There are numerous problems associated with using punishment or discipline to change behavior. Punishment creates negative effects in the workplace. To better understand this, work in your group to give an example of each of the following situations:

1. Punishment may not be applied to the person whose behavior you want to change.

2. Punishment applied over time may suppress the occurrence of socially desirable behaviors.

3. Punishment creates a dislike of the person who is implementing the punishment.

4. Punishment results in undesirable emotions such as anxiety and agressiveness.

5. Punishment increases the desire to avoid punishment.

6. Punishing one behavior does not guarantee that the desired behavior will occur.

7. Punishment follow-up requires allocation of additional resources.

8. Punishment may create a communication barrier and inhibit the flow of information.

Source: Adapted from class notes: Dr. Larry Michaelson, Oklahoma University.

EXERCISE 13

Tinker Toys

Contributed by Bonnie McNeely, Murray State University

Materials Needed
Tinker Toy sets.

Procedure
1. Form groups as assigned by the instructor. The mission of each group or temporary organization is to build the tallest possible Tinker Toy tower. Each group should determine worker roles: at least four students will be builders, some will be consultants who offer suggestions, and the remaining students will be observers who remain silent and complete the observation sheet provided below.

2. Rules for the exercise:
(a) Fifteen minutes allowed to plan the tower, but *only 60 seconds* to build.
(b) No more than two Tinker Toy pieces can be put together during the planning.
(c) All pieces must be put back in the box before the competition begins.
(d) Completed tower must stand alone.

Observation Sheet
1. What planning activities were observed?

Did the group members adhere to the rules?

2. What organizing activities were observed?

Source: Adapted from Bonnie McNeely, "Using the Tinker Toy Exercise to Teach the Four Functions of Management, *Journal of Management Education,* Vol. 18, No. 4 (November 1994), 468–472.

Was the task divided into subtasks? Division of labor?

3. Was the group motivated to succeed? Why or why not?

4. Were any control techniques observed?

Was a timekeeper assigned?

Were backup plans discussed?

5. Did a clear leader emerge from the group?

What behaviors indicated that this person was the leader?

How did the leader establish credibility with the group?

6. Did any conflicts within the group appear?

Was there a power struggle for the leadership position?

EXERCISE 14

Job Design Preferences

Procedure

1. Use the left column to rank the following job characteristics in the order most important *to you* (1—highest to 10—lowest). Then use the right column to rank them in the order you think they are most important *to others*.

____ Variety of tasks	____
____ Performance feedback	____
____ Autonomy/freedom in work	____
____ Working on a team	____
____ Having responsibility	____
____ Making friends on the job	____
____ Doing all of a job, not part	____
____ Importance of job to others	____
____ Having resources to do well	____
____ Flexible work schedule	____

2. Form workgroups as assigned by your instructor. Share your rankings with other group members. Discuss where you have different individual preferences and where your impressions differ from the preferences of others. Are there any major patterns in your group—for either the "personal" or the "other" rankings? Develop group consensus rankings for each column. Designate a spokesperson to share the group rankings and results of any discussion with the rest of the class.

My Fantasy Job

Contributed by Lady Hanson, California State Polytechnic University, Pomona

Procedure

1. Think about a possible job that represents what you consider to be your ideal or "fantasy" job. For discussion purposes, try to envision it as a job you would hold within a year of finishing your current studies. Write down a brief description of that job in the space below. Start the description with the following words—*My fantasy job would be . . .*

2. Review the description of the Hackman/Oldham model of Job Characteristics Theory offered in the textbook. Note in particular the descriptions of the core characteristics. Consider how each of them could be maximized in your fantasy job. Indicate in the spaces that follow how specific parts of your fantasy job will fit into or relate to each of the core characteristics.

   (a) Skill variety: _____

   (b) Task identity: _____

   (c) Task significance: _____

   (d) Autonomy: _____

   (e) Job feedback: _____

3. Form into groups as assigned by your instructor. In the group have each person share his or her fantasy job and the descriptions of its core characteristics. Select one person from your group to tell the class as a whole about her or his fantasy job. Be prepared to participate in general discussion regarding the core characteristics and how they may or may not relate to job performance and job satisfaction. Consider also the likelihood that the fantasy jobs of class members are really attainable—in other words: Can "fantasy" become fact?

Motivation by Job Enrichment

Contributed by Diana Page, University of West Florida

Procedure

1. Form groups of five to seven members. Each group is assigned one of the following categories:

(a) Bank teller

(b) Retail sales clerk

(c) Manager, fast-food service (e.g., McDonald's)

(d) Wait person

(e) Receptionist

(f) Restaurant manager

(g) Clerical worker (or bookkeeper)

(h) Janitor

2. As a group, develop a short description of job duties for the job your group has been assigned. The list should contain approximately four to six items.

3. Next, using job characteristics theory, enrich the job using the specific elements described in the theory. Develop a new list of job duties that incorporate any or all of the core job characteristics suggested by Richard Hackman and Greg Oldham, such as skill variety, task identity, and so on. Indicate for each of the new job duties which job characteristic(s) was/were used.

4. One member of each group should act as the spokesperson and will present the group's ideas to the class. Specifically describe one or two of the old job tasks. Describe the modified job tasks. Finally, relate the new job tasks the group has developed to specific job core characteristics such as skill variety, skill identity, and so on.

5. The group should also be prepared to discuss these and other follow-up questions:

(a) How would a manager go about enlarging but not enriching this job?

(b) Why was this job easy or hard?

(c) What are the possible constraints on actually accomplishing this enrichment in the workplace?

(d) What possible reasons are there that a worker would *not* like to have this newly enriched job?

EXERCISE 17

Annual Pay Raises

Procedure

1. Read the job descriptions below and decide on a percentage pay increase for each of the eight employees.

2. Make salary increase recommendations for each of the eight managers that you supervise. There are no formal company restrictions on the size of raises you give, but the total for everyone should not exceed the $10,900 (a 4 percent increase in the salary pool) that has been budgeted for this purpose. You have a variety of information on which to base the decisions, including a "productivity index" (PI), which Industrial Engineering computes as a quantitative measure of operating efficiency for each manager's work unit. This index ranges from a high of 10 to a low of 1. Indicate the percentage increase *you* would give each manager in the blank space next to each manager's name. Be prepared to explain why.

_____ *A. Alvarez*   Alvarez is new this year and has a tough workgroup whose task is dirty and difficult. This is a hard position to fill, but you don't feel Alvarez is particularly good. The word around is that the other managers agree with you. PI = 3. Salary = $33,000.

_____ *B. J. Cook*   Cook is single and a "swinger" who enjoys leisure time. Everyone laughs at the problems B.J. has getting the work out, and you feel it certainly is lacking. Cook has been in the job two years. PI = 3. Salary = $34,500.

_____ *Z. Davis* In the position three years, Davis is one of your best people, even though some of the other managers don't agree. With a spouse who is independently wealthy, Davis doesn't need money but likes to work. PI = 7. Salary = $36,600.

_____ *M. Frame* Frame has personal problems and is hurting financially. Others gossip about Frame's performance, but you are quite satisfied with this second-year employee. PI = 7. Salary = $34,700.

_____ *C.M. Liu* Liu is just finishing a fine first year in a tough job. Highly respected by the others, Liu has a job offer in another company at a 15 percent increase in salary. You are impressed, and the word is that the money is important. PI = 9. Salary = $34,000.

_____ *B. Ratin* Ratin is a first-year manager whom you and the others think is doing a good job. This is a bit surprising since Ratin turned out to be a "free spirit" who doesn't seem to care much about money or status. PI = 9. Salary = $33,800.

_____ *H. Smith* Smith is a first-year manager recently divorced and with two children to support as a single parent. The others like Smith a lot, but your evaluation is not very high. Smith could certainly use extra money. PI = 5. Salary = $33,000.

_____ *G. White* White is a big spender who always has the latest clothes and a new car. In the first year on what you would call an easy job, White doesn't seem to be doing very well. For some reason, though, the others talk about White as the "cream of the new crop." PI = 5. Salary = $33,000.

3. Convene in a group of four to seven persons and share your raise decision.

4. As a group, decide on a new set of raises and be prepared to report them to the rest of the class. Make sure that the group spokesperson can provide the rationale for each person's raise.

5. The instructor will call on each group to report its raise decisions. After discussion, an "expert's" decision will be given.

EXERCISE 18

Serving on the Boundary

Contributed by Joseph A. Raelin, Boston College

Procedure

The objective of this exercise is to experience what it is like being on the boundary of your team or organization and to experience the boundary person's divided loyalties.

1. As a full class, decide on a stake you are willing to wager on this exercise. Perhaps it will be 5¢ or 10¢ per person or even more.

2. Form into teams. Select or elect one member from your team to be an expert. The expert will be the person most competent in the field of international geography.

3. The experts will then form into a team of their own.

4. The teams, including the expert team, are going to be given a straightforward question to work on. Whichever team comes closest to deriving the correct answer will win the pool from the stakes already collected. The question is any one of the following as assigned by the instructor: (a) What is the airline distance between Beijing and Moscow (in miles)? (b) What is the highest point in Texas (in feet)? (c) What was the number of American battle deaths in the Revolutionary War?

5. Each team should now work on the question, including the expert team. However, after all the teams come up with a verdict, the experts will be allowed to return to their "home" team to inform the team of the expert team's deliberations.

6. The expert team members are now asked to reconvene as an expert team. They should determine their final answer to the question. Then, they are to face a decision. The instructor will announce that for a period of up to two minutes, any expert may either return to their home team (to sink or swim with the answer of the home team) or remain with the expert team. As long as two members remain in the expert team, it will be considered a group and may vie for the pool. Home teams, during the two-minute decision period, can do whatever they would like to do—within bounds of normal decorum—to try to persuade their expert member to return.

7. After the two minutes are up, teams will hand in their verdicts to the question, and the team with the closest answer (up or down) will be awarded the pool.

8. Class members should be prepared to discuss the following questions:
   (a) What did it feel like to be a boundary person (the expert)?
   (b) What could the teams have done to corral any of the boundary persons who chose not to return home?

EXERCISE 19

Eggsperiential Exercise

Contributed by Dr. Barbara McCain, Oklahoma City University

Materials Needed

1 raw egg per group

6 plastic straws per group

1 yard of plastic tape

1 large plastic jar

Procedure

1. Form into equal groups of five to seven people.
2. The task is to drop an egg from the chair onto the plastic without breaking the egg. Groups can evaluate the materials and plan their task for 10 minutes. During this period the materials may not be handled.
3. Groups have 10 minutes for construction.
4. One group member will drop the egg while standing on top of a chair in front of the class. One by one a representative from each group will drop their eggs.
5. Optional: Each group will name the egg.
6. Each group discusses their individual/group behav-

iors during this activity. Optional: This analysis may be summarized in written form. The following questions may be utilized in the analysis:
   (a) What kind of group is it? Explain.
   (b) Was the group cohesive? Explain.
   (c) How did the cohesiveness relate to performance? Explain.
   (d) Was there evidence of groupthink? Explain.
   (e) Were group norms established? Explain.
   (f) Was there evidence of conflict? Explain.
   (g) Was there any evidence of social loafing? Explain.

EXERCISE 20

Scavenger Hunt – Team Building

Contributed by Michael R. Manning and Paula J. Schmidt, New Mexico State University

Introduction

Think about what it means to be a part of a team—a successful team. What makes one team more successful than another? What does each team member need to do in order for their team to be successful? What are the characteristics of an effective team?

Procedure

1. Form teams as assigned by your instructor. Locate the items on the list below while following these important rules:

   a. Your team *must stay together at all times*—that is, you cannot go in separate directions.

   b. Your team must return to the classroom in the time allotted by the instructor.

   The team with the most items on the list will be declared the most successful team.

2. Next, reflect on your team's experience. What did each team member do? What was your team's strategy? What made your team effective? Make a list of the most important things your team did to be succesful. Nominate a spokesperson to summarize your team's discussion for the class. What items were similar between teams? That is, what helped each team to be effective?

Items for Scavenger Hunt

Each item is to be identified and brought back to the classroom.

1. A book with the word "team" in the title.
2. A joke about teams that you share with the class.
3. A blade of grass from the university football field.
4. A souvenir from the state.
5. A picture of a team or group.
6. A newspaper article about a team.
7. A team song to be composed and performed for the class.
8. A leaf from an oak tree.
9. Stationery from the dean's office.
10. A cup of sand.
11. A pine cone.
12. A live reptile. (*Note:* Sometimes a team member has one for a pet or the students are ingenious enough to visit a local pet store.)
13. A definition of group "cohesion" that you share with the class.
14. A set of chopsticks.
15. Three cans of vegetables.
16. A branch of an elm tree.
17. Three unusual items.
18. A ball of cotton.
19. The ear from a prickly pear cactus.
20. A group name.

(*Note:* Items may be substituted as appropriate for your locale.)

Source: Adapted from Michael R. Manning and Paula J. Schmidt, *Journal of Management Education,* Building Effective Work Teams: A Quick Exercise Based on a Scavenger Hunt (Thousand Oaks, CA: Sage Publications, 1995), pp. 392–398. Used by permission. Reference for list of items for scavenger hunt from C. E. Larson and F. M. Lafas, *Team Work: What Must Go Right/What Can Go Wrong* (Newbury Park, CA: Sage Publications, 1989).

EXERCISE 21

Work Team Dynamics

Introduction

Think about your course work team, a work team you are involved in for another course, or any other team suggested by the instructor. Indicate how often each of the following statements accurately reflects your experience in the team. Use this scale:

1 = Always   2 = Frequently   3 = Sometimes   4 = Never

_____ 1. My ideas get a fair hearing.

_____ 2. I am encouraged for innovative ideas and risk taking.

_____ 3. Diverse opinions within the team are encouraged.

_____ 4. I have all the responsibility I want.

_____ 5. There is a lot of favoritism shown in the team.

_____ 6. Members trust one another to do their assigned work.

_____ 7. The team sets high standards of performance excellence.

_____ 8. People share and change jobs a lot in the team.

_____ 9. You can make mistakes and learn from them on this team.

_____ 10. This team has good operating rules.

Procedure

Form groups as assigned by your instructor. Ideally, this will be the team you have just rated. Have all team members share their ratings, and make one master rating for the team as a whole. Circle the items on which there are the biggest differences of opinion. Discuss those items and try to find out why they exist. In general, the better a team scores on this instrument, the higher its creative potential. If everyone has rated the same team, make a list of the five most important things members can do to improve its operations in the future. Nominate a spokesperson to summarize the team discussion for the class as a whole.

Source: Adapted from William Dyer, _Team Building,_ 2nd ed. (Reading, MA: Addison-Wesley, 1987), pp. 123–125.

EXERCISE 22

Identifying Group Norms

Procedure

1. Choose an organization you know quite a bit about.

2. Complete the questionnaire below, indicating your responses using one of the following:

> (a) Strongly agree or encourage it.
> (b) Agree with it or encourage it.
> (c) Consider it unimportant.
> (d) Disagree with or discourage it.
> (e) Strongly disagree with or discourage it.

_If_ an employee in this organization were to . . . _Most other employees would:_

1. Show genuine concern for the problems that face the organization and make suggestions about solving them . . .   _____

2. Set very high personal standards of performance . . .   _____

3. Try to make the workgroup operate more like a team when dealing with issues or problems . . .   _____

4. Think of going to a supervisor with a problem . . .   _____

5. Evaluate expenditures in terms of the benefits they will provide for the organization . . .   _____

6. Express concern for the well-being of other members of the organization . . . ____
7. Keep a customer or client waiting while looking after matters of personal convenience . . . ____
8. Criticize a fellow employee who is trying to improve things in the work situation . . . ____
9. Actively look for ways to expand his or her knowledge to be able to do a better job . . . ____
10. Be perfectly honest in answering this questionnaire . . . ____

Scoring

A = +2, B = +1, C = 0, D = –1, E = –2

1. Organizational/Personal Pride
   Score ____
2. Performance/Excellence
   Score ____
3. Teamwork/Communication
   Score ____
4. Leadership/Supervision
   Score ____
5. Profitability/Cost-Effectiveness
   Score ____

6. Colleague/Associate Relations
   Score ____
7. Customer/Client Relations
   Score ____
8. Innovativeness/Creativity
   Score ____
9. Training/Development
   Score ____
10. Candor/Openness
   Score ____

EXERCISE 23

Workgroup Culture

Contributed by Conrad N. Jackson, MPC, Inc.

Procedure

1. The bipolar scales on this instrument can be used to evaluate a group's process in a number of useful ways. Use it to measure where you see the group to be at present. To do this, *circle* the number that best represents *how you see the culture of the group.* You can also indicate how you think the group *should* function by using a different symbol, such as a square (□) or a caret (^), to indicate how you saw the group at some time in the past.

2. (a) If you are assessing your own group, have everyone fill in the instrument, summarize the scores, then discuss their bases (what members say and do that has led to these interpretations) and implications. This is often an extremely productive intervention to improve group or team functioning.

(b) If you are assessing another group, use the scores as the basis for your feedback. Be sure to provide specific feedback on behavior *you have observed* in addition to the subjective interpretations of your ratings on the scales in this instrument.

(c) The instrument can also be used to compare a group's self-assessment with the assessment provided by another group.

1. Trusting	1 : 2 : 3 : 4 : 5	Suspicious
2. Helping	1 : 2 : 3 : 4 : 5	Ignoring, blocking
3. Expressing feelings	1 : 2 : 3 : 4 : 5	Suppressing feelings
4. Risk taking	1 : 2 : 3 : 4 : 5	Cautious
5. Authenticity	1 : 2 : 3 : 4 : 5	Game playing
6. Confronting	1 : 2 : 3 : 4 : 5	Avoiding
7. Open	1 : 2 : 3 : 4 : 5	Hidden, diplomatic

Source: Adapted from Donald D. Bowen, et al., *Experiences in Management and Organizational Behavior,* 4th ed. (New York: John Wiley & Sons, Inc.), 1997.

The Hot Seat

Contributed by Barry R. Armandi, SUNY–Old Westbury

Procedure

1. Form into groups as assigned by your instructor.
2. Read the following situation.

A number of years ago, Professor Stevens was asked to attend a departmental meeting at a university. He had been on leave from the department, but a junior faculty member discreetly requested that he attend to protect the rights of the junior faculty. The Chair, or head of the department, was a typical Machiavellian, whose only concerns were self-serving. Professor Stevens had had a number of previous disagreements with the Chair. The heart of the disagreements centered around the Chair's abrupt and domineering style and his poor relations with the junior faculty, many of whom felt mistreated and scared.

The department was a conglomeration of different professorial types. Included in the mix were behavioralists, generalists, computer scientists, and quantitative analysts. The department was embedded in the school of business, which had three other departments. There was much confusion and concern among the faculty, since this was a new organizational design. Many of the faculty were at odds with each other over the direction the school was now taking.

At the meeting, a number of proposals were to be presented that would seriously affect the performance and future of certain junior faculty, particularly those who were behavioral scientists. The Chair, a computer scientist, disliked the behaviorists, who he felt were "always analyzing the motives of people." Professor Stevens, who was a tenured full professor and a behaviorist, had an objective to protect the interests of the junior faculty and to counter the efforts of the Chair.

Including Professor Stevens, there were nine faculty present. The accompanying diagram below shows the seating

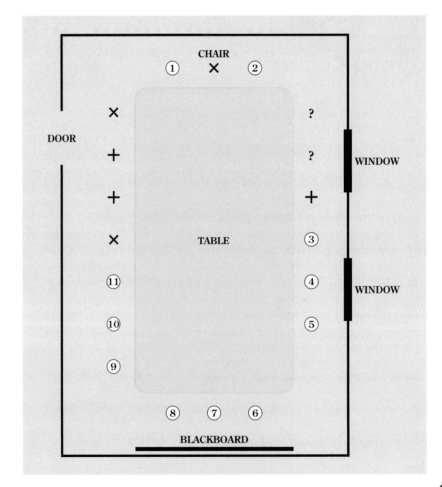

arrangement and the layout of the room. The ✕s signify those faculty who were allies of the Chair. The +s are those opposed to the Chair and supportive of Professor Stevens, and the **?**s were undecided and could be swayed either way. The circled numbers represent empty seats. Both **?**s were behavioralists, and the + next to them was a quantitative analyst. Near the door, the first ✕ was a generalist, the two +s were behavioralists, and the second ✕ was a quantitative analyst. The diagram shows the seating of everyone but Professor Stevens, who was the last one to enter the room. Standing at the door, Professor

Stevens surveyed the room and within 10 seconds knew which seat was the most effective to achieve his objective.

3. Answer the following questions in your group.
   (a) Which seat did Professor Stevens select and why?
   (b) What is the likely pattern of communication and interaction in this group?
   (c) What can be done to get this group to work harmoniously?

EXERCISE 25

Interview a Leader

Contributed by Bonnie McNeely, Murray State University

Procedure

1. Make an appointment to interview a leader. It can be a leader working in a business or nonprofit organization, such as a government agency, school, and so on. Base the interview on the form provided here, but feel free to add your own questions.
2. Bring the results of your interview to class. Form into groups as assigned by your instructor. Share the responses from your interview with your group and compare answers. What issues were similar? Different? Were the stress levels of leaders working in nonprofit organizations as high as those working in for profit firms? Were you surprised at the number of hours per week worked by leaders?
3. Be prepared to summarize the interviews done by your group as a formal written report if asked to do so by the instructor.

Interview Questionnaire

Student's Name _____ Date _____

1. Position in the organization (title):
2. Number of years in current position:
   Number of years of managerial experience:
3. Number of people directly supervised:
4. Average number of hours worked a week:
5. How did you get into leadership?
6. What is the most rewarding part of being a leader?
7. What is the most difficult part of your job?
8. What would you say are the *keys to success* for leaders?
9. What advice do you have for an aspiring leader?
10. What type of ethical issues have you faced as a leader?
11. If you were to enroll in a leadership seminar, what topics or issues would you want to learn more about?
12. (Student's question)
Gender: M____ F____ Years of formal education____
Level of job stress: Very high____ High____ Average____ Low____
Profit organization____ Nonprofit organization____
Additional information/Comments:

_____

Source: Adapted from Bonnie McNeely, "Make Your Principles of Management Class Come Alive," *Journal of Management Education,* Vol. 18, No. 2, May 1994, 246–249.

Leadership Skills Inventories

Procedure

1. Look over the skills listed below and ask your instructor to clarify those you do not understand.
2. Complete each category by checking either the "Strong" or "Needs Development" category in relation to your own level with each skill.
3. After completing each category, briefly describe a situation in which each of the listed skills has been utilized.
4. Meet in your groups to share and discuss inventories. Prepare a report summarizing major development needs in your group.

Instrument

	Strong	Needs Development	Situation
Communication	_____	_____	_____
Conflict management	_____	_____	_____
Delegation	_____	_____	_____
Ethical behavior	_____	_____	_____
Listening	_____	_____	_____
Motivation	_____	_____	_____
Negotiation	_____	_____	_____
Performance appraisal and feedback	_____	_____	_____
Planning and goal setting	_____	_____	_____
Power and influence	_____	_____	_____
Presentation and persuasion	_____	_____	_____
Problem solving and decision making	_____	_____	_____
Stress management	_____	_____	_____
Team building	_____	_____	_____
Time management	_____	_____	_____

Leadership and Participation in Decision Making

Procedure

1. For the 10 situations described below, decide which of the three styles you would use for that unique situation. Place the letter A, P, or L on the line before each situation's number.

   A—authority; make the decision alone without additional inputs.
   P—consultative; make the decision based on group inputs.
   L—group; allow the group to which you belong to make the decision.

Decision Situations

_____ 1. You have developed a new work procedure that will increase productivity. Your boss likes the idea and wants you to try it within a few weeks. You view your employees as fairly capable and believe that they will be receptive to the change.

_____ 2. The industry of your product has new competition. Your organization's revenues have been dropping. You have been told to lay off three of your ten employees in two weeks. You have been the supervisor for over one year. Normally, your employees are very capable.

_____ 3. Your department has been facing a problem for several months. Many solutions have been tried and have failed. You finally thought of a solution, but you are not sure of the possible consequences of the change required or its acceptance by the highly capable employees.

_____ 4. Flextime has become popular in your organization. Some departments let each employee start and end work whenever they choose. However, because of the cooperative effort of your employees, they must all work the same eight hours. You are not sure of the level of interest in changing the hours. Your employees are a very capable group and like to make decisions.

_____ 5. The technology in your industry is changing faster than the members of your organization can keep up. Top management hired a consultant who has given the recommended decision. You have two weeks to make your decision. Your employees are capable, and they enjoy participating in the decision-making process.

_____ 6. Your boss called you on the telephone to tell you that someone has requested an order for your department's product with a very short delivery date. She asked that you call her back with the decision about taking the order in 15 minutes. Looking over the work schedule, you realize that it will be very difficult to deliver the order on time. Your employees will have to push hard to make it. They are cooperative, capable, and enjoy being involved in decision making.

_____ 7. A change has been handed down from top management. How you implement it is your decision. The change takes effect in one month. It will personally affect everyone in your department. The acceptance of the department members is critical to the success of the change. Your employees are usually not too interested in being involved in making decisions.

_____ 8. You believe that productivity in your department could be increased. You have thought of some ways that may work, but you're not sure of them. Your employees are very experienced; almost all of them have been in the department longer than you have.

_____ 9. Top management has decided to make a change that will affect all of your employees. You know that they will be upset because it will cause them hardship. One or two may even quit. The change goes into effect in 30 days. Your employees are very capable.

_____ 10. A customer has offered you a contract for your product with a quick delivery date. The offer is open for two days. Meeting the contract deadline would require employees to work nights and weekends for six weeks. You cannot require them to work overtime. Filling this profitable contract could help get you the raise you want and feel you deserve. However, if you take the contract and don't deliver on time, it will hurt your chances of getting a big raise. Your employees are very capable.

2. Form groups as assigned by your instructor. Share and compare your choices for each decision situation. Reconcile any differences and be prepared to defend your decision preferences in general class discussion.

My Best Manager: Revisited

Contributed by J. Marcus Maier, Chapman University

Procedure

1. Refer to the list of qualities—or profiles—the class generated earlier in the course for the "Best Manager."
2. Looking first at your Typical Managers profile, suppose you took this list to 100 average people on the street (or at the local mall) and asked them whether ____ (Trait X, quality Y) was "more typical of men or of women in our culture." What do you think *most* of them would say? That ____ (X, Y etc.) is more typical of *women*? or of *men*? Or of neither/both?[1] Do this for every trait on your list(s). (5 minutes)
3. Now do the same for the qualities we generated in our Best Manager profile. (5 min.)
4. A straw vote is taken, one quality at a time, to determine the class's overall gender identification of each trait, focusing on the Typical Managers profile (10–15 min.). Then this is repeated for the Best Manager profile (10–15 min.).[2]
5. Discussion. What do you see in the data this group has generated? How might you interpret these results? (15–20 min.)

Source: Based on Maier's 1993 article, "The Gender Prism," *Journal of Management Education,* 17(3), 285–314. 1994 Fritz Roethlisberger Award Recipient for Best Paper (Updated, 1996).

[1] This gets the participants to move outside of their *own* conceptions to their awareness of *societal* definitions of masculinity and femininity.

[2] This is done by a rapid show of hands, looking for a clear majority vote. An "f" (for "feminine") is placed next to those qualities that a clear majority indicate are more typical of women, an "m" (for "masculine") next to those qualities a clear majority indicate would be more typical of men. (This procedure parallels the median-split method used in determining Bem Sex Role Inventory classifications.) If no clear majority emerges (i.e., if the vote is close), the trait or quality is classified as "both" (f/m). The designations "masculine" or "feminine" are used (rather than "men" or "women") to underscore the *socially constructed* nature of each dimension.

Active Listening

Contributed by Robert Ledman, Morehouse College

Procedure

1. Review active listening skills and behaviors as described in the textbook and in class.
2. Form into groups of three. Each group will have a listener, a talker, and an observer (if the number of students is not evenly divisible by three, two observers are used for one or two groups).
3. The "talkers" should talk about any subject they wish, but only *if* they are being actively listened to. Talkers should stop speaking as soon as they sense active listening has stopped.
4. The "listeners" should use a list of active listening skills and behaviors as their guide, and practice as many of them as possible to be sure the talker is kept

----

Source: Adapted from the presentation entitled "An Experiential Exercise to Teach Active Listening," presented at the Organizational Behavior Teaching Conference, Macomb, IL, 1995.

talking. Listeners should contribute nothing more than "active listening" to the communication.

5. The "observer" should note the behaviors and skills used by the listener and the effects they seemed to have on the communication process.

6. These roles are rotated until each student has played every role.

7. The instructor will lead a discussion of what the observers saw and what happened with the talkers and listeners. The discussion focuses on what behaviors from the posted list have been present, which have been absent, and how the communication has been affected by the listener's actions.

EXERCISE 30

Upward Appraisal

Procedure

1. Form workgroups as assigned by your instructor.
2. The instructor will leave the room.
3. Convene in your assigned workgroups for a period of 10 minutes. Create a list of comments, problems, issues, and concerns you would like to have communicated to the instructor in regard to the course experience to date. *Remember,* your interest in the exercise is twofold: (a) to communicate your feelings to the instructor and (b) to learn more about the process of giving and receiving feedback.
4. Select one person from the group to act as spokesperson in communicating the group's feelings to the instructor.
5. The spokespersons should briefly convene to decide on what physical arrangement of chairs, tables, and so forth is most appropriate to conduct the feedback session. The classroom should then be rearranged to fit the desired specifications.
6. While the spokespersons convene, persons in the remaining groups should discuss how they expect the forthcoming communications event to develop. Will it be a good experience for all parties concerned? Be prepared to critically observe the actual communication process.
7. The instructor should be invited to return, and the feedback session will begin. Observers should make notes so that they may make constructive comments at the conclusion of the exercise.
8. Once the feedback session is complete, the instructor will call on the observers for comments, ask the spokespersons for reactions, and open the session to discussion.

EXERCISE 31

360-Degree Feedback

Contributed by Timothy J. Serey, Northern Kentucky University

Introduction

The time of performance reviews is often a time of genuine anxiety for many organizational members. On the one hand, it is an important organizational ritual and a key part of the Human Resource function. Organizations usually codify the process and provide a mechanism to appraise performance. On the other hand, it is rare for managers to feel comfortable with this process. Often, they feel discomfort over "playing God." One possible reason for this is that managers rarely receive formal training about how to provide feedback.

From the manager's point of view, if done properly, giving feedback is at the very heart of his or her job as "coach" and "teacher." It is an investment in the professional development of another person, rather than the punitive element we so often associate with hearing from "the boss." From the subordinate's perspective, most people want to know where they stand, but this is usually tempered by a fear of "getting it in the neck." In many organizations, it is rare to receive straight, non-sugar-coated feedback about where you stand.

Procedure

1. Review the section of the book dealing with feedback before you come to class. It is also helpful if individuals make notes about their perceptions and feelings about the course *before* they come to class.
2. Groups of students should discuss their experiences, both positive and negative, in this class. Each group should determine the dimensions of evaluating the class itself *and* the instructor. For example, students might select criteria that include the practicality of the course, the way the material is structured and presented (e.g., lecture or exercises), and the instructor's style (e.g., enthusiasm, fairness).
3. Groups select a member to represent them in a subgroup that next provides feedback to the instructor before the entire class.
4. The student audience then provides the subgroup with feedback about their effectiveness in this exercise. That is, the larger class provides feedback to the subgroup about the extent to which students actually put the principles of effective feedback into practice (e.g., descriptive, not evaluative; specific, not general).

Source: Adapted from Timothy J. Serey, *Journal of Management Education,* Vol. 17, No. 2, May 1993. © 1993 by Sage Publications, Inc. Reprinted by permission of Sage Publications.

EXERCISE 32

Role Analysis Negotiation

Contributed by Paul Lyons, Frostburg State University

Introduction

A role is the set of various behaviors people expect from a person (or group) in a particular position. These role expectations occur in all types of organizations, such as one's place of work, school, family, clubs, and the like. Role ambiguity takes place when a person is confused about the expectations of the role. And sometimes, a role will have expectations that are contradictory—for example, being loyal to the company when the company is breaking the law.

The Role Analysis Technique, or RAT, is a method for improving the effectiveness of a team or group. RAT helps to clarify role expectations, and all organization members have responsibilities that translate to expectations. Determination of role requirements, by consensus—involving all concerned—will ultimately result in more effective and mutually satisfactory behavior. Participation and collaboration in the definition and analy-

Source: Adapted from Paul Lyons, "Developing Expectations with the Role Analysis Technique," *Journal of Management Education.* Vol. 17, No. 3, August 1993, pp. 386–389. © Sage Publications.

sis of roles by group members should result in clarification regarding who is to do what as well as increase the level of commitment to the decisions made.

Procedure

Working alone, carefully read the course syllabus that your instructor has given you. Make a note of any questions you have about anything for which you need clarification or understanding. Pay particular attention to the performance requirements of the course. Make a list of any questions you have regarding what, specifically, is expected of you in order for you to be successful in the course. You will be sharing this information with others in small groups.

EXERCISE 33

Lost at Sea

Introduction

Consider this situation. You are adrift on a private yacht in the South Pacific when a fire of unknown origin destroys the yacht and most of its contents. You and a small group of survivors are now in a large raft with oars. Your location is unclear, but you estimate being about 1000 miles south–southwest of the nearest land. One person has just found in her pockets five $1 bills and a packet of matches. Everyone else's pockets are empty. The following items are available to you on the raft.

	A	B	C
Sextant	___	___	
Shaving mirror	___	___	
5 gallons of water	___	___	
Mosquito netting	___	___	
1 survival meal	___	___	
Maps of Pacific Ocean	___	___	
Floatable seat cushion	___	___	
2 gallons oil-gas mix	___	___	
Small transistor radio	___	___	
Shark repellent	___	___	
20 square feet black plastic	___	___	
1 quart of 20-proof rum	___	___	
15 feet of nylon rope	___	___	
24 chocolate bars	___	___	
Fishing kit	___	___	

Source: Adapted from "Lost at Sea: A Consensus-Seeking Task," in *The 1975 Handbook for Group Facilitators.* Used with permission of University Associates, Inc.

Procedure

1. *Working alone,* rank in Column A the 15 items in order of their importance to your survival ("1" is most important and "15" is least important).
2. *Working in an assigned group,* arrive at a "team" ranking of the 15 items and record this ranking in Column B. Appoint one person as group spokesperson to report your group rankings to the class.
3. *Do not write in Column C* until further instructions are provided by your instructor.

EXERCISE 34

Entering the Unknown

Contributed by Michael R. Manning, New Mexico State University; Conrad N. Jackson, MPC, Inc., Huntsville, Alabama; and Paula S. Weber, New Mexico Highlands University

Procedure

1. Form into groups of four or five members. In each group spend a few minutes reflecting on members' typical entry behaviors in new situations and their behaviors when they are in comfortable settings.
2. According to the instructor's directions, students count off to form new groups of four or five members each.
3. The new groups spend the next 15–20 minutes getting to know each other. There is no right or wrong way to proceed, but all members should become more aware of their entry behaviors. They should act in ways that can help them realize a goal of achieving comfortable behaviors with their group.
4. Students review what has occurred in the new groups, giving specific attention to the following questions:
   (a) What topics did your group discuss (content)? Did these topics involve the "here and now" or were they focused on "there and then"?
   (b) What approach did you and your group members take to the task (process)? Did you try to initiate or follow? How? Did you ask questions? Listen? Respond to others? Did you bring up topics?
   (c) Were you more concerned with how you came across or with how others came across to you? Did you play it safe? Were you open? Did you share things even though it seemed uncomfortable or risky? How was humor used in your group? Did it add or detract?
   (d) How do you feel about the approach you took or the behaviors you exhibited? Was this hard or easy? Did others respond the way you had anticipated? Is there some behavior you would like to do more of, do better, or do less of?
   (e) Were your behaviors the ones you had intended (goals)?
5. Responses to these questions are next discussed by the class as a whole. (*Note:* Responses will tend to be mixed within a group, but between groups there should be more similarity.) This discussion helps individuals become aware of and understand their entry behaviors.
6. Optional individuals have identified their entry behaviors; each group can then spend 5–10 minutes discussing members' perceptions of each other:
   (a) What behaviors did they like or find particularly useful? What did they dislike?

(b) What were your reactions to others? What ways did they intend to come across? Did you see others in the way they had intended to come across?

(Alternatively, if there is concern about the personal nature of this discussion, ask the groups to discuss what they liked/didn't like without referring to specific individuals.)

EXERCISE 35

Vacation Puzzle

Contributed by Barbara G. McCain and Mary Khalili, Oklahoma City University

Procedure

Can you solve this puzzle? Give it a try and then compare your answers with those of classmates. Remember your communicative skills!

Puzzle

Khalili, McCain, Middleton, Porter, and Quintaro teach at Oklahoma City University. Each gets two weeks of vacation a year. Last year, each took his or her first week in the first five months of the year and his or her second week in the last five months. If each professor took each of his or her weeks in a different month from the other professors, in which months did each professor take his or her first and second week?

Here are the facts:

(a) McCain took her first week before Khalili, who took *hers* before Porter; for their second week, the order was reversed.
(b) The professor who vacationed in March also vacationed in September.
(c) Quintaro did not take her first week in March or April.
(d) Neither Quintaro nor the professor who took his or her first week in January took his or her second week in August or December.
(e) Middleton took her second week before McCain but after Quintaro.

Month	Professor
January	
February	
March	
April	
May	
June	
July	
August	
September	
October	
November	
December	

Source: Adapted to classroom activity by Dr. Mary Khalili.

The Ugli Orange

Introduction

In most work settings, people need other people to do their job, benefit the organization, and forward their career. Getting things done in organizations requires us to work together in cooperation, even though the ultimate objectives of those other people may be different from our own. Your task in the present exercise is learning how to achieve this cooperation more effectively.

Procedure

1. The class will be divided into pairs. One student in each pair will read and prepare the role of Dr. Roland, and one will play the role of Dr. Jones (role descriptions to be distributed by instructor). Students should read their respective role descriptions and prepare to meet with their counterpart (see Steps 2 and 3).
2. At this point the group leader will read a statement. The instructor will indicate that he or she is playing

the role of Mr. Cardoza, who owns the commodity in question. The instructor will tell you
(a) How long you have to meet with the other
(b) What information the instructor will require at the end of your meeting
After the instructor has given you this information, you may meet with the other firm's representative and determine whether you have issues you can agree to.

3. Following the meetings (negotiations), the spokesperson for each pair will report any agreements reached to the entire class. The observer for any pair will report on negotiation dynamics and the process by which agreement was reached.
4. Questions to consider:
(a) Did you reach a solution? If so, what was critical to reaching that agreement?
(b) Did you and the other negotiator trust one another? Why or why not?
(c) Was there full disclosure by both sides in each group? How much information was shared?
(d) How creative and/or complex were the solutions? If solutions were very complex, why do you think this occurred?
(e) What was the impact of having an "audience" on your behavior? Did it make the problem harder or easier to solve?

Source: Adapted from Hall et al., *Experiences in Management and Organizational Behavior,* 3rd ed. (New York: John Wiley and Sons, Inc.), 1988. Originally developed by Robert J. House. Adapted by D. T. Hall and R. J. Lewicki, with suggested modifications by H. Kolodny and T. Ruble.

Conflict Dialogues

Contributed by Edward G. Wertheim, Northeastern University

Procedure

1. Think of a conflict situation at work or at school and try to re-create a segment of the dialogue that gets to the heart of the conflict.
2. Write notes on the conflict dialogue using the following format

Introduction

- Background
- My goals and objectives

- My strategy
- Assumptions I am making

Dialogue (re-create part of the dialogue below and try to put what you were really thinking in parentheses).

Me:
Other:
Me:
Other, etc.

3. Share your situation with members of your group. Read the dialogue to them, perhaps asking someone to play the role of "other."
4. Discuss with the group:
    (a) The style of conflict resolution you used (confrontation, collaboration, avoidance, etc.)
    (b) The triggers to the conflict, that is, what really set you off and why
    (c) Whether or not you were effective
    (d) Possible ways of handling this differently
5. Choose one dialogue from within the group to share with the class. Be prepared to discuss your analysis and also possible alternative approaches and resolutions for the situation described.

EXERCISE 38

Force-Field Analysis

Procedure

1. Choose a situation in which you have high personal stakes (for example, how to get a better grade in course X; how to get a promotion; how to obtain a position).
2. Using a version of the Sample Force-Field Analysis Form on the next page, apply the technique to your situation.
    (a) Describe the situation as it now exists.
    (b) Describe the situation as you would like it to be.
    (c) Identify those "driving forces"—the factors that are presently helping to move things in the desired direction.
    (d) Identify those "restraining forces"—the factors that are presently holding things back from moving in the desired direction.
3. Try to be as specific as possible in terms of the above in relation to your situation. You should attempt to be exhaustive in your listing of these forces. List them all!
4. Now go back and classify the strength of each force as weak, medium, or strong. Do this for both the driving and the restraining forces.
5. At this point you should rank the forces regarding their ability to influence or control the situation.
6. In small groups share your analyses. Discuss the usefulness and drawbacks to using this method for personal situations and its application to organizations.
7. Be prepared to share the results of your group's discussion with the rest of the class.

Sample Force-Field Analysis Form

Current Situation:	Situation as You Would Like It to Be:
Driving Forces:	**Restraining Forces:**

EXERCISE 39

Organizations Alive!

Contributed by Bonnie L. McNeely, Murray State University

Procedure

1. Find a copy of the following items from actual organizations. These items can be obtained from the company where you now work, a parent's workplace, or the university. Universities have mission statements, codes of conduct for students and faculty, organizational charts, job descriptions, performance appraisal forms, and control devices. Some student organizations also have these documents. All the items do not have to come from the same organization. *Bring these items to class.*

   (a) Mission statement   (d) Job description
   (b) Code of ethics   (e) Performance appraisal form
   (c) Organizational chart   (f) Control device

2. Form groups in class as assigned by your instructor. Share your items with the group, as well as what you learned while collecting these items. For example, did you find that some firms have a mission, but it is not written down? Did you find that job descriptions existed, but they were not really used or had not been updated in years?

Source: Adapted from Bonnie L. McNeely, "Make Your Principles of Management Class Come Alive," *Journal of Management Education,* Vol. 18, No. 2, May 1994, 246–249.

EXERCISE 40

Fast-Food Technology

Contributed by D. T. Hall, Boston University, and F. S. Hall, University of New Hampshire

Introduction

A critical first step in improving or changing any organization is *diagnosing* or analyzing its present functioning.

Many change and organization development efforts fall short of their objectives because this important step was not taken or was conducted superficially. To illustrate this, imagine how you would feel if you went to your doctor complaining of stomach pains and he recommended surgery without conducting any tests, without obtaining any further information, and without a careful physical examination. You would probably switch doctors! Yet managers often attempt major changes with correspondingly little diagnostic work in advance. (It could be said that they undertake vast projects with half-vast ideas.)

In this exercise, you will be asked to conduct a group diagnosis of two different organizations in the fast-food business. The exercise will provide an opportunity to integrate much of the knowledge you have gained in other exercises and in studying other topics. Your task will be to describe the organizations as carefully as you can in terms of several key organizational concepts. Although the organizations are probably very familiar to you, try to step back and look at them as though you were seeing them for the first time.

Procedure

1. In groups of four or six people, your assignment is described below.

One experience most people in this country have shared is that of dining in the hamburger establishment known as McDonald's. In fact, someone has claimed that twenty-fifth-century archeologists may dig into the ruins of our present civilization and conclude that twentieth-century religion was devoted to the worship of golden arches.

Your group, Fastalk Consultants, is known as the shrewdest, most insightful, and most overpaid management consulting firm in the country. You have been hired by the president of McDonald's to make recommendations for improving the motivation and performance of personnel in their franchise operations. Let us assume that the key job activities in franchise operations are food preparation, order-taking and dealing with customers, and routine cleanup operations.

Recently the president of McDonald's has come to suspect that his company's competitors—such as Burger King, Wendy's, Jack-in-the-Box, Dunkin' Donuts, various pizza establishments, and others—are making heavy inroads into McDonald's market. He has also hired a market research firm to investigate and compare the relative merits of the sandwiches, french fries, and drinks served in McDonald's and the competitor, and has asked the market research firm to assess the advertising campaigns of the two organizations. Hence, you will not need to be concerned with marketing issues, except as they may have an impact on employee behavior. The president wants *you* to look into the *organization* of the franchises to determine the strengths and weaknesses of each. Select a competitor that gives McDonald's a good "run for its money" in your area.

The president has established an unusual contract with you. *He wants you to make your recommendations based upon your observations as a customer.* He does not want you to do a complete diagnosis with interviews, surveys, or behind-the-scenes observations. He wants your report in two parts. Remember, the president wants concrete, specific, and practical recommendations. Avoid vague generalizations such as "improve communications" or "increase trust." Say very clearly *how* management can improve organizational performance. Substantiate your recommendations by reference to one or more theories of motivation, leadership, small groups, or job design.

Part I

Given his organization's goals of profitability, sales volume, fast and courteous service, and cleanliness, the president of McDonald's wants an analysis that will *compare and contrast McDonald's and the competitor* in terms of the following concepts:

Organizational goals
Organizational structure
Technology
Environment
Employee motivation
Communication
Leadership style
Policies/procedures/rules/standards
Job design
Organizational climate

Part II

Given the corporate goals listed under Part I, what specific actions might McDonald's management and franchise owners take in the following areas to achieve these goals (profitability, sales volume, fast and courteous service, and cleanliness)?

Job design and workflow
Organizational structure (at the individual restaurant level)
Employee incentives
Leadership
Employee selection

How do McDonald's and the competition differ in these aspects? Which company has the best approach?

2. Complete the assignment by going as a group to one McDonald's and one competitor's restaurant. If possible, have a meal in each place. To get a more valid comparison, visit a McDonald's and a competitor located in the same area. After observing each restaurant, meet with your group and prepare your 10-minute report to the executive committee.

3. In class, each group will present its report to the rest of the class, who will act as the executive committee. The group leader will appoint a timekeeper to be sure

that each group sticks to its 10-minute time limit. Possible discussion questions include:

(a) What similarities are there between the two organizations?
(b) What differences are there between the organizations?
(c) Do you have any "hunches" about the reasons for the particular organizational characteristics you found? For example, can you try to explain why one organization might have a particular type of structure? Incentive system? Climate?
(d) Can you try to explain one set of characteristics in terms of some other characteristics you found? For example, do the goals account for structure? Does the environment explain the structure?

Alien Invasion

Procedure

This is an exercise in organizational culture. You will be assigned to a team (if you are not already in one) and instructed to visit an organization by your instructor.

1. Visit the site assigned as a team working under conditions set forth in the "situation" below.
2. Take detailed notes on the cultural forms that you observe.
3. Prepare a presentation for the class that describes these forms and draw any inferences you can about the nature of the culture of the organization—its ideologies, values, and norms of behavior.
4. Be sure to explain the basis of your inferences in terms of the cultural forms observed.

You will have 20 minutes to report your findings, so plan your presentation carefully. Use visual aids to help your audience understand what you have found.

Situation

You are Martians who have just arrived on Earth in the first spaceship from your planet. Your superiors have ordered you to learn as much about Earthlings and the way they behave as you can without doing anything to make them aware that you are Martians. It is vital for the future plans of your superiors that you do nothing to disturb the Earthlings. Unfortunately, Martians communicate by emitting electromagnetic waves and are incapable of speech, so you cannot talk to the natives. Even if you did, it is reported by the usually reliable Bureau of Interplanetary Intelligence that Earthlings may become cannibalistic if annoyed. However, the crash course in Earth languages taught by the bureau has enabled you to read the language.

Remember, these instructions limit your data collection to observation and request that you *not* talk to the "natives." There are two reasons for this instruction. First, your objective is to learn what the organization does when it is simply going about its normal business and not responding to a group of students asking questions. Second, you are likely to be surprised at how much you can learn by simply observing if you put your mind to it. Many skilled managers employ this ability in sensing what is going on as they walk through their plant or office area.

Since you cannot talk to people, some of the cultural forms (legends, sagas, etc.) will be difficult to spot unless you are able to pick up copies of the organization's promotional literature (brochures, company reports, advertisements) during your visit. Do not be discouraged, because the visible forms such as artifacts, setting, symbols, and (sometimes) rituals can convey a great deal about the culture. Just keep your eyes, ears, and antennae open!

Source: Adapted from Donald D. Bowen et al., *Experiences in Management and Organizational Behavior,* 4th ed. (New York: John Wiley & Sons, Inc.), 1997.

Power Circles

Contributed by Marian C. Schultz, University of West Florida

This exercise is designed to examine power and influence in the classroom setting. Specifically, it allows you to identify the combination of power bases used by your instructor in accomplishing his or her objectives for the course.

Procedure

1. Recall that the instructor's power includes the following major bases: (a) the authority that comes from the instructor's position (position power), (b) the knowledge, skill, and expertise of the instructor in the subject area (expert power), and (c) the regard in which you personally hold the instructor (referent power).

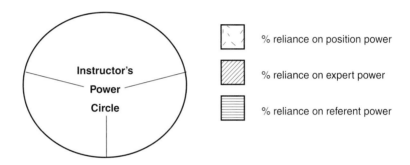

2. Indicate the configuration of power that is most evident in the way the instructor behaves in the course overall and according to the following "power circle." This circle can be filled in to represent the relative emphasis on the three power bases (e.g., 60 percent position, 30 percent expert, and 10 percent referent). Use the grid at the right to draw/fill in the circle to show the profile of instructor's power. The instructor will also complete a self-perceived power circle profile.
3. Consider also some possible special situations in which the instructor would have to use his or her power in the classroom context. Draw one power circle for each of the following situations, showing for each the power profile most likely to be used by the instructor to accomplish his or her goal.
   - Instructor wants to change the format of the final examination.
   - Instructor wants to add an additional group assignment to course requirements.
   - Instructor wants to have students attend a special two-hour guest lecture on a Saturday morning.
   - Instructor wants students to come to class better prepared for discussions of assigned material.
     The instructor will also complete a self-perceived power circle profile for each situation.
4. Share your power circles with those developed by members of your assigned group. Discuss the profiles and the reasons behind them in the group. Appoint one group member as spokesperson to share results in general class discussion. Discuss with the group the best way to communicate this feedback effectively to the instructor in the presence of all class members, and help prepare the spokesperson for the feedback session.

5. Have the instructor share his or her power profiles with the class. Ask the instructor to comment on any differences between the self-perceptions and the views of the class. Comment as a class on the potential significance to leaders and managers of differences in the way they perceive themselves and the ways they are perceived by others.
6. Discuss with the instructor and class how people may tend to favor one or more of the power bases (i.e., to develop a somewhat predictable power circle profile). Discuss as well how effective leaders and managers need to use power contingently, and modify their use of different power bases and power circle profiles to best fit the needs of specific influence situations.

SELF-ASSESSMENT INVENTORIES

Find online versions of many assessments at www.wiley.com/college/schermerhorn

Managerial Assumptions

Instructions

Read the following statements. Use the space to the left to write "Yes" if you agree with the statement, or "No" if you disagree with it. Force yourself to take a "yes" or "no" position for every statement.

1. Are good pay and a secure job enough to satisfy most workers?

2. Should a manager help and coach subordinates in their work?
3. Do most people like real responsibility in their jobs?
4. Are most people afraid to learn new things in their jobs?
5. Should managers let subordinates control the quality of their work?
6. Do most people dislike work?
7. Are most people creative?
8. Should a manager closely supervise and direct work of subordinates?

Source: Schermerhorn, John R. Jr., *Management*, 5th ed. (New York, John Wiley & Sons, Inc., 1996), p. 51. By permission.

9. Do most people tend to resist change?
10. Do most people work only as hard as they have to?
11. Should workers be allowed to set their own job goals?
12. Are most people happiest off the job?
13. Do most workers really care about the organization they work for?
14. Should a manager help subordinates advance and grow in their jobs?

Scoring

Count the number of "yes" responses to items 1, 4, 6, 8, 9, 10, 12; write that number here as [X = ____]. Count the number of "yes" responses to items 2, 3, 5, 7, 11, 13, 14; write that score here [Y = ____].

Interpretation

This assessment sheds insight into your orientation toward Douglas McGregor's Theory X (your "X" score) and Theory Y (your "Y" score) assumptions. You should review the discussion of McGregor's thinking in Chapter 1 and consider further the ways in which you are likely to behave toward other people at work. Think, in particular, about the types of "self-fulfilling prophecies" you are likely to create.

ASSESSMENT 2

A Twenty-First-Century Manager

Instructions

Rate yourself on the following personal characteristics. Use this scale.

> S = Strong, I am very confident with this one.
> G = Good, but I still have room to grow.
> W = Weak, I really need work on this one.
> ? = Unsure, I just don't know.

1. *Resistance to stress:* The ability to get work done even under stressful conditions.
2. *Tolerance for uncertainty:* The ability to get work done even under ambiguous and uncertain conditions.
3. *Social objectivity:* The ability to act free of racial, ethnic, gender, and other prejudices or biases.
4. *Inner work standards:* The ability to personally set and work to high-performance standards.
5. *Stamina:* The ability to sustain long work hours.
6. *Adaptability:* The ability to be flexible and adapt to changes.
7. *Self-confidence:* The ability to be consistently decisive and display one's personal presence.
8. *Self-objectivity:* The ability to evaluate personal strengths and weaknesses and to understand one's motives and skills relative to a job.
9. *Introspection:* The ability to learn from experience, awareness, and self-study.
10. *Entrepreneurism:* The ability to address problems and take advantage of opportunities for constructive change.

Scoring

Give yourself 1 point for each S, and 1/2 point for each G. Do not give yourself points for W and ? responses. Total your points and enter the result here [PMF = ____].

Interpretation

This assessment offers a self-described *profile of your management foundations* (*PMF*). Are you a perfect 10, or is your PMF score something less than that? There shouldn't be too many 10s around. Ask someone who knows you to assess you on this instrument. You may be surprised at the differences between your PMF score as self-described and your PMF score as described by someone else. Most of us, realistically speaking, must work hard to grow and develop continually in these and related management foundations. This list is a good starting point as you consider where and how to further pursue the development of your managerial skills and competencies. The items on the list are recommended by the American Assembly of Collegiate Schools of Business (AACSB) as skills and personal characteristics that should be nurtured in college and university students of business administration. Their success—and yours—as twenty-first-century managers may well rest on (1) an initial awareness of the importance of these basic management foundations and (2) a willingness to strive continually to strengthen them throughout your work career.

Source: See *Outcome Management Project,* Phase I and Phase II Reports (St. Louis: American Assembly of Collegiate Schools of Business, 1986 & 1987).

Turbulence Tolerance Test

Instructions

The following statements were made by a 37-year-old manager in a large, successful corporation. How would you like to have a job with these characteristics? Using the following scale, write your response to the left of each statement.

> 4 = I would enjoy this very much; it's completely acceptable.
>
> 3 = This would be enjoyable and acceptable most of the time.
>
> 2 = I'd have no reaction to this feature one way or another, or it would be about equally enjoyable and unpleasant.
>
> 1 = This feature would be somewhat unpleasant for me.
>
> 0 = This feature would be very unpleasant for me.

_____ 1. I regularly spend 30 to 40 percent of my time in meetings.

_____ 2. Eighteen months ago my job did not exist, and I have been essentially inventing it as I go along.

_____ 3. The responsibilities I either assume or am assigned consistently exceed the authority I have for discharging them.

_____ 4. At any given moment in my job, I have on the average about a dozen phone calls to be returned.

_____ 5. There seems to be very little relation in my job between the quality of my performance and my actual pay and fringe benefits.

_____ 6. About 2 weeks a year of formal management training is needed in my job just to stay current.

_____ 7. Because we have very effective equal employment opportunity (EEO) in my company and because it is thoroughly multinational, my job consistently brings me into close working contact at a professional level with people of many races, ethnic groups and nationalities, and of both sexes.

_____ 8. There is no objective way to measure my effectiveness.

_____ 9. I report to three different bosses for different aspects of my job, and each has an equal say in my performance appraisal.

_____ 10. On average about a third of my time is spent dealing with unexpected emergencies that force all scheduled work to be postponed.

_____ 11. When I have to have a meeting of the people who report to me, it takes my secretary most of a day to find a time when we are all available, and even then, I have yet to have a meeting where everyone is present for the entire meeting.

_____ 12. The college degree I earned in preparation for this type of work is now obsolete, and I probably should go back for another degree.

_____ 13. My job requires that I absorb 100–200 pages of technical materials per week.

_____ 14. I am out of town overnight at least one night per week.

_____ 15. My department is so interdependent with several other departments in the company that all distinctions about which departments are responsible for which tasks are quite arbitrary.

Source: Peter B. Vail, _Managing as a Performance Art: New Ideas for a World of Chaotic Change_ (San Francisco: Jossey-Bass, 1989), pp. 8–9. Used by permission.

_____ 16. In about a year I will probably get a promotion to a job in another division that has most of these same characteristics.

_____ 17. During the period of my employment here, either the entire company or the division I worked in has been reorganized every year or so.

_____ 18. While there are several possible promotions I can see ahead of me, I have no real career path in an objective sense.

——— 19. While there are several possible promotions I can see ahead of me, I think I have no realistic chance of getting to the top levels of the company.

_____ 20. While I have many ideas about how to make things work better, I have no direct influence on either the business policies or the personnel policies that govern my division.

_____ 21. My company has recently put in an "assessment center" where I and all other managers will be required to go through an extensive battery of psychological tests to assess our potential.

_____ 22. My company is a defendant in an antitrust suit, and if the case comes to trial, I will probably have to testify about some decisions that were made a few years ago.

_____ 23. Advanced computer and other electronic office technology is continually being introduced into my division, necessitating constant learning on my part.

_____ 24. The computer terminal and screen I have in my office can be monitored in my bosses' offices without my knowledge.

Scoring

Total your responses and divide the sum by 24; enter the score here [TTT = _____].

Interpretation

This instrument gives an impression of your tolerance for managing in turbulent times—something likely to characterize the world of work well into the [future]. In general, the higher your TTT score, the more comfortable you seem to be with turbulence and change—a positive sign. For comparison purposes, the average scores for some 500 MBA students and young managers was 1.5–1.6. The test's author suggests the TTT scores may be interpreted much like a grade point average in which 4.0 is a perfect A. On this basis, a 1.5 is below a C! How did you do?

ASSESSMENT 4

Global Readiness Index

Instructions

Rate yourself on each of the following items to establish a baseline measurement of your readiness to participate in the global work environment.

Rating Scale:

1 = Very Poor
2 = Poor
3 = Acceptable

Source: Developed from "Is Your Company Really Global," _Business Week_ (December 1, 1997).

4 = Good
5 = Very Good

_____ 1. I understand my own culture in terms of its expectations, values, and influence on communication and relationships.

_____ 2. When someone presents me with a different point of view, I try to understand it rather than attack it.

_____ 3. I am comfortable dealing with situations where the available information is incomplete and the outcomes unpredictable.

_____ 4. I am open to new situations and am always

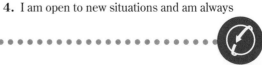

looking for new information and learning opportunities.

_____ 5. I have a good understanding of the attitudes and perceptions toward my culture as they are held by people from other cultures.

_____ 6. I am always gathering information about other countries and cultures and trying to learn from them.

_____ 7. I am well informed regarding the major differences in government, political, and economic systems around the world.

_____ 8. I work hard to increase my understanding of people from other cultures.

_____ 9. I am able to adjust my communication style to work effectively with people from different cultures.

_____ 10. I can recognize when cultural differences are influencing working relationships and adjust my attitudes and behavior accordingly.

Interpretation

To be successful in the twenty-first-century work environment, you must be comfortable with the global economy and the cultural diversity that it holds. This requires a *global mind-set* that is receptive to and respectful of cultural differences, *global knowledge* that includes the continuing quest to know and learn more about other nations and cultures, and *global work skills* that allow you to work effectively across cultures.

Scoring

The goal is to score as close to a perfect "5" as possible on each of the three dimensions of global readiness. Develop your scores as follows.

Items $(1 + 2 + 3 + 4)/4$

= _____ Global Mind-Set Score

Items $(5 + 6 + 7)/3$

= _____ Global Knowledge Score

Items $(8 + 9 + 10)/3$

= _____ Global Work Skills Score

ASSESSMENT 5

Personal Values

Instructions

Below are 16 items. Rate how important each one is to you on a scale of 0 (not important) to 100 (very important). Write the numbers 0–100 on the line to the left of each item.

Not important			Somewhat important			Very important		
0	10	20	30	40	50	60	70	80	90	100

_____ 1. An enjoyable, satisfying job.

_____ 2. A high-paying job.

_____ 3. A good marriage.

_____ 4. Meeting new people; social events.

_____ 5. Involvement in community activities.

_____ 6. My religion.

_____ 7. Exercising, playing sports.

_____ 8. Intellectual development.

_____ 9. A career with challenging opportunities.

_____ 10. Nice cars, clothes, home, etc.

_____ 11. Spending time with family.

_____ 12. Having several close friends.

_____ 13. Volunteer work for not-for-profit organizations, such as the cancer society.

Source: Robert N. Lussier, *Human Relations in Organizations,* 2nd ed. (Homewood, IL: Richard D. Irwin, 1993). By permission.

_____ 14. Meditation, quiet time to think, pray, etc.
_____ 15. A healthy, balanced diet.
_____ 16. Educational reading, TV, self-improvement programs, etc.

Scoring

Transfer the numbers for each of the 16 items to the appropriate column below, then add the two numbers in each column.

	Professional	Financial	Family	Social
	1. _____	2. _____	3. _____	4. _____
	9. _____	10. _____	11. _____	12. _____
Totals	_____	_____	_____	_____

	Community	Spiritual	Physical	Intellectual
	5. _____	6. _____	7. _____	8. _____
	13. _____	14. _____	15. _____	16. _____
Totals	_____	_____	_____	_____

Interpretation

The higher the total in any area, the higher the value you place on that particular area. The closer the numbers are in all eight areas, the more well-rounded you are. Think about the time and effort you put forth in your top three values. Is it sufficient to allow you to achieve the level of success you want in each area? If not, what can you do to change? Is there any area in which you feel you should have a higher value total? If yes, which, and what can you do to change?

·· ASSESSMENT 6 ··

Intolerance for Ambiguity

Instructions

To determine your level of tolerance (intolerance) for ambiguity, respond to the following items. PLEASE RATE EVERY ITEM; DO NOT LEAVE ANY ITEM BLANK. Rate each item on the following seven-point scale:

1	2	3	4	5	6	7
strongly disagree	moderately disagree	slightly disagree		slightly agree	moderately agree	strongly agree

Rating

_____ 1. An expert who doesn't come up with a definite answer probably doesn't know too much.

_____ 2. There is really no such thing as a problem that can't be solved.

_____ 3. I would like to live in a foreign country for a while.

_____ 4. People who fit their lives to a schedule probably miss the joy of living.

_____ 5. A good job is one where what is to be done and how it is to be done are always clear.

Source: Based on Budner, S. (1962) Intolerance of ambiguity as a personality variable, _Journal of Personality,_ Vol. 30, No. 1, 29–50.

_____ 6. In the long run it is possible to get more done by tackling small, simple problems rather than large, complicated ones.

_____ 7. It is more fun to tackle a complicated problem than it is to solve a simple one.

_____ 8. Often the most interesting and stimulating people are those who don't mind being different and original.

_____ 9. What we are used to is always preferable to what is unfamiliar.

_____ 10. A person who leads an even, regular life in which few surprises or unexpected happenings arise really has a lot to be grateful for.

_____ 11. People who insist upon a yes or no answer just don't know how complicated things really are.

_____ 12. Many of our most important decisions are based on insufficient information.

_____ 13. I like parties where I know most of the people more than ones where most of the people are complete strangers.

_____ 14. The sooner we all acquire ideals, the better.

_____ 15. Teachers or supervisors who hand out vague assignments give a chance for one to show initiative and originality.

_____ 16. A good teacher is one who makes you wonder about your way of looking at things.

_____ Total

Scoring

The scale was developed by S. Budner. Budner reports test–retest correlations of .85 with a variety of samples (mostly students and health care workers). Data, however, are more than 30 years old, so mean shifts may have occurred. Maximum ranges are 16–112, and score ranges were from 25 to 79, with a grand mean of approximately 49.

The test was designed to measure several different components of possible reactions to perceived threat in situations which are new, complex, or insoluble. Half of the items have been reversed.

To obtain a score, first *reverse* the scale score for the eight "reverse" items, 3, 4, 7, 8, 11, 12, 15, and 16 (i.e., a rating of 1 = 7, 2 = 6, 3 = 5, etc.), then add up the rating scores for all 16 items.

Interpretation

Empirically, low tolerance for ambiguity (high intolerance) has been positively correlated with:

- Conventionality of religious beliefs
- High attendance at religious services
- More intense religious beliefs
- More positive views of censorship
- Higher authoritarianism
- Lower Machiavellianism

The application of this concept to management in the 1990s is clear and relatively self-evident. The world of work and many organizations are full of ambiguity and change. Individuals with a *higher* tolerance for ambiguity are far more likely to be able to function effectively in organizations and contexts in which there is a high turbulence, a high rate of change, and less certainty about expectations, performance standards, what needs to be done, and so on. In contrast, individuals with a lower tolerance for ambiguity are far more likely to be unable to adapt or adjust quickly in turbulence, uncertainty, and change. These individuals are likely to become rigid, angry, stressed, and frustrated when there is a high level of uncertainty and ambiguity in the environment. High levels of tolerance for ambiguity, therefore, are associated with an ability to "roll with the punches" as organizations, environmental conditions, and demands change rapidly.

Two-Factor Profile

Instructions

On each of the following dimensions, distribute a total of 10 points between the two options. For example:

Summer weather	(7) ....(3)	Winter weather

1. Very responsible job (___) ....(___) Job security

2. Recognition for (___) ....(___) Good relations
   work accomplishments with co-workers

3. Advancement (___) ....(___) A boss who knows
   opportunities at work his/her job well

4. Opportunities to grow (___) ....(___) Good working
   and learn on the job conditions

5. A job that I can (___) ....(___) Supportive rules,
   do well policies of employer

6. A prestigious or (___) ....(___) A high base wage
   high-status job or salary

Scoring

Summarize your total scores for all items in the *left-hand column* and write it here: MF = ___.

Summarize your total scores for all items in the *right-hand column* and write it here: HF = ___.

Interpretation

The "MF" score indicates the relative importance that you place on motivating or satisfier factors in Herzberg's two-factor theory. This shows how important job content is to you. The "HF" score indicates the relative importance that you place on hygiene or dissatisfier factors in Herzberg's two-factor theory. This shows how important job context is to you.

Are You Cosmopolitan?

Instructions

Answer the questions below using a scale of 1 to 5: 1 representing "strongly disagree"; 2, "somewhat disagree"; 3, "neutral"; 4, "somewhat agree"; and 5, "strongly agree."

____ 1. You believe it is the right of the professional to make his or her own decisions about what is to be done on the job.

Source: Developed from Joseph A. Raelin, *The Clash of Cultures, Managers and Professionals* (Harvard Business School Press, 1986).

___ 2. You believe a professional should stay in an individual staff role regardless of the income sacrifice.
___ 3. You have no interest in moving up to a top administrative post.
___ 4. You believe that professionals are better evaluated by professional colleagues than by management.
___ 5. Your friends tend to be members of your profession.
___ 6. You would rather be known or get credit for your work outside rather than inside the company.
___ 7. You would feel better making a contribution to society than to your organization.
___ 8. Managers have no right to place time and cost schedules on professional contributors.

Scoring and Interpretation

A "cosmopolitan" identifies with the career profession, and a "local" identifies with the employing organization. Total your scores. A score of 30–40 suggests a cosmopolitan work orientation, 10–20 a "local" orientation, and 20–30 a mixed orientation.

ASSESSMENT 9

Group Effectiveness

Instructions

For this assessment, select a specific group you work with or have worked with; it can be a college or work group. For each of the eight statements below, select how often each statement describes the group's behavior. Place the number 1, 2, 3, or 4 on the line next to each of the 8 numbers.

Usually	Frequently	Occasionally	Seldom
1	2	3	4

___ 1. The members are loyal to one another and to the group leader.
___ 2. The members and leader have a high degree of confidence and trust in each other.
___ 3. Group values and goals express relevant values and needs of members.
___ 4. Activities of the group occur in a supportive atmosphere.
___ 5. The group is eager to help members develop to their full potential.
___ 6. The group knows the value of constructive conformity and knows when to use it and for what purpose.
___ 7. The members communicate all information relevant to the group's activity fully and frankly.
___ 8. The members feel secure in making decisions that seem appropriate to them.

Scoring

___ Total. Add up the eight numbers and place an X on the continuum below that represents the score.

Effective group   8 . . . 16 . . . 24 . . . 32   Ineffective group

Interpretation

The lower the score, the more effective the group. What can you do to help the group become more effective? What can the group do to become more effective?

Least Preferred Coworker Scale

Instructions

Think of all the different people with whom you have ever worked—in jobs, in social clubs, in student projects, or whatever. Next, think of the *one person* with whom you could work *least* well—that is, the person with whom you had the most difficulty getting a job done. This is the one person—a peer, boss, or subordinate—with whom you would least want to work. Describe this person by circling numbers at the appropriate points on each of the following pairs of bipolar adjectives. Work rapidly. There are no right or wrong answers.

Pleasant	8 7 6 5 4 3 2 1	Unpleasant
Friendly	8 7 6 5 4 3 2 1	Unfriendly
Rejecting	1 2 3 4 5 6 7 8	Accepting
Tense	1 2 3 4 5 6 7 8	Relaxed
Distant	1 2 3 4 5 6 7 8	Close
Cold	1 2 3 4 5 6 7 8	Warm
Supportive	8 7 6 5 4 3 2 1	Hostile
Boring	1 2 3 4 5 6 7 8	Interesting
Quarrelsome	1 2 3 4 5 6 7 8	Harmonious
Gloomy	1 2 3 4 5 6 7 8	Cheerful
Open	8 7 6 5 4 3 2 1	Guarded
Backbiting	1 2 3 4 5 6 7 8	Loyal
Untrustworthy	1 2 3 4 5 6 7 8	Trustworthy
Considerate	8 7 6 5 4 3 2 1	Inconsiderate
Nasty	1 2 3 4 5 6 7 8	Nice
Agreeable	8 7 6 5 4 3 2 1	Disagreeable
Insincere	1 2 3 4 5 6 7 8	Sincere
Kind	8 7 6 5 4 3 2 1	Unkind

Scoring

This is called the "least preferred coworker scale" (LPC). Compute your LPC score by totaling all the numbers you circled; enter that score here [LPC = _____].

Interpretation

The LPC scale is used by Fred Fiedler to identify a person's dominant leadership style. Fiedler believes that this style is a relatively fixed part of one's personality and is therefore difficult to change. This leads Fiedler to his contingency views, which suggest that the key to leadership success is finding (or creating) good "matches" between style and situation. If your score is 73 or above, Fiedler considers you a "relationship-motivated" leader; if your score is 64 and below, he considers you a "task-motivated" leader. If your score is between 65 and 72, Fiedler leaves it up to you to determine which leadership style is most like yours.

Source: Fred E. Fiedler and Martin M. Chemers. *Improving Leadership Effectiveness: The Leader Match Concept,* 2nd ed. (New York: John Wiley & Sons, Inc., 1984). Used by permission.

Leadership Style

Instructions

The following statements describe leadership acts. Indicate the way you would most likely act if you were leader of a workgroup, by circling whether you would most likely behave in this way:

> always (A); frequently (F); occasionally (O); seldom (S); or never (N)

A F O S N 1. Act as group spokesperson.
A F O S N 2. Encourage overtime work.
A F O S N 3. Allow members complete freedom in their work.
A F O S N 4. Encourage the use of uniform procedures.
A F O S N 5. Permit members to solve their own problems.
A F O S N 6. Stress being ahead of competing groups.
A F O S N 7. Speak as a representative of the group.
A F O S N 8. Push members for greater effort.
A F O S N 9. Try out ideas in the group.
A F O S N 10. Let the members work the way they think best.
A F O S N 11. Work hard for a personal promotion.
A F O S N 12. Tolerate postponement and uncertainty.
A F O S N 13. Speak for the group when visitors are present.
A F O S N 14. Keep the work moving at a rapid pace.
A F O S N 15. Turn members loose on a job.
A F O S N 16. Settle conficts in the group.
A F O S N 17. Focus on work details.
A F O S N 18. Represent the group at outside meetings.
A F O S N 19. Avoid giving the members too much freedom.
A F O S N 20. Decide what should be done and how it should be done.
A F O S N 21. Push for increased production.
A F O S N 22. Give some members authority to act.
A F O S N 23. Expect things to turn out as predicted.
A F O S N 24. Allow the group to take initiative.
A F O S N 25. Assign group members to particular tasks.
A F O S N 26. Be willing to make changes.
A F O S N 27. Ask members to work harder.
A F O S N 28. Trust members to exercise good judgment.
A F O S N 29. Schedule the work to be done.
A F O S N 30. Refuse to explain my actions.
A F O S N 31. Persuade others that my ideas are best.
A F O S N 32. Permit the group to set its own pace.
A F O S N 33. Urge the group to beat its previous record.
A F O S N 34. Act without consulting the group.
A F O S N 35. Ask members to follow standard rules.

              T _____   P _____

Scoring

1. Circle items 8, 12, 17, 18, 19, 30, 34 and 35.

2. Write the number 1 in front of a *circled item number* if you responded S (seldom) or N (never) to that item.

3. Write a number 1 in front of *item numbers not circled* if you responded A (always) or F (frequently).
4. Circle the number 1's which you have written in front of items 3, 5, 8, 10, 15, 18, 19, 22, 24, 26, 28, 30, 32, 34, and 35.
5. *Count the circled number 1's.* This is your score for leadership *concern for people.* Record the score in the blank following the letter P at the end of the questionnaire.
6. *Count the uncircled number 1's.* This is your score for leadership *concern for task.* Record this number in the blank following the letter T.

ASSESSMENT 12

"TT" Leadership Style

Instructions

For each of the following 10 pairs of statements, divide 5 points between the two according to your beliefs, perceptions of yourself, or according to which of the two statements characterizes you better. The 5 points may be divided between the a and b statements in any one of the following ways: 5 for a, 0 for b; 4 for a, 1 for b; 3 for a, 2 for b; 1 for a, 4 for b; 0 for a, 5 for b, but not equally (2 ½) between the two. Weigh your choices between the two according to the one that characterizes you or your beliefs better.

1. (a) As leader I have a primary mission of maintaining stability.
   (b) As leader I have a primary mission of change.
2. (a) As leader I must cause events.
   (b) As leader I must facilitate events.
3. (a) I am concerned that my followers are rewarded equitably for their work.
   (b) I am concerned about what my followers want in life.
4. (a) My preference is to think long range: what might be.
   (b) My preference is to think short range: what is realistic.
5. (a) As a leader I spend considerable energy in managing separate but related goals.
   (b) As a leader I spend considerable energy in arousing hopes, expectations, and aspirations among my followers.

6. (a) Although not in a formal classroom sense, I believe that a significant part of my leadership is that of teacher.
   (b) I believe that a significant part of my leadership is that of facilitator.
7. (a) As leader I must engage with followers at an equal level of morality.
   (b) As leader I must represent a higher morality.
8. (a) I enjoy stimulating followers to want to do more.
   (b) I enjoy rewarding followers for a job well done.
9. (a) Leadership should be practical.
   (b) Leadership should be inspirational.
10. (a) What power I have to influence others comes primarily from my ability to get people to identify with me and my ideas.
    (b) What power I have to influence others comes primarily from my status and position.

Scoring

Circle your points for items 1b, 2a, 3b, 4a, 5b, 6a, 7b, 8a, 9b, 10a and add up the total points you allocated to these items; enter the score here [**T** = _____]. Next, add up the total points given to the uncircled items 1a, 2b, 3a, 4b, 5a, 6b, 7a, 8b, 9a, 10b; enter the score here [T = _____].

Interpretation

This instrument gives an impression of your tendencies toward "transformational" leadership (your **T** score) and "transactional" leadership (your T score). You may want to refer to the discussion of these concepts in Chapter 15. Today, a lot of attention is being given to the transformational aspects of leadership—those personal qualities that inspire a sense of vision and desire for extraordinary accomplishment in followers. The most successful leaders of the future will most likely be strong in both "T"s.

Source: Questionnaire by W. Warner Burke, Ph.D. Used by permission.

Empowering Others

Instructions

Think of times when you have been in charge of a group—this could be a full-time or part-time work situation, a student workgroup, or whatever. Complete the following questionnaire by recording how you feel about each statement according to this scale.

> 1 = Strongly disagree
> 2 = Disagree
> 3 = Neutral
> 4 = Agree
> 5 = Strongly agree

When in charge of a group I find:

____ 1. Most of the time other people are too inexperienced to do things, so I prefer to do them myself.

____ 2. It often takes more time to explain things to others than just to do them myself.

____ 3. Mistakes made by others are costly, so I don't assign much work to them.

Source: Questionnaire adapted from L. Steinmetz and R. Todd, *First Line Management,* 4th ed. (Homewood, IL: BPI/Irwin, 1986), pp. 64–67. Used by permission.

____ 4. Some things simply should not be delegated to others.

____ 5. I often get quicker action by doing a job myself.

____ 6. Many people are good only at very specific tasks, and thus can't be assigned additional responsibilities.

____ 7. Many people are too busy to take on additional work.

____ 8. Most people just aren't ready to handle additional responsibilities.

____ 9. In my position, I should be entitled to make my own decisions.

Scoring

Total your responses; enter the score here [____].

Interpretation

This instrument gives an impression of your *willingness to delegate.* Possible scores range from 9 to 45. The higher your score, the more willing you appear to be to delegate to others. Willingness to delegate is an important managerial characteristic. It is essential if you—as a manager—are to "empower" others and give them opportunities to assume responsibility and exercise self-control in their work. With the growing importance of empowerment in the new workplace, your willingness to delegate is well worth thinking about seriously.

Machiavellianism

Instructions

For each of the following statements, circle the number that most closely resembles your attitude.

Statement	Disagree A Lot	A Little	Neutral	Agree A Little	A Lot
1. The best way to handle people is to tell them what they want to hear.	1	2	3	4	5
2. When you ask someone to do something for you, it is best to give the real reason for wanting it rather than reasons that might carry more weight.	1	2	3	4	5
3. Anyone who completely trusts someone else is asking for trouble.	1	2	3	4	5
4. It is hard to get ahead without cutting corners here and there.	1	2	3	4	5
5. It is safest to assume that all people have a vicious streak, and it will come out when they are given a chance.	1	2	3	4	5
6. One should take action only when it is morally right.	1	2	3	4	5
7. Most people are basically good and kind.	1	2	3	4	5
8. There is no excuse for lying to someone else.	1	2	3	4	5
9. Most people forget more easily the death of their father than the loss of their property.	1	2	3	4	5
10. Generally speaking, people won't work hard unless forced to do so.	1	2	3	4	5

Scoring and Interpretation

This assessment is designed to compute your Machiavellianism (Mach) score. Mach is a personality characteristic that taps people's power orientation. The high-Mach personality is pragmatic, maintains emotional distance from others, and believes that ends can justify means. To obtain your Mach score, add up the numbers you checked for questions 1, 3, 4, 5, 9, and 10. For the other four questions, reverse the numbers you have checked, so that 5 becomes 1; 4 is 2; and 1 is 5. Then total both sets of numbers to find your score. A random sample of adults found the national average to be 25. Students in business and management typically score higher.

The results of research using the Mach test have found: (1) men are generally more Machiavellian than women; (2) older adults tend to have lower Mach scores than younger adults; (3) there is no significant difference between high Machs and low Machs on measures of intelligence or ability; (4) Machiavellianism is not significantly related to demographic characteristics such as educational level or marital status; and (5) high Machs tend to be in professions that emphasize the control and manipulation of people—for example, managers, lawyers, psychiatrists, and behavioral scientists.

Source: From R. Christie and F. L. Geis, *Studies in Machiavellianism* (New York: Academic Press, 1970). By permission.

Personal Power Profile

Contributed by Marcus, Maier, Chapman University

Instructions

Below is a list of statements that may be used in describing behaviors that supervisors (leaders) in work organizations can direct toward their subordinates (followers). First, carefully read each descriptive statement, thinking in terms of *how you prefer to influence others*. Mark the number that most closely represents how you feel. Use the following numbers for your answers.

> 5 = Strongly agree
> 4 = Agree
> 3 = Neither agree nor disagree
> 2 = Disagree
> 1 = Strongly disagree

To influence others, I would prefer to:	Strongly Disagree	Disagree	Neither Agree nor Disagree	Agree	Strongly Agree
1. Increase their pay level	1	2	3	4	5
2. Make them feel valued	1	2	3	4	5
3. Give undesirable job assignments	1	2	3	4	5
4. Make them feel like I approve of them	1	2	3	4	5
5. Make them feel that they have commitments to meet	1	2	3	4	5
6. Make them feel personally accepted	1	2	3	4	5
7. Make them feel important	1	2	3	4	5
8. Give them good technical suggestions	1	2	3	4	5
9. Make the work difficult for them	1	2	3	4	5
10. Share my experience and/or training	1	2	3	4	5
11. Make things unpleasant here	1	2	3	4	5
12. Make being at work distasteful	1	2	3	4	5
13. Influence their getting a pay increase	1	2	3	4	5
14. Make them feel like they should satisfy their job requirements	1	2	3	4	5
15. Provide them with sound job-related advice	1	2	3	4	5
16. Provide them with special benefits	1	2	3	4	5
17. Influence their getting a promotion	1	2	3	4	5
18. Give them the feeling that they have responsibilities to fulfill	1	2	3	4	5
19. Provide them with needed technical knowledge	1	2	3	4	5
20. Make them recognize that they have tasks to accomplish	1	2	3	4	5

Source: Modified version of T. R. Hinken and C. A. Schriesheim, "Development and Application of New Scales to Measure the French and Raven (1959) Bases of Social Power." *Journal of Applied Psychology,* Vol. 74, 1989, 561–567.

Scoring

Using the grid below, insert your scores from the 20 questions and proceed as follows: *Reward power*—sum your response to items 1, 13, 16, and 17 and divide by 4. *Coercive power*—sum your response to items 3, 9, 11, and 12 and divide by 4. *Legitimate power*— sum your response to questions 5, 14, 18, and 20 and divide by 4. *Referent power*—sum your response to questions 2, 4, 6, and 7 and divide by 4. *Expert power*—sum your response to questions 8, 10, 15, and 19 and divide by 4.

Reward	Coercive	Legitimate	Referent	Expert
1 ____	3 ____	5 ____	2 ____	8 ____
13 ____	9 ____	14 ____	4 ____	10 ____
16 ____	11 ____	18 ____	6 ____	15 ____
17 ____	12 ____	20 ____	7 ____	19 ____
Total ____	____	____	____	____
Divide by 4 ____	____	____	____	____

Interpretation

A high score (4 and greater) on any of the five dimensions of power implies that you prefer to influence others by employing that particular form of power. A low score (2 or less) implies that you prefer not to employ this particular form of power to influence others. This represents your power profile. Your overall power position is not reflected by the simple sum of the power derived from each of the five sources. Instead, some combinations of power are synergistic in nature—they are greater than the simple sum of their parts. For example, referent power tends to magnify the impact of other power sources because these other influence attempts are coming from a "respected" person. Reward power often increases the impact of referent power, because people generally tend to like those who give them things that they desire. Some power combinations tend to produce the opposite of synergistic effects, such that the total is less than the sum of the parts. Power dilution frequently accompanies the use of (or threatened use of) coercive power.

ASSESSMENT 16

Your Intuitive Ability

Instructions

Complete this survey as quickly as you can. Be honest with yourself. For each question, select the response that most appeals to you.

1. When working on a project, do you prefer to:
   (a) Be told what the problem is but be left free to decide how to solve it?
   (b) Get very clear instructions about how to go about solving the problem before you start?
2. When working on a project, do you prefer to work with colleagues who are:
   (a) Realistic?

   (b) Imaginative?
3. Do you most admire people who are:
   (a) Creative?
   (b) Careful?
4. Do the friends you choose tend to be:
   (a) Serious and hard working?
   (b) Exciting and often emotional?
5. When you ask a colleague for advice on a problem you have, do you:
   (a) Seldom or never get upset if he or she questions your basic assumptions?
   (b) Often get upset if he or she questions your basic assumptions?
6. When you start your day, do you:
   (a) Seldom make or follow a specific plan?
   (b) Usually first make a plan to follow?

7. When working with numbers do you find that you:
   (a) Seldom or never make factual errors?
   (b) Often make factual errors?
8. Do you find that you:
   (a) Seldom daydream during the day and really don't enjoy doing so when you do it?
   (b) Frequently daydream during the day and enjoy doing so?
9. When working on a problem, do you:
   (a) Prefer to follow the instructions or rules when they are given to you?
   (b) Often enjoy circumventing the instructions or rules when they are given to you?
10. When you are trying to put something together, do you prefer to have:
    (a) Step-by-step written instructions on how to assemble the item?
    (b) A picture of how the item is supposed to look once assembled?
11. Do you find that the person who irritates you *the most* is the one who appears to be:
    (a) Disorganized?
    (b) Organized?
12. When an expected crisis comes up that you have to deal with, do you:
    (a) Feel anxious about the situation?
    (b) Feel excited by the challenge of the situation?

Scoring

Total the number of "a" responses circled for questions 1, 3, 5, 6, 11; enter the score here [A = _____]. Total the number of "b" responses for questions 2, 4, 7, 8, 9, 10, 12; enter the score here [B = _____]. Add your "a" and "b" scores and enter the sum here [A + B = _____]. This is your *intuitive score*. The highest possible intuitive score is 12; the lowest is 0.

Interpretation

In his book *Intuition in Organizations* (Newbury Park, CA: Sage, 1989), pp. 10–11, Weston H. Agor states: "Traditional analytical techniques . . . are not as useful as they once were for guiding major decisions. . . . If you hope to be better prepared for tomorrow, then it only seems logical to pay some attention to the use and development of intuitive skills for decision making." Agor developed the prior survey to help people assess their tendencies to use intuition in decision making. Your score offers a general impression of your strength in this area. It may also suggest a need to further develop your skill and comfort with more intuitive decision approaches.

ASSESSMENT 17

Decision-Making Biases

Instructions

How good are you at avoiding potential decision-making biases? Test yourself by answering the following questions:

1. Which is riskier:
(a) driving a car on a 400-mile trip?
(b) flying on a 400-mile commercial airline flight?

2. Are there more words in the English language:
(a) that begin with "r"?
(b) that have "r" as the third letter?

3. Mark is finishing his MBA at a prestigious university. He is very interested in the arts and at one time considered a career as a musician. Is Mark more likely to take a job:
(a) in the management of the arts?
(b) with a management consulting firm?

4. You are about to hire a new central-region sales director for the fifth time this year. You predict that the next director should work out reasonably well since the last four were "lemons" and the odds favor hiring at least one good sales director in five tries. Is this thinking
(a) correct?
(b) incorrect?

5. A newly hired engineer for a computer firm in the Boston metropolitan area has 4 years' experience and good all-around qualifications. When asked to estimate the starting salary for this employee, a chemist with very little knowledge about the profession or industry guessed an annual salary of $35,000. What is your estimate?
$_____ per year

Source: Incidents from Max H. Bazerman, *Judgment in Managerial Decision Making,* 3rd ed. (New York: John Wiley & Sons, Inc., 1994), pp. 13–14. Used by permission.

Scoring

Your instructor will provide answers and explanations for the assessment questions.

Interpretation

Each of the preceding questions examines your tendency to use a different judgmental heuristic. In his book *Judgment in Managerial Decision Making,* 3rd ed. (New York: John Wiley & Sons, 1994), pp. 6–7, Max Bazerman calls these heuristics "simplifying strategies, or rules of thumb" used in making decisions. He states, "In general, heuristics are helpful, but their use can sometimes lead to severe errors. . . . If we can make managers aware of the potential adverse impacts of using heuristics, they can then decide when and where to use them." This assessment offers an initial insight into your use of such heuristics. An informed decision maker understands the heuristics, is able to recognize when they appear, and eliminates any that may inappropriately bias decision making.

Test yourself further. Before hearing from your instructor, go back and write next to each item the name of the judgmental heuristic (see Chapter 3 text discussion) that you think applies.

Then write down a situation that you have experienced and in which some decision-making bias may have occurred. Be prepared to share and discuss this incident with the class.

ASSESSMENT 18

Conflict Management Styles

Instructions

Think of how you behave in conflict situations in which your wishes differ from those of one or more persons. In the space to the left of each statement below, write the number from the following scale that indicates how likely you are to respond that way in a conflict situation.

> 1 = very unlikely   2 = unlikely   3 = likely   4 = very likely

____ **1.** I am usually firm in pursuing my goals.
____ **2.** I try to win my position.
____ **3.** I give up some points in exchange for others.
____ **4.** I feel that differences are not always worth worrying about.
____ **5.** I try to find a position that is intermediate between the other person's and mine.
____ **6.** In approaching negotiations, I try to be considerate of the other person's wishes.
____ **7.** I try to show the logic and benefits of my positions.
____ **8.** I always lean toward a direct discussion of the problem.
____ **9.** I try to find a fair combination of gains and losses for both of us.
____ **10.** I attempt to work through our differences immediately.
____ **11.** I try to avoid creating unpleasantness for myself.
____ **12.** I try to soothe the other person's feelings and preserve our relationships.
____ **13.** I attempt to get all concerns and issues immediately out in the open.
____ **14.** I sometimes avoid taking positions that would create controversy.
____ **15.** I try not to hurt others' feelings.

Scoring

Total your scores for items 1, 2, 7; enter that score here [*Competing* = ____]. Total your scores for items 8, 10, 13; enter that score here [*Collaborating* = ____]. Total your scores

---

Source: Adapted from Thomas-Kilmann, *Conflict Mode Instrument,* Copyright © 1974, Xicom, Inc., Tuxedo, NY 10987. Used by permission.

for items 3, 5, 9; enter that score here [*Compromising* = ____]. Total your scores for items 4, 11, 14; enter that score here. [*Avoiding* = ____]. Total your scores for items 6, 12, 15; enter that score here [*Accommodating* = ____].

Interpretation

Each of the scores above corresponds to one of the conflict management styles discussed in Chapter 15. Research indicates that each style has a role to play in management but that the best overall conflict management approach is collaboration; only it can lead to problem solving and true conflict resolution. You should consider any patterns that may be evident in your scores and think about how to best handle conflict situations in which you become involved.

ASSESSMENT 19

Your Personality Type

Instructions

How true is each statement for you?

	Not True At All		Not True or Untrue		Very True
1. I hate giving up before I'm absolutely sure that I'm licked.	1	2	3	4	5
2. Sometimes I feel that I should not be working so hard, but something drives me on.	1	2	3	4	5
3. I thrive on challenging situations. The more challenges I have, the better.	1	2	3	4	5
4. In comparison to most people I know, I'm very involved in my work.	1	2	3	4	5
5. It seems as if I need 30 hours a day to finish all the things I'm faced with.	1	2	3	4	5
6. In general, I approach my work more seriously than most people I know.	1	2	3	4	5
7. I guess there are some people who can be nonchalant about their work, but I'm not one of them.	1	2	3	4	5
8. My achievements are considered to be significantly higher than those of most people I know.	1	2	3	4	5
9. I've often been asked to be an officer of some group or groups.	1	2	3	4	5

Scoring

Add all your scores to create a total score = ____.

Interpretation

Type A personalities (hurried and competitive) tend to score 36 and above. Type B personalities (relaxed) tend to score 22 and below. Scores of 23–35 indicate a balance or mix of Type A and Type B.

Source: From *Job Demands and Worker Health* (HEW Publication No. [NIOSH] 75–160), (Washington, DC: US Department of Health, Education and Welfare, 1975), pp. 253–254.

Time Management Profile

Instructions

Complete the following questionnaire by indicating "Y" (yes) or "N" (no) for each item. Force yourself to respond "yes" or "no". Be frank and allow your responses to create an accurate picture of how you tend to respond to these kinds of situations.

_____ 1. When confronted with several items of similar urgency and importance, I tend to do the easiest one first.

_____ 2. I do the most important things during that part of the day when I know I perform best.

_____ 3. Most of the time I don't do things someone else can do; I delegate this type of work to others.

_____ 4. Even though meetings without a clear and useful purpose upset me, I put up with them.

_____ 5. I skim documents before reading them and don't complete any that offer a low return on my time investment.

_____ 6. I don't worry much if I don't accomplish at least one significant task each day.

_____ 7. I save the most trivial tasks for that time of day when my creative energy is lowest.

_____ 8. My workspace is neat and organized.

_____ 9. My office door is always "open"; I never work in complete privacy.

_____ 10. I schedule my time completely from start to finish every workday.

_____ 11. I don't like "to do" lists, preferring to respond to daily events as they occur.

_____ 12. I "block" a certain amount of time each day or week that is dedicated to high-priority activities.

Scoring

Count the number of "Y" responses to items 2, 3, 5, 7, 8, 12. [Enter that score here ____.] Count the number of "N" responses to items 1, 4, 6, 9, 10, 11. [Enter that score here ____.] Add together the two scores.

Interpretation

The higher the total score, the closer your behavior matches recommended time management guidelines. Reread those items where your response did not match the desired one. Why don't they match? Do you have reasons why your behavior in this instance should be different from the recommended time management guideline? Think about what you can do (and how easily it can be done) to adjust your behavior to be more consistent with these guidelines. For further reading, see Alan Lakein, _How to Control Your Time and Your Life_ (New York: David McKay), and William Oncken, _Managing Management Time_ (Englewood Cliffs, NJ: Prentice Hall, 1984).

Source: Suggested by a discussion in Robert E. Quinn, Sue R. Faerman, Michael P. Thompson, and Michael R. McGrath, _Becoming a Master Manager: A Contemporary Framework_ (New York: John Wiley & Sons, Inc., 1990), pp. 75–76.

Organizational Design Preference

Instructions

To the left of each item, write the number from the following scale that shows the extent to which the statement accurately describes your views.

> 5 = strongly agree
>
> 4 = agree somewhat
>
> 3 = undecided
>
> 2 = disagree somewhat
>
> 1 = strongly disagree

I prefer to work in an organization where:

1. Goals are defined by those in higher levels.
2. Work methods and procedures are specified.
3. Top management makes important decisions.
4. My loyalty counts as much as my ability to do the job.

Source: John F. Veiga and John N. Yanouzas, _The Dynamics of Organization Theory: Gaining a Macro Perspective_ (St. Paul, MN: West, 1979), pp. 158–160. Used by permission.

5. Clear lines of authority and responsibility are established.
6. Top management is decisive and firm.
7. My career is pretty well planned out for me.
8. I can specialize.
9. My length of service is almost as important as my level of performance.
10. Management is able to provide the information I need to do my job well.
11. A chain of command is well established.
12. Rules and procedures are adhered to equally by everyone.
13. People accept authority of a leader's position.
14. People are loyal to their boss.
15. People do as they have been instructed.
16. People clear things with their boss before going over his or her head.

Scoring

Total your scores for all questions. Enter the score here [____].

Interpretation

This assessment measures your preference for working in an organization designed along "organic" or "mechanistic" lines. The higher your score (above 64), the more comfortable you are with a mechanistic design; the lower your score (below 48), the more comfortable you are with an organic design. Scores between 48 and 64 can go either way. This organizational design preference represents an important issue in the new workplace. Indications are that today's organizations are taking on more and more organic characteristics. Presumably, those of us who work in them will need to be comfortable with such designs.

ASSESSMENT 22

Which Culture Fits You?

Instructions

Check one of the following organization "cultures" in which you feel most comfortable working.

1. A culture that values talent, entrepreneurial activity, and performance over commitment; one that offers large financial rewards and individual recognition.
2. A culture that stresses loyalty, working for the good of the group, and getting to know the right people; one that believes in "generalists" and step-by-step career progress.
3. A culture that offers little job security; one that operates with a survival mentality, stresses that every individual can make a difference, and focuses attention on "turnaround" opportunities.
4. A culture that values long-term relationships; one that emphasizes systematic career development, regular

training, and advancement based on gaining of functional expertise.

Scoring

These labels identify the four different cultures: 1 = "the baseball team," 2 = "the club," 3 = "the fortress," and 4 = "the academy."

Interpretation

To some extent, your future career success may depend on working for an organization in which there is a good fit between you and the prevailing corporate culture. This assessment can help you learn how to recognize various cultures, evaluate how well they can serve your needs, and recognize how they may change with time. A risk taker, for example, may be out of place in a "club" but fit right in with a "baseball team." Someone who wants to seek opportunities wherever they may occur may be out of place in an "academy" but fit right in with a "fortress."

Source: Developed from Carol Hymowitz, "Which Corporate Culture Fits You?" *Wall Street Journal* (July 17, 1989), p. B1.

Notes

Case 2 References

1. Forbes.com/finance/lists on 9/5/04
2. Hook, B. and Stevenson, A., "Rising Dough," *Kiplinger's Personal Finance,* January, 2002, p. 71.
3. Ibid.
4. http://finance.yahoo.com/qcf?s=PNRA&annual, 9/5/04
5. Hoover's Company Records, #13703, available at lexus-nexus.com, 8/31/2004
6. Krantz, M. "Small Cap Stocks," *Business Week,* 4/2/2002, pp. 147-150.
7. Pethokouski, J.M. "Bye-Bye Burgers," *U.S. News & World Report,* 12/2/02, p. 36.
8. Ibid.
9. http://www.computerworld.com/mobiletopics/mobil/wifi/story/010801,95362,00.html, 8/ 30/ 2004.
10. www.panerabread.com_community_od.aspx, 8/30/ 2004.
11 http://www.panerabread.com/aboutfranchise.aspx, 8/ 30/ 2004

Case 10 References

1. Dodd, Annmarie. "The Fastest Sport on Earth—Fast-Moving and Fast-Growing, NASCAR Uses Its Loud, Folksy Appeal to Find New Racing Fans for the Future," *Daily News Record,* January 25, 1999.
2. Ibid.
3. Ibid.
4. Ibid.
5. Glick, Shav. "Dollar Signs: Sponsorships, Big Money Make NASCAR World Go 'Round," *Los Angeles Times,* February 14, 1999, p. D1.
6. Yost, Mark. "Companies Use NASCAR Races as Means to Rub Elbows, Boost Their Business," *Wall Street Journal,* February 22, 1999, p. B17B.
7. Dodd, op. cit.
8. "NASCAR Online: Jeff Gordon," http://www.nascar.com/winstoncup/drivers/GordJ01/index.html, February 19, 1999.
9. Cain, Holly. "Gordon Becomes Driving Force," *Seattle Times,* February 14, 1999, p. D1.
10. Glick, op. cit, p. D1.
11. Slater, Chuck. "Life in the Fast Lane," *Fast Company,* http://www.fastcompany.com/online/18/fastlane.html, October 1998.
12. Ibid.
13. Ibid.
14. Ibid.
15. Ibid.
16. Hinton, Ed. "Gordon's Gamble," *Sports Illustrated,* October 11, 1999.
17. Bechtel, Mark. "Like Old Times," *Sports Illustrated,* April 24, 2000.
18. Spencer, Lee. "Meet the Four-Time Champ—He's 30 Now," *Sporting News,* November 26, 2001.
Robbie Loomis
http://www.jeffgordon.com/team/bio_robbieloomis.html
record http://www.sportingnews.com/

Case 11 References

1. Mitchell, John. "Hoovers Industry Snapshot—Computer Software Industry," *Hoovers Online,* http://www.hoovers.com/features/industry/software1.html, February 5, 1999.
2. "Ross Perot Biography," *Perot Official World Wide Web Site,* http://www.perot.org/hrpbio.htm, December 17, 1998.
3. Ibid.
4. Myerson, Allan "Perot's Return to Business: The Vote's Not In," *New York Times,* February 22, 1998, p. 3:1.
5. Meyerson, Mort. "Everything I Thought I Knew About Leadership Is Wrong," *Fast Company,* April/May 1996, pp. 5–11.
6. Ibid.
7. Ibid.
8. Ibid.
9. Ibid.
10. Ibid.
11. Ibid.
12. Ibid.
13. Ibid.
14. "Perot Systems Homepage," http://www.perotsystems.com, February 17, 1999.
15. "Avis Selects Perot Systems for Imaging and Workflow Solution," *Business Wire,* April 8, 1996.
16. "Companies to Manage California Energy Grid," *Electric Light & Power,* September 1997, p. 28.

17. "Perot Systems Takes Major Stake in SwissAir Unit; Consulting Organization, Icarus, Serves European Airlines," *Business Wire*, March 4, 1997.
18. Meyerson, op. cit, pp. 10–11.
19. Zellner, Wendy and Himelstein, Linda. "Why Perot May Go with an IPO," *Business Week*, August 10, 1998, p. 65.
20. Meyerson, op. cit.
21. Ibid.
22. Ibid.
23. Ibid.
24. Cave, Andrew. "Perot Systems' Shares Leap 165. During Market Debut," *The Daily Telegraph*, February 3, 1999.
25. Mills, Mike. "MCI to Sell Unit to EDS," *Washington Post*, February 12, 1999, p. E01.

Case 12 References

1. *Harbour Report*, 1979–1989, p. 235.
2. *Harbour Report*, 1989–1992, p. 69.
3. While Bob Lintz was still at the Parma plant, it cost GM $795 more than Ford to produce a vehicle, $396 of which was attributed to GM's stamping plants. GM's contract with the International UAW, to which Parma and all GM's other facilities had to adhere, provided union members 95 percent of their take-home pay for up to three years in the event they were laid off. That would have cost the corporation $4 billion over the three-year agreement. In addition, UAW members received wage increases of 17 percent, bringing union wages and benefits to $36.60/hour.

Case 14 References

1. "Johnson and Johnson Homepage—1998 Fact Book," http://www.jnj.com/who_is_jnj/factbook/98fb_index .html, April 3, 1999.
2. Jones, Gladys Montgomery. "Framing the Future: How Johnson and Johnson Executives Keep in Touch with a Changing Marketplace—and One Another." *Continental Inflight Magazine*, March 1999, pp. 39–41.
3. "Johnson and Johnson Homepage—History," http://www.jnj.com/who_is_jnj/hist_index.html, April 3, 1999.
4. Hartley, Robert F. "Contrast—Johnson & Johnson's Tylenol: Great Crisis Management in Regaining Public Trust," *Management Mistakes and Successes*. New York: Wiley, pp. 330–344.
5. Ibid.
6. Langreth, Robert, and Winslow, Ron. "Johnson & Johnson Faces Question: Is It Merely an Unwieldy Anachronism?" *Wall Street Journal*, March 5, 1999, pp. B1, B4.
7. "Is KM Just Good Information Management?" *Financial Times* (London), March 8, 1999, p. 2.
8. www.hoovers.com.
9. Jones, op. cit.
10. Ibid.
11. Ibid.
12. Ibid.
13. Ibid.
14. Ibid.
15. Ibid.
16. Langreth and Winslow, op. cit.
17. Ibid.

Case 19 References

1. Canavan, Patrick. "Motorola: Agility for the Whole Organization," *Human Resource Planning*, September 1998, p. 13(1).
2. "Motorola Homepage—Timeline," http://www.mot.com/General/Timeline/timeln24.html, March 4, 1999.
3. "Managing People: Nicely Does It," *The Economist*, March 19, 1994, p. 84. "Motorola Homepage—Culture," http://www.mot.com/Employment/stand.htm, March 19, 1999.
4. "Organizational Culture Alignment," http://www.msdev.com/culture.htm, March 7, 1999.
5. Ibid.
6. Roth, Daniel. "From Poster Boy to Whipping Boy: Burying Motorola," *Fortune*, July 6, 1998, p. 28(2).
7. Ibid.
8. Cane, Alan. "Nokia Seizes Top Spot in Mobile Phones," *Financial Times* (London), February 8, 1999, p. 22.
9. Ibid.
10. Peltz, Michael. "Hard Cell," *Worth*, March 1999, pp. 45–47.
11. Mossberg, Walter. "Cures for PC Boredom: A Truly Global Phone and a Better Palm Pilot," *Wall Street Journal*, March 11, 1999, p. B1.
12. Peltz, op. cit.

References for Integrative Case

1. Karen Starr. "Dream On! Meet Joe Liemandt, http://www.trilogy.com/news-events/ar-detail.asp?id=77, *SellingPower*, October 1, 1997.
2. Robert Reich. "The Company of the Future," http://www.fastcompany.com/online/19/comfuture .html, *Fast Company*, November 1998.
3. Ibid.

4. Josh McHugh. "Holy Cow: No One's Done This," http://www.forbes.com/forbes/060396/mchugh.htm, *Forbes*, June 3, 1996.

5. Ibid.

6. Starr, op. cit.

7. Ibid.

8. McHugh, op. cit.

9. Ibid.

10. Starr, op. cit.

11. James Kim. "Software Pioneers Ease Pricing Process," http://www.trilogy.com/news-events/ar-detail.asp?id=74, *USA Today*, February 24, 1998.

12. Starr, op. cit.

13. McHugh, op. cit.

14. Starr, op. cit.

15. Ibid.

16. Ibid.

17. Ibid.

18. Ibid.

19. McHugh, op. cit.

20. Starr, op. cit.

21. Ibid.

22. Ibid.

23. Kim Girard. "Want to See that Desk in 3-D? Virtual Office Software May Boost Furniture Sales," *Computerworld*, April 6, 1998, p. 55.

24. Jim Kerstetter. "Trilogy Waves 'Buy-Buy,'" *PC Week*, September 14, 1998.

25. "Trilogy Homepage—Culture," http://www.trilogy.com/careers/college/culture.html, April 15, 1999.

26. Chuck Salter. "Insanity Inc.," http://www.fastcompany.com/online/21/insanityhtml, *Fast Company*, January 2, 1999.

27. Starr, op. cit.

28. Ibid.

29. Evan Ramstad. "How Trilogy Software Trains Its Recruits to Be Risk Takers," *Wall Street Journal*, September 21, 1998, p. A1, A10.

30. Michael A. Verespej. "Do Anything You Want," *Industry Week*, November 16, 1998, p. 14.

31. Salter, op. cit.

32. Ibid.

33. Ibid.

34. Ibid.

35. Ibid.

36. Ramstad, op. cit.

37. Salter, op. cit.

38. Ibid.

39. Ibid.

40. Ramstad, op. cit.

41. Ibid.

42. McHugh, op. cit.

43. Salter, op. cit.

44. Ramstad, op. cit.

45. Verespej, op. cit.

46. Salter, op. cit.

47. Ibid.

48. McHugh, op. cit.

49. "Baan Extends Its Reach: Sales Software to Join Manufacturing Suite," *Information Week*, December 2, 1996, p. 108.

50. McHugh, op. cit.

51. Ibid.

52. Daniel Lyons. "The Soul of a Gen-X Entrepreneur," *Forbes*, November 30, 1998.

53. Daniel Lyons. "The New Face of Artificial Intelligence," *Forbes*, November 30, 1998.

54. Lori Hawkins. "Trilogy Software Spins Off College Recruiting Program," *Knight Ridder/Tribune Business News*, January 13, 1999.

55. Barb Cole-Gomolski. "Web Service to Match IT Jobs, Grads," *Computerworld*, January 11, 1999, p. 20.

56. "Finding the Next Generation," *PC Week*, February 22, 1999, p. 98.

57. McHugh, op. cit.

58. Ibid.

Glossary

Ability A person's existing capacity to perform the various tasks needed for a given job.

Accommodation or **smoothing** Involves playing down differences and finding areas of agreement.

Achievement-oriented leadership Emphasizes setting challenging goals, stressing excellence in performance, and showing confidence in people's ability to achieve high standards of performance.

Action research The process of systematically collecting data on an organization, feeding it back for action planning, and evaluating results by collecting and reflecting on more data.

Active listening Encouraging people to say what they really mean.

Adhocracy An organizational structure that emphasizes shared, decentralized decision making; extreme horizontal specialization; few levels of management; the virtual absence of formal controls; and few rules, policies, and procedures.

Affective component The component of an attitude that reflects the specific feelings regarding the personal impact of the antecedents.

Agency theory Suggests that public corporations can function effectively even though its managers are self-interested.

Alternative dispute resolution Involves a neutral third party who helps others resolve negotiation impasses and disputes.

Anchoring and adjustment heuristic Bases a decision on incremental adjustments to an initial value determined by historical precedent or some reference point.

Aptitude The capability of learning something.

Arbitration When a neutral third party acts as judge with the power to issue a decision binding on all parties.

Artificial intelligence (AI) Studies how computers can be programmed to think like the human brain.

Associative choices Decisions which can be loosely linked to nagging continual problems but which were not specifically developed to solve the problem.

Attitude Predisposition to respond in a positive or negative way to someone or something in one's environment.

Attribution theory The attempt to understand the cause of an event, assess responsibility for outcomes of the event, and assess the personal qualities of the people involved.

Authoritarianism The tendency to adhere rigidly to conventional values and to obey recognized authority.

Authoritative command Uses formal authority to end conflict.

Authority decisions Made by the manager or team leader without involving others using information he or she possesses.

Automation Allows machines to do work previously accomplished by people.

Availability heuristic Bases a decision on recent events relating to the situation at hand.

Avoidance Involves pretending the conflict does not really exist.

Bargaining zone The zone between one party's minimum reservation point and the other party's maximum reservation point in a negotiating situation.

Behavioral component An intention to behave in a certain way based on a person's specific feelings or attitudes.

Behavioral decision theory Views decision makers as acting only in terms of what they perceive about a given situation.

Behavioral perspective Assumes that leadership is central to performance and other outcomes.

Behaviorally anchored rating scales (BARS) A performance appraisal approach that describes observable job behaviors, each of which is evaluated to determine good versus bad performance.

Beliefs Ideas about someone or something and the conclusions people draw about them.

Benefit cycle A pattern of successful adjustment followed by further improvements.

Brainstorming Generating ideas through "free-wheeling" discussion and without criticism.

Bureaucracy An ideal form of organization whose characteristics were defined by the German sociologist Max Weber.

Career planning Creates long-term congruence between individual goals and organizational career opportunities.

Career planning and development Working with managers and/or HR experts on career issues.

Career plateau A position from which someone is unlikely to move to advance to a higher level of responsibility.

Career stages Different points of work responsibility and achievement through which people pass during the course of their work lives.

Case study An in-depth analysis of one or a small number of settings.

Causality The assumption that change in the independent variable has caused change in the dependent variable.

Central tendency error Occurs when managers lump everyone together around the average, or middle, category.

Centralization The degree to which the authority to make decisions is restricted to higher levels of management.

Centralized communication networks Networks that link group members through a central control point.

Certain environments Provide full information on the expected results for decision-making alternatives.

Change agents People who take action to change the behavior of people and systems.

Changing The stage in which specific actions are taken to create a change.

Channels The pathways through which messages are communicated.

Charismatic leaders Those leaders who, by force of their personal abilities, are capable of having a profound and extraordinary effect on followers.

Classical conditioning A form of learning through association that involves the manipulation of stimuli to influence behavior.

Classical decision theory Views decision makers as acting only in terms of what they perceive about a given situation.

Coercive power The extent to which a manager can use the "right of command" to control other people.

Cognitive components The components of an attitude that are the beliefs, opinions, knowledge, or information a person possesses.

Cognitive dissonance Describes a state of inconsistency between an individual's attitude and behavior.

Cohesiveness The degree to which members are attracted to a group and motivated to remain a part of it.

Collaboration Involves recognition that something is wrong and needs attention through problem solving.

Collateral organization Involves a representative set of members in periodic small-group, problem-solving sessions.

Communication The process of sending and receiving symbols with attached meanings.

Communication channels The pathways through which messages are communicated.

Competition Seeks victory by force, superior skill, or domination.

Compressed work week A work schedule that allows a full-time job to be completed in less than five full workdays.

Compromise Occurs when each party involved in a conflict gives up something of value to the other.

Conceptual skill The ability to analyze and solve complex problems.

Confirmation trap The tendency to seek confirmation for what is already thought to be true, and to not search for disconfirming information.

Conflict Occurs when parties disagree over substantive issues or when emotional antagonisms create friction between them.

Conflict resolution Occurs when the reasons for a conflict are eliminated.

Confrontation meeting An OD intervention designed to help determine how an organization might be improved and to start action toward such improvement.

Conglomerates Firms that own several different unrelated businesses.

Consensus A group decision that has the expressed support of most members.

Consideration A highly considerate leader is sensitive to people's feelings and tries to make things pleasant for the followers.

Constructive stress Stress that has a positive impact on attitudes and performance.

Consultative decisions Decisions made by one individual after seeking input from or consulting with members of a group.

Content theories Profiles different needs that may motivate individual behavior.

Contingency approach Seeks ways to meet the needs of different management situations.

Continuous improvement The belief that anything and everything done in the workplace should be continually improved.

Continuous reinforcement A reinforcement schedule that administers a reward each time a desired behavior occurs.

Contrast effects Occur when an individual's characteristics are contrasted with those of others recently encountered who rank higher or lower on the same characteristics.

Control The set of mechanisms used to keep actions and outputs within predetermined limits.

Controlling Monitoring performance and taking any needed corrective action.

Coordination The set of mechanisms used in an organization to link the actions of its subunits into a consistent pattern.

Corporate governance The oversight of management decisions by Boards of Directors.

Countercultures Patterns of values and philosophies that outwardly reject those of the larger organization or social system.

Creativity Generates unique and novel responses to problems and opportunities.

Critical incident diary A method of performance appraisal that records incidents of unusual success or failure in a given performance aspect.

Cross-functional team Brings together persons from different functions to work on a common task.

Cultural intelligence The ability to identify, understand, and act effectively in cross-cultural situations.

Cultural relativism The suggestion that ethical behavior is determined by its cultural context.

Cultural symbol Any object, act, or event that serves to transmit cultural meaning.

Culture The learned and shared ways of thinking and acting among a group of people or society.

Decentralization The degree to which the authority to make decisions is given to lower levels in an organization's hierarchy.

Decentralized communication networks Networks that link all group members directly with one another.

Decision making The process of choosing a course of action to deal with a problem.

Deficit cycle A pattern of deteriorating performance that is followed by even further deterioration.

Delphi technique Involves generating decision-making alternatives through a series of survey questionnaires.

Demographic characteristics Background variables (e.g., age, gender) that help shape what a person becomes over time.

Destructive stress Stress that has a negative impact on both attitudes and performance.

Developmental approaches Systematic models of ways in which personality develops across time.

Directive leadership Spells out the what and how of subordinates' tasks

Distributed leadership The sharing of responsibility for meeting group task and maintenance needs.

Distributive justice The degree to which all people are treated the same under a policy.

Distributive negotiation Negotiation in which the focus is on positions staked out or declared by the parties involved who are each trying to claim certain portions of the available pie.

Diversity-consensus dilemma The tendency for diversity in groups to create process difficulties even as it offers improved potential for problem solving.

Divisional departmentation The grouping of individuals and resources by product, territories, services, clients, or legal entities.

Dogmatism Leads a person to see the world as a threatening place and regard authority as absolute.

Domestic multiculturalism Cultural diversity within a national population.

Dysfunctional conflict Works to the group's or organization's disadvantage.

Effective communication When the intended meaning equals the perceived meaning.

Effective groups Groups that achieve high levels of task performance, member satisfaction, and team viability.

Effective manager Leader of a team that consistently achieves high performance goals.

Efficient communication Communication that is low cost in its use of resources.

Emotional adjustment traits These traits measure how much an individual experiences emotional distress or displays unacceptable acts.

Emotional conflict Conflict that involves interpersonal difficulties that arise over feelings of anger, mistrust, dislike, fear, resentment, and the like.

Emotional intelligence The ability to manage oneself and one's relationships effectively.

Employee assistance programs Provide help for employees that are experiencing stressful personal problems.

Employee involvement teams Members of such teams meet regularly to examine work-related problems and opportunities.

Empowerment The process that allows individuals and groups to make decisions affecting themselves and their work.

Environmental complexity The magnitude of the problems and opportunities in the organization's environment as evidenced by the degree of richness, interdependence, and uncertainty.

Equity theory Adams' theory, which posits that people will act to eliminate any felt inequity in the rewards received for their work in comparison with others.

ERG theory Alderfer's theory, which identifies existence, relatedness, and growth needs.

Escalating commitment The tendency to continue a previously chosen course of action even when feedback suggests that it is failing.

ESOPs Like profit sharing, ESOPs are based on the total organization's performance, but measured in terms of stock price.

Ethical absolutism Assumption that a single moral standard applies to all cultures.

Ethical behavior Behavior that is morally accepted as "good" and "right."

Ethical dilemmas Situations that require a person to choose among actions that offer possible benefits while also violating ethical standards.

Ethics leadership Leadership with high moral standards.

Existence needs Desires for physiological and material well-being.

Expatriate A person who works and lives in a foreign country for an extended time.

Expectancy The probability that work effort will be followed by performance accomplishment.

Expectancy theory Vroom's theory that argues that work motivation is determined by individual beliefs regarding effort/performance relationships and work outcomes.

Expert power The ability to control another's behavior because of the possession of knowledge, experience, or judgment that the other person does not have but needs.

External adaptation Reaching goals and dealing with outsiders. Issues concerned are the tasks to be accomplished, the methods used to achieve the goals, and methods of coping with success and failure.

Extinction The withdrawal of the reinforcing consequences for a given behavior.

Extrinsic rewards Rewards given to the individual by some other person in the work setting.

Feedback The process of communicating how one feels about something another person has done or said.

Field survey A research design that relies on the use of some form of questionnaire for the primary purpose of describing and/or predicting some phenomenon.

FIRO-B theory Examines differences in how people relate to one another based on their needs to express and receive feelings of inclusion, control, and affection.

Flexible benefit plans Pay systems that allow workers to select benefits according to their individual needs.

Flexible manufacturing system Uses adaptive technology and integrated job designs to easily shift production among alternative products.

Flexible working hours Work schedules that give employees some daily choice in scheduling arrival and departure times from work.

Force-coercion strategy Uses authority, rewards, and punishments to create change.

Forced distribution A method of performance appraisal that uses a small number of performance categories, such as "very good," "good," "adequate," and "very poor" and forces a certain proportion of people into each.

Formal channels Communication pathways that follow the official chain of command.

Formal groups Officially designated groups for a specific organizational purpose.

Formalization The written documentation of work rules, policies, and procedures.

Functional conflict Results in positive benefits to the group.

Functional departmentation The grouping of individuals by skill, knowledge, and action yields.

Functional silos problem When persons working in different functions fail to communicate and interact with one another.

Fundamental attribution error The tendency to underestimate the influence of situational factors and to overestimate the influence of personal factors in evaluating someone else's behavior.

Gain sharing A pay system that links pay and performance by giving the workers the opportunity to share in productivity gains through increased earnings.

Garbage can model Views the main components of the choice process—problems, solutions, participants, and choice situations—as all mixed up together in the garbage can of the organization.

Glass ceiling effect A hidden barrier limiting advancement of women and minorities in organizations.

Globalization Involves growing worldwide interdependence of resource suppliers, product markets, and business competition.

Global manager A manager who has the international awareness and cultural sensitivity needed to work well across national borders.

Global organizational learning The ability to gather from the world at large the knowledge required for long-term organizational adaptation.

Global outsourcing Domestic jobs are replaced with contract workers hired in other countries.

Goal setting The process of developing and setting motivational performance objectives.

Grafting The process of acquiring individuals, units, and/or firms to bring in useful knowledge to the organization.

Grapevine The network of friendships and acquaintances that transfers information.

Graphic rating scale A scale that lists a variety of dimensions thought to be related to high-performance outcomes in a given job and that one is expected to exhibit.

Group decisions Decisions that are made by all members of the group.

Group dynamics The forces operating in groups that affect the ways members work together.

Groups Involves two or more people working together regularly to achieve common goals.

Groupthink The tendency of cohesive group members to lose their critical evaluative capabilities.

Growth needs Desires for continued personal growth and development.

Halo effect Occurs when one attribute of a person or situation is used to develop an overall impression of the person or situation.

Halo error Results when one person rates another person on several different dimensions and gives a similar rating for each one.

Heuristics Simplifying strategies or "rules of thumb" used to make decisions.

Hierarchy of needs theory Maslow's theory that offers a pyramid of physiological, safety, social, esteem, and self-actualization needs.

High-context cultures   Words convey only part of a message, while the rest of the message must be inferred from body language and additional contextual cues.

Higher-order needs   Esteem and self-actualization in Maslow's hierarchy.

High-performance organization (HPO)   An organization that is intentionally designed to bring out the best in people and produce sustainable organizational results.

Hindsight trap   A tendency to overestimate the degree to which an event that has already taken place could have been predicted.

Horizontal specialization   A division of labor through the formation of work units or groups within an organization.

House's path–goal theory of leadership   Assumes that a leader's key function is to adjust his or her behaviors to complement situational contingencies.

Human capital   The economic value of people with job-relevant abilities, knowledge, ideas, energies, and commitments.

Human resource strategic planning   The process of hiring capable, motivated people to carry out the organization's mission and strategy.

Human resources   The people who do the work that helps organizations fulfill their missions.

Human skill   The ability to work well with other people.

Hygiene factors   Factors in a job context, the work setting, that promote job dissatisfaction.

Inclusivity   The degree to which the culture respects and values diversity and is open to anyone who can perform a job, regardless of their diversity attributes.

Individualism-collectivism   The tendency of a culture's members to emphasize individual self-interests or group relationships.

Influence   A behavioral response to the exercise of power.

Informal channels   Do not follow the chain of command.

Informal groups   Unofficial groups that emerge to serve special interests.

Information power   Access to and/or control of information.

Information technology   The combination of machines, artifacts, procedures, and systems used to gather, store, analyze, and disseminate information to translate it into knowledge.

Initiating structure   This kind of leader is concerned with spelling out the task requirements and clarifying other aspects of the work agenda.

Innovation   The process of creating new ideas and putting them in practice.

Instrumental values   Values that reflect a person's beliefs about the means for achieving desired ends.

Instrumentality   The probability that performance will lead to various work outcomes.

Integrative negotiation   Negotiation in which the focus is on the merits of the issues, and the parties involved try to enlarge the available "pie" rather than stake claims to certain portions of it.

Intellectual capital   The sum total of knowledge, expertise, and energy available from organizational members.

Interactional justice   The degree to which people are treated with dignity and respect.

Interfirm alliances   Announced cooperative agreements of joint ventures between two independent firms.

Intergroup conflict   Occurs among groups in an organization.

Intergroup dynamics   Relationships between groups cooperating and competing with one another.

Intergroup team building   Helps groups improve their working relationships with one another and experience improved group effectiveness.

Intermittent reinforcement   A reinforcement schedule that rewards behavior only periodically.

Internal integration   The creation of a collective identity and way of working and living together within an organization.

Interorganizational conflict   Occurs between organizations.

Interpersonal conflict   Occurs between two or more individuals in opposition to each other.

Intrapersonal conflict   Occurs within the individual because of actual or perceived pressures from incompatible goals or expectations.

Intrinsic rewards Rewards received by the individual directly through task performance.

Intuition The ability to know or recognize quickly the possibilities of a situation.

Job analysis The procedure used to collect and classify information about tasks the organization needs to complete.

Job burnout Loss of interest in and satisfaction with a job due to stressful working conditions.

Job characteristics model Identifies five core job characteristics of special importance to job design—skill variety, task identity, task significance, autonomy, and feedback.

Job design The process of defining job tasks and the work arrangements to accomplish them.

Job enlargement Increases task variety by adding new tasks of similar difficulty to a job.

Job enrichment Increases job content by giving workers more responsibility for planning and evaluating duties.

Job migration The transferring of jobs from one country to another.

Job redesign Creates long-term congruence between individual goals and organizational career opportunities.

Job rotation Increases task variety by shifting workers among jobs involving tasks of similar difficulty.

Job satisfaction The degree to which individuals feel positively or negatively about their jobs.

Job sharing Allows one full-time job to be divided among two or more persons.

Job simplification Standardizes tasks and employs people in very routine jobs.

KISS principle Stands for "keep it short and simple."

Knowledge workers Employees whose major task is to produce new knowledge, typically through computer-oriented means.

Law of contingent reinforcement The view that, for a reward to have maximum reinforcing value, it must be delivered only if the desired behavior is exhibited.

Law of effect The observation that behavior which results in a pleasing outcome is likely to be repeated; behavior that results in an unpleasant outcome is not likely to be repeated.

Law of immediate reinforcement The more immediate the delivery of a reward after the occurrence of a desirable behavior, the greater the reinforcing effect on behavior.

Leader match training Leaders are trained to diagnose the situation to match their high and low LPC scores with situational control.

Leadership A special case of interpersonal influence that gets an individual or group to do what the leader wants done.

Leadership prototype An image people have in their minds of what a model leader should look like.

Leading Creates enthusiasm to work hard to accomplish tasks successfully.

Learning An enduring change in behavior that results from experience.

Least preferred coworker (LPC) scale A measure of a person's leadership style based on a description of the person with whom respondents have been able to work least well.

Legitimate power The extent to which a manager can use the "right of command" to control other people.

Leniency error The tendency to give relatively high ratings to virtually everyone.

Line units Work groups that conduct the major business of the organization.

Long-term/short-term orientation The degree to which a culture emphasizes long-term or short-term thinking.

Low-context cultures Cultures in which messages are expressed mainly by spoken and written words.

Low differentiation errors What occurs when raters restrict themselves to a small part of the rating scale.

Lower-order needs Physiological, safety, and social needs in Maslow's hierarchy.

Lump-sum increase A pay system in which people elect to receive their wage or salary increases in one or more "lump-sum" payments.

Maintenance activities Activities that support the emotional life of the group as an ongoing social system.

Management by objectives (MBO) A process of joint goal setting between a supervisor and a subordinate.

Management philosophy A philosophy that links key goal-related issues with key collaboration issues to come up with general ways by which the firm will manage its affairs.

Managerial mind-set An attitude or frame of mind about management.

Managerial script A series of well-known routines for problem identification and alternative generation and analysis common to managers within a firm.

Managers People who are formally responsible for supporting the work efforts of other people.

Masculinity-femininity The degree to which a society values assertiveness or relationships.

Matrix departmentation A combination of functional and divisional patterns wherein an individual is assigned to more than one type of unit.

MBWA Involves getting out of the office to directly communicate with others.

Mechanistic type (machine bureaucracy) Emphasizes vertical specialization and control with impersonal coordination and a heavy reliance on standardization, formalization, rules, policies, and procedures.

Mediation A neutral third party tries to engage the parties in a negotiated solution through persuasion and rational argument.

Merit pay A compensation system that bases an individual's salary or wage increase on a measure of the person's performance accomplishment during a specific time period.

Mimicry The copying of the successful practices of others.

Mission statements Written statements of organizational purpose.

Mixed messages Misunderstandings that occur when a person's words say one thing while his or her nonverbal cues say something else.

Monochronic culture Cultures in which people tend to do one thing at a time.

Motivating potential score The extent to which the core characteristics of a job create motivating conditions.

Motivation Forces within an individual that account for the level, direction, and persistence of effort expended at work.

Motivator factors In job content, the tasks people actually do, are sources of job satisfaction.

Multiculturalism Pluralism and respect for diversity in the workplace.

Multicultural workforces Include workers from diverse ethnic backgrounds and nationalities.

Multinational corporation A business with extensive international operations in more than one country.

Multiskilling Team members are trained in skills to perform different jobs.

Mum effect Occurs when people are reluctant to communicate bad news.

Need for achievement (nAch) The desire to do better, solve problems, or master complex tasks.

Need for affiliation (nAff) The desire for friendly and warm relations with others.

Need for power (nPower) The desire to control others and influence their behavior.

Negative reinforcement The withdrawal of negative consequences, which tends to increase the likelihood of repeating the behavior in similar settings; also known as avoidance.

Negotiation The process of making joint decisions when the parties involved have different preferences.

New leadership Emphasizes charismatic and transformational leadership approaches and various aspects of vision related to them, as well as self-directing work teams.

Noise Anything that interferes with the effectiveness of communication.

Nominal group technique Involves structured rules for generating and prioritizing ideas.

Nonprogrammed decisions Decisions created to deal uniquely with a problem at hand.

Nonverbal communication Communication that takes place through facial expressions, body movements, eye contact, and other physical gestures.

Norms Rules or standards for the behavior of group members.

Offshoring Contracting out or outsourcing to workers in foreign countries.

Open systems Systems that transform human and material resources into finished goods and services.

Operant conditioning The process of controlling behavior by manipulating, or "operating" on, its consequences.

Operations technology The combination of resources, knowledge, and techniques that creates a product or service output for an organization.

Organic type A professional bureaucracy that emphasizes horizontal specialization, extensive use of personal coordination, and loose rules, policies, and procedures.

Organization charts Diagrams that depict the formal structures of organizations.

Organizational behavior (OB) The study of individuals and groups in organizations.

Organizational behavior modification (OB Mod) The systematic reinforcement of desirable work behavior and the nonreinforcement or punishment of unwanted work behavior.

Organizational communication The process by which information is exchanged in the organizational setting.

Organizational (or corporate) culture The system of shared actions, values, and beliefs that develops within an organization and guides the behavior of its members.

Organizational design The process of choosing and implementing a structural configuration for an organization.

Organizational development (OD) The application of behavioral science knowledge in a long-range effort to improve an organization's ability to cope with change in its external environment and increase its problem-solving capabilities.

Organizational development interventions Activities initiated to support planned change and improve work effectiveness.

Organizational effectiveness Sustainable high performance in accomplishing mission and objectives.

Organizational governance The pattern of authority, influence, and acceptable managerial behavior established at the top of the organization.

Organizational learning The process of acquiring knowledge and using information to adapt to successfully changing circumstances.

Organizational myth A commonly held cause-effect relationship or assertion that cannot be empirically supported.

Organizational politics The management of influence to obtain ends not sanctioned by the organization or to obtain sanctioned ends through nonsanctioned means and the art of creative compromise among competing interests.

Organizational strategy The process of positioning the organization in the competitive environment and implementing actions to compete successfully.

Organizational transformation The redesign of organizations to streamline, gain flexibility, and utilize new technologies for high performance.

Organizations Collections of people working together to achieve a common purpose.

Organized anarchy A form or division in a firm in a transition characterized by very rapid change and a lack of a legitimate hierarchy.

Organizing Dividing up tasks and arranging resources to accomplish them.

Output controls Controls that focus on desired targets and allow managers to use their own methods for reaching defined targets.

Output goals The goals that define the type of business an organization is in.

Outsourcing jobs Occurs when people outside a firm are contracted to perform scheduled job activities.

Paired comparison A comparative method of performance appraisal whereby each person is directly compared with every other person.

Participative leadership Focuses on consulting with subordinates and seeking and taking their suggestions into account before making decisions.

Perception The process through which people receive, organize, and interpret information from their environment.

Performance appraisal A process of systematically evaluating performance and providing feedback on which performance adjustments can be made.

Performance gap A discrepancy between the desired and actual state of affairs.

Permanent part-time work Permanent work of fewer hours than the standard week.

Personal bias error Occurs when a rater allows specific biases, such as racial, age, or gender, to enter into performance appraisal.

Personality   Represents the overall profile or combination of characteristics that capture the unique nature of a person as that person reacts and interacts with others.

Personality dynamics   The ways in which an individual integrates and organizes social traits, values and motives, personal conceptions, and emotional adjustment.

Planned change   Intentional and occurs with a change agent's intentional direction.

Planning   Sets objectives and identifies the actions needed to achieve them.

Polychronic culture   A culture in which people tend to do more than one thing at a time.

Positive organizational behavior   The study and application of positively-oriented strengths and capacities.

Positive reinforcement   The administration of positive consequences that tend to increase the likelihood of repeating the behavior in similar settings.

Power   The ability to get someone else to do something you want done or the ability to make things happen or get things done the way you want.

Power distance   The willingness of a culture to accept status and power differences among its members.

Problem solving   Uses information to resolve disputes.

Procedural justice   The degree to which policies and procedures are properly followed.

Process consultation   Helps a group improve on such things as norms, cohesiveness, decision-making methods, communication, conflict, and task and maintenance activities.

Process controls   Controls that attempt to specify the manner in which tasks are to be accomplished.

Process innovations   Innovations introducing into operations new and better ways of doing things.

Process power   Control over methods of production and analysis.

Process reengineering   The total rethinking and redesign of organizational process to improve performance and innovation; involves analyzing, streamlining, and reconfiguring actions and tasks to achieve work goals.

Process theories   Theories that seek to understand the thought processes determining behavior.

Product innovations   Innovations that introduce new goods or services to better meet customer needs.

Profit-sharing plans   Reward employees based on the entire organization's performance.

Programmed decisions   Decisions that are determined by past experience as appropriate for a problem at hand.

Projection   The assignment of personal attributes to other individuals.

Punishment   The administration of negative consequences that tend to reduce the likelihood of repeating the behavior in similar settings.

Quality circle   Members of a quality circle meet regularly to find ways for continuous improvement of quality operations.

Quality of work life (QWL)   The overall quality of human experiences in the workplace.

Ranking   A comparative technique of performance appraisal that involves rank ordering of each individual from best to worst on each performance dimension.

Rational persuasion   The ability to control another's behavior because, through the individual's efforts, the person accepts the desirability of an offered goal and a reasonable way of achieving it.

Rational persuasion strategy   Uses facts, special knowledge, and rational argument to create change.

Realistic job previews   Previews which provide applicants with an objective description of a job and organization.

Recency error   A biased rating that develops by allowing the individual's most recent behavior to speak for his or her overall performance on a particular dimension.

Recruitment   The process of attracting the best qualified individuals to apply for a job.

Referent power   The ability to control another's behavior because of the individual's desire to identify with the power source.

Refreezing   The stage in which changes are reinforced and stabilized.

Reinforcement   The administration of a consequence as a result of behavior.

Reinforcement theories   They emphasize the means through which operant conditioning takes place.

Relatedness needs   Desires for satisfying interpersonal relationships.

Reliability   The consistency and stability of a score from a measurement scale.

Representative power   The formal right conferred by the firm to speak for and to a potentially important group.

Representativeness heuristic   Bases a decision on similarities between the situation at hand and stereotypes of similar occurrences.

Resistance to change   An attitude or behavior that shows unwillingness to make or support a change.

Restricted communication networks   Link subgroups that disagree with one another's positions.

Reward power   The extent to which a manager can use extrinsic and intrinsic rewards to control other people.

Risk environments   Business environments that provide probabilities regarding expected results for decision-making alternatives.

Rites   Standardized and recurring activities used at special times to influence the behaviors and understanding of organizational members.

Rituals   System of rites.

Role   A set of expectations for a team member or person in a job.

Role ambiguity   Occurs when someone is uncertain about what is expected of him or her.

Role conflict   Occurs when someone is unable to respond to role expectations that conflict with one another.

Role negotiation   A process through which individuals clarify expectations about what each should be giving and receiving as group members.

Role overload   Occurs when too much work is expected of the individual.

Role underload   Occurs when too little work is expected of the individual.

Romance of leadership   People attribute romantic, almost magical qualities to leadership.

Sagas   Embellished heroic accounts of the story of the founding of an organization.

Satisficing   Decision making that chooses the first alternative that appears to give an acceptable or satisfactory resolution of the problem.

Scanning   Looking outside the firm and bringing back useful solutions to problems.

Schemas   Cognitive frameworks that represent organized knowledge about a given concept or stimulus developed through experience.

Scientific method   A key part of the OB research foundations, which involves four steps: the research question or problem, hypothesis generation or formulation, the research design, and data gathering, analysis, and interpretation.

Selection   The series of steps from initial applicant screening to hiring.

Selective perception   The tendency to single out for attention those aspects of a situation or person that reinforce or emerge and are consistent with existing beliefs, values, and needs.

Self-concept   The view individuals have of themselves as physical, social, and spiritual or moral beings.

Self-directing work teams   Teams that are empowered to make decisions about planning, doing, and evaluating their work.

Self-fulfilling prophecy   The tendency to create or find in another situation or individual that which one has expected to find.

Self-managing teams   Same as self-directing work teams.

Self-monitoring   Reflects a person's ability to adjust his or her behavior to external, situational (environmental) factors.

Self-serving bias   The tendency to deny personal responsibility for performance problems but to accept personal responsibility for performance success.

Shamrock organizations   Firms that operate with a core group of permanent workers supplemented by outside contractors and part-time workers.

Shaping   The creation of a new behavior by the positive reinforcement of successive approximations to the desired behavior.

Shared-power strategy   Uses participative methods and emphasizes common values to create change.

Simple design   An organization configuration involving one or two ways of specializing individuals and units.

Situational control   The extent to which leaders can determine what their groups are going to do and what the outcomes of their actions and decisions are going to be.

Skill-based pay   A system that rewards people for acquiring and developing job-relevant skills in number and variety relevant to the organization's need.

Social capital   The performance potential represented in the relationships maintained among people at work.

Social facilitation   The tendency for one's behavior to be influenced by the presence of others in a group.

Social information processing theory   An approach that believes that individual needs and task perceptions result from socially constructed realities.

Social loafing   Occurs when people work less hard in groups than they would individually.

Social responsibility   The obligation of organizations to behave in ethical and moral ways.

Social traits   Surface-level traits that reflect the way a person appears to others when interacting in various social settings.

Socialization   Orienting new employees to the firm and its work units.

Societal goals   Goals that reflect the intended contributions of an organization to the broader society.

Sociotechnical systems   Organizational systems that integrate people and technology into high-performance work settings.

Sources and types of values   Parents, friends, teachers, and external reference groups can all influence individual values.

Span of control   The number of individuals reporting to a supervisor.

Staff units   Groups that assist the line units by performing specialized services for the organization.

Stakeholders   People and groups with an interest or "stake" in the performance of the organization.

Standardization   The degree to which the range of actions in a job or series of jobs is limited.

Status congruence   The consistency between a person's status within and outside of a group.

Stereotyping   When one thinks of an individual as belonging to a group or category and the characteristics commonly associated with the group or category are assigned to the individual.

Stimulus   Something that incites action.

Strategy   The process of positioning the organization in the competitive environment and implementing actions to compete successfully.

Stress   Tension from extraordinary demands, constraints, or opportunities.

Stress management   An active approach to deal with stress that is influencing behavior.

Stress prevention   Minimizing the potential for stress to occur.

Stressors   Things that cause stress.

Strictness error   The tendency to give everyone a low rating.

Structural redesign   Involves realigning the structure of the organization or major subsystem in order to improve performance.

Subcultures   Unique patterns of values and philosophies within a group that are not consistent with the dominant culture of the larger organization or social system.

Substantive conflict   Fundamental disagreement over ends or goals to be pursued and the means for their accomplishment.

Substitutes for leadership   Make a leader's influence either unnecessary or redundant in that they replace a leader's influence.

Supportive leadership   Focuses on subordinate needs, well-being, and promotion of a friendly work climate.

Survey feedback   Begins with the collection of data via questionnaires from organization members or a representative sample of them.

Sweatshops   Employ people that must work under adverse labor conditions

Synergy   The creation of a whole that is greater than the sum of its parts.

Systems goals   Goals concerned with conditions within the organization that are expected to increase its survival potential.

Task activities   Actions that directly contribute to the performance of important group tasks.

Task performance   The quantity and quality of work produced.

Team building   A collaborative way to gather and analyze data to improve teamwork.

Teams   People working actively together to achieve a common purpose for which they are all accountable.

Teamwork   Occurs when group members work together in ways that utilize their skills well to accomplish a purpose.

Technical skill   An ability to perform specialized tasks.

Telecommuting   Working at home or in a remote location that uses computer and telecommunication linkages with the office.

Temporary part-time work   Temporary work of fewer hours than the standard week.

Terminal values   A person's preferences concerning the "ends" to be achieved.

Theory   A set of systematically interrelated concepts, definitions, and hypotheses that are advanced to explain and predict phenomena.

360-degree evaluation   (also called 360-degree feedback) A comprehensive approach that uses evaluations of bosses, peers, and subordinates but also self-ratings, customer ratings, and others outside the work unit.

Total quality management (TQM)   A total commitment to high-quality results, continuous improvement, and meeting customer needs.

Training   Provides the opportunity to acquire and improve job-related skills.

Trait perspectives   Assume that traits play a central role in differentiating between leaders and nonleaders or in predicting leader or organizational outcomes.

Transactional leadership   Involves leader-follower exchanges necessary for achieving routine performance agreed upon between leaders and followers.

Transformational leadership   Occurs when leaders broaden and elevate followers' interests and followers look beyond their own interests for the good of others.

Transformational change   radically shifts the fundamental character of an organization.

Two-factor theory   Herzberg's theory that identifies job context as the source of job dissatisfaction and job content as the source of job satisfaction.

Type A orientation   A personality orientation characterized by impatience, desire for achievement, and perfectionism.

Type B orientation   A personality orientation characterized by an easygoing and less competitive nature than Type A.

Uncertain environments   Business environments that provide no information to predict expected results for decision-making alternatives.

Uncertainty avoidance   The cultural tendency to be uncomfortable with uncertainty and risk in everyday life.

Unfreezing   The stage of the change process at which a situation is prepared for change.

Unplanned change   Change that occurs spontaneously and without a change agent's direction.

Valence   The value to the individual of various work outcomes.

Validity   The degree of confidence one can have in the results of a research study.

Value congruence   Occurs when individuals express positive feelings upon encountering others who exhibit values similar to their own.

Value creation   The extent to which an organization satisfies the needs of strategic constituencies.

Values   Broad preferences concerning appropriate courses of action or outcomes.

Vertical specialization   A hierarchical division of labor that distributes formal authority.

Virtual groups   Groups that work together via computer networks.

Virtual organization   An ever-shifting constellation of firms, with a lead corporation, that pool skills, resources and experiences to thrive jointly.

Virtual team   A work team that convenes and operates with its members linked together electronically via networked computers.

Wellness   Maintaining physical and mental health to better deal with stress when it occurs.

Whistleblower   Someone within the organization who exposes the wrongdoings of others in order to preserve high ethical standards.

Workforce diversity   Differences based on gender, race and ethnicity, age, and able-bodiedness.

Work-life balance   Deals with the demands from one's work and personal affairs.

Zone of indifference   The range of authoritative requests to which a subordinate is willing to respond without subjecting the directives to critical evaluation or judgment.

Notes

Chapter 1

ENDNOTES

[1] See Jeffrey Pfeffer, *The Human Equation: Building Profits by Putting People First* (Boston: Harvard Business School Press, 1998); Charles O'Reilly III and Jeffrey Pfeffer, *Hidden Value: How Great Companies Achieve Extraordinary Results with Ordinary People* (Boston: Harvard Business School Press, 2000); information on Malden Mills from Ken Maguire, "Workers Stand Up for Malden Mills," *Associated Press* (December 21, 2001), www.mit.edu. Information from Marshall Hood, "An Investment in People," *Columbus Dispatch* (April 25, 2004), p. H1.

[2] For a general overview, see Jay W. Lorsch (ed.), *Handbook of Organizational Behavior* (Englewood Cliffs, NJ: Prentice Hall, 1987).

[3] Geert Hofstede, "Cultural Constraints in Management Theories," *Academy of Management Executive* 7 (1993):81–94.

[4] John Huey, "Managing in the Midst of Chaos," *Fortune* (April 5, 1993), pp. 38–48. See also Tom Peters, *Thriving on Chaos* (New York: Knopf, 1991); Jay R. Galbraith, Edward E. Lawler III, and Associates, *Organizing for the Future: The New Logic for Managing Organizations* (San Francisco: Jossey-Bass, 1993); William H. Davidow and Michael S. Malone, *The Virtual Corporation: Structuring and Revitalizing the Corporation of the 21st Century* (New York: HarperBusiness, 1993); Charles Handy, *The Age of Unreason* (Boston: Harvard Business School Press, 1990); Charles Handy, *The Age of Paradox* (Boston: Harvard Business School Press, 1994); Peter Drucker, *Managing in a Time of Great Change* (New York: Truman Talley, 1995); Peter Drucker, *Management Challenges for the 21st Century* (New York: Harper, 1999).

[5] See Daniel H. Pink, "Free Agent Nation," *Fast Company* (December 1997); 131ff; Tom Peters, "The Brand Called You," *Fast Company* (August/September 1997).

[6] Robert B. Reich, "The Company of the Future," *Fast Company* (November 1998): p. 124ff.

[7] Based on Jay A. Conger, *Winning 'Em Over: A New Model for Managing in the Age of Persuasion* (New York: Simon & Schuster, 1998), pp. 180–181; Stewart D. Friedman, Perry Christensen, and Jessica DeGroot, "Work and Life: The End of the Zero-Sum Game," *Harvard Business Review* (November/December 1998):119–129; C. Argyris, "Empowerment: The Emperor's New Clothes," *Harvard Business Review* (May/June 1998):98–105.

[8] For more on mission statements, see Patricia Jones and Larry Kahaner, Say It and Live It: The 50 Corporate Mission Statements that Hit the Mark (New York: Currency/Doubleday, 1995); John Graham and Wendy Havlick, *Mission Statements: A Guide to the Corporate and Nonprofit Sectors* (New York: Garland, 1995).

[9] These mission statements and others are found on corporate websites.

[10] James C. Collins and Jerry I. Porras, "Building Your Company's Vision," *Harvard Business Review* (September/October 1996):65–77.

[11] Reich (1998).

[12] See Michael E. Porter, *Competitive Strategy: Techniques for Analyzing Industries and Competitors* (New York: Free Press, 1980); *Competitive Advantage: Creating and Sustaining Superior Performance* (New York: Free Press, 1986); Gary Hamel and C. K. Prahalad, "Strategic Intent," *Harvard Business Review* (May/June 1989):63–76; Richard A. D'Aveni, *Hyper Competition: Managing the Dynamics of Strategic Maneuvering* (New York: Free Press, 1994).

[13] For a discussion of the Arthur Andersen case and related ethical issues, see Terry Thomas, John R. Schermerhorn Jr., and John W. Dinehart, "Strategic Leadership of Ethical Behavior in Business," *Academy of Management Executive* X (2004).

[14] Edgar Schein, *Organizational Culture and Leadership*, 2nd ed. (San Francisco: Jossey-Bass, 1997); Edgar Schein, *The Corporate Culture Survival Guide* (San Francisco: Jossey-Bass, 1999). See also Terrence E. Daeal and Alan A. Kennedy, *Corporate Cultures: The Rites and Rituals of Corporate Life* (Reading, MA: Addison Wesley, 1982).

[15] James Collins and Jerry Porras, *Built to Last* (New York: HarperBusiness, 1994).

[16] The foundation report on diversity in the American workplace is *Workforce 2000: Work and Workers in the 21st Century* (Indianapolis: Hudson Institute, 1987). For comprehensive discussions, see Martin M. Chemers, Stuart Oskamp, and Mark A. Costanzo, *Diversity in Organizations: New Perspectives for a Changing Workplace* (Beverly Hills: Sage, 1995); Robert T. Golembiewski, *Managing Diversity in Organizations* (Tuscaloosa: University of Alabama Press, 1995).

[17] See R. Roosevelt Thomas Jr. with Marjorie I. Woodruff, *Building a House for Diversity* (New York: AMACOM, 1999); R. Roosevelt Thomas, "From Affirmative Action to Affirming Diversity," *Harvard Business Review* (March/April 1990):107–117; R. Roosevelt Thomas, *Beyond Race and Gender: Unleashing the Power of Your Total Workforce by Managing Diversity* (New York: AMACOM, 1992).

[18] See W. Richard Scott, *Organizations: Rational Natural and Open Systems,* 4th Ed. (Englewood Cliffs, NJ: Prentice-Hall, 1998).

[19] See the discussion in Gaerth Jones, *Organizational Theory and Design*, 3rd ed. (Upper Saddle River, NJ: Prentice-Hall, 2001).

[20] See the discussion in James L. Gibson, John M. Ivancevich, and James H. Donnelly Jr., *Organizations: Behavior, Structure, Processes*, 5th ed. (Homewood, IL: Richard D. Irwin, 1991).

[21] For more on the management process, see John R. Schermerhorn Jr., *Management*, 8th ed. (New York: Wiley, 2005).

[22] The review is from Henry Mintzberg, *The Nature of Managerial Work* (New York: Harper & Row, 1973). For related and further developments, see Morgan W. McCall Jr., Ann M. Morrison, and Robert L. Hannan, *Studies of Managerial Work: Results and Methods*, Technical Report No. 9 (Greensboro, NC: Center for Creative Leadership, 1978); John P. Kotter, *The General Managers* (New York: Free Press, 1982); Fred Luthans, Stuart Rosenkrantz, and Harry Hennessey, "What Do Successful Managers Really Do?" *Journal of Applied Behavioral Science* 21(2) (1985):255–270; Robert E. Kaplan, *The Warp and Woof of the General Manager's Job*, Technical Report No. 27 (Greensboro, NC: Center for Creative Leadership, 1986); Fred Luthans, Richard M. Hodgetts, and Stuart A. Rosenkrantz, *Real Managers* (New York: HarperCollins, 1988).

[23] Mintzberg (1973). See also Henry Mintzberg, *Mintzberg on Management* (New York: Free Press, 1989); "Rounding Out the Manager's Job," *Sloan Management Review* (Fall 1994):11–26.

[24] Kotter (1982); John P. Kotter, "What Effective General Managers Really Do," *Harvard Business Review* 60 (November/December 1982): 161. See Kaplan (1986).

[25] Herminia Ibarra, Managerial Networks, Teaching Note: #9-495-039, Harvard Business School Publishing, Boston, MA.

[26] Jonathan Gosling and Henry Mintzberg, "The Five Minds of a Manager," *Harvard Business Review* (November 2003):pp. ...

[27] Ibid., p.

[28] Ibid., p.

[29] Robert L. Katz, "Skills of an Effective Administrator, *Harvard Business Review* 52 (September/October 1974):94. See also Richard E. Boyatzis, *The Competent Manager: A Model for Effective Performance* (New York: Wiley, 1982).

[30] Daniel Goleman, *Emotional Intelligence* (New York: Bantam, 1995); Daniel Goleman, *Working with Emotional Intelligence* (New York: Bantam, 1998). See also Daniel Goleman "What Makes a Leader," *Harvard Business Review* (November/December 1998): 93–102; and "Leadership That Makes a Difference," *Harvard Business Review* (March/April 2000):79–90, quote from p. 80.

[31] See Peter Senge, *The Fifth Discipline* (New York: Harper, 1990); D. A. Garvin, "Building a Learning Organization," *Harvard Business Review* (November/December 1991):78–91; Chris Argyris, *On Organizational Learning*, 2nd ed. (Malden, MA: Blackwell, 1999).

[32] For a recent discussion of experiential learning, see D. Christopher Kayes, "Experiential Learning and Its Critics: Preserving the Role of Experience in Management Learning and Education," *Academy of Management Learning and Education*, 1(2), (2002):pp. 137–149.

SOURCE NOTES

Information and quotes from Sharon Shinn, "Enterprise & Education," *BizEd* (March/April, 2004), pp. 22–26.

Information from Timothy D. Schellhardt, " An Idyllic Workplace Under a Tycoon's Thumb," Wall Street Journal (November 23, 1998), p. B1; corporate website: www. sas.com.

Fred Lager, *Ben & Jerry's: The Inside Scoop* (New York: Crown, 1994). Information from Amy Merrick, "Gap Offers Unusual Look at Factory Conditions," *Wall Street Journal* (May 12, 2004), pp. A1, A12.1

Chapter 2

ENDNOTES

[1] See Jeffrey Pfeffer, *The Human Equation: Building Profits by Putting People First* (Boston: Harvard Business School Press, 1998) and Charles O'Reilly III and Jeffrey Pfeffer, *Hidden Value: How Great Companies Achieve Extraordinary Results with Ordinary People* (Boston: Harvard Business School Press, 2000).

[2] Quote from Pfeffer.

[3] See Dave Ulrich, "Intellectual Capital = Competence – Commitment," *Harvard Business Review* (Winter 1998):15–26; Jeffrey Pfeffer and John F. Veiga, "Putting People First for Organizational Success," *Academy of Management Executive* 13 (May 1999):37–48.

[4] See, for example, Robert B. Reich, "The Company of the Future," *Fast Company* (November 1998):124ff; Robert Reich, *The Future of Success* (New York: A. Knopf, 2001).

[5] See Denise M. Rousseau, "Organizational Behavior in the New Organizational Era," *Annual Review of Psychology* 48 (1997):515–546; Peter Drucker, *Management Challenges for the 21st Century* (New York: Harper, 1999).

[6] Pfeffer (1998).

[7] Developed from conversations with Dr. Barry A. Macy, Texas Tech University, Fall 2001.

[8] One perspective on the stakeholder view is offered by Thomas Donaldson and Lee Preston, "The Stakeholder Theory of the Corporation," *Academy of Management Review* 20 (1995):65–91.

[9] Thomas A. Stewart, "Planning a Career Without Managers," *Fortune* (March 20, 1995):72–80.

[10] See, for example, Philip B. Crosby, *Quality Is Still Free: Making Quality Certain in Uncertain Times* (New York: McGraw-Hill, 1995); Robert E. Cole and W. Richard Scott (eds.) *The Quality Movement and Organization Theory* (Thousand Oaks, CA: Sage, 2000).

[11] "What Makes a Company Great?" *Fortune* (October 26, 1998), p. 218.

[12] See Pfeffer (1998).

[13] Ulrich (1998).

[14] Fortune survey.

[15] See P. S. Adlere and S. Kwon, "Social Capital: Prospects for a New Concept," *Academy of Management Review*, 27 (January 2002):17–40.

[16] Bradley L. Kirksman, Kevin B. Lowe, and Dianne P. Young, "The Challenge in High Performance Work Organizations," *Journal of Leadership Studies* (2) (Spring 1998):3–15.

[17] See Peter Senge, *The Fifth Discipline* (New York: Harper, 1990); D. A. Garvin, "Building a Learning Organization," *Harvard Business Review* (November/December 1991):78–91; Danny Miller, "A Preliminary Typology of Organizational Learning: Synthesizing the Literature," *Journal of Management*, (3) (1996):485–505; Chris Argyris, *On Organizational Learning*, 2nd ed. (Malden, MA: Blackwell, 1999).

[18] Quote from Nancy Dunne, "Turbulent Times as Companies Turn on a Dime," *Financial Times* (May 13, 2004), p. 26.

[19] Edgar H. Schein, "Organizational Culture," *American Psychologist* 45 (1990):109–119. See also Edgar H. Schein, *Organizational Culture and Leadership*, 2nd ed. (San Francisco: Jossey-Bass,

1997); and *The Corporate Culture Survival Guide* (San Francisco: Jossey-Bass, 1999).

[20] A classic work is Terrence E. Deal and Alan A. Kennedy, *Corporate Cultures: The Rites and Rituals of Corporate Life* (Reading, MA: Addison-Wesley, 1982); see also James Collins and Jerry Porras, *Built to Last* (New York: Harper Business, 1994).

[21] In *Corporate Culture and Performance* (New York: Macmillan, 1992), John P. Kotter and James L. Heskett make the point that strong cultures have the desired effects over the long term only if they encourage adaptation to a changing environment. See also Collins and Porras (1994).

[22] See the OCI and other resources at www.humansynergistics.com.

[23] Robert A. Cooke and J. L. Szumal, "Measuring Normative Beliefs and Shared Behavioral Expectations in Organizations: The Reliability and Validity of the Organizational Culture Inventory," *Psychological Reports* 72 (1993):1299–1330.

[24] Ibid; Robert A. Cooke and J. L. Szumal, "Using the Organizational Culture Inventory to Understand the Operating Cultures of Organizations," in N. M. Ashkanasy, C. P. M. Wilerom, and M.F. Peterson (eds.), *Handbook of Organizational Culture and Climate* (Thousand Oaks, CA: Sage, 2000), pp. 147–162.

[25] Lee Gardenswartz and Anita Rowe, *Managing Diversity: A Complete Desk Reference and Planning Guide* (Chicago: Irwin, 1993).

[26] R. Roosevelt Thomas Jr., *Beyond Race and Gender* (New York: AMACOM, 1992), p. 10; see also R. Roosevelt Thomas Jr., "From 'Affirmative Action' to 'Affirming Diversity,'" *Harvard Business Review* (November/December 1990):107–17; R. Roosevelt Thomas Jr., with Marjorie I. Woodruff, *Building a House for Diversity* (New York: AMACOM, 1999).

[27] The foundation report is *Workforce 2000: Work and Workers for the 21st Century* (Indianapolis: Towers Perrin/Hudson Institute, 1987).

[28] Information from Carol Hymowitz, "While Some Women Choose to Stay at Home, Others Gain Flexibility," *Wall Street Journal* (March 30, 2004), p. B1; "It's Time for Working Women to Earn Equal Pay," AFL-CIO (2004), retrieved from www.aflcio.org/yourjobeconomy/women/equalpay; Genara C. Armas, "Women's Pay Still Lags Men's, Census Shows," *Columbus Dispatch* (June 4, 2004), p. E1.

[29] For current information, see U.S. Census Bureau reports at www.factfinder.census.gov.

[30] For background, see Taylor Cox Jr., "The Multicultural Organization," *Academy of Management Executive* 5 (1991):34–47; *Cultural Diversity in Organizations: Theory, Research and Practice* (San Francisco: Berrett-Koehler, 1993).

[31] Thomas and Woodruff (1991).

[32] "Diversity Today: Corporate Recruiting Practices in Inclusive Workplaces," *Fortune* (June 12, 2000), p. S4.

[33] Information from "Racism in Hiring Remains, Study Says," *Columbus Dispatch* (January 17, 2003), p. B2.

[34] Stephanie N. Mehta, "What Minority Employees Really Want," *Fortune* (July 10, 2000), pp. 181–186.

[35] For discussions of the glass ceiling effect, see Ann M. Morrison, Randall P. White, and Ellen Van Velso, *Breaking the Glass Ceiling* (Reading, MA: Addison-Wesley, 1987); Anne E. Weiss, *The Glass Ceiling: A Look at Women in the Workforce* (New York: Twenty First Century, 1999); Debra E. Meyerson and Joyce K. Fletcher, "A Modest Manifesto for Shattering the Glass Ceiling," *Harvard Business Review* (January/February 2000).

[36] Judith B. Rosener, "Women Make Good Managers, So What?" *Business Week* (December 11, 2000), p. 24.

[37] Thomas (1992), p. 17.

[38] Thomas and Woodruff.

[39] Based on ibid., pp. 11–12.

[40] Survey reported in "The Most Inclusive Workplaces Generate the Most Loyal Employees," *Gallup Management Journal* (December 2001), retrieved from http://gmj.gallup.com/.

[41] Thomas Kochan, Katerina Bezrukova, Robin Ely, Susan Jackson, Aparna Joshi, Karen Jehn, Jonathan Leonard, David Levine, and David Thomas, "The Effects of Diversity on Business Performance: Report of the Diversity Research Network," reported in SHRM Foundation Research Findings, retrieved from www.shrm.org/foundation/findings.asp. Full article published in *Human Resource Management* (2003).

[42] These failures are described in L. W. Jeeter, *Disconnected: Deceit and Betrayal at WorldCom* (New York: Wiley, 2003); B. McClean & P. Elkind, *Smartest Guys in the Room: Amazing Rise and Scandalous Fall of Enron.* (New York: Portfolio, 2003); B. L. Toffler. *Final Accounting: Ambition, Greed and the Fall of Arthur Andersen* (New York: Broadway Books, 2003); S. Watkins & M. Swartz. *Power Failure: The Inside Story of the Collapse of Enron* (New York: Doubleday, 2003).

[43] For an overview, see Linda K. Trevino and K. Nelson, *Managing Business Ethics* (New York: Wiley, 1995).

[44] Archie B. Carroll, "In Search of the Moral Manager," *Business Horizons* (March/April 2001):7–15.

[45] Mahzarin R. Banagji, Max H. Bazerman, and Dolly Chugh, "How (Un)ethical are You?" *Harvard Business Review* (December 2003).

[46] Terry Thomas, John R. Schermerhorn Jr., and John W. Dinehart, "Strategic Leadership of Ethical Behavior in Business," *Academy of Management Executive* (2004).

[47] A good overview is available in Linda K. Trevino and Katherine J. Nelson, *Managing Business Ethics*, 2nd ed. (New York: Wiley, 1999).

[48] See Blair Sheppard, Roy J. Lewicki, and John Minton, *Organizational Justice: The Search for Fairness in the Workplace* (New York: Lexington Books, 1992); Jerald Greenberg, *The Quest for Justice on the Job: Essays and Experiments* (Thousand Oaks, CA: Sage, 1995); Robert Folger and Russell Cropanzano, *Organizational Justice and Human Resource Management* (Thousand Oaks, CA: Sage, 1998); Mary A. Konovsky, "Understanding Procedural Justice and Its Impact on Business Organizations," *Journal of Management* 26 (2000):489–511.

[49] Interactional justice is described by Robert J. Bies, "The Predicament of Injustice: The Management of Moral Outrage," in L. L. Cummings & B. M. Staw (eds.), *Research in Organizational Behavior* (Vol. 9) (Greenwich, CT: JAI Press, 1987), pp. 289–319. The example is from Carol T. Kulik and Robert L. Holbrook, "Demographics in Service Encounters: Effects of Racial and Gender Congruence on Perceived Fairness," *Social Justice Research*, Vol. 13 (2000), pp. 375–402.

[50] See Steven N. Brenner and Earl A. Mollander, "Is the Ethics of Business Changing?" *Harvard Business Review* 55 (January/February 1977):50–57; Saul W. Gellerman, "Why 'Good' Managers Make Bad Ethical Choices," *Harvard Business Review* 64 (July/August 1986):85–90; Barbara Ley Toffler, *Tough Choices: Managers Talk Ethics* (New York: Wiley, 1986); Justin G. Longnecker, Joseph A. McKinney, and Carlos W. Moore, "The Generation Gap in Busi-

ness Ethics," *Business Horizons* 32 (September/October 1989):9–14; John B. Cullen, Vart Victor, and Carroll Stephens, "An Ethical Weather Report: Assessing the Organization's Ethical Climate," *Organizational Dynamics* (Winter 1990):50–62; Dawn Blalock, "Study Shows Many Execs Are Quick to Write Off Ethics," *Wall Street Journal* (March 26, 1996), p. C1.

[51] Based on Gellerman (1986).

[52] Survey results from Del Jones, "48% of Workers Admit to Unethical or Illegal Acts," *USA Today* (April 4, 1997), p. A1.

[53] Information from Ethics Resource Center, "Major Survey of America's Workers Finds Substantial Improvements in Ethics": www.ethics.org/releases/nr_20030521_nbes.html.

[54] A classic book is Archie B. Carroll, *Business and Society: Managing Corporate Social Performance* (Boston: Little, Brown, 1981).

[55] See, for example, Sandra A. Waddock, C. Bodwell, and S. B. Graves, "Responsibility: The New Business Imperative," *Academy of Management Executive* 16 (May 2002):132–147.

[56] For research on whistleblowers, see Paula M. Miceli and Janet P. Near, *Blowing the Whistle* (New York: Lexington, 1992).

[57] A vast amount of material on the Enron and Andersen debacles is available in the press, with the *Wall Street Journal, Business Week, Fortune*, and others reporting and documenting the story.

[58] See the discussion by Thomas, Schermerhorn, and Dinehart (2004).

[59] For a broader discussion of compliance issues, see Linda K. Trevino, G. R. Weaver, D. G. Gibson, and Barbara Toffler, "Managing Ethics and Legal Compliance: What Works and What Hurts," *California Management Review* (Winter 1999):131–151.

[60] See Wayne F. Cascio, "Board Governance: A Social Systems Perspective," *Academy of Management Executive* 18(1) (2004):97–101; Lorin Letendre, "The Dynamics of the Boardroom," *Academy of Management Executive* 18(1) (2004):101–105.

[61] For a good practical overview, see Judith Burns, "Everything You Wanted to Know About Corporate Governance…But Didn't Know How to Ask," *Wall Street Journal* (October 27, 2003), pp. R1, R7.

[62] Ibid.

[63] See, for example "Pay for Performance Report," Institute of Management and Administration (December, 2003).

[64] Lynne S. Paine, "Managing for Organizational Integrity, *Harvard Business Review* (March/April, 1994):106–117.

[65] This case is reported in Jenny C. McCune, "Making Lemonade," *Management Review* (June 1997):49–53.

[66] David A. Nadler and Edward E. Lawler III, "Quality of Work Life: Perspectives and Directions," *Organizational Dynamics* 11 (1983):22–36; the discussion of QWL in Thomas G. Cummings and Edgar F. Huse, *Organizational Development and Change* (St. Paul, MN: West, 1990); Stewart D. Friedman, Perry Christensen, and Jessica DeGroot, "Work and Life: The End of the Zero-Sum Game," *Harvard Business Review* (November/December 1998):119–129.

[67] Douglas McGregor, *The Human Side of Enterprise* (New York: McGraw-Hill, 1960).

[68] Fred Luthans, "Positive Organizational Behavior: Developing and Managing Psychological Strengths," *Academy of Management Executive* 16(1) (2002):57–75.

[69] C. Rick Snyder and Shane J. Lopez (eds,), *Handbook of Positive Psychology* (London: Oxford University Press).

[70] See K. S. Cameron, J. E. Dutton, and R. E. Quinn (eds.), *Positive Organizational Scholarship* (San Francisco: Berrett-Koehler, 2003).

[71] See the discussion of the leadership applications of POB by William L. Gardner and John R. Schermerhorn Jr., "Unleashing Individual Potential: Performance Gains Through Positive Organizational Behavior and Authentic Leadership," *Organizational Dynamics* (in press).

[72] Kenichi Ohmae's books include *The Borderless World: Power and Strategy in the Interlinked Economy* (New York: Harper, 1989); *The End of the Nation State* (New York: Free Press, 1996); *The Invisible Continent: Four Strategic Imperatives of the New Economy* (New York: Harper, 1999).

[73] For a discussion of globalization, see Thomas L. Friedman, *The Lexus and the Olive Tree: Understanding Globalization* (New York: Bantam Doubleday Dell, 2000); John Micklethwait and Adrian Woodridge, *A Future Perfect: The Challenges and Hidden Promise of Globalization* (New York: Crown, 2000); Alfred E. Eckes Jr. and Thomas W. Zeiler, *Globalization and the American Century* (Cambridge, UK: Cambridge University Press, 2003).

[74] Michael E. Porter, *The Competitive Advantage of Nations: With a New Introduction* (New York: Free Press, 1998).

[75] Andrea Hopkins, "Outsourcing Causes 9% of U.S. Layoffs," June 10, 2004, posted at Reuters.com.

[76] See Daniel H. Pink, "Free Agent Nation," *Fast Company* (December 1997):131ff; Tom Peters, "The Brand Called You," *Fast Company* (August/September 1997).

[77] Charles Handy, *The Age of Unreason* (Boston: Harvard Business School Press, 1990). See also his later book, *The Age of Paradox* (Boston: Harvard Business School Press, 1994).

[78] See the Life Styles Inventory other resources at www.humansynergistics.com.

[79]Peters (1997).

SOURCE NOTES

Information and quotes from Sharon Shinn, "Luv, Colleen," *BizEd* (March/April, 2003):18–23; corporate Web site: www.southwestairlines.com.

Information from Mylene Mangalindan, "The Grownup at Google," *Wall Street Journal* (March 29, 2004), pp. B1, B5.

Information from Jennifer Koch Laabs, "Thinking Outside the Box at The Container Store," *Workforce* (March, 2001); and, "The Container Store at the Top of Fortune's '100 Best' for Fifth Year in a Row," corporate news release (December 29, 2003).

Information from Kathleen Hays, Valerie Morris, and Gerri Willis, "Applying Feng Shui to Workplace, *CNNFN, The Flipside* (August 21, 2003); Sallie Hofmeister, "Want a Corner Office? First Check the Chi," *Los Angeles Times* (March 21, 2004), p. C1.

Chubb Group: Information from Sue Shellenberger, "Amid Gay Marriage Debate, Companies Offer More Benefits to Same-Sex Couples," *Wall Street Journal* (March 18, 2004), p. D1. Whole Foods Market: Information from Andrew Blackman, "Putting a Ceiling on Pay," *Wall Street Journal* (April 12, 2004), p. R11.

Chapter 3

ENDNOTES

[1] "Wal Around the World," *Economist* (December 8, 2001), pp. 55–57; Corporate Web site: www.walmart.com.

[2] For a good discussion of executive views, see "In Search of Global Leaders," *Harvard Business Review* (August 2003).

[3] Kenichi Ohmae, *The Invisible Continent* (New York: Harper Business, 2000); Kenichi Ohmae *The Borderless World* (New York:

Harper Business, 1989); Peter F. Drucker, "The Global Economy and the Nation-State," *Foreign Affairs* (September/October 1997).

[4] See Michael Porter's three-volume series *The Competitive Advantage of Nations, Competitive Advantage,* and *Competitive Strategy* (New York: Free Press, 1998).

[5] Kenichi Ohmae, *The Evolving Global Economy* (Cambridge, MA: Harvard Business School Press, 1995); Kenichi Ohmae, "Putting Global Logic First," *Harvard Business Review* (January/February 1995):119–125; Jeffrey E. Garten, "Can the World Survive the Triumph of Capitalism?" *Harvard Business Review* (January/February, 1997):67–79.

[6] William B. Johnson, "Global Workforce 2000: The New World Labor Market," *Harvard Business Review* (March/April 1991):115–127.

[7] See Porter (1998); Kenichi Ohmae, *The End of the Nation State: The Rise of Regional Economies* (New York: Free Press, 1995); William Greider, *One World, Ready or Not: The Manic Logic of Global Capitalism* (New York: Free Press, 1998).

[8] See, for example, Michael E. Porter, "Clusters and the New Economics of Competition," *Harvard Business Review* (November/December, 1998).

[9] Mzamo P. Mangaliso and Mphuthumi B. Damane, "Building Competitive Advantage from Ubuntu: Management Lessons from South Africa," *Academy of Management Executive* 15 (2001):23–33.

[10] James A. Austin and John G. McLean, "Pathways to Business Success in Sub-Saharan Africa," *Journal of African Finance and Economic Development* 2 (1996):57–76; information from "International Business: Consider Africa," *Harvard Business Review* 76 (January/February 1998):16–18.

[11] "In Search of Global Managers."

[12] Ibid.

[13] Robert T. Moran and John R. Risenberger, *Making Globalization Work: Solutions for Implementation* (New York: McGraw-Hill, 1993); "Don't Be an Ugly-American Manager," *Fortune* (October 16, 1995), p. 225; "A Way to Measure Global Success," *Fortune* (March 15, 1999), pp. 196–197.

[14] "Don't Be an Ugly-American Manager"; Vanessa Houlder, "Foreign Culture Shocks," *Financial Times* (March 22, 1996), p. 12.

[15] Geert Hofstede, *Culture's Consequences: International Differences in Work-Related Values,* 2nd ed.(Beverly Hills, CA: Sage, 2001); Fons Trompenaars and Charles Hampden-Turner, *Riding the Waves of Culture: Understanding Cultural Diversity in Global Business,* 2nd ed. (New York: McGraw-Hill, 1998). For an excellent discussion of culture, see also "Culture: The Neglected Concept," in Peter B. Smith and Michael Harris Bond (eds.), *Social Psychology Across Cultures,* 2nd ed. (Boston: Allyn & Bacon, 1998). See also Michael H. Hoppe, "An Interview with Geert Hofstede," *Academy of Management Executive* 18 (2004): 75–79; Harry C. Triandis, "The Many Dimensions of Culture," *Academy of Management Executive* 18 (2004):88–93.

[16] Geert Hofstede, *Culture and Organizations: Software of the Mind* (London: McGraw-Hill, 1991).

[17] P. Christopher Earley and Randall S. Peterson, "The Elusive Cultural Chameleon: Cultural Intelligence as a New Approach to Intercultural Training for the Global Manager," *Academy of Management Learning and Education* 3(1) (2004):100–115.

[18] A good overview of the world's cultures is provided in Richard D. Lewis, *When Cultures Collide: Managing Successfully Across Cultures* (London: Nicholas Brealey, 1996).

[19] Benjamin L. Whorf, *Language, Thought and Reality* (Cambridge, MA: MIT Press, 1956).

[20] Edward T. Hall, *Beyond Culture* (New York: Doubleday, 1976).

[21] A classic work and the source of our examples is Edward T. Hall, *The Silent Language* (New York: Anchor Books, 1959).

[22] Allen C. Bluedorn, Carol Felker Kaufman, and Paul M. Lane, "How Many Things Do You Like to Do at Once?" *Academy of Management Executive* 6 (November 1992):17–26.

[23] The source of our examples and a classic reference is Edward T. Hall, *The Hidden Dimension* (New York: Anchor Books, 1969; Magnolia, MI: Peter Smith, 1990). See also Edward T. Hall, *Hidden Differences* (New York: Doubleday, 1990).

[24] The classic work is Max Weber, *The Protestant Ethic and the Spirit of Capitalism* (New York: Scribner, 1930). For a description of religious influences in Asian cultures, see S. Gordon Redding, *The Spirit of Chinese Capitalism* (New York: Walter de Gruyter, 1990).

[25] Hofstede (2001); Geert Hofstede and Michael H. Bond, "The Confucius Connection: From Culture Roots to Economic Growth," *Organizational Dynamics* 16 (1988):4–21.

[26] Hofstede (2001).

[27] Chinese Culture Connection, "Chinese Values and the Search for Culture-Free Dimensions of Culture," *Journal of Cross-Cultural Psychology* 18 (1987):143–164.

[28] Hofstede and Bond (1988); Geert Hofstede, "Cultural Constraints in Management Theories," *Academy of Management Executive* 7 (February 1993):81–94. For a further discussion of Asian and Confucian values, see also Jim Rohwer, *Asia Rising: Why America Will Prosper as Asia's Economies Boom* (New York: Simon & Schuster, 1995); Lewis (1996), ch 3.

[29] For an example, see John R. Schermerhorn Jr. and Michael H. Bond, "Cross-Cultural Leadership Dynamics in Collectivism + High Power Distance Settings," *Leadership and Organization Development Journal* 18 (1997):187–193.

[30] Nancy J. Adler, *International Dimensions of Organizational Behavior,* 2nd ed. (Boston: PWS-Kent, 1991).

[31] Trompenaars and Hampden-Turner (1998).

[32] Alvin Toffler, *The Third Wave* (New York: Morrow, 1980).

[33] "In Search of Global Managers."

[34] John Seybold, "Managing in Turbulent Times," *BizEd* (March/April, 2004):38–43.

[35] Ibid.

[36] See Hofstede (1993, 2001); Adler (1991).

[37] Adler (1991).

[38] See Rosalie Tung, "Expatriate Assignments: Enhancing Success and Minimizing Failure," *Academy of Management Executive* (May 1987):117–126; Adler (1991); J. Stewart Black and Hal B. Gregersen, "The Right Way to Manage Expats," *Harvard Business Review* (March/April 1999).

[39] Nancy J. Adler, "Reentry: Managing Cross-Cultural Transitions," *Group and Organization Studies* 6, (3) (1981):341–356; Adler (1991).

[40] For a discussion of international business ethics, see Thomas Donaldson and Thomas W. Dunfee, *Ties That Bind* (Boston: Harvard Business School Press, 1999); Thomas Donaldson, "Values in Tension: Ethics Away from Home," *Harvard Business Review* (September/October 1996):48–62; Debora L. Spar, "The Spotlight and the Bottom Line," *Foreign Affairs* (March/April 1998).

[41] Information from Council on Economic Priorities Accreditation Agency Web site: www.cepaa.org.

[42] Donaldson (1996).

[43] Ibid.; Thomas Donaldson and Thomas W. Dunfee, "Towards a Unified Conception of Business Ethics: Integrative Social Contracts Theory," *Academy of Management Review* 19 (1994):252–285; Donaldson and Dunfee (1999). For a related discussion, see John R. Schermerhorn Jr., "Alternative Terms of Business Engagement in Ethically Challenging Environment," *Business Ethics Quarterly* (1999):

[44] Geert Hofstede, "Motivation, Leadership and Organization: Do American Theories Apply Abroad?" *Organizational Dynamics* (1980):43+; Hofstede, (1993).

[45] Two classic works are William Ouchi, *Theory Z: How American Businesses Can Meet the Japanese Challenge* (Reading, MA: Addison-Wesley, 1981); Richard Tanner and Anthony Athos, *The Art of Japanese Management* (New York: Simon & Schuster, 1981).

[46] See J. Bernard Keys, Luther Tray Denton, and Thomas R. Miller, "The Japanese Management Theory Jungle—Revisited," *Journal of Management* 20 (1994):373–402; "Japanese and Korean Management Systems," in Min Chen (ed.), *Asian Management Systems* (New York: Routledge, 1995).

[47] Makoto Ohtsu, *Inside Japanese Business: A Narrative History, 1960-2000* (Armonk, N.Y.: M.E. Sharpe, 2002), pp. 39–41.

SOURCE NOTES

Council on Economic Priorities Accreditation Agency Web site: www.cepaa.org.

Information from "Latin Pop: A Low-Budget Cola Shakes Up Markets South of the Border," *Wall Street Journal* (October 27, 2003), pp. A1, A18.

Information from Thomas L. Friedman, "Ironic Similarities: Global Technology Fuels Entrepreneurs, Terrorists," *Columbus Dispatch* (March 16, 2004), p. A9.

Information from Leon de Kock, "Ubuntu at Work," *Sunday Times of South Africa* (October 12, 2003), p. 1. See also Mangaliso ad Damane, 2001, op. cit.

Information from Jamie Smyth, "Xerox's Chief Copies Good Practices, Not Past Mistakes," *Irish Times* (March 21, 2003), p. 24.

Information from William M. Bulkeley, "Bribery Case Tied to IBM Unit Triggers U.S. Inquiry in Korea," *Wall Street Journal* (January 6, 2004), p. B5.

Chapter 4

ENDNOTES

[1] "Bank of the Americas," *Fortune* (April 14, 2003), pp. 145–148.

[2] R. Jacob, "The Resurrection of Michael Dell," *Fortune* (August 1995), pp. 117–128.

[3] See N. Brody, *Personality: In Search of Individuality* (San Diego, CA: Academic Press, 1988), pp. 68–101; C. Holden, "The Genetics of Personality," *Science* (August 7, 1987), pp. 598–601.

[4] See Geert Hofstede, *Culture's Consequences: International Differences in Work-Related Values*, abridged ed. (Beverly Hills: Sage Publications, 1984).

[5] Chris Argyris, *Personality and Organization* (New York: Harper & Row, 1957); Daniel J. Levinson, *The Seasons of a Man's Life* (New York: Knopf, 1978); Gail Sheehy, *New Passages* (New York: Ballantine Books, 1995).

[6] Viktor Gecas, "The Self-Concept," in Ralph H. Turner and James F. Short, Jr. (eds.), Vol. 8, *Annual Review of Sociology* (Palo Alto, CA: Annual Review, 1982), p. 3. Also see Arthur P. Brief and Ramon J. Aldag, "The Self in Work Organizations: A Conceptual Review," *Academy of Management Review* (January 1981):75–88; and Jerry J. Sullivan, "Self Theories and Employee Motivation," *Journal of Management* (June 1989):345–363.

[7] Compare Philip Cushman, "Why the Self Is Empty," *American Psychologist* (May 1990): pp. 599–611.

[8] Based in part on a definition in Gecas (1982), p. 3.

[9] Suggested by J. Brockner, *Self-Esteem at Work* (Lexington, MA: Lexington Books, 1988), p. 144; John A. Wagner III and John R. Hollenbeck, *Management of Organizational Behavior* (Englewood Cliffs, NJ: Prentice-Hall, 1992), pp. 100–101.

[10] M. R. Barrick and M. K. Mount, "The Big Five Personality Dimensions and Job Performance: A Meta Analysis," *Personnel Psychology* 44 (1991):1–26; M. R. Barrick and M. K. Mount, "Autonomy as a Moderator of the Relationships Between the Big Five Personality Dimensions and Job Performance," *Journal of Applied Psychology* (February 1993):111–118.

[11] See Jim C. Nunnally, *Psychometric Theory*, 2nd ed. (New York: McGraw-Hill, 1978), ch. 14.

[12] See David A. Whetten and Kim S. Cameron. *Developing Management Skills*, 3rd ed. (New York: HarperCollins, 1995), p. 72.

[13] Raymond G. Hunt, Frank J. Krzystofiak, James R. Meindl, and Abdalla M. Yousry, "Cognitive Style and Decision Making," *Organizational Behavior and Human Decision Processes* 44(3) (1989):436–453. For additional work on problem-solving styles, see Ferdinand A. Gul, "The Joint and Moderating Role of Personality and Cognitive Style on Decision Making," *Accounting Review* (April 1984):264–277; Brian H. Kleiner, "The Interrelationship of Jungian Modes of Mental Functioning with Organizational Factors: Implications for Management Development," *Human Relations* (November 1983):997–1012; James L. McKenney and Peter G. W. Keen, "How Managers' Minds Work," *Harvard Business Review* (May/June 1974):79–90.

[14] Some examples of firms using the Myers–Briggs Type Indicators are given in J. M. Kunimerow and L. W. McAllister, "Team Building with the Myers-Briggs Type Indicator: Case Studies," *Journal of Psychological Type* 15 (1988):26–32; G. H. Rice Jr. and D. P. Lindecamp, "Personality Types and Business Success of Small Retailers," *Journal of Occupational Psychology* 62 (1989):177–182; B. Roach, *Strategy Styles and Management Types: A Resource Book for Organizational Management Consultants* (Stanford, CA: Balestrand, 1989).

[15] J. B. Rotter, "Generalized Expectancies for Internal versus External Control of Reinforcement," *Psychological Monographs* 80 (1966):1–28.

[16] Don Hellriegel, John W. Slocum Jr., and Richard W. Woodman, *Organizational Behavior*, 5th ed. (St. Paul, MN: West, 1989), p. 46.

[17] See Wagner and Hollenbeck (1992), ch. 4.

[18] Niccolo Machiavelli, *The Prince*, trans. George Bull (Middlesex, UK: Penguin, 1961).

[19] Richard Christie and Florence L. Geis, *Studies in Machiavellianism* (New York: Academic Press, 1970).

[20] See M. Snyder, *Public Appearances/Private Realities: The Psychology of Self-Monitoring* (New York: Freeman, 1987).

[21] Ibid.

[22] Adapted from R. W. Bonner, "A Short Scale: A Potential Measure of Pattern A Behavior," *Journal of Chronic Diseases* 22 (1969). Used by permission.

[23] See Meyer Friedman and Ray Roseman, *Type A Behavior and Your Heart* (New York: Knopf, 1974). For another view, see Wal-

ter Kiechel III, "Attack of the Obsessive Managers," *Fortune* (February 16, 1987), pp. 127–128.

[24] See P. E. Jacob, J. J. Flink, and H. L. Schuchman, "Values and Their Function in Decisionmaking," *American Behavioral Scientist* 5, Suppl. 9 (1962):6–38.

[25] See M. Rokeach and S. J. Ball Rokeach, "Stability and Change in American Value Priorities, 1968–1981," *American Psychologist* (May 1989):775–784.

[26] Milton Rokeach, *The Nature of Human Values* (New York: Free Press, 1973).

[27] See W. C. Frederick and J. Weber, "The Values of Corporate Managers and Their Critics: An Empirical Description and Normative Implications," in W. C. Frederick and L. E. Preston (eds.), *Business Ethics Research Issues and Empirical Studies* (Greenwich, CT: JAI Press, 1990), pp. 123–144.

[28] Gordon Allport, Philip E. Vernon, and Gardner Lindzey, *Study of Values* (Boston: Houghton Mifflin, 1931).

[29] Adapted from R. Tagiuri, "Purchasing Executive: General Manager or Specialist?" *Journal of Purchasing* (August 1967):16–21.

[30] Bruce M. Maglino, Elizabeth C. Ravlin, and Cheryl L. Adkins, "Value Congruence and Satisfaction with a Leader: An Examination of the Role of Interaction," unpublished manuscript (Columbia, SC: University of South Carolina, 1990), pp. 8–9.

[31] Maglino, Ravlin, and Adkins (1990).

[32] Daniel Yankelovich, *New Rules! Searching for Self-Fulfillment in a World Turned Upside Down* (New York: Random House, 1981); Daniel Yankelovich, Hans Zetterberg, Burkhard Strumpel, and Michael Shanks, *Work and Human Values: An International Report on Jobs in the 1980s and 1990s* (Aspen, CO: Aspen Institute for Humanistic Studies, 1983); William Fox, *American Values in Decline: What We Can Do* (Gainesville, FL: 1st Books Library, 2001).

[33] See D. Jamieson and Julia O'Mara, *Managing Workplace 2000* (San Francisco: Jossey-Bass, 1991), pp. 28–29.

[34] Compare Martin Fishbein and Icek Ajzen, *Belief, Attitude, Intention and Behavior: An Introduction to Theory and Research* (Reading, MA: Addison-Wesley, 1973).

[35] See A. W. Wicker, "Attitude Versus Action: The Relationship of Verbal and Overt Behavioral Responses to Attitude Objects," *Journal of Social Issues* (Autumn 1969): pp. 41–78.

[36] Leon Festinger, *A Theory of Cognitive Dissonance* (Palo Alto, CA: Stanford University Press, 1957).

[37] J. Laabs, "Interest in Diversity Training Continues to Grow," *Personnel Journal* (October 1993):p. 18.

[38] L. R. Gómez-Mejía, D. B. Balkin, and R. L. Cardy, *Managing Human Resources* (Englewood Cliffs, NJ: Prentice-Hall, 1995), p. 154.

[39] John P. Fernandez, *Managing a Diverse Workforce* (Lexington, MA: Heath, 1991); Jamieson and O'Mara (1991).

[40] Howard N. Fullerton Jr. and Mitra Toosi, "Labor Force Projections to 2010: Steady Growth and Changing Composition," *Monthly Labor Review*, (November 2001):21–30.

[41] Linda A. Krefting and Frank J. Kryzstofiak, "Looking Like America: Potential Conflicts Between Workplace Diversity Initiatives and Equal Opportunity Compliance in the U.S.," Working paper (Lubbock, TX: Texas Tech University, 1998), p. 10.

[42] Ibid.

[43] See L. Gardenswartz and A. Rowe, *Managing Diversity: A Complete Desk Reference and Planning Guide* (Homewood, IL: Business One Irwin, 1993),p. 405.

[44] See E. Macoby and C. N. Jacklin. *The Psychology of Sex Differences* (Stanford, CA: Stanford University Press, 1974); G. N. Powell, *Women and Men in Management* (Beverly Hills: Sage, 1988); T. W. Mangione, "Turnover—Some Psychological and Demographic Correlates," in R. P. Quinn and T. W. Mangione (eds.), *The 1969–70 Survey of Working Conditions* (Ann Arbor: University of Michigan Survey Research Center, 1973); R. Marsh and H. Mannan, "Organizational Commitment and Turnover: A Predictive Study," *Administrative Science Quarterly* (March 1977):57–75; R. J. Flanagan, G. Strauss, and L. Ulman, "Worker Discontent and Work Discontent and Work Place Behavior," *Industrial Relations* (May 1974):101–123; K. R. Garrison and P. M. Muchinsky, "Attitudinal and Biographical Predictions of Incidental Absenteeism," *Journal of Vocational Behavior* (April 1977):221–230; G. Johns, "Attitudinal and Nonattitudinal Predictions of Two Forms of Absence from Work," *Organizational Behavior and Human Performance* (December 1978):431–444; R. T. Keller, "Predicting Absenteeism from Prior Absenteeism, Attitudinal Factors, and Nonattitudinal Factors," *Journal of Applied Psychology* (August 1983):536–540.

[45] Gómez-Mejía, Balkin, and Cardy (1995), p. 171.

[46] "The Growing Influence of Women," *Workplace Visions* (September/October 1998):2.

[47] This discussion is summarized from Alice H. Eagly and Marloes L. Van Engen, "Women and Men as Leaders," in George R. Goethals, Georgia J. Sorenson, and James McGregor Burns (Eds.) *Encyclopedia of Leadership* (Vol. 4), (Great Barrington, MA/Thousand Oaks, CA: Berkshire/Sage 2004), pp. 1657–1663; Alice H. Eagly and Linda L. Carli, "Women and Men as Leaders", in John Antonakis, Anna T. Cianciolo, and Robert J. Sternberg (eds.), *The Nature of Leadership* (Thousand Oaks, CA: Sage, 2004), pp. 279–302; Alice H. Eagly and Linda L. Carli, "The Female Leadership Advantage: An Evaluation of the Evidence", *The Leadership Quarterly*, 14(6)(2003):807–834; Robert Vecchio, "Leadership and Gender Advantage," *The Leadership Quarterly*, (6)13 (2002):643–671.

[48] Fullerton and Toosi (2001), p. 22.

[49] Nina Monk, "Finished at Forty," *Fortune* (February 1, 1999), pp. 50–58.

[50] *Mosaics*, "Diversity News: Age Discrimination Unrest in Britain," 3(2) (March/April 1997), p. 3.

[51] Paul Mayrand, "Older Workers: A Problem or the Solution?" *AARP Textbook Authors' Conference Presentation* (October 1992), p. 29; G. M. McEvoy and W. F. Cascio, "Cumulative Evidence of the Relationship Between Employee Age and Job Performance," *Journal of Applied Psychology* (February 1989):11–17.

[52] See Fernandez (1991), p. 236; *Mosaics*, "Diversity News: Age Discrimination Unrest in Britain," 4(2)(March/April, 1998), p. 4.

[53] Fernandez (1991); *Mosaics*, Vol. 4, No. 2, Patrick Digh, "Finding New Talent in a Tight Market." *Mosaics* 4(2) (March/April, 1998), pp. 1, 4–6.

[54] See Taylor H. Co and Stacy Blake, "Managing Cultural Diversity: Implications for Organizational Competitiveness," *Academy of Management Executive* 5(3) (1991): p. 45.

[55] Literature covering this topic is reviewed in Stephen P. Robbins, *Organizational Behavior*, 8th ed. (Englewood Cliffs, NJ: Prentice-Hall, 1998), ch. 2.

[56] Ibid.

[57] Krefting and Krzystofiak (1998), p. 14.

[58] Larry L. Cummings and Donald P. Schwab, *Performance in Organizations: Determinants and Appraisal* (Glenview, IL: Scott, Foresman, 1973), p. 8.

[59] See J. Hogan, "Structure of Physical Performance in Occupational Tasks," *Journal of Applied Psychology* 76 (1991): pp. 495–507.

[60] H. W. Lane and J. J. DiStefano (eds.), *International Management Behavior* (Scarborough, Ontario: Nelson Canada, 1988), pp. 4–5; Z. Abdoolcarim, "How Women Are Winning at Work," *Asian Business* (November 1993):24–29.

[61] Gardenswartz and Rowe (1993), p. 405; Michelle N. Martinez, "Equality Effort Sharpens Bank's Edge," *HR Magazine* (January 1995):38–43.

[62] Michelle Neely Martinez, "Health Care Firm Seeks to Measure Diversity," *HR News* (October 1997): p. 6.

[63] Ibid.

[64] See www.shrm.org/surveys for surveys available to SHRM members.

[65] Jonathan Stutz and Randy Massengale, "Measuring Diversity Initiatives," *HR Magazine* (December 1997):84, 90.

SOURCE NOTES

Jordan Hyman, "Nicklaus Is Helping Kids Step Up to the First Tee," *Sports Illustrated* (October 28, 2002) p. 16.

Kenneth M. Thompson, "A Conversation with F. Bryon Nahser: Focusing on Values through Pragmatic Inquiry," *Journal of Leadership and Organizational Studies* 10(2) (2003):125–132.

Based on Tim Wedel, "A World Unto Itself", *USA Weekend* (April 16–18, 2004), p. 24.

Based on James Hannah, "For 84-year-old Blowers, Nothing Compares to Flying", *Lubbock Avalanche Journal* (December 25, 2003), p. B7.

Based on Associated Press, "Hi-Tech Aging", *Lubbock Avalanche-Journal* (March 23, 2003), p. D1.

Effective Manager information from Gary N. Powell, "One More Time: Do Male and Female Managers Differ?" *Academy of Management Executive* 4(3) (1995):74.

Continuum excerpted from Chris Argyris, *Personality and Organization* (New York: Harper & Row, 1957).

Problem-solving summary based on R. P. McIntyre and M. M. Capen, "A Cognitive Style Perspective on Ethical Questions," *Journal of Business Ethics* 12 (1993):631; D. Hellriegel, J. Slocum, and Richard Woodman, *Organizational Behavior*, 7th ed. (Minneapolis: West Publishing, 1995), ch. 4.

Summarized from Crayton Harrison, "Banks Finding Diversity Pays Off Several Ways," *Dallas Morning News* (August 13, 2000), p. 23L.

Based on M. Rokeach, *The Nature of Human Values* (New York: Free Press, 1973).

Effective Manager information from Michelle N. Martinez, "Health Care Firm Seeks to Measure Diversity," *HR News* (October 1997):6.

Chapter 5

ENDNOTES

[1] Based on Associated Press, "Dallas Attempts to Break away from J.R. Image," *Dallas Morning News* (April 17, 2004), p. B18.

[2] "Clark's Catch Engraved in NFL Lore," *Lubbock Avalanche-Journal* (January 11, 1992), p. D5.

[3] H. R. Schiffmann, *Sensation and Perception: An Integrated Approach*, 3rd ed. (New York: Wiley, 1990).

[4] Example from John A. Wagner III and John R. Hollenbeck, *Organizational Behavior*, 3rd ed. (Upper Saddle River, NJ: Prentice-Hall, 1998), p. 59.

[5] See M. W. Levine and J. M. Shefner, Fundamentals of Sensation and Perception, Georgia T. Chao and Steve W. J. Kozlowski, "Employee Perceptions on the Implementation of Robotic Manufacturing Technology," *Journal of Applied Psychology* 71 (1986): 70–76; Steven F. Cronshaw and Robert G. Lord, "Effects of Categorization, Attribution, and Encoding Processes in Leadership Perceptions," *Journal of Applied Psychology* 72 (1987):97–106.

[6] See Robert Lord, "An Information Processing Approach to Social Perceptions, Leadership, and Behavioral Measurement in Organizations," in B. M. Staw and L. L. Cummings (eds.), *Research in Organizational Behavior* (Vol. 7) (Greenwich, CT: JAI Press, 1985), pp. 87–128; T. K. Srull and R. S. Wyer, *Advances in Social Cognition* (Hillsdale, NJ: Erlbaum, 1988); U. Neisser, *Cognitive and Reality* (San Francisco: Freeman, 1976), p. 112.

[7] See J. G. Hunt, *Leadership: A New Synthesis* (Newbury Park, CA: Sage, 1991), ch. 7; R. G. Lord and R. J. Foti, "Schema Theories, Information Processing, and Organizational Behavior," in H. P. Simms Jr. and D. A. Gioia (eds.), *Thinking Organization* (San Francisco: Jossey-Bass, 1986), pp. 20–48; S. T. Fiske and S. E. Taylor, *Social Cognition* (Reading, MA: Addison-Wesley, 1984).

[8] See J. S. Phillips, "The Accuracy of Leadership Ratings: A Categorization Perspective," *Organizational Behavior and Human Performance* (Vol. 33) (1984), pp. 125–138; J. G. Hunt, B. R. Baliga, an M. F. Peterson, "Strategic Apex Leader Scripts and an Organizational Life Cycle Approach to Leadership and Excellence," *Journal of Management Development* 7 (1988):61–83.

[9] D. Bilimoria and S. K. Piderit, "Board Committee Membership Effects of Sex-Based Bias," *Academy of Management Journal*, 37 (1994):1453–1477.

[10] Dewitt C. Dearborn and Herbert A. Simon, "Selective Perception: A Note on the Departmental Identification of Executives," *Sociometry* 21 (1958):140–144.

[11] J. P. Walsh, "Selectivity and Selective Perception: An Investigation of Managers' Belief Structures and Information Processing," *Academy of Management Journal* 24 (1988):453–470.

[12] J. Sterling Livingston, "Pygmalion in Management," *Harvard Business Review* (July/August 1969):81–89.

[13] D. Eden and A. B. Shani, "Pygmalion Goes to Boot Camp," *Journal of Applied Psychology* 67 (1982):194–199.

[14] See B. R. Schlenker, *Impression Management: The Self-Concept, Social Identity, and Interpersonal Relations* (Monterey, CA: Brooks/Cole, 1980); W. L. Gardner and M. J. Martinko, "Impression Management in Organizations," *Journal of Management* (June 1988):332; R. B. Cialdini, "Indirect Tactics of Image Management: Beyond Banking," in R. A. Giacolini and P. Rosenfeld (eds.), *Impression Management in the Organization* (Hillsdale, NJ: Erlbaum, 1989), pp. 45–71.

[15] See H. H. Kelley, "Attribution in Social Interaction," in E. Jones et al. (eds.), *Attribution: Perceiving the Causes of Behavior* (Morristown, NJ: General Learning Press, 1972).

[16] See "Obese Women Finding Business Just Doesn't Pay," *Lubbock Avalanche-Journal* (January 28, 2001), p. 2D.

[17] See Terence R. Mitchell, S. G. Green, and R. E. Wood, "An Attribution Model of Leadership and the Poor Performing Subordinate," in Barry Staw and Larry L. Cummings (eds.), *Research in Organizational Behavior* (New York: JAI Press, 1981), pp. 197–234; John H. Harvey and Gifford Weary, "Current Issues in At-

tribution Theory and Research," *Annual Review of Psychology* 35 (1984):427–459.

[18] R. M. Steers, S. J. Bischoff, and L. H. Higgins, "Cross Cultural Management Research," *Journal of Management Inquiry* (December 1992):325–326; J. G. Miller, "Culture and the Development of Everyday Causal Explanation," *Journal of Personality and Social Psychology* 46 (1984):961–978.

[19] A. Maass and C. Volpato, "Gender Differences in Self-Serving Attributions About Sexual Experiences," *Journal of Applied Psychology* 19 (1989):517–542.

[20] See J. M. Crant and T. S. Bateman, "Assignment of Credit and Blame for Performance Outcomes," *Academy of Management Journal* (February 1993):7–27; E. C. Pence, W. E. Pendelton, G. H. Dobbins, and J. A. Sgro, "Effects of Causal Explanations and Sex Variables on Recommendations for Corrective Actions Following Employee Failure," *Organizational Behavior and Human Performance* (April 1982):227–240.

[21] See F. Fosterling, "Attributional Retraining: A Review," *Psychological Bulletin* (November 1985):496–512.

SOURCE NOTES

Based on K. C. Cole, "As Crew Cut Era Fades, Science Lets Its Hair Down", *Dallas Morning News* (April 18, 2004), p 31A.

Based on Lyric W. Winik, "Parade's Special Intelligence Report", *Parade Magazine* (October 5, 2003), p. 16.

Based on Rick Bragg, "Long Time Coming," *Sports Illustrated* (April 19, 2004), pp. 73–81.

Based on Janine Latus, "Ivan: The Charitable," *Continental* (July 2003):51–53.

Based on David Whitford, "Veeck Family Values." *Fortune* (September 15, 2003):191[D-H].

Based on Sarah Lyall, "He Came, He Sawed, He Freed My Car", *Dallas Morning News* (October 13, 2003). See p. 17A.

Data reported in Edward E. Lawler III, Allan M. Mohrman, Jr., and Susan M. Resnick, "Performance Appraisal Revisited," *Organizational Dynamics* 13 (Summer 1984):20–35.

Information from John R. Schermerhorn Jr., "Team Development for High Performance Management," *Training and Development Journal* 40 (November 1986):38–41.

Information from B. R. Schlinker, *Impression Management: The Self Concept, Social Identity, and Interpersonal Relations* (Monterey, CA: Brooks/Cole, 1980).

Chapter 6

ENDNOTES

[1] Based on Associated Press, "Get an A, Earn $50 for College," *Dallas Morning News* (April 18, 2004), p. 4A.

[2] See John P. Campbell, Marvin D. Dunnette, Edward E. Lawler III, and Karl E. Weick, Jr., *Managerial Behavior Performance and Effectiveness* (New York: McGraw-Hill, 1970), ch. 15.

[3] Geert Hofstede, "Cultural Constraints in Management Theories," *Academy of Management Executive* 7 (February 1993):81–94.

[4] Geert Hofstede, *Culture's Consequences: International Differences in Work-Related Values*, abridged ed. (Beverly Hills: Sage, 1984).

[5] Abraham Maslow, *Eupsychian Management* (Homewood, IL: Irwin, 1965); Abraham Maslow, *Motivation and Personality*, 2nd ed. (New York: Harper & Row, 1970).

[6] Lyman W. Porter, "Job Attitudes in Management: II. Perceived Importance of Needs as a Function of Job Level," *Journal of Applied Psychology* 47 (April 1963):141–148.

[7] Douglas T. Hall and Khalil E. Nougaim, "An Examination of Maslow's Need Hierarchy in an Organizational Setting," *Organizational Behavior and Human Performance* 3 (1968):12–35; Porter (1963); John M. Ivancevich, "Perceived Need Satisfactions of Domestic Versus Overseas Managers," *Journal of Applied Psychology* 54 (August 1969):274–278.

[8] Mahmoud A. Wahba and Lawrence G. Bridwell, "Maslow Reconsidered: A Review of Research on the Need Hierarchy Theory," *Academy of Management Proceedings* (1974):514–520; Edward E. Lawler III and J. Lloyd Shuttle, "A Causal Correlation Test of the Need Hierarchy Concept," *Organizational Behavior and Human Performance* 7 (1973):265–287.

[9] Nancy J. Adler, *International Dimensions of Organizational Behavior*, 2nd ed. (Boston: PWS-Kent, 1991), p. 153; Richard M. Hodgetts and Fred Luthans, *International Management* (New York: McGraw-Hill, 1991), ch. 11.

[10] Clayton P. Alderfer, "An Empirical Test of a New Theory of Human Needs," *Organizational Behavior and Human Performance* 4 (1969):142–175; Clayton P. Alderfer, *Existence, Relatedness, and Growth* (New York: Free Press, 1972); Benjamin Schneider and Clayton P. Alderfer, "Three Studies of Need Satisfaction in Organization," *Administrative Science Quarterly* 18 (1973):489–505.

[11] Lane Tracy, "A Dynamic Living Systems Model of Work Motivation," *Systems Research* 1 (1984):191–203; John Rauschenberger, Neal Schmidt, and John E. Hunter, "A Test of the Need Hierarchy Concept by a Markov Model of Change in Need Strength," *Administrative Science Quarterly* 25 (1980):654–670.

[12] Sources pertinent to this discussion are David C. McClelland, *The Achieving Society* (New York: Van Nostrand, 1961); David C. McClelland, "Business, Drive and National Achievement," *Harvard Business Review* 40 (July/August 1962):99–112; David C. McClelland, "That Urge to Achieve," *Think* (November/December 1966):19–32; G. H. Litwin and R. A. Stringer, *Motivation and Organizational Climate* (Boston: Division of Research, Harvard Business School, 1966), pp. 18–25.

[13] George Harris, "To Know Why Men Do What They Do: A Conversation with David C. McClelland," *Psychology Today* 4 (January 1971):35–39.

[14] David C. McClelland and David H. Burnham, "Power Is the Great Motivator," *Harvard Business Review* 54 (March/April 1976):100–110; David C. McClelland and Richard E. Boyatzis, "Leadership Motive Pattern and Long-Term Success in Management," *Journal of Applied Psychology* 67 (1982):737–743.

[15] P. Miron and D. C. McClelland, "The Impact of Achievement Motivation Training in Small Businesses," *California Management Review* (Summer 1979):13–28.

[16] The complete two-factor theory is well explained by Herzberg and his associates in Frederick Herzberg, Bernard Mausner, and Barbara Bloch Synderman, *The Motivation to Work*, 2nd ed. (New York: Wiley, 1967); Frederick Herzberg, "One More Time: How Do You Motivate Employees?" *Harvard Business Review* 46 (January/February 1968):53–62.

[17] From Herzberg (1968).

[18] See Robert J. House and Lawrence A. Wigdor, "Herzberg's Dual-Factor Theory of Job Satisfaction and Motivation: A Review of the Evidence and a Criticism," *Personnel Psychology* 20 (Winter 1967):369–389; Steven Kerr, Anne Harlan, and Ralph Stogdill,

"Preference for Motivator and Hygiene Factors in a Hypothetical Interview Situation," *Personnel Psychology* 27 (Winter 1974):109–124; Nathan King, "A Clarification and Evaluation of the Two-Factor Theory of Job Satisfaction," *Psychological Bulletin* (July 1970):18–31; Marvin Dunnette, John Campbell, and Milton Hakel, "Factors Contributing to Job Satisfaction and Job Dissatisfaction in Six Occupational Groups," *Organizational Behavior and Human Performance* (May 1967):143–174; R. J. House and L. Wigdor, "Herzberg's Dual Factor Theory of Job Satisfaction and Motivation: A Review of the Evidence and a Criticism," *Personnel Psychology* (Summer 1967):369–389.

[19] Adler (1991), ch. 6; Nancy J. Adler and J. T. Graham, "Cross Cultural Interaction: The International Comparison Fallacy," *Journal of International Business Studies* (Fall 1989):515–537; Frederick Herzberg, "Workers Needs: The Same Around the World," *Industry Week* (September 27, 1987), pp. 29–32.

[20] See, for example, J. Stacy Adams, "Toward an Understanding of Inequality," *Journal of Abnormal and Social Psychology* 67 (1963):422–436; J. Stacy Adams, "Inequity in Social Exchange," in L. Berkowitz (ed.), *Advances in Experimental Social Psychology* (Vol. 2) (New York: Academic Press, 1965), pp. 267–300.

[21] Adams (1965).

[22] These issues are discussed in C. Kagitcibasi and J. W. Berry, "Cross-Cultural Psychology: Current Research and Trends," *Annual Review of Psychology* 40 (1989):493–531.

[23] Victor H. Vroom, *Work and Motivation* (New York: Wiley, 1964).

[24] See ibid.

[25] See Terence R. Mitchell, "Expectancy Models of Job Satisfaction, Occupational Preference and Effort: A Theoretical, Methodological, and Empirical Appraisal," *Psychological Bulletin* 81 (1974):1053–1077; Mahmoud A. Wahba and Robert J. House, "Expectancy Theory in Work and Motivation: Some Logical and Methodological Issues," *Human Relations* 27 (January 1974):121–147; Terry Connolly, "Some Conceptual and Methodological Issues in Expectancy Models of Work Performance Motivation," *Academy of Management Review* 1 (October 1976):37–47; Terrence Mitchell, "Expectancy-Value Models in Organizational Psychology," in N. Feather (ed.), *Expectancy, Incentive and Action* (New York: Erlbaum & Associates, 1980).

[26] See Lyman W. Porter and Edward E. Lawler III, *Managerial Attitudes and Performance* (Homewood, IL: Irwin, 1968).

[27] See Adler (1991).

[28] For good overviews of reinforcement-based views, see W. E. Scott Jr. and P. M. Podsakoff, *Behavioral Principles in the Practice of Management* (New York: Wiley, 1985); Fred Luthans and Robert Kreitner, *Organizational Behavior Modification and Beyond* (Glenview, IL: Scott, Foresman, 1985).

[29] For some of B. F. Skinner's work, see his *Walden Two* (New York: Macmillan, 1948); *Science and Human Behavior* (New York: Macmillan, 1953); *Contingencies of Reinforcement* (New York: Appleton-Century-Crofts, 1969).

[30] E. L. Thorndike, *Animal Intelligence* (New York: Macmillan, 1911), p. 244.

[31] Adapted from Luthans and Kreitner (1985).

[32] This discussion is based on ibid.

[33] Both laws are stated in Keith L. Miller, *Principles of Everyday Behavior Analysis* (Monterey, CA: Brooks/Cole, 1975), p. 122.

[34] This example is based on a study by Barbara Price and Richard Osborn, "Shaping the Training of Skilled Workers," working paper (Detroit: Department of Management, Wayne State University, 1999).

[35] See John Putzier and Frank T. Novak, "Attendance Management and Control," *Personnel Administrator* (August 1989):59–60.

[36] Robert Kreitner and Angelo Kiniki, *Organization Behavior*, 2nd ed. (Homewood, IL: Irwin, 1992).

[37] These have been used for years; see K. M. Evans, "On-the Job Lotteries: A Low-Cost Incentive That Sparks Higher Productivity," *Compensation and Benefits Review* 20(4) (1988):63–74; A. Halcrow, "Incentive! How Three Companies Cut Costs," *Personal Journal* (February 1986):12.

[38] A. R. Korukonda and James G. Hunt, "Pat on the Back Versus Kick in the Pants: An Application of Cognitive Inference to the Study of Leader Reward and Punishment Behavior," *Group and Organization Studies* 14 (1989):299–234.

[39] See "Janitorial Firm Success Story Started with Cleaning Couple," *Lubbock Avalanche-Journal* (August 25, 1991), p. E7.

[40] Edwin A. Locke, "The Myths of Behavior Mod in Organizations," *Academy of Management Review* 2 (October 1977):543–553. For a counterpoint, see Jerry L. Gray, "The Myths of the Myths About Behavior Mod in Organizations: A Reply to Locke's Criticisms of Behavior Modification," *Academy of Management Review* 4 (January 1979):121–129.

[41] Robert Kreitner, "Controversy in OBM: History, Misconceptions, and Ethics," in Lee Frederiksen (ed.), *Handbook of Organizational Behavior Management* (New York: Wiley, 1982), pp. 71–91.

[42] W. E. Scott Jr. and P. M. Podsakoff, *Behavioral Principles in the Practice of Management* (New York: Wiley, 1985); also see W. Clay Hamner, "Reinforcement Theory and Contingency Management in Organizational Settings," in Richard M. Steers and Lyman W. Porters (eds.), *Motivation and Work Behavior*, 4th ed. (New York: McGraw-Hill, 1987), pp. 139–165; Luthans and Kreitner (1985); Charles C. Manz and Henry P. Sims Jr., *Superleadership* (New York: Berkeley, 1990).

SOURCE NOTES

Based on David Kirkpatrick, "Big-League R&D Gets Its Own eBay," *Fortune* (May 3, 2004) p. 74.

Based on Mike Hanes, "Wind Ensemble Journeys to England on Concert Tour," *Southern Alumni* (March 2004):16.

Based on Rick Gosselin, "Grabbing a Second Chance," *Dallas Morning News* (April 18, 2004), p. 4C.

Based on Associated Press, "Guidebooks Help Pastors Aid Jobless," *Lubbock Avalanche-Journal* (February 8, 2004), p. D5.

Based on Class Notes, "Life Member Named to Top 50 Technology List," *Southern Alumni* 66(1) (2004):16.

Based on Richard M. Hodgets and Thomas M. Tworoger, "A Conversation with AutoNation's President, Mike Maroone: Auto Retailing Where 'Retail is Detail,'" *Journal of Leadership and Organizational Studies* 9(4) (2003):87–95.

Chapter 7

ENDNOTES

[1] David Grainger, "One Truck a Minute", *Fortune* (April 5, 2004), pp. 252–258.

[2] See William E. Wymer and Jeanne M. Carsten, "Alternative Ways to Gather Opinions," *HR Magazine* 37(4) (April 1992):71–78.

[3] The Job Descriptive Index (JDI) is available from Dr. Patricia C. Smith, Department of Psychology, Bowling Green State University; the Minnesota Satisfaction Questionnaire (MSQ) is available from the Industrial Relations Center and Vocational Psychology Research Center, University of Minnesota.

[4] Barry M. Staw, "The Consequences of Turnover," *Journal of Occupational Behavior* 1 (1980):253–273; John P. Wanous, *Organizational Entry* (Reading, MA: Addison-Wesley, 1980).

[5] Charles N. Greene, "The Satisfaction-Performance Controversy," *Business Horizons* 15 (1972):31–41; Michelle T. Iaffaldano and Paul M. Muchinsky, "Job Satisfaction and Job Performance: A Meta-Analysis," *Psychological Bulletin* 97 (1985):251–273; Dennis Organ, "A Reappraisal and Reinterpretation of the Satisfaction-Causes-Performance Hypothesis," *Academy of Management Review* 2 (1977):46–53; Peter Lorenzi, "A Comment on Organ's Reappraisal of the Satisfaction-Causes-Performance Hypothesis," *Academy of Management Review* 3 (1978):380–382.

[6] Lyman W. Porter and Edward E. Lawler III, *Managerial Attitudes and Work Performance* (Homewood, IL: Irwin, 1968).

[7] Frederick W. Taylor, *The Principles of Scientific Management* (New York: Norton, 1967).
Information from "Building the S80: More Than a Sum of Its Parts," *Volvo S80* (1998); company Web site: www.volvo.com.

[8] Frederick Herzberg, "One More Time: How Do You Motivate Employees?" *Harvard Business Review* 46 (January/February 1968):53–62.

[9] Paul J. Champagne and Curt Tausky, "When Job Enrichment Doesn't Pay," *Personnel* 3 (January/February 1978):30–40.

[10] For a complete description, see J. Richard Hackman and Greg R. Oldham, *Work Redesign* (Reading, MA: Addison-Wesley, 1980).

[11] See J. Richard Hackman and Greg Oldham, "Development of the Job Diagnostic Survey," *Journal of Applied Psychology* 60 (1975): pp. 159–170.

[12] Hackman and Oldham (ibid). For forerunner research, see Charles L. Hulin and Milton R. Blood, "Job Enlargement, Individual Differences, and Worker Responses," *Psychological Bulletin* 69 (1968):41–55; Milton R. Blood and Charles L. Hulin, "Alienation, Environmental Characteristics and Worker Responses," *Journal of Applied Psychology* 51 (1967):284–290.

[13] Gerald Salancik and Jeffrey Pfeffer, "An Examination of Need-Satisfaction Models of Job Attitudes," *Administrative Science Quarterly* 22 (1977):427–456; Gerald Salancik and Jeffrey Pfeffer, "A Social Information Processing Approach to Job Attitude and Task Design," *Administrative Science Quarterly* 23 (1978):224–253.

[14] George W. England and Itzhak Harpaz, "How Working Is Defined: National Contexts and Demographic and Organizational Role Influences," *Journal of Organizational Behavior* (July 1990):253–266.

[15] William A. Pasmore, "Overcoming the Roadblocks to Work-Restructuring Efforts," *Organizational Dynamics* 10 (1982):54–67; Hackman and Oldham, op. cit. (1975).

[16] See William A. Pasmore, *Designing Effective Organizations: A Sociotechnical Systems Perspective* (New York: Wiley, 1988).

[17] "Robots," *The Economist* (October 17, 1998), p. 116.

[18] See "Robots Filling Many Duties in Hospitals," *Lubbock Avalanche-Journal* (July 7, 2004), p. D6.

[19] Peter Senker, *Towards the Automatic Factory: The Need for Training* (New York: Springer-Verlag, 1986).

[20] See Ramchandran Jaikumar, "Postindustrial Manufacturing," *Harvard Business Review* (1986):69–76.

[21] Michael Hammer, "Reengineering Work: Don't Automate, Obliterate," *Harvard Business Review* (July/August 1990):104–112.

[22] See Thomas M. Koulopoulos, *The Workflow Imperative: Building Real World Business Solutions* (New York: Van Nostrand Reinhold, 1995).

[23] For a good overview, see Michael Hammer and James Champy, *Reengineering the Corporation* (New York: HarperBusiness, 1993); Michael Hammer, *Beyond Reengineering* (New York: HarperBusiness, 1997).

[24] For overviews, see Allan R. Cohen and Herman Gadon, *Alternative Work Schedules: Integrating Individual and Organizational Needs* (Reading, MA: Addison-Wesley, 1978); and Jon L. Pearce, John W. Newstrom, Randall B. Dunham, and Alison E. Barber, *Alternative Work Schedules* (Boston: Allyn & Bacon, 1989). See also Sharon Parker and Toby Wall, *Job and Work Design* (Thousand Oaks, CA: Sage, 1998).

[25] B. J. Wixom Jr., "Recognizing People in a World of Change," *HR Magazine* (June 1995):7–8; "The Value of Flexibility," *Inc.* (April 1996):114.

[26] Information from Alan Krueger and Alexandre Mas, "Strikes, Scabs and Tread Separations: Labor Strife and the Production of Defective Bridgestone/Firestone Tires," Working Paper, Princeton University Industrial Relations Section (January 9, 2002); "The Hidden Cost of Labor Strife," *Wall Street Journal* (January 30, 2002), p. 1.

[27] C. Latack and L. W. Foster, "Implementation of Compressed Work Schedules: Participation and Job Redesign as Critical Factors for Employee Acceptance," *Personnel Psychology* 38 (1985):75–92.

[28] *Business Week* (December 7, 1998), p. 8.

[29] "Aetna Life & Casualty Company," *Wall Street Journal* (June 4, 1990), p. R35; (June 18, 1990), p. B1.

[30] Getsy M. Selirio, "Job Sharing Gains Favor as Corporations Embrace Alternative Work Schedule," *Lubbock Avalanche-Journal* (December 13, 1992), p. 2E.

[31] Ibid.

[32] "Making Stay-at-Homes Feel Welcome," *Business Week* (October 12, 1998), pp. 153–155.

[33] T. Davenport and K. Pearlson, "Two Cheers for the Virtual Office," *Sloan Management Review* (Summer 1998):51–64.

[34] "Making Stay-at-Homes Feel Welcome" (1998).

[35] Daniel C. Feldman and Helen I. Doerpinghaus, "Missing Persons No Longer: Managing Part-Time Workers in the '90s," *Organizational Dynamics* (Summer 1992): pp. 59–72.

SOURCE NOTES

Based on Rob Walker, "Brand Blue," *Fortune*, (April 28, 2003), pp. 118/B/–118/H/.

Based on Richard S. Chang, "He's Driven to Help Others," *Parade* (April 18, 2004), p. 20.

Based on Justin Pope, "Nuns Turn to Technology for Their Chocolate Business," *Lubbock Avalanche-Journal* (May 10, 2003), p. B5.

Based on Sal Ruibal, "Hospital Ready to be Hub for War's Wounded," *USA Today* (March 19, 2003), p. 8D.

Based on Ken Thompson, "A Conversation with Mark Sussor: Leadership in the Largest UPS Distribution Facility in the World," *The Journal of Leadership Studies* 8(2) (2001):145–159.

Based on Jeff Walker, "Global Recruiting for Tech Tennis Teams," *Lubbock Avalanche-Journal* (April 29, 2004) p. D1.

Figure 7.2 adapted from J. Richard Hackman and Greg R. Oldham, "Development of the Job Diagnostic Survey," *Journal of Applied Psychology* 60 (1975): p. 161. Used by permission.

Based on Edwin A. Locke and Gary P. Latham: "Work Motivation and Satisfaction: Light at the End of the Tunnel," *Psychological Science* 1(4) (July 1990):244.

Chapter 8

ENDNOTES

[1] David Tarrant, "Forging a Warrior," *Dallas Morning News* (April 27, 2003), pp 1E, 3E, 14E.

[2] Edwin A Locke, Karyll N. Shaw, Lise M. Saari, and Gary P. Latham, "Goal Setting and Task Performance: 1969–1980," *Psychological Bulletin* 90 (July/November 1981): 125–152; Edwin A Locke and Gary P. Latham, "Work Motivation and Satisfaction: Light at the End of the Tunnel," *Psychological Science* 1(4) (July 1990):240–246; Edwin A. Locke and Gary Latham, *A Theory of Goal Setting and Task Performance*, (Englewood Cliffs, NJ: Prentice Hall, 1990).

[3] Gary P. Latham and Edwin A. Locke, "Goal Setting—A Motivational Technique That Works," *Organizational Dynamics* 8 (Autumn 1979): 68–80; Gary P. Latham and Timothy P. Steele, "The Motivational Effects of Participation Versus Goal-Setting on Performance," *Academy of Management Journal* 26 (1983):406–417; Miriam Erez and Frederick H. Kanfer, "The Role of Goal Acceptance in Goal Setting and Task Performance," *Academy of Management Review* 8 (1983):454–463; R. E. Wood and E. A. Locke, "Goal Setting and Strategy Effects on Complex Tasks," in B. Staw and L. L. Cummings (eds.), *Research in Organizational Behavior* (Greenwich, CT: JAI Press, 1990).

[4] See E. A. Locke and G. P. Latham, "Work Motivation and Satisfaction," *Psychological Science* 1(4) (July 1990):241.

[5] Ibid.

[6] For a good review of MBO, see Anthony P. Raia, *Managing by Objectives* (Glenview, IL: Scott, Foresman, 1974).

[7] Ibid. Steven Kerr summarizes the criticisms well in "Overcoming the Dysfunctions of MBO." *Management by Objectives* 5(1), 1976.

[8] Michael Hammer, "Reengineering Work: Don't Automate, Obliterate," *Harvard Business Review* (July/August 1990):104–112.

[9] See Thomas M. Koulopoulos, *The Workflow Imperative: Building Real World Business Solutions* (New York: Van Nostrand Reinhold, 1995).

[10] For a good overview, see Michael Hammer and James Champy, *Reengineering the Corporation* (New York: Harper Business, 1993); Michael Hammer, *Beyond Reengineering* (New York: HarperBusiness, 1997).

[11] Information from "The Business Imperative for Workflow & Business Process Reengineering," *Fortune* (November 27, 1995), special advertising supplement.

[12] For more details, see G. P. Latham and K. N. Wexley, *Increasing Productivity through Performance Appraisal* (2nd ed.); Stephen J. Carroll and Craig E. Schneier, *Performance Appraisal and Review Systems* (Glenview, IL: Scott, Foresman, 1982).

[13] See George T. Milkovich and John W. Boudreau, *Personnel/Human Resource Management: A Diagnostic Approach*, 5th ed. (Plano, TX: Business Publications, 1988).

[14] For a detailed discussion, see S. J. Carroll and H. L. Tosi Jr., *Management of Objectives: Application and Research* (New York: Macmillan, 1976); Raia (1974).

[15] For discussion of many of these errors, see David L. Devries, Ann M. Morrison, Sandra L. Shullman, and Michael P. Gerlach, *Performance Appraisal on the Line* (Greensboro, NC: Center for Creative Leadership, 1986), ch. 3.

[16] E. G. Olson, "The Workplace Is High on the High Court's Docket," *Business Week* (October 10, 1988), pp. 88–89.

[17] Based on J. J. Bernardin and C. S. Walter, "The Effects of Rater Training and Diary Keeping on Psychometric Error in Ratings," *Journal of Applied Psychology* 61 (1977):64–69; see also R. G. Burnask and T. D. Hollman, "An Empirical Comparison of the Relative Effects of Sorter Response Bias on Three Rating Scale Formats," *Journal of Applied Psychology* 59 (1974):307–312.

[18] W. F. Cascio and H. J. Bernardin, "Implications of Performance Appraisal Litigation for Personnel Decisions," *Personnel Psychology* 34 (1981):221–222.

[19] See David Shar, "Comp Star Adds Efficiency and Flexibility to Performance Reviews," *HR Magazine* (October 1997):37–42.

[20] For complete reviews of theory, research, and practice, see Edward E. Lawler III, *Pay and Organizational Effectiveness* (New York: McGraw-Hill, 1971); Edward E. Lawler III, *Pay and Organizational Development* (Reading, MA: Addison-Wesley, 1981); Edward E. Lawler III, "The Design of Effective Reward Systems," in Jay W. Lorsch (ed.), *Handbook of Organizational Behavior* (Englewood Cliffs, NJ: Prentice-Hall, 1987), pp. 255–271.

[21] As an example, see D. B. Balkin and L. R. Gómez-Mejía (eds.), *New Perspectives on Compensation* (Englewood Cliffs, NJ: Prentice-Hall, 1987).

[22] Jone L. Pearce, "Why Merit Pay Doesn't Work: Implications from Organization Theory," in Balkin and Gómez-Mejía (1987), pp. 169–178; Jerry M. Newman, "Selecting Incentive Plans to Complement Organizational Strategy," in Balkin and Gómez-Mejía (1987), pp. 214–224; Edward E. Lawler III, "Pay for Performance: Making It Work," *Compensation and Benefits Review* 21 (1989):55–60.

[23] See Daniel C. Boyle, "Employee Motivation That Works," *HR Magazine* (October 1992):83–89; Kathleen A. McNally, "Compensation as a Strategic Tool," *HR Magazine* (July 1992):59–66.

[24] S. Caudron, "Master the Compensation Maze," *Personnel Journal* (June 1993):640–648.

[25] N. Gupta, G. E. Ledford, G. D. Jenkins, and D. H. Doty, "Survey Based Prescriptions for Skill-Based Pay," *American Compensation Association Journal* 1(1) (1992):48–59; L. W. Ledford, "The Effectiveness of Skill-Based Pay," *Perspectives in Total Compensation* 1(1) (1991):1–4.

[26] See Brian Graham-Moore, "Review of the Literature," in Brian Graham-Moore and Timothy L. Ross (eds.), *Gainsharing* (Washington, DC: Bureau of National Affairs, 1990), p. 20.

[27] S. E. Markham, K. D. Scott, and B. L. Little, "National Gainsharing Study: The Importance of Industry Differences," *Compensation and Benefits Review* (January/February 1992):34–45.

[28] L. R. Gómez-Mejía, D. B. Balkin, and R. L. Cardy, *Managing Human Resources* (Englewood Cliffs, NJ: Prentice-Hall, 1995), pp. 410–411.

[29] Ibid., pp. 409–410.

[30] C. O'Dell and J. McAdams, "The Revolution in Employee Benefits," *Compensation and Benefits Review* (May/June 1987):68–73.

[31] For a good discussion of human resource management strategy and its linkage to overall management strategy, see A. J. Templer and R. J. Cattaneo, "A Model of Human Resources Management Effectiveness," *Canadian Journal of Administrative Sciences* 12(1)(1995):77–88.

[32] See J. R. Schermerhorn Jr., *Management*, 5th ed. (New York: Wiley, 1996), ch. 12; summarized from G. M. Bounds, G. H. Dobbins, and O. S. Fowler, *Management: A Total Quality Perspective* (Cincinnati: South-Western, 1995), ch. 9; Gómez-Mejía, Balkin, and Cardy, (1995), chs. 2, 6.

[33] Bounds, Dobbins, and Fowler (1995), *Ibid.*

[34] Ibid., Gómez-Mejía, Balkin, and Cardy (1995), pp. 97–98.

[35] Summarized from Bounds, Dobbins, and Fowler (1995), pp. 319–321; Gómez-Mejía, Balkin, and Cardy (1995), ch. 6; Schermerhorn (1996), pp. 290–293.

[36] See "Blueprints for Service Quality: The Federal Express Approach," *AMA Management Briefing* (New York: AMA Publications, 1991).

[37] Based on A. Uris, *Eighty-Eight Mistakes Interviewers Make and How to Avoid Them* (New York: AMA Publications, 1988).

[38] G. C. Thornton, *Assessment Centers in Human Resource Management* (Reading, MA: Addison-Wesley, 1992).

[39] B. B. Gaugler, D. B. Rosenthal, G. C. Thornton, and C. Bentson, "Meta-Analysis of Assessment Center Validity," *Journal of Applied Psychology* 72 (1987):493–511.

[40] William Bommer, "The Iliad Assessment Center," unpublished manuscript, Cleveland State University, Spring 2004.

[41] P. M. Muchinsky, "The Use of Reference Reports in Personnel Selection: A Review and Evaluation," *Journal of Occupational Psychology* 52 (1979):287–297.

[42] Much of this discussion is derived from Daniel C. Feldman, "The Multiple Socialization of Organizational Members," *Academy of Management Review* 6(2) (1981):309–318.

[43] This training discussion is based on Bounds, Dobbins, and Fowler (1995), pp. 326–329; Schermerhorn (1996), pp. 294–295; S. R. Robbins, *Organizational Behavior*, 7th ed. (Englewood Cliffs, NJ: Prentice-Hall, 1996), pp. 641–644.

[44] See Rob Muller, "Training for Change," *Canadian Business Review* (Spring 1995):16–19.

[45] Much of the initial discussion in this section is based on Daniel C. Feldman, "Careers in Organizations: Recent Trends and Future Directions," *Journal of Management* 15 (June 1989):135–156; Irving Janis and Dan Wheeler, "Thinking Clearly About Career Choices," *Psychology Today* (May 1978):67; Walter Kiechel III, "How We Will Work in the Year 2000," *Fortune* (May 17, 1993), pp. 38–52.

[46] Charles Handy, *The Age of Unreason* (Boston: Harvard Business School Press, 1991).

[47] David Kirkpatrick, "The Net Makes it All Easier—Including Exporting U.S. Jobs," *Fortune* (May 26, 2003); Victor Godinez, "Overseas Outsourcing Expected to Continue", *Dallas Morning News* (August 17, 2003), 146–148; Daniel W. Drezner, "The Outsourcing Bogeyman," *Foreign Affairs* 83(3) (May/June 2004):22–34.

[48] This discussion combines earlier and later career development literature based on Janis and Wheeler, p. 67; Daniel J. Levinson, *The Seasons of a Man's Life* (New York: Knopf, 1978); Douglas T. Hall, *Careers in Organizations* (Santa Monica, CA: Goodyear, 1975); Lloyd Baird and Kathy Krim, "Career Dynamics: Managing the Superior–Subordinate Relationship," *Organization Dynamics* (Spring 1983):47; Paul H. Thompson, Robin Zenger Baker, and Norman Smallwood, "Improving Professional Development by Applying the Four-Stage Career Model," *Organization Dynamics* (Autumn 1986):49–62; Thomas P. Ference, James A. F. Stoner, and E. Kirby Warren, "Managing the Career Plateau." *Academy of Management Review* 2 (October 1977):602–612; Gail Sheehy, *New Passages: Mapping Your Life Across Time* (New York: Ballantine Books, 1995).

SOURCE NOTES

Based on Marianne Lawrence, "Publishing CEO Succeeds while Breaking Barriers along the Way," *Southern Alumni* (March 2004):30–33.

Based on Associated Press, "Manning Plans More Improvement,", *Lubbock Avalanche-Journal* (May 1, 2004), p. B8. Based on Anne Fisher, "Does Big Brother Software Treat Staff Like Kids?" *Fortune* (March 8, 2004), p. 68.

Christopher Tkaczyk, Ellen Florian, and Jaclyn Stemple, "Fifty Best Companies for Minorities", *Fortune* (July 7, 2003), pp. N03ff.

Based on Smith Barney Citigroup, "Youssou N'Dour," *Fortune* (May 3, 2004), special advertising feature.

Performance review form adapted from Andrew D. Szilagi Jr. and Marc J. Wallace Jr., *Organizational Behavior and Performance*, 3rd ed. (Glenview, IL: Scott, Foresman, 1983), pp. 393–394.

Adapted from J. P. Campbell, M. D. Dunnette, R. D. Arvey, and L. V. Hellervik, "The Development Evaluation of Behaviorally Based Rating Scales," *Applied Psychology* 57 (1973): 18. Copyright 1973 by the American Psychological Association. Reprinted by permission of publisher and authors.

The Effective Manager information from J. Zignon, "Making Performance Appraisal Work for Teams," *Training* (June 1994), pp. 58–63.

Chapter 9

ENDNOTES

[1] Information from David Kirkpatrick, "The Second Coming of Apple," *Fortune* (November 9, 1998), pp. 86–92. See also Brent Schlender, "The Three Faces of Steve," *Fortune* (November 9, 1998), pp. 96–104; www.apple.com.

[2] For a good discussion of groups and teams in the workplace, see Jon R. Katzenbach and Douglas K. Smith, "The Discipline of Teams," *Harvard Business Review* (March/April 1993):111–120; and Greg L. Stewart, Charles C. Mane, and Henry P. Sims, *Team Work and Group Dynamics* (New York: John Wiley & Sons, 1999).

[3] Harold J. Leavitt and Jean Lipman-Blumen, "Hot Groups," *Harvard Business Review* (July/August 1995):109–116.

[4] See, for example, Edward E. Lawler III, *High-Involvement Management* (San Francisco: Jossey-Bass, 1986).

[5] Marvin E. Shaw, *Group Dynamics: The Psychology of Small Group Behavior*, 2nd ed. (New York: McGraw-Hill, 1976).

[6] Bib Latané, Kipling Williams, and Stephen Harkins, "Many Hands Make Light the Work: The Causes and Consequences of Social Loafing," *Journal of Personality and Social Psychology* 37 (1978):822–832; E. Weldon and G. M. Gargano, "Cognitive Effort in Additive Task Groups: The Effects of Shared Responsibility on the Quality of Multi-Attribute Judgments," *Organizational Behavior and Human Decision Processes* 36 (1985):348–361; John M. George, "Extrinsic and Intrinsic Origins of Perceived Social Loafing in Organizations," *Academy of Management Journal* (March 1992):191–202; W. Jack Duncan, "Why Some People Loaf in Groups While Others Loaf Alone," *Academy of Management Executive* 8 (1994):79–80.

[7] D. A. Kravitz and B. Martin, "Ringelmann Rediscovered," *Journal of Personality and Social Psychology* 50 (1986):936–941.

[8] A classic article is by Richard B. Zajonc, "Social Facilitation," *Science* 149 (1965):269–274.

[9] Rensis Likert, *New Patterns of Management* (New York: McGraw-Hill, 1961).

[10] For a good discussion of task forces, see James Ware, "Managing a Task Force," Note 478-002, Harvard Business School, 1977.

[11] See D. Duarte and N. Snyder, *Mastering Virtual Teams: Strategies, Tools, and Techniques That Succeed* (San Francisco: Jossey-Bass, 1999).

[12] See, for example, Leland P. Bradford, *Group Development*, 2nd ed. (San Francisco: Jossey-Bass, 1997).

[13] J. Steven Heinen and Eugene Jacobson, "A Model of Task Group Development in Complex Organization and a Strategy of Implementation," *Academy of Management Review* 1 (October 1976):98–111; Bruce W. Tuckman, "Developmental Sequence in Small Groups," *Psychological Bulletin* 63 (1965):384–399; Bruce W. Tuckman and Mary Ann C. Jensen, "Stages of Small Group Development Revisited," *Group & Organization Studies* 2 (1977):419–427.

[14] See J. Richard Hackman, "The Design of Work Teams," in Jay W. Lorsch (ed.), *Handbook of Organizational Behavior* (Englewood Cliffs, NJ: Prentice Hall, 1987), pp. 343–357.

[15] David M. Herold, "The Effectiveness of Work Groups," in Steven Kerr (ed.), *Organizational Behavior* (New York: Wiley, 1979), p. 95; see also the discussion of group tasks in Stewart, Manz, and Sims, op. cit. (1999), pp. 142–143.

[16] Daniel R. Ilgen, Jeffrey A. LePine, and John R. Hollenbeck, "Effective Decision Making in Multinational Teams," in P. Christopher Earley and Miram Erez (eds.), *New Perspectives on International Industrial/Organizational Psychology* (San Francisco: New Lexington Press, 1997); Warren Watson, "Cultural Diversity's Impact on Interaction Process and Performance," *Academy of Management Journal* 16 (1993).

[17] L. Argote and J. E. McGrath, "Group Processes in Organizations: Continuity and Change," in C. L. Cooper and I. T. Robertson (eds.), *International Review of Industrial and Organizational Psychology* (New York: Wiley, 1993), pp. 333–389.

[18] See Ilgen, Le Piner, and Hollenbeck (1997), pp. 377–409.

[19] William C. Schultz, *FIRO: A Three-Dimensional Theory of Interpersonal Behavior* (New York: Rinehart, 1958).

[20] William C. Schultz, "The Interpersonal Underworld," *Harvard Business Review* 36 (July/August 1958):130.

[21] Katzenbach and Smith (1993).

[22] E. J. Thomas and C. F. Fink, "Effects of Group Size," in Larry L. Cummings and William E. Scott (eds.), *Readings in Organizational and Human Performance* (Homewood, IL: Irwin, 1969), pp. 394–408.

[23] Shaw (1976).

[24] George C. Homans, *The Human Group* (New York: Harcourt Brace, 1950).

[25] For a discussion of intergroup dynamics, see Edgar H. Schein, *Process Consultation* Volume I (Reading, MA: Addison-Wesley, 1988), pp. 106–115.

[26] "Producer Power," *The Economist* (March 4, 1995), p. 70.

[27] The concept of interacting, coacting, and counteracting groups is presented in Fred E. Fiedler, *A Theory of Leadership Productivity* (New York: McGraw-Hill, 1967).

[28] Research on communication networks is found in Alex Bavelas, "Communication Patterns in Task-Oriented Groups," *Journal of the Acoustical Society of America* 22 (1950): 725–730. See also "Research on Communication Networks," as summarized in Shaw (1976), pp. 137–153.

[29] The discussion is developed from Schein (1988), pp. 69–75.

[30] Ibid., p. 73.

[31] Developed from guidelines presented in the classic article by Jay Hall, "Decisions, Decisions, Decisions," *Psychology Today* (November 1971):55–56.

[32] Norman R.F. Maier, "Assets and Liabilities in Group Problem Solving," *Psychological Review* 74 (1967):239–249.

[33] Ibid.

[34] Irving L. Janis, "Groupthink," *Psychology Today* (November 1971):33–36; Irving L. Janis, *Groupthink*, 2nd ed. (Boston: Houghton Mifflin, 1982). See also J. Longley and D. G. Pruitt, "Groupthink: A Critique of Janis' Theory," in L. Wheeler (ed.), *Review of Personality and Social Psychology* (Beverly Hills, CA: Sage, 1980); Carrie R. Leana, "A Partial Test of Janis's Groupthink Model: The Effects of Group Cohesiveness and Leader Behavior on Decision Processes," *Journal of Management* 11(1) (1985):5–18. See also Jerry Harvey, "Managing Agreement in Organizations: The Abilene Paradox," *Organizational Dynamics* (Summer 1974):63–80.

[35] Janis (1982).

[36] Gayle W. Hill, "Group Versus Individual Performance: Are Two Heads Better Than One?" *Psychological Bulletin* 91 (1982):517–539.

[37] These techniques are well described in George P. Huber, *Managerial Decision Making* (Glenview, IL: Scott, Foresman, 1980); Andre L. Delbecq, Andrew L. Van de Ven, and David H. Gustafson, *Group Techniques for Program Planning: A Guide to Nominal Groups and Delphi Techniques* (Glenview, IL: Scott, Foresman, 1975); William M. Fox, "Anonymity and Other Keys to Successful Problem-Solving Meetings," *National Productivity Review* 8 (Spring 1989):145–156.

[38] Delbecq, Van de Ve, and Gustafson al., op. cit. (1975); Fox, op. cit. (1989).

[39] R. Brent Gallupe and William H. Cooper, "Brainstorming Electronically," *Sloan Management Review* (Fall 1993):27–36.

SOURCE NOTES

"What a Zoo Can Teach You," *Fortune* (May 18, 1992); Thomas Stewart, "The Search for the Organization of Tomorrow," *Fortune* (May 18, 1992); Nancy Austin, "Making Team Work," *Working Woman* (January 1993); Barbara Ettorre, "A Day in the Life: The Wild Life of a Manager—San Diego Zoo Animal Care Manager Curby Simerson," *Management Review* 84 (August 1995), p. 28; www.sandiegozoo.org.

Information and quotes from Richard Lapchick, "Robert L. Johnson, Founder/Chairman/CEO of Black Entertainment Television (BET) and Majority Owner of the NBA's Charlotte Bobcats, on Leading Talented People," *The Academy of Management Executive* 18 (1) (2004):114–119.

W. L. Gore & Associates: Information from Shelley Branch, "The 100 Best Companies to Work for in America," *Fortune* (January 11, 1999), p. 126.

Information from Stephen Baker and Manjeet Kripalani, "Will Outsourcing Hurt America's Supremacy?" *Business Week* (March 1, 2004), pp. 85–94.

See section on "commitment to U.S. manufacturing" on the corporate Web site: www.newbalance.com.

Chapter 10

ENDNOTES

[1] Information from Tom Redburn, "His Dream Is That We'll All Hear Little Voices," *New York Times* (September 23, 1998), p. 9; corporate Web site: www.audible.com.

[2] *Fortune* (May 7, 1990), pp. 52–60. See also Ronald E. Purser and Steven Cabana, *The Self-Managing Organization* (New York: Free Press, 1998).

[3] Susan Albers Mohrman, Jay R. Galbraith, Edward E. Lawler III, et al., *Tomorrow's Organization: Crafting Winning Capabilities in a Dynamic World* (San Francisco: Jossey-Bass, 1998).

[4] Jon R. Katzenbach and Douglas K. Smith, "The Discipline of Teams," *Harvard Business Review* (March/April 1993a):111–120; Jon R. Katzenbach and Douglas K. Smith, *The Wisdom of Teams: Creating the High-Performance Organization* (Boston: Harvard Business School Press, 1993b).

[5] Jay A. Conger, *Winning 'Em Over: A New Model for Managing in the Age of Persuasion* (New York: Simon & Schuster, 1998).

[6] Ibid., p. 191.

[7] Katzenbach and Smith (1993a and 1993b).

[8] See also Jon R. Katzenbach, "The Myth of the Top Management Team," *Harvard Business Review* 75 (November/December 1997):83–91.

[9] Katzenbach and Smith (1993a and 1993b).

[10] For a good overview, see Greg L. Stewart, Charles C. Manz, and Henry P. Sims, *Team Work and Group Dynamics* (New York: Wiley, 1999).

[11] Katzenbach and Smith (1993a), p. 112.

[12] Developed from ibid. (1993a), pp. 118–119.

[13] See Stewart, Manz, and Sims (1999), pp. 43–44.

[14] See Daniel R. Ilgen, Jeffrey A. LePine, and John R. Hollenbeck, "Effective Decision Making in Multinational Teams," in P. Christopher Earley and Miriam Erez (eds.), *New Perspectives on International Industrial/Organizational Psychology* (San Francisco: New Lexington Press, 1997), pp. 377–409.

[15] Ibid., Warren Watson, "Cultural Diversity's Impact on Interaction Process and Performance," *Academy of Management Journal* 16 (1993).

[16] For an interesting discussion of sports teams see Ellen Fagenson-Eland, "The National Football League's Bill Parcells on Winning, Leading, and Turning Around Teams," *Academy of Management Executive* 15 (August 2001):48–57; Nancy Katz, "Sports Teams as a Model for Workplace Teams: Lessons and Liabilities," *Academy of Management Executive*. 15 (August 2002):56–69.

[17] For a good discussion of team building, see William D. Dyer, *Team Building*, 3rd ed. (Reading, MA: Addison-Wesley, 1995).

[18] Developed from a discussion by Edgar H. Schein, *Process Consultation* (Reading, MA: Addison-Wesley, 1969), pp. 32–37; Edgar H. Schein, *Process Consultation* (Vol. I) (Reading, Ma: Addison-Wesley, 1988), pp. 40–49.

[19] The classic work is Robert F. Bales, "Task Roles and Social Roles in Problem-Solving Groups," in Eleanor E. Maccoby, Theodore M. Newcomb, and E. L. Hartley (eds.), *Readings in Social Psychology* (New York: Holt, Rinehart & Winston, 1958).

[20] For a good description of task and maintenance functions, see John J. Gabarro and Anne Harlan, "Note on Process Observation," Note 9-477-029 (Harvard Business School, 1976).

[21] See Daniel C. Feldman, "The Development and Enforcement of Group Norms," *Academy of Management Review* 9 (1984):47–53.

[22] See Robert F. Allen and Saul Pilnick, "Confronting the Shadow Organization: How to Select and Defeat Negative Norms," *Organizational Dynamics* (Spring 1973):13–17; Alvin Zander, *Making Groups Effective* (San Francisco: Jossey-Bass, 1982), ch. 4; Feldman (1984).

[23] For a summary of research on group cohesiveness, see Marvin E. Shaw, *Group Dynamics* (New York: McGraw-Hill, 1971), pp. 110–112, 192.

[24] Information from Stratford Shermin, "Secrets of HP's 'Muddled' Team," *Fortune* (March 18, 1996), pp. 116–120.

[25] See Jay R. Galbraith and Edward E. Lawler III, "The Challenges of Change: Organizing for Competitive Advantage," in Mohrman, Galbraith, Lawler, et al. (1998).

[26] See Kenichi Ohmae, "Quality Control Circles: They Work and Don't Work," *Wall Street Journal* (March 29, 1982), p. 16; Robert P. Steel, Anthony J. Mento, Benjamin L. Dilla, Nestor K. Ovalle, and Russell F. Lloyd, "Factors Influencing the Success and Failure of Two Quality Circles Programs," *Journal of Management* 11(1) (1985):99–119; Edward E. Lawler III and Susan A. Mohrman, "Quality Circles: After the Honeymoon," *Organizational Dynamics* 15(4) (1987):42–54.

[27] See Jay R. Galbraith, *Designing Organizations* (San Francisco: Jossey-Bass, 1998).

[28] Jerry Yoram Wind and Jeremy Main, *Driving Change: How the Best Companies Are Preparing for the 21st Century* (New York: Free Press, 1998), p. 135.

[29] Jessica Lipnack and Jeffrey Stamps, *Virtual Teams: Reaching Across Space, Time, and Organizations with Technology* (New York: Wiley, 1997).

[30] For a review of some alternatives, see Jeff Angus and Sean Gallagher, "Virtual Team Builders—Internet-Based Teamware Makes It Possible to Build Effective Teams from Widely Dispersed Participants," *Information Week* (May 4, 1998).

[31] R. Brent Gallupe and William H. Cooper, "Brainstorming Electronically," *Sloan Management Review* (Fall 1993):27–36.

[32] Ibid.

[33] For early research on related team concepts, see Richard E. Walton, "How to Counter Alienation in the Plant," *Harvard Business Review* (November/December 1972):70–81; Richard E. Walton, "Work Innovations at Topeka: After Six Years," *Journal of Applied Behavior Science* 13 (1977):422–431; Richard E. Walton, "The Topeka Work System: Optimistic Visions, Pessimistic Hypotheses, and Reality," in Zager and Rosow (eds.), *The Innovative Organization*, ch. 11.

SOURCE NOTES

Information from Carol Hymowitz, "The Best Leaders Have Employees Who Would Follow Them Anywhere," *Wall Street Journal* (February 10, 2004), p. B1; "Rudy Guiliani on Leadership," speech to the IHRSA convention in Las Vegas (March 23, 2004).

Information from Robert Imrie, "Monks Turn Over New Leaf in Business," *Columbus Dispatch* (March 5, 2004), p. E3.

Charles Schwab & Co.: Information from Eric Matson, "The Seven Sins of Deadly Meetings," *Fast Company Handbook of the Business Revolution* (New York: Fast Company, 1997), p. 31.

Information from Stephen Baker and Manjeet Kripalani, "Will Outsourcing Hurt America's Supremacy?" *Business Week* (March 1, 2004), pp. 85–95.

Greg L. Stewart, Charles C. Manz, and Henry P. Sims, *Team Work and Group Dynamics* (New York: Wiley, 1999), pp. 18–26.

Chapter 11

ENDNOTES

[1] Translated by Donald D. Davis, who also provides the basis for this leadership description. See Donald D. Davis, "The Tao of Leadership in Virtual Teams", *Organizational Dynamics* 33(1) (2004):47–62.

[2] See J. P. Kotter, *A Force for Change: How Leadership Differs from Management* (New York: Free Press, 1990).

[3] See Bernard M. Bass, *Bass and Stogdill's Handbook of Leadership*, 3rd ed. (New York: Free Press, 1990).

[4] See Alan Bryman, *Charisma and Leadership in Organizations* (London: Sage, 1992), ch. 5.

[5] Ralph M. Stogdill, *Handbook of Leadership* (New York: Free Press, 1974).

[6] Based on information from Robert J. House and Ram Aditya, "The Social Scientific Study of Leadership: Quo Vadis?" *Journal of Management* 23 (1997):409–474; Shelley A. Kirkpatrick and Edwin A. Locke, "Leadership: Do Traits Matter?" *The Executive* 5(2) (1991):48–60; Gary Yukl, *Leadership in Organizations*, 3rd ed. (Upper Saddle River, NJ: Prentice-Hall, 1998), ch. 10.

[7] Rensis Likert, *New Patterns of Management* (New York: McGraw-Hill, 1961).

[8] Bass (1990), ch. 24.

[9] Yukl (1998); George Graen, "Leader-Member Exchange Theory Development: Discussant's Comments," paper presented at the Academy of Management meeting, San Diego, August 1998.

[10] Yukl (1998); Peter G. Northouse, *Leadership Theory and Practice* (Thousand Oaks, CA: Sage, 1997), ch. 7.

[11] See M. F. Peterson, "PM Theory in Japan and China: What's in It for the United States?" *Organizational Dynamics* (Spring 1988):22–39; J. Misumi and M. F. Peterson, "The Performance-Maintenance Theory of Leadership: Review of a Japanese Research Program," *Administrative Science Quarterly* 30 (1985):198–223; P. B. Smith, J. Misumi, M. Tayeb, M. F. Peterson, and M. Bond, "On the Generality of Leadership Style Measures Across Cultures," paper presented at the International Congress of Applied Psychology, Jerusalem, July 1986.

[12] G. B. Graen and M. Uhl-Bien, "Relationship-Based Approach to Leadership: Development of Leader-Member Exchange (LMX) Theory of Leadership over 25 Years: Applying a Multi-Level Multi-Domain Perspective," *Leadership Quarterly* 6 (Summer 1995):219–247.

[13] House and Aditya (1997).

[14] Kirkpatrick and Locke (1991); Yukl (1998), ch. 10; J. G. Hunt and G. E. Dodge, "Management in Organizations," *Handbook of Psychology* (Washington, DC: American Psychological Association, 2000).

[15] This section is based on Fred E. Fiedler and Martin M. Chemers, *Leadership* (Glenview, IL: Scott, Foresman, 1974).

[16] This discussion of cognitive resource theory is based on Fred E. Fiedler and Joseph E. Garcia, *New Approaches in Effective Leadership* (New York: Wiley, 1987).

[17] See L. H. Peters, D. D. Harke, and J. T. Pohlmann, "Fiedler's Contingency Theory of Leadership: An Application of the Meta-Analysis Procedures of Schmidt and Hunter," *Psychological Bulletin* 97 (1985):274–285.

[18] Yukl (1998).

[19] F. E. Fiedler, M. M. Chemers, and L. Mahar, *Improving Leadership Effectiveness: The Leader Match Concept*, 2nd ed. (New York: Wiley, 1984).

[20] For documentation, see Fred E. Fiedler and Linda Mahar, "The Effectiveness of Contingency Model Training: A Review of the Validation of Leader Match," *Personnel Psychology* (Spring 1979):45–62; Fred E. Garcia, Cecil H. Bell, Martin M. Chemers, and Dennis Patrick, "Increasing Mine Productivity and Safety Through Management Training and Organization Development: A Comparative Study," *Basic and Applied Social Psychology* (March 1984):1–18; Arthur G. Jago and James W. Ragan, "The Trouble

with Leader Match Is That It Doesn't Match Fiedler's Contingency Model," *Journal of Applied Psychology* (November 1986):555–559.

[21] See Yukl (1998); R. Ayman, M. M. Chemers, and F. E. Fiedler, "The Contingency Model of Leadership Effectiveness: Its Levels of Analysis," *Leadership Quarterly* (Summer 1995):pp. 147–168.

[22] This section is based on Robert J. House and Terence R. Mitchell, "Path-Goal Theory of Leadership," *Journal of Contemporary Business* (Autumn 1977):81–97.

[23] Ibid.

[24] C. A. Schriesheim and L. L. Neider, "Path-Goal Theory: The Long and Winding Road," *Leadership Quarterly* 7 (1996):317–321; M. G. Evans, "Commentary on R. J. House's Path-Goal Theory of Leader Effectiveness," *Leadership Quarterly* 7 (1996):305–309.

[25] R. J. House, "Path-Goal Theory of Leadership: Lessons, Legacy, and a Reformulated Theory," *Leadership Quarterly* 7 (1996): 323–352.

[26] See the discussion of this approach in Paul Hersey and Kenneth H. Blanchard, *Management of Organizational Behavior* (Englewood Cliffs, NJ: Prentice Hall, 1988); Paul Hersey, Kenneth Blanchard, and Dewey E. Johnson, *Management of Organizational Behavior*, 8th ed. (Upper Saddle River, NJ: Prentice Hall, 2001).

[27] R. P. Vecchio and C. Fernandez, "Situational Leadership Theory Revisited," in M. Schnake (ed.), *1995 Southern Management Association Proceedings* (Valdosta, GA: Georgia Southern University, 1995), pp. 137–139; Claude L. Graeff, "Evolution of Situational Leadership Theory: A Critical Review," *Leadership Quarterly* 8 (1997):153–170.

[28] The discussion in this section is based on Steven Kerr and John Jermier, "Substitutes for Leadership: Their Meaning and Measurement," *Organizational Behavior and Human Performance* 22 (1978):375–403; Jon P. Howell, David E. Bowen, Peter W. Dorfman, Steven Kerr, and Phillip M. Podsakoff, "Substitutes for Leadership: Effective Alternatives to Ineffective Leadership," *Organizational Dynamics* (Summer 1990):21–38.

[29] Phillip M. Podsakoff, Peter W. Dorfman, Jon P. Howell, and William D. Todor, "Leader Reward and Punishment Behaviors: A Preliminary Test of a Culture-Free Style of Leadership Effectiveness," *Advances in Comparative Management* 2 (1989:95–138; T. K. Peng, "Substitutes for Leadership in an International Setting," unpublished manuscript, College of Business Administration, Texas Tech University (1990); P. M. Podsakoff and S. B. MacKenzie, "Kerr and Jermier's Substitutes for Leadership Model: Background, Empirical Assessment, and Suggestions for Future Research," *Leadership Quarterly* 8(2) (1997):117–132.

[30] See T. R. Mitchell, S. G. Green, and R. E. Wood, "An Attributional Model of Leadership and the Poor Performing Subordinate: Development and Validation," in L. L. Cummings and B. M. Staw (eds.), *Research in Organizational Behavior* (Vol. 3) (Greenwich, CT: JAI Press, 1981), pp. 197–234.

[31] James G. Hunt, Kimberly B. Boal, and Ritch L. Sorenson, "Top Management Leadership: Inside the Black Box," *Leadership Quarterly* 1 (1990):41–65.

[32] This discussion relies heavily on the work of Marcus W. Dickson, Deanne N. DenHartog, and Jacqueline K. Mitchelson, "Research on Leadership in a Cross-Cultural Context: Making Progress and Raising New Questions," *The Leadership Quarterly* 14(6) (2003):729–768.

[33] C. R. Gerstner and D. B. Day, "Cross-Cultural Comparison of Leadership Prototypes," *The Leadership Quarterly* (1994):122–134.

[34] Hunt, Boal, and Sorenson (1990).

[35] See J. Pfeffer, "Management as Symbolic Action: The Creation and Maintenance of Organizational Paradigms," in Cummings and Staw (1990), pp. 1–52.

[36] James R. Meindl, "On Leadership: An Alternative to the Conventional Wisdom," in Staw and Cummings (1990), pp. 159–203.

[37] Compare with Bryman (1992); also see James G. Hunt and Jay A. Conger (eds.), *The Leadership Quarterly* 10(2) (1999), special issue.

[38] See R. J. House, "A 1976 Theory of Charismatic Leadership," in J. G. Hunt and L. L. Larson (eds.), *Leadership: The Cutting Edge* (Carbondale: Southern Illinois University Press, 1977), pp. 189–207.

[39] R. J. House, W. D. Spangler, and J. Woycke, "Personality and Charisma in the U.S. Presidency," *Administrative Science Quarterly* 36 (1991):364–396.

[40] Pillai and E. A. Williams, "Does Leadership Matter in the Political Arena? Voter Perceptions of Candidates Transformational and Charismatic, Leadership and the 1996 U.S. Presidential Vote," *Leadership Quarterly* 9 (1998):397–416.

[41] See Jane M. Howell and Bruce J. Avolio, "The Ethics of Charismatic Leadership: Submission or Liberation," *Academy of Management Executive* 6 (May 1992):43–54.

[42] Jay Conger and Rabindra N. Kanungo, *Charismatic Leadership in Organizations* (San Francisco: Jossey-Bass, 1998).

[43] Ibid.

[44] Shamir, "Social Distance and Charisma: Theoretical Notes and an Exploratory Study," *The Leadership Quarterly* 6 (Spring 1995):19–48.

[45] See B. M. Bass, *Leadership and Performance Beyond Expectations* (New York: Free Press, 1985); Bryman (1992), pp. 98–99.

[46] B. M. Bass, *A New Paradigm of Leadership* (Alexandria, VA: U.S. Army Research Institute for the Behavioral and Social Sciences, 1996).

[47] Bryman (1992) ch. 6; B. M. Bass and B. J. Avolio, "Transformational Leadership: A Response to Critics," in M. M. Chemers and R. Ayman (eds.), *Leadership Theory and Practice: Perspectives and Directions* (San Diego, CA: Academic Press, 1993), pp. 49–80; Kevin B. Lowe, K. Galen Kroeck, and Nagaraj Sivasubramanium, "Effectiveness Correlates of Transformational and Transactional Leadership: A Meta-Analytic Review of the MLQ Literature," *Leadership Quarterly* 7 (1996):385–426.

[48] See Bradley L. Kirkman, Kevin B. Lowe, and Dianne P. Young, "The Challenge in High Performance Organizations," *The Journal of Leadership Studies* 5(2) (1998):3–15.

[49] This discussion relies heavily on that of Katrina A. Zalatan and Gary Yukl, "Team Leadership", in George R. Goethals, Georgia J. Sorenson, and James McGregor Burns, *Encyclopedia of Leadership* (Vol. A), (Great Barrington, MA, Berkshire/Sage, 2004), pp. 1529–1552.

[50] Bass (1996); Bass and Avolio (1993).

[51] See Jay A. Conger and Rabindra N. Kanungo, "Training Charismatic Leadership: A Risky and Critical Task," in Jay A. Conger, Rabindra N. Kanungo, and Associates (eds.), *Charismatic Leadership: The Elusive Factor in Organizational Effectiveness* (San Francisco: Jossey-Bass, 1988), ch. 11.

[52] See J. R. Kouzes and B. F. Posner, *The Leadership Challenge: How to Get Extraordinary Things Done in Organizations* (San Francisco: Jossey-Bass, 1991).

[53] Marshall Sashkin and Molly G. Sashkin, *Leadership That Matters* (San Francisco: Berrett-Koehler), ch. 10.

SOURCE NOTES

Based on Selwyn Crawford, "The Army Way", *Dallas Morning News* (February 1, 2004), p. 10E.

Based on "Meg and the Machine", *Fortune* (September 1, 2003), pp. 69–78.

Based on John Helyar, "Ride 'Em Cowboy," *Fortune* (September 29, 2003), pp. 59–70.

Based on Fred Vogelstein, "Mighty Amazon," *Fortune* (May 26, 2003), pp. 60–74.

Based on Kenneth R. Thompson, "A Conversation with Reverend Theodore Hesburgh: Building a World Class University," *The Journal of Leadership Studies* 7(1) (2000):116–128.

Based on Alex Taylor III, "The Americanization of Toyota," *Fortune* (December 8, 2003), pp. 165–170.

Trait-based information from Robert J. House and Ram Aditya, "The Social Scientific Study of Leadership: Quo Vadis?" *Journal of Management* 23 (1987):405–474; Shelby A. Kirkpatrick and Edwin A. Locke, "Leadership: Do Traits Matter?" *The Executive* 5(2) (1991):48–60; Gary Yukl, *Leadership in Organizations* (Upper Saddle River, NJ: Prentice Hall, 1998), ch. 10.

Summarized from Cheryl Hall, "Building Her Own Vision," *Dallas Morning News* (May 28, 2000), pp. 1H–2H.

Fiedler model based on F. E. Fiedler and M. M. Chemers, *Leadership and Effective Management* (Glenview, IL: Scott, Foresman, 1974).

Path–goal information adapted from Richard N. Osborn, James G. Hunt, and Lawrence R. Jauch, *Organizational Theory: An Integrated Approach* (New York: Wiley, 1980), p. 464.

From Paul Hersey and Kenneth H. Blanchard, *Management of Organizational Behavior* (Englewood Cliffs, NJ: Prentice Hall, 1988), p. 171. Used by permission.

Based on Steven Kerr and John Jermier, "Substitutes for Leadership: Their Meaning and Measurement," *Organizational Behavior and Human Performance* 22 (1978):387; Fred Luthans, *Organizational Behavior* 6th ed. (New York: McGraw-Hill, 1992), ch. 10.

Close and Distant based on Boas Shamir, "Social Distance and Charisma: Theoretical Notes and an Exploratory Study," *Leadership Quarterly* 6 (1995):19–48.

Effective Manager based on B. M. Bass, *Leadership and Performance Beyond Expectations* (New York: Free Press, 1985).

Effective Manager information from Jay A. Conger and Rabindra N. Kanungo, "Training Charismatic Leadership: A Risky and Critical Task," in J. A. Conger, R. N. Kanungo, et al. (eds.), *Charismatic Leadership: The Elusive Factor in Organizational Effectiveness* (San Francisco: Jossey-Bass, 1988), ch 11.

Chapter 12

ENDNOTES

[1] www.northwesternmutual.com.

[2] We would like to thank Janice M. Feldbauer, Michael Cart, Judy Nixon, and Romuald Stone for their comments on the organization of this chapter and the emphasis on a managerial view of power.

[3] Rosabeth Moss Kanter, "Power Failure in Management Circuit," *Harvard Business Review* (July/August 1979):65–75.

[4] John R. P. French and Bertram Raven, "The Bases of Social Power," in Dorwin Cartwright (ed.), *Group Dynamics Research and Theory* (Evanston, IL: Row, Peterson, 1962), pp. 607–623.

[5] We have added process, information, and representative power to the French and Raven list.

[6] John P. Kotter, "Power, Success, and Organizational Effectiveness," *Organizational Dynamics* 6 (Winter 1978):27; David A. Whetten and Kim S. Cameron, *Developing Managerial Skills* (Glenview, IL: Scott, Foresman, 1984), pp. 250–259.

[7] David Kipinis, Stuart M. Schmidt, Chris Swaffin-Smith, and Ian Wilkinson, "Patterns of Managerial Influence: Shotgun Managers, Tacticians, and Bystanders," *Organizational Dynamics* 12 (Winter 1984):60, 61.

[8] Ibid., pp. 58–67; David Kipinis, Stuart M. Schmidt, and Ian Wilkinson, "Intraorganizational Influence Tactics: Explorations in Getting One's Way," *Journal of Applied Psychology* 65 (1980):440–452.

[9] Warren K. Schilit and Edwin A. Locke, "A Study of Upward Influence in Organizations," *Administrative Science Quarterly*, 27 (1982):304–316.

[10] Ibid.

[11] Stanley Milgram, "Behavioral Study of Obedience," in Dennis W. Organ (ed.), *The Applied Psychology of Work Behavior* (Dallas: Business Publications, 1978), pp. 384–398. Also see Stanley Milgram, "Behavioral Study of Obedience," *Journal of Abnormal and Social Psychology* 67 (1963):371–378; Stanley Milgram, "Group Pressure and Action Against a Person," *Journal of Abnormal and Social Psychology* 69 (1964):137–143; Stanley Milgram, "Some Conditions of Obedience and Disobedience to Authority," *Human Relations* 1 (1965):57–76; Stanley Milgram, *Obedience to Authority* (New York: Harper & Row, 1974).

[12] Chester Barnard, *The Functions of the Executive* (Cambridge, MA: Harvard University Press, 1938).

[13] Ibid.

[14] See Steven N. Brenner and Earl A. Mollander, "Is the Ethics of Business Changing?" *Harvard Business Review* 55 (February 1977):57–71; Barry Z. Posner and Warren H. Schmidt, "Values and the American Manager: An Update," *California Management Review* 26 (Spring 1984):202–216.

[15] Useful reviews include a chapter in Robert H. Miles, *Macro Organizational Behavior* (Santa Monica, CA: Goodyear, 1980); Bronston T. Mayes and Robert W. Allen, "Toward a Definition of Organizational Politics," *Academy of Management Review* 2 (1977):672–677; Gerald F. Cavanagh, Dennis J. Moberg, and Manuel Velasquez, "The Ethics of Organizational Politics," *Academy of Management Review* 6 (July 1981):363–374; Dan Farrell and James C. Petersen, "Patterns of Political Behavior in Organizations," *Academy of Management Review* 7 (July 1982):403–412; D. L. Madison, R. W. Allen, L. W. Porter, and B. T. Mayes, "Organizational Politics: An Exploration of Managers' Perceptions," *Human Relations* 33 (1980):92–107.

[16] Mayes and Allen (1977), p. 675.

[17] Jeffrey Pfeffer, *Power in Organizations* (Marshfield, MA: Pitman, 1981), p. 7.

[18] Michael Sconcolfi, Anita Raghavan, and Mitchell Pacelle, "All Bets Are Off: How the Salesmanship and Brainpower Failed at Long Term Capital," *Wall Street Journal* (November 16, 1998), pp. 1, 18–19.

[19] B. E. Ashforth and R. T. Lee, "Defensive Behavior in Organizations: A Preliminary Model," *Human Relations* (July 1990):621–648; personal communication with Blake Ashforth, December 1998.

[20] Developed from James L. Hall and Joel L. Leldecker, "A Review of Vertical and Lateral Relations: A New Perspective for Managers," in Patrick Connor (ed.), *Dimensions in Modern Management*, 3rd ed. (Boston: Houghton Mifflin, 1982), pp. 138–146, which was based in part on Leonard Sayles, *Managerial Behavior* (New York: McGraw-Hill, 1964).

[21] Ibid.

[22] Pamela L. Perrewe, Gerald R. Ferris, Dwight D. Frink, and William P. Anthony, "Political Skill: An Antidote for Workplace Stressors," *Academy of Management Executive* 14(3) (2001):115–120.

[23] Amy J. Hillman and Michael A. Hitt, "Corporate Political Strategy Formulation: A Model of Approach Participation and Strategy Decisions," *Academy of Management Review* 24(3) (1999):825–842.

[24] See Karen Masterson and Rachel Graves, "Congress Approves Airline Bailout" *Houston Chronicle,* September 23 (2001):1–2; Douglas A. Schuler, "Corporate Political Strategy and Foreign Competition: The Case of the Steel Industry," *Academy of Management Journal* 29(3) (1996):720–732.

[25] Hillman and Hitt (1999).

[26] See Jeffrey Pfeffer, *Organizations and Organization Theory* (Boston: Pitman, 1983); Jeffrey Pfeffer and Gerald R. Salancik, *The External Control of Organizations* (Englewood Cliffs, NJ: Prentice-Hall, 1978); Pfeffer (1981); M. M. Harmon and R. T. Mayer, *Organization Theory for Public Administration* (Boston: Little, Brown, 1984); W. Richard Scott, *Organizations: Rational, Natural and Open Systems* (Englewood Cliffs, NJ: Prentice-Hall, 1987).

[27] J. M. Ivancevich, T. N. Deuning, J. A. Gilbert, and R. Konopaske, "Deterring White-Collar Crime," *Academy of Management Executive* 17 (2003):114–128.

[28] C. Daily, D. Dalton, and A. A. Cannella Jr., "Corporate Governance: Decades of Dialog and Data," *Academy of Management Review* 28 (2003):371–383.

[29] D. Dalton, C. Daily, A. E. Ellstrand, and J. L. Johnson, " Meta-Analysis of Financial Performance and Quality: Fusion or Confusion?" *Academy of Management Journal* 46 (1998):13–26.

[30] T. A. Kochan, "Addressing the Crisis in Confidence in Corporations: Root Causes, Victims, and Strategies for Reform," *Academy of Management Executive* 16 (2002):139–142.

[31] Ibid.

[32] Ibid.

[33] See Pfeffer (1983).

[34] See the early work of James D. Thompson, *Organizations in Action* (New York: McGraw-Hill, 1967) and more recent studies by R. N. Osborn and D. H. Jackson, "Leaders, Riverboat Gamblers, or Purposeful Unintended Consequences in Management of Complex Technologies," *Academy of Management Journal* 31 (1988):924–974; M. Hector, "When Actors Comply: Monitoring Costs and the Production of Social Order," *Acta Sociologica* 27 (1984):161–183; T. Mitchell and W. G. Scott, "Leadership Failures, the Distrusting Public and Prospects for the Administrative State," *Public Administration Review* 47 (1987):445–452.

[35] J. J. Jones, *The Downsizing of American Potential* (New York: Raymond Press, 1996).

[36] This discussion is based on Cavanagh, Moberg, and Velasquez (1981); and Manuel Velasquez, Dennis J. Moberg, and Gerald Cavanagh, "Organizational Statesmanship and Dirty Politics: Ethical Guidelines for the Organizational Politician," *Organizational Dy-*

namics 11 (1983):65–79, both of which offer a fine treatment of the ethics of power and politics.

SOURCE NOTES

www.microsoft.com; "Microsoft and the Browser Wars," *Seattle Times* (November 18, 1998), pp. C1–C3: "ASAP Interview with Bill Gates," *Forbes ASAP* (1992), p. 84; "Identity Crises," *Forbes Magazine* (May 25, 1992), p. 82; "Microsoft Aims Its Arsenal at Networking," *Business Week* (October 12, 1992), pp. 88–89; "The PTC and Microsoft," *Business Week* (December 28, 1992), p. 30; "The PC Wars Are Sweeping into Software," *Business Week* (July 13, 1992), p. 132; Top 10 reasons to get Windows XP Home Edition, www.microsoft.com/windowsxp; Eric Wildstrom, "Microsoft: How it Became Stronger than Ever," businessweek.com/magazine/content/01-23/63735001.htm.
www.Dell.com/uslen/gen/corporate; www.dell.com/.
www.melita.com
www.littlecaesars.com

Chapter 13

ENDNOTES

[1] Information and quotes from Sue Shellenbarger, "More Managers Find a Happy Staff Leads to Happy Customers," *Wall Street Journal* (December 28, 1998), p. B1; Robert D. Hoff, "Sun Power: Is the Center of the Computing Universe Changing?" *Business Week* (January 18, 1999).
[2] Surveys reported online at the American Management Association Web site (www.amanet.org): "The Passionate Organization" (September 26–29, 2000) and "Managerial Skills and Competence" (March/April 2000).
[3] Baseline survey reported in Lucent Technologies, 1998 Annual Report.
[4] See Angelo S. DeNisi and Abraham N. Kluger, "Feedback Effectiveness: Can 360-Degree Appraisals Be Improved?" *Academy of Management Executive* 14 (2000):129–139.
[5] Networking is considered an essential managerial activity by Kotter (1982).
[6] Thomas J. Peters and Robert H. Waterman, Jr., *In Search of Excellence* (New York: Harper & Row, 1983).
[7] See Robert H. Lengel and Richard L. Daft, "The Selection of Communication Media as an Executive Skill," *Academy of Management Executive* (August 1998):225–232.
[8] Portions of this section are adapted from John R. Schermerhorn Jr., *Management*, 5th ed. (New York: Wiley, 1996), pp. 375–378. Used by permission.
[9] *Business Week* (May 16, 1994), p. 8.
[10] See Axelrod (1996).
[11] See Richard L. Birdwhistell, *Kinesics and Context* (Philadelphia: University of Pennsylvania Press, 1970).
[12] Edward T. Hall, *The Hidden Dimension* (Garden City, NY: Doubleday, 1966).
[13] See D. E. Campbell, "Interior Office Design and Visitor Response," *Journal of Applied Psychology* 64 (1979):648–653; P. C. Morrow and J. C. McElroy, "Interior Office Design and Visitor Response: A Constructive Replication," *Journal of Applied Psychology* 66 (1981):646–650.
[14] M. P. Rowe and M. Baker, "Are You Hearing Enough Employee Concerns?" *Harvard Business Review* 62 (May/June 1984):127–135.

[15] This discussion is based on Carl R. Rogers and Richard E. Farson, "Active Listening" (Chicago: Relations Center of the University of Chicago).
[16] Modified from an example in ibid.
[17] See C. Barnum and N. Woliansky, "Taking Cues from Body Language," *Management Review* 78 (1989):59; S. Bochner (ed.), *Cultures in Contact: Studies in Cross-Cultural Interaction* (London: Pergamon, 1982); A. Furnham and S. Bocher, *Culture Shock: Psychological Reactions to Unfamiliar Environments* (London: Methuen, 1986); "How Not to Do International Business," *Business Week* (April 12, 1999); Yori Kagegama, "Tokyo Auto Show Highlights," Associated Press (October 24, 2001).
[18] Quotes from "Lost in Translation," *Wall Street Journal* (May 18, 2004), pp. B1, B6.
[19] See Gary P. Ferraro, "The Need for Linguistic Proficiency in Global Business," *Business Horizons* 39 (May/June 1966):39–46.
[20] This example is from Richard V. Farace, Peter R. Monge, and Hamish M. Russell, *Communicating and Organizing* (Reading, MA: Addison-Wesley, 1977), pp. 97–98.
[21] The statements are from *Business Week* (July 6, 1981), p. 107.
[22] See A. Mehrabian, *Silent Messages* (Belmont, CA: Wadsworth, 1981).
[23] This research is reviewed by John C. Athanassiades, "The Distortion of Upward Communication in Hierarchical Organizations," *Academy of Management Journal* 16 (June 1973):207–226.
[24] F. Lee, "Being Polite and Keeping MUM: How Bad News is Communicated in Organizational Hierarchies," *Journal of Applied Social Psychology* 23 (1993):1124–1149.
[25] Waterman (1983).
[26] Information from Alison Overholt, "Intel's Got (Too Much) Mail," *Fortune* (March 2001):56–58.
[27] Information from Michael Totty, "The Path to Better Teamwork," *Wall Street Journal* (May 24, 2004), p. R4.
[28] Ibid.
[29] Reported in "Big Brother Inc.," www.pccomputing.com (March 2000), p. 88. See "My Boss, Big Brother," *Business Week* (January 22, 1996), p. 56.
[30] Deborah Tannen, *Talking 9 to 5* (New York: Avon, 1995).
[31] Deborah Tannen, *You Just Don't Understand: Women and Men in Conversation* (New York: Ballantine, 1991).
[32] Deborah Tannen, "The Power of Talk: Who Gets Heard and Why," *Harvard Business Review* (September/October, 1995): 138–148.
[33] Reported by *Working Woman* (November 1995), p. 14.
[34] Ibid.
[35] For an editorial opinion, see Jayne Tear, "They Just Don't Understand Gender Dynamics," *Wall Street Journal* (November 20, 1995), p. A14.

SOURCE NOTES

Information from "Entrepreneurs Speak at HBS," *Harvard Business School Bulletin* (February 1999):6; corporate Web site: www.virgin.com.
Monsanto: Information from Timothy D. Schellhardt, "Monsanto Best on Box Buddies," *Wall Street Journal* (February 23, 1999), p. B1.
Information from "How They Feel," *Columbus Dispatch* (February 20, 2004), p. D1.

Information from Mei Fong, "Chinese Charm School," *Wall Street Journal* (January 13, 2004), pp. B1, B6.

Information from Riva Richmond, "It's 10 A.M. Do You Know Where Your Workers Are?" *Wall Street Journal* (January 12, 2004), pp. R1, R4.

Chapter 14

ENDNOTES

[1] www.plantemorand.com.

[2] For concise overviews, see Susan J. Miller, David J. Hickson, and David C. Wilson, "Decision-Making in Organizations," in Stewart R. Clegg, Cynthia Hardy, and Walter R. Nord (eds.), *Handbook of Organizational Studies* (London: Sage Publications, 1996), pp. 293–312; George P. Huber, *Managerial Decision Making* (Glenview, IL: Scott, Foresman, 1980).

[3] This section is based on Michael D. Cohen, James G. March, and Johan P. Olsen, "The Garbage Can Model of Organizational Choice," *Administrative Science Quarterly* 17 (1972):1–25; and James G. March and Herbert A. Simon, *Organizations* (New York: Wiley, 1958), pp. 137–142.

[4] See KPMG, "Enterprise Risk Management Services," www.kpmg.com.

[5] This traditional distinction is often attributed to Herbert Simon, *Administrative Behavior* (New York: Free Press, 1945), but an available source is Herbert Simon, *The New Science of Management Decision* (New York: Harper & Row, 1960).

[6] Ibid.

[7] Also see Mary Zey (ed.), *Decision Making: Alternatives to Rational Choice Models* (Thousand Oaks, CA: Sage Publications, 1992).

[8] Simon (1945).

[9] For discussions, see Cohen, March, and Olsen (1972); Miller, Hickson, and Wilson (1996); Michael Masuch and Perry LaPontin, "Beyond Garbage Cans: An AI Model of Organizational Choice," *Administrative Science Quarterly* 34 (1989):38–67.

[10] Weston H. Agor, *Intuition in Organizations* (Newbury Park, CA: Sage Publications, 1989).

[11] Henry Mintzberg, "Planning on the Left Side and Managing on the Right," *Harvard Business Review* 54 (July/August 1976):51–63.

[12] See Weston H. Agor, "How Top Executives Use Their Intuition to Make Important Decisions," *Business Horizons* 29 (January/February 1986):49–53; Agor (1989).

[13] The classic work in this area is found in a series of articles by D. Kahneman and A. Tversky, "Subjective Probability: A Judgment of Representativeness," *Cognitive Psychology* 3 (1972):430–454; "On the Psychology of Prediction," *Psychological Review* 80 (1973):237–251; "Prospect Theory: An Analysis of Decision Under Risk," *Econometrica* 47 (1979):263–291; "Psychology of Preferences," *Scientific American* (1982):161–173; "Choices, Values, Frames," *American Psychologist* 39 (1984):341–350.

[14] Definitions and subsequent discussion based on Max H. Bazerman, *Judgment in Managerial Decision Making*, 3rd ed. (New York: Wiley, 1994).

[15] Cameron M. Ford and Dennis A. Gioia, *Creative Action in Organizations* (Thousand Oaks, CA: Sage Publications, 1995).

[16] G. Wallas, *The Art of Thought* (New York: Harcourt, 1926). Cited in Bazerman (1994).

[17] E. Glassman, "Creative Problem Solving," *Supervisory Management* (January 1989):21–26; B. Kabanoff and J. R. Rossiter, "Recent Developments in Applied Creativity," *International Review of Industrial and Organizational Psychology* 9 (1994):283–324.

[18] I. L. Thompson and L. Brajkovich, "Improving the Creativity of Organizational Work Groups," *Academy of Management Journal* 17 (2003):96–115.

[19] Ibid.

[20] For further discussion of these factors, see R. W. Woodman, J. E. Sawyer, and R. W. Griffin, "Toward a Theory of Organizational Creativity," *Academy of Management Review* 18(1993):293–321; M. A. Glyn, "Innovative Genius: A Framework for Relating Individual and Organizational Intelligences to Innovation," *Academy of Management Review* 21 (1996); 1081–1111; C. M Ford, "A Theory of Individual Creativity in Multiple Social Domains, *Academy of Management Review* 21(1196):1112–1134.

[21] R. Drazen, M. Glenn, and R. Kazanjian, "Multilevel Theorizing About Creativity in Organizations: A Sensemaking Perspective," *Academy of Management Review* 24 (1999):286–307.

[22] Ibid.

[23] Ibid.

[24] For recent studies, see J. Perry-Smith and C. Shalley, "The Social Side of Creativity: A Static and Dynamic Social Network Perspective," *Academy of Management Review* 28 (2003):89–01; S. Taggar, "Individual Creativity and Group Ability to Utilize Individual Creative Resources: A Multilevel Model," *Academy of Management Journal* 45 (2002):315–330.

[25] Ibid.

[26] Information from Kenneth Labich, "Nike vs. Reebok," *Fortune* (September 18, 1995), pp. 90–106.

[27] James A. F. Stoner, *Management*, 2nd ed. (Englewood Cliffs, NJ: Prentice-Hall, 1982), pp. 167–168.

[28] Paul C. Nutt, "Surprising but True: Half the Discussions in Organizations Fail," *Academy of Management Executive* 13(4) (1999):75–90.

[29] Ibid.

[30] Victor H. Vroom and Philip W. Yetton, *Leadership and Decision Making* (Pittsburgh: University of Pittsburgh Press, 1973); Victor H. Vroom and Arthur G. Jago, *The New Leadership* (Englewood Cliffs, NJ: Prentice-Hall, 1988).

[31] Barry M. Staw, "The Escalation of Commitment to a Course of Action," *Academy of Management Review* 6 (1981):577–587; Barry M. Staw and Jerry Ross, "Knowing When to Pull the Plug," *Harvard Business Review* 65 (March/April 1987):68–74. See also Glen Whyte, "Escalating Commitment to a Course of Action: A Reinterpretation," *Academy of Management Review* 11 (1986):311–321.

[32] Joel Brockner, "The Escalation of Commitment to a Failing Course of Action: Toward Theoretical Progress," *Academy of Management Review* 17 (1992):39–61; J. Ross and B. M. Staw, "Organizational Escalation and Exit: Lessons from the Shoreham Nuclear Power Plant," *Academy of Management Journal* 36 (1993):701–732.

[33] Bazerman (1994), pp. 79–83.

[34] See Brockner (1992); Ross and Staw (1993); J. Z. Rubin, "Negotiation: An Introduction to Some Issues and Themes," *American Behavioral Scientist* 27 (1983):135–147.

[35] See "Computers That Think Are Almost Here," *Business Week* (July 17, 1995):68–73.

[36] A. R. Dinnis and J. S. Valacich, "Computer Brainstorms: Two Heads Are Better Than One," *Journal of Applied Psychology* (February 1994):77–86.

37 For an expanded discussion of such ethical frameworks for decision making, see Linda A. Travino and Katherine A. Nelson, *Managing Business Ethics* (New York: Wiley, 1995).

38 B. Kabanoff and J. R. Rossiter, "Recent Developments in Applied Creativity," *International Review of Industrial and Organizational Psychology* 9 (1994):283–324.

39 Fons Trompenaars, *Riding the Waves of Culture: Understanding Cultural Diversity in Business* (London: Nicholas Brealey Publishing, 1993), p. 6.

40 Ibid., pp. 58–59.

41 For a good discussion of decision making in Japanese organizations, see Min Chen, *Asian Management Systems* (New York: Routledge, 1995).

42 Nancy J. Adler, *International Dimensions of Organizational Behavior*, 2nd ed. (Boston: PWS-Kent, 1991).

43 See Miller, Hickson, and Wilson (1996).

44 We would like to thank Kristi M. Lewis for emphasizing the importance of identifying criteria and weighing criteria and urging us to include this section on ethics.

45 For an expanded discussion of ethical frameworks for decision making, see Linda A. Travino and Katherine A. Nelson, *Managing Business Ethics* (New York: Wiley, 1995); Saul W. Gellerman, "Why 'Good' Managers Make Bad Ethical Choices," *Harvard Business Review* 64 (July/August 1986):85–90; Barbara Ley Toffler, *Tough Choices: Managers Talk Ethics* (New York: Wiley, 1986).

46 Stephen Fineman, "Emotion and Organizing," in Clegg, Hardy, and Nord, (1996), *Handbook of Organizational Studies*, pp. 542–580.

SOURCE NOTES

www.nokia.com.

www.REI.com.

www.chase.com.

www.Pella.com.

S.S. Harrington, "What Corporate America Is Teaching About Ethics," *Academy of Management & Education* 11 (1991):21–30; Don Hellriegel, John Slocum, and Richard Woodman, *Organizational Behavior* (Minneapolis: West Publishing, 1999). Reprinted from Victor H. Vroom and Arthur G. Jago, *The New Leadership* (Englewood Cliffs, NJ: Prentice-Hall, 1988), p. 184. Used by permission of the author.

www.banksterling.com.

www.freshexpress.com.

www.jackinthebox.com.

www.chase.com.

CHAPTER 15

ENDNOTES

1 Information from "From 'Blank Looks' to Blank Checks," *Business Week Enterprise* (December 7, 1998), pp. Ent 18–20; Organization Web site: www.capitalacrossamerica.org.

2 See, for example, Henry Mintzberg, *The Nature of Managerial Work* (New York: Harper & Row, 1973); John R. P. Kotter, *The General Managers* (New York: Free Press, 1982).

3 One of the classic discussions is by Richard E. Walton, *Interpersonal Peacemaking: Confrontations and Third-Party Consultation* (Reading, MA: Addison-Wesley, 1969).

4 Kenneth W. Thomas and Warren H. Schmidt, "A Survey of Managerial Interests with Respect to Conflict," *Academy of Management Journal* 19 (1976):315–318.

5 For a good overview, see Richard E. Walton, *Managing Conflict: Interpersonal Dialogue and Third Party Roles*, 2nd ed. (Reading, MA: Addison-Wesley, 1987); Dean Tjosvold, *The Conflict-Positive Organization: Stimulate Diversity and Create Unity* (Reading, MA: Addison-Wesley, 1991).

6 Walton (1969).

7 Ibid.

8 Information from Hal Lancaster, "Performance Reviews: Some Bosses Try a Fresh Approach," *Wall Street Journal* (December 1, 1998), p. B1.

9 Richard E. Walton and John M. Dutton, "The Management of Interdepartmental Conflict: A Model and Review," *Administrative Science Quarterly* 14 (1969):73–84.

10 Geert Hofstede, *Culture's Consequences: International Differences in Work-Related Values* (Beverly Hills, CA: Sage Publications, 1980), and Geert Hofstede, "Cultural Constraints in Management Theories," *Academy of Management Executive* 7 (1993):81–94.

11 These stages are consistent with the conflict models described by Alan C. Filley, *Interpersonal Conflict Resolution* (Glenview, IL: Scott, Foresman, 1975); and Louis R. Pondy, "Organizational Conflict: Concepts and Models," *Administrative Science Quarterly* (September 1967): pp. 269–320.

12 Information from Ken Brown and Gee L. Lee, "Lucent Fires Top China Executives," *The Wall Street Journal* (April 7, 2004), p. A8.

13 Walton and Dutton (1969).

14 Rensis Likert and Jane B. Likert, *New Ways of Managing Conflict* (New York: McGraw-Hill, 1976).

15 Information from "Saturday Morning Fever," *Economist* (December 8, 2001): 56.

16 See Jay Galbraith, *Designing Complex Organizations* (Reading, MA: Addison-Wesley, 1973); David Nadler and Michael Tushman, *Strategic Organizational Design* (Glenview, IL: Scott, Foresman, 1988).

17 E. M. Eisenberg and M. G. Witten, "Reconsidering Openness in Organizational Communication," *Academy of Management Review* 12 (1987):418–426.

18 R. G. Lord and M. C. Kernan, "Scripts as Determinants of Purposeful Behavior in Organizations," *Academy of Management Review* 12 (1987):265–277.

19 See Filley (1975); L. David Brown, *Managing Conflict at Organizational Interfaces* (Reading, MA: Addison-Wesley, 1983).

20 Ibid., pp. 27, 29.

21 For discussions, see Robert R. Blake and Jane Strygley Mouton, "The Fifth Achievement," *Journal of Applied Behavioral Science* 6 (1970):413–427; Kenneth Thomas, "Conflict and Conflict Management," in M. D. Dunnett (ed.), *Handbook of Industrial and Organizational Behavior* (Chicago: Rand McNally, 1976), pp. 889–935; and Kenneth W. Thomas, "Toward Multi-Dimensional Values in Teaching: The Examples of Conflict Behaviors," *Academy of Management Review* 2 (1977):484–490.

22 See, for example, Valerie Patterson, "How to Negotiate Pay in a Tough Economy," *The Wall Street Journal* (March 29, 2004), p. R7.

23 For an excellent overview, see Roger Fisher and William Ury, *Getting to Yes: Negotiating Agreement Without Giving In* (New York: Penguin, 1983). See also James A. Wall Jr., *Negotiation: Theory and Practice* (Glenview, IL: Scott, Foresman, 1985).

[24] Roy J. Lewicki and Joseph A. Litterer, *Negotiation* (Homewood, IL: Irwin, 1985), pp. 315–319.

[25] Ibid., pp. 328–329.

[26] For a good discussion, see Michael H. Bond, *Behind the Chinese Face* (London: Oxford University Press, 1991); and Richard D. Lewis, *When Cultures Collide*, Ch. 23 (London: Nicholas Brealey Publishing, 1996).

[27] The following discussion is based on Fisher and Ury (1983); and Lewicki and Litterer (1985).

[28] This example is developed from Max H. Bazerman, *Judgment in Managerial Decision Making*, 2nd ed. (New York: Wiley, 1991), pp. 106–108.

[29] For a detailed discussion, see Fisher and Ury (1983); and Lewicki and Litterer (1985).

[30] Developed from Bazerman (1991), pp. 127–141.

[31] Fisher and Ury (1983), p. 33.

[32] Lewicki and Litterer (1985), pp. 177–181.

SOURCE NOTES

Information from "Capitalizing on Diversity: Navigating the Seas of the Multicultural Workforce and Workplace," *Business Week*, Special Advertising Section (December 4, 1998).

HRM News: Information from Carol Kleiman, "Performance Review Comes 'Full Circle,'" *Columbus Dispatch* (January 31, 1999), p. 291.

Information from BC cycle, Associated Press (January 8, 2004); and Loch Adamson, "Roxanne Quimby for Governor!" *Fast Company* (December 2003):112.

Information and quotes from Carol Hymowitz, "Home Depot's CEO Led a Revolution, but Left Some Behind," *Wall Street Journal* (March 16, 2004), p. B1.

CHAPTER 16

ENDNOTES

[1] See Robert Reich, "The Company of the Future," *Fast Company* (November 1998):124.

[2] Michael Beer and Nitin Mitra, "Cracking the Code of Change," *Harvard Business Review* (May/June, 2000):133.

[3] Tom Peters, *Thriving on Chaos* (New York: Random House, 1987); Tom Peters, "Managing in a World Gone Bonkers," *World Executive Digest* (February 1993):26–29; Tom Peters, *The Circle of Innovation* (New York: Knopf, 1997).

[4] See David Nadler and Michael Tushman, *Strategic Organizational Design* (Glenview, IL: Scott, Foresman, 1988); Noel M. Tichy, "Revolutionize Your Company," *Fortune* (December 13, 1993), pp. 114–118.

[5] Jerry I. Porras and Robert C. Silvers, "Organization Development and Transformation," *Annual Review of Psychology* 42 (1991):51–78.

[6] The classic description of organizations on these terms is by Harold J. Leavitt, "Applied Organizational Change in Industry: Structural, Technological and Humanistic Approaches," in James G. March (ed.), *Handbook of Organizations* (Chicago: Rand McNally, 1965). This application is developed from Robert A. Cooke, "Managing Change in Organizations," in Gerald Zaltman (ed.), *Management Principles for Nonprofit Organizations* (New York: American Management Association, 1979). See also David A. Nadler, "The Effective Management of Organizational Change," in Jay W. Lorsch (ed.), *Handbook of Organizational Behavior* (Englewood Cliffs, NJ: Prentice-Hall, 1987), pp. 358–369.

[7] Beer and Mitra (2000), p. 133.

[8] John P. Kotter, "Why Transformation Efforts Fail," *Harvard Business Review* (March/April 1995):59–67.

[9] Kurt Lewin, "Group Decision and Social Change," in G. E. Swanson, T. M. Newcomb, and E. L. Hartley (eds.), *Readings in Social Psychology* (New York: Holt, Rinehart & Winston, 1952), pp. 459–473.

[10] Noel M. Tichy and Mary Anne Devanna, *The Transformational Leader* (New York: John Wiley & Sons, 1986), p. 44.

[11] The change strategies are described in Robert Chin and Kenneth D. Benne, "General Strategies for Effecting Changes in Human Systems," in Warren G. Bennis, Kenneth D. Benne, Robert Chin, and Kenneth E. Corey (eds.), *The Planning of Change*, 3rd ed. (New York: Holt, Rinehart & Winston, 1969), pp. 22–45.

[12] Example developed from an exercise reported in J. William Pfeiffer and John E. Jones, *A Handbook of Structural Experiences for Human Relations Training* (Vol. II) (La Jolla, CA: University Associates, 1973).

[13] Ibid.

[14] Ibid.

[15] Donald Klein, "Some Notes on the Dynamics of Resistance to Change: The Defender Role," in Bennis et al. (1969), pp. 117–124.

[16] See Everett M. Rogers, *Communication of Innovations*, 3rd ed. (New York: Free Press, 1993).

[17] Ibid.

[18] John P. Kotter and Leonard A. Schlesinger, "Choosing Strategies for Change," *Harvard Business Review* 57 (March/April 1979): 109–112.

[19] A classic work in this area is Peter F. Drucker, *Innovation and Entrepreneurship* (New York: Harper, 1985).

[20] Edward B. Roberts, "Managing Invention and Innovation," *Research Technology Management* (January/February 1988):1–19. For an extensive case study, see John Clark, *Managing Innovation and Change* (Thousand Oaks, CA: Sage, 1995). For a comprehensive update on innovation in industry, see "Innovation in Industry," *The Economist* (February 20, 1999), pp. 5–18.

[21] Quotes from Kenneth Labich, "The Innovators," *Fortune* (June 6, 1988), pp. 49–64; Bill Breen, "The Thrill of Defeat," *Fast Company* (June, 2004), p. 78.

[22] Arthur P. Brief, Randall S. Schuler, and Mary Van Sell, *Managing Job Stress* (Boston: Little, Brown, 1981).

[23] A review of research is available in Steve M. Jex, *Stress and Job Performance* (Thousand Oaks, CA: Sage, 1998).

[24] "Couples Dismayed at Long Workdays, New Study Finds," *Columbus Dispatch* (January 23, 1999), p. 5A.

[25] See Orlando Behling and Arthur L. Darrow, *Managing Work-Related Stress* (Chicago: Science Research Associates, 1984).

[26] Meyer Friedman and Ray Roseman, *Type A Behavior and Your Heart* (New York: 1974).

[27] See H. Selye, *The Stress of Life*, rev. ed. (New York: McGraw-Hill, 1976).

[28] Jeffrey Pfeffer, *The Human Equation: Building Profits by Putting People First* (Boston: Harvard Business School Press, 1998).

[29] Quotes are from Alan M. Webber, "Danger: Toxic Company," *Fast Company* (November 1998):152.

[30] See John D. Adams, "Health, Stress, and the Manager's Life Style," *Group and Organization Studies* 6 (September 1981):291–301.

[31] Information from Mike Pramik, "Wellness Programs Give Businesses Healthy Bottom Line," *Columbus Dispatch* (January 18, 1999), pp. 10–11.

[32] Ibid.

[33] Pfeffer, op cit. (1998).

SOURCE NOTES

Information and quotes from Amy Taso and Jane Black, "Where Will Carly Fiorina Take HP?" *Business Week On-Line* (June 11, 2003); Dan Thanh Dang, "Hewlett-Packard Chief Speaks to University of Maryland Students, Executives," *Baltimore Sun* (October 11, 2003).

Information from Ken Brown and Gee L. Lee, "Lucent Fires Top China Executives," *Wall Street Journal* (April 7, 2004), p. A8.

Lonnie Johnson: Information from Patricia J. Mays, "Gun Showers Wealth on Inventor," *Columbus Dispatch* (January 24, 1999), p. 6B.

Information from Bernard Wysocki Jr., "To Fix Health Care, Hospitals Take Tips from the Factory Floor," *Wall Street Journal* (April 9, 2004), pp. A1, A6.

Pitney Bowes: See Scott Kirsner, "Designed for Innovation," *Fast Company* (November 1998), pp. 54+.

Information from Chris Warren, "Do You Want Organic Fries with That?" *Southwest Airlines Spirit* (May 2004):32–41.

The Josephson Institute: Information from organizational Web site: http://www.josephsoninstitute.org/about.htm.

Chapter 17

ENDNOTES

[1] The bulk of this chapter was originally based on Richard N. Osborn, James G. Hunt, and Lawrence R. Jauch, *Organization Theory: Integrated Text and Cases* (Melbourne, FL: Krieger, 1985). For a more recent but consistent view, see Lex Donaldson, "The Normal Science of Structural Contingency Theory," in Stewart R. Clegg, Cynthia Hardy, and Walter R. Nord (eds.), *Handbook of Organizational Studies* (London: Sage Publications, 1996), pp. 57–76.

[2] For more information about Fifth Third and its CEO, see www.53.com.

[3] The view of strategy provided here is a combination of perspectives drawn from several sources, including Alfred D. Chandler, *The Visible Hand: The Managerial Revolution in America* (Cambridge, MA: Belknap, 1977); Michael E. Porter, *Competitive Strategy* (New York: Free Press, 1980); L. R. Jauch and R. N. Osborn, "Toward an Integrated Theory of Strategy," *Academy of Management Review* 6 (1981): 491–498; B. Wernefelt, "A Resource-Based View of the Firm," *Strategic Management Journal* 5 (1984): 171–180; J. B. Barney, "Firm Resources and Sustained Competitive Advantage," *Journal Management* 17 (1991): 99–120; Michael A. Hitt, R. Duane Ireland, and Robert E. Hoskisson, *Strategic Management: Competition and Globalization* (Cincinnati, OH: Southwestern, 2001).

[4] H. Talcott Parsons, *Structure and Processes in Modern Societies* (New York: Free Press, 1960).

[5] See Terri Lammers, "The Effective and Indispensable Mission Statement," *Inc.* (August 1992): 1, 7, 23; and I. C. MacMillan and A. Meshulack, "Replacement Versus Expansion: Dilemma for Mature U.S. Businesses," *Academy of Management Journal* 26 (1983):708–726.

[6] L. Larwood, C. M. Falbe, M. Kriger, and P. M. Miesing, "Structure and Meaning of Organizational Vision," *Academy of Management Journal* 38 (1995):740–770.

[7] See Stewart R. Clegg and Cynthia Hardy, "Organizations, Organization and Organizing," in Clegg, Hardy, and Nord (eds.) (1996), pp. 1–28; William H. Starbuck and Paul C. Nystrom, "Designing and Understanding Organizations," in P. C. Nystrom and W. H. Starbuck (eds.), *Handbook of Organizational Design: Adapting Organizations to Their Environments* (New York: Oxford University Press, 1981).

[8] See Jeffery Pfeffer, "Barriers to the Advance of Organization Science," *Academy of Management Review* 18(4) (1994): 599–620; Richard M. Cyert and James G. March, *A Behavioral Theory of the Firm* (Englewood Cliffs, NJ: Prentice-Hall, 1963). A good discussion of organizational goals is also found in Charles Perrow, *Organizational Analysis: A Sociological View* (Belmont, CA: Wadsworth, 1970); Richard H. Hall, "Organizational Behavior: A Sociological Perspective," in Jay W. Lorsch (ed.), *Handbook of Organizational Behavior* (Englewood Cliffs, NJ: Prentice-Hall, 1987), pp. 84–95.

[9] See Osborn, Hunt, and Jauch (1985) for the historical rates; for differences in survival rates by time of formation in the development of a technology, see R. Agarwal, M. Sarkar, and R. Echambadi, "The Conditioning Effect of Time on Firm Survival: An Industry Life Cycle Approach," *Academy of Management Journal* 25 (2002):971–985.

[10] Janice Beyer, Danta P. Ashmos, and R. N. Osborn, "Contrasts in Enacting TQM: Mechanistic vs. Organic Ideology and Implementation," *Journal of Quality Management* 1 (1997):13–29; for an early treatment, see Paul R. Lawrence and Jay W. Lorsch, *Organization and Environment* (Homewood, IL: Irwin, 1969).

[11] Chandler (1977).

[12] For reviews, see Osborn, Hunt, and Jauch (1985); Clegg, Hardy, and Nord (1996).

[13] See Prashant C. Palvia, Shailendra C. Palvia, and Edward M. Roche, *Global Information Technology and Systems Management: Key Issues and Trends* (Nashua, NH: Ivy League Publishing, 1996).

[14] For instance, see J. E. M. McGee, M. J. Dowling, and W. L. Megginson, "Cooperative Strategy and New Venture Performance: The Role of Business Strategy and Management Experience," *Strategic Management Journal* 16 (1995):565–580; James B. Quinn, *Intelligent Enterprise: A Knowledge and Service Based Paradigm for Industry* (New York: Free Press, 1992).

[15] See L.F. Cranor and S. Greenstein (eds.), *Communications Policy and Information Technology: Promises, Problems and Prospects* (Cambridge, MA: MIT Press, 2002); P. Candace Deans, *Global Information Systems and Technology: Focus on the Organization and Its Functional Areas* (Harrisburg, PA: Ideal Group Publishing, 1994); Osborn, Hunt, and Jauch (1985).

[16] Haim Levy and Deborah Gunthorpe, *Introduction to Investments*, 2nd ed. (Cincinnati, OH: South-Western, 1999); Cranor and Greenstein (2002).

[17] William G. Ouchi and M. A. McGuire, "Organization Control: Two Functions," *Administrative Science Quarterly* 20 (1977):559–569.

[18] This discussion is adapted from W. Edwards Deming, "Improvement of Quality and Productivity Through Action by Management," *Productivity Review* (Winter 1982):12, 22; W. Edwards Deming, *Quality, Productivity and Competitive Position* (Cambridge, MA: MIT Center for Advanced Engineering, 1982).

[19] For related reviews, see W. Richard Scott, *Organizations: Rational, Natural, and Open Systems*, 2nd ed. (Englewood Cliffs, NJ: Prentice-Hall. 1987); Osborn, Hunt, and Jauch (1985); Clegg, Hardy, and Nord (1996).

[20] See Osborn, Hunt, and Jauch (1985), pp. 273–303, for a discussion of centralization/decentralization.

[21] Ibid.

[22] For reviews of structural tendencies and their influence on outcomes, also see Scott (1987); Clegg, Hardy, and Nord (1996).

[23] Ibid.

[24] For a good discussion of the early use of matrix structures, see Stanley Davis, Paul Lawrence, Harvey Kolodny, and Michael Beer, *Matrix* (Reading, MA: Addison-Wesley, 1977).

[25] See P. R. Lawrence and J. W. Lorsch, *Organization and Environment: Managing Differentiation and Integration* (Homewood, IL: Richard D. Irwin, 1967).

[26] See Osborn, Hunt, and Jauch (1985).

[27] Max Weber, *The Theory of Social and Economic Organization*, translated by A. M. Henderson and H. T. Parsons (New York: Free Press, 1947).

[28] These relationships were initially outlined by Tom Burns and G. M. Stalken, *The Management of Innovation* (London: Tavistock, 1961).

[29] See Henry Mintzberg, *Structure in Fives: Designing Effective Organizations* (Englewood Cliffs, NJ: Prentice-Hall, 1983).

[30] Ibid.

[31] Ibid.

[32] See Osborn, Hunt, and Jauch (1985) for an extended discussion.

[33] See Peter Clark and Ken Starkey, *Organization Transitions and Innovation—Design* (London: Pinter Publications, 1988).

SOURCE NOTES

www.Stericycle.com

www.NBBJ.com

www.landolakesinc.com

M. A. Boland, and J. P. Katz. "Jack Gherty, President and CEO of Land O'Lakes, on Leading a Branded Food and Farm Supply Cooperative," *Academy of Management Executive.* 17(3) (2003): 24–34.

www.noblecorp.com

Chapter 18

ENDNOTES

[1] See www.IBM.com, CEO's comments on 2000 and 2003 financial performance.

[2] R. N. Osborn, J. G. Hunt, and L. Jauch, *Organization Theory Integrated Text and Cases* (Melbourne, FL: Krieger, 1984), pp. 123–215.

[3] The view of strategy as a process of co-evolution was drawn from several sources, including Alfred D. Chandler, *The Visible Hand: The Managerial Revolution in America* (Cambridge, MA: Belknap, 1977); Michael E. Porter, *Competitive Strategy* (New York: Free Press, 1980); L. R. Jauch and R. N. Osborn, "Toward an Integrated Theory of Strategy," *Academy of Management Review* 6 (1981):491–498; B. Wernefelt, "A Resource-Based View of the Firm," *Strategic Management Journal* 5 (1984):171–180; J. B. Barney, "Firm Resources and Sustained Competitive Advantage," *Journal Management* 17 (1991):99–120; Ross Marion, *The Edge of Organization: Chaos and Complexity Theories of Formal Social Systems* (London: Sage, 1999); Arie Lewin, Chris Long, and Timothy Caroll, "The Coevolution of New Organizational Forms," *Organization Science* 10 (1999):535–550; Michael A. Hitt, R. Duane Ireland, and Robert E. Hoskisson, *Strategic Management: Competition and Globalization* (Cincinnati, OH: Southwestern, 2001).

[4] See Henry Mintzberg, *Structure in Fives: Designing Effective Organizations* (Englewood Cliffs, NJ: Prentice-Hall, 1983).

[5] For a comprehensive review, see W. Richard Scott, *Organizations: Rational, Natural, and Open Systems*, 2nd ed. (Englewood Cliffs, NJ: Prentice-Hall, 1987).

[6] See Peter M. Blau and Richard A. Schoenner, *The Structure of Organizations* (New York: Basic Books, 1971); Joan Woodward, *Industrial Organization: Theory and Practice* (London: Oxford University Press, 1965).

[7] Ibid.

[8] Gerardine DeSanctis, "Information Technology," in Nigel Nicholson (ed.), *Blackwell Encyclopedic Dictionary of Organizational Behavior* (Cambridge, MA: Blackwell, 1995), pp. 232–233.

[9] James D. Thompson, *Organization in Action* (New York: McGraw-Hill, 1967).

[10] Woodward (1965).

[11] For reviews, see Osborn, Hunt, and Jauch (1984); Louis Fry, "Technology-Structure Research: Three Critical Issues," *Academy of Management Journal* 25 (1982), pp. 532–552.

[12] Mintzberg (1983).

[13] Charles Perrow, *Complex Organizations: A Critical Essay*, 3rd ed. (New York: Random House, 1986).

[14] Mintzberg (1983).

[15] Prashant C. Palvia, Shailendra C. Palvia, and Edward M. Roche, *Global Information Technology and Systems Management: Key Issues and Trends* (Nashua, NH: Ivy League Publishing, 1996).

[16] DeSanctis (1995).

[17] P. Candace Deans, *Global Information Systems and Technology: Focus on the Organization and Its Functional Areas* (Harrisburg, PA: Ideal Group Publishing, 1994).

[18] Osborn, Hunt, and Jauch (1984).

[19] David A. Nadler and Michael L. Tushman, *Competing by Design: The Power of Organizational Architecture* (New York: Oxford University Press, 1997).

[20] David Lei, Michael Hitt, and Richard A. Bettis, "Dynamic Capabilities and Strategic Management," *Journal of Management* (1996): pp. 547–567.

[21] Melissa A. Schilling, "Technological Lockout: An Integrative Model of the Economic and Strategic Factors Driving Technological Success and Failure," *Academy of Management Review* 23(2) (1998):267–284.

[22] Jack Veiga and Kathleen Dechant, "Wired World Woes: www.help," *Academy of Management Executive* 11(3) (1997):73–79.

[23] Jaana Woiceshyn, "The Role of Management in the Adoption of Technology: A Longitudinal Investigation," *Technology Studies* 4(1) (1997):62–99.

[24] See M. L. Markus, B. Manville, and C. E. Agres, "What Makes a Virtual Organization Work," *MIT Sloan Management Review* 42 (2002):13–27; Janice Beyer, Danta P. Ashmos, and R. N. Osborn, "Contrasts in Enacting TQM: Mechanistic vs Organic Ideology and Implementation," *Journal of Quality Management* 1 (1997):13–29.

[25] Veiga and Dechant (1997).

[26] Hitt, Ireland, and Hoskisson (2001).

27. This section is based on R. N. Osborn and J. G. Hunt, "The Environment and Organization Effectiveness," *Administrative Science Quarterly* 19 (1974):231–246; Osborn, Hunt, and Jauch (1984).

28. See R. N. Osborn and C. C. Baughn, "New Patterns in the Formation of U.S. Japanese Cooperative Ventures," *Columbia Journal of World Business* 22 (1988):57–65.

29. This section is based on R. N. Osborn, *The Evolution of Strategic Alliances in High Technology*, working paper (Detroit: Department of Management, Wayne State University, 2001); also see Shawn Tully, "The Modular Corporation," *Fortune* (February 8, 1993):27–32.

30. For a more extended discussion, see P. Kenis and D. Knoke, "How Organizational Field Networks Shape Interorganizational Tie-Formation Rates," *Academy of Management Journal* 27 (2002):275–294.

31. The discussion of the virtual organization is based on B. Hedgerg, G. Hahlgren, J. Hansson, and N. Olve, *Virtual Organizations and Beyond* (New York: Wiley, 2001).

32. This treatment of the boundaryless organization is based on R. Ashkenas, D. Ulrich, T. Jick, and S. Kerr, *The Boundaryless Organization: Breaking the Chains of Organizational Structure* (San Francisco: Jossey-Bass, 1995). For earlier discussion, also see R. Golembiewski, *Men, Management and Morality* (New Brunswick, NJ: Transaction, 1989). For a critical review, see R. Golembiewski, "The Boundaryless Organization: Breaking the Chains of Organizational Structure, A Review," *International Journal of Organizational Analysis* 6 (1998): 267–270.

33. This set of prescriptions is drawn from S. Kerr and D. Ulrich, "Creating the Boundaryless Organization: The Radical Reconstruction of Organization Capabilities," *Planning Review* 23 (1995):41–46.

34. G. Huber, "Organizational Learning: The Contributing Process and the Literature," *Organization Science* 2(1) (1991):88–115.

35. J. W. Myer and B. Rowan, "Institutionalized Organizations: Formal Structure as Myth and Ceremony," *American Journal of Sociology* 83 (1977):340–363.

36. A. Bandura, *Social Learning Theory* (Englewood Cliffs, NJ: Prentice-Hall, 1977).

37. See, for example, A. M. Morrison, R. P. White, and E. Van Velsor, *Breaking the Glass Ceiling* (Reading, MA: Addison-Wesley, 1987); J. D. Zalesny and J. K. Ford, "Extending the Social Information Processing Perspective: New Links to Attitudes, Behav[ior] and Perceptions," *Organizational Behavior and Human De[cision] Processes* 47 (1990):205–246; M. E. Gist, C. Schwoerer [and B.] Rosen, "Effects of Alternative Training Methods of S[elf-Efficacy] and Performance in Computer Software Training," *J[ournal of Ap]plied Psychology* 74 (1989):884–91; D. D. Sutton a[nd R.] man, "Pygmalion Goes to Work: The Effects of [Expec]tations in a Retail Setting," *Journal of Ap[plied Psychology]* (1989):943–950; M. E. Gist, "The Influence [of] Self-Efficacy and Idea Generation Amon[g] *Psychology* 42 (1989):787–805.

38. See M. E. Gist, "Self Efficacy: Implications [for] havior and Human Resource Management," *Aca[demy of Manage]ment Review* 12 (1987):472–485; A. Bandura, "Self-E[fficacy] nisms in Human Agency," *American Psycho[logist]* (1987):122–147.

39. J. March, *Decisions and Organizations* (Oxford: Blackw[ell,] 1988).

40. R. N. Osborn and D. H. Jackson, "Leaders, Riverboat Gamblers, or Purposeful Unintended Consequences in the Management of Complex Technologies," *Academy of Management Journal* 31 (1988):924–947.

41. See R. Lord and M. Kernan, "Scripts as Determinants of Purposeful Behavior in Organizations," *Academy of Management Review* 12 (1987):265–278; A. L. Stinchcombe, *Economic Sociology* (New York, Academic Press, 1983).

42. Osborn and Jackson (1988).

43. Ibid.

44. O. P. Walsch and G. R. Ungson, "Organization Memory," *Academy of Management Review* 16 (1) (1991):57–91.

45. A. A. Marcus, *Business and Society: Ethics, Government and World of Economy* (Homewood, IL: Richard D. Irwin, 1993).

46. Ibid.

SOURCE NOTES

www.Millennium.com.

Warner-Lambert Annual Report 1997, p. 24.

www.cisco.com.

M. L. Markus, B. Manville, and C. E. Agres, "[ ] Organization Work," *MIT Sloan M[anagement Review]* (2002):13–27.

www.monster.com

www.corning.com/inside.

Chapter 19

ENDNOTES

1 This description and [ ]

2 Edgar Schein, "Or[ ] 45 (1990):109–119

ership (San Fran[cisco]

3 Schein (199[0]

4 See www[ ]

5 This ex[ ] "Corp[ ] (Ma[ ]

6 [ ]

[15] Schein (1985), pp. 52–57.

[16] Schein (1990).

[17] For early work, see T. Deal and A. Kennedy, *Corporate Culture* (Reading, MA: Addison-Wesley, 1982); T. Peters and R. Waterman, *In Search of Excellence* (New York: Harper & Row, 1982). More recent studies are summarized in Joanne Martin and Peter Frost, "The Organizational Culture War Games: The Struggle for Intellectual Dominance," in Stewart R. Clegg, Cynthia Hardy, and Walter R. Nord (eds.), *Handbook of Organization Studies* (London: Sage Publications, 1996), pp. 599–621.

[18] Schein (1990).

[19] H. Gertz, *The Interpretation of Culture* (New York: Basic Books, 1973).

[20] Beyer and Trice (1987).

[21] H. M. Trice and J. M. Beyer, "Studying Organizational Cultures Through Rites and Ceremonials," *Academy of Management Review* 3 (1984):633–669.

[22] J. Martin, M. S. Feldman, M. J. Hatch, and S. B. Sitkin, "The Uniqueness Paradox in Organizational Stories," *Administrative Science Quarterly* 28 (1983):438–453; *Business Week* (November 1992), p. 117.

Trice and Beyer (1984).

N. Osborn and D. Jackson, "Leaders, River Boat Gamblers, or Useful Unintended Consequences," *Academy of Management* 31 (1988):924–947.

Feldman, Hatch, and Sitkin (1983).

and Beyer (1984).

tion is based on R. N. Osborn and C. C. Baughn, *An Assessment of the State of the Field of Organizational Design* VA: U.S. Army Research Institute, 1994).

Frost (1996).

stede and M. H. Bond, "The Confucius Connection: Roots to Economic Growth," *Organizational Dynamics* :4–21.

[30] Warner Burke, *Organization Development* (Reading, MA: Addison-Wesley, 1987); Wendell L. French and Cecil H. Bell Jr., *Organization Development*, 4th ed. (Englewood Cliffs, NJ: Prentice-Hall, 1990); Edgar F. Huse and Thomas G. Cummings, *Organization Development and Change*, 4th ed. (St. Paul, MN: West, 1989).

[31] Warren Bennis, "Using Our Knowledge of Organizational Behavior," in Lorsch, pp. 29–49.

[32] Excellent overviews are found in Huse and Cummings (1989), pp. 32–36, 45; and French and Bell (1990).

[33] Richard Beckhard, "The Confrontation Meeting," *Harvard Business Review* 45 (March/April 1967):149–155.

[34] See Dale Zand, "Collateral Organization: A New Change Strategy," *Journal of Applied Behavioral Science* 10 (1974):63–89; Barry A. Stein and Rosabeth Moss Kanter, "Building the Parallel Organization," *Journal of Applied Behavioral Science* 16 (1980):371–386.

[35] J. Richard Hackman and Greg R. Oldham, *Work Redesign* (Reading, MA: Addison-Wesley, 1980).

SOURCE NOTES

www.ethicsquality.com.

www.hermanmiller.com.

www.cantorusa.com; Helen Dunne, Andrew Cave, and Dan Sabbagh, "Broker Traces Six of 1,000 Staff." www.news.telegraph.co.uk; September 13, 2001; Edleman Public Relations Worldwide, "Cantor Fitzgerald and eSpeed to Expedite Bonus Distributions for Families of Employees Lost in the World Trade Center Tragedy," www.cantorusa.com.press.php, October 10, 2001.

www.wamu.com

Figure 19.2 reprinted from *California Management Review* 12(2) (1996):26, Figure 1, by permission of the Regents. Copyright 1969 by the Regents of the University of California.

Photo Credits

Chapter 1

Opener: Susan C. Bourgoin/Foodpix/PictureArts Corp. Page 3: Reprinted with permission Black Enterprise Magazine, New York, NY. All rights reserved. Page 4: Dennis O'Clair/Stone/Getty Images. Page 7: Photo courtesy SAS Institute Inc. Page 9: ©AP/Wide World Photos. Page 13: Randy Faris/Corbis Images. Page 15: Justin Sullivan/Getty Images.

Chapter 2

Opener: Dan Lim/Masterfile. Page 27: ©AP/Wide World Photos. Page 31: Chirstine Chew/UPI/Landov. Page 34: Stephen Chernin/Getty Images. Page 35: ©AP/Wide World Photos. Page 39: Photo courtesy of The Container Store. Page 40 (top): Courtesy SAS Institute, Inc. Page 40 (bottom): Neo Vision/Photonica.

Chapter 3

Opener: David Sutherland/Stone/Getty Images. Page 53: Bob Abraham/Corbis Stock Market. Page 54: Indranil Mukherjee/AFP/Getty Images. Page 55: Courtesy Vukani-Ubuntu Community Development Projects. Page 57: Courtesy Social Accountability International. Page 61: Stefan Zaklin/Getty Images News and Sport Services. Page 62: Ric Ergenbright/Corbis Images. Page 64: Chung Sung-Jun/Getty Images.

Chapter 4

Opener: Ricardo Funari/Age Fotostock America, Inc. Page 77: Richard Hamilton Smith/Corbis Images. Page 83: Courtesy F. Byron Nahser. Page 88: Eriko Sugita/Reuters/Landov. Page 90: Courtesy Herbert K. Sloane. Page 91: ©AP/Wide World Photos.

Chapter 5

Opener: New Vision/Photonica. Page 101: Warren Bolster/Stone/Getty Images. Page 105: ©AP/Wide World Photos. Page 106: Viktor Korotayev/Reuters/Landov. Page 107: Justin Sullivan/Getty Images. Page 109: Lawrence Lucier/Getty Images. Page 111: Courtesy Jonathan Player.

Chapter 6

Opener: Dimitri Lundt/Corbis Images. Page 121: Courtesy InnoCentive. Page 124: ©AP/Wide World Photos. Page 125: Photo by Mike Hanes, Director of Bands, Southern Illinois University Carbondale. Page 129: ©AP/Wide World Photos. Page 133: Courtesy Dr. Dhyana Ziegler, Host and Co-Producer of the Delta SEE Connection; photo by Jefferson Walker IV. Page 136: Courtesy AutoNation.

Chapter 7

Opener: Justin Pumfrey/Taxi/Getty Images. Page 143: Tim Mosenfelder/Corbis Images. Page 144: Joe Raedle/Getty Images. Page 150: Courtesy Donna Terek. Page 152: ©AP/Wide World Photos. Page 154: Courtesy Mark Susor. Page 158: Robin O'Shaughnessy/Lubbock Avalanche Journal.

Chapter 8

Opener: Vince Streano/Corbis Images. Page 166: Photo by David J. Swift, provided courtesy of Carol Arne Decker. Page 170: ©AP/Wide World Photos. Page 184: Photodisc Blue/PhotoDisc, Inc./Getty Images. Page 187 (top): Courtesy Imke Lass. Page 187 (bottom): Getty Images News and Sport Services.

Chapter 9

Opener: Patrik Giardino/Corbis Images. Page 195: Photo by Zoological Society of San Diego/Getty Images. Page 197: ©AP/Wide World Photos. Page 198: Courtesy W. L. Gore & Associates, Inc. Page 202: Courtesy DaimlerChrysler Corporation. Page 203: Indranil Mukherjee/AFP/Getty Images. Page 210: ©AP/Wide World Photos.

Chapter 10

Opener: Graham French/Masterfile. Page 219: Reuters/Gregory Heisler for TIME/Handout/Landov. Page 221: Photo courtesy LaserMonks. Page 222: Steven Peters/Stone/Getty Images. Page 224: Bruce Ayres/Stone/Getty Images. Page 231: Pixtal/Age Fotostock America, Inc. Page 232: Getty Images News and Sport Services.

Chapter 11

Opener: David Muir/Masterfile. Page 242: ©Dallas Morning News. Page 244: Kim Kulish/Corbis. Page 249: ©AP/Wide World Photos. Page 255: Dan Lamont/Corbis. Page 256: Photo by Time Life Pictures/Time Magazine, ©Time Inc./Time Life Pictures/Getty Images. Page 258: Courtesy Toyota Motor North America, Inc. Page 259: Courtesy Parkland Health and Hospital System.

Chapter 12

Opener: Gary Cralle/The Image Bank/Getty Images. Page 268: Courtesy Texas Instruments. Page 271: Courtesy Avocent Corporation. Page 272: Courtesy Melita International. Page 277: Courtesy Dell Computer. Page 281: Bloomberg New/Landov. Page 282: ©AP/Wide World Photos. Page 284: Courtesy Little Caesar Enterprises, Inc.

Chapter 13

Opener: Bruno Morandi/Age Fotostock America, Inc. Page 296: ©Markel/Liaison Agency, Inc./Getty Images. Page 299: Corbis Images. Page 303: Chuck Savage/Corbis Images. Page 304: Courtesy SRC Holdings Corp. Page 305: Courtesy Alibaba.com. Page 307: Photo by Timothy Greenfield-Sanders; provided courtesy of American Express. Page 308: Joe Raedle/Getty Images.

Chapter 14

Opener: Owen Franken/Corbis Images. Page 316: Corbis Images. Page 319: Courtesy Sterling Bank. Page 320: Courtesy Pella Windows and Doors. Page 323: Courtesy Nokia Corporation. Page 324: Courtesy Jack in the Box Restaurants. Page 325: Antonio M. Rosario/The Image Bank/Getty Images. Page 330: Courtesy Fresh International.

Chapter 15

Opener: PhotoDisc, Inc./Getty Images. Page 340: Gaillarde Raphael/Gamma-Presse, Inc. Page 344: Ken Fisher/Stone/Getty Images. Page 349: Klaus Hackenberg/Stone/Getty Images. Page 352: Courtesy Ogilvy and Mather. Page 353: Kwame Zikomo/SUPERSTOCK. Page 354: OH/AFP/Getty Images.

Chapter 16

Opener: Dan Lim/Masterfile. Page 361: Chris Farina/Corbis. Page 362: Steve Allen/Getty/Brand X Pictures. Page 367: SUPER SOAKER is a trademark of Larami, Ltd., a division of Hasbro and is used with permission. ©2004 Hasbro. All Rights Reserved. Page 368: Corbis Images. Page 370: Pascal Le Segretain/Getty Images. Page 371: Courtesy Josephson Institute of Ethics. Page 373: Courtesy O'Naturals.

Chapter 17

Opener: Burke/Triolo/Getty/Brand X Pictures. Page 382: Getty Images News and Sport Services. Page 384: Jeff Greenberg/Age Fotostock America, Inc. Page 387: Courtesy Noble Corporation. Page 393: Layne Kennedy/Corbis. Page 397: ©Tim Hursley.

Chapter 18

Opener: David Madison/The Image Bank/Getty Images. Page 410: ©PhotoDisc. Page 412: Courtesy Millenium Chemicals. Page 414: Provided courtesy of Monster.com. Page 420: Firefly Productions/Corbis Stock Market. Page 422: Courtesy Corning, Inc. Page 428: ©AP/Wide World Photos.

Chapter 19

Opener: Greg Pease/Stone/Getty Images. Page 437: Courtesy Ethics Quality, Inc. Page 440: Courtesy The Body Shop, Inc. Page 441: ©AP/Wide World Photos. Page 445: Erin Patrice O'Brien/Taxi/Getty Images. Page 446: Courtesy Herman Miller, Inc. Page 447: Courtesy Washington Mutual Bank.

Organizations Index

Name Index

Subject Index

Terms in **boldface** are glossary terms.